CIMA

PROFESSIONAL COMPETENCE LEVEL

PAPER T4

TEST OF PROFESSIONAL COMPETENCE IN MANAGEMENT ACCOUNTING

STUDY TEXT

In this edition:

- Exam-centred topic coverage, directly linked to CIMA's learning outcomes, syllabus content and assessment matrix
- Exam focus points showing you what the examiner will want you to do
- Practice papers for you to work through and develop your exam skills

VALID FOR EXAMS UP TO NOVEMBER 2013

BPP LEARNING MEDIA

First edition January 2010
Third edition June 2012

ISBN 9781 4453 9613 2
(Previous ISBN 9780 7517 9484 7)

e-ISBN 9781 4453 9289 9

British Library Cataloguing-in-Publication Data
A catalogue record for this book
is available from the British Library

Published by

BPP Learning Media Ltd
BPP House, Aldine Place
London W12 8AA

www.bpp.com/learningmedia

Printed in the United Kingdom

Your learning materials, published by BPP Learning Media Ltd, are printed on paper sourced from sustainable, managed forests.

All our rights reserved. No part of this publication may be reproduced, stored in a retrieval system or transmitted, in any form or by any means, electronic, mechanical, photocopying, recording or otherwise, without the prior written permission of BPP Learning Media Ltd.

We are grateful to the Chartered Institute of Management Accountants for permission to reproduce past examination questions. The suggested solutions have been prepared by BPP Learning Media Ltd.

©
BPP Learning Media Ltd
2012

A note about copyright

Dear Customer

What does the little © mean and why does it matter?

Your market-leading BPP books, course materials and e-learning materials do not write and update themselves. People write them: on their own behalf or as employees of an organisation that invests in this activity. Copyright law protects their livelihoods. It does so by creating rights over the use of the content.

Breach of copyright is a form of theft – as well as being a criminal offence in some jurisdictions, it is potentially a serious breach of professional ethics.

With current technology, things might seem a bit hazy but, basically, without the express permission of BPP Learning Media:

- Photocopying our materials is a breach of copyright
- Scanning, ripcasting or conversion of our digital materials into different file formats, uploading them to facebook or emailing them to your friends is a breach of copyright

You can, of course, sell your books, in the form in which you have bought them – once you have finished with them. (Is this fair to your fellow students? We update for a reason.) But the e-products are sold on a single user licence basis: we do not supply 'unlock' codes to people who have bought them second-hand.

And what about outside the UK? BPP Learning Media strives to make our materials available at prices students can afford by local printing arrangements, pricing policies and partnerships which are clearly listed on our website. A tiny minority ignore this and indulge in criminal activity by illegally photocopying our material or supporting organisations that do. If they act illegally and unethically in one area, can you really trust them?

Contents

	Page
Introduction	iv

Part A Tackling the case study

1	The Test of Professional Competence in Management Accounting (TOPCIMA)	3
2	How you will be marked: the assessment matrix	11
3	Technical knowledge	31
4	The BPP approach (1): approach and explore the case situation	53
5	The BPP approach (2): synthesise what you know	91
6	Report writing and the TOPCIMA paper	105
7	The exam	117

Part B Teaching case: Zubinos

8	Zubinos: pre-seen data	125
9	Zubinos: approach and explore the case situation	139
10	Zubinos: synthesise what you know	161
11	Zubinos: unseens and requirements	173
12	Zubinos: answer	187

Part C Practice T4 (TOPCIMA) cases

BeeZed Construction Services (BZCS)

13	BZCS: pre-seen data	201
14	BZCS: some help from BPP	215
15	BZCS: unseen and requirements	267
16	BZCS: answer	279

Papy - supermarket chain

17	Papy: pre-seen data	297
18	Papy: some help from BPP	313
19	Papy: unseen and requirements	369
20	Papy: answer	379

Jot toys

21	Jot toys: pre-seen data	395
22	Jot toys: some help from BPP	411
23	Jot toys: unseen and requirements	473
24	Jot toys: answer	483

Specimen Exam Paper (Pilot paper)

25	EGC: Specimen exam paper	501

The Test of Professional Competence in Management Accounting (TOPCIMA)

The Test of Professional Competence in Management Accounting (TOPCIMA) comprises **two component parts** that must both be achieved in order to pass the test.

Part A is **work based practical experience**. **Part B** is the TOPCIMA **case study examination**.

You are awarded credits rather than marks, and to pass the TOPCIMA, you must achieve at least **75 credits** across the two parts of the test.

These 75 credits must comprise **50 credits from Part A** and a minimum of **25 credits for Part B** (out of a maximum of 50 credits).

The overall result for the TOPCIMA can only be given when both component parts have been completed. Therefore you are advised to take Part A and Part B concurrently, although they can be taken in any order once the all the strategic level examinations (E3, P3 & F3) have been completed.

Part A

Work Based Practical Experience – 50 credits

You must prepare and submit a 'CIMA Career Profile' demonstrating work based practical experience and skills development.

You must gain a minimum of three years' relevant work based practical experience, drawn from the three areas shown in the table below. A minimum of 18 months experience must be drawn from the 'Core experience' area.

Area 1 – Basic experience	Area 2 – Core experience	Area 3 – Supplementary experience
1a. Preparing and maintaining accounting records	2a. Preparation of management accounts	3a. Financial strategy
1b. Statutory and regulatory reporting	2b. Planning, budgeting and forecasting	3b. Corporate finance
1c. IT desktop skills	2c. Management reporting for decision making	3c. Treasury management
1d. Systems and procedure development	2d. Product and service costing	3d. Taxation
	2e. Information management	3e. Business evaluation and appraisal
	2f. Project appraisal	3f. Business strategy
	2g. Project management	3g. External relationships
	2h. Working capital control	
	2i. Risk management and business assurance	

You may have gained some or all of the required experience before you registered as a CIMA student.

You can find full details of the practical experience requirements, and how to complete the CIMA Career Profile, in the 'Practical experience' section of the CIMA website www.cimaglobal.com.

Once your Career Profile is approved, you will be awarded the 50 credits you need to pass Part A of the TOPCIMA.

Part B

Case Study Examination

You must sit a **three hour examination**, based on a mixture of **pre-seen** and **unseen material**. This examination is based upon a case study which provides an integrated test of syllabus content from across the full CIMA syllabus. The case study examination has no specific syllabus content of its own, but it will draw heavily on ideas you have covered in the three strategic level papers – E3, F3 and P3.

Although the organisations in the case study will be fictional, they will be based on a real industry or business.

You need to score a minimum of 25 credits in this examination (out of 50) in order to pass the Test of Professional Competence in Management Accounting.

To pass the exam you will need to apply strategic management accounting techniques to analyse and evaluate information and recommend solutions. You will also need to communicate your ideas and solutions clearly to your reader.

This study text is designed to show you how to approach the case study examination, and to maximise your chances of passing it.

How the BPP Learning Media Study Text can help you pass the Case Study Examination

Aims of this Study Text

This Study Text has been written for the Test of Professional Competence in Management Accounting (TOPCIMA) case study examination.

- It is written at the **right level.**
- It is targeted to the **exam**. We have taken note of past papers, questions put to the examiners, the assessment methodology, and the cases set to date under the previous syllabus.

You may be studying at home on your own until the date of the exam, or you may be attending a full-time course. BPP has material to suit both options. The key to the case is to **prepare** and to **practise.**

Work through this Study Text before CIMA issues the pre-seen data. Then use the BPP Learning Media **TOPCIMA Toolkit**. Written around the real pre-seen data, the Toolkit contains analyses and exercises to get you thinking, as well as a number of 'mock' unseens to prepare you for the real thing.

Recommended use

Six to two months before the exam	**This Study Text** This Study Text shows you a step by step approach to tackling the TOPCIMA exam and gives you the opportunity to practise on previous case studies with unseens and full answers.
Two months before the exam	**BPP Learning Media TOPCIMA Toolkit** **CIMA** posts the pre-seen part of the case on its website about six weeks before the exam. The BPP Learning Media TOPCIMA Toolkit is written by BPP Learning Media authors and tutors around the real pre-seen. It many exercises and practice exams to help you pass. Look on our website for details. **BPP Professional Education TOPCIMA discussion board** Join the study discussion board. Here you can send TOPCIMA-related messages to other TOPCIMA students and to BPP Professional Education's team of tutors and BPP Learning Media authors. For more details visit: www.bpp.com/cima

Suggested study approach

Throughout the BPP Learning Media series, we offer advice on how to study. The TOPCIMA exam is different from all other exams in that it does not require any specialist knowledge, more the ability to apply knowledge you have gained from all the other CIMA papers, particularly those at Strategic Level.

This is how we help you through your study for the case.

Key steps	Activity
Chapter 1	Describes the case in detail, with questions bringing some of the key issues into perspective.
Chapter 2	Describes the marking scheme in depth. It is **vital** that you understand this so that you can focus your efforts.
Chapter 3	Gives a brief overview of some important technical knowledge areas.
Chapters 4–5	**Suggests** a structured sequence of tasks to take you through the two months before the exam. (Throughout you are given the opportunity to practise your written communication skills.) These are **tools** to help you through. You do not have to use all of them.
Chapter 6	Gives you some hints and tips on report writing.
Chapter 7	Describes how you should approach exam day.
Chapter 8	Your first case to practise on: Zubinos.
Chapters 9–10	A step-by-step analysis through Zubinos, applying the approach outlined in Chapters 4–5.
Chapters 11–12	The unseen data from Zubinos with an answer for you to consider.
Chapters 13–24	Three further practice case studies. It is important that you get an idea of the variety of approaches that could be taken. We have added some analysis to help you work through these exams.

Syllabus: learning aims and outcomes

Learning aims

The aim of the TOPCIMA examination is to ensure that candidates have the competences required for them to become qualified accountants. As such, there is a requirement that CIMA members:

- Have a sound technical knowledge of the specific subjects within the curriculum
- Can apply technical knowledge in an analytical and practical manner
- Can extract, from various subjects, the knowledge required to solve many-sided or complex problems
- Can solve a particular problem by distinguishing the relevant information from the irrelevant, in a given body of data
- Can, in multi-problem situations, identify the problems and rank them in the order in which they need to be addressed
- Appreciate that there can be alternative solutions and understand the role of judgement in dealing with them
- Can integrate diverse areas of knowledge and skills
- Can communicate effectively with users, including formulating realistic recommendations in a concise and logical fashion
- Can identify, advise on and/or resolve ethical dilemmas.

Rationale

The TOPCIMA will provide an integrated test of syllabus content that is mainly included within the three Strategic level papers (E3, P3 and F3). However, it will also draw upon content covered within the six papers at Managerial and Operational Level.

The TOPCIMA will require the student to deal with material in less structured situations than that encountered in previous Strategic level papers, and to integrate a variety of tools in arriving at a recommended solution. It is unlikely that there will be a single right answer to a complex business problem and students will be expected to recognise the possible alternatives in dealing with a problem.

The emphasis will be on assessing candidates' capabilities and competence in the practical use of appropriate, relevant knowledge; the ability to demonstrate the application of the higher level skills of synthesis, analysis and evaluation; and skill in presenting and communicating information effectively to users.

Learning outcomes

Students will be required to go through the following stages to prepare for, and to answer, the requirement of the case set within the TOPCIMA.

A – Preparatory to the TOPCIMA exam

- Analyse the context within which the case is set
- Analyse the current position of the organisation
- Identify and analyse the issues facing the organisation

Note: These preparatory activities should be undertaken using the published 'pre-seen' case study materials.

B – During the exam

- Analyse the current position of the organisation
- Identify, analyse and prioritise the issues facing the organisation
- Identify, evaluate and discuss possible feasible options and courses of action available to the organisation
- Recommend a course of action
- Prepare and present information in a format suitable for presentation to senior management, and to an appropriate standard.

Note: These activities during the exam will be undertaken using both the pre-seen material and the unseen case study materials.

The exam

Obtaining the exam paper

The 'exam' paper effectively comes in two sections.

- At least six weeks before the exam CIMA will post the **pre-seen** data on its website. You are expected to become familiar with this, and undertake preparatory analysis on it.

- In the exam, you are given a fresh copy of the pre-seen, and up to six pages of 'unseen' data that you have not seen before. This 'unseen' material will introduce further developments which will need to be discussed. It will also identify the question requirement.

When the pre-seen material is published on the CIMA website, CIMA will also publish a 'Case Study Assessment Matrix.' This will identify the assessment criteria and scoring system which will be used to mark students' performance in the TOPCIMA examination.

It is vital that you review the assessment matrix as well as the pre-seen material as part of your preparation for the examination.

The need for Internet access

CIMA will not distribute the pre-seen case study data by post. Instead, you will be told when the material is available on CIMA's website, and you will be able to download it. The material is likely to be in PDF format, readable by Adobe Acrobat software. This is free software and is available from CIMA's (and BPP's) website.

If you do **not** have Internet access, CIMA advises you to contact CIMA's local office or the Student Services Centre.

Taking TOPCIMA

There are two ways of taking TOPCIMA

1   **Computer-based exam**

    In this approach you sit the exam on specially modified computers at an exam centre. You will use Word and Excel. This option is available for all four sittings (March, May, September and November).

2   **Conventional paper-based exam**

    You will write your report on paper in the traditional way at an exam centre. This option is only available for the May and November sittings.

The following has been extracted from details about the syllabus on CIMA's website.

'There will be a written examination paper of **three hours plus 20 minutes of pre-examination question paper reading time**. The paper will have a limited number of questions (requirements). They will normally be answered using a report and/or presentation, with further supporting documents, to a variety of users. The questions will be based upon a case study (pre-seen material) which will be published on the CIMA website at least six weeks in advance of the examination. This will provide an opportunity before the examination, to undertake preparatory analysis based upon the pre-seen material. The volume of pre-seen material is likely to be between 10 and 20 sides of A4 paper. Further information regarding the case (unseen material) will be added as part of the examination paper. This will allow further developments to be explained and additional issues to be raised. The volume of unseen material is likely to be between three and six sides of A4 paper.

Questions will test the student's capabilities and competence in the application of appropriate knowledge, and the processes undertaken in dealing with the problems identified in the examination, together with the ability to present and communicate information in a variety of formats'.

Please note that the additional 20 minutes reading time at the start of the examination means there will be a total of 200 minutes of exam room time.

Requirement

There will be one overall requirement but it **will contain two elements**.

The main element of the requirement is likely to be write a **report**, but this will then be supplemented with a second element: to produce some supporting Powerpoint slides, a memo, or a graph, for example. The mark allocation will be split **90 marks** for the main element of the requirement (the report) and **10 marks** for the supporting documents (slides, memo, email etc).

Although there is no requirement that TOPCIMA exams have to include a report, past experience suggests this is likely to be the case. If you need to write a report, this should follow a standard layout (see Chapter 6).

Under the 2005 (old) syllabus, TOPCIMA exams usually asked students to take on a role as an external consultant and write their report from that perspective. However, under the current (2010) syllabus you could be asked to take on a role *either* as an employee of the organisation in the case study *or* as an external consultant.

The specimen exam paper for the 2010 syllabus asked students to prepare a report from the perspective of a divisional management accountant. We expect that you will need to **write a report from an internal perspective** (for example, as a senior management accountant) rather then from an external perspective (for example, a consultant).

Specimen exam paper (Pilot paper)

The Pilot paper concerned a nationalised electricity generating corporation, with a bureaucratic culture and a centralised organisation structure. The corporation has historically benefited from significant levels of government funding.

However, there are now increasing pressures for nationalised industries in its country to improve their productivity and returns on assets. There are also calls for electricity companies to move towards using more efficient and renewable forms of power generation.

The unseen data explained organisational changes which have led to a new, divisionalised structure and the creation of a new management board. It is clear the corporation has to undergo cultural change to become more efficient and accountable.

Candidates were required to place themselves in the position of the management accountant of one of the divisions in the corporation, and present a report that prioritised, analysed and evaluated the issues facing the division, and made appropriate recommendations. There were up to 90 marks available for this report.

Candidates were also required to prepare two slides summarising the case for investing in new equipment to increase fuel efficiency and reduce harmful emissions from two power stations. There were up to 10 marks available for these slides.

The Specimen exam paper is included at Chapter 25 in this text.

Exam advice in overview

The following is a summary of TOPCIMA exam advice taken from the examiners' comments on previous exam sittings.

General overview

The TOPCIMA exam is designed to test higher level skills. Candidates need to be able to **apply** their technical knowledge and understanding of the business setting in which the case is set. It is essential that this is applied to the new data supplied in the unseen material on the exam day. Candidates will need to use their **judgement** to solve multi-faceted problems given in the pre-seen and unseen material and to 'think on their feet'.

Candidates need to research the business setting in which a case is set and have a good understanding and familiarity with the **pre-seen material**, but must discuss the **unseen material** on the exam day and answer the requirement that has been set. An open mind will be much more useful on exam day than pre-prepared answers.

Candidates should ensure that their answers cover all of the criteria of the TOPCIMA assessment matrix (see Chapter 2 for detailed guidance). Candidates will need to clearly identify the key issues and discuss them in a priority order, justifying the choice of priority. Fully justified, well reasoned recommendations are required, covering all areas of the report, preferably at the end. To score well, candidates not only need to recommend a course of action as required but to justify the recommendations they have made.

It is suggested that candidates use 'check-lists' of issues to be discussed and the recommendations for each issue.

Key tasks to improve your performance

(a) Before the exam, thoroughly research the business setting for the case you will be sitting, and make sure you are totally familiar with the pre-seen material.

(b) Revise relevant business strategies and techniques (including strategic management accounting techniques) and be able to apply them.

(c) Familiarise yourself with the TOPCIMA assessment matrix, to ensure your answer covers all of the criteria.

(d) In the exam itself, identify the relevant key issues in the unseen material, and ensure your report covers these issues. Being able to prioritise issues is one of the most important skills being tested in TOPCIMA.

(e) Time management. The TOPCIMA exam is very time pressured, so good time management is crucial to success.

TACKLING THE CASE STUDY

Part A

The Test of Professional Competence in Management Accounting (TOPCIMA)

TOPCIMA is the culmination of all the work you have put into your CIMA qualification so far. Although you have completed scenario questions in other Strategic level papers, paper T4 – TOPCIMA is a totally different type of exam.

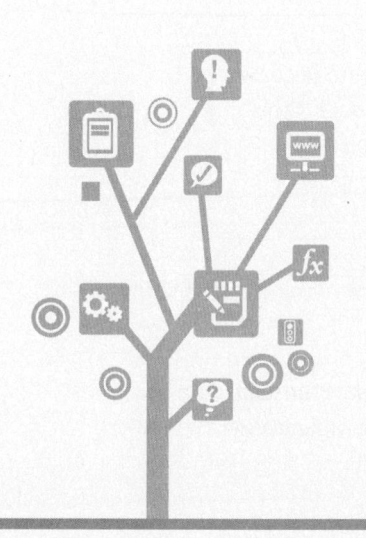

topic list

1 TOPCIMA paper: what it is and what it's for

2 The TOPCIMA paper and other exams

3 Getting hold of the case

4 How to use this Study Text

5 Other help from BPP

1 TOPCIMA paper: what it is and what it's for

TOPCIMA tests your ability to apply all the skills and knowledge you have acquired throughout your CIMA studies to the type of practical business situation you may be asked to deal with as a chartered management accountant. TOPCIMA requires a sound understanding of a variety of **business and financial techniques**, coupled with **commercial understanding** and the ability to **apply your knowledge** to the situation presented to you. TOPCIMA tests your ability to apply your knowledge to the case.

However, you do not have to learn any new theories specifically for the TOPCIMA exam.

1.1 What it is

The Test of Professional Competence in Management Accounting (TOPCIMA) is the culmination of your CIMA studies. It is unlike any other exam. Here are the main features in outline.

1.1.1 Before the exam

About **six weeks** before the exam you will access CIMA's website and download between 15 and 20 pages of **'pre-seen'** data (plus supplementary background information, possibly).

The pre-seen data:

- Contains a description of an organisation
- Identifies some issues about the organisation and its context
- Shows you what the examiner will be looking for

You must use the two months before the exam to become **familiar** with the organisation in the pre-seen data. (This BPP Study Text will show you some techniques for becoming familiar with the organisation in the case.) Why?

Memory

You **cannot take anything** you have prepared into the exam room.

AND

Challenge

You will be given **more 'unseen' data in the exam** about the organisation and its environment.

PART A TACKLING THE CASE STUDY 1: The Test of Professional Competence in Management Accounting (TOPCIMA) | 5

1.1.2 The exam

You cannot take your analysis with you, and you will have to leave any notes or analysis you have prepared in advance at the door.

In the exam room this is what you will be given.

Data
- A clean copy of all the **pre-seen material**: this should be identical; if not you will be told where to find the differences.
- New **unseen** material.
- Relevant mathematical tables.

Requirement

There will be a requirement describing **one or more tasks** that you must complete in a given format (eg report format; PowerPoint slides; Memo; email)

Answer booklet or computer

You must write or type your answer here. In the computer based exam you will use Word and Excel.

Effectively, you have **three hours** to write in your **answer booklets or on your PC** the answer to a relatively short, possibly unstructured, question.

1.1.3 After the exam

Your answer to the requirement will be reviewed against the **assessment matrix** you will have seen, and the markers will be looking at how well you have performed against the matrix.

1.2 What is the case for?

The case is specially designed to test what CIMA calls **higher level skills**. These skills do not comprise the ability to remember facts or formulae but relate directly to the type of business situation you might, having qualified though CIMA, encounter as a management accountant in practice at strategic level. These higher level skills are shown in the table below.

Synthesis	Analysis	Evaluation	Presentation and communication
Gathering together diverse items of data, getting the big picture	Manipulating data to find useful information	Making an informed judgement as to the information	Communication of information to an audience

Mainly before the exam ─────────────────────────→ Mainly during the exam

The case study enables you to show that you have these skills. They are treated in more depth on the **assessment matrix** which we discuss in Chapter 2, but here is a brief example.

1.3 Example: higher level skills in miniature

This is a very simple exercise to show what we mean by higher level skills. You have the following data on your desk.

- A request from A Co's marketing staff to extend the credit period they offer to A Co's customers
- A Co's sales ledger (which has 100 customers)
- A letter from A Co to its customers saying that it has increased its prices by 20%
- Recent financial statements of B Co, a customer accounting for 10% of A Co's turnover
- An article from the *Financial Times* describing new competition in B Co's market

How might skills of synthesis, analysis, evaluation and communication be applied here?

Skill	What it is	A Co
Synthesis	Gathering together diverse items of data. Getting the big picture	B Co is facing competition and a huge increase in costs. If B Co goes out of business, A Co loses 10% of its turnover.
Analysis	Manipulating data to find useful information	You could use B Co's accounts to calculate profit margins and cash position, and hence whether it is a good credit risk.
Evaluation	Making an informed judgement	You might suggest that extending the credit period to B Co is risky for A Co, but you need to consider the potential advantages or disadvantages of doing so.
Presentation and Communication	Communication of information to an audience	You might have to present a report to the Finance Director, and summarise key points on a Powerpoint slide.

To test these skills, you may be required to carry out a number of tasks.

Synthesise	Analyse	Evaluate	Communicate

Task

In the case study:

- Analyse and identify the current position of an organisation
- Identify and analyse the relevant issues facing an organisation
- Evaluate possible feasible courses of action available
- Evaluate a range of specific proposals
- Make appropriate recommendations
- Produce information in a suitable format for presentation to management

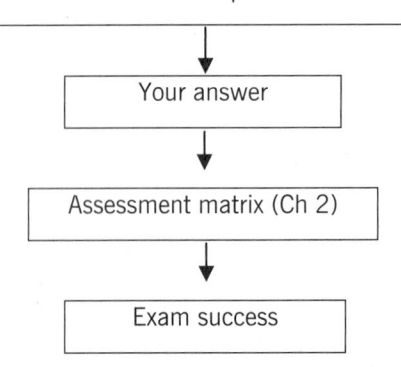

↓

Your answer

↓

Assessment matrix (Ch 2)

↓

Exam success

2 The TOPCIMA paper and other exams

How is the TOPCIMA paper different from all the other CIMA exams?

There is no real **syllabus**.	BUT	You have to show **higher level** skills.
You do not have to learn anything new. It is **not a test of knowledge**.	BUT	You have to **use your knowledge** of all the strategic level syllabus and your CIMA studies.
There is **no single 'right' answer**.	BUT	How you show you tackle the case (the process) is as important as the actual recommendations you make.
The business situation and data is **unstructured**.	BUT	You need to use a number of tools to make sense of it.
You will see a lot of the material in advance.	BUT	You will be presented with **new** data in the exam and you cannot take anything you have done into the exam.
You have plenty of time to prepare.	BUT	You cannot question-spot.
There is not a marking scheme.	BUT	You will be judged on an **'assessment matrix'**.

3 Getting hold of the case

To maximise your chances of passing TOPCIMA you need to prepare thoroughly for it. Your preparation should include a detailed analysis of the pre-seen scenario. Your analysis must enable you to understand the industry featured in the case study, and the issues facing the company described in the pre-seen material. From this, you should prepare real-life examples which you could use to support the arguments you make in your report.

3.1 What is the pre-seen material?

About six weeks in advance of the sitting, you will obtain the case and the assessment matrix from CIMA's website *www.cimaglobal.com*. If you do not have Internet access, you should contact your CIMA local office or Student Services Centre as a matter of urgency because CIMA will not distribute the pre-seen case study by post.

CIMA has stated that the CIMA **pre-seen material** will consist of the following.

Feature	Description
A list of contents	
An introductory scenario	This sets the scene for the case study
A series of 'exhibits' (documents) relevant to the scenario	These could be: • Organisation charts • Biographies of key personnel • Memorandum or report • Minutes of a meeting • Notes made by a colleague • Published accounts • Management accounts • Brochure • Press article • Academic or professional journal article

4 How to use this Study Text

4.1 The design

This Study Text for the TOPCIMA has been designed to familiarise you with the case study format and methodology. We suggest some useful tools to help you make sense of the data and offer a structured approach.

Clearly, if you are taught in a class, your lecturer may want to deal with it in a different way, with good reason. **Your lecturer knows best.** Each case is different, so our approach is non-prescriptive: we offer you tools, not instructions.

4.2 The assessment matrix: Chapter 2

Given that the TOPCIMA exam is so very different from other exams, the first thing you need to do is examine **how it will be marked**. This is the purpose of Chapter 2, where we show you the **assessment matrix** and test you with questions covering each element so you know what the **examiners are expecting**. Knowledge alone is not enough to pass TOPCIMA; you need to apply your knowledge as required.

4.3 Technical knowledge: Chapter 3

The examiner has stated that candidates should be familiar with techniques and theories learned in the strategic level subjects and should be able to use them to solve some of the business problems facing the organisation in the case.

Chapter 3 has a brief revision of a range of business and financial techniques that you should use and incorporate in your answers. However, the techniques we cover in Chapter 3 are not an exhaustive list of the techniques you may need to use in your TOPCIMA exam. You should be prepared to use **any** of the models or theories you have learned during your **CIMA studies as a whole**, but especially during your **strategic level** studies.

4.4 The BPP approach: Chapter 4

Chapter 4 describes our **suggested** approach to tackling TOPCIMA.

(a) We have broken the six weeks between receipt of the case and the exam into a **structured sequence of tasks**. This is **not** meant to be **completely prescriptive** – after all, every case is **different**. However, preparing for the case is like doing a project. It is an axiom of **project management** that establishing a **work breakdown structure is vital for success.** This is what we do in Chapter 4.

(b) The tasks are designed to focus on the **individual criteria** of the assessment matrix, as well as to stimulate your thought processes about the case, so that you become thoroughly familiar with the business situation. However, the tasks **are a set of tools. You do not have to do all of them.**

(c) When faced with the real case, you may **adapt** the BPP approach. Indeed, **always follow your tutor's or lecturer's advice** on this, as each case situation is very different.

(d) We feel that a structured sequence of tasks will reduce your **analytical work to manageable proportions**.

As in Chapter 2, most stages of the approach are accompanied by useful questions and examples to get you thinking, and equally importantly, to give you practice in communication.

PART A TACKLING THE CASE STUDY 1: The Test of Professional Competence in Management Accounting (TOPCIMA)

4.5 Part B: Teaching case: Zubinos

As well as suggesting an approach for you to take, we apply our approach in practice.

We apply **each tool** in the BPP approach to a past case study – Zubinos – and provide examples of 'good' and 'not so good' responses to the data. Then, to enable you to practise your skills on the unseen data, there is the material from a past exam. You will be able to mark your own efforts and compare them with ours.

4.6 Part C: Practice T4 TOPCIMA cases

We reproduce three more cases, with BPP's analysis, the actual unseens and requirements, and suggested answers. Exam practice is vital preparation for TOPCIMA, because you need to build the skills required to write a good answer.

5 Other help from BPP

5.1 Further resources

The **BPP Learning Media T4 TOPCIMA Toolkit** contains a detailed analysis of the pre-seen for your exam, many activities covering all areas of the assessment matrix, and mock unseens with full answers. The Toolkit is developed by BPP's authors and tutors and is available about three weeks **after the pre-seen material is issued**. Our website (www.bpp.com/cima) will contain details. CIMA also offers **on-line case resources** to students.

If you need to revise your **knowledge**, for example when sitting the case study six months after sitting the other strategic level subjects, then **BPP Learning Media Passcards** are the ideal solution.

How you will be marked: the assessment matrix

This chapter covers the most important thing you need to know: the **criteria** by which you will be assessed.

We show you the TOPCIMA guidance on the mark breakdown that will apply to your exam.

We then go through each criterion of the matrix, with brief exercises to get you thinking.

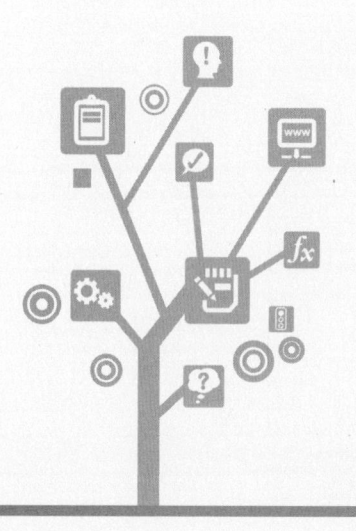

topic list

1 Marking the case study

2 The assessment matrix in detail

1 Marking the case study

1.1 The assessment matrix

The case study is not like a normal exam, and it is not marked like a normal exam either. You know that the requirement (or requirements) may be relatively unstructured. You cannot expect to get 20 marks for Section (a) followed by another ten marks for (b) and so forth. If there is one requirement, you have to consider your performance in the examination as a whole.

A great deal of your success in the exam depends on the quality of the preparation that you do – and this preparation must be targeted at the key issues the examiners are looking for.

It is not easy for the examiners either. How do they assess the higher level skills of synthesis, analysis, evaluation and communication? These all seem quite subjective.

To deal with this problem, CIMA has devised an **assessment matrix**, which will be used to judge your script. This is shown below. Look at it carefully, because an important part of your preparation for the TOPCIMA is identifying how to write an answer which will earn marks against each of the criteria in the matrix. (We will discuss how marks are allocated shortly.)

Criterion	Maximum marks available
Analysis of issues	**(25 marks)**
Technical	5
Application	15
Diversity	5
Strategic choices	**(35 marks)**
Focus	5
Prioritisation	5
Judgement	20
Ethics	5
Recommendations	**(40 marks)**
Logic	30
Integration	5
Ethics	5
Total	**100**

Exam skills

The mark allocations we have shown here are taken from the assessment matrix for the Specimen Paper for the 2010 syllabus, and for the exams to date under this syllabus. Although the headings and marks available are expected to remain constant, the exact mark allocation may change from one exam to another. Make sure you check the exact mark allocation for your exam as part of your preparation. The Assessment criteria is included at the end of the pre-seen material for each exam.

1.2 Awarding the marks

In order to succeed in TOPCIMA, you need to:

1. Use **analytical techniques** to help you analyse the issues in the unseen with relevant reference to the pre-seen material and the industry setting as well as real life parallels of the issues; you will also need to apply your technical knowledge.

2. **Prioritise** the issues and discuss the impact these issues may have on the organisation in the case; you will then need to suggest a range of alternative actions that the organisation could undertake to address the issues. You will need to discuss the impact these issues may have on the organisation. In doing this, you also need to recognise any relevant **ethical implications** of the issues.

3. Make **recommendations** for how to deal with each of the prioritised issues you have discussed earlier.

Marks are awarded for fulfilling each of the three stages according to the criteria shown below.

Analysis of Issues		
Technical	Use relevant theoretical techniques and frameworks and perform relevant calculations to help you to analyse the case material and support your arguments.	5
Application	Use the techniques, frameworks and calculations you have produced to support your analysis of the issues and your choices of actions.	15
Diversity	Display knowledge of relevant real life situations within the same or a similar context as that in which the case is set. Additionally, display knowledge of real life commercial or organisational issues relevant to the situation in the case. These may occur in the industry or organisational setting in which the case is set or in different industries or settings.	5
Total for analysis		25

Strategic Choices		
Focus	Select the issues you feel to be the most important and make sure that you properly address these issues in the report you produce.	5
Prioritisation	Rank the key issues, stating clearly and concisely your rationale to justify your ranking. Issues should be given high priority primarily because of their impact on the organisation in the case. Their urgency may also be a factor. Also, state the issues that you feel deserve a lower priority ranking and give your reasons.	5
Judgement	Exercise commercial and professional judgement to discuss the key issues. Discuss the impact the priority issues have on the organisation. Discuss alternative courses of action, with reasons, that the organisation could take to resolve these issues. Your analysis should include relevant supporting financial analysis.	20

Strategic Choices		
Ethics	Using your judgement, highlight and analyse the ethical issues in the case and state why you consider these issues to have ethical implications. Discuss alternative courses of action that the organisation could take to resolve the issues.	5
Total for strategic choices		35

Recommendations		
Logic	Make clear, well justified recommendations for each of the prioritised issues and ensure the reasoning for the recommended courses of action is clearly stated. The recommendations should follow on logically from the weight of the arguments and choices of actions given earlier in the report.	30
Ethics	Make clear, well justified recommendations for each of the ethical issues and ensure the reasoning for the recommended courses of action is clearly stated. The recommendations should follow on logically from the weight of the arguments you make in your report.	5
Integration	Produce a well-structured report in an appropriate format and linguistic style. These marks are awarded holistically according to the overall quality and functionality of your report.	5
Total for recommendations		40
		100

Exam skills

The total 100 marks will be split 90:10 between main element of the requirement (report) and the second part (slides, memo, e-mail, graph etc.) The second part will be marked as a separate question, and all 10 marks will be given for **logic**.

2 The assessment matrix in detail

2.1 Technical

Although the TOPCIMA is primarily a test of your 'higher skills' of judgement and logic, you do still need to display sound technical knowledge. TOPCIMA directly rewards your technical knowledge and the examiner expects to see it displayed in the exam.

Technical Skills: 'Use relevant theoretical techniques and frameworks and perform relevant calculations to help you analyse the case material and support your arguments.' You have the relevant **detailed subject knowledge** from throughout your earlier CIMA studies, particularly at Strategic Level.

You may need to refresh your knowledge of the important technical areas and these are covered in Chapter 3 of this Text.

Relevant theories that could feature in TOPCIMA exams include:

- SWOT analysis
- PEST analysis (Political, Economic, Social, Technological)
- Porter's five forces
- Porter's generic strategies (Cost Leadership, Differentiation, Focus)
- Porter's value chain
- Industry life cycle (Introductory, Growth, Shakeout, Mature, Decline)
- Ansoff's growth vector matrix
- BCG matrix
- Stakeholder analysis (Mendelow's matrix)
- The balanced scorecard (Financial, Customer, Business Process, Innovation and Learning perspectives)
- Suitability, Acceptability and Feasibility model for strategic option evaluation
- Ratio analysis
- Project appraisal
- Make or buy decisions
- Cash flow forecasts
- Net present value analysis
- Business valuations
- Change management models (force field analysis; unfreeze-change-freeze; growth models)
- Project management techniques

Marks are awarded for the breadth of technical theories you present. But writing out theory takes a long time for very few extra marks.

Exam skills

Ensure you:

- Select technical theories that make a contribution to your reader's understanding of the situation of the firm. Technical marks can also be awarded for the use of numerical techniques (such as NPV or cash flow forecasts) in this respect.

- Limit yourself to two or three pieces of technical theory – because the mark allocation is too little to justify spending more time than this

- Present technical theories as **Appendices** to your report, eg Appendix 1 – SWOT Analysis, Appendix 2 – Stakeholder analysis, Appendix 3 – Cash flow forecast. However, make sure you cross-reference these Appendices to the main body of your report.

The quality and inclusion of relevant calculations will gain additional marks under the application criteria.

2.2 Application

Application 'Use the techniques, frameworks and calculations you have produced to support your analysis of the issues and your choices of actions.' You can demonstrate how to **use** technical knowledge.

This criterion overlaps the Technical Knowledge criterion. BPP's belief is that in practice they are assessed together.

The main skills rewarded are:

- Ability to conduct financial analysis of issues in the case
- Ability to apply the technical theory above to shed light on the case

Financial analysis could involve, for example:

- Calculation of NPV of projects, often with probabilities
- Ratio analysis (eg calculating gearing)
- Updating a cash flow or profit forecast
- Preparing or commenting on a business valuation

Non-financial applications could include:

- Relating analysis of issues, options and recommendations to elements in the SWOT analysis
- Explaining falling profitability in terms of the intensification of the 5 Forces (Porter)
- Warning of the risks of an overseas venture by reference to PEST analysis
- Applying Balanced Scorecard to developing a performance related pay scheme

Numerical skills are an important part of the T4 exam, and it may be possible to score 15 marks in the 'Application' criteria for numerical analysis alone. The techniques required will all be techniques that you have learnt already, so the key issues here are these:

(a) Do calculations that are **relevant** to your analysis and conclusions, and that **add value** (eg by clarifying the position or evaluating solutions).

(b) Explain your calculations and present your workings clearly.

Exam skills

(a) Don't waste time doing detailed, unnecessary calculations at the expense of discussion. Make sensible assumptions to save time and cover any lack of knowledge of more complex techniques eg WACC is 10%.

(b) The case study fundamentally tests higher level skills, not arithmetic. **So, can you afford to get your sums wrong?**

Yes and No. Although marks aren't specifically allocated for numerical skills, if your numerical skills are poor, this will **reflect badly** on your **overall ability to present sensible, well argued conclusions** – in other words you will not be fit to be let loose on unsuspecting businesses as a chartered management accountant.

As you have come this far in your exams, this is unlikely. Any errors of this nature are likely to be caused by panic.

As the case study draws on all strategic level papers, you may need to apply some knowledge of financial management.

In your **preparation** for the exam, and in your review of the 'pre-seen' material, you need to use your numerical skills to become properly acquainted with the organisation's situation and financial position. We will provide a checklist of the type of questions you should be asking in Chapter 5.

Exam skills

To make the point again. 'While numerical skills are important, being able to comment on the significance of the figures is even more important.' Remember also that it will not be necessary to try to study the entire CIMA syllabus again, as you will be able to identify any relevant knowledge areas from the pre-seen material.

Ensure you:

- Refer to your technical theory appendices in the main body of your report (if you are asked to write a report)
- Provide a formal numerical analysis of options, cash flow forecasts etc
- Present your financial workings as separate appendices to your report
- Refer in the main body of the report to the key figures and conclusions from your financial analysis
- Remember that you are not permitted to conduct calculations during the 20 minutes reading time allowed

Question — Using numerical data

Iolinda Co is a biotechnology company about to be listed on a stock market. It has used genetic manipulation (GM) technology to generate a species of rose that is impervious to being attacked by insects, such as aphids. The company is very confident that the new rose will be a huge market success, but needs to conduct trials in plant nurseries. Of course, these trials may have unintended consequences. There is a risk that the trials may fail and/or that environmentalists will disrupt them. Iolinda does have some other valuable patents, in GM technology for farmers, but this is the first time it will market directly to consumers as opposed to other businesses. Consumers and the gardening public will, in effect, be propagating GM plants.

The venture capital firms which have financed Iolinda want to recover their investment by selling shares. Other biotechnology companies have no difficulties in raising equity. However, the share prices of biotechnology firms have been quite volatile in relation to the market as a whole, with some spectacular successes and failures. Iolinda intends to float whatever the outcome of the rose project.

Required

In this question, you are going to **adopt the role of the examiner**. What **numerical analysis** would you like to see done, if you gave the student the following information?

(1) Historic data on likely success/failure of trials of GM products (ie failure rate pre-launch)

(2) Cash flows required for the trials pre-launch

(3) Proposed pricing strategy (eg penetration or skimming strategies) and sales forecast; distribution and marketing costs assuming launch is successful; comparative volumes in relation to other products

(4) Projected EPS for the company as a whole, or similar information from the prospectus

(5) Interest rates

(6) Market values, dividend levels and yields, and betas of similar companies

> **Solution**

The examiner might expect you to investigate the following.

The **historic success rate** for GM product trials might give an idea of **risk**. You may also need to consider the risk that the **political climate** opposed to GM products may significantly reduce the sales turnover. All this will be relevant to **investment appraisal**.

If significant cash flows are involved, you may be required to prepare **cash budgets.**

The proposed pricing strategy will give an idea of what cash flows might be expected and hence you could estimate the significance of the rose trial in the **overall product portfolio**.

With suitable information you might analyse the **risk** of the project, and use the **beta**, if it meets the relevant tests.

2.3 Diversity

KEY TERM

Diversity: 'Display knowledge of relevant real life situations within the same or a similar context as that in which the case is set. Additionally, display knowledge of real life commercial or organisational issues relevant to the situation in the case. These may occur in the industry or organisational setting in which the case is set or in different industries or settings'. A wide range of views and knowledge is reflected. Remember that the T4 TOPCIMA exam is designed as a multi-disciplinary case study.

This criterion rewards you bringing for (relevant) real-life examples into your final report and requires you to have an understanding of the industry setting, ie **business awareness.**

Real life examples can include:

- Knowledge of legislation or other factors affecting the industry featured in the Pre-seen
- Illustration of issues by reference to real-world firms in the same industry
- Discussion of general business issues by reference to other firms

Exam skills

To gain marks under this criterion you should:

- Mention the names of real-world firms in the same industry, their real-world customers and suppliers, and the laws and policies they face
- Establish the relevance to the issues in the exam of any real-world fact you bring in
- Avoid excessive name dropping just for the sake of it

There will probably be one mark available per comment so five marks for diversity will require five good comments.

Why is **business awareness** relevant to the case study?

(a) The case study is normally set in an **industry context**, such as manufacturing or services. Each business context poses different questions. Remember that most of the developed economies in the western world are heavily orientated round the **service sector**.

(b) Case studies will be **realistic and representative** of the industry sector under consideration. **They do not, however, have to be based on a real company.**

(c) The **case study may not be set in an identified country.** This decision is entirely CIMA's, so that students will not be prejudiced if they do not live in the country where the case is set. So, you are likely to encounter imaginary countries such as Veeland, Aland, etc. However, be aware the use of imaginary countries could limit your ability to cite political or social factors if you do not have sufficient information about the country or context of the question.

How can you attain business awareness?

(a) **In general**

- Read the business press, such as the *Economist*, the *Financial Times* or the business pages of papers such as the *Times*, the *Guardian*, the *Independent* or the *Daily Telegraph*
- Read *Financial Management* and other CIMA magazines
- Look at websites such as bbc.co.uk, timesonline.co.uk, www.bized.co.uk

(b) **For the TOPCIMA exam**

- Use the Internet to research the industry and similar organisations (once you've seen the pre-seen and know what industry and organisation you're dealing with)
- Take a look at any specialist trade journals
- Obtain a company report from a firm in the industry
- See Chapter 4 for more detail about how to explore the case study scenario

Exploiting business awareness

(a) So what to do with all this knowledge? At the very least:

- Try to understand the main **cost** and **revenue drivers** of the industry
- Do a brief **five forces** analysis (Porter)
- Who are the main customers of the industry's products (consumers or organisations)?

(b) Be sensitive to the **size** of the business. A corner shop with two people is very different from a large supermarket.

(c) What **terminology** does the industry use? For example lawyers have 'clients'. From the case data, or from your research, you should be able to identify any generic terms.

(d) Remember that most business decisions are **uncertain**. You will only have limited information and, if a lack of information means decisions will be riskier, you should say so. However, you will always be given enough information on the key issues.

(e) Make sure your examples are relevant.

Exam skills

In order to score marks, your examples must be specifically relevant to the case, and applied to the case: for example, to indicate how the issue in your example could influence a recommendation you are making in your answer. However, simply listing lots of unconnected examples and failing to apply them to the case will not earn you marks.

2.4 Focus

Focus: 'Select the issues you feel to be the most important and make sure that you properly address these issues in the report you produce'.

KEY TERM

Remember that a lot of the pre-seen and unseen material will turn out to be **irrelevant to the key issues**. You need to identify the relevant key data and issues in the case material, ie what really matters.

In the exam you will face ten or so problems from which you must select and focus on four or five. You should not waste time talking too much about the rest.

The issues to focus on break down into:

(a) One or more **short-term 'emergency' issues** that must be dealt with quickly, eg:

- Imminent strike action that will halt production and let down valuable clients
- Running out of a key supply that will leave shelves empty and lose customer goodwill
- Fire that destroys capacity, delivery inventories and financial records
- A public relations disaster that must be headed off quickly
- A hostile approach by a predator company
- Loss of a key member of management
- Loss of key contract that means firm must cut costs quickly
- Potential breaching of borrowing limits with the bank that may lead to foreclosure.

These are usually introduced in the Unseen material.

(b) **Investment or other strategic options** that must be evaluated in relation to deeper background issues affecting the ability of the firm to prosper in the future, eg intensifying competition destroying margins in the industry:

- Firm lacks the finance and management structure and skills to grow
- Inappropriate portfolio of businesses that need to be scaled down to a core business

These background issues can often be seen in the Pre-seen material and the decisions presented in the Unseen are there to test your appreciation of them.

(c) Some **ethical issues** that management should be alerted to, eg:

- Discovery that managers have been bribing people to win contracts or get legal favours
- Mistreatment of staff over pay, or of dismissals
- Misleading statements made to customers
- Unsafe or socially undesirable manufacturing processes
- Products issues of Corporate Social Responsibility (CSR) affecting the business

Exam skills

To gain marks under the Focus criterion you must:

- Cover these key issues in more depth in your answer rather than spreading your coverage equally across all the issues
- Explain the significance of these issues, ie why they are key
- Make clear recommendations on what to do about these issues

The examiner recommends setting up a 'check list' of report headings, to ensure that all of the key data and issues in the case material have been discussed.

Question — Knowledge

Bovine Burgers (BB) is a chain of fast food restaurants with branches across the whole world. BB are considering changing their burger-manufacturing system from **heating** the burgers on a flat hotplate to **flame grilling** them. This will mean a significant change to the way the firm prepares and sells burgers, and a change to the equipment in each shop. BB must purchase and distribute this equipment. BB denotes each shop as a profit centre.

Your boss has asked for your views as to the strategic management accounting implications of the switch in burger-making technology.

PART A TACKLING THE CASE STUDY 2: How you will be marked: the assessment matrix

Required

Identify which of the following concepts are relevant to Bovine Burgers and why.

Technical	Application: Relevant? Yes/Perhaps?/No	Focus: Why is it relevant (or not)?
Transfer pricing		
ABC		
WACC		
Marketing mix		
DCF		
JIT		
5 Forces		
McFarlan matrix		
SWOT		
ROI		
TQM		

Solution

Technical	Application: Relevant? Yes/Perhaps?/No	Focus: Why is it relevant (or not)?
Transfer pricing	Perhaps	Head office will be transferring equipment over the world to divisions.
ABC	Yes	New grilling method involves new cooking activities and possibly different cost drivers.
WACC	No	Unless you are asked to do a project appraisal and are given WACC as the discount rate, you can ignore this.
Marketing mix	Perhaps	The change to the new grill may require more marketing spend, hence a different focus.
DCF	Perhaps	You may use DCF for appraising the strategy.
JIT	No	Fast food is already just in time, and JIT is not really relevant to this context.

Technical	Application: Relevant? Yes/Perhaps?/No	Focus: Why is it relevant (or not)?
5 Forces	No	Not relevant to **what you have been asked to do** – no competitors are mentioned.
McFarlan matrix	No	Nothing at all about the use of information systems.
SWOT	No	Too generic and high level for this question.
ROI	Yes	Each shop is a profit centre.
TQM	Perhaps	A brand such as Bovine Burgers needs to offer **consistent** product and service quality.

Refresh your knowledge of these concepts from Chapter 3 if you need to.

2.5 Prioritisation

Prioritisation – 'Rank the key issues, stating clearly and concisely your rationale to justify your ranking.

Issues should be given high priority primarily because of their **impact** on the organisation in the case. Their **urgency** may also be a factor. Also, state the issues that you feel deserve a lower priority ranking and give your reasons.'

In short, to prioritise is to put items in a **logical order of importance, based on a clear rationale**. For example, if you are washed up on a desert island from a shipwreck, the underlying **rationale** for anything you do, initially, will be survival. Assuming you have no injuries, your first priority will be to find clean drinking water, and then food: this is because human beings can go without food for longer than without drinking water.

Exam skills

The examiner will have identified which issues he or she considers to be key, and will expect to see these in the first few issues of your prioritised report. Although there is no 'right' or 'wrong' answer in the context of TOPCIMA overall, if you fail to prioritise the key issues it will be more difficult to pass the paper. Prioritisation is a difficult skill to master, and you should practise prioritisation of issues in as many case studies as possible.

CIMA have indicated that if a candidate fails to identify as major issues those issues which the examiner ranks as 1st or 2nd priority, that candidate will find it difficult to score a pass mark overall.

In order to gain good marks your answer must be prioritised throughout.

At the beginning of your report (assuming you are asked to write a report)

- Identify and state the **key issues** in priority order
- Explain **why** they are key issues and why you have put them in the order they appear
- You should aim to identify **FOUR KEY ISSUES** in the main report.

In the body of your report

- Discuss each issue in a separate section so that your answer demonstrates depth of analysis
- Save time and keep focus by not wasting time writing lots about issues that are not priorities
- Keep Ethics issues in a section of their own

At the end of your report

- Give recommendations on what to do about the most important issues
- State **why** you have made your recommendations. Do not just list them: **justify** them

2.5.1 Elements to consider (possible bases for prioritising issues)

Timescale:	Short-term	Long-term
Scale of impact:	Significant	Not significant
Risk:	High	Low

Exam skills

Note that a short-term problem (running out of cash) can have a significant impact and be a high risk. Anything fundamental to the survival of the business is important.

Remember **impact** and **urgency** are the key tests for prioritisation, as illustrated in the following

PART A TACKLING THE CASE STUDY

2: How you will be marked: the assessment matrix

importance / urgency matrix:

	Strategic importance Low	Strategic importance High
Urgency High	Lower priority	Highest priority (major issues)
Urgency Low	Other issues (lowest priority)	High priority (but not as high as major issues)

Question — Prioritisation

In 2000, BMW pulled out of car manufacturing in the UK. It sold most of its investment in Rover Cars to another firm, with the Land Rover division going to Ford.

Here are some of the factors and issues surrounding the decision.

- Rover lost £750m in 1999.

- £150m of aid from the UK government to BMW was under threat from the European commission, given its concern over state subsidies.

- At the time, the pound sterling exchange rate was very high compared to the euro, making goods exported from the UK to Europe very expensive for European buyers.

- 10,000 jobs in Rover were at risk, as were 40,000 supplier jobs in the West Midlands. BMW spent a lot of time and money on 'the English patient' since buying it.

- BMW had invested in Rover to enable BMW to become a volume car manufacturer as opposed to a niche maker of executive cars.

- BMW is the 14th largest motor manufacturer in an industry that has been consolidating recently.

- It was uncertain if the UK would abandon the pound sterling and adopt the Euro as its currency.

- Rover lost market share in the UK from 13.5% to 6% over the 5 years up to 2000. Too few British buyers were buying Rover Cars.

- BMW could be vulnerable to a takeover.

- The main BMW brand was suffering at the time.

What might have been BMW's priorities in reaching the decision? Show a rationale.

Solution (1) Clear pass

Rationale

Survival of BMW. BMW's management wished to preserve BMW as a successful, independent company, and considered that future involvement with Rover would jeopardise this aim.

Key issues underlying the decision:

Priority – importance	Justification
1 Stem losses: no prospect of future profitability	**Future**. BMW had invested a lot in Rover, but what concerned them was the future – future incremental cash flows were negative. Rover had been losing market share in the UK. Exports had tailed off because of the high level of sterling. New products had not been successful.
2 Concentrate on BMW brand	**External**. Too much management attention had been focused on Rover. No evidence existed that this had hit BMW brand yet, but managers were concerned about this.
3 Compete elsewhere: consolidation of motor industry	**External**. Motor firms are merging into larger groups – the reason why BMW bought Rover.

The answer above has a clear rationale and the relative importance of each item is shown.

Solution (2) Clear fail

- Rover lost £750m in 1999.
- The exchange rate was not favourable and so cars were expensive.
- Rover had been losing market share.
- BMW wanted to concentrate on building the BMW brand.

This answer is a clear fail because it does not clearly specify the **rationale** behind the decision, which is that Rover will be a **future** drain of cash for BMW, and that investing in Rover will prevent BMW from protecting its brand.

The first three bullet points are background information not priorities. **Priorities involve taking action**.

If you have difficulty, use the grid below as a guide to prioritisation (with some possible applications to the BMW example above).

	Important	Not important
Urgent (must be done now)	Top priority (stem cash losses)	Mid-priority (state aid?)
Not urgent (can be done later)	Mid-priority (eg protect BMW brand)	Bottom priority (eg UK not participating in Single Currency)

Exam skills

In BPP's experience, most students are weak in the 'prioritisation' area, and they struggle to separate key issues from less important ones.

Being able to prioritise and make recommendations is vitally important to passing TOPCIMA. The key strategic issues in a case should be clearly identified and discussed in a priority order, and you should **justify** your choice of priority.

Remember, you should aim to identify **four main issues** from the case to prioritise and discuss. However, you should keep any purely **ethical issues separate**, and discuss them in the 'Ethical issues' section of your report.

2.6 Judgement

Judgment: 'Exercise commercial and professional judgement to discuss the key issues. Discuss the impact the priority issues have on the organisation. Discuss alternative courses of action, with reasons, that the organisation could take to resolve these issues. Your analysis should include relevant supporting financial analysis.'

Focus and prioritisation concern issues. You show judgement by coming up with **solutions** to the issues raised. You will be rewarded for **breadth** of discussion and a 'business sense' of what is being said.

Judgement can be seen as the link between the discussion of the issues and the recommendations.

(a) When identifying strategic options, you might
    (i) Pick out clues from the case
    (ii) Use strategic models to develop ideas

(b) When it comes to evaluating and ranking choices, you could assess them in terms of their

    Suitability, acceptability and feasibility; incorporating
    (i) SWOT
    (ii) cost-benefit analysis
    (iii) stakeholder mapping

(c) You need to demonstrate a good commercial understanding of how the organisation in the case could enhance shareholder value.

Exam skills

To display good judgement in your answer you should:

- Evaluate options using the terms suitability, acceptability and feasibility explicitly
- Ensure each recommendation is justified by showing how it addresses the problems you explained in your analysis of the issues
- Justify your recommendations by reference to the experiences of real-world firms or practical examples
- Write your report (or whatever form of communication is required) using a depth of explanation and language appropriate to the situation of the people it is addressed to.

2.7 Logic

Logic: 'Make clear, well justified recommendations for each of the prioritised issues and ensure the reasoning for the recommended courses of action is clearly stated. The recommendations should follow on logically from the weight of the arguments and choices of actions given earlier in the report.'

To get good marks under this criterion ensure:

- **Recommendations appear at the end of the report** not at the end of each sub-section 'because a recommendation cannot be made until all of the other issues are discussed and assessed, as many are competing for the same scarce resources – manpower and finance'

- **Recommendations include a justification**. The reason for recommending the course of action should be justified by reference back to the urgency of the issue and the analysis you have presented of it

- Each recommendation you make should include:
    - **What** to do (action)
    - **Why** to do it (justification), and
    - **How** to do it.

Sometimes you may also need to comment **when** a recommendation should be implemented, **who** should be responsible for implementing it, and what **impact** it will have on the organisation.

- **Recommendations must deal with the priority issues** at least

Note that although there are 30 marks available in total for 'logic', these are split into 20 for the main report and 10 for the supplementary elements (slides, memo, e-mail etc.)

2.7.1 Logic – Question 2 (10 marks)

The second part of the requirement (worth 10 marks) will be marked as a separate entity. All the marks will be awarded for logic.

To score well here, you need to provide a clear and succinct analysis of the issue identified in the requirement. Marks will be awarded for the **clarity** and **relevance** of the analysis you provide.

Make sure you use the format prescribed by the question (eg slides, memo, email, graph or chart), and show any calculations as an appendix. In particular, avoid putting too much detail on a slide; if it is going to be presented to an audience it needs to be clear for the audience to read.

Exam skills

The issue which forms the basis of part (b) of the requirement will be one of the top four issues prioritised in part (a) of the report.

2.8 Ethics

Ethics refer to notions of 'right' and 'wrong'. In a business context, the impact of a company's strategic decisions will have an ethical implication (eg child labour, pollution, wage rates, dealing openly and fairly with stakeholders, suppliers, customers etc). The concept of 'corporate social responsibility' (CSR) is particularly relevant.

CIMA has published its own Code of Ethics for Professional Accountants which applies to all CIMA members and students from 1st January 2006. There are five fundamental principles in the Code: **integrity; objectivity; professional competence and due care; confidentiality;** and **professional behaviour**. Full details of the Code are available on CIMA's website (www.cimaglobal.com).

You will need to **identify** the ethical issues and then briefly justify **why** the issue has an ethical dimension. You should then offer **realistic advice** on how to resolve the ethical issues.

Ethical issues may include (but are not limited to) the following:

- **Personal and professional ethics:** obligations as a Chartered Management Accountant (as highlighted in CIMA's Code of Ethics)

- **Business ethics:** duty to shareholders, duty to other stakeholders, commercial tactics, treatment of customers, treatment of employees and responsibility for their safety, and responsibility for impact of business on society at large through pollution, unemployment, or denial of access to essential services

- **Corporate governance:** the quality and behaviour of the Board. It also involves things like the integrity of the management accounting control system, existence of internal controls and the quality of the management and staff

- **Corporate social responsibility:** beyond simply meeting the needs of shareholders to embrace wider social responsibilities. This might involve impact on future generations, responsibility for public safety, need to give opportunities to less-advantaged groups in society. The issue of **sustainability** could also be important here.

- **Ethical systems**: whether the organisation has adequate systems in place for detection of significant ethical issues and ensuring compliance with internal and external codes of conduct.

It is most likely that there will be 2-3 ethical issues in your exam, although CIMA has indicated that there could only be one.

It is vital that you **distinguish between the ethical issues and the commercial issues** which the organisation in your exam is facing. Ethical issues can usually be described as issues under the following moral principles:

- **Fairness**: this means treating someone as they deserve to be treated or as you would wish to be treated if you were in their position. Therefore discrimination, poor pay, summary dismissal, or refusal of reasonable requests for assistance are unfair. Deliberately distorting competition or taking advantage of a customer's ignorance or desperate position is unfair. Some of these are also illegal, and many would give rise to commercially-damaging publicity. However, these things happen. But society recognises the practices as ethically wrong and wants to stamp them out.

- **Justice**: this means going through a proper process, involving weighing up the evidence and arguments and coming to a balanced decision and a measured response. Therefore things like sacking someone without hearing what they have to say, or ignoring their side of the story, is unjust. So is punishing someone harshly for a minor wrong, even if the rules lay down that punishment. In such a case, the rules and the punishment are both unjust. Justice and Fairness overlap so don't waste time in the exam trying to distinguish them.

- **Honesty and straightforwardness**: this is as basic as telling the truth and not withholding important information, or trying to use loopholes to escape responsibilities. It also covers taking assets or value belonging to other people. This principle covers things like corruption, misrepresentation, deliberately misleading wording, and selling someone something unsuitable.

- **Duty, responsibility and integrity**: as a citizen you have duties - such as to obey the law, report crime and so on. As an employee you take on other duties that flow from your job and you are paid to do them and put in a position of trust by your superiors or the people that voted you into the post. Therefore you must put personal interest aside and act as the role requires you to do. Any attempt by you to make someone else forget their duty and responsibility, such as by making bribes or threats, is also an unethical action by you too.

Question — Ethics

The notion of 'corporate social responsibility' suggests that organisations should consider the good of the wider community (both global and local) within which they operate (ie not just the interests of customers and profitability). The notion of 'corporate citizenship' is also becoming increasingly important. Why are consumers looking for businesses to demonstrate a wider ethical commitment to society?

Solution

Here are a few suggestions. Ethics in business has been described as a 'bandwagon' gaining momentum.

- Consumers are increasingly aware of the issues eg fair trade, child labour, advertising standards
- High profile ecological problems, highlighting issues around environmental sustainability
- Consumers tend to be cynical of big business claims — ethical 'badges' need to be genuine
- Treatment of employees is a high-profile area
- Human resource management policies often embrace the application of ethical principles

- Word-of-mouth is becoming very important, especially in the Internet age: many people will recommend (or avoid) a company because of its ethically responsible (or otherwise) reputation
- Government pressure

Exam skills

You should have noted from the assessment matrix we showed earlier that five marks are available for **identifying** the ethical issues and five marks for making **recommendations** on how to deal with them.

To gain good marks from the Ethics section of the assessment matrix you should:

- Identify the ethical issues along with other issues at the start of your report
- Cover 'Ethical issues' as a separate section of your report. Do not include discussion of ethical issues amongst the discussion of priority issues.
- Ensure you state the issue (eg dismissal of a sick employee) and the ethical principle (eg 'fairness of treatment')
- Discuss the implications of the issue (eg who would suffer as a result of it)
- Advise management on the options available to them to resolve the issue, and make appropriate recommendations about the course of action to take
- Make recommendations on ethical matters in the 'Ethical issues' section of your report rather than in the main recommendations section

2.9 Integration

Integration: 'Produce a well-structured report in an appropriate format and linguistic style.

These marks are awarded holistically according to the overall quality and functionality of your report.

This means that you have considered the diverse issues seriously and critically, have elaborated on them and combined them into a sensible whole. It overlaps other criteria such as Technical, Application, Judgement and Logic.

Key data calculated or presented in appendices must be discussed further in the main body of the report. The report should flow well and be in a logical sequence. This allows markers to use their discretion based on the 'professional feel' of the overall report and its fitness for purpose.

2.9.1 Structuring business communications

Too often, you can be let down by poor communication. Throughout this Study Text, you will be given opportunities to practise your skills in this respect.

We will cover the format and structure of **reports** in Chapter 6 but here are some things to keep in mind. The examiner has proposed the following structure for any business communication, whatever the format.

Introduction: be brief

Contents: identification of issues and evaluation of each issue from all relevant perspectives

Conclusions: cross reference these back to the appropriate section

Recommendations: This is the most important section, making clear and justified recommendations on all of the issues identified.

Appendices: detailed calculations and supporting analysis, cross referenced to the appropriate section.

PART A TACKLING THE CASE STUDY   2: How you will be marked: the assessment matrix

Question
Conclusions

You're the examiner!

Context

Bastable Co is a firm specialising in the manufacture of balloons for recreational use and advertising. The firm is now considering manufacturing airships, filled with helium, as an environmentally-friendly alternative to airplanes. Each airship will offer berths for forty people, competing with sea cruises. Airship manufacture will involve raising money from investors. Bastable is facing competition in its core markets, mainly from firms which exploit new materials to produce lighter balloons that are cheaper to operate.

Two conclusions to student scripts ended as follows.

Script 1

> *Conclusion*
>
> Choices available to Bastable
>
> 1   Manufacture airships alone
> 2   Go into a joint venture with another manufacturer to manufacture airships
>
> *Recommendation*
>
> Option 1 is chosen. It generates a positive NPV and opens up new markets and business opportunities, without the firm sacrificing these benefits to a joint venture partner.

Script 2

> Bastable should not manufacture airships. Even if a joint venture partner is chosen, the NPV of the project does not look attractive enough in relation to the other option which is to focus on balloons and on the competitive threats.

As the examiner, how would you mark them?

Solution

Neither of the scripts would indicate a clear pass, for the micro-case situation we have described, but for different reasons.

Script 1 – does not judge all the alternatives – one of which is not to go ahead. The positive NPV is not compared with other uses of the funds. There is a problem with content and analysis. However, in terms of presentation, the options are clearly numbered, and the recommendation is clear, separately identified and justified.

Script 2 – does actually address the alternatives: manufacture or not manufacture airships, and shows evidence of greater judgement in comparing all the options. However it mixes up a conclusion and a recommendation and is not presented well.

Exam skills

To gain marks under the integration criterion you should ensure:

- Anything you cite as an issue, an opportunity or a threat also appears in your SWOT analysis
- The recommendations section has a sub-section of several paragraphs dealing with each of the main issues in the Unseen and Pre-seen material
- Your detailed calculations and analysis in the appendices are referred to in the main body of the report

Although we cannot guarantee you will have to produce your answer in a report format, evidence from past papers suggests it is highly likely that you will.

We will look at how to write a report in Chapter 6.

Technical knowledge

This chapter is for you to use if you need a reminder of any key knowledge areas from your previous CIMA studies.

It is designed as a brief reminder and if there are any areas you find difficult, you should refer to the relevant textbooks you have used previously.

Please note, however, that TOPCIMA does not rely solely on the Strategic Level syllabus to provide the appropriate techniques and models which you could use in your answer. You could be expected to use techniques and models from across your CIMA studies as a whole.

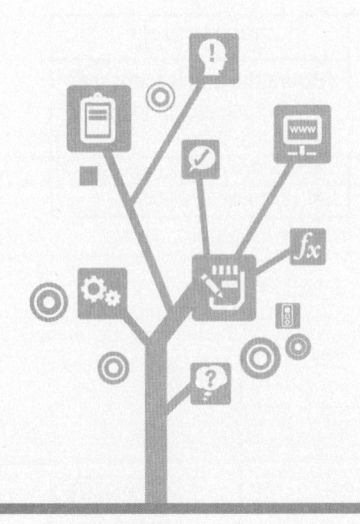

topic list

1 Technical knowledge in TOPCIMA

2 Business strategy (Enterprise strategy)

3 Risk and control strategy (Performance strategy)

4 Financial strategy

1 Technical knowledge in TOPCIMA

We explained in Chapter 2 that TOPCIMA directly rewards your technical knowledge and the examiner expects to see it displayed in the exam.

However, remember you will only be given marks if technical knowledge is **relevant** to your analysis and recommendations and **applied** in an analytical and practical way.

The topics in this chapter have been selected based on requirements from past TOPCIMA Case Study exams. However, we must stress that the analysis you may need to do in your exam may not be limited to these topics or models. You should be prepared to apply any of the techniques and models you have learned during your CIMA studies as a whole.

2 Business strategy (Enterprise strategy)

2.1 The rational model of strategic planning

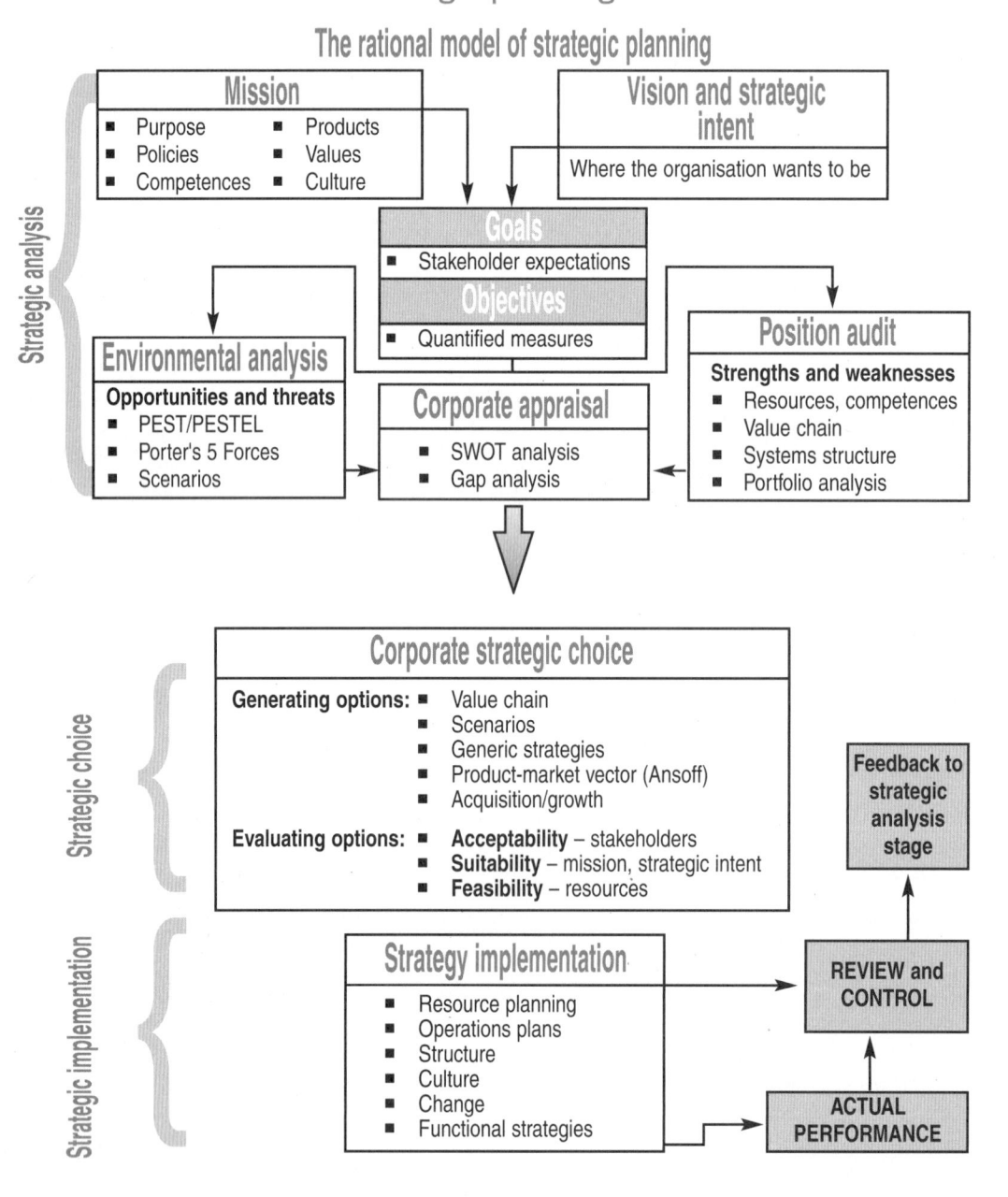

The rational model of strategic planning

Strategic analysis

Mission
- Purpose
- Policies
- Competences
- Products
- Values
- Culture

Vision and strategic intent
- Where the organisation wants to be

Goals
- Stakeholder expectations

Objectives
- Quantified measures

Environmental analysis
Opportunities and threats
- PEST/PESTEL
- Porter's 5 Forces
- Scenarios

Corporate appraisal
- SWOT analysis
- Gap analysis

Position audit
Strengths and weaknesses
- Resources, competences
- Value chain
- Systems structure
- Portfolio analysis

Strategic choice

Corporate strategic choice

Generating options:
- Value chain
- Scenarios
- Generic strategies
- Product-market vector (Ansoff)
- Acquisition/growth

Evaluating options:
- **Acceptability** – stakeholders
- **Suitability** – mission, strategic intent
- **Feasibility** – resources

Strategic implementation

Strategy implementation
- Resource planning
- Operations plans
- Structure
- Culture
- Change
- Functional strategies

REVIEW and CONTROL

ACTUAL PERFORMANCE

Feedback to strategic analysis stage

2.2 Industry analysis

2.2.1 PEST analysis

A framework for analysing the environment is PEST.

Political/legal factors

Many aspects of business activity are subject to legal regulation:

- Contract
- Health and safety
- Data protection
- Employment
- Tax
- Consumer protection

Other aspects are regulated by supervisory bodies. The EU is a significant influence.

Economic factors

These operate in both a national and international context. Relevant factors include:

- Inflation rates
- Employment rates
- Interest rates
- Capital markets
- Savings levels
- Exchange rates
- The business cycle
- International trade

Government policy
- Fiscal policy (taxes, borrowing, spending)
- Monetary policy (interest rates, exchange rates)
- Size and scope of the public sector

Social factors

Demography is the study of human population and population trends

Demographic factors such as birth rate, average age, ethnicity, death rate, family structure have clear implications for patterns of demand and availability of labour.

Culture in society is as important as organisational culture in a business

Cultural factors include language, religion, custom, music and literature. TV is a vital aspect in culture. Business must be particularly aware of **cultural change**.

Technological factors

Many strategies are based on exploiting technological change (eg Internet trading). Others are defences against such change (eg emphasising service or quality when a competitor introduces a major technical development).

Technological developments affect all aspects of business (especially IT developments)

- New products and services become available
- New methods of production and service provision
- Improved handling of information in sales and finance
- New organisation structures to exploit technology
- New media for communication with customers and within the business (eg Internet)

2.2.2 Porter's Five Forces Analysis

Porter says that **five forces** together determine the long term profit potential of an **industry**

Bargaining power of suppliers

Depends on:
- Number of suppliers
- Threats to suppliers industry
- Number of customers in the industry
- Scope for substitution
- Switching costs
- Selling skills

Suppliers seek **higher prices**

Threat of new entrants

This is limited by **barriers to entry**
- Scale economies
- Switching costs
- Patent rights
- Product differentiation
- Access to distribution
- Access to resources

Rivalry among current competitors

Depends on:
- Market growth
- Spare capacity
- Uncertainty about competitor's strategy
- Buyers ease of switching
- Exit barriers

Threat from substitute products

A substitute is produced by a different industry but satisfies the same needs

Bargaining power of customers

Depends on:
- Volume bought
- Scope for substitution
- Switching costs
- Purchasing skills
- Importance of quality

Customers seek **lower prices**

2.2.3 Globalisation

Changes in the world market place
- Globalisation of business and customers
- Science and technology developments
- Mergers, acquisitions and alliances
- Scrutiny of business decisions
- Changing business practices and relationships

Caused by
- Liberalisation of trade
- International capital markets
- Newly industrialised countries
- Regional groupings, eg EU
- Developing countries

Effects
- Lower barriers to entry
- Opportunities to compete abroad
- Opportunities to invest abroad
- Opportunities to raise finance overseas

2.2.4 Industry life cycle

	Introduction	Growth	Maturity/shakeout	Decline
Products	Basic, no standards established	Better, more sophisticated, differentiated	Superior, standardised	Varied quality but fairly undifferentiated
Competitors	None to few	Many entrants	Competition increases, weaker players leave	Few remain. Competition may be on price
Buyers	Early adopters, prosperous, curious must be induced	More customers attracted and aware	Mass market, brand switching common	Enthusiasts, traditionalists, sophisticates
Profits	Negative – high first mover advantage	Increasing, as sales increase rapidly	High, but beginning to decline	Falling, as sales and prices have fallen
Objectives & Strategy	Build product awareness Dominate market, build quality	Try to maximise market share React to competitors with marketing spend	Maximise profit while defending market share Cost reductions sought	Control costs Possibly harvest or divest

PART A TACKLING THE CASE STUDY 3: Technical knowledge

2.3 Resource analysis

2.3.1 Position audit

Position audit

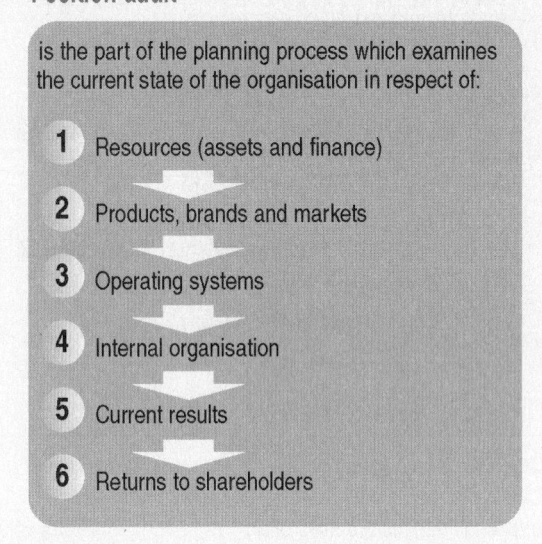

is the part of the planning process which examines the current state of the organisation in respect of:

1. Resources (assets and finance)
2. Products, brands and markets
3. Operating systems
4. Internal organisation
5. Current results
6. Returns to shareholders

2.3.2 The Ms model

This divides the items in a position audit into factors beginning with 'M'.

Resource	Example
Machinery	Age. Condition and utilisation of assets. Technologically up-to-date? Cost. Patents. Goodwill. Brands.
Make-up	Culture and structure. Brands. Patents.
Management	Skills, experience and vision of senior management. Loyalty. Career progression. Structure.
Management information	Ability to generate and disseminate ideas. Information systems (including databases; data warehouses.) Availability of information to support strategic decision-making.
Markets	Products and customers. Markets and market segments the organisation operates in. Position of the organisation and its products/services in those markets.
Materials	Relationships with suppliers. Quality and reliability of inputs. Waste. New materials. Cost. Availability. Future provision. Security of supply.
Men and women	Human resources. Number of staff. Skills. Wage costs (as a proportion of total costs.) Efficiency. Labour turnover. Industrial relations. Staff morale.
Methods	How are activities carried out? Outsourcing, networking, JIT.
Money	What is the organisation's cash position? Credit and turnover periods. Cash surpluses/deficits. Short term and long term finance. Gearing levels. Investment plans.

2.3.3 SWOT analysis

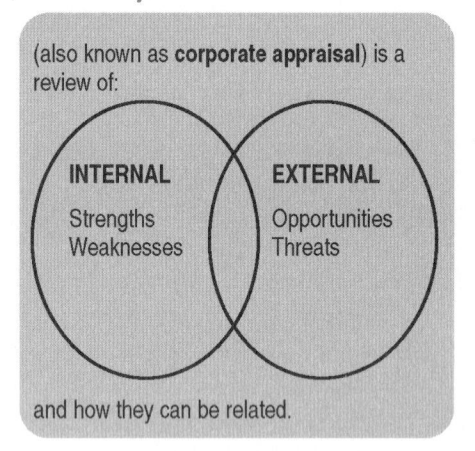

SWOT analysis (also known as **corporate appraisal**) is a review of:

- **INTERNAL**: Strengths, Weaknesses
- **EXTERNAL**: Opportunities, Threats

and how they can be related.

The results can be combined in the SWOT framework.

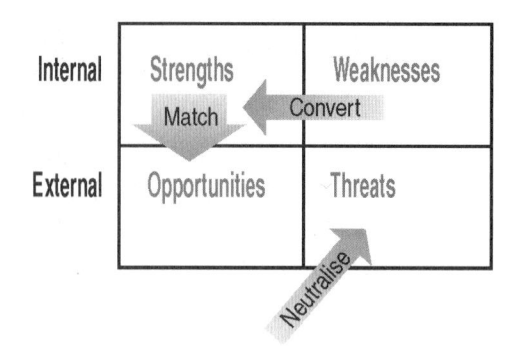

	Strengths	Weaknesses
Internal	Match ←	Convert
External	Opportunities	Threats
		↗ Neutralise

2.3.4 Value chain analysis

Porter grouped the various activities of an organisation into a **value chain**.

A firm's value chain is connected to what Porter calls a **value system**.

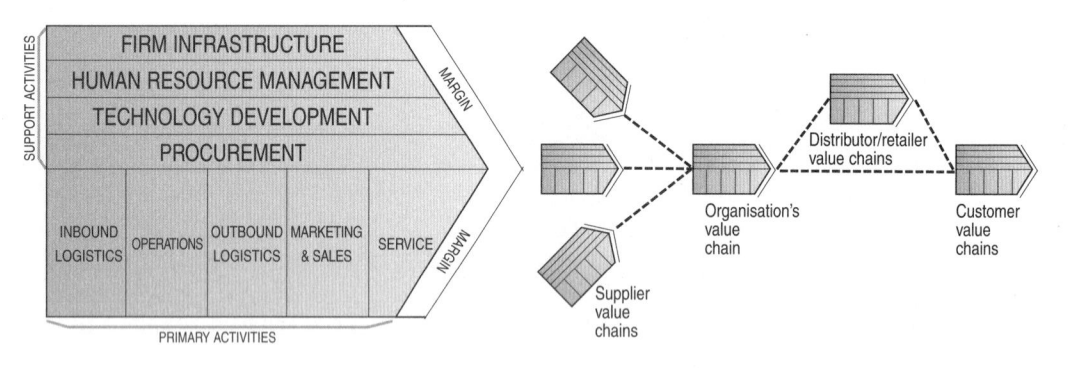

Value chain (primary activities): Inbound Logistics, Operations, Outbound Logistics, Marketing & Sales, Service

Support activities: Firm Infrastructure, Human Resource Management, Technology Development, Procurement

Value system: Supplier value chains → Organisation's value chain → Distributor/retailer value chains → Customer value chains

The **margin** is the excess the customer is prepared to **pay** over the **cost** to the firm of obtaining resource inputs and providing value activities. It represents the **value created** by the **value activities** themselves and by the **management of the linkages** between them. **Linkages** connect the activities in the value chain. The activities affect one another and therefore must be co-ordinated.

Using the value chain. A firm can secure competitive advantage in several ways.

- Invent new or better ways to do activities
- Combine activities in new or better ways
- Manage the linkages in its own value chain
- Manage the linkages in the value system

2.3.5 The product portfolio

The company's offerings to the market are fundamental to its success. They must be kept under review so that there is a suitable mix. The **product life cycle** is an important concept and strategies must be appropriate to the stage in the life cycle. But product life cycle must be applied with care. We can distinguish 3 aspects of 'product'.

- **Product class** (or **generic product**) – a broad category
- **Product form** – type within the category
- **Brand** – The specific product

Product life cycle

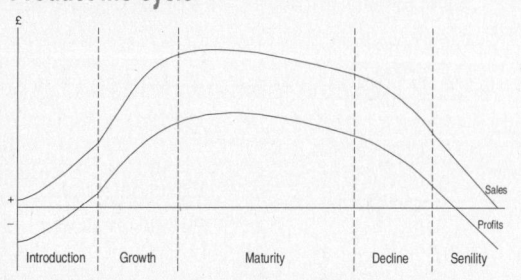

Stages: Introduction | Growth | Maturity | Decline | Senility (showing Sales and Profits curves)

Introduction: development, marketing and production costs high; sales volume low; loss maker; negative cash flow.

Growth: sales volumes accelerate, profits rise, but cash flow likely to remain negative; competitors enter the market. High advertising costs.

Maturity: longest period; profits good, but low market growth. Cash flow positive; reminder promotion

Decline: many causes; sales fall, over-capacity in industry; some players leave market

Senility: profit negligible; product may be retained in niche

Portfolio analysis is applicable to products, market segments and SBUs. There are four basic strategies:

- **Build** – Invest for market share growth
- **Hold** – Maintain current position
- **Harvest** – Manage for profit in the short term
- **Divest** – Release resources for use elsewhere

The BCG Matrix

Market growth	High (share)	Low (share)
High	Star	Question mark
Low	Cash cow	Dog

Relative market share

Stars – build
Cash cows – hold or harvest
Question marks – build or harvest
Dogs – divest or hold

Problems with the BCG matrix

- Rather simplistic
- Ignores innovation
- Dogs and question marks may be needed to complete a range
- Ignores competitors other than market leader
- Does not indicate overall best mix or *how* to build stars and question marks.

2.3.6 Competences and critical success factors

Competences can be divided into two types:

- An organisation must achieve **threshold** competences in all activities
- **Core competences** are those where it out performs the competition *and* that are difficult to imitate

Critical success factors are performance requirements that are fundamental to competitive success. They are underpinned by **key tasks**. Key tasks must be prioritised.

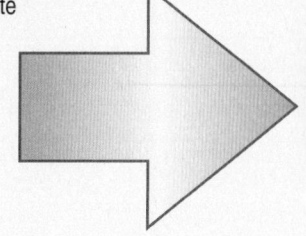

> A *competence* provides an organisation with the ability to achieve its *critical success factors*

2.4 Organisational and management analysis

You should understand the current organisational structure of the organisation in the unseen material and look for any improvements or changes that could be made to make it more effective.

2.4.1 Greiner's stage model of growth

PHASE 3
PHASE 4
PHASE 5
Large
Evolution stages
Revolution stages
Size of organisation
Small
5: Crisis of ?
4: Crisis of RED TAPE
5: Growth through COLLABORATION
3: Crisis of CONTROL
4: Growth through COORDINATION
2: Crisis of AUTONOMY
3: Growth through DELEGATION
1: Crisis of LEADERSHIP
2: Growth through DIRECTION
1: Growth through CREATIVITY
Young
Age of organisation
Mature

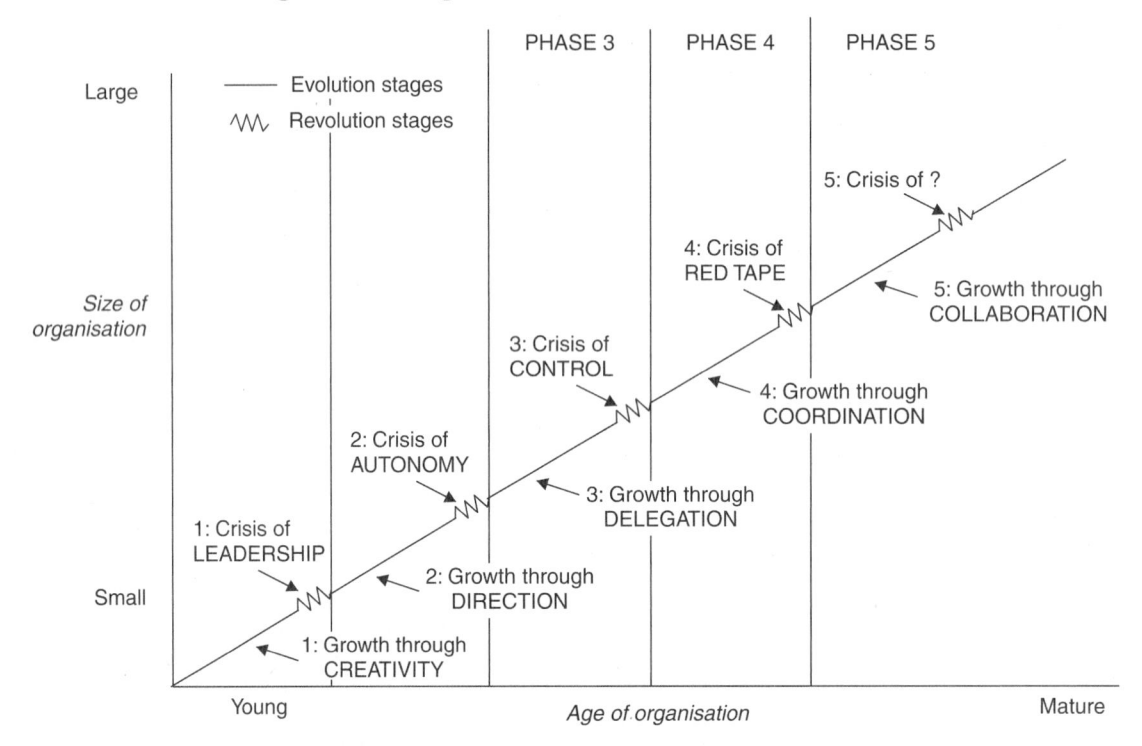

2.4.2 Organisational structures

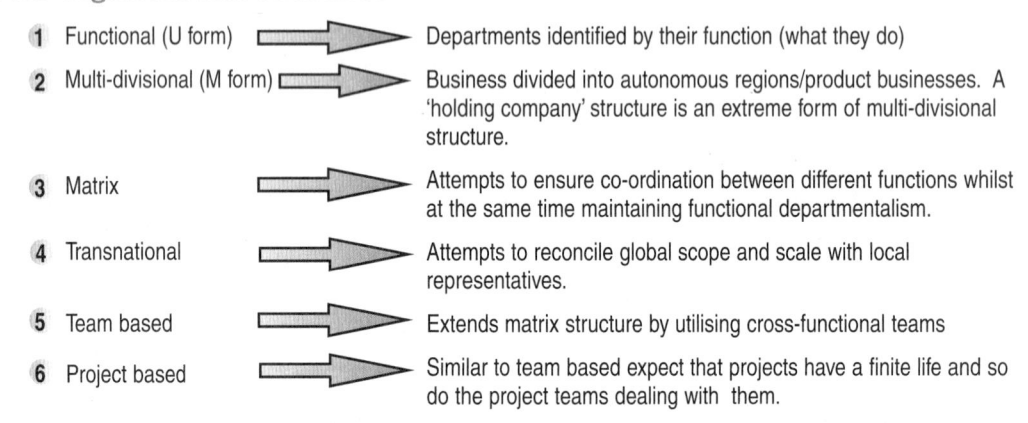

1 Functional (U form)	Departments identified by their function (what they do)
2 Multi-divisional (M form)	Business divided into autonomous regions/product businesses. A 'holding company' structure is an extreme form of multi-divisional structure.
3 Matrix	Attempts to ensure co-ordination between different functions whilst at the same time maintaining functional departmentalism.
4 Transnational	Attempts to reconcile global scope and scale with local representatives.
5 Team based	Extends matrix structure by utilising cross-functional teams
6 Project based	Similar to team based expect that projects have a finite life and so do the project teams dealing with them.

2.5 Strategic options

2.5.1 Competitive strategies

The purpose of competitive strategy is to create a position within an industry which copes successfully with the five competitive forces and thereby yields a superior return on investment for the firm. A firm can use its value chain to help design its competitive strategy.

Cost leadership
Aims to be the lowest cost producer in the industry as a whole

Aspects of cost
- Economies of scale
- Use the newest production technology
- Learning curve effect
- Productivity improvement
- Minimisation of overheads
- Favourable access to inputs
- Use IT to monitor costs

Differentiation
Aims to exploit a product or service perceived as unique within the industry as a whole

Aspects of differentiation
- **Breakthrough** products – radical performance advantage
- **Improved** products – more cost-effective
- **Competitive** products – unique combinations of features
  - Brand image
  - Special product features
  - Unique combination of **value activities**

Focus
Activity is restricted to a particular **segment** of the market. Either cost leadership or differentiation strategy is then pursued. Such concentrated effort can be more effective, but the segment may be attacked by a larger firm.

Generic strategies and the five competitive forces

Competitive force	Advantages – Cost leadership	Advantages – Differentiation	Disadvantages – Cost leadership	Disadvantages – Differentiation
New entrants	Economies of scale raise entry barriers	Brand loyalty and perceived uniqueness are entry barriers		
Substitutes	Firm not as vulnerable to the threat of substitutes as its less cost-effective competitors.	Customer loyalty is a weapon against substitutes		
Customers	Customers cannot drive down prices further than the next most efficient competitor	Customers have no comparable alternative. Brand loyalty should lower price sensitivity	Very internally focused. Ignores customers' needs.	Customers may no longer need the differentiating factor. Sooner or later, customers become price sensitive
Suppliers	Flexibility to deal with cost increases	Higher margins can offset vulnerability to supplier price rises	Increase in input costs can reduce price advantages	
Industry rivalry	Firm remains profitable when rivals collapse through excessive price competition	Unique features reduce direct competition	Technological change will require capital investment, or make production cheaper for competitors. Competitors learn via imitation. Cost concerns ignore product design or marketing issues	Imitation narrows differentiation. Differentiating factors may be undermined if rivals develop significantly better technology.

2.5.2 Product market strategies

Ansoff described four possible growth strategies in the **growth vector matrix**.

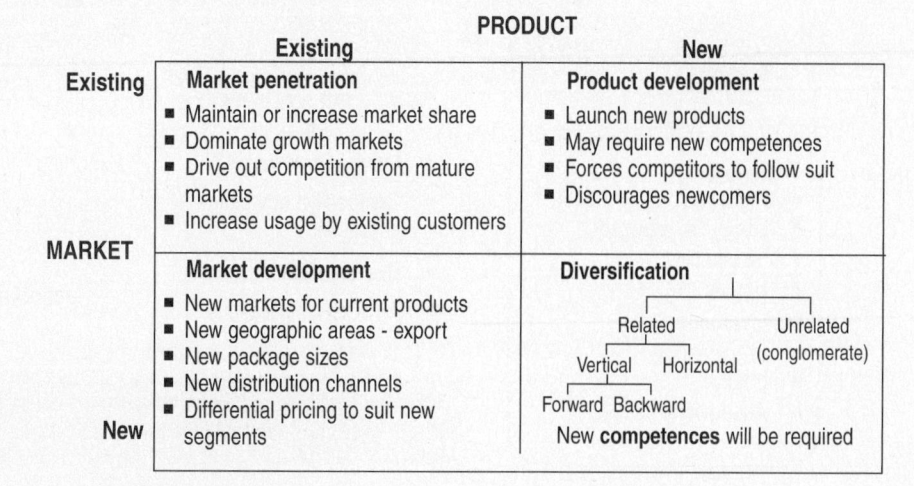

PRODUCT / MARKET

	Existing Product	New Product
Existing Market	**Market penetration** - Maintain or increase market share - Dominate growth markets - Drive out competition from mature markets - Increase usage by existing customers	**Product development** - Launch new products - May require new competences - Forces competitors to follow suit - Discourages newcomers
New Market	**Market development** - New markets for current products - New geographic areas - export - New package sizes - New distribution channels - Differential pricing to suit new segments	**Diversification** Related (Vertical – Forward, Backward; Horizontal) / Unrelated (conglomerate) New **competences** will be required

Horizontal integration

Development into activities that are competitive with or complementary to present activities; eg electricity companies selling gas. Offers economies of scale.

Conglomerate diversification

- Spreads risk
- May obtain synergy (eg acquiring tax losses, utilising distribution channels, pooling R+D.)

However:
- Unfamiliarity with new segments increases risk
- More opportunities to go wrong
- Cultural and management integration mismatches

Vertical integration

The organisation becomes its own supplier (backward vertical integration) or distributor (forward vertical integration).
- Secures supplies
- Stronger relationship with end-users
- Profits from all parts of value system
- Creates barriers to entry

However:
- 'More eggs in same end-market basket' (*Ansoff*) – more vulnerable to a single market
- Does not offer significant economies of scale

Other strategies

- Withdrawal
- Demerger
- Divestment

2.5.3 Choosing a method of growth

Organic growth

The development of internal resources
- Supports **learning** and is supported by it
- Encourages innovation as source of growth
- Consistent culture and management style
- Provides economies of scale
- Ease of control

However:
- Can be slow
- Not good for dealing with barriers to entry
- Firm has to bear all risks internally

Mergers and acquisitions

- Provides access to a variety of resources: products; managers; suppliers; production facilities; technology and skills; distribution facilities; marketing advantages; cash; tax losses
- Can overcome barriers to entry
- Can spread risk
- Can defend against predators

However, many acquisitions fail to enhance shareholder value.
- Cost: the price is often too high
- Cultural problems, especially in management
- Top management egos can warp judgement
- Professional advisers drive the market
- Customers may be disturbed by changes

2.5.4 International expansion

Key decisions for international expansion

1. Whether to market abroad at all?
2. Which markets to enter?
3. Mode of entry?

Advantages
- Higher sales and profits
- Life cycle extended
- Seasonality
- Spread risk

Disadvantages
- Less control
- Costly
- Adaptations needed

- Market attractiveness
- Competitive advantage possessed
- Risk (political, business)
- Any CSR implications

- Exporting
- Contract manufacture; licence
- Overseas divisions or subsidiaries

Before getting involved, the company must consider both **strategic** ('Does it fit?') and **tactical** ('Can we do it?') issues.

2.5.5 Joint ventures, alliances, franchising

Joint ventures are arrangements between firms to pool their interests on a project. The mechanism is to create a new firm under joint control.

Alliances aim to complement technology, geography, markets and so on.

Advantages
- Coverage of a larger number of markets
- Reduced risk of government intervention
- Closer control over operations
- Local knowledge
- Spreading of risk and costs
- Learning from partners

However, there can be major conflicts of interest, and disagreements over:
- Profit sharing
- Investment levels
- Management
- Marketing strategy

Other arrangements include co-operative methods such as:

1. Licensing – the licenser provides rights, advice and know how in return for a royalty
2. Franchising – the franchiser provides expertise and brand, the franchisee provides capital and is responsible for day-to-day operations
3. Sub-contracting – enhanced access to resources, reduce overheads

2.5.6 Divestment

Firms can also divest themselves of businesses in declining sectors or non-core activities.

Reasons for divestment
- To rationalise a business and concentrate resources on core activities
- To sell off subsidiaries at a profit
- To make a profit by buying and selling companies
- To get out while the going is good
- To raise funds to invest elsewhere

Demergers and management buyouts have become more common as conglomerates go out of fashion.

2.6 Change management

2.6.1 Lewin's 3 stage (ice cube) model

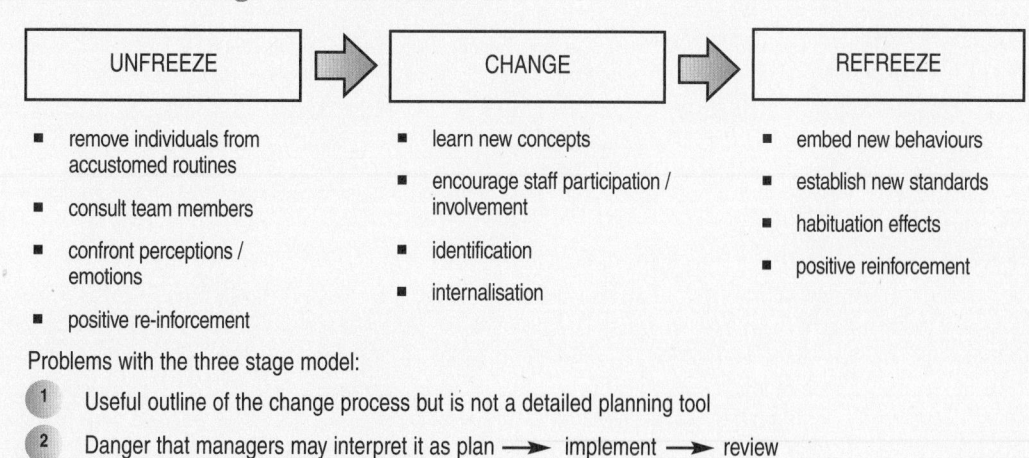

UNFREEZE	CHANGE	REFREEZE
- remove individuals from accustomed routines - consult team members - confront perceptions / emotions - positive re-inforcement	- learn new concepts - encourage staff participation / involvement - identification - internalisation	- embed new behaviours - establish new standards - habituation effects - positive reinforcement

Problems with the three stage model:

1. Useful outline of the change process but is not a detailed planning tool
2. Danger that managers may interpret it as plan ⟶ implement ⟶ review
3. Ignores the fundamental issue that people will only change if they feel and appreciate the need to do so

2.6.2 Force field analysis

Force field analysis: identifying the factors that promote or hinder change.

For change to be successfully implemented:

- Exploit promoting forces
- Reduce hindering forces

so that driving forces outweigh resisting forces

Forces driving change
- Improving quality
- Improving efficiency
- Potential savings
- Legislation/legal requirements

The status quo

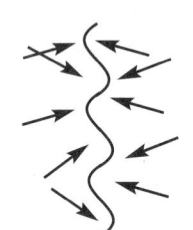

Forces holding back change
- Individual concerns. eg
  - fear of the unknown
  - dislike of uncertainty
  - potential loss of power
  - potential loss of rewards
  - potential lack or loss of skills
- Cost/budget constraints
- Existing system sufficient

Force field analysis **doesn't give any insights into the detail of how to manage change**, or how to overcome the resistence to change.

2.6.3 Resistance to change

People resist change due to to fear of the unknown

- Confronts apathy / forces people out of comfort zones
- Reduces stability
- Can result in restructure (job changes / losses)
- May present technological challenges

Kotter and Schlesinger's approaches to resistance

1. Education and communication
2. Participation and involvement
3. Facilitation and support
4. Negotiation and agreement
5. Manipulation and co-optation
6. Coercion, implicit and explicit

Underlying theme: **communication** is critical in overcoming resistance to change.

3 Risk and control strategy (Performance strategy)

3.1 Information systems strategy

Information strategy
Information strategy is the long-term plan concerned with exploiting IS and IT either to support business strategies or create new strategic options.

Information systems (IS)
IS strategy aims to use information systems to support the organisation's objectives.

Information management (IM)
IM is the approach an organisation has for managing its systems including planning developments, organisational environment, control and technology.

The key element of IM is making sure the **right** information is communicated to the **right** and **not** the **wrong** people.

Strategic IS
Strategic IS are systems that change goals, processes, products, services or environmental relationships with the aim of gaining competitive advantage.

Information technology (IT)
IT strategy means ensuring systems operated satisfy the organisation's information needs. It involves balancing supply and demand of funds and facilities, and development of programmes.

Strategy for IS/IT
A strategy for IS/IT is justified on the grounds that it:
- Involves high costs
- Is critical to the success of many organisations
- Can be used as a source of competitive advantage
- Impacts on customer service
- Affects all levels of management
- Affects the way management information is created and presented
- Requires effective management to obtain maximum benefit
- Involves many stakeholders eg, other business users, governments, IT manufacturers, consumers and employees

Developing a strategy for IS/IT
An IS/IT strategy must deal with deal issues:
- The organisation's business needs and business objectives
- The organisation's current use of IS/IT: identify gaps in system coverage
- How these gaps will be closed

Benefits of technological change
- Cutting production costs
- Developing better quality products and services
- Developing new products and services
- Providing products and services more quickly
- Freeing staff from repetitive work

Strategic grid
McFarlan and McKenney devised a matrix to show four levels of dependence on IS/IT in an organisation.

Applications portfolio
Peppard developed the strategic grid into the **applications portfolio** to show the potential impact of current individual applications.

Strategic importance of **planned** information systems		Low	High
	High	Turnaround	Strategic
	Low	Support	Factory

Strategic importance of **current** information systems

Strategic importance of individual applications in the predicted **future** competitive environment		Low	High
	High	High potential	Strategic
	Low	Support	Key operational

Strategic importance of individual applications in the **current** competitive environment

Developing an information strategy

Earl's three leg analysis

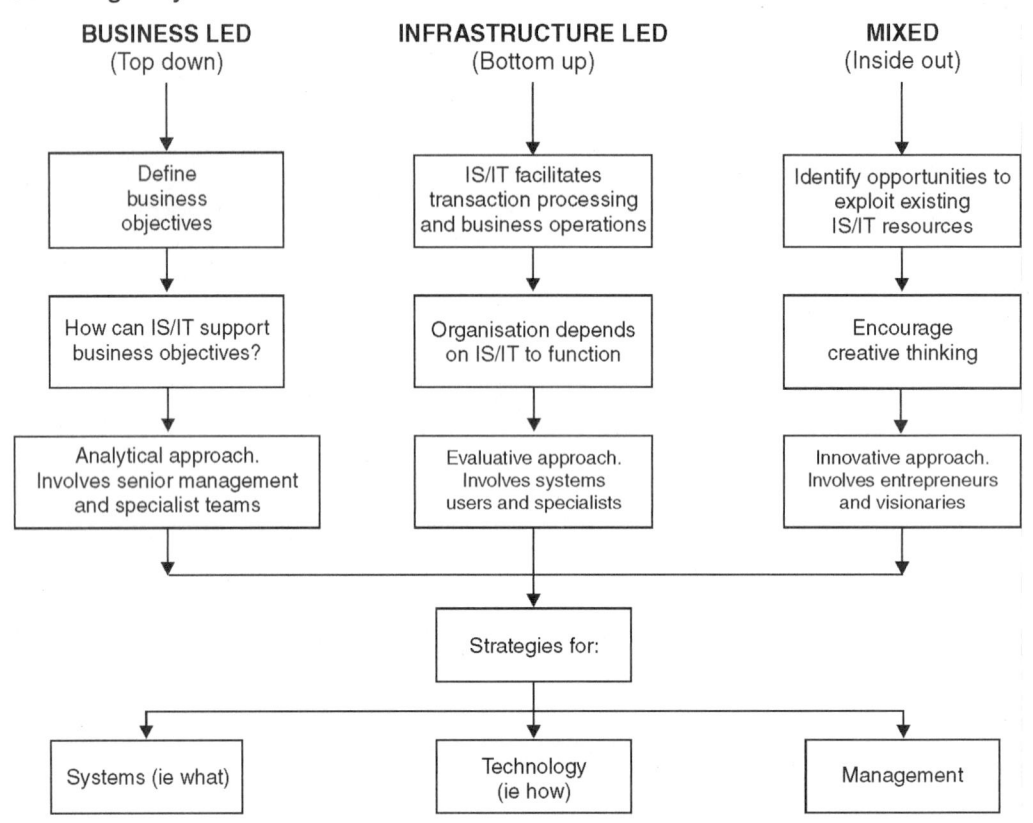

BUSINESS LED (Top down)
- Define business objectives
- How can IS/IT support business objectives?
- Analytical approach. Involves senior management and specialist teams

INFRASTRUCTURE LED (Bottom up)
- IS/IT facilitates transaction processing and business operations
- Organisation depends on IS/IT to function
- Evaluative approach. Involves systems users and specialists

MIXED (Inside out)
- Identify opportunities to exploit existing IS/IT resources
- Encourage creative thinking
- Innovative approach. Involves entrepreneurs and visionaries

Strategies for:
- Systems (ie what)
- Technology (ie how)
- Management

3.2 Outsourcing

Outsourcing is the contracting out of specified operations or services to an external vendor.

Types of outsourcing

- Ad-hoc: short-term need for more IS/IT skills
- Project management: a particular project is outsourced
- Partial: some IT/IS services are outsourced
- Total: external suppliers provide the IT/IS services

Outsourcing organisations

- Facilities management (FM) companies - usually all equipment remains with the client, but the responsibility for providing and managing the specified services rests with the FM company.
- Software houses - concentrate on the provision of 'software services' eg, feasibility studies, systems analysis and design, and application programming.
- Consultancy firms - can be involved in strategic and specialist studies, project management, body-shopping and recruitment.
- Hardware manufacturers and suppliers - will also contract for maintenance of the equipment.

Advantages of outsourcing	Disadvantages of outsourcing
☑ No uncertainty about cost: services are specified in advance for a fixed price. ☑ Long-term contracts encourage planning for the future. ☑ Outsourcing can bring economies of scale. ☑ A specialist organisation is able to retain skills and knowledge. ☑ New skills and knowledge become available. ☑ Flexibility.	☒ IS may be too important to be contracted out. Information is at the heart of management. ☒ Risky in commercial and/or legal terms where confidential information is available to outsiders. ☒ IS can be used to gain competitive advantage. Opportunities may be missed and any new technology devised by the third party could be available to competitors. ☒ An organisation may be locked into an unsatisfactory contract. ☒ FM does not encourage awareness of the potential costs and benefits of IS/IT.

3.3 Corporate risk

3.3.1 Types of risk

Risk classification
- **Fundamental** - affect society in general
- **Particular** - individual in control
- **Speculative** - good or bad consequences
- **Pure** - only outcomes harmful

Benefits of risk management
- Predictability of cash flows
- Limitation of bad events
- Increased shareholder confidence
- Weigh v costs

General business risks	Volatility of profits caused by the nature and type of business operations • Industries/markets • Product life cycle • Economy • Inputs • Competitors • Production process
Property risks	Risks from damage, destruction or theft of property
Trading risks	Physical risk - risk of goods going astray Credit risk - payment default Trade risk - risk of customer refusing to accept goods Liquidity risk - inability to finance credit
Cultural risk	Trading problems caused by different customs, laws and language leading to differences in expected manner in which transactions conducted
Legal risk	Risks of incurring legal penalties and costs
Political risk	Risk that political action will affect position and value. Examples of actions include exchange controls, tax regulations and asset appropriation
Currency and interest rate risk	Possibility of loss or gain due to future changes in exchange or interest rates
Technological risk	Risks include computer malfunction, security breaches and technological progress making products obsolete
Fraud risk	Loss through fraudulent activities of staff or management

3.3.2 Risk management

A framework of enterprise risk management involves.

- Cost environment
- Objective setting
- Event identification
- Risk assessment
- Risk response
- Control activities
- Information and communication
- Monitoring

4 Financial strategy

4.1 Maximisation of shareholder wealth.

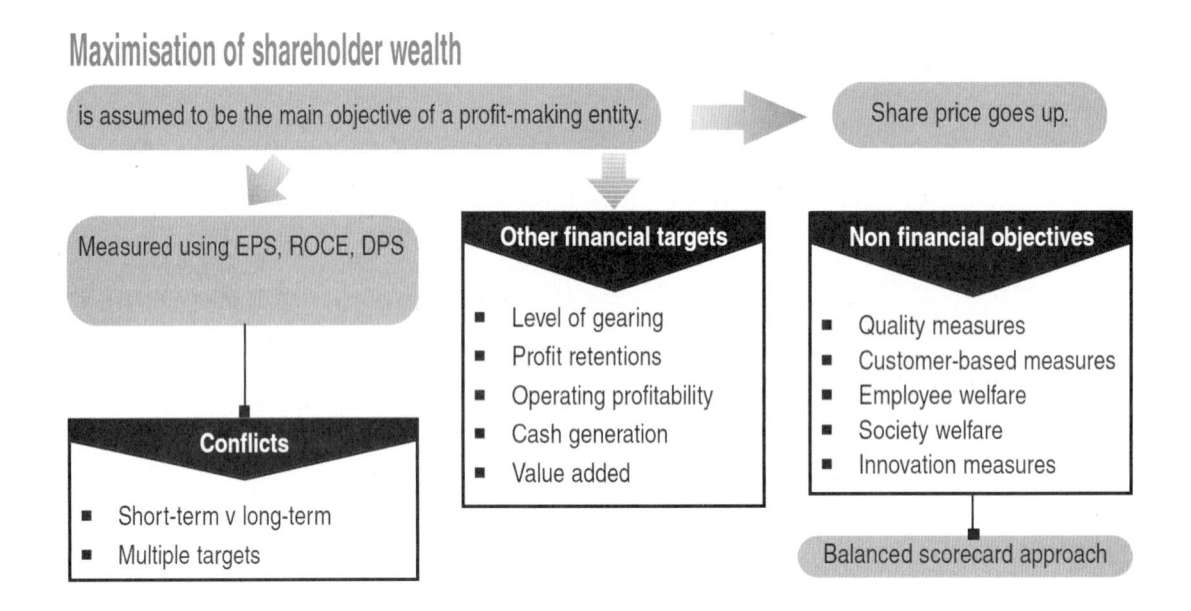

Maximisation of shareholder wealth is assumed to be the main objective of a profit-making entity. → Share price goes up.

Measured using EPS, ROCE, DPS

Conflicts
- Short-term v long-term
- Multiple targets

Other financial targets
- Level of gearing
- Profit retentions
- Operating profitability
- Cash generation
- Value added

Non financial objectives
- Quality measures
- Customer-based measures
- Employee welfare
- Society welfare
- Innovation measures

Balanced scorecard approach

4.2 Ratio analysis

Remember!
Consider carefully the requirements of the question and the contents of the scenario before calculating ratios. The examiner will be looking for relevant ratios accompanied by meaningful comments.

Profitability and return
- Return on capital employed
- Profit margin
- Asset turnover

Liquidity ratios
- Current ratio
- Acid test ratio
- Inventory turnover
- Payables days
- Receivables days

Debt and gearing
- Debt ratio (Total debts: Assets)
- Gearing (Proportion of debt in long-term capital)
- Interest cover
- Cash flow ratio (Cash inflow: Total debts)

Stock market ratios
- Dividend yield
- Interest yield
- Earnings per share
- Dividend cover
- Price/earnings ratio

Comparisons with previous years
- % growth in profit
- Sales
- Changes in gearing ratio
- Changes in current/quick ratios
- Changes in asset turnover
- Changes in EPS, market price, dividend

Comparisons with other companies in same industry
These can put improvements into perspective if other companies are doing better, and provide evidence of general trends.
- Growth rates
- Retained profits
- Non-current asset levels

Comparisons with companies in different industries
Investors need to know differences between sectors.
- Sales growth
- Profit
- ROCE
- P/E ratios
- Dividend yields

Problems with ratio analysis
- Use of comparable information
- Out-of-date information
- Ratios not definitive
- Careful interpretation
- Manipulation
- Comparisons with other information

4.3 Information in accounts

Non-current assets
- Valuation methods
- Asset age and nature

Share capital and reserves
- New share issue
- Level of profits retained
- Scrip issues/dividends

Financial obligations
- Redeemable debt
- Earn-out arrangements (see below)
- Potential/contingent liabilities

ACCOUNTING INFORMATION

Loans
- Whether loans secured
- Closeness of redemption/repayment date
- Interest rates

Contingencies
- Guarantees
- Uncalled share liabilities
- Lawsuits and claims

Post balance sheet events
- Mergers/acquisitions
- Asset sales
- New/closed trading activities

4.4 Cost of capital

Elements of cost of capital

Risk free rate of return	Return required from a completely risk free investment eg yield on government securities
Business risk premium	Increase in required rate of return due to uncertainty about future and business prospects
Financial risk premium	Danger of high debt levels, variability of equity returns

Private companies

No market values available.

- Use cost of capital for similar public companies, adding premiums for business and financial risk
- Take risk-free rate of return and add premiums for business and financial risk

Cost of capital if constant dividends paid

$$k_e = \frac{d}{P_0}$$ *Exam formula*

where P_0 is price at time
 d is dividend
 k_e is cost of equity or preference capital

Dividend growth model

$$k_e = \frac{d_0(1+g)}{P_0} + g = \frac{d_1}{P_0} + g$$ *Exam formula*

where d_0 is dividend at time 0
 d_1 is dividend at time 1
 g is dividend growth rate

Estimating growth rate

Use experience or formula (Gordon's growth model)

$$g = bR$$

where R is accounting return on capital employed
 b is proportion of earnings retained

$$g = \sqrt[n]{\frac{\text{dividend in year x}}{\text{dividend in year x} - n}} - 1$$

WACC

$$WACC = k_e \left[\frac{V_E}{V_E + V_D}\right] + k_d(1-t)\left[\frac{V_D}{V_E + V_D}\right]$$ *Exam formula*

k_e is cost of equity V_E is market value of equity
k_d is cost of debt V_D is market value of debt

Use market values rather than book values unless market values unavailable (unquoted company)

4.5 Business valuations

Net assets valuation method

Value of shares in class = Net assets attributable to class / No of shares in class

Possible bases of valuation

Historic basis (unlikely to be realistic)

Replacement basis (asset used on ongoing basis)

Realisable basis (asset sold/ business broken up)

Price - earnings ratio

P/E ratio = Market value / EPS

Market value = EPS × P/E ratio

Have to decide suitable P/E ratio.

Factors to consider:
- Industry
- Status
- Marketability
- Shareholders
- Asset backing and liquidity
- Nature of assets
- Gearing

Dividend valuation model

$$P_0 = \frac{d}{k_e}$$

Where P_0 is price at time 0
d is Dividend (constant)
k_e is cost of equity

$$P_0 = \frac{d_1}{k_e - g}$$ **Exam formula**

Where d_1 is dividend in year 1
g is dividend growth rate

Uses of net asset valuation method

- As measure of security in a share valuation
- As measure of comparison in scheme of merger
- As floor value in business that is up for sale

Problems in valuation

- Need for professional valuation
- Realisation of assets
- Contingent liabilities
- Market for assets

Accounting rate of return

Value of business = Estimated future profits / Required return on capital employed

In a takeover bid, there may be adjustments required for new levels of directors' remuneration, interest charges and rationalisation. ARR is used to decide maximum amount to pay in a takeover.

Earnings yield valuation model

Market value = Earnings / Earnings yield

Assumptions

- Dividends from new projects of same risk type as existing operations
- No increase in cost of capital
- Perfect information
- Shareholders have same marginal capital cost
- Ignore tax and issue expenses

Problems

- Companies that don't pay dividends don't have zero values
- Need enough profitable projects to maintain dividends
- Dividend policy likely to change on takeover

Discounted cash flows method

Value investment using expected after-tax cash flows of investment and appropriate cost of capital.

Free cash flow

Value of company is sum of future free cash flows.

- Revenues
- – Operating costs
- + Depreciation
- + Interest (1 – tax rate)
- – Taxes
- – Debt repayment
- – Working capital
- – Investment expenditure

Shareholder value analysis

Analysis focuses on key decisions affecting value and risk. Decisions depend on value drivers (eg profit margin, working capital, required return).

Problems with cash flow methods

- Difficult to select appropriate cost of capital
- Unreliable estimates of future cash flows
- Not best method for minority interests who lack influence on cash flows

4.6 Sources of business finance

4.6.1 Equity finance

Stock market listing:
- Access to wider pool of finance
- Improved marketability of shares
- Transfer of capital to other uses
- Enhancement of company image
- Facilitation of growth by acquisition

Disadvantages of obtaining listing

- Loss of control
- Vulnerability to takeover
- More scrutiny
- Greater restrictions on directors
- Compliance costs

Retained earnings

Obtaining cash by retaining funds within the business rather than paying dividends.

- Flexible source of finance
- Same pattern of shareholdings
- Opportunity costs of lost dividend income

Offer for sale

The company sells shares to the public at large. Offer for sale by tender means allotting shares at the highest price they will be taken up.

Placing

Placing means arranging for most of an issue to be bought by a small number of institutional investors. It is cheaper than an offer for sale.

Costs of share issues

- Underwriting costs
- Stock Exchange listing fees
- Issuing house, solicitors, auditors, public relation fees
- Printing and distribution costs
- Advertising

Pricing share issues

- Price of similar companies
- Current market conditions
- Future trading prospects
- Premium on launch
- Price growth after launch
- Higher price means fewer shares and less earnings dilution

Rights issue

is an offer to existing shareholders enabling them to buy new shares.

Offer price will be lower than current market price

Advantages of rights issue
- Lower issue costs than offer for sale
- Shareholders acquire shares at discount
- Relative voting rights unaffected

Scrip dividend

is a dividend payment in the form of new shares, not cash.

Value of rights
Theoretical ex-rights price – Issue price

Scrip issue/bonus issue

is an issue of new shares to current shareholders, by converting equity reserves.

Theoretical ex-rights price

$$\frac{1}{N+1} ((N \times \text{cum rights price}) + \text{issue price}) \quad \text{Exam formula}$$

where N = number of shares required to buy one new share

4.6.2 Debt finance

(a) **Overdrafts and loans**

Overdrafts and loans

Overdrafts are used for short-term financing needs. A maximum facility is granted; the bank will want any long-term balance reduced. Overdrafts are repayable on demand; security may be specific assets or over the whole business.

Loans are medium and long-term. The organisation won't be subject to the publicity requirements or costs of a loan stock issue on the stock exchange. Security or restrictive covenants may be imposed.

Overdrafts
- Designed for day to day help
- Only pay interest when overdrawn
- Bank has flexibility to review
- Can be renewed
- Won't affect gearing calculation

Overdrafts v loans

Loans
- Medium-term purposes
- Interest and repayments set in advance
- Bank won't withdraw at short notice
- Shouldn't exceed asset life
- Can have loan-overdraft mix

(b) **Loan stock**

Loan stock (Debentures)

The stock has a nominal value, the debt owed by the company, and interest is paid on this amount. Security may be given.

Fixed charge (specific assets, can't dispose without lender's consent)

Floating charge (class of assets, can dispose until default)

Deep discount bonds are issued at a large discount to nominal value of stock.

Zero coupon bonds are issued at a discount, with no interest paid on them.

(c) **Leasing**

This is a contract between the lessor and lessee for the hire of a specific asset.

Operating leases
- Lessor bears most of risk and rewards
- Lessor responsible for servicing and maintenance
- Period of lease short, less than useful economic life of asset
- Asset not shown on lessee's balance sheet

Finance leases
- Lessee bears most of risks and rewards
- Lessee responsible for servicing and maintenance
- Primary period of lease for asset's useful economic life, secondary (low-rent) period afterwards
- Asset shown on lessee's balance sheet

(d) **Trade credit**

4.6.3 Venture capital

Venture capital is risk capital normally provided in return for an equity stake and possibly board representation.

- Business startups
- Development of new products/markets
- Management buyouts
- Realisation of investments

Investment considerations
- Nature of product
- Production expertise
- Management expertise
- Markets
- Profit expectations
- Risk borne by current owners
- Innovation
- Ability to out-perform competitors

Information required by venture capitalists
- Business plan
- Finance needs
- Recent trading capital
- Cash and profit forecasts
- Management and shareholders
- Current sources of finance

The BPP approach (1): approach and explore the case situation

In Chapters 1 and 2, we explained what the case exam is for and how you can expect to be marked. To repeat, can obtain the 'pre-seen' material from CIMA's website at least 6 weeks before the exam. You must use these six weeks before the exam to do as much research about the industry and the organisation as possible. However, remember you will not be able to bring any analysis notes or crib-sheets into the exam room so it is important you have committed the key findings from your research to memory so that you can use them as necessary in the exam itself.

A key objective of the pre-seen data is that you become familiar with the company – the big picture as well as the detail. How does this chapter help you?

- Your objective: become familiar with the company in the case situation.
- You have to consider 'all the angles'
- You have to remember your analysis in the exam

We break down this process into a **sequence of stages** to structure your time.

- Approach the case
- Explore the case situation
- Synthesise what you know

In each case there are tasks that can be done: think of these as a resource of techniques for that stage. (You will not need to do all of them.)

A note for students

Every case is different, and this **suggested** generic approach may need to be supplemented, adapted, or radically recast depending on the case situation.

- You will benefit from **sharing your ideas with other students**.
- **Your lecturer or tutor will know best.**

topic list

1 The BPP approach in outline

2 Approach the case

3 Explore the case situation

4 Conclusion

1 The BPP approach in outline

1	Tools to approach the case: Chapter 4	Time	Criteria of the assessment matrix
1.1	Read the case quickly twice without taking notes	1 hour	
1.2	Quickly re-read the case after a day	30 mins	
1.3	Mark up the case slowly, taking notes	2 hours	
1.4	Summarise the data in précis	1 hour	Diversity, Logic, Judgement
1.5	Carry out an information audit	1 hour	Diversity, Integration, Prioritisation
1.6	Research the industry and company	Depends	Diversity
1.7	Identify relevant technical knowledge	30 mins	Technical, Application, Focus, Diversity

2	Tools to explore the case situation: Chapter 4		
2.1	Analyse the numbers	Depends	Technical, Application, Focus, Logic, Diversity
2.2	General environmental analysis (PEST) and trends	1 hour	Diversity, Technical, Application, Focus, Logic, Ethics
2.3	Analyse the business environment and competitive strategy	1.5 hours	Diversity, Technical, Application, Focus, Logic, Ethics
2.4	Audit the product/service portfolio	1 hour	Technical, Application, Focus, Logic, Ethics, Diversity
2.5	How does the business add value?	1 hour	Integration, Ethics
2.6	Identify information systems and processes	1 hour	Technical, Application, Focus, Diversity
2.7	Identify key issues in structure, culture and personnel including management and internal control	1 hour	Technical, Application, Focus, Prioritisation, Ethics, Diversity
2.8	Identify investor objectives, capital structure and other stakeholder objectives	1 hour	Technical, Application, Focus, Ethics, Diversity
2.9	Identify and analyse possible business projects	1 hour	Integration, Technical, Application, Focus, Ethics, Diversity

3	Tools to synthesise what you know: Chapter 5		
3.1	Summarise your findings in an interim position statement	1 hour	Prioritisation, Logic, Judgement, Technical, Application, Focus, Diversity
3.2	Draw up a mission statement for the current business from the pre-seen data	30 mins	Logic, Prioritisation
3.3	Relate the business's distinctive competences to the critical success factors for the industry	30 mins	Logic, Judgement, Prioritisation
3.4	Identify and analyse risks, internal and external	1 hour	Diversity, Technical, Application, Focus, Prioritisation, Ethics
3.5	Carry out a graded SWOT analysis	1 hour	Prioritisation
3.6	Identify key business issues	1 hour	Prioritisation, Integration, Diversity, Ethics
3.7	Draw up a balanced scorecard	1 hour	Integration, Logic, Judgement, Prioritisation
3.8	Prepare a one page business summary	1 hour	Logic, Judgement, Prioritisation, Diversity, Integration

4	Practise report writing before the exam: Chapter 6	
5	The exam – three hours + 20 minutes reading: Chapter 7	Time
5.1	The night before: review your business summary and the pre-seen	
5.2	In the exam itself: • Review the unseen and requirement • Skim read the data • Read the requirement carefully, making a mental note of the recipient of the report, the required format and what you have to do	Reading time 20 mins
5.3	Read the unseen data in depth. Be sure to identify what has changed. Make notes on the question paper identifying the key issues.	
5.4	Consider the big picture and plan your answer. Do the calculations	40 mins
5.5	Draw up the appendices, terms of reference and introduction	10 mins
5.6	Prioritise the issues: 4 key issues and 'other issues'	15 mins
5.7	Write the main body of the report	50 mins
5.8	Write the ethics section	15 mins
5.9	Write up your recommendations	30 mins
5.10	Write the conclusion and review your work	5 mins
5.11	'Question 2': Use format required and keep answer succinct. Refer to calculations.	15 mins

2 Approach the case

Objectives of stage 1: Approach the Case

- Absorb the case without getting bogged down in detail
- Provide a sound basis for further analysis
- Identify information needs and deficiencies

Step 1.1 Read the case study quickly twice without taking notes

CIMA will put the case on its **website.** (CIMA will tell you when: keep this date in your diary.) To download the case, you will of course, need Internet access and Adobe Acrobat software: (this is free software, and you can obtain it from CIMA's website or BPP's). You will also need your student login or registration details.

Don't panic when you first look at the case, but **don't ignore** it for weeks. You have to **get to know the case situation** and its background industry, and the best way is to get started sooner rather than later. You do have around six weeks, however, and BPP can help you. Before you do anything, however, **TAKE A PHOTOCOPY**, in case you lose the case, spill a drink over it, or whatever. We advise you to photocopy the case on to large A3 paper (this book is A4) so you will have plenty of space to write on it **when the time comes.**

(a) Book a **quiet, uninterrupted hour** into your diary, when you know you can read the case. (You might find that **gentle background music** makes your brain more receptive. Scientific tests have shown that for many people certain types of music – mainly classical – can relax the brain.)

(b) **Read the case twice**, **quickly, without taking notes**. Speed-reading twice can improve memory retention, and you do not want to get overwhelmed by the detail. So, do not take notes at this stage – sit in an armchair, rather than at your desk, if you need this discipline.

Step 1.2 Quickly re-read the case after a day

Briefly reviewing information on a regular basis can help you absorb and remember it. However, don't take notes this time. This re-reading session is just to refresh your mind.

Step 1.3 Mark up the case and take notes

Read the case more slowly, highlighting key points, introducing numbered paragraphs or drawing a mind map. The purpose of this stage is still to help you get a broad overview, and the **result of this will be a précis**, summarising the data in the case to fix it in your mind.

(a) At your desk, lay out your A3 copy of the case study. This will give you a lot of space to mark up the material or make notes.

(b) Give each paragraph of the case a **separate paragraph reference** – you will find it easier to refer to paragraphs later if they are numbered.

(c) With a **highlighter** pen, highlight key facts – **do not analyse them for the time being**. Alternatively, you can note down if a fact is important on the side of the paper.

(d) Another technique is to do a **spider diagram** or **mind map**. Starting from the centre of the page, you can link issues in steps. Mind maps are excellent for linking different items of data together or fixing them in your brain. You will find examples throughout this Workbook.

(e) You may also consider what you should do with the separate **Exhibits or Appendices**. These will certainly contain useful information.

Financial data	This will need to be analysed
People involved	These indicate some issues relating to 'internal politics'
Links	Sometimes they take the story forward, and contain valuable information

Step 1.4 Summarise the data in a précis

What is a précis? A concise summary of essential facts. In other words it is short, comprehensive (it summarises), focused, relevant (essential) and based on facts. **It does not incorporate analysis or opinions**. So what's the point of writing out a summary of a case you have read several times, taken notes on, and by now you know fairly well? There are two reasons for doing a précis.

(a) You will start testing your **written business communication skills** – as you have seen already these are a major part of how you will be assessed in this case.

(b) It is a fact that putting things into your own words **can help you absorb and understand the data.**

You should also include key issues arising from the **Exhibits** or **Appendices** in the pre-seen.

PART A TACKLING THE CASE STUDY   4: The BPP approach(1): approach and explore the case situation

Question
Summarise

Here is some data from an old newspaper article. Précis it into 100 words. Give yourself a time limit.

Financial Times	Précis
Halifax, the mortgage bank, has agreed to pay £760m for a controlling stake in St James's Place Capital (SJPC), the holding company for J Rothschild Assurance, in a deal designed to pull the upmarket life assuror into the internet age.	
Halifax bought 17 per cent of the company from Prudential late on Tuesday at 300p a share, a premium of 70p to Tuesday's closing price. It will now extend the offer to up to 60 per cent of the shares, leaving SJPC with a separate listing.	
The bid is the latest move in Halifax's aggressive internet strategy, which began when it poached Jim Spowart from Standard Life bank to set up Intelligent Finance (IF), an online bank due to launch this summer.	
It hopes to add £5bn of assets to IF by selling a St James's-branded private banking service, run by IF, through SJPC's 1,000-strong salesforce.	
'This is an absolutely cracking business,' said James Crosby, Halifax chief executive. 'It increases the scale of our distribution operation in long-term savings and will assist our drive for diversification (away from mortgages).'	
Sir Mark Weinberg, chairman of SJPC, said the company had decided last year to seek a strategic partner to help it use the internet to extend its product range, and began talks with Prudential, which then owned 29 per cent of the shares. 'It became clear that their vision and our vision were not parallel to the extent that there wasn't the opportunity for a value-creating partnership,' he said.	
Analysts said the deal, which is expected to be earnings-enhancing in the first year, would help IF as long as the product, still under wraps, is as exciting as the bank claims.	
The SJPC salesforce own about 8 per cent of the company and have options on another 8 per cent.	

BPP LEARNING MEDIA

Helping hand

Financial Times	Précis
Halifax, the mortgage bank, has agreed to pay £760m for a controlling stake in St James's Place Capital, the holding company for J Rothschild Assurance, in a deal designed to pull the upmarket life assurer into the internet age.	Halifax, the mortgage bank, has spent £760m to control St James's Place Capital (SJPC), a life assurer with Internet potential.
Halifax bought 17 per cent of the company from Prudential late on Tuesday at 300p a share, a premium of 70p to Tuesday's closing price. It will now extend the offer to up to 60 per cent of the shares, leaving SJPC with a separate listing.	Halifax acquired the controlling stake from Prudential Insurance in two stages.
The bid is the latest move in Halifax's aggressive internet strategy, which began when it poached Jim Spowart from Standard Life bank to set up Intelligent Finance (IF), an online bank due to launch this summer.	The bid forms part of Halifax's strategy to develop internet businesses, such as Intelligent Finance (IF) an online bank.
It hopes to add £5bn of assets to IF by selling a St James's-branded private banking service, run by IF, through SJPC's 1,000-strong salesforce.	The acquisition should bring cross-selling opportunities.
'This is an absolutely cracking business,' said James Crosby, Halifax chief executive. 'It increases the scale of our distribution operation in long-term savings and will assist our drive for diversification (away from mortgages).'	There are economies of scale in distribution and opportunities for diversification.
Sir Mark Weinberg, chairman of SJPC, said the company had decided last year to seek a strategic partner to help it use the internet to extend its product range, and began talks with Prudential, which then owned 29 per cent of the shares. 'It became clear that their vision and our vision were not parallel to the extent that there wasn't the opportunity for a value-creating partnership,' he said.	SJPC had been looking for a partner to develop its Internet business for some time.
Analysts said the deal, which is expected to be earnings-enhancing in the first year, would help IF as long as the product, still under wraps, is as exciting as the bank claims.	The deal will help IF and it is expected to increase earnings.
The SJPC salesforce own about 8 per cent of the company and have options on another 8 per cent.	

Solution

Answer (1)

Here is a possible précis

Halifax, the mortgage bank, paid £760m (in two stages) to Prudential Insurance to control St James's Place Capital (SJPC) a life assurer with internet potential. The bid formed part of Halifax's strategy to develop internet businesses, such as Intelligent Finance, an on-line bank. The deal offered cross selling opportunities, economies of scale in distribution and opportunities for diversification. SJPC had been

PART A TACKLING THE CASE STUDY   4: The BPP approach(1): approach and explore the case situation

looking for a partner to develop its internet business for some time. The deal was intended to help IF as it was intended to increase earnings.

What do you think? Could it be improved? It appears a bit unstructured.

Answer (2)

1   Halifax paid £760m to Prudential to acquire St James's Place Capital.

2   Rationale

(a) Halifax and SJPC both wanted to develop an internet business and felt they would make good partners.

(b) Other benefits included cross selling opportunities, economies of scale in distribution, and diversification, and increased earnings

Debrief

Answer 2 is probably too concise. It misses out the fact that Halifax is to launch an on-line bank, a key area of its strategy. However, it is clearer in terms of structure, because it adopts report format and has a heading ('rationale').

Whatever your précis, you have summarised the initial case situation in your own words, and you will then be in a position to analyse it further.

Step 1.5 Carry out an information audit

Now that you have summarised the case, you have an idea of what information you **have** and the information you **do not have**. Look at the checklists starting on the page after next.

(a) **Rationale**

(i) Conceivably it could form part of the **unseen** element – but this is unlikely. You will be able to classify the data.

(ii) You can **derive information by further** analysis – it will feed into Stage 2 Explore the Case Situation.

(iii) You will become more familiar with the case.

(iv) It will help your analysis if you can relate different types of information to each other.

(b) **Process**

You almost certainly will need to do a further analysis but this will feed into Stage 2 Explore the Case Situation.

Tick: yes, we have the data   ✓
P: we have some data   P
Cross: no, we don't have this data   X

Alternatively, it may help you to use **colour highlighting** pens to shade each box so you get a visual overview of where you are lacking data.

(c) Notes about the checklist

(i) It is organised **according to business function;** however, the data may not be presented in this way. We suggest you clarify it by identifying where your data lands on the grid below. (Many decisions need to be taken on the basis of **forecast events** or performance. You may be given forecast statements of financial position (balance sheets) and income statements, or only forecast market data.)

		Orientation	
		Historic	*Future*
Focus	Internal	Internal historic For example: past financial data, existing corporate culture, past decisions, sunk costs, operating constraints, existing customer contracts	Internal future For example: new products planned, new projects, projected future costs or investments, forecasts
	External	External historic For example: past trends, history of regulation	External future For example: market trends, likely economic outrun, potential competitors

(ii) We also suggest you add paragraph references as you go through, especially useful when making connections between different areas.

(d) You will be preparing one of these sheets for 'Zubinos' which we are using as a teaching case in Part B of this Study Text (Chapters 8 – 12). **We suggest you photocopy these sheets on to A3.**

(e) The checklist is a suggestion. Add to it if necessary.

Step 1.6   Research the industry and company

Researching the industry is a vital component of your **knowledge**. Very soon you should be able to get an idea of recent developments, key issues and so on.

Exam skills

The industry under review varies from paper to paper. Case studies in past TOPCIMA exams have ranged from clothes shops, coffee shops, airlines, resort hotels and supermarkets (which should be relatively easy for most people in the developed world to identify with) to a recycling company, a construction company and a children's toy manufacturer. However, whatever the industry identified in your pre-seen, it is important you do as much research on it as you can.

Research the industry

In addition to **trade** and **business magazines**, here are some pointers.

www.cimaglobal.com

CIMA students can access the students' page after logging in. It includes case study details, a message board, and discussion threads about the case.

www.ft.com

Some content requires you to subscribe, but this site can give you a wealth of information about different industries and financial/commercial issues.

www.economist.com

Articles and discussions about business and finance issues

You can also try the websites of relevant trade associations. Sometimes, a websearch using an engine such as *Google* can produce good results.

Note down – or suggest – critical success factors for the industry. You may need them later.

	Focus Int/Ext		Orientation		Notes (eg links, implications, possible calculations)
	Int ref	Ext ref	Hist ref	Fut ref	
Date of case scenario					
Managing director					
Your boss					
Financial data					
Balance sheet					
Income statement					
Cash flow statement					
Notes to accounts					
Further management accounting data					
Product/service costs					
Revenue details					
Contribution					
Performance measures					
Budget vs actual data					
How the firm appraises projects and investments (eg payback, DCF)					
Planning					
Mission and objectives					
Planning process					
Risk management					
Operations data					
Location					
Plant and equipment					
Capacity					
Outsourcing					
Organisation					
Structure					
Culture					
Power					
Key personnel					
Management assumptions					
Systems					
Management info systems					
Mgt reports - content and format					
IT deployment					
Internal controls					
Funding data					
Equity shares					
Long term debt, and repayment schedules					
Working capital					
Cost of capital					
Interest rates					

	Focus Int/Ext		Orientation		Notes (eg links, implications, possible calculations)
	Int ref	Ext ref	Hist ref	Fut ref	
Product service					
Range					
Features					
Competitors					
Quality					
Demand					
Marketing mix					
• Product					
• Price					
• Place (distribution)					
• Promotion					
• People					
• Processes					
• Physical evidence					
Performance measures					
Customers					
Market share					
Market size					
Key customers					
Market research					
Market strategy					
Environment					
Political					
Legal					
Economic					
Social					
Cultural					
Technological					
Ecological/ethical					
Stakeholders					
Competition					
Current					
Potential					
Suppliers					
Current					
Potential					

Step 1.7 Identify relevant technical knowledge

You should by now have refreshed your technical knowledge.

You have to **apply** your knowledge and a good way is to **jot down**, as you go through the case, any areas of knowledge that come to mind and **why** they might be relevant. Do **not** try to use everything you know in the case – it will not all be relevant. The vast majority of the marks on the assessment matrix do not address specific technical knowledge but rather its **use**.

Conclusion

In this stage, we have covered a lot of ground. You've read the case without taking notes, you've read the case whilst taking notes, and you've marked up the case and written down the information – without doing any other work.

This preparation has been essential. There is a lot of data to absorb, and you cannot easily question spot. As stated earlier, the purpose of this stage is to get you familiar with the case data in outline. Then you can analyse it.

3 Explore the case situation

> **Objective of stage 2: Explore the Case Situation**
>
> You should have soundly assessed the fundamentals of the case study scenario in Stage 1 *Approach the Case*.
>
> Now you need to start to apply your knowledge, analytical techniques and lateral thinking skills to what you know, so as to tease out more information from the case.
>
> We suggest a number of models you can consider to help you analyse the data. Again, you need to do this systematically.
>
> REMEMBER:
>
> (1) EVERY CASE SITUATION IS UNIQUE SO YOU MAY HAVE TO ADAPT THE TECHNIQUES SUGGESTED HERE.
>
> (2) YOU HAVE THE ASSESSMENT MATRIX SO YOU CAN FOCUS YOUR EFFORTS ON THE TECHNIQUES THAT ARE MOST RELEVANT.

Step 2.1 Analyse the numbers

Why should you do this now?

(a) Unlike case studies offered by other professional bodies, CIMA's case aims to integrate what you have learned in a **management accounting** context. In your career, one of the skills you will have to offer to future employers is numerical literacy, and the ability to present, mark up and explain the implications and significance of financial data.

(b) The financial data in the case is only **part** of the story, although it is an important part. It will enable you to put other aspects of the case in context. For example, if you work out the cost of capital, you will be able to use it as a discount rate for project evaluation, perhaps.

(c) Remember that you have to say why your analysis is meaningful. What do the numbers mean?

(d) As an accountant, don't be tempted to solve everything by numbers, to the exclusion of other analyses – but numerical analysis should underpin your conclusions.

(e) If you have access to a spreadsheet programme such as Excel, you could do some **simple financial modelling**. How sensitive, for example, is profit to changes in assumptions as to inflation or to any new projects envisaged?

This is good practice if you are taking the exam on computer.

(f) You may find numerical data in a number of contexts.

STEP 1 Review your information audit for the numerical data you have.

STEP 2 From **internal company data**, calculate key ratios if possible, and identify trends in past, current and forecast data.

STEP 3 Apply numerical analysis to **external data** where available, eg market growth rate.

STEP 4 Analyse your data for reasonableness. Are internal growth objectives realistic in the light of market and competitor conditions? What about the cost base needed to generate these revenues?

STEP 5 Write a report on the financial position. You will write a report because you **need practice** and you need to tease out the **meaning of the data.**

Below is a possible checklist you could use. Only calculate relevant ratios, and **invent your own if they are meaningful.** If you do invent ratios, note down what you are calculating and what you are trying to prove. Whose viewpoint are you taking: The managers'? Shareholders'?

Analytical tool	Issues	Other areas
Actual vs forecast	Identify trends: will they continue?	Comparable companies Competitors
Revenue	Price, volume and mix of products Limiting factors	PEST, business environment Pricing Market share (eg output volume) Forecast market share
Cost of sales	Step costs Learning curve impact Operational gearing (fixed and variable costs)	Production capacity Labour rates Suppliers Money-saving opportunities
Gross profit percentage	Useful marker – given market conditions	Competitor costs for comparison
Expenses	Activity based costing	Can relate to advertising costs used to purchase market share
Net profit	Useful to help forecast cash flows Sensitivity to changes in revenue, and costs	Company valuation (eg discounted future profits) if a take-over target
Interest cover	Cost of borrowing Project appraisal	Bank, investors, PEST analysis
Dividend cover	Shareholders' expectations Policy	

Analytical tool	Issues	Other areas
ROE (Return on equity)	Gives the investor's viewpoint	
ROCE (Return on capital employed)	Accounting measures, easy to manipulate You may need to take a nuanced approach to 'capital' employed for a company financed in part by long-term debt; reviewing **operating** performance by reference only to equity shareholders may not be 'helpful'.	Other firms
Retained profit/assets employed	Future investment in the business	
Non-current assets (gross and net)	Age and valuation (eg at cost) Valuation (historic vs market)	Capacity utilisation
Revenue/non-current assets		Compare with other firms
Revenue periods • Inventory • Receivables • Payables	Establish operating cycle, as cash can be released from working capital if managed more tightly	
Working capital/assets employed	Liquidity? Financing costs?	
Current/quick ratio	Working capital cash flows and timing	
Gearing	Can be calculated in a number of different ways	
Debt/equity	Timing of cash flows	
Earnings per share	Shareholders	
Price/earnings ratio	Company valuation	
WACC	Project appraisal financing	
Trends in share price	Shareholder concerns. Raising money	

Question

Presenting financial data

In the case study, you will be required to present financial information, which may well be written for a non-financial manager. You will need to avoid jargon or making too many assumptions as to what the manager might know. You will also need to explain what it means and what implications it has. We reproduce here a question from an exam of a previous CIMA syllabus.

In a number of cities, music societies, which are charitable organisations, provide classical music concerts by operating concert halls and supporting orchestras employing full-time musicians. Earned income arises mainly from giving concerts, with additional earned income from catering activities, ancillary sales programmes, CDs and downloads, souvenirs, and hiring out the concert hall facilities. The earned income is much less than the cost of running the orchestras and concert halls, which are also supported by subsidies in the form of annual grants from local government authorities and the central government, and from business sponsorship, which is a form of corporate public relations expenditure.

The broad aims of the music societies are to provide the best possible standard of live performance of classical music in their home cities (supported by grants from their local government authority) and in other areas of the country (supported by grants from the central government), and to encourage new music and musicians.

As they are charities, music societies do not aim to make a profit. Any surpluses are invested in improvements to the concert halls and spent on additional musicians.

Costs are largely fixed and are broadly 75% orchestral and 25% concert hall and administration (mostly staff). Levels of remuneration, especially for musicians, are low, considering the skills and training required.

The scope for increases in income is very limited. Grants will not increase, and may decrease. The orchestras (allowing for rehearsal time) are fully occupied. Fees for engagements elsewhere in the country and abroad are falling due to the competition from orchestras from other countries.

The chairman of the manufacturing company for which you are a management accountant has recently become a non-executive director of the local music society (X Music), which owns the concert hall and employs the orchestra. His first impressions are that the music is probably excellent, though he is no expert, but that the data available on operations is very limited.

Some comparisons are available with another music society (Y Music) in a smaller city: these are given below.

Required

On the basis of the available data, prepare a report for the chairman, comparing the key features of the business and financial performance of X Music with that of Y Music.

Comparative data

			20X2		20W7	
	20X7		(5 years ago)		(10 years ago)	
Number of performances	X	Y	X	Y	X	Y
Concerts in home city	74	84	77	91	75	91
Other concerts in home country	63	26	88	38	81	52
Overseas concerts	8	8	15	–	11	–
TV/radio/recording	5	11	9	5	14	9
Total	150	129	189	134	181	152
Income						
Concerts in home city	698	1,043	540	717	410	459
Other concerts in home country	916	762	697	361	518	371
Overseas concerts	282	333	154	–	100	–
TV/radio/recording	70	210	72	128	53	118
Other earned income	466	133	76	41	56	22
Business sponsorship	397	607	141	135	56	44
Total earned income	2,829	3,088	1,680	1,382	1,193	1,014
Grant – central government	1,300	1,500	900	1,000	500	900
Grant – local government authority	655	950	150	750	400	500
Total income	4,784	5,538	2,730	3,132	2,093	2,414
Total costs	4,872	5,356	2,703	3,147	2,059	2,402
Surplus/(deficit)	(88)	182	27	(15)	34	12
Cumulative surplus/(deficit)	(686)	311	80	(26)	141	62

> **Solution**

REPORT

To: The Chairman

From: Management Accountant   Date: 3 July 20X8

Subject: Comparison of the performances of X Music and Y Music

This report provides a comparison of the key features of the business and financial performance of X Music and Y Music.

1 **EXECUTIVE SUMMARY**

1.1 **X Music's** results for **20X7** show a **marked deterioration** in financial performance. The society reported a **deficit** of £88,000 in 20X7 (compared with surpluses of £27,000 and £34,000 in 20X2 and 20W7 respectively) and a worrying cumulative deficit of £686,000 (compared with cumulative surpluses of £80,000 in 20X2 and £141,000 in 20W7).

1.2 **Y Music**, on the other hand, was **more successful** and reported a **surplus** of £182,000 and a cumulative surplus of £311,000 in 20X7. A deficit of £15,000 in 20X2 and a surplus of £12,000 in 20W7, and a cumulative deficit in 20X2 (£26,000) and a cumulative surplus in 20W7 (£62,000) point to the possibility that the society's **results have been fluctuating widely** over the last decade, however.

1.3 An analysis of business and financial data for the two societies highlights a number of factors which may well have played their part in these results.

2 **NUMBER OF PERFORMANCES**

2.1 Since 20W7, the **number of performances** given by **X Music** has **dropped** by 17% (from 181 to 150), while the number given by **Y Music** has **dropped** by 15% (from 152 to 129). The similarity in these figures tends to suggest that both societies have been **affected to a similar degree by competition from foreign orchestras**. Despite this fall, however, Y Music has reported both a surplus and a cumulative surplus in 20X7.

2.2 The **number of performances of all types of concert** given by **X Music** in **20X7** have **dropped** from those in 20W7 and 20X2. The number of concerts in other areas of the country (not the home city) in particular has dropped by over 28% to 63 from the 88 reported in 20X2. The number of performances in the home city has remained fairly constant (75 in 20W7 and 74 in 20X7).

2.3 **Y Music** has seen a significant **fall in the number of concerts played elsewhere in the home country** (a drop of 50% from 52 in 20W7 to 26 in 20X7). From playing no concerts abroad in 20X2, Y Music played 8 in 20X7 (as did X Music), and made 11 TV/radio/recording appearances in 20X7, compared with only five in 20X2.

2.4 In 20X7, **Y Music** gave 84 **concerts in its home city**, 10 **more than** the number of performances by **X Music** in its home city. This is **surprising** given that Y Music is based in a smaller city with, one assumes, a smaller concert-going population. **Overall**, however, **X Music** gave 150 performances in 20X7, 21 **more than Y Music**, principally because it made 63 performances in other areas of the country. X Music's disappointing results cannot therefore be attributed to the number of concerts it performed.

3 INCOME

3.1 **Both societies** have reported a **significant increase** in total earned income over the ten-year period. X Music's earned income was 137% higher in 20X7 (£2,829,000) compared with that in 20W7 (£1,193,000). Y Music's was 205% higher (£3,088,000) compared with £1,014,000). It is, however, the **income per concert** that has **led to X Music's poor financial performance**, as illustrated by the following figures for 20X7.

	20X7	
	X Music	Y Music
Income per concert in home city	£9,432	£12,417
Income per concert in home country	£14,540	£29,308
Income per overseas concert	£35,250	£41,625
Income per TV/radio/recording event	£14,000	£19,091

3.2 X Music achieves a significantly lower income per performance for all types of performance than that achieved by Y Music. The difference is most marked when comparing **concerts in the home country**, with **Y Music's income per performance being over double that of X Music's**. This could be because audience sizes are smaller at X Music's performances or ticket prices may be lower, but on the basis of the data provided it is not possible to state definite causes. If you were able to provide me with attendance figures and information about ticket prices I could provide you with a more detailed analysis.

3.3 **X Music's other earned income** of £466,000 in 20X7 (16% of total earned income) is significantly **higher than that of Y Music** (£133,000, representing 4% of total earned income) and hence its catering and merchandising activities are probably considerably more effective than those of Y Music. X Music's figure also compares well with the £56,000 earned ten years previously.

3.4 On the other hand, **business sponsorship** appears to have been extremely **lucrative for Y Music** in 20X7, bringing in £607,000, almost the same income as that earned from concerts in other parts of the country. X Music's business sponsorship at £397,000 was only 65% of Y Music's, although both societies have shown significant increases from the levels in 20W7 (X Music £56,000; Y Music £44,000) and 20X2 (X Music £141,000; Y Music £135,000).

3.5 The **grants** from both central government and the local authority **awarded to Y Music** in 20W7, 20X2 and 20X7 were **higher than those awarded to X Music**. In 20X7, grants represented 44% of Y Music's total income, compared with 41% of X Music's, with Y Music receiving £2,450,000 in grants compared with £1,955,000 by X Music. **Y Music's committee** appear to be **far more effective** in **applying for grants** and X Music's committee should be encouraged to actively pursue this source of income.

4 COSTS

4.1 Despite the fact that X Music put on more performances than Y Music in 20W7, 20X2 and 20X7, **X Music's costs have always been lower**. In 20X7, X Music's costs per performance were £32,480 (£4,872,000/150) whereas Y Music's were £41,519 (£5,356,000/129). Given that one would expect overseas concerts to be the most expensive to put on, and both societies gave eight overseas concerts, this cost difference **may highlight particular cost control skills at X Music** (or alternatively, of course, particularly poor cost control at Y Music). On the other hand, because 75% of the costs are related to the orchestra, it **could point to lower quality performances by X Music** (which might explain X Music's lower income per performance) **or to different forms of performance** by the two societies, the two forms requiring different numbers of musicians.

5 RECOMMENDATION

5.1 Given that X Music's total costs were not covered by total income in 19X7, and that there is no guaranteed level of grant income, X Music should carry out a detailed review of expenditure.

Signed: Management Accountant

Comment on answer

This answer is a very thorough examination of the issues. In terms of format, some of the comparative data could have been put into tables, rather than being incorporated in the narrative.

Exam skills

It is quite possible that the financial data you will receive in the pre-seen or unseen will be incomplete and you may need to make assumptions. If necessary, state clearly any assumptions you have made.

Step 2.2 General environmental analysis (PEST) and trends

PEST analysis and its variants (such as SLEPT or PESTEL) should be familiar to you from the **Enterprise Management (E2)** and **Enterprise Strategy (E3)** papers, and the key issue here is to ensure that you have covered and prioritised everything that you can. You have already identified the information you have. To help you prioritise, you might wish to grade your PEST into order of importance (High, Medium, Low) perhaps with justifications.

Para in case	Type of factor	Comment and significance	Likely importance H, M, L
	Political		
	Legal		
	Economic		
	Social		
	Cultural		

PART A TACKLING THE CASE STUDY   4: The BPP approach(1): approach and explore the case situation   **71**

Para in case	Type of factor	Comment and significance	Likely importance H, M, L
	Technological		
	Ecological		
	Stakeholders		

Question   PEST

Airbus has built the world's largest passenger plane, the A380 ('super-jumbo'), seating between 550 and 650 people, challenging the Boeing 747. In December 2004, Airbus' main shareholder EADS, which has an 80% stake, revealed that the project was £1.6 billion over budget, at more than £8.4 billion. The UK's BAE systems owns 20% of Airbus. The UK government offered launch aid of £530m to get it started. This is a large plane, to be marketed at the major airlines. Airbus promises a 15% to 20% fall in aircraft operating costs. The terms of the launch aid were secret. (However, many years ago, the EU and US agreed on a formula for assessing state aid to their relative industries. American aircraft makers enjoyed indirect support thanks to the demands of the arms industry. Boeing and the US government are concerned that the launch aid breaches this agreement.)

Boeing is developing a smaller plane, the Dreamliner. Airbus and Boeing differ on the respective markets for these aircraft. Airbus believes that there will be a market for large jets flying between central hubs, where people will change planes for onward journeys. Boeing believes that the market for smaller, point-to-point aircraft is larger.

Below are some PEST factors, taken at random.

(a) Classify them as of High, Medium or Low importance to Airbus (for the purposes of this Workbook).

(b) Write a report about what the issues are.

(c) Comment on the suggested report prepared by BPP for (b) above.

Factor

1   Better video-conferencing, eg via the Internet

2   More working at home

3   Greater demand in rich countries for tailor-made holidays

4   Genetically modified food

5   EU-US disputes at the World Trade Organisation

6   Deregulation in air markets (in terms of destination served)

7   Ageing population in western world

8   Political instability in Asia (N Korea; Thailand) and Middle East (Libya; Egypt)

9   Air traffic is projected to rise 5% pa to 2030

10 Stricter asylum and immigration laws applied over Europe

11 Continued expansion of high speed train networks in Europe

12   Short-term reduction in passenger numbers due to global recession

13   Disruption to travel as a result of natural hazards (eg earthquakes, volcanoes)

14   Growth of 'low cost' airlines in Europe flying to obscure airports

15   Airports will have to change

Solution

(a)   Classification of importance

You may well disagree with these. This is to be expected. There is no 'right' answer, but you need a rationale to support your classification.

High

5. May well affect financing of the project and Airbus's status as a company.

6. Firms can compete on different routes. This may restrain demand for jumbo jets and build demand for the dreamliner: but this might be overridden by overall growth.

9. A huge increase. Airports cannot expand fast enough and there is only so much space: bigger aircraft are one solution.

11. High speed trains compete with aircraft for speed and are often more convenient; more relevant to short haul flights than long distance flights.

15. Airports need to be big enough to take the planes

Medium

1. May reduce demand for business travel.

3. Affects destinations people want to fly to, and the market for scheduled and chartered flights: perhaps people will prefer smaller planes.

8. May slow demand for air traffic, or increase economic problems in the region.

12. Airlines may be reluctant to order new planes if passenger numbers are falling, and their profits are also falling. However, in the longer term passenger numbers are expected to carry on rising, so recession is unlikely to lead to a permanent fall in demand for air travel.

13. It is hard to assess the impact of any natural hazards, but they are unlikely to have any significant long term impact.

14. Low cost carriers like cheap planes; perhaps the A380 is too big.

Low

2. Affects other transport firms but not airlines, as this deals with normal domestic commuting more than international business trips.

4. Nothing to do with Airbus at all!

7. Demand can come from elsewhere; population is getting wealthier in Asia.

10. Affects airline operations but not overall demand.

(b) REPORT

To: A manager
From: Consultant
Date:
Re: Environmental influences on Airbus

1 Introduction

1.1 Airbus is one of the world's largest manufacturers of aircraft. It received £530m from the British government in launch aid for the new A380 super-jumbo jet, to compete directly with the Boeing 747.

2 Political factors

2.1 Airbus has always been a controversial feature of the political landscape, owing to its funding arrangements. The US government believes the funding is anti-competitive and potentially damaging to Boeing. Airbus counters that US companies benefit from huge defence contracts and state grants, which act as hidden subsidies.

2.2 The EU and USA are in dispute over other trade issues, and so there may be some further political fallout as a result of the proposed funding arrangements.

2.3 Political factors may also affect the stability of the Asian market, one of the world's growth areas. There is a risk that political instability in these areas will adversely affect the growth of the industry.

3 Economic factors

3.1 Airbus's proposal for the A380 was based on predictions of increased demand for air travel, fuelled by overall prosperity and economic growth.

3.2 Much of this travel is discretionary, such as business or holiday travel. Therefore, in the short term, global recession will undermine this predicted growth.

3.3 Governments may have limited money to spend on increasing airport size. Super-jumbos, by carrying more people, can reduce the need for extra flights.

3.4 The effect of deregulation may be to undermine the business model on which Airbus depends.

4 Social and cultural factors

4.1 Air travel is scheduled to grow; however, evidence seems to suggest that holidaymakers prefer individual holidays to particular destinations rather than general packages. This might reduce demand for mass travel between hubs.

4.2 Natural hazards and social unrest may affect popular perceptions of the riskiness of overseas travel.

5 Technological factors

5.1 Airbus might be interested in other technologies, but technology can influence underlying customer demand. Will video and internet conferencing reduce the underlying demand for business travel? Will supersonic travel be preferred?

6 Conclusion

6.1 Airbus is investing a lot of money, taking a calculated risk that economic and market conditions will justify airplanes of this size.

6.2 The launch aid financing is also at risk owing to political factors.

(c) *Comment on the report*

1 Some **relevant** items are mentioned which did not appear on the list – this shows **business awareness.**

2 Rightly, the report does not cover the items which we classified as '**low**' on the list. They are just not relevant.

3 The factors are classified in logical order. However, more could be done to draw out the interrelationships between them.

4 There is a useful conclusion summarising the environmental factors affecting the product **concept** and the **launch aid**.

Step 2.3 Analyse the business environment and competitive strategy

The technical **knowledge** required should be familiar to you from the **Enterprise Strategy** paper (E3), but the tools employed are relevant to structuring your analysis of the case study. You will be using these tools to obtain a deeper understanding of the case and the context.

(a) The key issues are: customers, suppliers, and competitors, and how they impact on the business – the important issue is to identify or bring to light key issues hinted at or stated directly in the case data.

(b) What is the industry's stage of development? Is it an **emergent industry**, a **mature industry** or a **declining industry**?

(c) You may have to deal with a **conglomerate** or a firm operating on a number of different industry sectors (eg Virgin: planes, trains, personal finance, recorded music, soft drinks). Each sector might have different characteristics.

(d) We also suggest you carry out a **five forces analysis**. Classify each force as High, Medium or Low (H, M, L) in impact.

(e) What is the firm's competitive strategy?

Five forces and industry analysis

(a) **Identify the type of industry(s)**

	What industries does the company operate in?	Classify as emergent, mature, or declining
1		
2		
3		

(b) **Threat of new entrants. (Add others if you wish.)**

	Item	Comment
1	High capital costs to enter?	
2	Is there a strong brand?	
3	Is the industry attractive?	
4	Does the case suggest new entrants?	
5	Ease of exit (if declining sector)	
	Threat of new entrants: high, medium or low (H, M, L)?	

(c) **Substitute products**

	Item	Comment
1	Can other industries provide the same benefit?	
2	Does the case evidence any threats?	
3	Other considerations	
	Threat from substitute products: high, medium, low (H, M, L)?	

(d) **Customer bargaining power and marketing issues**

	Item		Comment
1	Consumer or business to business? If B-to-B, any issues in customers' own markets?		
2	Total turnover		
3	Market size		Current and new markets
4	Market share		Compared to major competitors
5	Does the organisation really understand its customers and their needs?		
6	Can key segments be identified in the data? If yes, what are they and what percentage of turnover do they represent?		
	Segment 1 2 3 4 5 6	Percentage turnover	Do they have different needs?
7	Trends in turnover and other sales performance indicators		
8	Does the case identify any Key Customers who account for a significant proportion of turnover? • If Yes, note details • Is it possible to do a customer profitability analysis? • Are there some customers who are not profitable?		Are they profitable, loyal, happy?
9	Are current customers loyal or are they beginning to defect?		
10	Are customers price sensitive?		
11	Does the case identify customers and markets not served?		
12	Can customers obtain the same benefits easily elsewhere? How easy is it for them to switch supplier?		
13	Does the organisation have a coherent marketing strategy based on the 7Ps? Product – Price – Promotion – Place – People – Process – Physical evidence		
14	Does the organisation consider building long-term customer relationships?		

	Item	Comment
15	What is the branding policy?	
	Customer bargaining power: high, medium, low (H, M, L)?	

(e) **Suppliers and resources**

	Item	Comment
1	Supplier industries – what resources does the business consume?	
2	Does the case detail suppliers?	
3	Trends in input costs – and volatility	
4	Are key suppliers identified? If so, whom? How close is the relationship?	
5	Ease of sourcing supplies from other/new suppliers	
6	Can firm easily pass on increases in input prices to customers?	
7	Is the supply chain managed strategically?	
	Supplier bargaining power: high, medium, low (H, M, L)?	

(f) **Competitors**

	Item	Comment
1	Does the case identify **particular** current competitors? If yes: • What are the competitors? • What are the competitors' competitive strategy?	
2	Does the case suggest potential new competitors in the current industry? Substitute products?	
	Competitive rivalry: high, medium, low (H, M, L)?	

(g) **Identify the current competitive strategy**

Cost leadership indicators	Differentiation indicators
• Price competitive • Production efficiencies	• Evidence of special products/ services • Higher prices • R&D department

Cost focus indicators	Differentiation focus indicators
• Segmentation • Cheapest for segment • Conscious decision to restrict customer base	• Conscious decision to restrict customer base • Needs of segments consciously identified and incorporated in decision making

Summarise the business environment by combining your '5 forces' analysis and PEST in a report or mind map.

To prepare yourself for **this** case study exam, we recommend you use a variety of techniques to stimulate your thinking. So far, we've given checklists and asked you to write reports. However because all the elements of the business environment are interconnected, we suggest you draw a simple **mind-map** or **spider diagram**.

- Start at the centre of the page
- Work outwards linking ideas with lines

Question

Environment

More about Airbus. Review your PEST analysis of Airbus, and consider the data below.

There are relatively few aircraft makers in the world. Airbus's main competitor is Boeing. Airbus has given up its status as a consortium in which each participant (Aerospatiale of France, BAe of the UK, DA of Germany and Casa of Spain) had the right to make part of the plane. Airbus is now a single company, and a subsidiary of EADS, a global aerospace and defence corporation. Governments have a great interest in the aerospace manufacturing industry for defence reasons, and Aerospatiale is part owned by the French government. Aircraft engines are supplied by Rolls Royce, Pratt and Whitney and GE. Furthermore, whilst Airbus is going ahead with a super-jumbo, Boeing has indicated it will not compete. Instead Boeing is seeking orders for a new supersonic plane.

The business model underpinning A380 assumes that people will fly from hub airport to hub airport and change on to connecting flights.

Boeing is developing a fast, supersonic plane, the Dreamliner, holding fewer passengers than the Airbus A380. It will, however, fly from 'point' to 'point'.

Required

Draw a mind-map of the general and competitive environment.

Solution

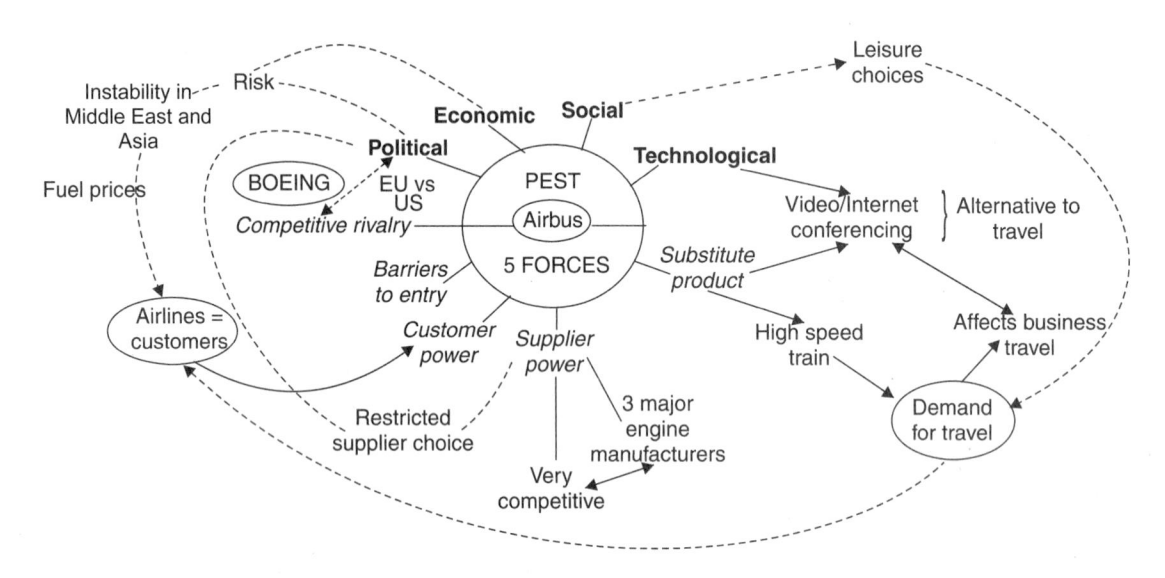

[Mind map diagram combining PEST and 5 Forces analysis centered on Boeing/Airbus:
- Political: EU vs US, Instability in Middle East and Asia (Risk)
- Economic: Fuel prices
- Social: Leisure choices
- Technological: Video/Internet conferencing, High speed train (Alternative to travel, Affects business travel)
- 5 Forces: Competitive rivalry, Barriers to entry, Customer power (Airlines = customers), Supplier power (3 major engine manufacturers, Very competitive, Restricted supplier choice), Substitute product
- All linking to Demand for travel]

Demand for flights

The mind map technique, as you will see, enables you to make connections and see things as a whole. Note the environmental influences on Airbus's customers, who have significant power. You will also note the interconnection between technological factors and substitute products. Doubtless you could develop this further.

In practice, we have moved to the synthesis stage.

Step 2.4 Audit the product/service portfolio

Again, drawing on **Business Strategy**, you need clearly to define what is it the business does. As you are analysing the case study, you need to think a bit more deeply than just 'widgets' or products, but to try to link it with the customer analysis you have done earlier.

STEP 1 Define the product in terms of customer needs satisfied.
- Customers buy a benefit: this can have a physical and a service component.
- Are customers' needs being satisfied in terms of the features offered by the product?

The purpose of doing this is that it can help enrich your understanding of substitute products that satisfy the same needs.

STEP 2 Identify product and service elements.

STEP 3 Use the BCG matrix to identify how the product or service is positioned.

STEP 4 Use your numerical skills to identify and analyse product costs and profitability.

Question
Products and services

Fireclown Software produces and sells computer software that deals with timesheets and project management. The firm makes versions for a Microsoft Access database and also an SQL server database. Charges start at £2,400 per user on a declining scale, so with 10 users (the maximum recommended for the ACCESS version), the fee per user works out at £1,600, or £16,000 in total. The firm will charge extra for installation, and will offer either a standard shell, or tailor solutions to clients' individual needs. The firm charges 20% of the initial purchase costs per year for on-line support, and offers free upgrades. The typical Fireclown client is a firm that uses job production, that requires people in different departments to work together effectively, and that bills costs to clients, hence the importance of the timesheet software. The average 'age' of Fireclown's clients is ten years, and the average number of users per client is five.

Required

Audit the product/service portfolio.

STEP 1 What is Fireclown offering?

Customers need to co-ordinate, plan and monitor complex projects and to bill their clients. Fireclown Software offers a **solution** to these needs.

STEP 2 Product and service elements

The 'product' is the software, and the 'services' are the after-sales support, the installation, and so on.

STEP 3 Fireclown's product portfolio

In the case, you may apply like models such as the **BCG matrix**. Here, there is not enough information for you to do so. What data would you need for this?

- Old and new products identified
- Old and new markets identified
- Cash flow, profit and growth data

STEP 4 Identify product costs and/or customer profitability, if possible.

In Fireclown's case, if a customer stays for more than five years, the annual service fee of 20% of initial installation cost will be worth more to Fireclown than the initial software cost.

For example, take a customer with **five** users and **ten** years' service.

1 user £2,400
10 users – cost per user £1,600 } 5 users, say £2,000 per user

Initial fee 5 users @ £2,000 = £10,000 initial revenue

Service contract = £10,000 @ 20% over 10 years = £20,000

From this, we can hazard a guess that 2/3rds of Fireclown's revenue is from **service** income **if the average customer 'age' is ten years**.

STEP 5 Competitive strategy – see next question.

Step 2.5 How does the business add value?

Here, you can apply your knowledge of **value chain analysis**, say, and other techniques such as **functional cost analysis** to identify what is special about the business.

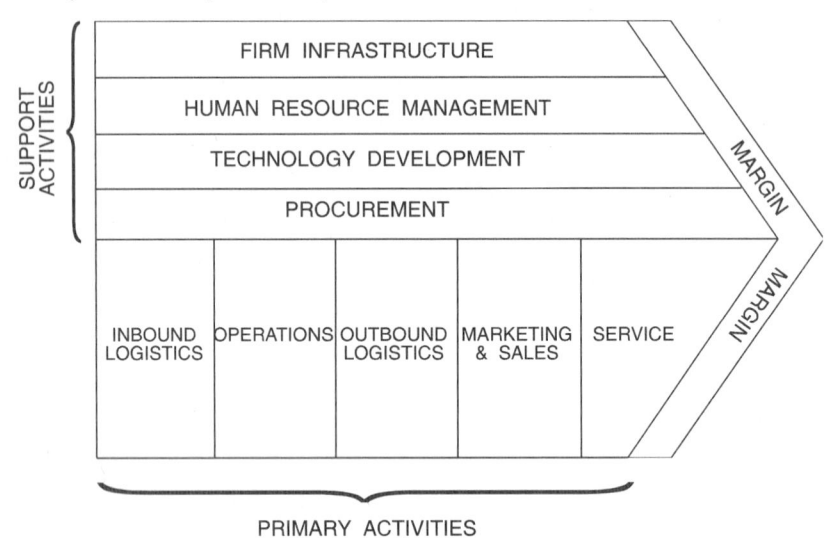

```
                    ┌─ FIRM INFRASTRUCTURE ─────────────┐
         SUPPORT    │  HUMAN RESOURCE MANAGEMENT        │  MARGIN
         ACTIVITIES │  TECHNOLOGY DEVELOPMENT           │
                    └─ PROCUREMENT ─────────────────────┘
                    │INBOUND │OPERATIONS│OUTBOUND│MARKETING│SERVICE│ MARGIN
                    │LOGISTICS│         │LOGISTICS│& SALES │       │
                           PRIMARY ACTIVITIES
```

You can then comment on each area of the value chain.

Question — Value adding

Fireclown continued

How does Fireclown add value and what is its competitive strategy?

Solution

Inputs are minimal as Fireclown is in the business of creating, selling and servicing intellectual property. **Technology development** is perhaps the most significant aspect of its operations. **Outbound logistics** are likely to be relatively minimal but, as we have seen, **after-sales service** is a critical element of its revenue.

As for **competitors**, you might like to jot down what you consider its current competitive strategy to be. Fireclown, arguably, is pursuing a strategy of focus (based on size of user base) and differentiation.

Step 2.6 Identify information systems management controls and processes

Here you will need to draw on your knowledge of **Risk and Controls**, as this could form an aspect of the case study requirement. This deals with the information and control systems available to the organisation in the case study. Here is a checklist.

	Issue	Comment
1	**Information technology**	
1.1	What are the structural arrangements for IT? (eg IT department, delegated to users, information, outsourced)	
1.2	Who looks after IT strategy and security?	

	Issue	Comment
1.3	What is the role of IT in the development of the company? (McFarlan's grid) • Factory • Support • Turnaround • Strategic	
1.4	Is IT use considered within the business strategy and is its implementation harmonised with it?	
1.5	Is e-commerce relevant and does the firm have a stance towards this development?	
1.6	Main systems • Operational reporting • Corporate reporting	
2	**Knowledge and information**	
2.1	What internal communication systems are in use – eg paper, email, intranet? Is this advisable?	
2.2	Do managers receive good information in terms of the performance of the business	
2.3	Knowledge management – is information shared or hoarded?	
3	**Risk**	
3.1	Does current IT set up expose the firm to risk?	
4	**Management and internal control systems**	
4.1	How are activities and resources controlled in the organisation?	
4.2	Is the management accounting system well designed and managed?	
4.3	Who sets performance targets, and are they effective?	
4.4	What is the extent of centralisation versus divisionalisation?	
4.5	Is reporting timely?	
4.6	Are management accounting and information systems regularly audited?	
4.7	Generally, are principles of good corporate governance followed?	
4.8	Is the business susceptible to fraud (computer-based or otherwise)?	

Question
Indicators

EF Co is a long-established company which manufactures a large range of computers, from mainframe to portable, on a single site. Its turnover is about £500 million per annum. The company has recently undergone a major information systems change involving the following.

(a) Capital expenditure of £50 million over three years (the NPV will be £7 million)

(b) Workforce cut from 10,000 to 7,000 employees

(c) Radical changes to work practices, both in the manufacturing systems (use of CAD/CAM) and reorganisation of managerial and administrative functions

The new Managing Director needs to identify and understand some indicators which can be used to evaluate the success or otherwise of this change.

Required

Recommend to the Managing Director up to five key indicators that he can use and explain why each is relevant to his requirements.

Solution

REPORT

To: The Managing Director, EF Co

From: Accountant

Date: 23 November 20X5

Subject: Recommendations for key indicators

In evaluating the effect of the recent changes within EF Co the following indicators can be recommended.

(a) **Added value per employee** is useful as a possible measure of **productivity.** This could, for example, be defined as sales income less bought in services (including finance charges) and material, divided by the number of employees.

The company has proceeded down the route of replacing personnel with capital equipment. The productivity of the remaining workforce should therefore be significantly greater than before.

The **information** for this indicator is readily available from the **usual management accounting sources**. Knowing the cost of capital, the savings in payroll costs, and the budgeted throughput, a target added value per employee can be calculated that represents breakeven on the financial effect of the changes.

A **weakness** with this indicator is that certain elements are susceptible to **changes in economic conditions** as well as to internal changes.

Any business process re-engineering of this nature should bring about significant gains in productivity by **eliminating inefficient and outdated processes** altogether. New procedures should reflect **best practice** in the industry, and, for this reason, some use of **benchmarking against competitors** in the industry is also recommended.

(b) **Responsiveness** to customers and the marketplace is vital.

The purpose of the changes is not simply to save money, but to enable the company to **react speedily to consumer needs**. The information technology industry is becoming a prime example of 'relationship marketing', wherein the supplier is attempting to become closer to each customer. This is a means of seeking competitive advantage. Thus the organisation will be trying to behave as if it were 'lean and mean' and provide fast response to each customer, not simply manufacturing 'boxes'. Hence the introduction of CAD/CAM.

An **important indicator** therefore, as an example of speed of reaction, is the **speed at which bespoke customer needs are met**. To make this indicator consistent, project times from agreement of customer specification to delivery need to be measured.

A **problem** with this is that the size of the project will affect the speed of delivery. Perhaps project times could be divided by the sales margin for comparability and consistency. The lower the ratio the better. A company target figure should be established as a yardstick.

(c) **Financial** indicators, such as **management accounting ratios** (credit risk, receivables days, WIP turnround etc) should also be used. Although **care** is needed in **interpretation**, because of distortions caused by accounting policies and the need for consistency from period to period, the **traditional measures** of working capital efficiency (summarised perhaps as 'working capital days', namely receivables days plus inventory days less supplier days) are **as relevant as ever** to modern industry.

The improvement in the **manufacturing systems** will have included measures designed to improve **inventory management** and **financial control**, probably one of the variants of JIT (just-in-time) and perhaps ABM (activity based management) or other relevant costing/management systems. The effect on cash flow should be dramatic once the new systems are in place.

These cost savings can be set against the capital costs incurred in developing new systems. Standard **investment appraisal** techniques can be used here: current thinking suggests that a balanced measure, incorporating NPV, payback and IRR gives the most rounded view. In addition **project management measures** relating to budget, timetables and quality (availability, response etc) can be used.

(d) **Strategic direction** is extremely difficult to assess as it involves such long-term factors. Major systems change of the type undertaken is certainly part of a strategic process and its success can only be seen by reference to the **overall market position** of the company and its **reputation**. The value of the **brand name** may be measured, but such measures are **subjective**. Better is a **long-term tracking of share price** and **market share**.

Although **strategic planning is long-term**, IT can sit awkwardly with this, as so much **technology is short-term** in nature, with manufacturers reducing product life cycles in their quest for competitive advantage. This means that IT-based decisions may need to be changed within the life of a particular strategy. This problem can to some extent be addressed by a formal **Information Systems Planning** exercise, which creates a framework for development, providing guidelines over a period of time to ensure that activities fit into strategic criteria.

(e) **Critical success factors** can be used. Each CSF will already have been ascribed one or more performance indicators. CSFs are fundamental to the strategic direction of the company. Here, the changes to be evaluated are more than just small improvements to individual parts of the company, they are a fundamental change to the very nature and shape of the organisation.

The ultimate measure of their effectiveness could be said to be in the **bottom line results** of EF Ltd; however, other factors will also be relevant, for example, **reliability indicators**. This might take the form of warranty claims/sales, or claims/number of products supplied, or may be based on customer surveys measuring the elusive characteristic of 'customer satisfaction'. The reputation of the company, and thus its potential to generate future cash flows – the definition of the value of the enterprise – depends on the quality of its service. It is important to know that the reduction in personnel numbers, and the introduction of automation have not compromised quality.

The above should be read in the light of the assumption that **systems development** is undertaken in general to **meet business needs** and **fulfil organisational objectives**. These might be categorised as:

- Reductions in cost base
- Investment in IT infrastructure
- Responding to, or anticipating, changing market conditions
- Ensuring that IT supports strategic plans

It is only by setting **appropriate performance indicators**, such as the above, that the success of systems development can be **measured**.

In conclusion, the measurement of the key components of the strategy of the company are vital to the **control and updating** of that strategy as it links **'hard'** cost/benefit analysis with **'softer'** areas which are difficult to quantify and often subjective.

Signed: Accountant

Step 2.7 Identify key issues in structure, culture and personnel

Structure and culture can be either a strength or a weakness, especially as senior management sets the tone. Although you only have so much information to go on, it is useful to have a reasoned opinion in your own mind. This may only be an opinion, but it will give you an underlying rationale for any changes.

(a) **Structure**

Issue	Comment
Step 1 Draw an organisation chart, if the case has not already provided you with one.	
Step 1.1 What sort of departmentation approach is used (eg functional, matrix)?	
Step 2 Does the case data indicate any problems with the current organisation structure, such as reporting/communication, co-ordination, corporate governance, focus on the business?	
Step 3 Does the case data offer opportunities for you to benchmark the performance of different departments with other firms? If so, how does the firm compare?	
Step 4 Identify any outsourcing arrangements currently in force, and arrive at a reasoned judgement as to how effective they are in terms of operations, risk and financial security.	
Step 5 Identify any possible opportunities for outsourcing and note feasibility.	
Step 6 In your opinion, is the structure a strength or a weakness in the light of the situation facing the business and why?	
Step 7 Recommend improvements: what structure (in brief) would you consider better?	

(b) **Culture**

Issue	Comment
Step 1 What does the case tell you about the culture of the organisation and its management? Classify it, if you can, according to a framework used in your earlier studies.	
Step 2 Is it a strength or a weakness?	

(c) **Personnel and human resources management (HRM)**

Issue	Comment
Step 1 Who are the key people?	
Step 2 Do they have objectives which can affect the performance of the firm?	
Step 3 What influence do they have: • Internally? • Externally?	
Step 4 Does the firm have a succession plan?	
Step 5 Is there any evidence of poor industrial relations?	
Step 6 Is there a strategy for HRM and is it aligned with the business strategy?	
Step 7 What are its employment policies (contracts, rewords, performance appraisal)?	
Step 8 Does the firm invest in training?	
Step 9 Is there evidence of high staff turnover?	
Step 10 Does the firm have skills and competences base needed for the future?	
Step 11 What is the quality of the management team, given the challenges facing the business?	
Step 12 Do managers have a shared vision?	
Step 13 Do they understand their rules and responsibilities under corporate governance regulations (eg UK Corporate Governance Code)?	

Step 2.8 Identify investor objectives, capital structure and other stakeholder objectives

	Investors	Comment
Step 1	Identify share owning structure: • Privately owned? • Publicly traded?	
Step 2	Note information as to the return shareholders and investors are expecting from the company – use comparative information.	
Step 3	Note trends in the share price, if this information is given.	
Step 4	If you have a P/E ratio and a market value, calculate a **possible value for the business**.	
Step 5	Do you have information to calculate the WACC? If yes, do so.	
Step 6	Note comparative information about other companies for a benchmark as to shareholder expectations.	
Step 7	Note data as to the risk of the company (eg the beta).	
Step 8	Review gearing ratios.	
Step 9	Would you invest in this company?	
Step 10	**Managers** Objectives Remuneration Performance	
Step 11	**Employees** Objectives	
Step 12	Lenders Exposure Relationship	
Step 13	Government (central and local) Relationship Power to influence	
Step 14	Customers and suppliers See '5 forces' analysis	
Step 15	Community Pressure groups etc	

The purpose of this exercise is to indicate to you the possible objectives of the actors in the case.

Exam skills

The issues of Betas, WACC and so on may come up, and it is possible you may have to prepare a company valuation. The March 2005 case required candidates to prepare a valuation in connection with a takeover bid.

Question
Market values

PMS is a private limited company with intentions of obtaining a stock market listing in the near future. The company is wholly equity financed at present, but the directors are considering a new capital structure prior to it becoming a listed company.

PMS operates in an industry where the average asset beta is 1.2. The company's business risk is estimated to be similar to that of the industry as a whole. The current level of earnings before interest and taxes is £400,000. This earnings level is expected to be maintained for the foreseeable future.

The rate of return on riskless assets is at present 10% and the return on the market portfolio is 15%. These rates are post-tax and are expected to remain constant for the foreseeable future.

PMS is considering introducing debt into its capital structure by one of the following methods.

(a) £500,000   10% Debentures at par, secured on land and buildings of the company
(b) £1,000,000 12% Unsecured loan stock at par

The rate of corporation tax is expected to remain at 33% and interest on debt is tax deductible.

Required

Calculate, for *each* of the *two* options:

(a) Values of equity *and* total market values
(b) Debt/equity ratios
(c) Cost of equity

Solution

The first step is to calculate the present cost of equity using the **capital asset pricing model** (CAPM):

$$K_e = R_f + [R_m - R_f]\beta$$

where K_e = cost of equity (expected % return)
        R_f = risk free rate of return (10%)
        β = beta value (1.2)
        R_m = market rate of return (15%)

In this case: K_e = 10% + (15 − 10)% × 1.2
              = 16%

This cost of equity can now be applied in the **dividend valuation model** to find the **total market value of the firm**. It is assumed that all earnings are distributed as dividend; earnings and therefore dividends do not grow.

$$p_0 = d_0/K_e$$

where p_0 = market value
        d_0 = current level of dividends (post tax)
        K_e = cost of equity
        p_0 = £0.4m × 0.67/0.16
             = £1.675m

(a) The situation under the different scenarios can be summarised as follows.

	Current £'000	Scen 1 £'000	Scen 2 £'000
Profit before interest and tax	400.0	400.0	400.0
Less interest	(0.0)	(50.0)	(120.0)
	400.0	350.0	280.0
Less tax at 33%	(132.0)	(115.5)	(92.4)
Distributable profits	268.0	234.5	187.6

According to the basic theory of capital structure developed by **Modigliani and Miller**, the market value of a firm is independent of capital structure. When tax is introduced into the calculations, the market value of the firm will increase as debt is added to the capital mix because of the present value of the **tax shield** on interest payments. This can be expressed as:

$$V_g = V_u + DT_c$$

where V_g = market value of the geared company
 V_u = market value of the ungeared company
 D = market value of debt
 T_c = rate of corporation tax

In this case:

	Current £'000	Scen 1 £'000	Scen 2 £'000
V_u	1,675	1,675	1,675
D	0	500	1,000
T_c	33%	33%	33%
$D \times T_c$	0	165	330
Total market value (V_g)	1,675	1,840	2,005

The value of the equity can now be found:

$$E = V_g - D$$

Scenario 1: £1.84m – £0.5m = £1.34m

Scenario 2: £2.005m – £1.0m = £1.005m

(b) The ratio of **debt to equity** is given by D/E:

Scenario 1: 500/1,340 = 37.3%
Scenario 2: 1,000/1,005 = 99.5%

(c) Assuming that all distributable profits are paid as dividends, the **cost of equity** can be found using:

$$K_e = d_0/p_0$$

where K_e = cost of equity
 d_0 = dividend (distributable profit above)
 p_0 = market value of equity

Scenario 1: 234.5/1,340 = 17.5%
Scenario 2: 187.6/1,005 = 18.7%

Step 2.9 Identify and analyse possible business projects

The case data may provide you with information about business projects.

(a) By this, we mean, for example, **new product development**, a proposed **acquisition**, new **information systems**. There could be projects currently in progress or being proposed. You may be given numerical data to evaluate the project. **Remember decision-making** (eg theory about sunk costs, money already spent). Your **technical skills** could be beneficial here.

(b) A project could on the other hand be an **opportunity** in the market, or something crying out from the data. (It could be a project suggested by a deficiency in current operations, for example, which could be dealt with by improving the information system.) This is an examination of your ability to think critically.

(c) We suggest you note down possible business projects in a schedule, with a rationale.

No	Project – rationale	Main para refs in case
1		
2		

Question — Projects

Clothes Rus a UK retail chain, is facing difficulties, for a variety of reasons, and a programme of change has been put in place. This has included the appointment of a new chief executive and chairman, and the appointment of top staff from other retailers. The company faces a takeover. One cause is that Clothes Rus is alleged to have failed to respond appropriately to customer needs. At one time the inventory for each store were determined centrally. Every store was supposed to stock goods in pre-determined quantities, on the basis of **store size alone** (not patterns of actual consumer purchases). If a particular store ran out, in the past people would have driven to the next nearest Clothes Rus store, perhaps in another town. In recent years, however, they have just gone to another retailer, such as Next.

Can you identify any 'business projects' from the data above?

> **Solution**

This is based on a real life example, the key issues being inventory and purchase information. From the data, the information system is at fault in that inventory decisions are taken **centrally** and not related to the individual buying patterns of each store. With data mining software, Clothes Rus would be able to identify store buying patterns and be able to respond more quickly.

In the schedule proposed, you could have analysed this as follows. If you had been provided with financial data, then you could have identified some of the cashflows.

No.	Project – rationale	Main para refs in case
1	Data mining • Protect/increase turnover by retaining customers • Provide information to ensure no stock-outs	x.1

It is quite possible that the case will provide you with details of current projects. You may be able to do a DCF analysis on these.

4 Conclusion

Keep in mind the following issues.

> 1. Who are the key players in each company and who is the most important?
>
> 2. What do you think is the key strategic problem facing each company?
>
> 3. What is the main element of each company's plans for the future?
>
> 4. What is the biggest immediate problem facing each company?
>
> 5. What are the main features of the companies' statements of financial position (balance sheets) at the most recent year end?
>
> 6. What are the main SWOT points for each company?
>
> 7. What information have you been given in the pre-seen (in overall terms); what information might you be given in the unseen and why?
>
> 8. Write down your approach for the exam, step by step, from start to finish.
>
> 9. Write down the nine areas in the assessment matrix and what you have to do to get marks for each area.
>
> 10. Compare your approach to the exam with the nine areas, and make sure that you include ways in your technique of doing what CIMA requires of you.

We have now done most of the analysis we want to do. You may feel awash with data and ideas. In the next chapter, we help you pull together all you have done, so you have a clear understanding of the business – in other words, so that it makes sense to you. You will then have a solid foundation to deal with what the examiner might throw at you in the exam.

The BPP approach (2): synthesise what you know

In the last chapter, analysis was relatively easy. All you had to do was to apply what you already know. In **this chapter**, we **give you tools to help you** to synthesise this data into a coherent structure. In other words, we want to get you to understand the sinews of the business and the issues facing it.

- You will then find it easier to deal with the unexpected in the unseen.

- Remember, you are explicitly advised not to question spot. There are unlikely to be questions lurking away in the data.

- It will help you a great deal to talk over the issues with someone else doing the paper, to see what perspectives their analysis has brought to the situation. And remember, too, that your **lecturer can offer vital guidance** - each case is different, and your **lecturer will know best**.

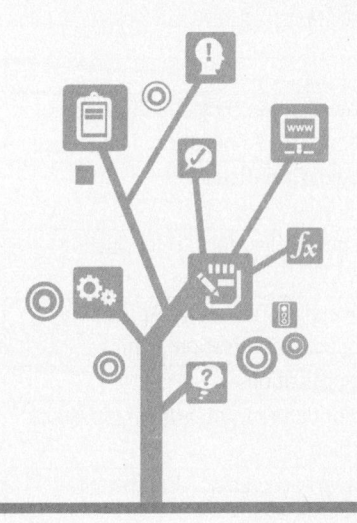

topic list

1 Synthesise what you know

1	Tools to approach the case: Chapter 4	Time	Criteria of the assessment matrix
1.1	Read the case quickly twice without taking notes	1 hour	
1.2	Quickly re-read the case after a day	30 mins	
1.3	Mark up the case slowly taking notes	2 hours	
1.4	Summarise the data in précis	1 hour	Diversity, Logic, Judgement
1.5	Carry out an information audit	1 hour	Diversity, Integration, Prioritisation
1.6	Research the industry and company	-	Diversity
1.7	Identify relevant knowledge	30 mins	Technical, Application, Focus

2	Tools to explore the case situation: Chapter 4		Technical, Application, Focus, Logic
2.1	Analyse the numbers	Depends	Diversity, Technical, Application, Focus, Logic, Ethics
2.2	General environmental analysis (PEST) and trends	1 hour	Diversity, Technical, Application, Focus, Logic, Ethics
2.3	Analyse the business environment and competitive strategy	1.5 hours	Technical, Application, Focus, Logic, Ethics
2.4	Audit the product/service portfolio	1 hour	
2.5	How does the business add value?	1 hour	Integration, Ethics
2.6	Identify **information systems** and processes	1 hour	Technical, Application, Focus
2.7	Identify key issues in structure, culture and personnel	1 hour	Technical, Application, Focus, Prioritisation, Ethics
2.8	Identify investor objectives, capital structure and other stakeholder objectives	1 hour	Technical, Application, Focus, Ethics
2.9	Identify and analyse possible business projects	1 hour	Integration, Technical, Application, Focus, Ethics

3	Tools to synthesise what you know: Chapter 5		
3.1	Summarise your findings in an interim position statement	1 hour	Prioritisation, Logic, Judgement, Technical, Application, Focus
3.2	Draw up a mission statement for the current business from the pre-seen data	30 mins	Logic, Prioritisation
3.3	Relate the business's distinctive competences to the critical success factors for the industry	30 mins	Logic, Judgement, Prioritisation
3.4	Identify and analyse risks, internal and external	1 hour	Diversity, Technical, Application, Focus, Prioritisation, Ethics
3.5	Carry out a graded SWOT analysis	1 hour	Prioritisation
3.6	Identify key business issues	1 hour	Prioritisation, Integration, Diversity, Ethics
3.7	Draw up a balanced scorecard	1 hour	Integration, Logic, Judgement, Prioritisation
3.8	Prepare a one page business summary	1 hour	Logic, Judgement, Prioritisation, Diversity, Integration

4	Practise report writing before the exam: Chapter 6		

5	The exam – three hours: Chapter 7	Time
5.1	The night before: review your business summary and the pre-seen	
5.2	In the exam itself: • Review the unseen and requirement • Skim read the data • Read the requirement carefully, making a mental note of the recipient of the report, the required format and what you have to do	Reading time 20 mins
5.3	Read the unseen data in depth. Be sure to identify what has changed. Make notes on the question paper identifying the key issues.	
5.4	Consider the big picture and plan your answer. Do the calculations	40 mins
5.5	Draw up the appendices, terms of reference and introduction	10 mins
5.6	Prioritise the issues: 4 key issues and 'other issues'	15 mins
5.7	Write the main body of the report	50 mins
5.8	Write the ethics section	15 mins
5.9	Write up your recommendations	30 mins
5.10	Write the conclusion and review your work	5 mins
5.11	'Question 2': use format required and keep answer succinct. Refer to calculations.	15 mins

1 Synthesise what you know

Objective of stage 3: Synthesise what you know

In Stages 1 and 2, you were becoming familiar with the broad outline of the case and you were exploring some of the issues, and teasing out some of the relationships between different items of data. The purpose of Stage 3 is to describe a number of techniques to bring all this thinking together into a coherent framework. All the tools in this stage try to help you integrate your knowledge into a few key issues.

Step 3.1 Summarise your findings in an interim position statement

It may feel as is all we are suggesting you do is produce different types of summary. But that is not the case. You started off by doing a précis, and after that you did a lot of analysis to tease out key issues in the case study. Some issues may still be uncertain, of course, but you have come quite far. **You should now be able to reach genuine conclusions as a result of your analysis**. Whereas, with the initial précis, you were supposed just to review the data, this **position statement** should incorporate some of the results of your analysis.

(a) Ideally, your statement should be a page long.

(b) This is meant to help you draw your breath, so to speak.

(c) You could use your précis as a basis for this statement and re-write it or add to it with the results of your analysis.

(d) Try to build connections between the data you have identified in the case. **Here's a tip:** if you are unsure how to **link items,** use the **value chain** model.

Question

Synthesis

Here are some facts about Obsidian plc.

- Founded 1879, Sheffield UK

- Business: generalist stainless steel cutlery manufacture (80% turnover, 60% gross profit) plus luxury cutlery (20% sales, 40% gross profit)

- Net profit margin: 15% after overheads (no further analysis by department)

- Return on assets: 10% (the bare minimum needed, according to the chairman)

- Warranties and refunds: 1% of sales

- Competitors: low cost producers from China have captured two key accounts for mass produced cutlery

- Customers: UK supermarkets and department stores

- New product development: luxury silver cutlery, handcrafted for the US market, Obsidian plc's first attempt at exporting

- Factory workforce: 500 (of which 250 work in the speciality cutlery section)

- Capacity utilisation: 85%

- The website established 2 years ago receives 100 hits a month in 20X0 rising to 1000 a month in 20X1, showing some customer interest in the luxury cutlery

- Number of accounts: mass production, 100; speciality, 200

Required

Summarise this business situation. Do not be afraid to come to some initial conclusions.

Solution

1 **Introduction**

Obsidian plc is a long-established manufacturer of specialist and mass market cutlery, based in the UK, dealing mainly with UK customers.

2 **Customers and markets**

2.1 Obsidian has been losing business to competitors from China, perhaps due to a combination of price and quality problems. Obsidian spends 1% of turnover on warranties, and has recently lost two accounts.

2.2 Obsidian's luxury business has fared better, successfully exporting to the US. Most interest expressed from website contacts has been for the luxury manufactured cutlery. In two years, website hits have gone up by a factor of ten.

3 **Products and production**

3.1 There are two types of cutlery; products for the mass market and those produced for the luxury market.

3.2 The mass produced cutlery account for 80% of turnover but only 60% of gross profit suggesting thin margins. The specialist cutlery accounts for 20% of turnover but 40% of gross profit.

3.3 The specialist craft workforce is about 50% of the total, and there are many more accounts that need to be serviced in smaller quantities. (Perhaps activity based costing should be used to see how overheads are incurred.) The firm combines, possibly, mass production with job production.

3.4 The financial position will suffer – the firm has lost two major accounts (2% of its mass-production customer base, probably worth more by value).

4 **Financial position**

4.1 ROCE is 10%, and net profit is 15% of turnover.

Comment

This answer is a lot longer than a bald list of facts – and it does summarise **relationships** between them and draws out a narrative. For example, it **links** the **loss** of two accounts with **overseas competition** (your business awareness should tell you that China is a low-cost manufacturing centre) and with possible quality problems.

You could have organised this very differently, of course.

Step 3.2 Draw up a mission statement for the current business

In practice, **mission statements** can often be so much hot air, promising everything to everybody, and easily mocked.

(a) However, the reason why your are doing this **now** is to ensure that you have a clear idea of the current business – it is a device simply to integrate your **thinking and understanding of the case**.

(b) The unseen data in the case may suggest a quite **different mission** or data inconsistent with the mission.

(c) Try to keep it to a **few lines.**

(d) **Do not get tied up making objectives** – unless, say, it is clearly stated in the data that shareholders want a return. This is **just to help you grasp** the business's current position.

Question   Mission

Draw up a mission statement for Obsidian plc (see Question 1).

Solution

Obsidian plc seeks to satisfy shareholders by making and selling cutlery, in hand crafted and mass produced format, in the UK and overseas.

Comment

Note that we have put in 'shareholders' first of all before getting carried away by what the business does. Some firms might quantify these objectives.

Step 3.3 Relate the firm's distinctive competences to the critical success factors for the industry

(a) A **distinctive competence** is what a firm does uniquely or better than other firms do. Of course, some firms do not have a distinctive competence as such, although they might have unique features.

(b) A **critical success factor** is what you have to achieve to be successful in the long term. It can be applied to an industry or a project.

Here is quite a tricky example.

Question
Competences

The *Virgin Group* runs diverse activities: airlines (Virgin Atlantic); holidays (Virgin Holidays); a music and entertainment store (Virgin Megastore); health clubs (Virgin Active); a drinks business (Virgin Drinks); financial services (Virgin money); telecommunications (Virgin Mobile); radio (Virgin Radio); an online casino (Virgin Games); a rail company (Virgin Trains) and even a Formula 1 racing team (Virgin Racing).

(a) What do you think is the **distinctive competence** of the Virgin Group?

(b) Identify relevant **critical success factors**.

Solution

(a) The founder of the Virgin Group, Sir Richard Branson, has described himself as a 'branded venture capitalist' investing in a variety of businesses. Perhaps Virgin has a genuinely distinctive competence in **branding**.

(b) **Critical success factors** for the Virgin group **as a whole** are hard to identify – there are separate factors for success in different industries. For example, music retailing is not the same as rail transport. Arguably a CSF for the Virgin Group is that **its brand is easily recognisable and held in high esteem** and that it has a profitable image in each business (eg retailing, transportation, financial services). Other possible CSFs are that Virgin offers value for money for customers and improves the customer's experience through innovation.

Below are possible critical success factors for Virgin's **airline** business.

Success factors might be:

(1) Ability to attract **profitable** customers
(2) Ability to fill seating **capacity**
(3) **Safety and conformance** with regulatory requirements
(4) **Delivery** of services promised

Safety, factor (3), is **necessary** to be in the industry **at all**, so it is not critical to **success** in commercial terms. For **success** in the industry, factors such as profitable customers and seating capacity, supported by the delivery on the service promised, are more important.

Step 3.4 **Identify and analyse and quantity risks, internal and external, to the business and its stakeholders**

The purpose of doing a risk assessment **now** is that it forces you to integrate different areas of the business, the environment and stakeholders. (You could just as easily do this as part of your analysis work, but it does synthesise some issues.)

(a) For the purposes of the case study, we can say that **a risk** is any event that is uncertain and that could have significant consequences for the business, its performance operations or its stakeholders.

(b) This might have consequences for the **long-term survival** of the business or aspects of it. We have already analysed the **external** environment as a source of risks, but **internally,** risks could be caused by factors such as:

- Strike action
- Breakdown
- **Information systems** crashing (especially if operationally important)
- Customer response

(c) Risk can be **quantified** or be given a **value**. Boards need to consider any risks and their likelihood, acceptability and potential impact. **Internal control systems** could assist with this risk management process.

(d) Risk may be viewed by different stakeholders in different ways. You may incorporate risk into **project appraisal**.

(e) You should have enough data from your previous analysis and working papers.

(f) Here is a checklist.

Risk type	Consequences (quantify if useful)	Possible cost	Importance, likelihood and seriousness H = over 70% M = 30–70% L = up to 30%
Business			
Political			
Financial			
Exchange			
Operational gearing			
Other			

(g) Obviously, something that affects the long-term survival of the business is highly important. The reason for identifying the stakeholders affected is that the objectives of stakeholders differ. If you are given probabilistic data, you may use **decision trees**.

Question — Business risks

Here is some data about *Boo.com*.

Boo.com was an **Internet-based** fashion and sports goods retailer which invested $120m of venture capital. Set up by two young entrepreneurs, Boo hired staff from university, but apparently had difficulty holding on to its Finance Director. Boo developed an innovative website and hoped to introduce its services at once in 18 different countries. There was a strong corporate culture, but staff numbers expanded rapidly.

Required

Identify business risks in Boo.com.

Solution

Fact	Risk?
Most of Boo.com's staff were fresh from university	Little management experience, although lots of good ideas.
Boo.com wanted to sell in 18 countries at once	The risk was that Boo.com would **fail** to fulfil on its promises to its customers. Few normal retailers would be so ambitious. The mechanics of fulfilment, such as delivery and logistics, were as critical as the front end.
Staff were highly paid and hard working, but staff numbers were growing all the time	These were probably not used effectively.
Fashion	This industry can be inherently volatile.
New, innovative technology	Boo's website only really started to work five months after launch.
No finance director	Poor controls over the cash – many internet companies have gone into receivership (as Boo.com itself did in 2000!)

Step 3.5   Carry out a graded SWOT analysis

SWOT is another useful framework to integrate and synthesise the different elements of the case study and the results of your analysis. This is invariably subjective, but it enables you to prioritise effectively.

(a)   Strengths and weaknesses are internal. Opportunities and threats are external.

(b)   A strength can turn into a weakness in some circumstances. For example, organisational culture can be a strength, but it can be inappropriate in the wrong environmental conditions.

(c)   Categorise all items by areas of the business. It might then emerge that there may be particular weaknesses in particular areas (eg weak in production, strong in marketing).

(d)   You can use other business models to help you determine what are opportunities for example. The Ansoff matrix from the Enterprise Strategy paper can structure your thinking here.

(e)   You should indicate whether these are high, medium or low in importance.

STRENGTHS	Ref	Function	WEAKNESSES	Ref	Function
1			1		
2			2		
3			3		
4			4		
5			5		
6			6		
7			7		
8			8		
9			9		
10			10		

OPPORTUNITIES	Ref	Function	THREATS	Ref	Function
1			1		
2			2		
3			3		
4			4		
5			5		
6			6		
7			7		
8			8		
9			9		
10			10		

Step 3.6 List key business issues

You should be able to identify six to ten **key issues** for the business, ranked in order of significance. Why?

(a) They reflect what is of concern to the business, irrespective of what turns up in the unseen. For example if **cash flow** is a key issue (from Step 2.1 Analyse the numbers), you will be alert for cash flow implications in the unseen data in the exam room. You can also mention some key business projects.

(b) A list will be easy to remember and it will help you prioritise.

(c) It might help you a great deal if you are able to compare notes with a colleague.

(d) Finally, you need to give the key issues a time horizon, to differentiate between **urgency** and **importance**.

Issue in order of importance	Description	Time scale (years)
1		
2		
3		
4		
5		
6		
7		
8		
9		
10		

Question — Key issues

Let us return briefly to the example of Virgin (see Question on Competences). Obviously, the management has an objective for each of the businesses, but these also link to issues for the **Virgin group** as a whole. Here are some facts.

In September 2007, Richard Branson sold his UK chain of Virgin record stores to a group of senior staff in the business, who subsequently rebranded the stores as 'Zavvi'.

The deal ended Branson's 30 year involvement with High Street music retailing, and highlights the problems music retailers are facing as sales have fallen dramatically following the advent of digital music downloads.

Nonetheless, Zavvi's management team believed the business had a bright future, despite the problems facing the sector.

They felt they could deliver a new brand that "lives and breathes" entertainment, and delivers high quality, enthusiastic service to existing and new customers.

However, in December 2008, following the collapse of its largest supplier Zavvi, went into administration, because it was unable to source stock in its usual way. Zavvi had attempted to buy supplies from alternative suppliers, but experienced difficulties in obtaining stock on favourable credit terms or acceptable prices.

As a result, the company's working capital was placed under intense pressure and it was unable to pay its quarterly rents when they became due in December.

Identify the key issues from the data above.

Solution

For Zavvi, the key issue was being able to generate enough cash to pay bills. This was both urgent and important, because it led to the collapse of the company.

For Richard Branson and Virgin the industry life cycle was a key issue. Virgin decided that music retailing was a declining sector and was no longer profitable, which is why the business was sold.

Although Zavvi's management team believed the business had a bright future, the problems which HMV (the last remaining major high street music retailer in the UK) is currently suffering suggest they might have been too optimistic, and changes in technology have fundamentally reshaped the music retailing industry.

Step 3.7 Draw up a balanced scorecard

The balanced scorecard is another technique you can use to draw your analysis together. It identifies key performance measures – perhaps you could relate these to critical success factors and the links between them. **Remember that there are four perspectives.** Again, the issue is to identify the linkages between factors.

↑ market share ⇒ ↑ capacity utilisation

Financial	Internal process
- Profitability - ROCE - Cash flow - Share price, P/E ratio	- Efficiency - Capacity utilisation
Customer	Innovation and learning
- Market share - Complaints	- New product/service development

Linking issues

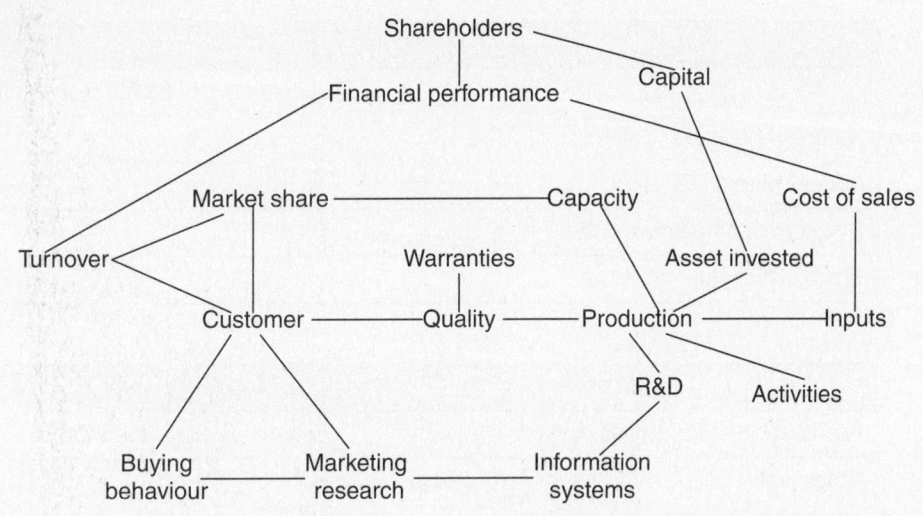

```
                    Shareholders
                         |              Capital
           Financial performance
              /          |       \
         /               |         \
   Market share ——— Capacity        Cost of sales
    /    \            |      \        /
Turnover  \         Warranties  Asset invested
          Customer ——— Quality ——— Production ——— Inputs
           /    |    \                  |   \
          /     |     \                R&D   Activities
       Buying  Marketing  Information
     behaviour research    systems
```

Step 3.8   Prepare a one-page business summary

This step requires you to **synthesise** and select the really **key data** of all the work you have done so far – the data which, in the exam room, you would be kicking yourself if you had forgotten or had to re-calculate or re-analyse – in other words, items of **high importance**. Remember that **synthesis** is a higher level skill.

(a) A **final synthesis of all the work** you have done so far in one document.

(b) **A one page note of all the key facts** and issues that you need to remember so that you are **not completely taken aback by the unseen data** and forget all the analysis you have done. **In the exam, you will have the case data, but none of your notes.** A lot depends on how thorough your preparation has been and your ability to remember key facts.

(c) A suggested format for the summary is given but you **should invent your own**, depending on the circumstances of the case and how easy it is **for you** to remember.

(d) Only transfer those items you think to be of **high** importance to the summary document. This does not mean that everything else is irrelevant – far from it – but you should really try to remember the key lessons you have drawn from the exercise.

(e) Alternatively you can draw a **mind map**, similar to that given in the section covering the environmental analysis. The key is to **get everything on to one page** which you can easily revise from.

BUSINESS SUMMARY: Name of company			
Nature of business (2.4):........................	Turnover	CFSs for success in industry	
		•	
Current mission (3.2)		•	
Distinctive competence (3.3)			
Major stakeholder objective			

ANALYSIS BACKUP				
Key financial data: trends (2.1)		External (2.2, 2.3): 5 forces		
Gross profit	Estimated value of business	P		1 Barriers
Net profit		E		2 Substitutes
ROCE		S		3 Customers
Other		T		4 Suppliers
				5 Company
Gearing		Internal (2.6, 2.7)		
Cash		• Capacity		
Operating cycle		• Structure		
Worrying indicators		• Information		
		• Other		
Competitive strategy: Cost leadership/Differentiation/Focus/'stuck in the middle'				
Customers – Key data				

SYNTHESIS				
SWOT (Items of high importance)			RISKS: (High importance)	Time
0	0		1	
1	1		2	
2	2		3	
3	3			
Weaknesses	Threats			
1	1		4	
2	2			
3	3		5	
Key issues (3.6) (High importance)		Time	Selection of possible business projects (2.8) (High importance)	
1			1	
2			2	
3			3	
4			4	
5			5	
6			Possible discount rate	

Report writing is so important we are going to give it a chapter on its own.

Report writing and the TOPCIMA paper

You really do need to practise here. Your ability to communicate clearly in writing is vital to your success in the TOPCIMA exam.

You need to be able to communicate your ideas and solutions, or recommendations, clearly to your reader.

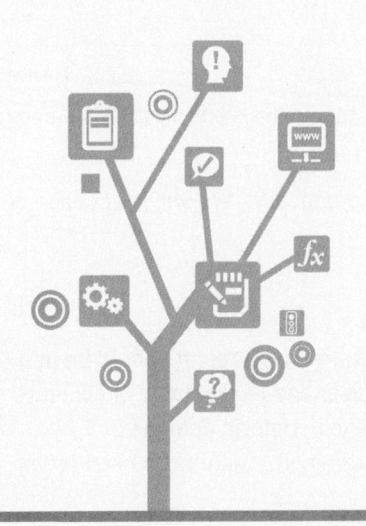

topic list

1 Report writing and the assessment matrix
2 Structure
3 Language
4 Example report
5 Other formats

1 Report writing and the assessment matrix

1.1 The report format

You may be required to present your answer in a number of formats but a **report format is the most likely**. Even when not specifically asked for, report format is still a good idea, as it focuses your mind on structure and layout, and makes your answer easier to mark. However, read the **question requirement** carefully to make sure you understand exactly what you are being asked to do.

Question — Report format

Put what follows into report format.

'The first criterion is whether this will be profitable over the estimated life cycle of product A. Another criterion which is related to the first criterion is that of estimated volume sales at the proposed price. A third criterion which needs to be considered when deciding whether or not to launch Product A is....'

Solution

(a) Decision criteria in rank order

    (i) Profit (ROI) over product life cycle

    (ii) Sales volume at proposed price

    (iii) ...

This is just an example. We have tried to get you to use report format in the analysis and synthesis stages at various times.

When writing a report, there is a clear need for appendices, workings and structure. We will cover each of these, but here is a step by step guide.

Exam skills

The examiner has given some guidance on reports. The key requirements are that a report should be in a recognisable format and should be easy to navigate. There should be a clear and logical table of contents and each part of the report should be clearly headed and identified. Detailed strategic analysis or calculations should be included as appendices, but referred to within your report. There is no need for an executive summary if time is short.

Finally:

'DO NOT WASTE TIME ON EXCESSIVE PRESENTATION AT THE EXPENSE OF THE CONTENT OF YOUR REPORT'

2 Structure

2.1 A design suggestion

Although you may be required to write your report from an external perspective (eg as a consultant hired to advise the Board of a company) or from an internal perspective (eg as a management accountant of the company advising the Board), it is more likely you will have to adopt an **internal perspective**.

Make sure the technical knowledge you display (eg management accounting, business strategy etc.) is appropriate to the context in which you are writing the report.

A report written by a strategic consultant advising the Board would be expected to focus on the big decisions affecting the long-term development on the business.

An internal report prepared by the management accountant is more likely to have to look at management accounting issues, although in writing the report the management accountant should also be prepared to include advice about the strategic or longer-term implications of the issues facing the business or recommendations he / she makes.

The exact structure of your report must reflect the requirement given in your exam, but the following is a suggested approach for the overall design for your report. (Page numbers are indicative only.)

Page 1	**Title block** • Who the report is written for (eg 'Board of XYZ plc') • Who has written the report (eg Independent Consultant') • Date • Title
	Table of contents • Outline the contents of the report in numbered sections • Give titles of Appendices • Can be used to manage your time by allocating minutes to each section/subsection you plan to include within your report.
Page 2	**Section 1 – Introduction** • A brief introduction (between 5-10 lines maximum) on the background situation of the organisation and the issues it faces. Incorporate Unseen data if it changes the situation • Avoid explaining or evaluating issues **Section 2 – Terms of reference** • Two or three lines to set the scene of who you are (eg management accountant or external consultant), who the report was commissioned by, and who it is aimed at. Can almost be a paraphrase of question requirement.
Pages 3 to 4	**Section 3 – Review and prioritisation of main issues facing the management of the organisation** • Based on SWOT analysis in Appendix 1 • Place top **four** issues in priority order with numbered subheadings (eg '3.1 Cash Flow Crisis – Priority 1') • Justify the sequence of priorities in terms of consequences for organisation • Less important issues grouped as 'other issues' at end • Refer to 'Ethical Issues' in section 5, but do not include them here • Do not explain the background to the issues nor provide recommendations.

Few potential marks
• Integration
• Diversity

Crucial section that carries up to 30% of marks
• Focus
• Judgement
• Prioritisation
20% of script length

Pages 5 to 8	**Section 4 – Discussion of the main issues facing the management of the organisation**
	Numbered paragraphs each dealing with an issue from Section 3 (eg 4.1 Cash Flow Crisis – Priority 1')
	- In the same sequence as issues in Section 3
	- For each main issue, explain the background and the potential consequences it has for the organisation
	- Issues should be supported by analysis in the Appendices
	- Numerical values stated and referenced to Appendix where they can be found (eg 'the maximum amount that should be paid for the new business has been calculated at £3.6bn (Appendix 3 line 7)'
	- Reference to technical theories in Appendix (eg 'XYZ plc is following a stuck in the middle strategy – see Appendix 2')
	- Discuss possible alternative actions to overcome issues but **avoid putting recommendations here**
	- Analyse alternatives using 'Suitability, acceptability, feasibility'
	- Use real-life examples to support your discussions – but only if they are directly relevant
	- Less important issues shown under 'other issues' heading, but only written about if time allows
Pages 9 to 10	**Section 5 – Ethical issues to be addressed by the management of the organisation**
	- Identify three issues and rank in priority order
	- State the ethical principles and duties involved
	- Recommend appropriate action for each
Pages 11 to 13	**Section 6 – Recommendations**
	Regarded by the Examiner as *'the most important part of the report'*
	- Numbered sections corresponding to each of the numbered sections from Section 4 (eg '6.1 Dealing with cash flow crisis')
	- Each section states **what decision you recommend**, explains **why you recommend it**, and then **tells management how to do it** (eg *'This report recommends management rejects the new contract in its present form. The contract is insufficiently profitable and has the following unacceptable features ... etc. A formal letter should be sent to the management of XYZ Ltd rejecting the contract and stating the areas of concern This would leave the door open to XYZ Ltd submitting an improved offer'*)
	- As a minimum, recommendations must be given for each of the four prioritised issues identified in Section 3
	- It is **not** acceptable to avoid making recommendations on grounds such as 'need more information' or 'firm needs a strategic plan to deal with this'. You **must** make recommendations

Section 4 notes: Important section that carries up to 30% of marks
- Technical
- Application
- Focus
- Judgement
- Diversity

40% of script

Section 5 notes: Mini report within a report. 10% of marks, majority for recommendations

Section 6 notes: Most important section worth up to 30% of the marks
- Logic
- Integration
- Judgement

Page 13	**Section 7 – Conclusion** • Brief two or three lines for closing comments	Very few marks here
Pages 14 to 18	**Appendices** Put at back of answer booklet/Word document and on Excel spreadsheets Appendix 1: SWOT analysis Appendix 2: other theories from business strategy (PEST, 5 forces, Ansoff, Stakeholder Map) Appendix 3 etc: numerical workings Key data and analysis given in appendices should also be discussed within the body of the report	Essential for justification of analysis and recommendations • Technical • Application Up to 15 marks
Page 19	**Section 8 – Question 2** Produce your answer to Question 2. • Use the prescribed format • Refer to supporting calculations in the appendices to the main report • Keep answer brief: do not include unnecessary detail	• Logic Up to 10 marks

Exam skills

As we have noted above, the Examiner regards the 'Recommendations' section as the most important section of the report: the actions you recommend are what gives your report value to its readers. Make sure you allow yourself plenty of time (at least 30 minutes) to make your recommendations.

There is a danger that because the 'Recommendations' are the penultimate section of your report, you will run out of time before you get to them if you haven't managed your time properly.

For example, don't spend too long on the 'Introduction' and 'Terms of Reference' which will score very few marks. In fact, you should only be looking to spend about 5 minutes on them, leaving you more time for the main mark-scoring sections of the report.

Exam skills

Although diagrams can be used in the Appendices, and should be used for the SWOT analysis, the diagrams themselves are not essential for other models or theories. As long as you refer to the relevant theory, this will score a technical mark, with further credit for applying the theory to your analysis or discussion of the issues in the case.

3 Language

3.1 Stylistic requirements

Consider the following actual extract from an exam script submitted for a past exam paper for the Chartered Institute of Marketing. Note in particular the writing times.

> (a) Proposals for change in the organisational structure
> (b) Creation of 'strategic business units' centred around each terminal
>
> This would allow each terminal to be represented at board level with each managers having his own operational and commercial staff beneath him. This will involve a huge restructuring of the organisation and individual job roles/responsibilities, however this move is necessary in order that commercial and operations staff work alongside each other and cooperate to solve problems in the most effective way, to the benefit of EAL in serving the needs of its customers. All commercial versus operations conflicts would be solved lower down the hierarchy which will in turn be flattened out as a result of restructuring. Each terminal general manager must have beneath him his appropriate support staff for his commercial and operations roles: eg catering manager, retail operations manager, quality control engineers.
>
> Total words = c 140   **Total time = 8 minutes**

Keeping the same heading, we might change the section to read as follows:

> Each terminal to become an SBU under a general manager with his own support staff (catering, retail operations, quality control etc).
>
> BENEFIT
>
> Although requiring much restructuring and reformulation of job descriptions:
>
> (a) Commercial and operations staff would work together in meeting the needs of the customer
> (b) All commercial v operations conflicts would be solved lower down the hierarchy
> (c) Each terminal would be represented at board level
>
> Total words = c 70   **Total time = 4 minutes**

The re-wording cuts the original word length in half.

- It is easier to understand and mark.
- It takes half the time to write. There would be extra time to make extra points and gain extra marks.

3.2 'Less is More'

Rule	Example No	Example Yes
Keep words simple	Expenditure vs	Cost
	Aggregate vs	Total
Short words are quicker to write	Terminate vs	End
Avoid words you don't need to write	I would be grateful	Please
	Due to the fact that	Because
	In the not too distant future	Soon (better: say when!)
	At this point in time	Now (or currently)
	In the majority of instances	In most cases
	It is recommended that A Ltd should consider	A Ltd should consider
Total	36 words (55 syllables)	14 words (18 syllables)

Be careful of jargon: jargon is technical language with a precise meaning and therefore has its uses. Bear in mind the needs of your audience. If your report is addressed to the finance director you can make more use of accounting jargon than you would to the marketing director. Remember that some industries have their own jargon.

Be precise. Be careful of 'very', 'fairly', 'partly', unless you are unable to state facts.

Do not criticise the reader. Your reports will be advising management or others, who may not be financial specialists. You will have no friends if you say to them they are useless or incompetent. That will blind them to your message. After all, if they are seeking your advice, they know that there are issues to be investigated.

Remember your audience. Remember who the report is directed to.

Remember also that an external report is more likely to focus on high level strategic issues (eg potential acquisition, company valuations) whereas an internal report is likely to have a greater focus on operational issues with strategic overtones (for example, organisation structures; change management; and improving management information or information systems).

4 Example report

You are the management accountant of a company which specialises in producing dairy products for the slimming market. The results of your latest research have just been published (see below).

Data

Market Research Results

This research was carried out from January to June 20X9, using in-depth interviews in the respondents' homes, recorded on tape and interpreted by ourselves, 'The XYZ Research Agency', specialists in market research for the food industry.

Sample size: 500
Age range: 15-55
Socio-economic groups: ABC1*
Locations: Bristol, Manchester and Greater London
Sex: Males and Females

Three broad categories were tested and the results are as follows:

Motives for wanting to lose weight	*% of respondents with weight problems mentioning*
To feel good physically	68
For health reasons	67
To stay fit	43
Because I want to live longer	25
To stay mentally alert	23
To be more attractive	21
To be more popular	15
Methods for weight control	
Avoid certain foods, eat 'slimming items'	32
Eat and drink less	23
Play sports, keep 'fit'	22
'Have certain diet days'	7
Take medicines, stimulants	3

Food which people dislike giving up	% of respondents with weight problems mentioning
Cakes, pies, bakery products	31
Sweets, sugar	23
Beer, alcoholic beverages	17
Meat, sausages etc	15
Chocolate	13
Cream	9
Fruit juices	9
Potatoes	9
Pasta	9

In general, the comments also revealed that dieting means a loss of pleasure at mealtimes, causes problems when one can't eat the same as the family and also one is regarded as being 'ill' when dieting.

---

* Socio-economic groupings:

A   Higher managerial, Chief Executives etc
B   Managerial, Executives etc
C1   Higher clerical, Supervisory etc

Required

Write a short formal report to the marketing director, Mr David Forsythe, highlighting the conclusions drawn from this research. Your recommendation will be used to help identify new products for possible development in this market

---

To: Marketing Director

From: Management Accountant

Date:

REPORT ON NEW PRODUCT DEVELOPMENT

1   The survey

2   Findings

2.1   Motives for losing weight

2.2   Methods of weight control

2.3   Foods respondents disliked giving up

2.4   General comments

3   Conclusions

4   Recommendations

Appendix A: Motives for weight loss

Appendix B: Methods of weight control

Appendix C: Foods which people dislike giving up

1   THE SURVEY

1.1   This report has been compiled from research findings designed to show:

    (a)   Respondents' motives for losing weight
    (b)   Respondents' methods of weight control
    (c)   Foods which respondents were reluctant to give up

1.2   Respondents were a sample group of 500 ABC1s aged 15-55 of both sexes in the Bristol, Manchester and Greater London areas. In-depth interviews were recorded in the respondents' homes, and analysed by XYZ Research: see Appendix A.

2 FINDINGS

2.1 *Motives for losing weight* (see Appendix A)

Most respondents expressed their motives for losing weight as the desire for physical well-being (68%), health (67%) and fitness (43%), with related concerns, such as longevity and mental alertness, also scoring over 20%.

Perhaps unexpectedly, the motives most commonly associated with 'slimming' – increased attractiveness and popularity – scored comparatively low, with 21% and 15% respectively.

2.2 *Methods of weight control* (see Appendix B)

The most frequently-stated method of weight control (32%) was based on food selection: consuming 'slimming items' and avoiding certain foods. Reduced consumption in general (23%) and increased physical activity (22%) featured strongly, however, compared to the use of medicines and stimulants, mentioned by only 3% of respondents.

2.3 *Foods respondents disliked giving up* (see Appendix C)

A significant proportion of respondents were reluctant to give up foods in the high-calorie 'snack' categories: cakes, pies and bakery products (31%), sweets and sugar (23%). Alcohol (17%), meat (15%) and chocolate (13%) also featured significantly, compared to the more 'healthy' food groups such as fruit juice, potatoes and pasta (9% each). Cream was the only dairy product mentioned, (9%).

2.4 General comments

Respondents experienced 'dieting' as a loss of pleasure, an inconvenience when it comes to family meals, and a social stigma.

3 CONCLUSIONS

The prime reason for losing weight was health and fitness, mainly achieved through regulated food intake and increased activity. However, respondents felt deprived in general by the dieting process, and particularly disliked giving up snack foods and food generally regarded as 'unhealthy': processed foods, high in fats and sugars, low in fibre.

4 RECOMMENDATIONS

These findings present opportunities in several areas.

4.1 In order to maximise sales of our existing products, we should reappraise our promotional strategy in the light of these findings, to ensure that:

 (a) The health rather than the cosmetic benefits of our products
 (b) That our products are tasty, convenient and normal: not like dieting

4.2 We may also be able to widen the market for our existing products. Since health and well-being was the most common reason for losing weight, we might extend our marketing message to include non-dieters: emphasising the healthy image of dairy products in general and low-fat alternatives in particular.

4.3 Respondents' desire to eat normally while dieting suggests a continuing market for low-fat, low-calorie adaptations, especially of those food which people dislike giving up. Since dairy products currently feature quite low on this list, however, we should consider diversifying into the most significant areas highlighted by the research. Chocolate products may be an initial avenue, being closest to our existing product portfolio, but we may need to look at bakery and confectionery products. This would offer the potential to develop a more extensive brand, and to capture a larger share of the wider slimming market.

APPENDIX A: MOTIVES FOR WEIGHT LOSS

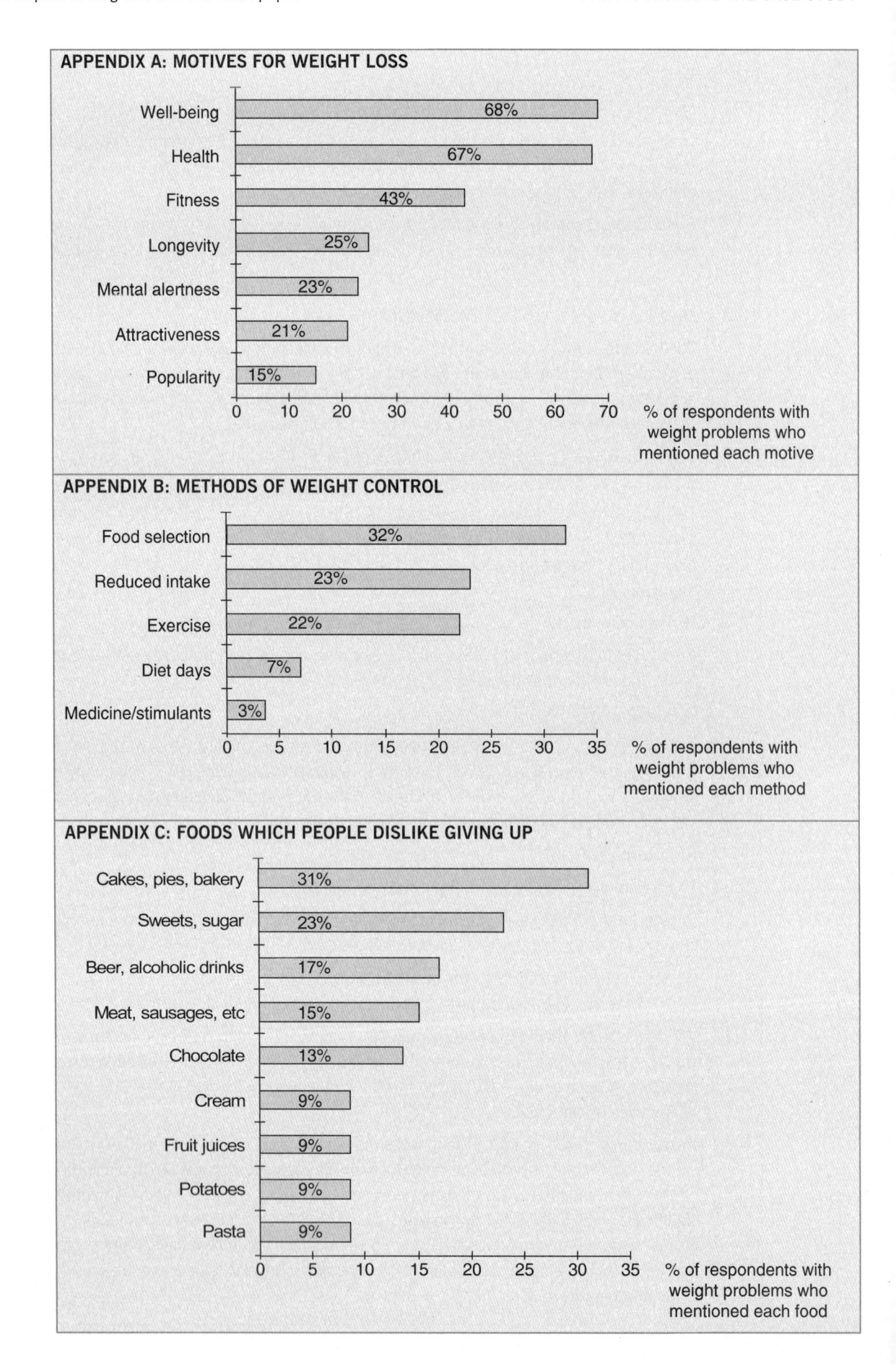

Motive	%
Well-being	68%
Health	67%
Fitness	43%
Longevity	25%
Mental alertness	23%
Attractiveness	21%
Popularity	15%

% of respondents with weight problems who mentioned each motive

APPENDIX B: METHODS OF WEIGHT CONTROL

Method	%
Food selection	32%
Reduced intake	23%
Exercise	22%
Diet days	7%
Medicine/stimulants	3%

% of respondents with weight problems who mentioned each method

APPENDIX C: FOODS WHICH PEOPLE DISLIKE GIVING UP

Food	%
Cakes, pies, bakery	31%
Sweets, sugar	23%
Beer, alcoholic drinks	17%
Meat, sausages, etc	15%
Chocolate	13%
Cream	9%
Fruit juices	9%
Potatoes	9%
Pasta	9%

% of respondents with weight problems who mentioned each food

Debrief. What did you think of the report?

(a) Note that the report writer had constructed a graph of the data. You **may** be given graph paper in the exam and you **may** use it to make clear your points.

(b) Note that the conclusion and recommendations are different and are separate.

5 Other formats

As we have already mentioned, it is likely that you will be asked to produce a report (either internal or external) but you may also need to employ other formats in your answer.

Remember, there will also be a second part to the requirement worth 10 marks: question 1 (b).

This will assess your ability to communicate a particular issue from the main report effectively.

This second requirement is unlikely to be in a report format, so you should expect to have to use more than one format for communicating your answer. For example, the requirements in the specimen paper (Pilot Paper) were: to produce an internal report (worth up to 90 marks) and then prepare two slides (worth up to 10 marks).

5.1 Briefing notes

These are more informal than a report – but, as a rule of thumb, help yourself maintain the overall structure by numbering the paragraphs.

Structure	Features
• Heading/title • From/To/Date • Indication of content • Summary of key points/recommendations • Suggested agenda (if addressee is preparing for a meeting) • Main text of document • Concluding paragraph • Appendices	• Informal • Short sentences, short paragraphs • Concise • Not necessarily numbered

5.2 Letter

It is far less likely that you will have to produce a letter than a report, but if you are, make sure your answer follows the structure of a business letter:

Structure	Features
• Letter heading • Introductory paragraph outlining purpose of the letter and indicating content • Summary of key point/recommendations • References to detailed text in attachments • Concluding paragraph indicating the next action to be taken • Sign off • Attachments/appendices	• Formal address • Unlikely to have paragraph numbering • Report may be attached • Generally for external communication

5.3 PowerPoint/Slides

You could be asked to produce **slides**, or **notes for a presentation**. Again you need to keep track of where you are and to show that your data is organised clearly.

Structure	Features
• Title • Summary • Topic slides in a recognisable sequence • Conclusion plus notes	• Slides themselves should be brief: eg a list of no more than six points • Most slide presentations feature the slides and supporting notes offering more detail

5.4 Memo

Structure	Features
• Distribution (To/From/Date) • Special features (eg confidential) • Topic sections (emphasised by paragraph headings)	• For internal use, and much less formal than a report • A very flexible means of communication – from simple paragraphs to detailed prescriptions (eg instructions) • Should finish with a conclusion or recommendation

5.5 Email

It is also possible you might be asked to prepare an email (in conjunction with a report) highlighting the key points in a report.

If you are, you should aim to key your email brief and make sure you focus only on the key points.

5.6 Graphs and charts

You shouldn't expect the 10 mark requirement in Question 1(b) necessarily to be a written document. You could also be asked to prepare a graph, histogram or bar chart as if they were attachments to an email or a report.

In the 'Useful articles' section for T4 on CIMA's website (www.cimaglobal.com) there is a 'Student support guide' focusing on the 10 mark part (b) requirement. This article provides some examples of the type of requirement you could expect to see in part (b) of your exam. You are strongly advised to look at these before you sit your exam.

Exam skills

If you have to prepare slides as part of your answer, (for example, summarising the business case for an investments proposal), the examiner is likely to only want to see the 5 or 6 most important points on the slides.

The assessment criteria of logic, judgement, and prioritisation in particular could all be important here, but remember the 10 marks in Question 1(b) are all included within the '**Logic**' in the Assessment Matrix.

The exam

You have three hours (after 20 minutes reading time) to satisfy the examiner that you have achieved the requisite standard as required by the assessment matrix.

- You will be faced with some unfamiliar information when you sit the exam.
- You will have to integrate this with what you already know about the business.

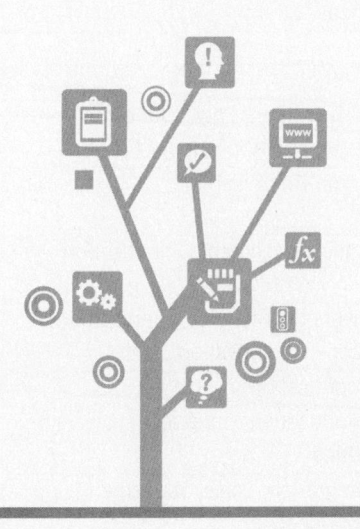

7

topic list

1 Before the exam (Step 5.1)

2 The reading time (Steps 5.2 to 5.3)

3 Your answer (Steps 5.4 to 5.9)

1	Tools to approach the case: Chapter 4	Time	Criteria of the assessment matrix
1.1	Read the case quickly twice without taking notes	1 hour	
1.2	Quickly re-read the case after a day	30 mins	
1.3	Mark up the case slowly, taking notes	2 hours	
1.4	Summarise the data in précis	1 hour	Diversity, Logic, Judgement
1.5	Carry out an information audit	1 hour	Diversity, Integration, Prioritisation
1.6	Research the industry and company	-	Diversity
1.7	Identify relevant knowledge	30 mins	Technical, Application, Focus

2	Tools to explore the case situation: Chapter 4		Technical, Application, Focus, Logic
2.1	Analyse the numbers	Depends	Diversity, Technical, Application, Focus, Logic, Ethics
2.2	General environmental analysis (PEST) and trends	1 hour	Diversity, Technical, Application, Focus, Logic, Ethics
2.3	Analyse the business environment and competitive strategy	1.5 hours	Technical, Application, Focus, Logic, Ethics
2.4	Audit the product/service portfolio	1 hour	
2.5	How does the business add value?	1 hour	Integration, Ethics
2.6	Identify information systems and processes	1 hour	Technical, Application, Focus
2.7	Identify key issues in structure, culture and personnel	1 hour	Technical, Application, Focus, Prioritisation, Ethics
2.8	Identify investor objectives, capital structure and other stakeholder objectives	1 hour	Technical, Application, Focus, Ethics
2.9	Identify and analyse possible business projects	1 hour	Integration, Technical, Application, Focus, Ethics

3	Tools to synthesise what you know: Chapter 5		
3.1	Summarise your findings in an interim position statement	1 hour	Prioritisation, Logic, Judgement, Technical, Application, Focus
3.2	Draw up a mission statement for the current business from the pre-seen data	30 mins	Logic, Prioritisation
3.3	Relate the business's distinctive competences to the critical success factors for the industry	30 mins	Logic, Judgement, Prioritisation
3.4	Identify and analyse risks, internal and external	1 hour	Diversity, Technical, Application, Focus, Prioritisation, Ethics
3.5	Carry out a graded SWOT analysis	1 hour	Prioritisation
3.6	Identify key business issues	1 hour	Prioritisation, Integration, Diversity, Ethics
3.7	Draw up a balanced scorecard	1 hour	Integration, Logic, Judgement, Prioritisation
3.8	Prepare a one page business summary	1 hour	Logic, Judgement, Prioritisation, Diversity, Integration

4	Practise report writing before the exam: Chapter 6		

5	The exam – three hours: Chapter 7	Time
5.1	The night before: review your business summary and the pre-seen	
5.2	In the exam itself: • Review the unseen and requirement • Skim read the data • Read the requirement carefully, making a mental note of the recipient of the report, the required format and what you have to do	Reading time 20 mins
5.3	Read the unseen data in depth. Be sure to identify what has changed. Make notes on the question paper identifying the key issues.	
5.4	Consider the big picture and plan your answer. Do the calculations	40 mins
5.5	Draw up the appendices, terms of reference and introduction	10 mins
5.6	Prioritise the issues: 4 key issues and 'Other issues'	15 mins
5.7	Write the main body of the report	50 mins
5.8	Write the ethics section	15 mins
5.9	Write up your recommendations	30 mins
5.10	Write the conclusion and review your work	5 mins
5.11	'Question 1(b)': Use format required and keep answer succinct. Refer to calculations	15 mins

1 Before the exam

The three hours of the TOPCIMA exam itself is the culmination of all the work you have put in over the past six weeks, analysing the preseen material. You have done a great deal of analysis and synthesis, using a number of different techniques. You should be able to live and breathe the life of the company in the pre-seen material.

In the exam, **you cannot take any notes with you**. All you will see is the case study data you received before your work began, some new data (unseen) and the requirement.

Step 5.1   **Review your business summary and the 'pre-seen' material**

It is vital, therefore, that before you go into the exam, you review the **business summary** as this contains all the work you have done already in a brief form. Even if you can remember **one** fact, such as the ROCE for the latest year, you will not have to recalculate it in the exam.

Also, have another look at the 'pre-seen' material before you go into the exam. You will encounter it again, in its unanalysed form, in the exam itself. You might want to link it, in your mind, to the business summary.

By now, you should be well versed in taking exams and should not need any further advice about getting to the exam hall in good time, making sure that your calculator works and so on. We would, however, advise you to bring **coloured highlighter pens.**

2 The reading time (Steps 5.2–5.3)

In the exam room you will find:

- A **copy of the pre-seen case** data you have been working on in the past six weeks
- Up to six sides (A4) of other data – the **unseen** data
- A **requirement**, which will describe one or more tasks you must complete
- A blank answer booklet for your answer and another one for appendices **or** a computer, specially adapted for the exam.

You cannot bring textbooks, notes or other materials into the room.

Step 5.2   Review the unseen and read the requirement

Firstly, don't panic. You have spent the last six weeks looking at the data, and analysing it thoroughly. However, it is quite possible that the new 'unseen' data will surprise you or seem unfamiliar. It might put you off. You cannot question spot from the case so the new material and the requirement may not be what you expect at all.

You have 20 minutes reading time, and you need to use it wisely. The TOPCIMA exam is **very time-pressured**, so using the reading time productively will be crucial to your chances of success.

Just as at the start of the pre-seen, you need to **skim read the new information** to get an idea of what it is telling you, before going into the detail.

Then read the requirement thoroughly and make a mental note of the role you must adopt, what you have to do, the required format of your answer, and who the recipients are (eg Board, shareholders etc).

(a)   What will the requirement look like?

CIMA has said that the requirement will contain **two overall tasks**. As we have said before, you are likely to have to write a **report** (for 90 marks), but this will be coupled with a **second, shorter task** (for 10 marks).

(b)   You are also asked to **adopt a particular role**. This is important to keep in mind, as it will determine the type of report you will write and how you present your data.

(c)   To make absolutely sure, use the requirements to head up your report. Here's an example.

Requirement

Hugh Mountolive the Chief Executive Officer can see both sides of the arguments presented by Melissa and Clea regarding closing down the Alexandria factory and moving to Port Said, but is uncertain about how to evaluate such an important issue.

He has asked you, Justine Nessim, the management accountant, to write a report covering all the major factors that need to be considered in relation to the closure and move, with a recommendation.

You can turn this into **a title page,** as follows.

To: Hugh Mountolive, Chief Executive Officer

From: Justine Nessim, management accountant

Date:

Re: Analysis and recommendations regarding the proposed closure of the factory in Alexandria and the move to Port Said

---

You have clearly identified the recipient of the report (the managing director), the role you must adopt (management accountant), and what you have to do.

PART A TACKING THE CASE STUDY 7: The exam

(d) If you analyse the requirement in (c) above this is what you might infer:

		Implications
Your role	Justine Nessim Management accountant	Adjudicating between Clea and Melissa?
Recipient	Hugh Mountolive	He cannot make up his mind and wants you to make a recommendation.
All the **major** factors		Not just financial issues but other considerations. **Major** factors are asked for, so you will have to prioritise here.
In relation to the **closure** and **move**		Two separate items are under review.
With a recommendation		This implies a choice between options, and your own recommendation. You will need a rationale for this.

> **KEY POINT**
> The main requirement is likely to be 'Prepare a report that prioritises, advises and evaluates the main issues facing [XYZ Co] and makes appropriate recommendations'.

Step 5.3 **Read the unseen data in depth**

Now you have firmly fixed in your mind what you have to do, you can start to read through the unseen data, looking for key words.

(a) As you go through the unseen data, **highlight key facts** and mark them as High, Medium or Low importance. You are aiming to create an **issue list.**

(b) **Then identify further information that you might need**. You may have to calculate some more ratios, for example, from the data provided.

(c) If new financial data is given, think about how you will use it.

(d) Think about which business strategy models you will use.

(e) Consider any real-life examples you could use.

(f) Remember, you need to be clear in your mind about **what has changed**. (What new details have emerged from the unseen materials?) It is vital that you take this on board.

3 Your answer

Step 5.4 Consider the big picture and **plan**

(a) Decide on the four key issues, the rationale and justification for your choice.

(b) You might benefit from drawing a spider diagram or mind map, identifying the key issues and the implications of them.

(c) Do the calculations. These will be included in the appendices. Make your assumptions very clear and do not get too involved, you do not have much time. The maximum amount of time you should spend will depend on the technical marks available, but more than 20 minutes will be too much.

(d) Plan your recommendations.

(e) Plan your writing time. Give approximate timings to each section of the report.

Exam skills

Make sure that, at the planning stage, you think about real life examples and the impact of one issue on others.

Step 5.5 **Draw up the appendices, terms of reference and introduction.**

(a) Produce your appendices. You should start with a SWOT analysis with all four key issues included.

(b) Write one sentence for the terms of reference.

(c) Write the introduction. Identify and prioritise the main issues facing the organisation, showing the top four items in order of priority.

Step 5.6 **Prioritise the issues**

Write the section on the prioritisation of the issues.

(a) Prioritise the top four issues. Remember to justify your choices: 'this is important because....'

(b) The remaining issues should be listed as bullet points.

(c) Make sure you refer to the business strategy models you have included in the appendices eg SWOT, PEST.

Step 5.7 **Write up the main body of the report and the ethics section**

(a) Write up the main discussion sections using technical knowledge, real life examples and calculations to illustrate your points in sufficient **depth**.

(b) Make sure you follow your plan.

(c) Write up your ethics section.

Step 5.8 **Write up your recommendations**

Exam skills

You must allow yourself 30 minutes to make recommendations and produce an exit strategy. You **will not pass** this exam **without making detailed recommendations** which are consistent with your analysis of the key issues.

(a) You need to write a recommendation for **each** issue.

(b) The main issues should have a number of recommendations.

(c) All recommendations must have a **justification**. '**Because**' is essential: "The company should do 'X' because.....".

(d) Recommendations must be sensible, commercial, practical and cover human resources, information technology and operational issues.

Step 5.9 **Write the conclusion and review your work**

Have you written a commercial, comprehensive report?

TEACHING CASE: ZUBINOS

Part B

Zubinos: pre-seen data

This chapter includes the pre-seen case study data for the case that we are looking at in detail.

The case study is taken from a real, past TOPCIMA exam.

Note that when this exam was sat (in 2006) there was only one element of the requirement, rather than the two that you will face in your exam.

However, the case study illustrates the length and style of material you can expect to have to deal with in your exam which is why we are using it as the basis for this teaching case.

You will see that we have numbered the paragraphs and have shaded various key words and phrases in the data. This indicates the sort of highlighting that you are likely to do while carrying out your in depth read-through and analysis.

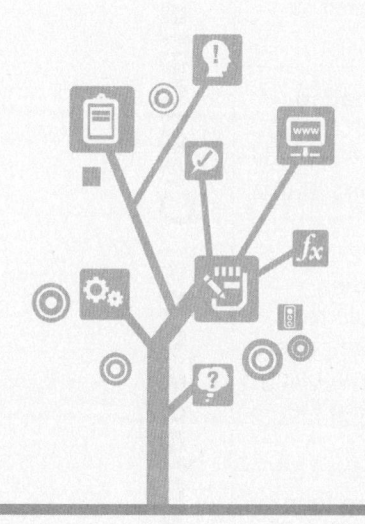

CIMA

Test of Professional Competence in Management Accounting
Monday 6 March 2006

PRE-SEEN MATERIAL, PROVIDED IN ADVANCE FOR PREPARATION AND STUDY FOR THE EXAMINATION TO BE HELD ON MONDAY 6 MARCH
INSTRUCTIONS FOR POTENTIAL CANDIDATES
This booklet contains the pre-seen case material for the March 2006 examination. It will provide you with the contextual information that will help you prepare yourself for the examination on Monday 6 March.
The TOPCIMA Assessment Matrix, which your script will be marked against, is available as a separate document which will also be e-mailed to you.
You may not take this copy of the pre-seen material into the examination hall. A fresh copy will be provided for you in the examination hall.
Unseen material will be provided for the examination: this will comprise further context and the examination question.
The examination will last for three hours. You will be allowed 20 minutes reading time **before the examination begins** during which you should read the question paper and, if you wish, make annotations on the question paper. However, you will **not** be allowed, **under any circumstances**, to begin using your computer to produce your answer, or to use your calculator during the reading time.
You will be required to answer ONE question which may contain more than one element.

Contents of this booklet:

Pre-seen material – Zubinos coffee shops

Appendix 1

Appendix 2

Appendix 3

Appendix 4

© The Chartered Institute of Management Accountants 2006

Zubinos Coffee Shops

Market overview

1 The number of chains of coffee shops in the UK has increased four-fold in the last five years, with thousands of branded coffee shops now operating around the UK. The total turnover for all branded coffee shops in the UK exceeded £1 billion (£1 billion is equal to £1,000 million) during 2005. Over the last few years a number of UK based branded coffee shops have emerged to compete with the internationally recognised coffee shop brands.

2 A further shift in the market growth is that the coffee bar culture has extended beyond the UK's major cities and is now successfully penetrating smaller towns. This has mainly been driven by the larger of the coffee shop brands. Consumer awareness of branded coffee shops has also increased in the last few years.

3 The range of products offered has also changed over the last few years and branded coffee shops are now meeting customer demand for a larger range of foods and better quality products by using premium ingredients. Furthermore, branded coffee shops are able to command a higher average price for their products by using quality and service as differentiators, as price appears not to be a particularly sensitive factor.

4 In addition to the branded coffee shops, there is a large number of non-specialist food and beverage outlets including department stores, supermarkets and bookshops, which continue to expand their own cafes. They are enjoying the success of the 'coffee culture' that has been established by the branded coffee shops.

5 Market research is very important in this fast moving consumer driven marketplace and the over-riding factor that continues to be the most important reason that consumers select a coffee shop is its convenience of location. There were over 500 branded coffee shops in London at the end of 2005.

Zubinos' personnel

6 The career histories of Zubinos' Directors and key employees are shown in **Appendix 1** starting on page 10.

The first Zubinos coffee shop

7 On returning to the UK in early 2001, Luis Zubino, the founder of Zubinos, bought a flat in London and set about locating suitable premises for his new business venture. His original plan was to have over five coffee shops opened within five years and he wanted the cash generated from each coffee shop to finance the opening costs for the next coffee shop. He had put together a business plan to get a personal loan, which was secured on both his own flat and his parents' house. This loan, together with his savings, was used to acquire £300,000 of equity in Zubinos.

8 Zubinos was formed in March 2001 with 2 million authorised shares of £1 each, of which 300,000 shares were allocated to Luis Zubino and these shares were fully paid up at par value in March 2001. At the time these shares were issued, £1 per share at par value was considered a fair value.

9 Luis Zubino opened the first Zubinos shop in June 2001 in London, in rented premises. He fully understood that it was location and convenience that would be critical to the success of the coffee shop. He had been lucky in being able to rent a large corner shop on a busy junction, which was surrounded by offices and on the route to nearby public transport, thereby having the benefit of many passers by. Luis Zubino hired a large number of staff to ensure good customer service and to minimise waiting times during peak busy periods such as lunch breaks.

10 Most coffee shops only serve a selection of hot and cold drinks and a small range of snacks and cakes. What distinguished Zubinos from many of the other branded coffee shops back in 2001, was that Zubinos also sold a range of freshly made sandwiches, with high quality fillings and other food items. Zubinos also sold a specialised brand of ice cream, which Luis Zubino imported from Italy, as he considered that the quality and taste was far superior to many other ice cream brands available in the UK. He was convinced that ice cream, which is a product that is kept frozen, could generate high margins, as it would have very little waste and none of the problems associated with the short shelf life of other foods.

11 Within six months, the first Zubinos shop was generating a high turnover and had established a high level of repeat business. Zubinos became a popular meeting place. The level of profitability was below plan as more staff had been employed to meet demand and Luis Zubino considered that he did not want to lose customers' goodwill by increasing waiting times to be served. By December 2001, he handed the day-to-day management of the shop to Val Pline, who had proved herself to be the hardest working and most trustworthy of all the staff employed at the coffee shop.

12 Luis Zubino briefed Val Pline on his plans for the shop for the next few months and agreed to pay bonuses to her when the turnover reached a certain level and again when net profit (after staff and fixed costs) reached £100,000 in any financial year. Val Pline was impressed with the business plan and her new responsibilities. Only six months previously, she had joined a coffee shop with limited experience and now she found herself running the coffee shop with the possibility of earning bonuses when it became even more successful.

The growth of Zubinos

13 Within two and a half years, by the end of 2003, Luis Zubino had opened a further five coffee shops, which was twice as fast as his original business plan had envisaged. All five shops were in rented premises to reduce the initial set-up costs, but Luis Zubino had not reduced the level of expenditure on the coffee shops design and fittings. The atmosphere that the coffee shop design had created was good, and was attractive to the target market of young people. Early on, from his market research, and from personal experience in his parents' business, Luis Zubino wanted his coffee shops to appeal to the 20-to-35 year old age range. This was for several reasons:

- The target age range market segment has more time and more disposable money;
- They attracted other people of similar ages into the coffee shops, as they become the place to meet up;
- The target age range would be attracted to the 'trendy' atmosphere that Luis Zubino has created at Zubinos.

14 Luis Zubino wanted to expand the number of Zubinos coffee shops, but could not find suitable premises to rent in the locations he wanted. By mid-2004 he appointed a management consultancy firm for financial planning advice on how he could expand the business. Zubinos had only been in existence, at that stage, for fewer than four years.

15 The consultant with whom he dealt with was George Shale, and the two quickly established good rapport and worked well together. It was George Shale's idea to open only a few more Zubinos coffee shops in the London area where sites were difficult to obtain and rent very expensive. George Shale recommended that Zubinos should start to expand into towns and cities elsewhere in the UK where shop location would not be such a problem, rather than continue to expand within the fiercely competitive London market.

16 When Jane Thorp joined Zubinos in early 2003, she could immediately see the large potential of the Zubinos brand. By the end of 2003, Zubinos had six shops operational with plans for four further shop openings in 2004. Eight further shops were opened in 2005, resulting in eighteen coffee shops in total operational by the end of 2005. The geographical split of Zubinos coffee shops was ten in London and eight coffee shops outside of London. Zubinos has not had any problems with building up its customer base after each new shop opening in the smaller towns and cities into which it had expanded.

17 George Shale also suggested that Zubinos could consider opening Zubinos coffee shops on the premises of another retailer. He undertook to try to locate a chain of retailers who would rent out part of their shop space. This has been done with other coffee shop chains, which have coffee shops located in motorway service areas and chains of bookshops. Luis Zubino liked the idea of a Zubinos coffee shop in a chain of other shops and a search for a suitable retail chain started in May 2004. However, with the expansion of Zubinos into eight provincial towns and cities, Zubinos has not yet pursued the identification of a suitable retail chain into which it could open Zubinos coffee shops.

18   The Zubinos business has a high turnover. However, profitability was still lower than some of its competitors, for several reasons as follows:
   - High rental costs for three of the ten London coffee shops;
   - High staff costs, as good customer service remains a high priority for Zubinos;
   - Lower than average gross margins on some products due to the higher than average procurement cost of the quality ingredients that Luis Zubino has selected;
   - Lower margins on coffee products as over 80% of its coffee beans are procured from suppliers who deal only with 'Fair Trade' coffee producers (see below).

Staffing issues and performance related bonuses

19   Luis Zubino was kept very busy with expanding the Zubinos business and left each of the coffee shop managers alone to run each Zubinos coffee shop. Most management responsibilities were devolved to the shop managers, who were responsible for local procurement of food supplies, staff recruitment and day-to-day staff management.

20   Vivien Zubino, Luis Zubino's wife, managed one of the London Zubinos coffee shops after they married in 2002. She also undertook much of the procurement of coffee supplies, together with Jane Thorp, until the full time Procurement Director, Maria Todd, joined Zubinos in September 2004. However, there were often duplication of orders or gaps in delivery of supplies as both Jane Thorp and Vivien Zubino were constantly busy with other responsibilities.

21   Payroll was operated by an out-sourced agency centrally and Luis Zubino managed all other staff issues. It was only with the appointment of Anita Wiseman in November 2004, that human resource (HR) matters were undertaken centrally. Zubinos employed over 360 staff (some part time) by 31 December 2005.

22   Anita Wiseman wants to formalise job responsibilities and recruitment and ensure that staff are offered promotion in newly opened branches of Zubinos. Following on from the dismissal of three employees during 2005 for minor thefts, of both produce and cash, she also suspected that staff management and the required control procedures were not in place in the coffee shops. Coffee is a high value product and one employee was dismissed for selling stolen bags of coffee beans. This theft was only identified because he had been foolish enough to steal, and then sell, the bags of coffee beans on the premises of the Zubinos coffee shop in which he worked. A fellow employee had reported the incident to Luis Zubino.

23   Anita Wiseman has introduced quarterly performance related bonuses for all employees based on the sales revenue and the net margin for each coffee shop. The bonus is paid quarterly to recognise the previous quarter's results and to motivate staff to stay with Zubinos, so reducing the high staff turnover. However, the bonuses paid for the last two quarters of 2005 were lower than previously paid, as the targets were more challenging. Some coffee shop managers and other employees were disappointed with their reduced bonus payments despite working as hard as ever over the Christmas 2005 period.

Fair Trade produce

24   Luis Zubino, having a strong social conscience, felt that the coffee beans that Zubinos coffee shops should use should be bought from suppliers of Fair Trade coffee. Additionally, from his initial research into the industry, he was convinced that Zubinos could charge a price premium for the use of Fair Trade coffee.

25   Fair Trade benefits 800,000 farmers worldwide selling a wide variety of products. Farmers are organised into small co-operatives, whereby products are procured at an agreed minimum price, which is above the price that some small independent farmers would be able to achieve for their crops on the open market. Fair Trade produce is successfully breaking the cycle of poverty for farmers in many countries and the coffee industry is one where Fair Trade has been very successful. Luis Zubino felt strongly that in today's world where consumers are demanding more humane and more environmentally sensitive products, the use of Fair Trade coffee in Zubinos coffee shops is a responsible and sensible choice of supply.

26 From the opening of the first Zubinos in 2001, Luis Zubino bought 100% of all coffee from Fair Trade suppliers. As the range of coffees expanded in Zubinos coffee shops, he found that some coffee and cocoa beans were unavailable through Fair Trade suppliers. On average, Zubinos procures over 80% of its produce from Fair Trade suppliers. Luis Zubino would still like this to be 100%. When Maria Todd joined in September 2004, Luis Zubino requested her to increase the proportion of coffee supplies procured from Fair Trade suppliers. This necessitated a change from some of its current suppliers to achieve this objective. The extensive use of Fair Trade coffee is used in some of Zubinos' marketing literature, and it has raised the profile and awareness of Fair Trade with some of its customers.

IT development

27 Jane Thorp commissioned an IT company in early 2005 to completely update the Zubinos website. The total cost of this IT work was forecast to be £220,000, but the final cost was a little over £300,000 including new hardware equipment. The new website has helped to create stronger brand awareness. The new Zubinos website also has an on-line communications area which allows users to 'chat' on line. Since November 2004, a range of Zubinos merchandise can also be ordered on-line. This range of merchandise includes coffee machines and coffee supplies, which have been selling well, despite little direct publicity.

28 George Shale is continuously frustrated by the lack of financial and business information in a usable format. The company had grown fast and he has prepared several proposals requesting that a new database financial forecasting system is implemented. He also wants the shop managers to be more involved in sales and profit forecasting and the system that he had proposed would allow shop managers to input their data for consolidation. However, Luis Zubino felt that the shop managers are already under a heavy workload and that the quality of the data that they could input into the proposed system would be little better than that currently submitted by e-mail to Zubinos Head Office. The current standard of forecasting by shop managers is not very good and has generally underestimated the growth in sales. The database proposal has been turned down previously on cost grounds, as Luis Zubino considers that the cost does not justify the slightly improved level of forecasting.

29 However, a new IT system to capture sales and product analysis data at source, which will also help with stock control, was commissioned in October 2005. This project has been scaled down from the original specification and is forecast to cost £110,000.

Introduction of a business investor

30 By summer 2004, Zubinos had eight coffee shops open and had found suitable locations for two more. However, Zubinos' bankers, Kite Bank, were reluctant to increase the level of loans. At the end of June 2004, Zubinos had three loans in place, totalling £600,000. All loans were at 12% interest per year. These were:

- An initial five-year loan for £300,000 taken out in December 2001;
- A second five-year loan for £200,000 taken out in December 2002 to fund further expansion;
- A third five-year loan taken out in April 2004 for £100,000, to cover a shortfall in working capital due to all cash resources being used for expansion.

31 Instead, the bank introduced Luis Zubino to the manager of the bank's private equity provider, who is Carl Martin. Carl Martin and Luis Zubino established a good working relationship early on in their business meetings and Carl Martin was impressed with the business plan and the growth of the Zubinos business in the last few years. He felt confident that if Kite Private Equity (KPE) were to invest in the Zubinos business, the additional private equity finance, together with less expensive loan finance, would allow the Zubinos business to expand far more rapidly.

32 After many discussions and the preparation of additional, more detailed business plans, KPE agreed to invest in the Zubinos business in January 2005.

33 KPE invested £2·4 million in equity finance initially, but the agreement was to also provide loan finance when required by expansion plans. The agreed value of loan finance was up to £5·0 million over the next 4 years at an annual interest rate of 10% per annum, secured against Zubinos assets. KPE appointed Carl Martin as its representative on the Board of Zubinos.

34 The balance sheet, income statement and statement of changes in equity for Zubinos for the last two financial years are shown in **Appendix 2**.

Shareholdings at December 2005

35 Since the formation of Zubinos in 2001, other Directors have purchased shares in Zubinos. They have paid between £2 and £5 per share, based on the agreed fair value at the time they acquired shares.

36 Luis Zubino and the rest of the Zubinos shareholders welcomed KPE into the business. KPE purchased 400,000 shares at £6 each (£1 each plus a share premium, based on an agreed fair value, of £5 per share). The shareholdings at 31 December 2005 are shown below.

	Number of shares	% shareholding %
Luis Zubino	300,000	30.0
Vivien Zubino	120,000	12.0
Jane Thorp	30,000	3.0
Maria Todd	24,000	2.4
Anita Wiseman	36,000	3.6
George Shale	90,000	9.0
KPE	400,000	40.0
Total shareholdings	1,000,000	100.0

37 The Zubinos Board comprises the above six shareholders plus Carl Martin, KPE's nominated representative. Luis Zubino is Chairman of the Board in addition to his role as Managing Director.

Analysis of gross margin

38 George Shale commissioned a new IT system in October 2005 that will capture and analyse sales and cost of sales data without all of the manual intervention and spreadsheet analysis that is currently required to produce management information. The system is due to be operational in early 2006.

39 The analysis of the gross margin across the eighteen Zubinos coffee shops for the year to 31 December 2005 is shown as follows. It should be noted that the figures below are for all eighteen Zubinos coffee shops, but eight of them were operational for only part of 2005.

	Coffee products £'000	Other drinks £'000	Sandwiches £'000	Ice-cream £'000	Other foods £'000	Total £'00
Sales revenue	4,734	1,344	3,584	896	3,360	13,91
Cost of food and drinks	926	642	1,260	182	1,962	4,97
Gross margin	3,808	702	2,324	714	1,398	8,94
Gross margin %	80%	52%	65%	80%	42%	64%

Zubinos' expansion plans

40 The current five-year plan was approved by KPE, and subsequently the Zubinos Board, in December 2005. This plan includes the expansion of Zubinos to 75 coffee shops by the end of 2010. An extract from this current five-year plan is shown in **Appendix 3**.

41 Much of the expansion planned is due to be financed by cash generated by operations, as well as additional loan finance from KPE. The amount of loan finance will be determined by whether the new openings will be in rented premises or whether the company will be required to purchase the site. Much will depend on the location selected and the alternatives available in each town or city targeted for expansion.

42 During 2005, eight new Zubinos coffee shops were opened. Up to the end of 2004, all coffee shops, except one, were in rented premises. Zubinos has previously purchased one property in London in 2003, in which it has its head office above the coffee shop. During 2005, two of the newly opened Zubinos coffee shops were in large premises that had been purchased, as Luis Zubino was unable to locate a suitable site that could be rented. The cost of the two coffee shops that were purchased were over £1 million each, including the shop fitting costs.

43 Jane Thorp uses a number of criteria for the selection of new sites for future Zubinos coffee shops. These include:

   1. *Competition* – the strength of the competition in the proposed market place and whether the competition will stimulate growth, but not be too strong so as to restrict profits.
   2. *Resources.* Whether there are adequate resources, staff and supply links to set up a new coffee shop.
   3. *Consumer demand.* Is there sufficient demand for a Zubinos coffee shop and what is the current level of demand and how is it being met? A further issue is whether the area has the income to create profitable demand for Zubinos.

44 Some relevant factors in the Zubinos expansion plan are the population size and the population density. When population becomes concentrated it often tends to take on a different character. Urbanisation produces the need for a higher level of products and services. Jane Thorp uses a number of easy measures such as the presence, or absence, of well-known chains of clothes retailers, to determine the potential for a new coffee shop location.

45 Jane Thorp had prepared a paper for the December 2005 Zubinos Board meeting, proposing that each Zubinos coffee shop should have a few computers available for customers' use, for browsing on the internet or for passing business people to send e-mails. The proposal is for the computers to be available free of charge for all customers. The Board considered the proposal, but decided against it for several reasons, not just on cost grounds, but on space considerations and also concerns over damage or theft. Luis Zubino stated that Zubinos did not need to offer its customers such facilities, as Zubinos coffee shops already were very busy at peak times. Jane Thorp is confident that this innovative free service is a good way of retaining customer loyalty and for attracting new customers.

Labelling of foods

46 One of the London-based Zubinos coffee shops had just broken the barrier of sales of £1 million in a rolling 12 month period. The manager at this coffee shop decided to try to increase sales further by introducing additional nutritional data for some food and drink products. The coffee shop manager decided, without consulting anyone, to display the calorie information as a ploy to improve sales. However, when she calculated and displayed the calorie content of many of the coffee products and foods, she was disappointed to find the calorie content very high. Many customers were also very surprised and switched to other drinks and did not purchase any cakes or pastries. This led to a small reduction of sales revenue.

47 This Zubinos coffee shop manager then started a new initiative during summer 2005 in the Zubinos coffee shop in which she manages. She introduced a small range of low fat and low calorie snacks and meals, which proved to be very popular. However, when this was discussed with Jane Thorp in Marketing, a major disagreement arose concerning the range of foods that Zubinos should be offering, and Jane Thorp's view that there should be a standard menu at all Zubinos coffee shops. The manager was furious that Zubinos Head Office had not welcomed her low calorie meal initiative.

Other recent developments in the Zubinos business

48 In April 2005, Zubinos introduced its first delivery service from three of its central London coffee shops. This delivery service to local businesses provides coffee and a catering service on customers' premises. Customers place orders on-line to their local Zubinos coffee shop. Despite a few initial problems, the delivery service is working well, although sales are still very low. Customers are automatically invoiced after delivery, instead of the usual cash payments in the coffee shops. There has been some additional work caused by payments received not matching with the invoiced amounts, and shop managers have simply written off the small differences. There is no system yet in place to chase up payment for deliveries if the customer does not pay within Zubinos' 30-day terms.

49 Zubinos wants to continue to be innovative and to be ahead of its competitors in terms of the types of foods offered. Jane Thorp and Maria Todd are in contact with a number of food manufacturers to explore offering a wider range of foods. They need to ensure that any new food ranges fit in with Zubinos' current pricing and food quality levels.

Proposed expansion of Zubinos overseas

50 Jane Thorp and Luis Zubino believe that during 2007, when Zubinos plans to have over 26 shops open in the UK, it will be in a position where it could consider expanding overseas. Already, a number of contacts of Luis Zubino, who live in Europe, are keen to operate Zubinos coffee shops in Europe.

PART B TEACHING CASE: ZUBINOS

51 The current five-year plan, which was approved by KPE and the Zubinos Board in December 2005, is based on operating 50 coffee shops in the UK by 2010 and 25 coffee shops in Europe.

52 However, Luis Zubino would like to have more than 25 coffee shops operating in Europe by 2010. There are a number of reasons why Zubinos should consider expanding abroad and these include:

- Saturated home market where competition is so intense that it can no longer gain any significant market share improvement
- Competition may be less intense in a different market
- Comparative advantage in product against local competition, particularly in areas dominated by British people living and holidaying abroad, which is becoming increasingly popular in some areas of Europe, especially Spain

Appendix 1

Zubinos' personnel

Luis Zubino – Chairman and Managing Director

Luis Zubino, now 29, had worked in his parents' café for two years after he left school. He did not want to go to university and instead saved enough money to travel extensively. He is an intelligent man, who has his father's entrepreneurial spirit. After spending several years abroad, he returned to the UK in 2001 and established Zubinos.

Vivien Zubino – Director

Vivien Zubino, now aged 30, married Luis Zubino in 2002, after the opening of the first Zubinos shop. She is a director of Zubinos and now works part time at one of the Zubinos coffee shops in London. She has assisted her husband in achieving his ambitious plans and has helped to create the designs for the Zubinos coffee shops and also some of the innovative menus available at Zubinos coffee shops. She has always supported her husband and his ideas, which has contributed to the high growth achieved to date. Vivien Zubino purchased shares in Zubinos during 2002.

Jane Thorp – Marketing Director

Jane Thorp was the first professional appointment that Luis Zubino made in early 2003. He knew by then that Zubinos had the potential to be successful, and understood the importance of branding, and the company needed a strong Marketing Director. Jane Thorp had previously worked in marketing for a mobile phone company and more recently for a leading high street fast food chain, which she did not like. Jane Thorp, aged 32, relished the challenges that Zubinos posed and was determined to help both Luis and Vivien Zubino to create a successful business. She invested personal funds into the company in 2003 when she bought 30,000 shares, which was then nearly 7% of the issued share capital.

Maria Todd – Procurement Director

Maria Todd, now 35, had worked in procurement for an international food retailer and was frustrated with the lack of initiative she was allowed to use. She had extensive procurement and contract experience and welcomed the challenges that a growing company, such as Zubinos, could offer her. Maria Todd invested £120,000 of personal funds to buy shares in the company.

Maria Todd joined Zubinos in September 2004 and is based in its Head Office, which is located above one of the London Zubinos coffee shops. The first floor above the shop accommodates around 28 employees including two junior procurement staff. Prior to Maria Todd joining Zubinos, most of the procurement decisions were made by a variety of people. She is frustrated by the lack of discipline in the company, as many coffee shop managers still order some supplies from local food wholesalers to meet demand. The coffee shop managers state that they need this flexibility to provide customers with the foods in demand. However, Maria Todd considers that the coffee shop managers are simply not planning their food ordering very well and are continuously running out of a variety of products. One shop even ran out of the specially mixed Zubinos coffee beans recently.

Anita Wiseman – Human Resources Director

Anita Wiseman, now 29, has known Luis Zubino since their school days. She has a degree in Human Resource management and has worked in human resources (HR) for a chain of department stores before joining Zubinos in November 2004. Prior to Anita Wiseman joining the company, much of the HR management work had been out-sourced or handled by Luis Zubino, who had delegated authority for hiring new employees to each coffee shop manager.

George Shale – Finance Director

George Shale, aged 39, had worked for a leading audit group for over 10 years before he moved into management consultancy. Zubinos appointed the consultancy firm that George Shale worked for in mid 2004 for financial planning advice. George Shale was the consultant in charge of the Zubinos case and worked closely with Luis Zubino on a new five-year plan. George Shale was so convinced by the business plan that he had helped to produce, and in Luis Zubino's ability to grow the Zubinos business, that he joined Zubinos in December 2004. He bought 90,000 shares in Zubinos. Prior to George Shale joining the company, much of the finance work was managed by Zubinos' external auditors, and supplemented by temporary finance staff. Since joining Zubinos, George Shale has recruited a small team and has taken all accounting and finance matters in-house.

Bob West – Business Planning Manager

Bob West, aged 35, used to work for George Shale at the management consultants and was recruited by George Shale to fill the new post of Business Planning Manager at Zubinos in June 2005. Bob West has always worked as a consultant and been involved with many young start-up business ventures, and has a lot of experience. However, he has not been involved in the food retailing business before joining Zubinos.

Jack Rayfield – Shop management and security

Jack Rayfield, aged 52, joined Zubinos in 2003 having worked in retail management for the past 20 years. He was recruited by Luis Zubino who considered him to be a reliable hard working manager who could take care of the day-to-day operations involved with the shops. Since Jack Rayfield joined, he has introduced many new procedures and tightened up some poor business practices. One of the procedures that he has introduced is daily banking of cash and reconciliations to records of revenue for each shop.

Jack Rayfield is very good on HR matters and has played an active role with shop managers in the recruitment of staff, particularly for new Zubinos coffee shops. However, recently he has clashed with Anita Wiseman over many issues.

Val Pline and Sally Higgins – Zubinos' Area Managers

Both Val Pline and Sally Higgins had originally joined Zubinos in junior supervisory roles in its early days and then progressed to coffee shop managers. In September 2005, they were both appointed to the new roles of area managers. Val Pline is responsible for all London and the South East-based Zubinos coffee shops and Sally Higgins has responsibility for all other UK coffee shops.

They have both received management training and have been rewarded with performance related bonuses linked to sales revenue and net margins. They are now responsible for the recruitment and management of all staff for the coffee shops that they manage. Due to high staff turnover, which is not unusual in this business sector, they have spent much time on staff recruitment and on staff training issues.

Carl Martin – Investment Director, Kite Private Equity (KPE)

Carl Martin, aged 39, is the liaison manager at KPE who is responsible for a range of clients into which KPE has invested equity and loan finance. The companies that KPE has invested in vary greatly and are operating in a wide range of industries, including manufacturing, service and retail sectors. Carl Martin was appointed to the Zubinos Board in January 2005, to manage KPE's shareholding.

Due to Carl Martin's demanding role in many other companies, he has left the Zubinos management team to manage the Zubinos business. He is content that the monthly sales and profits that had been achieved during 2005 were ahead of the agreed forecast. Therefore, he has not been as 'hands on' as he would have been if targets had not been met. Carl Martin gets on very well with Luis Zubino, and they both have much mutual respect for each other's roles. Luis Zubino appreciates that Zubinos would not have been able to grow as quickly without the KPE finance and is very pleased that Carl Martin has not really interfered with the way that Zubinos is run.

Appendix 2

Zubinos' Balance Sheet, Income Statement and Statement of changes in equity

Note. All data in this appendix is presented in international financial reporting format

Balance Sheet

	As at 31 December 2005 £'000	As at 31 December 2005 £'000	As at 31 December 2004 £'000	As at 31 December 2004 £'000
Non-current assets (net)		7,025		2,958
Current assets				
Inventory	420		395	
Trade receivables and rent prepayments	209	124		
Cash and short term investments	391		85	
		1,020		604
Total assets		8,045		3,562
Equity and liabilities				
Equity				
Paid in share capital	1,000		600	
Share premium reserve	2,630		630	
Retained profits	1,751		854	
		5,381		2,084
Non-current liabilities				
Loans				
Bank loan at 12% (repayable in 2006)	300		300	
Bank loan at 12% (repayable in 2007)	200		200	
Bank loan at 12% (repayable in 2009)	100		100	
KPE loan at 10% (repayable in 2010)	300		–	
		900		600
Current liabilities				
Trade payables	1,367		689	
Tax	283	160		
Accruals	114		29	
		1,764		878
Total equity and liabilities		8,045		3,562

Note. Paid in share capital represents 1 million shares of £1.00 each at 31 December 2005

Income Statement

Year ended 31 December

	2005 £'000	2004 £'000
Revenue	13,918	7,962
Total operating costs	12,651	7,225
Operating profit	1,267	737
Finance costs	(87)	(69)
Tax expense (effective tax rate is 24%)	(283)	(160)
Profit for the period	897	508

Statement of changes in equity

	Share capital £'000	Share premium £'000	Retained earnings £'000	Total £'000
Balance at 31 December 2004	600	630	854	2,084
New shares issued during 2005	400	2,000	–	2,400
Profit for the period	–	–	897	897
Dividends paid	–	–	–	–
Balance at 31 December 2005	1,000	2,630	1,751	5,381

Note. For the purpose of the case, it should be assumed that the accounts for the year ended 31 December 2005 are final and have been audited.

Appendix 3

Extracts from Zubinos 5-year plan

	Actual 2005	Plan 2006	Plan 2007	Plan 2008	Plan 2009	Plan 2010
Number of coffee shops:						
Start of the year	10	18	26	36	48	60
New openings	8	8	10	12	12	15
End of the year	**18**	**26**	**36**	**48**	**60**	**75**
Average number of coffee shops for the year	14	22	31	42	54	68
Analysis of new shop openings:						
UK	8	8	9	5	5	5
Overseas	–	–	1	7	7	10
	£'000	£'000	£'000	£'000	£'000	£'000
Coffee shops revenue	13,498	22,176	37,072	57,378	82,553	110,751
Revenue from new product launches in each year	420	1,560	2,200	2,900	3,800	4,800
Total revenue	13,918	23,736	39,272	60,278	86,353	115,551
Pre-tax operating profit	1,267	2,160	3,613	5,606	8,203	10,977
Capital expenditure	4,800	2,700	3,400	3,800	4,100	5,000

Note. The extracts from the 5-year plan shown above were approved by KPE and the Zubinos Board in December 2005.

Appendix 4

UK National News
TUESDAY DECEMBER 20 2005

ZUBINOS is winning a share of the coffee wars

THE coffee shops chain, Zubinos, renowned for its choice of coffees and fresh foods, today opened its eighteenth coffee shop and is now expanding nationwide.

Managing Director, Luis Zubino commented 'our customers are very important to us and we provide them with the coffees that they want and a wide variety of top quality foods in an appealing atmosphere'.

Zubinos has eight coffee shops outside the capital. They are much larger than many of its competitors' coffee shops. Zubino stated, 'our customers want to feel as if they are at home and we have created the authentic European coffee house atmosphere. Our sales are growing rapidly, which confirms to us that our customers like what we provide'.

It is forecast that sales for 2005 will be over £14 million, which is nearly 75% up from sales of around £8 million during 2004.

Zubinos appears to have managed to compete effectively against the many coffee shops chains, most of which have nationwide coverage. However, as Zubinos expands, the market expects there to be some consolidation. A leading UK coffee shop chain, Café Café, recently bought 12 coffee shops from the global coffee shop chain Whistle.

When asked about Zubinos expansion plans, Luis Zubino stated, 'it is our intention to continue to expand within the UK and to open Zubinos coffee shops overseas in the next few years'.

KPE, the private equity arm of Kite Bank, is financing much of the Zubinos expansion. KPE is quoted as being 'very pleased with Zubinos operational and financial performance to date'.

End of pre-seen material

Zubinos: approach and explore the case situation

This chapter covers steps 1 and 2 of the case study approach that we discussed in Chapter 4 of this Study Text.

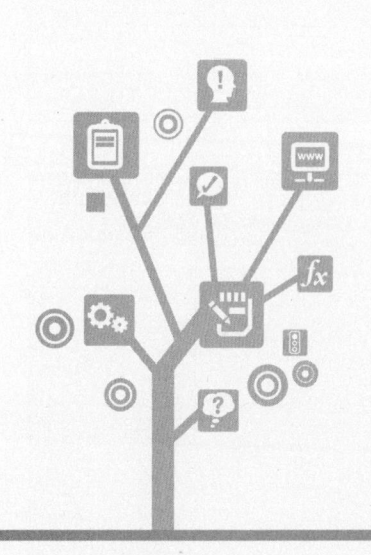

topic list

1. Approach Zubinos (Steps 1.1 to 1.7)
2. Analyse the numbers (Step 2.1)
3. General environmental analysis (PEST) and trends (Step 2.2)
4. Analyse the business environment and competitive strategy (Step 2.3)
5. Audit the product/service portfolio (Step 2.4)
6. How does the business add value? (Step 2.5)
7. Identify information systems and processes (Step 2.6)
8. Identify key issues in structure, culture and personnel (Step 2.7)
9. Identify investor objectives, capital structure and other stakeholder objectives (Step 2.8)
10. Identify and analyse possible business projects (Step 2.9)

1 Approach Zubinos (Steps 1.1 to 1.7)

Read, re-read and mark up the case (Steps 1.1 to 1.3)

This is just a reminder – **skim reading** the case twice at the outset enables you to get a better grasp of the big picture.

Quickly re-read the case after a time (Step 1.2) – perhaps the day after you first received it – an important part of the review process.

Mark up the case slowly, taking notes (Step 1.3), is your first detailed reading of the case. The purpose of this stage is to get you set up for writing a précis. You are not going into decision making mode here, just noting and summarising the data so you make sure you are covering everything. So, put away your calculator.

Summarise the data in a précis (Step 1.4)

In Chapter 4, we showed you how to do a précis. Go back to Chapter 4 Step 1.4 for the details. Once you have refreshed your memory, write your précis of Zubinos.

(a) **Look at our précis below**. Do you think it is any good? Yours may well be better.

(b) **Sample précis 1**. Give marks out of ten to your précis and ours. Someone else you know who is doing the exam may also be willing to mark it.

Give marks out of ten	Your précis	Our précis
Q1 Does the précis cover the key points at the right level of detail?		
Q2 Does the précis avoid analysis at this stage?		
Q3 Is the précis clearly structured?		
Q4 Is the précis well written?		

BPP précis	Paragraph reference
Market overview	1-5
Zubinos is a UK chain of coffee shops. Service marketing is an important consideration. There is strong competition and low barriers to entry. Location is critical, brands enable higher prices to be charged and coffee is an 'affordable luxury' purchase.	
The first Zubinos coffee shop	
Luis invested £300,000, using his own savings and borrowing money. Later investors have had to pay more for their shares, suggesting that wealth is being generated.	8
Luis knows the importance of location and convenience, although he later understands the significance of the **brand** for further expansion.	9
Note that demand peaks at different times: time of day could be used for **segmentation**.	
Zubinos' strategy of offering freshly made sandwiches and ice cream **differentiated** it against other branded coffee shops. There is a high level of repeat business.	10-11
People joining at the bottom could be given management positions quickly.	12
The growth of Zubinos	
There has been rapid expansion. **Segmentation** and **targeting** are mentioned with the 20 to 35 market. The main objective is growth. The rapid expansion shows evidence of low entry barriers.	13-15

BPP précis	Paragraph reference
By appointing George Shale, Luis is professionalising the management of the business. George recommends a strategy of market development (Ansoff), believing that other parts of the UK are less competitive.	
Jane Thorp is marketing director. She sees the potential of the **brand**.	6
Zubinos could consider opening coffee shops on the premises of another retailer.	17
Profitability is lower than some of its competitors.	18
Staffing issues and performance related bonuses	
Is Zubinos going through a crisis of delegation?	19-23
Zubinos is centralising certain management functions, such as procurement, marketing and HRM, thereby reducing the autonomy of local shops and instituting stricter control measures.	
The performance related bonuses seem to rely on financial measures. Lower bonus payments may be demotivating.	
Fair trade produce	
Luis believes coffee beans should be bought from Fair Trade suppliers, justifying a price premium and the policy is marketed.	24-26
IT development	
Zubinos is building a 'community' of people using its website, which might build loyalty. Also, the website allows brand extension – sale of coffee direct – a type of product development	27
There is a lack of financial and business information in a usable format. A new IT system will cost £110,000.	28-29
Introduction of a business investor	
The loan finance of 12% is expensive. Zubinos has been astute in obtaining long term investment resources to put its finances on a more secure footing 10% is still high.	30-34
Although the third 5-year loan is supposed to fund 'working capital', in effect it replaces money used for expansion. The expansion is to be rapid: this creates certain kinds of risk, eg overtrading. However, the professional management structure seems designed to take the company forward.	
Shareholdings at December 2005	
KPE paid £6 per share. This effectively values the company at £6m, or £5.4m if we deduct the loans. KPE has 40% of the shares but, critically, is offering a line of credit. This investor has power.	35-37
Luis and his wife own 42% of the shares. Luis is Chairman and Managing director.	
Analysis of gross margin	
A new MIS is planned to be operational in early 2006.	38
Only 34% of turnover is made up by coffee products or only 43.6% for all drinks. Drinks provide just over 50% of the gross margin, however. Even so, more than half of revenue, and just under half of gross margin, is accounted for by food.	39
Zubinos expansion plans	
The five year plan involves rapid expansion, financed by cash generated from operations and additional loan finance from KPE.	40-41

BPP précis	Paragraph reference
There is a problem with finding suitable properties to rent so shops have been purchased at over £1m.	42
Criteria for the selection of new sites are strength of competition, adequate resources and sufficient consumer demand. Presence of well-known chains is another factor.	43-44
Jane Thorp has proposed setting up cyber cafes.	45
Labelling of food	
There are no formal procedures for innovation and for piloting new products. Local initiatives have been discouraged. There is a potential market for low calorie products	46-47
Other recent developments	
A delivery service to local businesses has been started.	48
Zubinos could offer a wider range of foods.	49
Proposed expansion overseas	
Luis has European contacts keen to operate Zubinos coffee shops, growth overseas is included in the 5 year plan.	50-52
Reasons for expansion overseas include a saturated home market, less intense competition and comparative advantage against local competition.	
Appendix 1 Personnel	
There is no organisation chart.	
Luis is young and appears committed to the business.	
Vivien has been at the heart of new product development although she only works part time.	
Jane is used to consumer marketing and knows about fast food chains.	
Maria is in charge of procurement which Zubinos has had problems with. Local managers need help in forecasting.	
Anita has taken HR back in-house, there is no strategy for HRM.	
George helped put together the business plan and is emotionally committed to it. Accounting and finance matters have been taken back in-house.	
Bob knows about startups, although not about food retailing.	
Jack has introduced new procedures but has clashed with Anita on HR issues.	
Val and Sally are area managers for coffee shops – defined as 'new roles'. They are also responsible for recruitment and management of all staff.	
Carl represents 40% of the shares. He will get more involved if Zubinos does not hit its target.	
Appendix 4 Newspaper reports	
Zubinos coffee shops are larger than their competitors.	
Zubinos competes effectively: yet the industry is consolidating and other firms are growing by acquisition.	
KPE is pleased with 'operational and financial performance'	

So, what do you think about the précis above? Remember the point of the exercise is to assimilate information.

Carry out an information audit (Step 1.5)

We suggest you enlarge and photocopy the schedules already provided in Chapter 4 and mark them up (✓, X or P) with the information you have. The purpose of this is to go over again what you have after your précis, and to analyse more precisely what you are missing. It also enables you to start classifying the information into frameworks that can be used.

Research the industry (Step 1.6)

We chose Zubinos for our teaching case because it is the most accessible of the case studies to date. You can visit coffee shops and read about them very easily. You may already have a good knowledge of the business sector in which they operate, how they sell their products and how they compete.

You can use the internet to look up information on their likely rivals in the real world and topical issues such as fair trade.

Identify relevant technical knowledge (Step 1.7)

The following table lists possible technical knowledge issues for you to consider. Not all of these will need pursuing further. Most of these are covered in the other steps in the BPP approach.

Knowledge area
- Objectives and goal congruence
- Internal controls
- Ways to deal with risk:
    - Accept, insure, control, manage, transfer
- Greiner's organisational life cycle
- Service marketing mix
- Ansoff matrix
- Shareholder value analysis
- 5 forces/competitive strategies
- Corporate governance
- Ethics
    - Personal/professional ethics as a management accountant
    - Business ethics
    - Corporate social responsibility
- Project appraisal techniques
- Benchmarking
- Customer profitability analysis
- Supply chain management
- Motivation theory
- Mendelow's stakeholder matrix
- Sources of finance
- Business valuation
- e-commerce and McFarlan's grid
- Branding
- WACC
- Segmentation
- BCG matrix

In practice, most of the knowledge elements you cover will be drawn out from the specific steps we take to explore the case, analyse the case and synthesise our results.

2 Analyse the numbers (Step 2.1)

In the exam, you will only have a limited amount of time, so try to get to the heart of the data now. In our guide to the BPP approach, we gave a **checklist** of possible items to be considered, but **you should always add other numerical analysis that you consider useful.** You are very interested in future trends, which is why Zubinos' five year plan is useful.

Below we have calculated a table of ratios. We have not calculated every ratio in the list in Chapter 4 and we have added a few others. **You may have calculated a different set of ratios or gone into more detail.** Remember, you are using ratio analysis to **become more familiar with the case** – all the knowledge and technical abilities you now possess are tools to use.

Table of ratios

Actual vs forecast	The forecast is ambitious. There is no evidence yet that it is not being met, the 2005 figures are favourable.
Turnover	Turnover rose 75% last year Turnover is forecast to rise at 56% pa over the next 5 years There is no breakdown of turnover growth by store or product
Cost of sales	Gross margin in 2005 (weighted for sales mix) was 64.3%. Net margin in 2005 was 9.1%. Therefore, overheads to sales in 2005 was 55.2%.
Gross profit percentage	64.3% overall in 2005. No year to year comparators are available.
Expenses	Not separately available.
Net profit	There has been a slight reduction in net margin from 9.3% in 2004 to 9.1% in 2005. The pre-seen suggests this may be due to new stores.
Interest cover	Loans at between 10% and 12% Interest cover in 2005 = 14.56 times
Dividend cover	No dividends have been paid since 2001.
ROCE	Taking profits pre interest and tax over equity plus loans: 2004 = 737/2,684 = 27% 2005 = 1,267/6,281 = 20% Although falling, the ROCE is in excess of the cost of debt, at least. Also, ROCE will be low due to the expensive stores purchased during the year and the fact that new stores do not have the benefit of an entire year's earnings.
Retained profit/assets employed	Zubinos retains all its profits at present.
Non-current assets	In 2004 Zubinos generated £2.69 or revenue per £1 of non-current assets. In 2005 it generated £1.98 per £1. Could suggest that it overpaid for the most recent shops, certainly a worrying trend if more shops are to be acquired.
Turnover/current assets	2004 = £13.18 2005 = £13.64 This is a marginal improvement but not significant

Turnover periods Inventory, Receivables, Payables	Main point here is the greater use of trade credit. 2004 = 31.59 days 2005 = 35.8 days As the number of shops increase so does the amount of credit (from £689,000 in 2004 to £1,367,000 in 2005). It can be seen that credit taken is being extended too although it is not excessive.
Working capital/assets employed	Not relevant
Current/quick ratio	2004 = 0.23 2005 = 0.34 Given that this is a cash business this apparent lack of solvency is not an issue and is common in retail businesses.
Gearing	2004 = 600/(2,084 + 600) = 22% 2005 = 900/(5,381 + 900) = 14% Zubinos is low geared.
Earnings per share	2004 = 508,000/600,000 = £0.85 2005 = 897,000/1,000,000 = £0.90 Forecast EPS 2010 = (10,977000 × 0.76)/1,000,000 = £8.34
Price/earnings ratio	Not available using market values. KPE paid (2.4/0.4) £6 per share in 2005 which, using 2004 EPS, gives PE of 7.
Cost of capital	Not possible to calculate without making complex assumptions about future dividends.

These ratios are a useful starting point but we need to look at some areas of the financial data in more depth.

Gross margin analysis

	Coffee products	Other drinks	Sandwiches	Ice-cream	Other foods	Total
Sales revenue £'000	4,734	1,344	3,584	896	3,360	13,918
% of sales revenue	34%	10%	26%	6%	24%	100%
Gross margin £'000	3,808	702	2,324	714	1,398	8,946
Gross margin %	80%	52%	65%	80%	42%	64%
% contribution to gross margin	42%	8%	26%	8%	16%	100%

Valuation of shares

(a) **Net assets method**

On the basis of 2005 figures $\frac{\text{Equity}}{\text{Number of shares}} = \frac{5,381,000}{1,000,000} = £5.38$ per share

(b) **Price/earnings method**

Post tax earnings = £897,000

P/E Sector ratio = 20

Adjustment for Zubinos not being listed = 1/3

$$\text{Valuation} = \frac{897{,}000 \times 20 \times (1-1/3)}{1{,}000{,}000} = £11.96 \text{ per share}$$

(c) **Earnings flow valuation**

	2006 £'000	2007 £'000	2008 £'000	2009 £'000	2010 £'000
Pre-tax operating profit	2,160	3,613	5,606	8,203	10,977
Less: tax 24%	(518)	(867)	(1,345)	(1,969)	(2,634)
Post-tax earnings	1,642	2,746	4,261	6,234	8,343
Discount factor 12%	0.893	0.797	0.712	0.636	0.567
Discounted earnings	1,466	2,189	3,034	3,965	4,730

Value of discounted earnings = 15,384,000

$$\text{Value per share} = \frac{15{,}384}{1{,}000} = £15.38 \text{ per share}$$

2.1 Financial analysis report

You are the business adviser of Charles Frere, a rich friend of Vivien Zubino. Vivien has discussed with Charles the possibility of Charles purchasing 50,000 of the unissued shares of Zubinos, at a price of £7 per share. Charles is unsure whether this price is really a fair price and would like your comments on a fair valuation for the company, also the company's future prospects and financial risks.

Requirement

Prepare a report for Charles, discussing the principal features of Zubinos' most recent accounts and forecasts and advising him on a range of possible values per share. Your report should indicate what further information would be helpful for your analysis.

Report

This report comments on the main features of the most recent accounts and forecasts, suggests possible fair values under a range of methods and lists further information that would assist in valuing Zubinos.

1 **2005 accounts**

   (a) **Profitability and returns**

   Zubinos' **profit margin** and **increases in revenue and profit** appear to be **much better** than for many other coffee shop chains. Despite the significant increase in shop numbers, revenues, costs and operating profits have all increased at roughly the same rate in 2005, indicating that the expansion in 2005 appears to have been **well-controlled**. The breakdown of gross margins indicates that coffee sales only contribute about a third of revenues, though just over 40% of profits due to high mark-up. The amount of revenues generated by food may have implications for the forecasts (discussed below).

   The significant increase in earnings has boosted **earnings per share** by 6%, but the overall increase in finance has caused **return on capital employed** to drop from 27% to 20%. This figure is dependent on how much extra capital will be required over the next couple of years. Revenues generated by non-current assets have fallen significantly due to the investments in freehold rather than leasehold property in 2005.

   (b) **Liquidity and working capital**

   Both **current and quick ratios** are low, although for a consumables retailer this is not uncommon. The **fall in the current ratio** has been largely due to the much smaller increase in inventory (6%) than would be suggested by the expansion of shops, suggesting better control. The **increase in receivables** will mostly be due to prepayments on rentals, but may be partly due to problems collecting debts on the delivery service.

The main concern is the **rapid increase** in **trade payables**, with Zubinos now taking somewhat over a month on average to pay suppliers. Further increases may not only jeopardise Zubinos' **relations** with its suppliers, but also Zubinos' **reputation** as a Fair Trade customer. Zubinos' dependence on short-term finance appears to be increasing, which is rather worrying as the last bank loan was required to cover **increases in working capital.** Another concern is how well shop managers are carrying out **cash flow planning.**

(c) **Gearing**

It seems that Zubinos has potential to obtain extra loan finance as gearing at 14% has fallen as a result of the **venture capital investment** and the venture capitalist is happy to provide more loan capital. The interest cover of 14.6 suggests there is no problem meeting commitments.

However over the next couple of years retained cash earnings will not be enough to meet capital expenditure requirements and monies will be required to repay the loans repayable in 2006 and 2007. As mentioned above, **reliance on short-term finance** appears to be **increasing**. In addition the directors may intend Zubinos to start paying dividends; if it does, this will limit the retained funds available for investment.

2 **2006 – 2010 Forecast**

The rapid expansion planned makes the production of a reliable forecast very difficult. The forecast produced represents only one set of figures, based upon a number of assumptions some of which are **not clear** (see further information required) and which may differ significantly from the actual figures. In addition the company's forecasting has not been **very accurate** in the past, with under-estimation of the expansion in the early years, and the failure of staff to meet targets in late 2005 possibly being the result of over-optimistic recent forecasts.

In addition Zubinos' ability to meet the forecast will not only depend on the predicted demand levels being reached, but also the **finance** being available to support the required expansion and the **management and infrastructure** being further developed.

The following areas of the forecasts are particularly significant.

(a) **Revenues – coffee shops**

Most of the forecast growth is dependent upon the success of the new coffee shops opened after 2005. The figures suggest that saturation point will not have been reached in the **UK market** by 2010 as Zubinos is continuing to open shops in the UK up until that date. However the company appears to be expecting a **peak** to **be reached** in 2007, as the number of UK openings and the rate of growth in revenue per shop fall after that. This may reflect **expectations of UK market trends** that may not be very predictable, also expectations that shops opened abroad will have to **limit prices** whilst Zubinos establishes itself. Also by 2007 Zubinos may be located in all places with **most potential** in the UK, and after then will be choosing from locations with less promise.

In addition the forecast increases will also depend on being able to increase revenues from the product range in existing and new shops. As the products Zubinos already offers appear to be well-diversified, there may not be much scope for introducing new high-revenue earning products, even though the possibility of offering a wider range of foods is currently being investigated. Thus Zubinos' ability to increase revenue per shop appears to be dependent on its ability to **increase prices** without suffering a fall in demand, the effect of which matches or outweighs the rise in prices.

(b) **Revenues – other products**

The forecast suggests a very major expansion in new products over the next year or so with significant increases in following years. It is difficult to say how realistic these expectations are, as there is no detailed information about what these products are likely to be, or whether the category includes products that will be sold in coffee shops or is limited to products sold by other means. The forecast may be based on expansion of **on-line merchandise**, with the increase in sales fuelled by better publicity as well as more products.

(c) **Costs and profit margins**

Although operating profit margin dropped between 2004 and 2005, the directors expect that margins will gradually improve between 2005 and 2010. This suggests that the board expects **costs** to be kept under **reasonable control**, even if the increase in margins is mainly driven by enhanced revenues.

Costs may be limited by **centralising activities** such as **ordering**, also **rentals** on shops outside London being lower than for shops within the city. In addition the board appears to be taking a cautious attitude to initiatives involving significant expenditure, refusing to invest in on-line facilities for the cafes and scaling down the level of IT expenditure.

However there are a number of reasons why Zubinos may have difficulties limiting expenditure, although some of the items listed below will be capitalised rather than affecting profit margins.

(i) Zubinos is continuing to rely on **Fair Trade suppliers**

(ii) Zubinos has historically operated a policy of **significant investment** in **staff** and **fixtures and fittings**, and commercial pressures are likely to mean that this policy has to continue

(iii) **Increased expenditure** on **central functions** such as human resources will be necessary as the company expands

(iv) **Further investment** in **information technology** may also be required

(v) **Distribution costs** may **increase** significantly as Zubinos expands over the UK and into Europe

(d) **Capital expenditure**

The predicted level of capital expenditure per new shop opened drops significantly from £600,000 in 2005 to between £317,000 and £342,000 over the 2006 – 2010 period. In 2005 significant expenditure was needed to acquire the two freehold sties. The assumption appears to be that the great majority of new shops will be **leasehold sites**, but this will depend on what is available in the desired locations. It is also unclear how much capital expenditure will be needed to **refit** and **upgrade** existing stores, or how capital expenditure will be financed, as post-tax operating profits (and presumably retained cash) will not exceed capital expenditure until 2008.

3 **Valuation methods**

(a) **Net assets method**

The net assets method is based on the **current book value** of assets and takes no account of the future earnings potential of the company. It is generally used as a floor value in share purchase and acquisition negotiations. However the most recent value of shares in 2005 at £6.00 was rather closer to the net assets value of £5.38 based on the 2005 accounts than the other methods based on **earnings potential** that give higher values.

(b) **Price-earnings ratio**

This value has been calculated on the following basis.

(i) Taking **Zubinos' earnings in 2005**

(ii) Multiplying by a broad **average price-earnings ratio** of 20 for listed companies in the beverages sector

(iii) **Scaling down the valuation by 1/3** to take account of the fact that Zubinos' shares are not listed and hence are more difficult to sell

This method suggests a fair value of about £12 per share, and suggests the asking price of £7 is an undervalue. However, the following points should be kept in mind.

(i) The 2005 earnings figure is a snapshot in the middle of a period when Zubinos is expanding rapidly.

(ii) 20 is an **average** that does not take into account wide variations in the sector; other data suggests that the sector is becoming increasingly polarised between companies that are doing very well and companies that are seriously struggling.

(iii) More **sector-specific data** than for the whole beverages sector would be useful.

(iv) The **reduction of 1/3 in value** is fairly **arbitrary**.

(c) **Earnings methods**

This method takes operating earnings after tax and discounts them at a factor reflecting the company's weighted average cost of capital to approximate to a present value of future cash earnings. The forecast figures up to 2010 have been used; the cost of capital used is 12% on the basis that the **cost of debt** is lower than the interest rates charged because of tax relief on debt, but the **cost of equity** is rather higher than the cost of debt, because equity investment is riskier.

The value calculated per share, £15.38, is more than double the existing asking price. However there are a number of problems with this figure.

(i) It is dependent upon the **quality** of the **forecasts**.

(ii) The cost of capital figure chosen is an **approximation**, and a true figure might be higher, implying a lower valuation.

(iii) No account has been taken of earnings flows after 2010.

(iv) The figures have not been adjusted for **depreciation** or for **capital expenditure**.

(d) **Other comments**

The following **other reservations** apply to the valuation exercise.

(i) The **dividend valuation model** cannot be used to value the shares because Zubinos has not paid any dividends. The dividend valuation model is argued to be often the best method of valuing small % holdings of shares since shareholders holding small quantities of shares have **little control** over the **policies that determine earnings**.

(ii) Bringing **risk** into the valuation exercise is difficult but there clearly are risks in investing, as many companies in this sector are in financial difficulties, and if problems arise the bank and venture capital company will have first claim on the company's assets.

(iii) At present it appears that any **returns** from the shares will have to be realised in the form of **capital gains** as Zubinos is not paying any dividends. These can best be realised by Zubinos being listed on a stock exchange, but at present there are no plans to seek a listing.

4 **Other information required**

There are a number of issues concerning the forecasts on which more information would be helpful. It would be useful to know the **sources** of the data used, as if the forecasts were largely based on data supplied by **current shops**, these forecasts have not always been very accurate in the past. Another key issue is whether the forecasts are based on the assumption that growth will continue to be **organic** (that is not boosted by acquisitions) and new shops opened mainly in **leasehold** premises, also whether the forecasts assume that some of the new shops will be in the premises of another retailer.

More details would be helpful in the following areas.

(a) What will the impact, if any, on the forecasts of any predicted economic/ industry/ market/ social **trends** over the next five years?

> (b) The UK locations or geographical areas into which Zubinos is likely to expand in the next couple of years need to be considered. Bear in mind that the shops opened during this time period are expected to deliver **high growth**, despite **competition** that Zubinos is likely to face in those locations.
>
> (c) From 2008, what will be the **split in** expected revenues and profits **between** UK and overseas **shops**?
>
> (d) Any **expected changes** in the **product mix** offered by the shops need to be factored in?
>
> (e) Which **new products** are meant to be the most substantial contributors to the growth in new products?
>
> (f) Will there be any changes in the way the company operates that will have a **significant influence on cost patterns**? Examples include quality standards, staffing of new shops, use of suppliers and development of centralised functions.
>
> (g) Is capital expenditure is solely expected to be on **new shops**? or will existing fixtures and fittings will have to be replaced or a larger refit be required in order to maintain Zubinos' reputation for being trendy?
>
> (h) Is Zubinos is likely to pay any **dividends** over the next few years?
>
> 5 **Conclusion**
>
> The value of the investment depends on how the forecasts are viewed. Whilst Zubinos has exceeded forecasts in the past, its forecast expansion over the next few years is on a much greater scale than before. The price asked for appears reasonable in the light of what the venture capitalist paid a year ago and Zubinos' results in 2005. However I recommend that further details should be sought about the assumptions made in the forecast before a final decision is taken on whether to invest.
>
> **Appendices**
>
> *Note that the financial data that we have included earlier in this section would be inserted as appendices to a report.*

3 General environmental analysis (PEST) and trends (Step 2.2)

PEST analysis should already be familiar to you from your previous CIMA studies, but is a good test of your commercial awareness. PEST feeds into the **analysis of the risks** the business is facing.

> **PEST**
>
> **Political and legal factors**
>
> General 'political' factors have very little impact on Zubinos. Its main resource, coffee, is widely available and is a traded commodity. However, government decisions on personal and business taxation, employment regulation and so on will affect Zubinos, as is the case with other business.
>
> Legal and regulatory factors have a significant impact. Environmental health and food safety are enforced by local government through inspection. Local government officials can order Zubinos to close its coffee shops if the premises are not clean. Local authorities also grand planning permission (eg if a building's use changes) and, should Zubinos wish to sell alcohol, grant licenses.
>
> Because Zubinos is a limited company, it is regulated by company law. It must keep suitable accounting records. It collects VAT (sales tax) and PAYE for the government.
>
> Government regulations on labour may differ from market to market. When expanding into France and Spain, full account needs to be taken of local employment laws, which vary from country to country. The growth of the EU should make it easier to do business in these countries.
>
> If the company decides to float on a Stock Exchange, then the regulatory burden will grow.

> **Economic factors**
>
> As a discretionary purchase, coffee might be affected by a downturn in the economy. If people have less to spend, for example if interest rates on mortgages rise, they are likely to give up luxuries or switch to cheaper products. If unemployment rises, fewer people will visit Zubinos on the way to work. On the other hand, there will be downward pressure on wages, so the firm will be able to contain its costs.
>
> The exchange rate might affect the cost of some inputs. Net margins are relatively low, so a significant rise in input costs – unlikely though this is – could hurt margins.
>
> Local economic factors, as suggested in the case, are very important for each shop.
>
> **Social and cultural factors**
>
> This is critical. The company is targeting a demographic segment, and so needs to be in tune with the feelings and aspirations of that segment. To what extent is the coffee culture a permanent feature of the UK landscape? Other branded formats have flourished and declined owing to changing fashions and change in buyer behaviour. Fewer people are visiting pubs, for example, that was the case 20 years ago.
>
> People are becoming more health conscious, and if caffeine is associated with ill health, Zubinos will have to respond: but there are alternative beverages, decaffeinated versions and so on. (Green tea, for example, is being promoted as a healthy beverage.)
>
> **Technology**
>
> It is unlikely that there will be any replacement for 'eating out' or cafés. However, as suggested in the case, Internet access can be an additional service that is offered to customers. Technology can be used for marketing (eg website, text messages on mobile phones and so on).
>
> Technology is also influential in the operational management of the business, and the collection of management information. Developments in this respect (eg linking the stores to a central procurement system, perhaps linked electronically to suppliers) will be helpful.

4 Analyse the business environment and competitive strategy (Step 2.3)

Compare your completed checklists below with ours and summarise them in a five forces analysis.

4.1 Five forces and industry analysis

Step 1 **Identify the type of industry**

	What industries does the company operate in?	Classify as **emergent**, **mature** or **declining**
1	Coffee shops	Mature
2		
3		

Step 2 **Threat of new entrants**

	Item	Comment
1	High capital costs to enter	No
2	Is there a strong brand?	No
3	Is the industry attractive?	Yes
4	Does the case suggest new entrants?	Yes
5	Ease of exit (if declining sector)	Yes
	Threat of new entrants: high, medium or low (H/M/L)?	H

Step 3 Substitute products

	Item	Comment
1	Can other industries provide the same benefit?	Yes
2	Does the case evidence any threats?	Yes
3	Other considerations	
	Threat of substitute products: high, medium or low (H/M/L)?	H

Step 4 Customer bargaining power (and marketing issues)

	Item	Comment
1	Consumer or business to business?	Both
	If B-to-B, any issues in customers' own markets?	
2	Total revenue	£13.9 m
3	Market size	£1 bn
4	Market share	Small
5	Does the organisation really understand its customers and their needs?	Yes
6	Can key segments be identified in the data? If yes, what are they and what percentage of sales do they represent?	No
7	Trends in revenue and other sales performance indicators	Rapid growth
8	Does the case identify any Key Customers who account for a significant proportion of revenue? If Yes, note details Is it possible to do a customer profitability analysis? If so, are there some customers who are not profitable?	Yes 20-35 age group seen as the target market • No • Not known
9	Are current customers loyal or beginning to defect? How serious is this?	Customer loyalty is likely to be low given the number of substitutes
10	Are customers price sensitive?	Possibly
11	Does the case identify customers and markets not served?	Outside the UK
12	Can customers obtain the same benefits elsewhere?	Probably
13	Does the organisation have a coherent marketing strategy based on the 7Ps? Product – Price – Promotion – Place – People – Process – Physical evidence	Probably
14	Does the organisation consider building long-term customer relationships?	Possibly
15	What is the branding policy?	Brand is important but hard to compete with other global brands
	Customer bargaining power? high, medium or low (H/M/L)?	H

Step 5 **Suppliers and resources**

	Item	Comment
1	Supplier industries – what resources does the business consume?	Coffee, other foodstuffs
2	Are key suppliers identified? How close is the relationship?	No
3	Trends in input costs – and volatility See analysis of ratios	Not known
4	Is there a supply policy?	No
5	Ease of sourcing supplies from others/new suppliers	There are problems with supply
6	Can firm easily pass on increases in prices to customers?	No
7	Is the supply chain managed strategically?	No
	Supplier bargaining power: high, medium or low (H/M/L)?	M

Step 6 **Questions about competitors**

	Item	Comment
1	Does the case identify particular current competitors? If yes What are their goals and competitive strategy?	No Coffee shops are very competitive, but competition is very local
2	Does the case suggest potential competitors in the current industry?	Yes
	Competitive rivalry: high, medium or low (H/M/L)?	H

Now let us produce a specific competitive forces checklist.

Competitive forces checklist

Existing competition and competitive rivalry: intense

- There is intense competition
- Further differentiation is difficult to secure (quality and ethics are already catered for)
- The saturated home market may lead to consolidation in the industry
- Economies of scale enjoyed by large global brands may be difficult to match

New entrants

- Barriers to entry are low (Luis started successfully with a £300,000 loan)
- Bookshops, pubs, even petrol stations (BP's 'Wild Bean café') can offer coffee
- While it is easy to open a coffee shop, building a **brand** is harder
- Sandwich bars can compete

Substitutes

- Flasks – people can make coffee or other drinks at home
- Vending machines are getting better (Klix)
- Free water dispensers are provided in many offices
- Other meeting places include pubs and clubs for entertainment

Buyers

- Individuals exercise buying power through choice
- Companies (deliveries) may have high buying power

> **Suppliers**
> - Coffee is a widely traded commodity so supplier power is low: hence fair trade
> - Suppliers of rental property have high buying power
>
> The industry would appear to offer low profitability: brand building and scale economies would appear crucial for the long term.

5 Audit the product/service portfolio (Step 2.4)

Step 1   Define the product in terms of customer needs satisfied

Customers want to buy coffee and food products in a convenient location in shops with a good atmosphere. They are increasingly demanding a wide range of foods using premium products.

Step 2   **Identify product and service elements**

Product	Good coffee and food with an emphasis on Free Trade ingredients
Price	Premium pricing due to association with coffee culture and ambiance of shops
Promotion	Only the website is mentioned
Place	Key criterion in growth is the selection of sites in proximity to travel hubs and offices employing the target customers
People	Given that production of the drinks and management of the shops must take place with customers present, it is vital that the appearance and manner of the staff communicates the service values of Zubinos.
Physical	The appearance of the shops, their layout, furnishings, lighting and music will all be critical to making them somewhere that people want to meet, or to relax. To a lesser extent the crockery and cartons in which food and drink is provided will be an element here
Process	For take-away customers the speed of service is likely to be a key criterion. For the eat-in customer it is likely that an ability to linger will be important. Blending these two different service requirements will be essential

Step 3   **Use the BCG matrix to identify how the product or service is positioned**

Not presently relevant as Zubinos has only one line of business. Clearly individual stores may be classed as cash cows or problem children to assess cash flows in the company. The low relative share of Zubinos can be interpreted through the matrix as a possible weakness due to lack of economies or scale, lack of experience effects and lack of brand penetration.

Step 4   **Product costs and profitability**

We know that in December 2001, profitability was lower than that of its rivals. In Paragraph 18 of the pre-seen, we note that profitability was lower than **some** of its competitors, not all.

The gross margin is 64% (Para 39), the operating profit margin before tax is 9.1% (£1,267/£13,918). Costs in 2005 were £12,651, of which food and drink accounted for £4,972. The other expenses must relate to premises costs and overheads, including depreciation, or over 60% of total costs. 42.5% of the gross margin is accounted for by coffee (Para 39: £3,808/£8,946).

6 How does the business add value? (Step 2.5)

The value chain is another useful model for identifying what the business does and its strengths and weaknesses.

Value chain	Strengths	Weaknesses
Inbound logistics	• Quality ice cream • Fair trade coffee beans	• Duplicated/inconsistent ordering (customers do not receive high quality as standard) • Only 80% of the coffee is 'fair trade'. This undercuts the positioning. • There is a lack of planning and discipline in procurement.
Operations	• Staffing levels are suitable • Locations are good • Expensive fixtures/fittings • Internet access/ordering	• Thefts – possible stock-outs/disruption to service • Low-cost 'scaled down' internal IT systems • No customer focused innovations allowed
Outbound logistics	Delivery service/catering	No post-sale liaison with customers re: payment for deliveries
Marketing	Little known	Little known
Service	Incorporated above	Incorporated above

7 Identify information systems and processes (Step 2.6)

	Issue	Comment
1	**Information technology**	
1.1	What are the structural arrangements for IT? (eg IT department, delegated to users, information centre, outsourced)	Not clear
1.2	Who looks after IT strategy and security?	No clear role but Jane Thorp and George Shale have an input
1.3	What is the role of IT in the development of the company? (McFarlan's grid) • Factory • Support • Turnround • Strategic	Support
1.4	Is IT use considered within the business strategy and is it implementation harmonised with it?	No
1.5	Is e-commerce relevant and does the firm have a stance towards this development?	Yes, Zubinos website recently updated On line chat room: possible application of Web 2.0 technologies; analysing customer comments/suggestions?

	Issue	Comment
1.6	Main packages • Operational reporting • Corporate reporting	Unknown
2	**Knowledge and information**	
2.1	What internal communication systems are in use – eg paper, email, intranet?	Unknown
2.2	Do managers receive good information in terms of the performance of the business?	No
2.3	Knowledge management – is information shared or hoarded?	Unknown
3	**Risk**	
3.1	Does current IT set up involve business or security risk?	Yes • Lack of appropriate management information • Risks from website
4	**Management and internal control systems**	
4.1	How are activities and resources controlled in the organisation?	Rather chaotic with weaknesses apparent in internal control
4.2	Is the management accounting system well designed and operated?	No
4.3	Who sets performance targets, and are they effective?	There is a bonus scheme but it has caused problems
4.4	What is the extent of centralisation versus decentralisation?	Some attempt at centralisation but not particularly effective
4.5	Is reporting timely?	No
4.6	Are management accounting and information systems regularly audited?	No evidence.
4.7	Generally, are principles of good corporate governance followed (eg separation of chairman and chief executive?)	No
4.8	Is the business susceptible to fraud (computer-based or otherwise?)	Yes

8 Identify key issues in structure, culture and personnel (Step 2.7)

Fill in the checklist in Chapter 4 to marshal your thoughts.

(a) **Structure**

Item	Comment
Step 1 Draw an organisation chart, if the case has not already provided you with one.	
Step 1.1 What sort of departmentation approach is used (eg functional, matrix)?	Functional but with some overlaps of responsibility for recruitment
Step 2 Does the case data indicate any problems with the current organisation structure, such as reporting/communication, corporate governance, co-ordination, focus on the business?	Yes • Corporate governance • Weaknesses in internal controls
Step 3 Does the case data offer opportunities for you to benchmark the performance of different departments with other firms? If so, how does the firm compare?	Yes With 18 shops already there are opportunities for identifying and disseminating best practice.
Step 4 Identify any outsourcing arrangements currently in force, and arrive at a reasoned judgement as to how effective they are in terms of operations, risk and financial security.	Payroll No information on effectiveness
Step 5 Identify any possible opportunities for outsourcing and note feasibility.	IT?
Step 6 In your opinion, is the structure a strength or a weakness in the light of the situation facing the business and why?	Lack of clarify of roles is a weakness.
Step 7 Recommend improvements: what structure (in brief) would you consider better?	Need to adopt a formal structure suitable for their strategy.

(b) **Culture**

Item	Comment
Step 1 What does the case tell you about the culture of the organisation and its management? Classify it, if you can, according to a framework used in your earlier studies.	A mix of the rational model, freewheeling opportunism and incrementalist
Step 2 Is it a strength or a weakness?	

(c) **Personnel**

Item	Comment
Step 1 Who are the key people?	Luis Zubinos and a committed management team
Step 2 Do they have objectives which can affect the performance of the firm?	Luis is an entrepreneur, driven by a sense of mission
Step 3 What influence do key personnel have? • Internally • Externally	Extremely influential
Step 4 Does the firm have a succession plan?	No
Step 5 Is there any evidence of poor industrial relations?	Bonus scheme is not motivating and is not rewarding performance.
Step 6 Is there a strategy for HRM and is it aligned with the business strategy?	No. HR policy is vague and there are overlapping responsibilities
Step 7 What are its employment policies (contracts, rewards, performance appraisal)?	Relatively high staff costs. Problems with the bonus scheme
Step 8 Does the firm invest in training?	Area managers have had management training
Step 9 Is there evidence of high staff turnover?	Nothing in the case.
Step 10 Does the firm have skills base and competences needed for the future?	No current evidence of problems.
Step 11 What is the quality of the management team, given the challenges facing the business?	Good
Step 12 Do managers have a shared vision?	
Step 13 Do they understand their rules and responsibilities under corporate governance regulations?	No evidence

9 Identify investor objectives, capital structure and other stakeholder objectives (Step 2.8)

Fill in the checklist below.

	Investors	Comment
Step 1	Identify share owning structure: • Privately owned? • Publicly traded?	A private limited company with 40% of equity externally owned by KPE
Step 2	Note information as to the return shareholders and investors are expecting from the company – use comparative information?	Rapid expansion is planned. Possible future exit strategy for KPE but no details

	Investors	Comment
Step 3	Note trends in the share price, if this information is given.	NA
Step 4	If you have a P/E ratio and a market value, calculate a possible value for the business.	Post tax earnings = £897,000 P/E Sector ratio = 20 Adjustment for Zubinos not being listed = 1/3 Valuation = $\dfrac{897{,}000 \times 20 \times (1 - 1/3)}{1{,}000{,}000}$ = £11.96 per share
Step 5	Do you have information to calculate the WACC? If yes, do so.	No.
Step 6	Note comparative information about other companies for a benchmark as to shareholder expectations.	None
Step 7	Note data as to the risk of the company (eg the beta)	No data available.
Step 8	Review gearing ratios	2004 = 600/(2,084 + 600) = 22% 2005 = 900/(5,381 + 900) = 14% Zubinos has a low gearing ratio.
Step 9	Would you invest in this company?	
Step 10	Objectives Remuneration Performance	Already shareholders Bonus scheme issues
Step 11	*Employees* Objectives	*Comment* Unknown
Step 12	*Lenders* Exposure Relationship	*Comment* KPE are happy to provide more loan capital
Step 13	*Government* Power of influence	*Comment* Low
Step 14	*Customers and suppliers*	*Comment* See '5' forces analysis
Step 15	*Community*	*Comment* Ethical trading – Fair Trade issues

10 Identify and analyse possible business projects (Step 2.9)

The overall impression of Zubinos is that of a young company under-going rapid growth. The key question is how should the business expand further? This is possibly the nearest you will get to question spotting.

No.	Project – rationale	Main para refs in case
1	New shop openings in UK	15–17, 40–45
2	New product launches	49
3	Overseas expansion	50–52

Zubinos: synthesise what you know

This chapter completes the work you will be doing on the pre-seen material.

Do remember that each case is different, there may be further analysis or synthesis work you could do suggested by the data in each individual case.

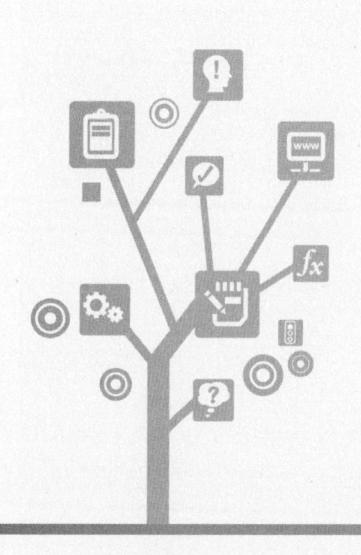

topic list

1. Summarise your findings in a position statement (Step 3.1)
2. Draw up a mission statement (Step 3.2)
3. Relate the business's distinctive competences to the critical success factors for the industry (Step 3.3)
4. Identify and analyse risks (Step 3.4)
5. Carry out a graded SWOT analysis (Step 3.5)
6. Identify the key business issues (Step 3.6)
7. Draw up a balanced scorecard (Step 3.7)
8. Prepare a one-page business summary (Step 3.8)

1 Summarise your findings in a position statement (Step 3.1)

As described earlier, this stage may involve updating your précis and summarising your analysis so far. It is your first chance to start identifying connections between the various aspects of the case. You may prefer to do so using a mind map.

Note that one of the purposes for doing this is to enable you to tell yourself a story to fix the case situation in your mind. Here is a possible position statement for Zubinos.

What Zubinos does and how its structured

Zubinos Coffee Houses is a five year old private company that presently operates 18 coffee houses. There are 10 shops in London and the South East of England and a further eight in the rest of the country.

It has featured very rapid growth with store openings accelerating from the original plan of one a year to eight new stores during 2005.

Zubinos has few distinctive characteristics to set it apart from rivals. One potential factor is its use of Fair Trade produce which accounts for 80% of its produce. (*BPP comment: by 'produce' we assume the pre-seen means just coffee and cocoa beans and does not include foods and ice cream*).

The operation of the coffee houses was regionalised in mid-2005 with two Area Managers, Val Pline and Sally Higgins, taking responsibility for London and South East and Regions respectively. The responsibilities of Area Managers are not stated clearly beyond those of assisting store managers with recruitment.

Senior management is structured by function, seemingly following consultancy advice in 2003 with several appointments being made in 2004. The functional responsibilities of Marketing, Procurement, Human Resources and Finance are covered, but there are no board level directors of operations nor information technology.

The board features six directors of whom four have functional responsibilities. There are two Non-Executive Directors, Carl Martin, nominee of Kite Private Equity, and Vivien Zubino, wife of the Luis Zubino the CEO. Neither of these NEDs can be regarded as independent. Luis Zubino combines the roles of Chairman and CEO.

Zubinos is 42% owned by Luis and Vivien Zubino and 40% owned by Kite Private Equity (KPE) with the remaining 18% of shares spread between the remaining directors. KPE will presumably be looking for an exit route to realise the capital gain on its shares.

Zubinos' present financial and competitive performance

In London, Zubinos has 10 out of the 500 branded shops operating, a market share (by location) of 2%. Therefore compared to major operators, it is very small.

Zubinos is profitable. Post tax profits grew 76% in 2005 against turnover growth of 74%. ROCE fell in 2005 to 15.7% compared to 20.7% for 2004 although this may be distorted by many of the eight shops opened in 2005 and included in year-end assets not having yielded a full year's earnings.

Capital gearing has fallen from 22% in 2004 to 14% in 2005 due the present policy of not paying a dividend and instead retaining profits.

Gross margins are strongest in coffee and ice cream (80%) but lower on sandwiches (65%), other drinks (52%) and other foods (42%). The wastage rate on perishable products may be a contributory factor here. However at present Zubinos margins are less than those of its rivals.

Key issues faced by Zubinos: its opportunities and its problems

The main issue facing Zubinos is how to realise the targets in its five year plan in a market that may be becoming mature. This plan shows ambitious growth over the next five years of **outlets** from 18 to 75 (417%), **turnover** by 830% and **profits** by 867%.

PART B TEACHING CASE: ZUBINOS   10: Zubinos: synthesise what you know   **163**

> The methods by Zubinos will do this have yet to be confirmed. Options include the following.
>
> - Expanding the range of products sold in the shops (for which there is a separate revenue line showing that the percentage of revenue from new products will grow from 3% to in excess of 4% in future years).
> - Striking a deal to open Zubinos branches inside the stores of other retail chains.
> - Opening more branches in London but also throughout the country, these are included in the 5 year forecast. Part of this issue is whether to rent or buy freehold properties in future.
> - Opening stores outside the UK of which the plan forecasts 25 by 2010.
> - Increasing its web-based business.
>
> Decisions need to be taken on these issues.
>
> There are problems in forecasting business which is leading unplanned procurements and other costs being incurred.
>
> There seem to be some **overlaps in responsibilities** that could cause tensions. One is in the hiring of staff which presently involves the HR director (Anita Wiseman) and the Area Managers. Another is between Anita Wiseman and Jack Rayfield (shop management and security).
>
> There could be some control problems. Financial control seems weak and one fraud has been discovered already.
>
> **Information or meetings forthcoming which may affect Zubinos' future.**
>
> These are the main outstanding issues.
>
> - The new IT system commissioned in 2005 is due to become operational during 2006. The management information provided by this may help Zubinos to assess the profitability of its stores and products better. It may also improve margins by allowing better forecasting.
> - Luis Zubino has been in discussions with other retail outlets to develop shop-in-store opportunities. The results of these discussions are still outstanding.

Debrief

- You have to make judgements. You have only so much data to go on.
- You will be able to develop your thinking when you draw up your business summary. A mind map can help link the issues.

2 Draw up a mission statement (Step 3.2)

The purpose of drawing up a mission statement is to **guide your decision-making** when looking at the unseen data and to **help you prioritise.**

You should be able to say with confidence what the business is for, or who it is for. Your mission statement should reflect the actual mission of the organisation.

Here is a possible **mission statement** for Zubinos.

We aim to provide excellent coffee shops in the UK and Europe, delighting our customers with food as well. We aim to be the best, being welcoming as well as selling the best coffee and food. We support ethical treatment of our suppliers, staff and other stakeholders.	What is missing? (a) Financial targets (b) Behaviour standards and values

3 Relate the business's distinctive competences to the critical success factors for the industry (Step 3.3)

These two models can get you thinking in broad terms about the business and the industry.

Current distinctive competences

A **distinctive** competence has to be distinctive – in other words, something unusual in the market place. It is difficult to see that Zubinos has distinctive competences nor that it has unique resources other than its locations.

CSFs

	CSFs	Does Zubinos have the competences to satisfy them?
1	Brand awareness	Marketing director has experience but needs a congruent strategy.
2	Human resource management	Individuals have human resources capability but needs a clear structure and policy.
3	Supply chain management	No procurement or information systems in place.

Debrief

You may disagree with our assessments of the CSFs in this industry.

4 Identify and analyse risks (Step 3.4)

Risk type	Consequences (quantify if useful)	Importance, likelihood and seriousness
Business		
1 Competitor action	• Increased competition in the locations in which the company operates shops, or changes in the products or facilities offered by existing competitors • Mergers resulting in competitors becoming larger and being able to benefit more from economies of scale, and being in a stronger negotiating position with suppliers	H
2 Property costs	Having to invest in freehold property (and hence incurring higher costs than currently planned) in order to be able to open shops in desirable areas	M
3 Falling returns	From shops in areas experiencing economic downturn, particularly in the retail sector	M
Operational		
1 Procurement problems	Shops could run out of inventory	H
2 Health and safety	Shops could be closed or products not offered	M
3 Quality issues	Failure of products to reach required quality standards could lead to loss of business	M
4 Staffing problems	Dissatisfied staff providing a lower standard of service and increased staff turnover resulting in more mistakes being made by inexperienced staff	H
5 Fraud	Vulnerable to losses because of employee theft of stock or cash	M

Risk type	Consequences (quantify if useful)	Importance, likelihood and seriousness
Financial		
1 Cash shortages	May require finance at possibly high cost to resolve cash shortages arising from expenditure required to finance expansion	M
2 Loss of supply sources	Supplier dissatisfaction may result from length of time taken to pay bills	M
3 Credit risk	Loss of revenue from delivery service through smaller amounts being collected than billed, and customers not paying at all because there is no system for chasing up slow paying debtors.	M
4 Interest rate risk	Zubinos will suffer increased finance costs if interest rates rise, and it has to take out new loans at higher fixed rates or take out loans at floating rates.	M
Exchange		
1 Currency	• If the £ moves adversely against the currencies of the countries where its significant suppliers are located • Currency risk if it expands into Europe and receives revenues in currencies other than £	M
Other		
Information risks	• Inappropriate decisions may be made because of the information systems not providing sufficient information or providing poor quality information • At a shop level, consequences could include ordering insufficient inventory; at a company level inaccurate information about profit margins and unrealistic forecasting could result in poor decisions being made about which products to offer and what prices to charge • Poor information could also lead to underestimates of the amount of cash that will be required, leading to an increased risk of cash shortages	H
Information technology risks	• Problems with the website could result in customers being unable to order products online and being unable to use the chatroom • Unauthorised users may be able to access customer data	M
Economic risks	• Changes in the economic environment such as an economic downturn leading to a fall in demand for expensive coffee as a luxury good • Fall in profits if there was an increase in commodity prices	M

Risk type	Consequences (quantify if useful)	Importance, likelihood and seriousness
Legal risks	• Stricter employment regulation may limit the hours employees can work and enhancing the protection employees have • Tougher health and safety regulations result in increased compliance costs and legal costs if Zubinos does transgress • New food labelling laws may force Zubinos to label products with nutritional data and threaten demand, as has happened in one London coffee shop • Changes in local planning laws may restrict what Zubinos can do with its buildings	M
Social and cultural risks	• Pubs are open for longer hours, leading to pubs rather than coffee shops being seen as places to congregate during the day • Changes in taste may lead to an increased demand for lower calorie foods than Zubinos is currently offering • Decreases in demand for coffee may result from increased fears of the consequences of excessive caffeine intake • As Zubinos has built its business on being fashionable, failing to keep up with changes in fashion, for example in terms of the 'look' of its coffee shops	M
Reputation risks	• Breaches of health and safety regulations and consequent legal action leading to customers believing that Zubinos' products are unhealthy • The ethical stance it has taken over Fair Trade; its marketing literature could be seen as misleading if it decides to use more suppliers who are not Fair Trade, or if it is believed to be exploiting Fair Trade suppliers, for example by slow payments of amounts owed	H

Debrief

(1) You may need to revisit your views in the light of the unseen data in the exam. The fact that a risk is **low** does not mean that it won't happen. It is just to help your decisions regarding your estimation of the **likely** risk.

(2) There is **no probabilistic data** in the pre-seen material so you cannot do more than a fairly simple analysis.

5 Carry out a graded SWOT analysis (Step 3.5)

The list below was the result of a brainstorming session. You may have thought of others.

Strengths	Weaknesses
1 Some good locations, some owned shops bigger than competitors' so higher peak usage capacity	1 There is confusion in the management structure
2 Financial position	2 Poor financial controls
3 Top management commitment, improved team	3 Poor planning, poor inventory control
	4 Lower profits than competitors

PART B TEACHING CASE: ZUBINOS 10: Zubinos: synthesise what you know

Strengths	Weaknesses
4 Better service formula than competitors (App 4) 5 Bigger shops, hence more flexible 6 Good reputation (press release) as a coffee bar 7 Brand, potentially, with strong values (fair trade) 8 Website is successful 9 Some dynamic staff. 10 A variety of food/drink is offered 11 Increasing profitability 12 Zubinos is not running the risk of overtrading, as it is investing and can use long term loan 13 Zubinos has a generic strategy (differentiation, not clear, location) – but this is not fleshed out (eg targets), not detailed 14 Place – good locations 15 Product assortment, seasonality 16 Price premium 17 Promotion/marketing; word-of-mouth 18 People 19 Process: in store, the customers are happy 20 Physical evidence. Ambience is good 21 Repeat business is achieved (but not measured)	5 Difficulties in managing growth. There is internal conflict: head office vs shops, there is conflict within senior management; centralisation stifles local initiative: poor management of innovation 6 Still small, few scale economies of scale 7 Bonus scheme is not motivating, and is not rewarding performance 8 Not diversified (BUT sticking to the knitting) 9 High interest on bank loans 10 Poor systems and IT– no strategic view, of this resource; not spending enough, given expansion plans 11 HR policies/practices: vague, overlapping responsibilities 12 It is not clear about the ability to finance FUTURE growth, from existing stores 13 No contingency plans 14 The assumptions in business plan are unclear
Opportunities	**Threats**
1 Alliance with another retail outlet 2 Internet café 3 Industry consolidation in UK (eg take over a company) 4 Overseas – growth for branded coffee shops 5 Expatriates in Spain/France 6 Locations outside London & SE 7 Franchising! 8 Non-food products (eg Starbucks offers music downloads) 9 Alcohol: 24 hours opening 10 Food innovation 11 Website 12 Railway stations (growing passenger numbers). 13 Shopping malls.	1 Property costs; lease price hike (upwards only) 2 Industry consolidation: strong venture capitalist wanting to exit in 2010? 3 Downturn in economy: cut in discretionary consumer spend 4 Commodity pricing (minor threat) 5 Employment regulation (eg opt out) in UK and EU 6 Local planning regulations, zoning 7 Low barriers to entry 8 'No logo' protests 9 Different food cultures 10 Food scares, faddishness, diet, substitutes 11 Changing lifestyle habits of target segments 12 Do city centres thrive? 13 Substitutes eg resurgent pubs 14 Falling retail sales 15 Competition: Whitbred, Starbucks have lot more shops

BPP LEARNING MEDIA

Prioritise your SWOT

You might well have considered different strengths to be priorities. (The numbers are drawn from the brainstormed list above.)

Key SWOT item	Justification
Strengths	2 **Financial position.** Unusually perhaps for a coffee chain, Zubinos has a strong financial position, underpinned by a supportive private equity firm, whose representative has agreed and approved the five year expansion plan. Without this long term financial support, Zubinos growth would be much slower.
	3 **Top management commitment.** The senior management team appear to be fairly young, and committed, with a smattering of experienced older hands such as Jack Rayfield, Carl Martin and George Shale who provide useful perspective.
Weaknesses	1 **Confusion in management structure.** Many new, professional members of the management team have been introduced in the past few years, but responsibility for recruitment, innovation and even forecasting is not clear.
	5 Related to (1) above there are, potential **difficulties in managing growth**, given evidence of conflict between senior managers and between the centralising tendencies and local initiative: Failure to manage this will lead to demotivated staff and poor management: in a service business, staff processes are vital and staff in the shops themselves are probably much closer to customers than those secluded in head office.
Opportunities	3 **Industry consolidation in the UK.** This suggests some chains will close and there are opportunities for acquisitions: although this is not covered in Zubinos' business plan. If Zubinos has a winning formula – supported by its large shops with higher capacity – it might expect to increase market share.
	4 **Overseas growth for branded coffee shops.** Franchising – the obvious choice – does not get a mention in the case. Perhaps branded coffee shops will not do so well overseas if the concept is not established. McDonalds proves it is possible to build a business based on standard service offerings. Focusing on expatriate Britons, however, displays a poverty of ambition. Countries **other** than France, with its established coffee culture, and Spain might offer a better opportunity.
Threats	3 **Downturn in the economy** and a cut in discretionary consumer spending. The UK economy had enjoyed a sustained period of growth from the late 1990s into the start of the 21st century, and within this overall growth there was also a growing service sector. [Note: This case was set in 2006]. However, as the global recession of 2008 –2009 has illustrated, discretionary purchases such as restaurant meals tend to suffer in a recession as people focus on essentials. This links to other changes in consumer behaviour, for example if people find other sources of entertainment, or pubs rebuild themselves.
	15 **Competition.** Barriers to entry are low as far as new entrants are concerned. Competition might also push up rents if there is competition for the best locations. Starbucks has many stores and other firms such as Costa have the flexibility to expand by franchising. Zubinos does offer other benefits, such as ice cream and fresh food, so it may be slightly better off.

6 Identify the key business issues (Step 3.6)

Issue in order of importance	Description
1	**Consolidating industry in the UK** Zubinos still has growth objectives in the UK, but other chains are consolidating. The competitive environment could become less favourable.
2	**Management practices, organisation structure and systems** Maintaining consistent product and service quality across the expanded business requires change in management. Luis has already assembled a senior management team to manage growth, but there is still plenty of work to do. Better systems (for IT) and procedures (for HR etc) need to be in place.
3	**Ability to manage and finance growth** Growth is financed partly by loans and partly by cash generated from operations. The business will become more complex and harder to manage. The company needs to learn how to balance local flexibility with central control.
4	**Possible cash withdrawals** Loans must be repaid, sooner or later dividends will be expected, and most of the management team have borrowed heavily.

7 Draw up a balanced scorecard (Step 3.7)

Financial perspective	Customer perspective
• Growth in the number of shops from 18 to 75 in five years • 830% increase in turnover • Profits of $10.98 million by 2010	• Increase in market share from current 2% • Take up of new products as % of turnover • Broaden segmental attractiveness
Internal process perspective	**Innovation and learning perspective**
• New IT system • Supply chain management • Operational management of stores	• Overseas development • New product development • Increasing web-based business

8 Prepare a one-page business summary (Step 3.8)

We proposed a format of the business summary in Chapter 4. Again, there is no need for you to follow this slavishly – it just depends on the circumstances of the case. You may feel you want to add a lot more (or less) data than what we have here.

Remember that the business summary should be **Key facts/ideas** that you have to remember, as you will not be allowed to bring this into the exam. You will have the case itself, but you will have to remember all your analysis.

BUSINESS SUMMARY: USE THIS FOR YOUR ANALYSIS AND SYNTHESIS			
Nature of business (Step 2.4): Coffee shops Current mission (Step 3.2)	CFSs for success in industry (Step 3.3)		
^	Brand awareness		Supply chain mgmt
^	Human resource mgmt		
Distinctive competence (Step 3.3)			
Major stakeholder objectives: Growth; new product development			
ANALYSIS BACKUP			
Key financial data: trends (Step 2.1)	External (Steps 2.2, 2.3): 5 forces/industry		
Turnover up 75% last yr Net margin 9.1% Gross margin 64.3% ROCE 20% Est value of business (Step 2.8) £5.38 – £15.38 per share Gearing 14% Worrying indicators: Use of trade credit increasing	P Regulations E Disposable incomes S Fashion, health T Internet, MIS	1 New entrants: high 2 Substitutes: high 3 Customer B/P: high 4 Supplier B/P medium 5 Rivalry high	
^	^	Industry: Mature	
^	Internal • Lack of management information • Internal control issues		
Competitive strategy: differentiation-focus			
Customers (Step 2.3): target age segment 20 – 35 years			
SYNTHESIS			
SWOT (Items of **high** importance) (Step 3.5)			RISKS (High importance) (Step 3.4)
Strengths 1 Financial position 2 Top management commitment	Opportunities 1 Industry consolidation in the UK 2 Overseas growth		1 Competitor action 2 Procurement problems 3 Staff problems 4 Reputation
Weaknesses 1 Confusion in management structure 2 Difficulties in managing growth	Threats 1 Downturn in economy 2 Competition		

Key issues (Step 3.6) (High importance)	Selection of possible business projects (Step 2.9)
1 Consolidating industry in UK	1 New shop openings in UK
2 Management practices, organisation structure and systems	2 New product launches
	3 Overseas expansion
3 Ability to finance and manage growth	
4 Possible cash withdrawals	

Zubinos: unseens and requirements

This chapter contains the unseen material and requirements from the Zubinos case study (the real March and May 2006 exams under the old syllabus).

We have included both the March and May unseen material to show how the same pre-seen material can be used to produce two very different case studies, which is why you must not try to question spot.

However, we have only used the March 2006 unseen as the basis of our illustration for how to tackle the unseen material, and we expect this to be the exam you focus on.

Accordingly, we have only produced an answer to the Zubinos March exam in Chapter 12.

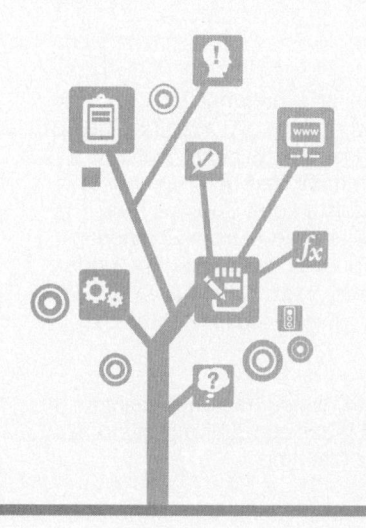

topic list

1. Before tackling the unseen material
2. Unseen material, requirement and assessment matrix (March 2006 unseen)
3. Review the unseen and requirement (Step 5.2)
4. Read the unseen data in depth (Step 5.3)
5. Writing your report (Steps 5.4 to 5.9)
6. May 2006 unseen (for illustrative purposes only)

1 Before tackling the unseen material

1.1 You have three hours and twenty minutes

Firstly, don't panic. You have a lot of time, and you have the pre-seen data – without your analysis – in front of you. (CIMA will tell you if they have amended the pre-seen data in any way.)

Bear in mind that the case is not designed to help you question spot. Therefore, do not be surprised if there are issues in the unseen that you have not thought of – you have done all the analysis that you can, but you **cannot second guess the examiner**. Therefore you should **EXPECT THE UNEXPECTED**.

Now **skim read** the unseen data and read the requirement.

2 Unseen material, requirement and assessment matrix

> **Introduction**
> This is the unseen material which was presented in the March 2006 exam.

Zubinos coffee shops – Unseen material provided on examination day

Read this information before you answer the question

Bad publicity for Zubinos

There have been several adverse national newspaper reports, as well as a national TV consumer programme, reporting that several of Zubinos' healthy food options are not what they seem. It has been reported that some of these foods, which have a low calorie count and are low in fat, contain high levels of salt, sugar and some additives which have had bad press over possible health concerns. Additionally, the calorie count on some foods sold at Zubinos has been shown incorrectly on its food label. The press has carried various reports from Zubinos' public relations (PR) company stating that "the adverse comments about Zubinos' healthy foods are mainly incorrect and minor problems have been vastly over-stated". Luis Zubino is also concerned that one of Zubinos' competitors could be trying to counter the success of Zubinos, by spreading incorrect rumours.

Zubinos out-sources its quality control to a leading food agency, QAIF, which has an excellent reputation. This agency also advises Zubinos' suppliers on the food labelling requirements and assists them with labelling when Zubinos procures food items for the first time.

The UK's Food Standards Organisation (FSO), which is responsible for all foods sold in the UK, is currently sampling a number of Zubinos food items following the recent bad press. The FSO has recently visited several Zubinos coffee shops and identified that there were several items being sold that did not have any food labels on and other food items that had incorrect or misleading data for ingredients and calorific values. Luis Zubino spoke very harshly to Maria Todd about these problems.

Maria Todd has been working very long hours and has been struggling to identify new suppliers for the planned shop openings in 2006, and was very upset by the way Luis Zubino reprimanded her over the food labelling problems. She feels that she can no longer cope with her growing role and is considering resigning.

A further embarrassing event for Zubinos occurred in early February 2006. Jane Thorp had approved each of the adverts in a routine advertising campaign promoting Zubinos. One of the adverts had stated, *"All coffee sold in Zubinos is Fair Trade coffee"*. However, a former Zubinos Head Office employee, who had been dismissed for theft, recently stated in the national press that only around 60% of Zubinos coffee was procured from Fair Trade suppliers. Even though the ex-employee's claim was not totally correct, as Zubinos use around 82% of Fair Trade coffee, the press picked up on the story. The employee also claimed that he was wrongly dismissed. His story had led to much negative publicity for Zubinos. The Advertising Standards body has investigated the false claim in Zubinos adverts and Zubinos has had to admit that the claim that all of its coffee was Fair Trade coffee was incorrect. However, the damage has been done and in February 2006, sales across all Zubinos shops were down by around 7%.

Offer to operate Zubinos coffee shops in Jibbs stores

Jibbs plc (Jibbs) is a listed company, which operates 140 do-it-yourself (DIY) retail stores in the UK and around Europe. Most of Jibbs stores in the UK are located on large out-of-town retail parks. For a number of reasons, Jibbs has seen its revenue and its EPS decline slightly over the last few years. The Jibbs Board has decided on a number of innovative ways to try to stop the decline in its business and improve the outlook for the future. This has included selling some of its smaller stores, and it also has plans for a major refit of its stores, which will be followed by advertising campaigns. Jibbs is trying to make its stores more appealing to its customers. The Jibbs Board has also decided to rent out space in its stores to a small number of other retailers and it has approached Zubinos with a proposal to open Zubinos coffee shops in some of its stores.

Jibb's Marketing Director, Jenny Wright, has put the following proposal to Zubinos, inviting it to open Zubinos coffee shops in a minimum of 20 stores, over the next 6 months. The proposal is to open Zubinos coffee shops for a two-year trial period, at a fixed rental fee of £50,000 per store per year. Zubinos average rental costs are over £100,000 per annum, but the rental space on offer in Jibbs' store is about 30% smaller than most of the existing Zubinos coffee shops, which would preclude Zubinos from offering its full range of foods and drinks.

At the end of the two-year trial period, Jibbs will decide whether to invite Zubinos to open more coffee shops in its other stores. However, Jibbs reserves the right to decline to renew the rental agreement, which would result in Zubinos having to remove all of its equipment and fixtures and fittings. It was also agreed that the rental cost would not be increased by more than the rate of inflation after the two-year trial, assuming that the trial was successful. Jibbs would not take any share of revenues, but would only charge for rent. All other costs, such as water charges and electricity, would be separately billed directly to Zubinos.

The forecast capital expenditure would be lower than currently spent on new Zubinos shops, and is forecast to be £180,000 per Jibbs store. The forecast market value of fittings at the end of the two-year trial is £90,000 per Jibbs store.

Jane Thorp has prepared the following post-tax cash flow forecast, based on twenty Zubinos coffee shops. These figures exclude capital expenditure.

Based on a total of 20 Zubinos coffee shops in Jibbs' stores	Year 1	Year 2
	£000	£000
Post-tax operating cash flows	1,250	1,500

Note: These post-tax operating cash flows include the rental fees of £50,000 per store per year.

George Shale considers a suitable risk adjusted cost of capital, for this particular proposed project, to be 14% post-tax. Jack Rayfield considers that the proposed expansion into Jibbs' stores is an easy way for Zubinos to expand its number of outlets, and could save management time that is currently spent on locating and negotiating rental agreements for High Street rented premises. Also the cost of the rent is lower. Luis Zubinos has expressed his doubts as to the validity of the cash flow forecasts prepared by Jane Thorp, which are based on throughput data provided by Jibbs.

Recent events

New HR Director
In December 2005, Anita Wiseman, Zubinos HR Director resigned and left Zubinos at the end of January 2006. She had been with the company for only a little over one year. She resigned following a series of disagreements with Luis Zubino and her frustrations with developing a workable HR policy for the company. Also, she found the overlap with the roles of the Area Managers to be conflicting with her overall HR responsibilities. She has not yet disposed of her shares in Zubinos, but **only** other Directors have a right to buy the shares from her, at a negotiated price. Until she has sold her shares in Zubinos, she has voting rights.

Zubinos has recruited a new HR Director, Kingsley Nu, who joined Zubinos in the middle of February 2006, but he has not yet bought any shares in Zubinos. Kingsley Nu immediately met with all of the coffee shop managers in the London area and is due to meet the remaining shop managers in March 2006. Kingsley Nu is impressed by the loyalty and hard work put in by almost all employees, which in most cases is far in excess of their job contracts.

He proposes that a company share ownership scheme is launched and that a monthly reward scheme for outstanding customer service is commenced. He considers that the working environment, the lack of rest periods and the poor facilities for staff should be improved immediately. He has presented Luis Zubino with a draft of some of his proposals, in advance of preparing a paper for the April 2006 Zubinos Board meeting. The proposals include the recruitment of additional staff (to reduce the hours worked by existing staff, many of which are unpaid hours worked in addition to their contracted hours). He also wants to improve staff facilities. The forecast annual cost of the proposals presented is estimated by Kingsley Nu to be around £300,000 per year, at current staffing levels. Luis Zubino's immediate reaction was that some of the proposals are a luxury that a small company like Zubinos simply cannot afford. He also considers this cost to be similar to the amount required to open a further Zubinos coffee shop, and he does not want to spend finance on staff issues which could slow down the expansion programme.

Zubinos loyalty card
Following Zubinos Board approval in January 2006, Jane Thorp is planning to shortly launch a Zubinos loyalty card. This scheme will award customers points each time they spend money at Zubinos shops and present their loyalty card to the cashier. When a regular customer has saved enough points they can be redeemed against purchases. This scheme is forecast to cost Zubinos 2% of its revenues for those customers who regularly use their loyalty card. It is expected that less than 50% of Zubinos revenue will be generated by customers with a loyalty card.

Expansion into Europe
With the successful opening of three new Zubinos shops in cities around the UK in January and February 2006, Luis Zubino is enthusiastic about opening the first Zubinos coffee shop in Europe. One of Luis Zubino's contacts has located a prime city centre site in a European city and wants to operate the shop for Zubinos. The rental agreement for this shop is currently being negotiated. The first European Zubinos coffee shop opening has been brought forward and is now forecast to open in July 2006, which is an advance of its current five-year plan.

Proposed acquisition of Zubinos

The Whistle Coffee Bar (WCB) has 180 coffee shops in the UK and 140 in Europe and is trading profitably with a P/E ratio of 18. It is listed in the UK and has a current share price of £16·80.

WCB's Business Development Director for the UK, Matt Jenkins, has contacted Luis Zubino and requested a meeting. At first, Luis Zubino thought that WCB wanted to meet to discuss the site selection for new Zubinos coffee shops. Zubinos has been successful in obtaining rented sites for the most recent three Zubinos coffee shops, despite having to outbid WCB for the locations that they were also trying to secure. This has resulted in Zubinos getting the required rental location, albeit at a slightly higher rent than was originally forecast.

Luis Zubino, George Shale and Carl Martin attended the meeting with WCB, which was held at the end of February 2006. Matt Jenkins of WCB stated that they have followed the successful expansion of Zubinos with interest and that they would like to acquire Zubinos for a cash price of £15·00 per Zubinos share. Additionally, WCB stated that it would be willing to offer senior management positions in WCB (but not WCB Board positions) to many of the Zubinos management team. Matt Jenkins made a very attractive offer of a senior finance position to George Shale, if the take-over of Zubinos is successful.

Carl Martin of KPE considers this could be a possible exit route for KPE, and has taken the acquisition proposal back to his superiors at KPE.

Luis Zubino is adamant that he does not wish to sell his shares to WCB and wants to prepare a sound case to KPE to convince it (and other Zubinos shareholders) not to sell its shares to WCB either. He stated to Carl Martin of KPE that he considered that WCB had only contacted them as Zubinos had become more successful in some city suburbs and other towns than the local WCB coffee shops.

Forecast cash flows

The forecast post-tax cash flows for the next five years, based on the agreed current five-year plan, given in **Appendix 3** to the pre-seen material, is as follows:

Approved 5-year plan cash flows	2006 £000	2007 £000	2008 £000	2009 £000	2010 £000
Operating post-tax cash flows	2,500	4,100	6,200	8,900	11,700

Note: These operating post-tax cash flows are cash generated from operations and do NOT include capital expenditure on new coffee shops and also do NOT include loan repayments.

Similar businesses to Zubinos, which are listed, have a P/E ratio of around 16. George Shale considers Zubinos overall cost of capital, to be 12%, post-tax.

Following the meeting with WCB, George Shale and Luis Zubino met and discussed how the five-year plan could be improved. Following their discussion, George Shale has prepared a draft of a new five-year plan which Luis Zubino has now discussed with other shareholders, including Carl Martin at KPE. The updated five-year plan includes a higher growth rate in sales than in the original plan and higher gross margins, based on Zubinos possible ability to negotiate further cost reductions from suppliers because of its increased level of purchasing. This revised plan also has a slightly higher growth of new Zubinos coffee shops, with a total of 80, instead of 75, by 2010.

However, the cost reductions factored into this forecast are rather optimistic as George Shale is aware that coffee prices are due to increase over the next year. Furthermore, George Shale is aware that Zubinos is likely to have an adverse currency exposure in 2006, due to changes in exchange rates, which have not been included in this updated forecast.

The post-tax cash flows generated by this updated forecast are shown below:

Updated five-year plan cash flows	2006 £000	2007 £000	2008 £000	2009 £000	2010 £000
Post-tax cash flows	2,900	5,100	7,400	11,400	14,700

Appointment of a consultant

At the Zubinos Board meeting in early March 2006, it was agreed that a consultant would be appointed to prepare a report, which prioritises and discusses the issues facing Zubinos and makes appropriate recommendations.

Requirement

You are the consultant appointed by the Zubinos Board.

Prepare a report that prioritises and discusses the issues facing Zubinos and makes appropriate recommendations.

KEY POINT

The Zubinos case has a single requirement – to produce a report.

However, the requirement in your exam will have **two parts**:

The main part (worth 90 marks) is likely to require a report; but the second part (worth 10 marks) is likely to require slides, a memo, an email, or a graph or chart.

Assessment Matrix for TOPCIMA – Zubinos

Criterion	Marks	Clear Pass	Pass	Marginal Pass	Marginal Fail	Fail	Clear Fail
Technical	5	Thorough display of relevant technical knowledge. **5**	Good display of relevant knowledge. **4**	Some display of relevant technical knowledge. **3**	Identification of some relevant knowledge, but lacking in depth. **2**	Little knowledge displayed, or some misconceptions. **1**	No evidence of knowledge displayed, or fundamental misconceptions. **0**
Application	10	Knowledge clearly applied in an analytical and practical manner. **9-10**	Knowledge applied to the context of the case. **6-8**	Identification of some relevant knowledge, but not well applied. **5**	Knowledge occasionally displayed without clear application. **3-4**	Little attempt to apply knowledge to the context. **1-2**	No application of knowledge displayed. **0**
Diversity	5	Most knowledge areas identified, covering a wide range of views. **5**	Some knowledge areas identified, covering a range of views. **4**	A few knowledge areas identified, expressing a fairly limited scope. **3**	Several important knowledge aspects omitted. **2**	Many important knowledge aspects omitted. **1**	Very few knowledge aspects considered. **0**
Focus	15	Clearly distinguishes between relevant and irrelevant information. **13-15**	Information used is mostly relevant. **9-12**	Some relevant information ignored, or some less relevant information used. **8**	Information used is sometimes irrelevant. **5-7**	Little ability to distinguish between relevant and irrelevant information. **1-4**	No ability to distinguish between relevant and irrelevant information. **0**
Prioritisation	10	Issues clearly prioritised in a logical order and based on a clear rationale. **9-10**	Issues prioritised with justification. **6-8**	Evidence of issues being listed in order of importance, but rationale unclear. **5**	Issues apparently in priority order, but without a logical justification or rationale. **3-4**	Little attempt at prioritisation or justification or rationale. **1-2**	No attempt at prioritisation or justification. **0**
Judgement	15	Clearly recognises alternative solutions. Judgement exercised professionally. **13-15**	Alternative solutions or options considered. Some judgement exercised. **9-12**	A slightly limited range of solutions considered. Judgement occasionally weak. **8**	A limited range of solutions considered. Judgement sometimes weak. **5-7**	Few alternative solutions considered. Judgement often weak. **1-4**	No alternative solutions considered. Judgement weak or absent. **0**
Integration	10	Diverse areas of knowledge and skills integrated effectively. **9-10**	Diverse areas of knowledge and skills integrated. **6-8**	Knowledge areas and skills occasionally not integrated. **5**	Knowledge areas and skills sometimes not integrated. **3-4**	Knowledge areas and skills often not integrated. **1-2**	Knowledge areas and skills not integrated. **0**
Logic	20	Communication effective, recommendations realistic, concise and logical. **16-20**	Communication mainly clear and logical. Recommendations occasionally weak. **11-15**	Communication occasionally unclear, and/or recommendations occasionally illogical. **10**	Communication sometimes weak. Some recommendations slightly unrealistic. **5-9**	Communication weak. Some unclear or illogical recommendations, or few recommendations. **1-4**	Very poor communication, and/or no recommendations offered. **0**
Ethics	10	Excellent evaluation of ethical aspects. Clear and appropriate advice offered. **9-10**	Good evaluation of ethical aspects. Some appropriate advice offered. **6-8**	Some evaluation of ethical aspects. Advice offered. **5**	Weak evaluation of ethical aspects. Little advice offered. **3-4**	Poor evaluation of ethical aspects. No advice offered. **1-2**	No evaluation of ethical aspects. Unethical, or no, advice offered. **0**
TOTAL	100						

© CIMA – January 2006

PART B TEACHING CASE: ZUBINOS

KEY POINT

> The format of the assessment matrix has changed slightly under the new syllabus compared to this. (See Chapter 2 for more detail on the assessment criteria.)
>
> However, it is possible that the maximum marks available for each criteria could vary slightly from one exam to the next. Make sure you take note of the marks available for each criterion in the exam you are sitting.

3 Review the unseen and requirement (Step 5.2)

Remember don't panic. You have three hours and twenty minutes and you have done a lot of preparation. You have also done a great deal of report practice. We are not going to cover report writing here in any more detail.

4 Read the unseen data in depth (Step 5.3)

Step 5.3   **Mark up and analyse the unseen data**

Read the unseen data carefully and mark up key points.

What has changed?

(a) What is the unseen telling us about the firm's internal conditions?

Item	Jot down new information here
• Internal structure	
• Personnel	
• Financing	
• Resources	
Strengths	
Weaknesses	

(b) Is the unseen telling us something new about the firm's external conditions?

Item	Jot down new information here

5 Writing your report (Steps 5.4 to 5.9)

(a) Produce your appendices. Start with a SWOT analysis and then do the necessary calculations.

(b) You need to choose the **key issues** and **prioritise** them.

5.1. Prioritising the key issues

On a number of occasions, we have stressed the importance of identifying the key issues in the case study and then prioritising them in your report.

We suggest a good way of identifying the key issues raised by the case study is to consider their **strategic importance** and the **urgency** with which they must be addressed.

We can illustrate this using an importance / urgency matrix:

	Low	High
High Urgency	**Lower priority** — List issues but don't discuss unless you have time	**High priority** — Comment in detail as one of the top 2 issues
Low Urgency	**Other issues** — List issues, but don't discuss	**High priority** — Comment in detail, but *after* the top 2 issues

The key issues (and therefore the ones you need to prioritise and discuss first in your report) are those which are both strategically important to the organisation and need to be addressed urgently.

An issue may be strategically important due to:

- Its high potential financial impact and risk
- Its impact on the long-term survival of the organisation
- Its potential to change the business model
- Its impact on the management team of the organisation (eg it will lead to changes in the senior management of the organisation)

An issue may be urgent because:

- Financial loss will occur if it is not dealt with soon
- There is limited time to make a decision before a deadline

> **Note**: Because the Zubinos case study had a single requirement, (as was the norm under the old syllabus) students have to choose five key issues.
>
> However, under the new syllabus, because the requirement has two parts, you now only have to choose four key issues to prioritise.

In our suggested answer presented in Chapter 12, the five key issues identified are:

(1) Adverse publicity
(2) Proposed acquisition
(3) The Jibbs offer
(4) Expansion overseas
(5) Human resources strategy

Do you agree with the issues chosen?

You also need to consider the **ethical issues** to discuss.

(c) Produce an answer plan

Possible answer plan

Section	Suggested content
1	Terms of reference
2	Introduction and key issues
3	Adverse publicity
4	Proposed acquisition
5	The Jibbs offer
6	Expansion overseas
7	Human resources strategy
8	Ethics
9	Recommendations
10	Conclusions

(d) Write an introduction, the terms of reference and the rationale for the prioritisation of the key issues.

(e) Develop the key issues under each heading from your contents table.

(f) Write your recommendations and conclusions.

6 May 2006 unseen

Zubinos coffee shops – Unseen material provided on examination day

Read this information before you answer the question

Success of new product line

In early September 2005, Sally Higgins, a Zubinos area manager, introduced a range of low calorie snacks and meals in one of the shops in which she manages. This initiative had caused quite a disagreement between Sally Higgins and Jane Thorp, who had not been consulted regarding the new food and drink items, which Sally Higgins had procured from a small local supplier.

By October 2005, it was clear that the new low calorie product line was very popular and accounted for 8% of the turnover for September 2005 in the one shop in which it was introduced. After some discussion, Luis Zubino and Jane Thorp agreed that the low calorie product line appealed to Zubinos customers and to offer this new low calorie food range in all Zubinos coffee shops. Maria Todd was requested to organise central procurement for all the low calorie food and drink products. Jane Thorp recommended that a suitable marketing strategy for the low calorie foods would be to have a range of takeaway calorie-controlled meal boxes, under the brand name of *"Zubinos Light"* retailing at £3·00 each.

The first *"Zubinos Light"* meal boxes were available in all eighteen Zubinos coffee shops during November 2005 and immediately became popular. Furthermore, some limited market research of the customers who bought the *"Zubinos Light"* meal boxes established that over 95% of these customers were new Zubinos customers. Jane Thorp was delighted that this new product was also bringing new customers into Zubinos.

In January 2006, a major advertising campaign, using radio and posters, was commenced, and was due to run to the end of June 2006 at a total cost of £425,000. By the end of February 2006, Zubinos found that it had become the victim of its own success. All eighteen shops were almost always sold out of the *"Zubinos Light"* meal boxes and Maria Todd had been having numerous procurement problems. The original supplier, ART, was unable to increase the quantity beyond its contract level of 2,000 boxes a day. A new supplier, BBK, was introduced in late January 2006, despite Maria Todd's concern over quality. By the end of April 2006, it was estimated that over 5,000 boxes per day were in demand and Zubinos was again almost always sold out. (Note: it should be assumed that there are only 20 days per month for which *"Zubinos Light"* meal boxes will have this level of demand, to coincide with normal working patterns).

A further two suppliers are being considered, CCV and DTY. The results from the initial inspections by Maria Todd and Zubinos' food agency, and the cost per box quotes, are shown below, compared to existing suppliers:

Supplier	*ART*	*BBK*	*CCV*	*DTY*
Food quality	Excellent	Below expectations	Below expectations	Excellent
Cleanliness of food preparation areas	Excellent	Below expectations	Very good	Excellent
Cost per meal box	£1·20	£1·60	£1·10	£2·00
Maximum daily capacity	2,000	2,000	5,000	8,000
Initial contract period	12 months	6 months	6 months	3 months

Supplier CCV would be only able to supply meal boxes to Zubinos in one geographic area of the UK, whereas DTY has a supply chain established for nationwide delivery. Maria Todd has not identified any other suppliers at this time and needs to urgently select a further supplier for the "Zubinos Light" meal boxes.

Luis Zubino's planned three month absence

Luis Zubino informed his fellow directors at the end of April 2006 that he is planning to take a three-month break from the business, following his recent split from his wife, whom he married four years ago. Luis Zubino's absence from the business is planned for June, July and August 2006.

Luis Zubino was clearly upset with the break-up of his marriage, which he felt was partly due to the very long hours that he has spent building up the Zubinos business. Luis Zubino discussed with George Shale his concern, that if his marriage is not reconciled, his ex-wife could demand a payment potentially amounting to several million pounds, if they were to get divorced. Any divorce settlement is likely to be sometime within the next two years.

Management Information

George Shale and Bob West are continually frustrated by the lack of management information in a usable format. Over the past two years a few new IT systems have been introduced but there are several inconsistencies between the systems. The monthly management accounts are prepared using financial data for each shop, but there is little statistical information on customers, such as repeat customers and customer profile. Also the analysis between main product types (coffees, food, ice creams, "Zubinos Light" meal boxes) cannot easily be obtained. George Shale recruited two accountants, on six-month contracts, at the end of March 2006 to analyse information on a weekly basis, so that trends in customer spending can be tracked.

Bob West has discussed with Luis Zubino several times the introduction of a data based management information system that would capture all of the required information at source. However, the proposed cost of the database is over £800,000 and Luis Zubino considers that the cost could escalate to over £1,000,000 and he is adamant that the administration systems, although basic, can manage at present.

Staff issues and extended opening hours

Due to the rapid expansion and the popularity of Zubinos, many of the staff have been working very hard and working long hours and they report that they feel under too much pressure. Furthermore, due to the popularity of Zubinos, it was decided to extend the opening hours, into the evening and instead of closing at 7pm, they are now open until 11pm each night, seven days a week. Many of Zubinos staff have complained about later working and this has resulted in some employees leaving the company, despite Zubinos pay being a little higher than the market rate.

Over the last few months, Zubinos has employed many European Union (EU) immigrants on temporary short-term contracts. Zubinos is paying below the market rate in this industry for these employees, but slightly above the legal minimum wage rate. The cost of these employees is approximately 12% below other Zubinos staff. The EU immigrants are also prepared to work long hours. The EU immigrant workers have accepted the shift patterns given to them, which often involve early morning shifts to accept deliveries from 5 o'clock in the morning. While these employees are given time off during the day, they are often scheduled to work a further shift later in the day, right up to closing time. Some of the EU immigrant employees choose to work straight through from early morning to closing time with very few breaks. These employees speak English poorly and offer poor customer service. Many Zubinos coffee shop managers have now noticed that the level of customer complaints has increased.

There have been several complaints and some adverse press coverage concerning disturbances to neighbours and people whose flats are above Zubinos coffee shops because of Zubinos' later closing time at night. However, the rental agreements for the rented shops allow this late closing time. Another factor that has caused problems to Zubinos' neighbours is the deliveries from its food suppliers between 5 and 6 o'clock in the morning to Zubinos coffee shops in some city centres. The parking of large delivery vehicles and the noise caused by unloading has led to several complaints, including a pending legal action for noise nuisance.

New Zubinos coffee shops in 2006

Luis Zubino wanted to open the planned eight new coffee shops in 2006, partly financed from the approved £5.0 million loan finance that KPE has made available to Zubinos. During January to May 2006, there have only been two new coffee shops opened. There are plans already in place for a further two openings later this year. The number of new Zubinos coffee shops has fallen behind schedule, as Luis Zubino, who plays a crucial role in the site selection process, has not pursued the expansion programme, as he usually would have done, due to his personal problems with his marriage breakdown.

Bob West is now trying to secure rental agreements on a further four shops. He has been unable to find suitable rental sites for two of them. He has drafted a proposal for the June 2006 Zubinos Board meeting, requesting approval to purchase two retail premises at a total cost of £2.2 million for both sites.

The capital cost and shop fitting costs are also forecast to exceed the current planned capital expenditure budget during 2006, due to two reasons:

- All four of the new coffee shops that have been opened or are currently being prepared for opening, are in larger premises, with higher fittings costs;

- The latest, more expensive, refrigerated display units have been ordered for the new Zubinos shop openings in 2006, which are far superior to those in other Zubinos shops.

The average capital expenditure for each new Zubinos coffee shop in 2006 is now forecast to be £330,000, compared to an average of £250,000 in 2005.

The latest forecast for 2006, prepared at the end of April 2006, assumes a total of only 6 new shops opening during 2006. The forecast cash which will be generated from operations for 2006 is £2.2 million. This will be used to partially fund the planned capital expenditure which is currently forecast for 2006 to be £4.7 million (and this capital expenditure forecast assumes the purchase of the two retail premises, as detailed above).

Operating costs

In an attempt to reduce operating costs, Maria Todd has chosen to change a few suppliers who are providing high cost food items, and has managed to procure very similar food items at a lower cost. She has also chosen to procure a higher proportion of coffee from UK wholesalers, which has resulted in large cost savings.

The cost savings have been achieved due to two reasons. Firstly, the coffee beans are purchased from UK wholesalers who bulk buy and the cost per kilogram is lower than the Fair Trade coffee that Zubinos had previously purchased. Most of these new coffee purchases are not Fair Trade coffee. Secondly, Zubinos pays for these new coffee purchases in UK sterling and is not exposed to any risk of currency movements.

Zubinos is now considering whether its marketing literature should be changed to reflect that only 60% of its coffee purchases is now Fair Trade coffee, whereas previously it was over 80% Fair Trade.

Franchising proposal

An international franchising company, GlobalFranch (GF) has approached Luis Zubino at the end of April 2006 with a proposal to assist Zubinos to expand via franchising. The proposal was presented to the Zubinos Board in May 2006, and Luis Zubino's initial response is favourable.

GF has stated that it has over thirty franchisees ready to open franchised outlets and it considers that the Zubinos business could be a very successful franchised business. GF has also stated that it is considering offering its franchise service to two other coffee shop chains, which are based in Europe, but has decided to allow Zubinos to have first refusal. GF has therefore stated that it needs a final decision by the end of June 2006.

GF's proposal is to franchise out the Zubinos coffee shop brand and expand both in the UK and overseas, particularly in the rapidly growing Far Eastern market. GF would like to offer its services and its experience to recruit and manage franchisees, which would then operate franchised Zubinos coffee shops in the UK, Europe and the Far East. GF insists on a minimum contract period of 5 years, with a one-year notice period. GF also stipulates that in order to allow the franchisees to build up their business, Zubinos should limit the number of its coffee shops which it operates to no more than 40% of the planned franchised coffee shops by the end of 2009.

The financial forecast shown below is based on the following number of franchised shops:

Number of forecast franchised shops	2007	2008	2009	2010	2011
New openings in year	20	30	50	80	120
Cumulative franchised shops	20	50	100	180	300

The proposal is that for each new franchised shop, Zubinos would receive 9% of the gross sales revenue. Zubinos would also supply all of its regular coffees and own brand product lines to franchised shops at agreed prices, which would include a mark up of around 6% on cost.

GF has stated that its fees for locating franchisees and managing the franchising business for Zubinos would be a fee of £20,000 for each new shop opened plus a fee of 6% of the franchised revenue for the first year of each shop opening. After the first year of each shop opening GF would charge a flat fee of 2% of the franchised revenue for the contract period. GF has prepared the following forecast cash flows (pre-tax) for the next 5 years:

Franchise income payable to Zubinos:	2007 £million	2008 £million	2009 £million	2010 £million	2011 £million
Revenue	0.9	3.5	8.2	16.9	31.9
Mark up on supplies to franchisees	0.2	0.7	1.5	2.7	4.4
Total Franchise income	1.1	4.2	9.7	19.6	36.3
Franchise fees payable by Zubinos to GF:					
£20,000 for each new shop	0.4	0.6	1.0	1.6	2.4
6% of revenue for first year	0.6	1.6	2.8	5.0	8.5
2% of total franchised revenue	0.0	0.2	0.9	2.1	4.3
Total franchise fees payable	1.0	2.4	4.7	8.7	15.2

Zubinos exclusive coffee machines

Jane Thorp launched a new product line in November 2004, selling exclusive coffee machines to customers for their homes or offices. These are sold on Zubinos website and also in Zubinos coffee shops. Until the summer of 2005, they were not well-marketed, but following a promotional campaign, the coffee machines have sold particularly well, and customers have repeatedly bought further coffee supplies from Zubinos.

The coffee machines have been procured from a leading coffee machine manufacturer on an exclusive contract for Zubinos. The coffee machines use specially designed sachets of coffee that can only be bought from Zubinos coffee shops, or available from Zubinos website. The unique selling point is that customers can enjoy their favourite type of Zubinos cup of coffee in the comfort of their own homes. The projected cash flows for the next three years for the sale of the coffee machines and coffee supplies are as follows:

	2006 £million	2007 £million	2008 £million
Sales - Coffee machines	1·1	1·3	1·7
- Coffee supplies	1·1	2·9	7·1
Costs - Coffee machines	1·2	1·4	1·9
- Coffee supplies	0·2	0·6	1·4

There have been a significant number of dissatisfied customers who have returned faulty machines over the last few months. Originally, as a gesture of goodwill, Jane Thorp had instructed all shop managers to give customers with faulty machines, a free replacement machine and free samples of coffee sachets. However, the number of faulty machines has increased in March and April 2006. The manufacturer has examined a number of returned machines, and has identified a design fault. All new manufactured coffee machines from May 2005 will have this fault corrected.

Appointment of a consultant

At the Zubinos Board meeting in the middle of May 2006, it was agreed that a consultant would be appointed to advise the Board on the issues facing Zubinos.

Zubinos: answer

This answer to the **March** 2006 exam was written by a TOPCIMA student under exam conditions in 3 hours. All the analysis was her own. You might, on reading this answer, find material you had not considered or may disagree with some aspects. This is as it should be: everyone will approach the case in a different way, and the way the TOPCIMA exam is marked reflects this.

Remember, however, that when this exam was set there was a single requirement – to produce a report. Therefore the expectation was to identify five high priority issues. However, in your exam you should only aim to identify four high priority issues.

We have included a suggested marking scheme developed by BPP Learning Media from the Post Exam Guides and Script Reviews following the exam, showing how marks could been earned for each aspect of the assessment

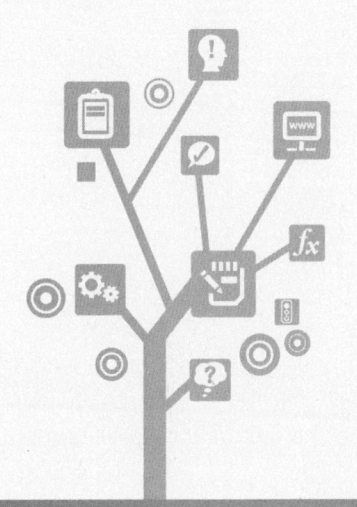

1 Report

To   Zubinos Board
From   Consultant
Subject   Issues facing Zubinos
Date   xx xx 2006

Section	Content
1	Terms of reference
2	Introduction and key issues
3	Adverse publicity
	3.1 Quality control
	3.2 Fair Trade coffee
4	Proposed acquisition
5	The Jibbs offer
	5.1 The strategic fit of Jibbs and Zubinos
	5.2 The financial aspects
6	Expansion overseas
	6.1 European expansion
	6.2 Other overseas expansion
7	Human resources strategy
	7.1 Policies and procedures
	7.2 Reward scheme
8	Ethics
	8.1 Fair Trade
	8.2 Inflated forecast
	8.3 Competitor rumours
9	Recommendations
10	Conclusion

Appendices

1 Terms of reference

This report has been prepared for the Board of Zubinos to prioritise and discuss the issues facing Zubinos and make appropriate recommendations.

2 Introduction and key issues

Appendix 1 shows the inherent strengths and weaknesses of Zubinos and the opportunities and threats currently facing them. From this it can be seen that a key strength identified is the Zubinos brand image and the threat from the adverse publicity, together with the weaknesses in procurement and quality control, is therefore the first priority issue to be addressed.

The proposed acquisition by WCB is identified as the main threat to the current senior management and is therefore the next issue to be dealt with in this report.

The Jibbs offer is the most significant opportunity currently identified and requires careful consideration by the Board. Another business opportunity is the proposed expansion into Europe and this is also analysed and evaluated.

Lastly, the problems with human resources are identified as a weakness in Appendix 1 and this report will suggest how these can be overcome.

3 Adverse publicity

It can be argued that there are a number of key reasons why consumers choose to spend their money at Zubinos. The shops are in prime locations and have an agreeable ambience, the service is good and the coffee and other products sold are perceived to be of a high quality and from Fair Trade sources.

However, there are numerous competitors as evidenced by a recent newspaper article concerning the 17 places where it is possible to buy coffee in Fleet Street, London. Bad publicity will therefore have an adverse impact on sales as customers may quickly choose to spend their money elsewhere. The bad publicity has not only been in newspapers, but also on a national TV consumer programme and such programmes have considerable influence and power over consumer choices. Sales have already fallen by 7% in February and this decline must be halted as a matter of urgency if financial and growth targets are to have any chance of being met. There are two distinct areas of concern.

3.1 Quality Control

The UK Food Standards Organisation has identified problems with quality control so action does need to be taken urgently. This area is outsourced to QAIF, which has an excellent reputation. However, Zubinos may have been relying on its reputation and not properly controlling and auditing its activities. Luis has blamed Maria Todd, but should perhaps be focusing more on QAIF and ensuring that proper systems of control are in place.

Maria Todd is overloaded and in need of support. Procurement in a business such as Zubinos is a key function and should be given more of a priority. There is an urgent need to find new suppliers, particularly of Fair Trade coffee.

3.2 Fair Trade coffee

It is clear that Zubinos have made a false claim in recent advertising claiming that 'all' of their coffee is sourced from Fair Trade suppliers. This is a hot topic as Marks and Spencer have been running a big campaign concerning their use of 100% Fair Trade coffee in their Café Revive shops and their commitment to increased availability of Fair Trade products. This has led to numerous newspaper articles on the subject.

Zubinos should have been in an ideal position to capitalise on this publicity instead of having to deal with the embarrassment and negative impact of their incorrect adverts. Immediate action needs to be taken to counteract this negative publicity.

4 Proposed acquisition

Appendix 1 identifies the bid from WCB as a threat to the current management team, and Luis Zubino is adamant that he does not want to sell his shares to WCB. Presumably, but not necessarily, his wife Vivien agrees with his views and their joint 42% holding of Zubinos shares is a bigger holding than anybody else's. However, KPE holds 40% of the shares and their main objective is to achieve growth in the value of their shares. The recently departed HR Director, Anita Wiseman, still has voting rights over her 36,000 shares and if she were to side with KPE, their joint 43.6% holding will be bigger than that of Luis and Vivien Zubino. It is therefore crucial to analyse whether shareholder value will be maximised by accepting the £15 per share offer or by continuing with the present management.

Appendix 2 contains an updated cash flow forecast from which an estimated valuation of £8.71 per share has been derived. The figures used are from the original 5 year plan, which was approved by KPE and the Zubinos Board, with downwards adjustments of 10% in 2006 made for the recent fall in revenue. It has been assumed that the more optimistic predictions of growth, revenue and cost reduction made by George Shale will be counteracted by the effects of the negative publicity, coffee price increases and adverse exchange rate movements. This method does not consider free cash flow arising from trading activities beyond the period of the 5-year plan, therefore it can be viewed as a very prudent estimate of share price.

An alternative valuation can be made using an adjusted P/E ratio of 11 multiplied by the 2005 post-tax profit to give £9.87 per share.

A third valuation of £5.38 could be given by the net assets method but this ignores the significant value of the intangible assets, for example staff, brand, location, in a service organisation such as Zubinos.

WCB's offer therefore looks to be acceptable. However, the assumptions behind all of these valuations can be questioned and much higher growth could be achieved under the management of Luis Zubino than that of WCB. It is worth noting that WCB have recently sold 12 coffee shops to a rival chain so it seems strange that they should be seeking to expand by acquiring Zubinos. It could be a defensive strategy as Zubinos has become more successful in some areas and has outbid WCB in location acquisitions.

KPE would make a profit on their investment at this price but their expected exit was 2010 and they may be prepared to take an optimistic longer term view of Zubinos' growth prospects under Luis Zubino.

A realistic and achievable 5 year plan should be developed and agreed with KPE with assumptions clearly explained.

5 Jibbs offer

Jibbs is a chain of DIY stores who have proposed that Zubinos open coffee shops inside its retail park stores. Jibbs has seen its revenue and EPS decline recently and is looking for ways to halt this decline. There are two key issues to be examined.

5.1 The fit of Jibbs with Zubinos

The average customer of an out-of-town DIY store is likely to be time pressured and cost conscious. The stores are not designed for customers to linger, although there are plans for major refits. The rental space on offer is 30% lower than the existing Zubinos shops. The desired customer at Zubinos is prepared to pay a premium for its products and views the larger than average shops and the ambience as a reason to choose to purchase. The fit of these two organisations is therefore questionable.

5.2 The financial aspects

The post-tax cash flow forecast has been prepared by Jane Thorp, a marketing specialist, and is based on throughput data provided by Jibbs. It is therefore likely to be over optimistic.

There is a significant risk involved in this project, which George has recognised in his higher risk adjusted cost of capital of 14%. At the end of the two-year trial period, Jibbs could decline to renew the rental agreement and Zubinos would incur a loss of £1.8 million on the fittings, together with the costs of their removal. The assumed residual value of £90,000 per store for fittings may be an over-optimistic estimate of the realisable value. This is a large amount for a company whose current annual post-tax profit is only £897,000.

These factors mean that the Jibbs offer should be rejected and Zubinos should continue to look for a more acceptable retail chain in which to open coffee shops.

6 Expansion overseas

Luis Zubino has identified overseas expansion as a potential area for growth.

6.1 European expansion

A contact has located a prime site in a European city and wants to operate the shop for Zubinos. A rental agreement is being negotiated but all aspects of this transaction need to be carefully examined and evaluated.

The proposal is effectively a franchise agreement, as the contact will be operating the shop. This is potentially a lucrative engine for growth and a strategy for franchising should be developed. Aspects such as protection of the brand, procurement and control should be looked at as well as the financial implications. The European contact can then be used as a pilot and if it proves successful, franchising could be used as a future growth strategy.

6.2 Other overseas expansion

Europe is a mature market for coffee shops with established competitors who would have excellent knowledge of local customs and culture. Zubinos should consider other countries with more rapid economic growth and potential for a new entrant to establish themselves. Starbucks are looking to expand into China and India and Zubinos could consider following them, a strategy which can often be lucrative in emerging markets.

7 Human resources strategy

Appendix 1 identifies the lack of coherent human resources policies and procedures as a key weakness of Zubinos. In a service sector business, well motivated and trained quality staff are an essential intangible asset that needs to be nurtured and controlled. Human resources have not been a priority as evidenced by Anita Wiseman's resignation following a series of disagreements with Luis. Two aspects for consideration in particular can be identified.

7.1 Policies and procedures

A disgruntled former employee has created bad publicity for Zubinos and is claiming wrongful dismissal. Dismissal is a legal minefield and procedures need to be carefully followed to avoid such a problem. Effective recruitment and following up of references will help to avoid the employment of dishonest employees.

Zubinos needs to have an agreed human resources strategy, policy and associated procedures to ensure that such problems are avoided in the future.

7.2 Reward scheme

The current reward scheme is based on the achievement of financial targets and has proved problematic. The new HR director has proposed a share ownership scheme. This however is unlikely to achieve increased employee motivation as Zubinos shares cannot be traded in an open market and no dividends are paid.

A reward scheme based on balanced scorecard measures such as customer satisfaction, speed of service and so on would be more effective and should be developed.

It is essential that Luis Zubino recognises the vital role of human resource management and supports Kingsley Nu in his new role.

8 Ethics

There are three areas where ethical issues need to be analysed.

8.1 Fair Trade

Consumers increasingly expect companies to be socially responsible and will be very unimpressed if a company is found to have made incorrect ethical claims. As mentioned in section 3.2, Fair Trade is a hot topic, which is gaining a great deal of publicity, and the number of Fair Trade suppliers is increasing. Zubinos should capitalise on this publicity and source 100% of its products from Fair Trade suppliers.

8.2 Inflated forecasts

Senior managers of a company have a duty to ensure that forecasts and other financial information are accurate and reliable. The updated five-year plan looks to be over optimistic and should be re-examined to ensure it is presenting a true and fair picture of Zubinos' prospects to its stakeholders.

8.3 Competitor rumours

Luis is concerned that a competitor has been spreading incorrect rumours. This is unethical behaviour and should be investigated. The way to counter-act such rumours is with positive publicity and the temptation to compete via the same underhand methods should be avoided.

9 Recommendations

To remedy the difficulties identified in this report and exploit the opportunities presented, the Board is advised to action the following recommendations. They are presented in accordance with prioritisation rationale expressed in the introduction to the report:

1. To avoid any recurrence of quality control and incorrect labelling of products sold Zubinos should immediately initiate an audit of the services provided by QAIF and take immediate action to resolve problems identified. Following this a robust system of performance monitoring and internal controls of the outsourcing contract with QAIF needs to be established, effectively managed and periodically reviewed.

2. To alleviate the pressure of work currently suffered by Maria Todd, the firm should recruit an experienced assistant for her. The prime function of this new role should be to identify more suppliers, particularly of Fair Trade coffee, thus allowing the Procurement Director to focus on the more strategic aspects of supply chain management and inventory control. Only when 100% Fair Trade coffee sources can be established and supplies guaranteed should this fact be advertised widely.

3. The acquisition offer from WCB should be rejected, for the reasons identified in the report. A more realistic and achievable 5 year plan should be produced, based on reliable and authoritative planning assumptions, which should be presented to the Board and KPE at the first opportunity.

    The plan should be able to illustrate that the growth potential of Zubinos over the next 5 years (and beyond) makes the £15 share price offer from WCB less attractive to those viewing their interest in Zubinos as a long term investment.

4. The Jibbs offer should be rejected as the business risks involved are too great, there is no recognisable strategic fit, and the financial returns are unsubstantiated. However Zubinos should still continue to identify other more acceptable retail chains where profitable joint development opportunities to open coffee shops can be identified.

5. In order to expand into the European market Zubinos should establish a franchising strategy, and use the European contact identified as a pilot. Franchising represents a low risk market development opportunity for Zubinos, and if successful could establish the Zubinos brand across Europe very rapidly and with a relatively low investment required.

    Over the next year it would be advisable to examine the suitability of other countries as potential locations for coffee shops, so that the franchising strategy could be directed most effectively and profitably.

6. Zubinos being a service business, and one that has experienced a number of personnel problems, needs to develop coherent human resource policies and procedures. This will help retain staff and motivate them to deliver better performance. The implementation of a new employee reward scheme using balanced scorecard performance measures rather than short term financial results may help to achieve this.

10 Conclusion

Zubinos is in a strong position but faces a number of significant threats, which need to addressed as a matter of urgency. Several internal weaknesses have also been identified and action suggested to overcome them. Acting on the recommendations contained in this report will then allow the company to capitalise on the opportunities presented and achieve its targets for growth.

Appendix 1: SWOT Analysis

Strengths	Weaknesses
• Zubinos Brand • Good shop locations • Retail space larger than average • Loyal staff • Entrepreneurial leadership • Strong finances	• Procurement problems • Quality control issues • Lack of human resources policies and procedures • Ineffective internal controls
Opportunities	**Threats**
• Jibbs offer • Expansion into Europe and potential franchising • New product innovation	• Bad publicity • Hostile takeover bid • Increase in coffee prices • Adverse currency movements • KPE selling its shares

Appendix 2: Zubinos business valuation

	2006	2007	2008	2009	2010
	£'000	£'000	£'000	£'000	£'000
Post tax cash flows	2,250	4,100	6,200	8,900	11,700
Capital expenditure	(2,700)	(3,400)	(3,800)	(4,100)	(5,000)
Free cash flow	(450)	700	2,400	4,800	6,700
Discount factor @ 12%	0.893	0.797	0.712	0.636	0.567
Present value	(402)	558	1,709	3,053	3,799

Total present value	£8,717,000
No of shares	1,000,000
Share price	£8.71

Assumptions

1 Post tax cash flows in 2006 (£2,500,000) will be 10% lower than originally forecast due to the adverse publicity

2 This fall will be reversed in 2007 and revenue will then be as per the original 5 year plan

2 Suggested marking scheme for Zubinos March 2006

Note: this would be marked slightly differently under the new assessment matrix which applies under the 2010 syllabus (see Chapter 2).

Criteria	Issues to be discussed	Marks	Total Marks available for criterion
Technical	SWOT/PEST/Ansoff/Porter's 5 forces/Porter's generic strategies/ Mendelow/Suitability, Acceptability, Feasibility/BCG matrix/ Balanced Scorecard/Life cycle analysis 1 mark for EACH technique displayed *Note.* 0 marks for simply naming techniques without explaining the relevant technique	1 each	5 marks
Application	SWOT – to get full 3 marks must include WCB bid in Threats	1–3	
	PEST	1–2	
	Other Technical Knowledge applied to case material in a meaningful relevant way – on merit	1–2	
	Calculations		
	NPV analysis of Jibbs proposal	1–2	
	Valuations of Zubinos in respect of WCB bid:		Max = 10
	• Based on cash flows	1–2	
	• Additional marks for cash flows into perpetuity	1–2	
	• Valuation based on P/E ratio	1–2	
	Other relevant calculations, such as loyalty card	1	
	Relevant ratios (1 mark for calcs + 1 mark for discussion of relevance of ratio)	1–2	
	Total available marks (but max = 10)	**18**	
Diversity	Display of sound business awareness and relevant real life examples	1–3 on merit	
	Relevant discussion on exit strategies for KPE	1–2 on merit	Max = 5
	Other relevant knowledge displayed	1–2 on merit	
	Total available marks (but max = 5)	**7**	

PART B TEACHING CASE: ZUBINOS   12: Zubinos: answer

Criteria	Issues to be discussed	Marks	Total Marks available for criterion
Focus	**Issues to be discussed**		
	Discussion on WCB bid	1–4	
	Discussion on KPE view of the WCB bid	1–2	
	Discussion of HR issues	1–2	
	Discussion on bad publicity and falling sales in Feb 2006	1–2	
	Discussion on Jibbs proposal	1–2	
	Discussion on overseas expansion	1	Max = 15
	Discussion on other relevant issues (on merit) • Loyalty card • Control of operating costs • Zubinos Board • Whether Zubinos should consider franchising	1–2 each up to max of 6	
	Total marks available (but max = 15)	19	
Prioritisation	Full 10 marks if 5 issues prioritised and rationale for ranking good and top priority of WCB is included in top 2 priorities.	Full 10	
	The WCB bid should be in top 2 priorities on the basis that there is no greater threat to a company's very existence than a hostile take-over bid. OR		Max = 10
	6–9 marks if top priority of WCB bid is in top 2 priorities but ranking rationale is weak OR	6–9	
	4 marks maximum (marginal fail) if WCB bid is not in top 2 priorities (irrespective of quality of rationale for ranking of other priorities)	Up to 4	
Judgement	**8 key issues requiring analysis in this case:**		
	Marks on merit based on depth of analysis and commercially realistic comments (not just 1 mark for each point made). Full marks could be awarded even if all of the issues listed have not been analysed, although it is unlikely that high marks would be awarded if the analysis did not include most of the issues shown below.		
	1. WCB bid Analysis to include that the £15 is an initial bid an that there could be higher offers or other bidders, the trade off of risk of high values in the future versus cash now and that Zubinos shareholders are looking for substantially higher gains in the future	1–4	Max = 15
	2. Need to stop current downfall in revenues Analysis that identifies that urgent action is required to stop revenue decline & need to be customer focussed	1–2	
	3. HR issues and quality of customer service Analysis to include a clear understanding between HR issues and the quality of customer service provided. Max 1 mk if customer service not discussed.	1–3	

Criteria	Issues to be discussed	Marks	Total Marks available for criterion
	4. Jibbs proposal Analysis of the proposal should include identification that this is not a good strategic fit for Zubinos, that it is a different target audience and that the investment would not be a good use of the scarce loan facilities (as it would require £3.6 million of the total loan of £5 million)	1–3	
	5. Zubinos 5 year plan and the need to achieve this to keep investors content	1–2	
	6. Advice to the Zubinos Board on the timing and alternative exit strategies for KPE (this could include a MBO or a listing around 2009)	1–2	
	7. Recognition of possibility of other take-over bids in the future.	1–2	
	8. Franchising – recognition that this is a common method of expansion in this industry	1–2	
	Total marks available (but max = 15)	**20**	
Integration	Judge script holistically and whether recommendations follow on logically from analysis of the issues in the report and refers to data in appendices	1–4 if weak or 6–10 if good	10
Logic	General presentation and EFFECTIVE business communication. If report format and business English is good and all data in appendices are fully discussed in the report = full 5 marks. More usual to award 3 or 4 marks, depending on quality of report format and communication skills.	1–5	Max = 20
	Recommendations (Marks on merit. Max 1 mark if only an unjustified recommendation is given)		
	Accept or reject WCB bid with supporting reasons	1–4	
	Ways to increase revenues after bad publicity	1–2	
	HR issues	1–2	
	Jibbs proposal (Max = 1 if rec is to accept)	1–2	
	Ways to achieve 5 year plan	1–2	
	Whether to franchise in future	1–2	
	KPE exit plans	1–2	
	Other recs (on merit)	Up to 5	
	Total marks available (but max = 20)	**26**	

Criteria	Issues to be discussed	Marks	Total Marks available for criterion
Ethics	**Ethical issues in case include:** Unhealthy low calorie foods Wrong labelling Incorrect marketing of volume of Fair Trade coffee HR issues including long hours worked Overstated 5 year plan is misleading to investors 1–5 marks (on merit) for each ethical issue including detailed advice on each ethical issue as follows: • 1–2 marks for identification and justification of why an issue has an ethical dimension • +1–3 marks for detailed recommendations of actions (including when and by whom) to overcome the ethical dilemma Therefore if an ethical issue is fully discussed and clear recommendations made = full 5 marks for each ethical issue, although if the identification of the ethical aspect of the issue is not well discussed and the recommendations are weak, marks will be 2–3 for each issue. However, maximum of 4 marks overall (marginal fail) if several ethical issues discussed but no meaningful or sensible advice given.	1–5 each including advice Max = 4 if no advice	Max = 10
Total			**100**

PRACTICE TOPCIMA CASES

Part C

BeeZed Construction Services (BZCS): Pre-seen data

This chapter includes the 'pre-seen' data for BeeZed Construction Services, examined in March and May 2011.

However, please note the **paragraph numbering has been added by BPP** for ease of reference. The 'real' pre-seen material you will get from CIMA for your exam will not have the paragraphs numbered.

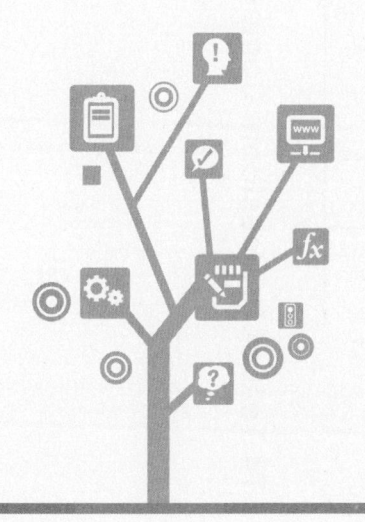

CIMA

T4 – Part B Case Study Examination

For examinations on Tuesday 1 March 2011 and on Thursday 26 May 2011

PRE-SEEN MATERIAL, PROVIDED IN ADVANCE FOR PREPARATION AND STUDY FOR THE EXAMINATIONS IN MARCH AND MAY 2011.
INSTRUCTIONS FOR POTENTIAL CANDIDATES
This booklet contains the pre-seen case material for the above examinations. It will provide you with the contextual information that will help you prepare yourself for the examinations.
The Case Study Assessment Criteria, which your script will be marked against, is included on page 13.
You may not take this copy of the pre-seen material into the examination hall. A fresh copy will be provided on the examination day.
Unseen material will be provided on the examination day; this will comprise further context and the examination question.
The examination will last for three hours. You will be allowed 20 minutes reading time **before the examination begins** during which you should read the question paper and, if you wish, make annotations on the question paper. However, you will **not** be allowed, **under any circumstances**, to either begin writing or using your computer to produce your answer or to use your calculator during the reading time.
You will be required to answer ONE question which may contain more than one element.
PC examination only: Your computer will contain two blank files – one Word and an Excel file. Please ensure that you check that the file names for these two documents correspond with your candidate number.

Contents of this booklet:	Page
Pre-seen material – BZCS construction case	2
Pre-Seen Appendices 1 - 4	9
Case Study Assessment Criteria	13

© The Chartered Institute of Management Accountants 2011

BeeZed Construction Services (BZCS) case

Construction industry background

1. Due to the current economic climate, the demand for building work in Europe has fallen overall by over 10% from 2008 levels. Furthermore, it is forecasted that the volume of construction work will not increase until the start of 2011. Many companies in the construction industry have suffered falls in profits as a direct result of the slowdown in new contracts being awarded.

2. Many European construction companies are involved in a large range of projects in many countries worldwide. Few large construction companies (except some house building companies) operate only within their national boundaries. Most construction companies have established a range of expertise in specific types of project, such as construction of office buildings, hospitals, airports, roads or schools. This expertise allows the construction companies to use their skills and reputation to bid for, and win, further projects in Europe and in other countries around the world.

3. Many large construction projects are financed using Private Finance Initiatives (PFI). PFI is defined as private finance being used to fund public infrastructure work. Private finance is defined as finance provided mainly by banks, institutional investors and pension funds. The Private Finance Initiative (PFI) is a way of creating Public Private Partnerships (PPP). PPP is defined as agreements between public bodies or central governments and private construction companies to deliver the agreed projects. Examples of public infrastructure works are road building and construction of new schools. PFI projects also involve the private sector construction company taking on responsibility for providing an on-going service. This typically includes maintaining and managing the project over the life of the building or for a fixed term of 20 years or longer. Therefore, PFI projects generate revenue streams for the construction company for the initial construction project as well as for long-term maintenance and management of the asset. PFI projects involve the private construction company as a partner in the project and this has generated favourable outcomes in respect of the percentage of projects completed on time and completed to the agreed budget.

In the construction industry there are 3 main types of contract, which are:

4. 1. Fixed price contracts – this is where the revenue for the private construction company is fixed at the contract stage, subject to changes in specifications agreed during construction.

5. 2. "Cost plus" contracts – this is where the revenue for the private construction company will comprise all of the actual costs of the project plus an agreed profit element.

6. 3. Long-term PFI projects – this is where the revenue for the private construction company will include the contracted construction revenue as well as revenues for on-going maintenance and property management for a long-term project, typically 20+ years.

7. The process for private construction companies to win a new contract for a large construction project is summarised in the following steps:

    1. A company or government body will invite tenders
    2. The construction company will tender for the contract by preparing a detailed bid
    3. A company or government body will select its "preferred contractor"
    4. The bid price and the contract details will be negotiated and agreed
    5. Contracts are then signed
    6. Selection and appointment by the construction company of suppliers for manpower resources (sub-contractors), as well as for materials
    7. Work commences

8   It should be noted that during construction work, there are often many requests for changes to the original contract specifications or design which are submitted to the construction company. These changes usually affect costs and manpower. All of these change requests have to be negotiated and additional revenues agreed before the changes can be made.

BeeZed

9   BeeZed is a construction and property management company listed on a European stock exchange.

10 BeeZed has 3 wholly owned subsidiary companies which are:

- BeeZed Construction Services (BZCS) – concerned with a wide range of construction projects
- BeeZed Professional Services (BZPS) – concerned with offering consultancy services
- BeeZed Building Support Services (BZBSS) – concerned with property management and maintenance services.

11 In respect of PFI projects, the parent company, BeeZed, will sign the overall contract for the project. BZCS will be involved only with the construction work and BZBSS will manage the ongoing maintenance and property management work. When a PFI contract is signed, the parent company, BeeZed, will agree on how the revenues will be split between BZCS and BZBSS.

12 This case study is concerned ONLY with BeeZed Construction Services (BZCS).

BZCS

13 BZCS has many construction projects around the world, ranging from road building, construction of public sector buildings, including hospitals, schools and university buildings to commercial contracts for office buildings. Some of the construction projects that BeeZed is involved with are financed by PFI. However, only the revenue related to the construction project is allocated to BZCS. The revenue relating to the ongoing maintenance and property management work is allocated to BZBSS and is <u>not</u> included in this case study. BZCS has a good reputation in this industry for quality and safety as well as its ability to deliver projects on time. These are all critical success factors for keeping its existing customers content and for providing a basis for winning future business.

14 BZCS has 6 divisions, which are:

1. Office Buildings Division – includes building bespoke office buildings for specific company orders, as well as speculative construction of office buildings in city centres or on business park complexes.

2. Sports Facilities Division – includes the construction of large sports stadiums as well as the construction of small regional sports facilities.

3. Environmental Projects Division – includes the construction of water treatment facilities, the construction of sophisticated waste management facilities and marine projects, including the construction of container terminals and marinas.

4. Infrastructure Projects Division – includes road building and airport construction.

5. Community Projects Division – includes the construction of hospitals and smaller healthcare facilities as well as schools and university facilities.

6. Energy Projects Division – includes the construction of gas storage facilities and power stations.

15 Each of these 6 divisions is headed by a Commercial Director who is responsible for all of the projects undertaken by that division.

16 A summary of the organisational structure for BZCS, effective from 1 January 2011, is shown in **Appendix 1** on page 9.

17 In the year ended 30 September 2010, BZCS generated total revenues of €1,267 million and operating profit of €34.7 million.

18 BZCS is a wholly owned subsidiary of BeeZed. An extract from the accounts for BZCS is shown in **Appendix 2** on page 10.

19 All of the non-current liabilities represent inter-company long-term loans from its parent company, BeeZed. BeeZed has a range of non-current liabilities with several external bodies including bank loans.

20 BZCS's cash flow statement for the year ended 30 September 2010 is shown in **Appendix 3** on page 11.

Geographical analysis of revenues

21 BZCS currently has construction projects operational throughout Europe, the USA, the Middle East and in some other countries, mainly in Asia.

22 The geographical analysis of the total construction services revenue of €1,267 million for the year ended 30 September 2010 was as follows:

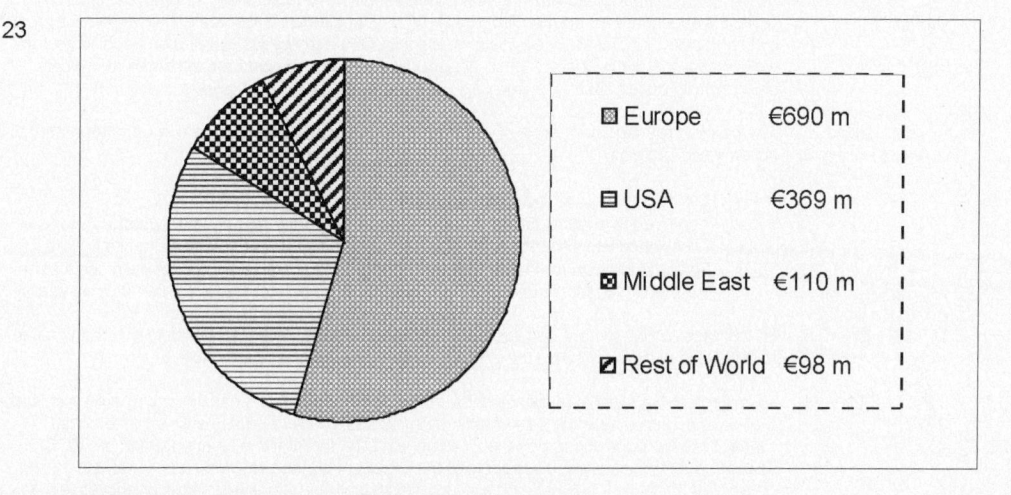

23

Region	Revenue
Europe	€690 m
USA	€369 m
Middle East	€110 m
Rest of World	€98 m

Analysis of revenues and operating profit by division

24 The revenues and operating profit for each of BZCS's 6 divisions for the year ended 30 September 2010 are shown in a table on the next page:

25

	Revenue	Operating profit
	€ million	€ million
Office buildings	220.0	8.5
Sports facilities	145.2	3.4
Environmental projects	193.1	4.2
Infrastructure projects	365.2	16.8
Community projects	213.6	1.3
Energy projects	129.9	0.5
Total	1,267.0	34.7

Financials

26   The operating profit margins achieved by BZCS are low, as is the norm for this industry. However, for some of BZCS's PFI construction projects, BZBSS, which is part of the BeeZed group, earns additional revenues for a further 10 to 30 years for the ongoing maintenance and property management of the PFI projects.

27   Whilst BZCS prepares annual financial accounts, all of the accounting for each construction project is accounted for on a project basis. All direct costs are allocated to the respective project, including salary and associated costs for all of BZCS's employees working on each project as well as sub-contractor costs. All non-project based overhead costs are allocated to projects using activity based costing techniques based on appropriate cost drivers.

28   The monthly management accounts show the following information for all on-going operational construction projects:

- Contract revenues and costs
- Approved change requests to contracts and amended revenues and costs
- Cumulative costs to date for the project (spanning current and past financial years)
- Forecast of costs for the remainder of the project (which are split between costs to be incurred in the current financial year and costs to be incurred in future financial years)

29   BZCS uses a project management system called BZPM. Each Project Manager is responsible for all direct costs incurred on the project for which he / she is responsible.

30   Each Project Manager is responsible for presenting the projects' financial and operational issues that have occurred for each project on a monthly basis. These presentations are to senior management groups chaired by the Commercial Director for the relevant division of BZCS. These presentations cover all aspects of the project, including safety issues, forecasts for the delivery of the project against plan and any significant operational problems or successes. If there is a significant problem, the Project Manager will be expected to travel to BZCS's Head Office to present the information to the BZCS Board. Where there are no operational or financial concerns, the Project Manager conducts his monthly presentation by video conferencing.

Order book

31   At 30 September 2010 BZCS had an order book valued at over €2,400 million. This is 30% higher than the level of BZCS's order book at the 30 September 2009. The order book represents the value of contracts signed which have either not yet been commenced or are currently in progress.

Project Management

32 BZCS uses a project management system to plan each project, called BZPM. The contract details and agreed key stages are set up in BZPM when the contract is signed for each new construction project. A Project Manager is appointed for each project. He or she is responsible for controlling all stages of the project using BZPM. This includes control of resources, both BZCS employees and outsourced sub-contractors, timings for each stage of the project, project planning and managing contract change requests. The Project Manager is also responsible for control and reporting of costs against the original contract and the updated budget for the project.

33 The finance system interfaces directly with BZPM allowing data on payments for materials and sub-contractors, payroll costs and revenues to be directly allocated to each stage of the relevant project. The Project Manager and his team, assisted by the Finance Department, prepare monthly accruals based on activities undertaken in the month, which have not been invoiced. BZPM is able to generate reports on all aspects of each project, including forecast timings for all activities and costs, by the end of day 3 after each month end.

Corporate Social Responsibility

34 BZCS takes its Corporate Social Responsibility (CSR) very seriously. The BZCS Board is committed to safety on all projects and also to the reduction of waste from sites and the reduction of carbon emissions. It is also very aware of environmental concerns and works closely with the communities in which it operates.

35 BZCS's commitment to health and safety and environmental issues is shown below.

36 *Health and Safety*
Health and safety is a top priority for BZCS. BZCS continues to enhance its culture of safety throughout the company and its supply chain, to ensure that its employees, sub-contractors and the public are safe. BZCS also ensures that environmental safety is adhered to, so as to try to ensure that the communities in which it operates are not damaged or polluted.

37 BZCS, like all construction companies, adheres to all Health and Safety legislation and BZCS goes beyond what is required by law. It trains all of its employees to ensure their competency and full understanding of what and why safety is so important in all aspects of the company. This training covers all aspects of health and safety, from construction work at building sites to transportation of materials and disposal of waste. BZCS continues to measure its performance against a range of key Health and Safety indicators.

38 BZCS's annual accident frequency rate has fallen over the last 7 years and is currently 0.16 accidents per 100,000 work hours. This is the lowest accident rate ever achieved by BZCS and is amongst the lowest of the top construction companies globally. 20,000 person days of Health and Safety training has been provided by BZCS during the last financial year ended 30 September 2010.

39 BZCS recognises that it is also important that its supply chain is fundamental to the safe delivery of all construction projects and it works closely with the companies in its supply chain. It tries to ensure that best practice is promoted and that a positive safety culture is created. BZCS provides Health and Safety awareness training to its key suppliers to ensure that they meet BZCS's challenging Health and Safety requirements. BZCS also conducts audits of its suppliers. Recently some suppliers' contracts were not renewed as they did not meet the criteria set by BZCS for Health and Safety standards.

Environmental issues
40 BZCS is committed to complying with a European Union (EU) wide programme to reduce the volume of waste that goes to landfill sites. Where possible waste from construction sites is sorted by category of material (such as earth, packaging or materials which can be recycled) and is recycled or disposed of in a safe way. BZCS has a range of waste management contractors which manage the safe disposal of site waste. They have demonstrated their

41. abilities to divert waste from landfill sites. Last year, ended 30 September 2010, BZCS's target was to dispose of, or recycle, 60% of site waste that would otherwise have ended up in landfill sites. BZCS exceeded this target and disposed of, or recycled, 62% of its waste from its construction sites.

41. BZCS is committed to reducing its carbon footprint and to minimising its impact on the environment. BZCS uses the latest technology on its construction projects so that new buildings are able to operate in an environmentally responsible way and utilise efficient electrical fittings. Many of the buildings contracted by European government departments, such as schools and hospitals, use renewable energy sources and BZCS works closely with the architects to ensure that the buildings will help to deliver planned reductions in carbon emissions.

42. BZCS's Mission Statement and CSR initiatives are shown in **Appendix 4** on page 12.

Contracts

43. BZCS is continuously working on bids for possible new contracts. It has specialised teams headed up by Bid Managers in each of BZCS's 6 divisions. When a bid has been won and a contract signed, then a Project Manager is appointed to manage the project. Sometimes, on a particularly complicated project, the initial Bid Manager will become the Project Manager.

44. Each of BZCS's 6 divisions usually has between 1 and 5 projects in progress at any point in time. Furthermore, each of the 6 divisions is usually involved in the bid preparation and the bidding process for several other proposed projects. Whilst BZCS has been the preferred supplier for some European government departments in the past for infrastructure projects and community projects, these large customers are now imposing increasingly strict criteria for suppliers to meet. Bids need to be competitive in the current challenging economic climate. Therefore, BZCS, like many other construction companies, is not successful in winning all of the projects for which it bids for.

45. In order to balance the risk of relying on specific construction sectors and a relatively small customer base, BZCS tries to win contracts from a wide selection of organisations. These include government and private sector customers. BZCS also undertakes a wide range of different types of construction project.

46. BZCS has secured some construction projects for the London 2012 Olympic Games.

47. At any point in time BZCS usually has between 12 and 20 projects in progress, with bid preparations taking place for a further 10 or more projects. The bid value of a contract varies greatly, ranging from €5 million to over €800 million for individual contracts. Contract duration often spans more than 2 years.

48. As at the end of December 2010, BZCS has 14 projects currently operational, of which 10 are due for completion during 2011 and the remaining 4 are due to be completed in 2012.

Bid tendering process

49. In the UK, the Government's regulator, the Office of Fair Trading (OFT) has been undertaking investigations of "bid-rigging" in the construction industry. The OFT has established that there is widespread evidence of construction companies which have been involved in manipulating the bidding process. This has allowed specific companies to win Government awarded construction projects at higher prices than could be achieved through a fair competitive bidding process. This on-going investigation has involved the OFT accessing paperwork for over 100 contracts from 20 construction companies. It will also impact on the ways that construction companies, including BZCS, bid for new projects in the future.

50. In order to be treated leniently, BZCS has advised the OFT that it did have discussions with some other construction companies concerning the level of its bid for a UK hospital construction project that it won the contract for in 2008. The project is proceeding on time and it is forecast that it will not over-run the agreed fixed price budget.

51 BZCS is waiting to hear the outcome of the OFT's investigation into this specific contract. BZCS has included a provision for a contingent liability, for a possible fine, in the accounts for the current financial year ending 30 September 2011.

Re-structuring of BZCS

52 During 2009 and the early part of 2010, BZCS underwent a re-structuring process to enable it to become more competitive following the downturn in construction projects due to the current economic environment. The Board of BZCS recognised the need to become more flexible and to sub-contract a greater volume of its core construction work. Following a Board decision in March 2009, BZCS reduced the number of its employees by 1,800 within 1 year. At the end of September 2010, BZCS had 10,100 employees. Many of BZCS's ex-employees have joined some of BZCS's supply chain companies, which are BZCS's sub-contractors. Therefore some of these people work on the same project as previously but now are employed by sub-contractors or have become short-term freelance contractors to BZCS.

53 BZCS has also focused on winning a wider range of private construction projects as many European governments have cut the budgets on public sector projects and bidding is more competitive than ever.

54 A summary of the organisational structure for BZCS, effective from 1 January 2011, is shown in **Appendix 1** on page 9.

55 Within each division, the Commercial Director has responsibility for each of the Project Managers who are each responsible for one operational project. Projects that are operational are defined as a project in which the contracts have been signed but construction is not complete. Each division also has Bid Managers responsible for preparing bids or tenders for new projects and Sales and Marketing Managers for selling to, and liaising with, customers. Additionally there is a Post Completion Manager responsible for all projects that have ongoing problems or require minor rectification work after the project has been completed.

56 *Re-structuring of the Procurement Department*
Before the re-structuring of BZCS, each division was responsible for the procurement for each of the projects under its control. Effective from 1 January 2011, there is a new central Procurement Department for the whole of BZCS. This is under the direct control of an experienced Procurement Director, who reports directly to BZCS's Managing Director. The new Procurement Director was recruited from a rival construction company and joined BZCS in October 2010.

57 The employees who worked in the procurement departments within each of BZCS's 6 divisions have been brought together in one centralised Procurement Department, based in Europe. This should help to facilitate better control over purchases and achieve higher bulk discounts, especially for some raw materials. On an operational level, all of BZCS's Project Managers at construction sites in each country will now make all purchases through the new centralised Procurement Department. They will be given limited authority to purchase goods locally where no global contract is in place for particular materials.

58 The new centralised Procurement Department is in the process of selecting "preferred suppliers" within each country in which it operates. Where possible, the preferred supplier will be another large international company that can provide materials to BZCS in many of the countries in which BZCS has on-going construction projects. The Finance Department is working closely with the Procurement Director in the selection and appointment of new and existing suppliers. The re-structuring of BZCS's Procurement Department has resulted in an overall reduction in headcount in procurement employees. The new centralised Procurement Department will help meet BZCS's target for Head Office cost savings.

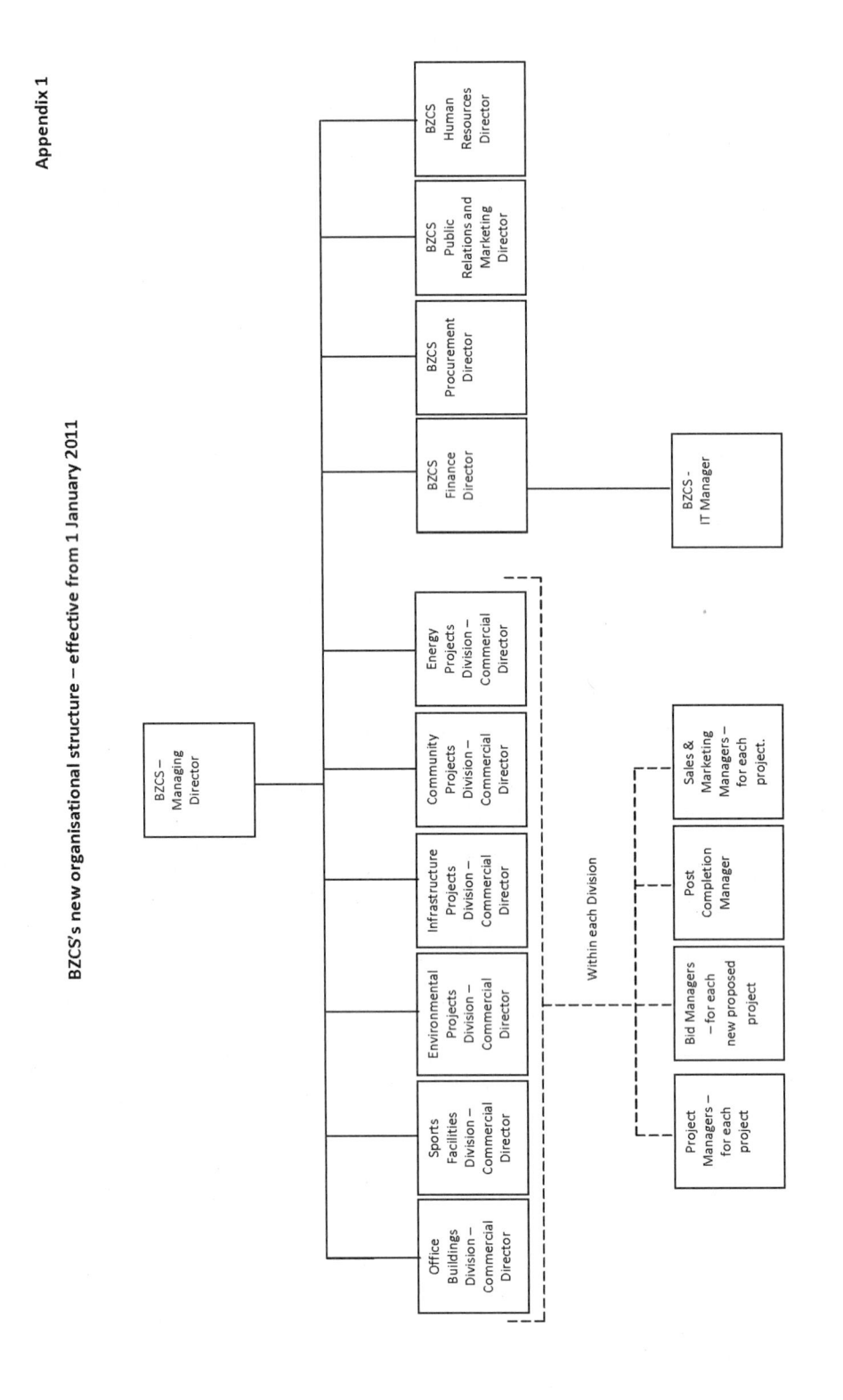

13: BeeZed Construction Services (BZCS): pre-seen data

Appendix 1

BZCS's new organisational structure – effective from 1 January 2011

```
                                    BZCS –
                               Managing Director
                                       |
    ┌──────────┬──────────┬──────────┬──────────┬──────────┬──────────┬──────────┬──────────┬──────────┐
  Office     Sports   Environmental Infrastructure Community  Energy      BZCS       BZCS        BZCS       BZCS
 Buildings  Facilities   Projects     Projects    Projects   Projects   Finance   Procurement  Public     Human
  Division  Division –   Division –   Division –  Division – Division – Director   Director    Relations  Resources
     –     Commercial   Commercial   Commercial  Commercial Commercial              and        Director
Commercial  Director     Director     Director    Director   Director               Marketing
 Director                                                                           Director
                                                                  |
                                                                BZCS –
                                                              IT Manager
```

Within each Division:
- Project Managers – for each project
- Bid Managers – for each new proposed project
- Post Completion Manager
- Sales & Marketing Managers – for each project

BZCS: some help from BPP

In Chapter 4 we mentioned the importance of working through the case in detail, analysing the information contained in each paragraph, before summarising the data in a précis.

This chapter is designed to help you as you work through the unseen material, and highlights the sort of questions you should be asking as you do.

However, remember that as you work through the case, you should also be preparing a more general strategic analysis of BeeZed: in particular, SWOT analysis and stakeholder analysis.

And don't forget that once you have worked through the pre-seen material, you should then synthesise what you know, as we did for Zubinos in Chapter 10. You should ultimately be aiming to summarise the findings of your analysis of the pre-seen material into a one-page business summary.

Finally, remember that the BPP Learning Media toolkit for your paper will provide you with detailed activities which help you analyse the pre-seen material specifically related to your exam.

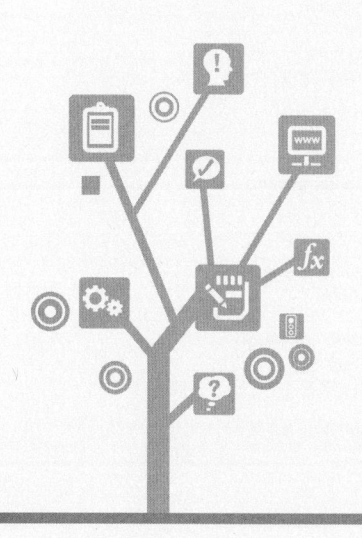

topic list

1 Reading the case in detail

2 Analysis from BPP Learning Media

1 Reading the case in detail

BeeZed Construction Services (BZCS) case

Construction industry background

1. Due to the current economic climate, the demand for building work in Europe has fallen overall by over 10% from 2008 levels. Furthermore, it is forecasted that the volume of construction work will not increase until the start of 2011. Many companies in the construction industry have suffered falls in profits as a direct result of the slowdown in new contracts being awarded.

2. Many European construction companies are involved in a large range of projects in many countries worldwide. Few large construction companies (except some house building companies) operate only within their national boundaries. Most construction companies have established a range of expertise in specific types of project, such as construction of office buildings, hospitals, airports, roads or schools. This expertise allows the construction companies to use their skills and reputation to bid for, and win, further projects in Europe and in other countries around the world.

3. Many large construction projects are financed using Private Finance Initiatives (PFI). PFI is defined as private finance being used to fund public infrastructure work. Private finance is defined as finance provided mainly by banks, institutional investors and pension funds. The Private Finance Initiative (PFI) is a way of creating Public Private Partnerships (PPP). PPP is defined as agreements between public bodies or central governments and private construction companies to deliver the agreed projects. Examples of public infrastructure works are road building and construction of new schools. PFI projects also involve the private sector construction company taking on responsibility for providing an on-going service. This typically includes maintaining and managing the project over the life of the building or for a fixed term of 20 years or longer. Therefore, PFI projects generate revenue streams for the construction company for the initial construction project as well as for long-term maintenance and management of the asset. PFI projects involve the private construction company as a partner in the project and this has generated favourable outcomes in respect of the percentage of projects completed on time and completed to the agreed budget.

In the construction industry there are 3 main types of contract, which are:

4. 1. Fixed price contracts – this is where the revenue for the private construction company is fixed at the contract stage, subject to changes in specifications agreed during construction.

5. 2. "Cost plus" contracts – this is where the revenue for the private construction company will comprise all of the actual costs of the project plus an agreed profit element.

6. 3. Long-term PFI projects – this is where the revenue for the private construction company will include the contracted construction revenue as well as revenues for on-going maintenance and property management for a long-term project, typically 20+ years.

7. The process for private construction companies to win a new contract for a large construction project is summarised in the following steps:

   1. A company or government body will invite tenders
   2. The construction company will tender for the contract by preparing a detailed bid
   3. A company or government body will select its "preferred contractor"
   4. The bid price and the contract details will be negotiated and agreed
   5. Contracts are then signed
   6. Selection and appointment by the construction company of suppliers for manpower resources (sub-contractors), as well as for materials
   7. Work commences

Page 2 of the Pre-seen

Paras	
1	What are the implications of this paragraph for interpreting the financial information in Appendices 2 & 3 of the Pre-seen material?
2	Are construction firms like BZCS exposed to the recession in Europe?
3	What is the reason for the increased popularity of undertaking construction using Private Finance Initiatives (PFI)?
	How does a PFI work?
	What problems do PFI/PPP arrangements encounter?
	What impact do PFI projects have on the Statement of Comprehensive Income and the Statement of Financial Position of a firm like BZCS?
4-6	How do the risks of the contractor vary between these three forms of contract?
7	Why is a bid price agreed only at Step 4 given that the detailed bid was prepared at Step 2?
	What techniques have you studied in your CIMA exams so far that might be used by contractors during this process?
	What management accounting information will the contractor require from its management accountants?
	What ethical issues may be raised during the process described?

8 It should be noted that during construction work, there are often many requests for changes to the original contract specifications or design which are submitted to the construction company. These changes usually affect costs and manpower. All of these change requests have to be negotiated and additional revenues agreed before the changes can be made.

BeeZed

9 BeeZed is a construction and property management company listed on a European stock exchange.

10 BeeZed has 3 wholly owned subsidiary companies which are:

- BeeZed Construction Services (BZCS) – concerned with a wide range of construction projects
- BeeZed Professional Services (BZPS) – concerned with offering consultancy services
- BeeZed Building Support Services (BZBSS) – concerned with property management and maintenance services.

11 In respect of PFI projects, the parent company, BeeZed, will sign the overall contract for the project. BZCS will be involved only with the construction work and BZBSS will manage the ongoing maintenance and property management work. When a PFI contract is signed, the parent company, BeeZed, will agree on how the revenues will be split between BZCS and BZBSS.

12 This case study is concerned ONLY with BeeZed Construction Services (BZCS).

BZCS

13 BZCS has many construction projects around the world, ranging from road building, construction of public sector buildings, including hospitals, schools and university buildings to commercial contracts for office buildings. Some of the construction projects that BeeZed is involved with are financed by PFI. However, only the revenue related to the construction project is allocated to BZCS. The revenue relating to the ongoing maintenance and property management work is allocated to BZBSS and is not included in this case study. BZCS has a good reputation in this industry for quality and safety as well as its ability to deliver projects on time. These are all critical success factors for keeping its existing customers content and for providing a basis for winning future business.

14 BZCS has 6 divisions, which are:

1. Office Buildings Division – includes building bespoke office buildings for specific company orders, as well as speculative construction of office buildings in city centres or on business park complexes.

2. Sports Facilities Division – includes the construction of large sports stadiums as well as the construction of small regional sports facilities.

3. Environmental Projects Division – includes the construction of water treatment facilities, the construction of sophisticated waste management facilities and marine projects, including the construction of container terminals and marinas.

4. Infrastructure Projects Division – includes road building and airport construction.

5. Community Projects Division – includes the construction of hospitals and smaller healthcare facilities as well as schools and university facilities.

6. Energy Projects Division – includes the construction of gas storage facilities and power stations.

Paras	
8	How might the information in this paragraph be used in the exam?
9	What is the significance of BZCS being part of a listed company?
10-12	What potential significance can be attached to the Examiner telling us about the two other divisions of BeeZed if these are not going to be the subject of the exam?
13	What new information is introduced in this paragraph?
14	How does the balance of business in this paragraph affect our assessment of the likely risks and returns of BZCS?

15 Each of these 6 divisions is headed by a Commercial Director who is responsible for all of the projects undertaken by that division.

16 A summary of the organisational structure for BZCS, effective from 1 January 2011, is shown in **Appendix 1** on page 9.

17 In the year ended 30 September 2010, BZCS generated total revenues of €1,267 million and operating profit of €34.7 million.

18 BZCS is a wholly owned subsidiary of BeeZed. An extract from the accounts for BZCS is shown in **Appendix 2** on page 10.

19 All of the non-current liabilities represent inter-company long-term loans from its parent company, BeeZed. BeeZed has a range of non-current liabilities with several external bodies including bank loans.

20 BZCS's cash flow statement for the year ended 30 September 2010 is shown in **Appendix 3** on page 11.

Geographical analysis of revenues

21 BZCS currently has construction projects operational throughout Europe, the USA, the Middle East and in some other countries, mainly in Asia.

22 The geographical analysis of the total construction services revenue of €1,267 million for the year ended 30 September 2010 was as follows:

23

Region	Revenue
Europe	€690 m
USA	€369 m
Middle East	€110 m
Rest of World	€98 m

Analysis of revenues and operating profit by division

24 The revenues and operating profit for each of BZCS's 6 divisions for the year ended 30 September 2010 are shown in a table on the next page:

Paras	
15	Does your role in this exam mean you will be reporting to one of these 6 Commercial Directors?
16-20	What new information is introduced in these paragraphs?
21-23	What might the Examiner have had in mind by including data on geographical analysis of revenues?

25

	Revenue	Operating profit
	€ million	€ million
Office buildings	220.0	8.5
Sports facilities	145.2	3.4
Environmental projects	193.1	4.2
Infrastructure projects	365.2	16.8
Community projects	213.6	1.3
Energy projects	129.9	0.5
Total	1,267.0	34.7

Financials

26 The operating profit margins achieved by BZCS are low, as is the norm for this industry. However, for some of BZCS's PFI construction projects, BZBSS, which is part of the BeeZed group, earns additional revenues for a further 10 to 30 years for the ongoing maintenance and property management of the PFI projects.

27 Whilst BZCS prepares annual financial accounts, all of the accounting for each construction project is accounted for on a project basis. All direct costs are allocated to the respective project, including salary and associated costs for all of BZCS's employees working on each project as well as sub-contractor costs. All non-project based overhead costs are allocated to projects using activity based costing techniques based on appropriate cost drivers.

28 The monthly management accounts show the following information for all on-going operational construction projects:

- Contract revenues and costs
- Approved change requests to contracts and amended revenues and costs
- Cumulative costs to date for the project (spanning current and past financial years)
- Forecast of costs for the remainder of the project (which are split between costs to be incurred in the current financial year and costs to be incurred in future financial years)

29 BZCS uses a project management system called BZPM. Each Project Manager is responsible for all direct costs incurred on the project for which he / she is responsible.

30 Each Project Manager is responsible for presenting the projects' financial and operational issues that have occurred for each project on a monthly basis. These presentations are to senior management groups chaired by the Commercial Director for the relevant division of BZCS. These presentations cover all aspects of the project, including safety issues, forecasts for the delivery of the project against plan and any significant operational problems or successes. If there is a significant problem, the Project Manager will be expected to travel to BZCS's Head Office to present the information to the BZCS Board. Where there are no operational or financial concerns, the Project Manager conducts his monthly presentation by video conferencing.

Order book

31 At 30 September 2010 BZCS had an order book valued at over €2,400 million. This is 30% higher than the level of BZCS's order book at the 30 September 2009. The order book represents the value of contracts signed which have either not yet been commenced or are currently in progress.

Paras	
25	How profitable is BZCS? Are its profits sufficient?
26	Does this paragraph have any impact on how we evaluate the 6 divisions of BZCS?
27-30	Why has the Examiner included this detail on costing and management accounting?
	What issues are raised by the allocation of non-project based overhead costs?
	What cost drivers might be used to allocate the non-project based overhead costs?
	What is the potential significance to your examination of the monthly reporting described in paragraph 30?
31	Is BZCS set for growth in 2011?

Project Management

32 BZCS uses a project management system to plan each project, called BZPM. The contract details and agreed key stages are set up in BZPM when the contract is signed for each new construction project. A Project Manager is appointed for each project. He or she is responsible for controlling all stages of the project using BZPM. This includes control of resources, both BZCS employees and outsourced sub-contractors, timings for each stage of the project, project planning and managing contract change requests. The Project Manager is also responsible for control and reporting of costs against the original contract and the updated budget for the project.

33 The finance system interfaces directly with BZPM allowing data on payments for materials and sub-contractors, payroll costs and revenues to be directly allocated to each stage of the relevant project. The Project Manager and his team, assisted by the Finance Department, prepare monthly accruals based on activities undertaken in the month, which have not been invoiced. BZPM is able to generate reports on all aspects of each project, including forecast timings for all activities and costs, by the end of day 3 after each month end.

Corporate Social Responsibility

34 BZCS takes its Corporate Social Responsibility (CSR) very seriously. The BZCS Board is committed to safety on all projects and also to the reduction of waste from sites and the reduction of carbon emissions. It is also very aware of environmental concerns and works closely with the communities in which it operates.

35 BZCS's commitment to health and safety and environmental issues is shown below.

36 *Health and Safety*
Health and safety is a top priority for BZCS. BZCS continues to enhance its culture of safety throughout the company and its supply chain, to ensure that its employees, sub-contractors and the public are safe. BZCS also ensures that environmental safety is adhered to, so as to try to ensure that the communities in which it operates are not damaged or polluted.

37 BZCS, like all construction companies, adheres to all Health and Safety legislation and BZCS goes beyond what is required by law. It trains all of its employees to ensure their competency and full understanding of what and why safety is so important in all aspects of the company. This training covers all aspects of health and safety, from construction work at building sites to transportation of materials and disposal of waste. BZCS continues to measure its performance against a range of key Health and Safety indicators.

38 BZCS's annual accident frequency rate has fallen over the last 7 years and is currently 0.16 accidents per 100,000 work hours. This is the lowest accident rate ever achieved by BZCS and is amongst the lowest of the top construction companies globally. 20,000 person days of Health and Safety training has been provided by BZCS during the last financial year ended 30 September 2010.

39 BZCS recognises that it is also important that its supply chain is fundamental to the safe delivery of all construction projects and it works closely with the companies in its supply chain. It tries to ensure that best practice is promoted and that a positive safety culture is created. BZCS provides Health and Safety awareness training to its key suppliers to ensure that they meet BZCS's challenging Health and Safety requirements. BZCS also conducts audits of its suppliers. Recently some suppliers' contracts were not renewed as they did not meet the criteria set by BZCS for Health and Safety standards.

40 *Environmental issues*
BZCS is committed to complying with a European Union (EU) wide programme to reduce the volume of waste that goes to landfill sites. Where possible waste from construction sites is sorted by category of material (such as earth, packaging or materials which can be recycled) and is recycled or disposed of in a safe way. BZCS has a range of waste management contractors which manage the safe disposal of site waste. They have demonstrated their

Paras	
32-33	How is financial control exercised in BZCS?
	What implications may the information in this paragraph have for your exam?
34-42	How comprehensive is BZCS' commitment to Corporate Social Responsibility?
	Will CSR benefit the business of BZCS?

41 abilities to divert waste from landfill sites. Last year, ended 30 September 2010, BZCS's target was to dispose of, or recycle, 60% of site waste that would otherwise have ended up in landfill sites. BZCS exceeded this target and disposed of, or recycled, 62% of its waste from its construction sites.

41 BZCS is committed to reducing its carbon footprint and to minimising its impact on the environment. BZCS uses the latest technology on its construction projects so that new buildings are able to operate in an environmentally responsible way and utilise efficient electrical fittings. Many of the buildings contracted by European government departments, such as schools and hospitals, use renewable energy sources and BZCS works closely with the architects to ensure that the buildings will help to deliver planned reductions in carbon emissions.

42 BZCS's Mission Statement and CSR initiatives are shown in **Appendix 4** on page 12.

Contracts

43 BZCS is continuously working on bids for possible new contracts. It has specialised teams headed up by Bid Managers in each of BZCS's 6 divisions. When a bid has been won and a contract signed, then a Project Manager is appointed to manage the project. Sometimes, on a particularly complicated project, the initial Bid Manager will become the Project Manager.

44 Each of BZCS's 6 divisions usually has between 1 and 5 projects in progress at any point in time. Furthermore, each of the 6 divisions is usually involved in the bid preparation and the bidding process for several other proposed projects. Whilst BZCS has been the preferred supplier for some European government departments in the past for infrastructure projects and community projects, these large customers are now imposing increasingly strict criteria for suppliers to meet. Bids need to be competitive in the current challenging economic climate. Therefore, BZCS, like many other construction companies, is not successful in winning all of the projects for which it bids for.

45 In order to balance the risk of relying on specific construction sectors and a relatively small customer base, BZCS tries to win contracts from a wide selection of organisations. These include government and private sector customers. BZCS also undertakes a wide range of different types of construction project.

46 BZCS has secured some construction projects for the London 2012 Olympic Games.

47 At any point in time BZCS usually has between 12 and 20 projects in progress, with bid preparations taking place for a further 10 or more projects. The bid value of a contract varies greatly, ranging from €5 million to over €800 million for individual contracts. Contract duration often spans more than 2 years.

48 As at the end of December 2010, BZCS has 14 projects currently operational, of which 10 are due for completion during 2011 and the remaining 4 are due to be completed in 2012.

Bid tendering process

49 In the UK, the Government's regulator, the Office of Fair Trading (OFT) has been undertaking investigations of "bid-rigging" in the construction industry. The OFT has established that there is widespread evidence of construction companies which have been involved in manipulating the bidding process. This has allowed specific companies to win Government awarded construction projects at higher prices than could be achieved through a fair competitive bidding process. This on-going investigation has involved the OFT accessing paperwork for over 100 contracts from 20 construction companies. It will also impact on the ways that construction companies, including BZCS, bid for new projects in the future.

50 In order to be treated leniently, BZCS has advised the OFT that it did have discussions with some other construction companies concerning the level of its bid for a UK hospital construction project that it won the contract for in 2008. The project is proceeding on time and it is forecast that it will not over-run the agreed fixed price budget.

Paras	
43	Does having a separate Bid Manager and Project Manager raise any control issues for BZCS?
44	What implications would failing to gain government contracts have for BZCS?
45-46	Has BZCS spread its risks effectively?
47-48	Does BZCS have sufficient new contracts to sustain its business?
49-51	What may the impacts of the OFT investigation be on BZCS and its industry?

51 BZCS is waiting to hear the outcome of the OFT's investigation into this specific contract. BZCS has included a provision for a contingent liability, for a possible fine, in the accounts for the current financial year ending 30 September 2011.

Re-structuring of BZCS

52 During 2009 and the early part of 2010, BZCS underwent a re-structuring process to enable it to become more competitive following the downturn in construction projects due to the current economic environment. The Board of BZCS recognised the need to become more flexible and to sub-contract a greater volume of its core construction work. Following a Board decision in March 2009, BZCS reduced the number of its employees by 1,800 within 1 year. At the end of September 2010, BZCS had 10,100 employees. Many of BZCS's ex-employees have joined some of BZCS's supply chain companies, which are BZCS's sub-contractors. Therefore some of these people work on the same project as previously but now are employed by sub-contractors or have become short-term freelance contractors to BZCS.

53 BZCS has also focused on winning a wider range of private construction projects as many European governments have cut the budgets on public sector projects and bidding is more competitive than ever.

54 A summary of the organisational structure for BZCS, effective from 1 January 2011, is shown in **Appendix 1** on page 9.

55 Within each division, the Commercial Director has responsibility for each of the Project Managers who are each responsible for one operational project. Projects that are operational are defined as a project in which the contracts have been signed but construction is not complete. Each division also has Bid Managers responsible for preparing bids or tenders for new projects and Sales and Marketing Managers for selling to, and liaising with, customers. Additionally there is a Post Completion Manager responsible for all projects that have ongoing problems or require minor rectification work after the project has been completed.

56 *Re-structuring of the Procurement Department*
Before the re-structuring of BZCS, each division was responsible for the procurement for each of the projects under its control. Effective from 1 January 2011, there is a new central Procurement Department for the whole of BZCS. This is under the direct control of an experienced Procurement Director, who reports directly to BZCS's Managing Director. The new Procurement Director was recruited from a rival construction company and joined BZCS in October 2010.

57 The employees who worked in the procurement departments within each of BZCS's 6 divisions have been brought together in one centralised Procurement Department, based in Europe. This should help to facilitate better control over purchases and achieve higher bulk discounts, especially for some raw materials. On an operational level, all of BZCS's Project Managers at construction sites in each country will now make all purchases through the new centralised Procurement Department. They will be given limited authority to purchase goods locally where no global contract is in place for particular materials.

58 The new centralised Procurement Department is in the process of selecting "preferred suppliers" within each country in which it operates. Where possible, the preferred supplier will be another large international company that can provide materials to BZCS in many of the countries in which BZCS has on-going construction projects. The Finance Department is working closely with the Procurement Director in the selection and appointment of new and existing suppliers. The re-structuring of BZCS's Procurement Department has resulted in an overall reduction in headcount in procurement employees. The new centralised Procurement Department will help meet BZCS's target for Head Office cost savings.

Paras	
52	What will be the effect on the costs, profits and CSR of BZCS making greater use of subcontractors?
53	What are the implications for the marketing activities if BZCS of seeking more private sector contracts?
54	What may be the reasons for the Examiner setting January 1st 2011 as the date for the new structure to come into effect?
55	How many Project Managers did BZCS need at the end of 2010?
56-58	What benefits will BZCS expect to get from centralised procurement? What difficulties may BZCS experience from centralised procurement? How could the role of the Procurement Department be improved?

Appendix 1

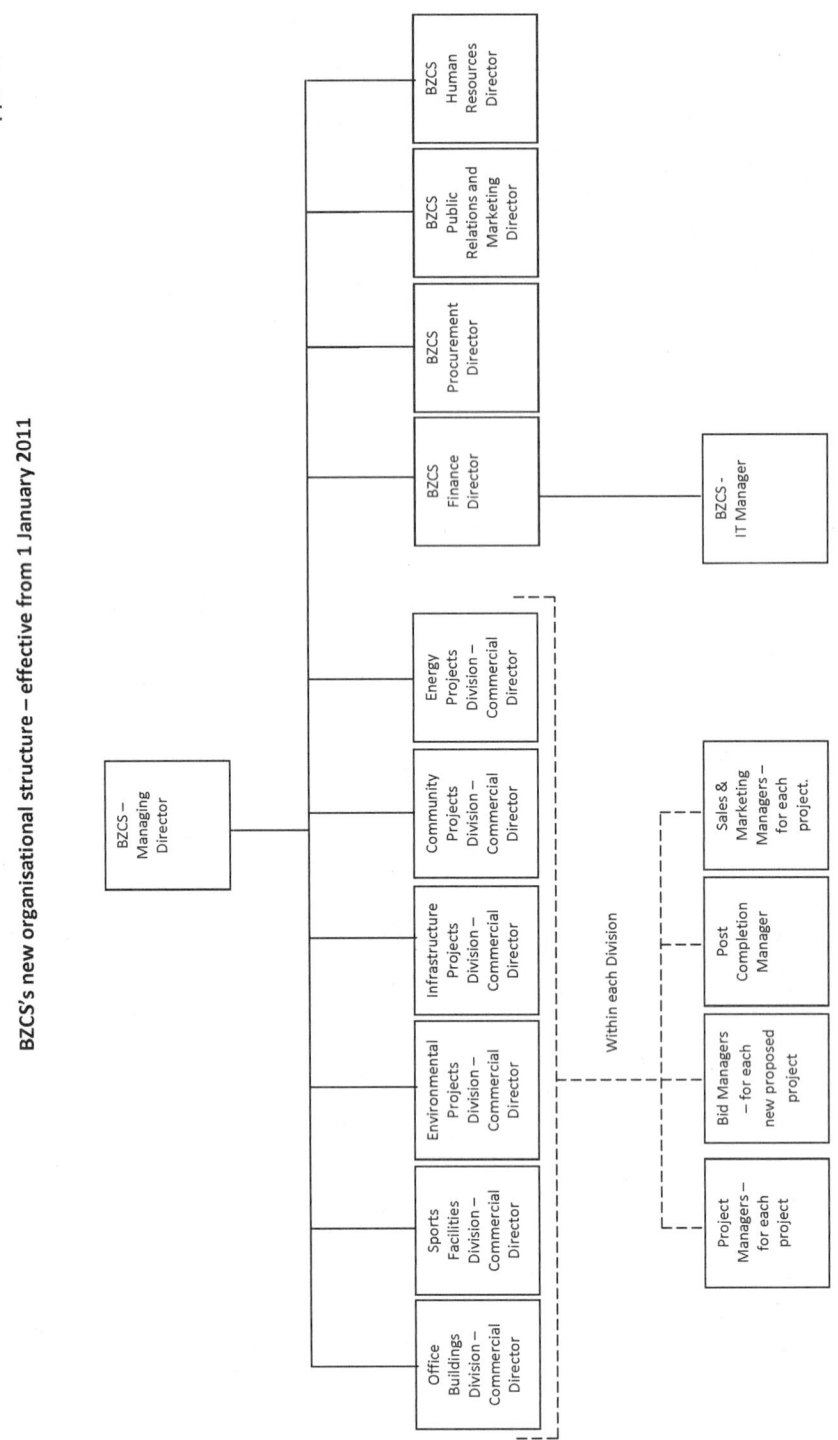

BZCS's new organisational structure – effective from 1 January 2011

```
                                    BZCS –
                                   Managing
                                   Director
        ┌──────────┬──────────┬──────────┬──────────┬──────────┬──────────┐                    ┌──────────┬──────────┬──────────┬──────────┐
   Office      Sports    Environmental Infrastructure Community   Energy                     BZCS       BZCS         BZCS           BZCS
  Buildings  Facilities   Projects      Projects      Projects   Projects                   Finance   Procurement  Public Relations Human
  Division – Division –   Division –    Division –    Division – Division –                 Director   Director    and Marketing    Resources
  Commercial Commercial   Commercial    Commercial    Commercial Commercial                                        Director         Director
  Director   Director     Director      Director      Director   Director                       │
                                                                                              BZCS –
                                                                                             IT Manager

                      Within each Division
   ┌──────────┬──────────┬──────────┬──────────┐
  Project    Bid Managers  Post       Sales &
  Managers –  – for each   Completion  Marketing
  for each   new proposed  Manager    Managers –
  project    project                  for each
                                      project.
```

Appx	
1	Why has the case writer introduced these changes from January 1st 2011?
	What further improvements could be made to this new organisational structure?

Appendix 2

**Extracts from BZCS's Statement of Comprehensive Income,
Statement of Financial Position and Statement of Changes in Equity**

Statement of Comprehensive Income	Year ended 30 September 2010	Year ended 30 September 2009
	€ million	€ million
Sales revenue	1,267.0	1,280.0
Cost of sales	1,210.3	1,222.0
Gross profit	56.7	58.0
Administrative expenses	22.0	22.8
Operating profit	34.7	35.2
Finance income	0.2	0.3
Finance expense	7.5	8.7
Profit before tax	27.4	26.8
Tax expense (effective tax rate is 20%)	5.5	5.4
Profit for the period	21.9	21.4

Statement of Financial Position	As at 30 September 2010		As at 30 September 2009	
	€ million	€ million	€ million	€ million
Non-current assets (net)		241.0		234.0
Current assets				
Inventory	3.1		3.4	
Trade receivables	167.0		167.8	
Cash and cash equivalents	23.4		31.2	
		193.5		202.4
Total assets		434.5		436.4
Equity and liabilities				
Equity				
Share capital	10.0		10.0	
Retained earnings	176.0		154.1	
		186.0		164.1
Non-current liabilities				
Inter-company loan (provided by parent company BeeZed)		125.0		145.0
Current liabilities				
Trade payables	118.0		121.9	
Tax payables	5.5		5.4	
		123.5		127.3
Total equity and liabilities		434.5		436.4

Note: Paid in share capital represents 10 million shares of €1.00 each at 30 September 2010 which are 100% owned by parent company BeeZed

Statement of Changes in Equity	Share Capital	Share premium	Retained earnings	Total
	€ million	€ million	€ million	€ million
Balance at 30 September 2009	10.0	-	154.1	164.1
Profit	-	-	21.9	21.9
Dividends paid	-	-	-	-
Balance at 30 September 2010	**10.0**	**-**	**176.0**	**186.0**

Appendix 3

Cash Flow Statement

	Year ended 30 September 2010	
	€ million	€ million
Cash flows from operating activities:		
Profit before taxation (after Finance costs (net))		27.4
Adjustments:		
Depreciation	88.0	
Finance costs (net)	7.3	
		95.3
(Increase) / decrease in inventories	0.3	
(Increase) / decrease in trade receivables	0.8	
Increase / (decrease) in trade payables (excluding taxation)	(3.9)	
		(2.8)
Cash generated from operations		119.9
Finance costs (net) paid	(7.3)	
Tax paid	(5.4)	
		(12.7)
Cash generated from operating activities		107.2
Cash flows from investing activities:		
Purchase of non-current assets	(95.0)	
Cash used in investing activities		(95.0)
Cash flows from financing activities:		
Repayment of inter-company loans	(20.0)	
Cash flows from financing activities		(20.0)
Net decrease in cash and cash equivalents		(7.8)
Cash and cash equivalents at 30 September 2009		31.2
Cash and cash equivalents at 30 September 2010		23.4

March and May 2011   T4 – Part B Case Study

Appendix 4

BZCS's Mission Statement and CSR initiatives

BZCS's mission statement is:

"To be the preferred supplier for quality construction projects and to strive to implement a long-term relationship with our customers based on safety, quality and a timely service"

BZCS has the following CSR initiatives:

Prudent use of natural resources:
- Reducing waste
- Improving design
- Improving the use of resources
- Improving its supply chain
- Increasing the use of locally sourced resources

Environmental issues:
- Reducing water pollution
- Reducing emissions into the atmosphere
- Reducing waste going to landfill sites

Social issues:
- Improving Health and Safety for our employees and sub-contractors
- Supporting our employees
- Giving due consideration to the communities in which we work
- Developing the skills of our employees

Economic growth
- Investing in the communities in which we operate
- Rewarding our shareholders
- Satisfying our customers
- Managing our risks

End of pre-seen material

Your script will be marked against the T4 Part B Case Study Assessment Criteria shown on the next page.

Assessment Criteria

Criterion	Maximum marks available
Analysis of issues (25 marks)	
Technical	5
Application	15
Diversity	5
Strategic choices (35 marks)	
Focus	5
Prioritisation	5
Judgement	20
Ethics	5
Recommendations (40 marks)	
Logic	30
Integration	5
Ethics	5
Total	**100**

2 Analysis from BPP Learning Media

In this section, we provide an analysis of the pre-seen material: in effect, providing answers to the questions we have raised in the previous section.

Para 1 **What are the implications of this paragraph for interpreting the financial information in Appendices 2 & 3 of the Pre-seen material?**

The financial information in Appendices 2 & 3 cover the period 1st October 2008 to 30th September 2010. The 10% fall in building work since 2008 may have contributed to BZCS's

- fall in sales revenue from €1,280m to €1,267m (1%)
- fall in operating profit from €35.2m to €34.7m (1.5%)

This suggests less work in a more competitive market.

It also opens the possibility that if the forecast increase in volumes of construction work in 2011 materialises, the examiner could present a more favourable outlook for BZCS in the Unseen information on exam day. However it should be remembered that construction projects are long-term. Construction work cannot be turned on and off like a tap.

This means there may be a considerable time lag between at an upturn in tenders and an upturn in the revenues of construction firms like BZCS. Para 7 below shows the steps in such projects with work commencing only following 6 stages of non-revenue generating activity.

It also means that BZCS's 2009 and 2010 results may have been flattered by the tail of existing projects commissioned before the fall since 2008. This means that 2011 may still be a tough year for BZCS.

Para 2 **Are construction firms like BZCS exposed to the recession in Europe?**

Paragraph 1 says that the 10% fall in construction work occurred in Europe. Paragraph 2 alludes to building firms having contracts worldwide. Para 13 later confirms that BZCS 'has many construction projects around the world' and paragraphs 22-23 demonstrate that 54.4% of BZCS's revenues came from Europe (€690m/€1,267m).

European construction projects are presently being curtailed by two factors:

1. *Reduced bank lending to business*, and to the construction sector in particular, as a consequence of the credit crunch and consequently the bank reluctance to be exposed further to the property market.

2. *Tighter public spending* due to governments seeking to repay national debt by cutting their expenditure. This has come as a consequence of *European Contagion*: the falling credit ratings of the sovereign debt of some high borrowing EU member states that threatens to raise the interest paid by all European governments on their debt.

Therefore construction firms like BZCS may diversify some of the risk of decline in Europe by their work elsewhere, for example Middle East, India and Far East.

For example the construction sector in India has exhibited a compound annual growth rate of 20% pa over the past 5 years, China 12.6% and Saudi Arabia about 5% (*source www.constructionweekonline.com*)

Para 3 **What is the reason for the increased popularity of undertaking construction using Private Finance Initiatives (PFI)?**

PFI initiatives are in effect a form of 'lend-lease agreement' or off-balance sheet financing for public sector projects. They were first operated in Australia in the 1980s and adopted in the UK from 1992. The UK is a major user of PFI in the World and in 2010 it remains the UK government's preferred method of financing public infrastructure investment. The World Bank advocates Public Private Partnerships (PPP) arrangements and is using these to promote education and telecoms investments in many countries, including India. The main arguments for them are that they

- Enabled public sector to benefit from the greater cost efficiencies and project management skills of private sector construction firms. The argument holds that professional building firms are specialists in construction, project management and facilities management and so can do it cheaper than public bodies. Also they may enjoy economies of scale and cost reductions from vertical integration that public bodies will not.

- Permitted public sector organisations to afford capital investment without breaking their budgets. Most public sector organisations adopt a form of cash flow accounting which makes no distinction between capital expenditure and income expenditure. Therefore buying a new hospital or school had to be afforded from the current years incomes, despite the benefits of the new building lasting for 15 or 20 years in the future. This severely limited the amount of new investment that took place.

- Reduced the levels of government spending and borrowing necessary to obtain new hospitals, roads, schools and so on. The public finance convention is to charge the entire cost of the project to the year in which it was paid for rather than capitalising it as a private firm would do. This has the effect of seeming to raise government spending in the year the projects are undertaken. Also they are conventionally paid for by the issue of government securities to the financial markets, ie an increase in government borrowing. Both of these are frowned-on by financial markets which see 'borrow and spend' policies by governments as a sign of poor public sector financial management.

- Transfers risk to the private sector where it can be managed more effectively. This can include over-runs on project costs, excessive costs of maintenance, or subsequent decisions to abandon use of the asset. Proponents of PFI argue that private construction firms can mitigate these risks by their greater expertise in managing such projects (ie that a construction firm build things all the time whereas hospital management are rarely involved in such projects), but also they would be more able to find alternative uses for the asset in the event that the public body wished to abandon it (for example if they closed a hospital the PFI-built nurses home could be turned into residential accommodation for the elderly by the private contractor without too much fuss).

Governments wishing to provide better public infrastructure but without placing an immediate burden on the public purse used PFIs to bridge the gap. Similar lend-lease arrangements are used by private sector firms too. One UK construction firm, Bovis, has a specialist division seeking such contracts internationally (www.bovislendlease.com).

How does a PFI work?

- A PFI normally starts with the creation of a Single Purpose Vehicle (SPV – or sometimes *Special Purpose Company SPC*) to design, finance, build and operate the project and the resulting asset (termed a *DFBO concession*). This is usually a company set up by the contractor, or sometimes by several contractors together where one is an expert in constriction and another in facilities management say.

- The SPV will manage the building of the asset and looks after all the contracts. These are usually a construction contract, for building it, and a facilities management contract for running it for up to 20 years thereafter.

- The SPVC owns the asset, for example a new hospital building, and charges the government body a fee for its use. This is called a unitary charge, and is levied on the basis of usage, for example per patient bed/day. Thus the government avoids the capital cost of the new hospital, but it signs a commitment to 20 years of payments instead.

- The ownership of the asset at the end of the period may pass to the government, or may stay with the SPV, depending on the PPP agreement.

What problems do PFI/PPP arrangements encounter?

PFI/PPP are used by some countries, but have also be very publicly abandoned by others.

Public criticism: the general public and sections of the media regularly complain that PPP is a back-door route to giving away public services to the profit-making sector and expecting future generations to pay for them. The argument is made that a PPP asset has to return a profit to the SPV in excess of the cost of capital tied up in it, whereas if it were provided by the state directly this profit would no be required. Added to this is the point that the cost of capital to a private firm must be higher than it is to a government borrower. Taken together the conclusion is that the hospital or school will ultimately cost more if undertaken by PPP.

- *Poor drafting of contracts*: a PPP contract sets the framework for up to 20 years ahead. Public sector bodies are not experts in drafting such contracts and frequently found themselves caught in a restrictive contract that did not meet their evolving requirements. This often led to them paying high fees to the partner in order to terminate the contract.
- *Loss of private finance in credit crunch*. Since the banking crisis of 2007-2010 banks have been generally unwilling to lend, and this has included to PPP projects. This has made it difficult for new projects to be undertaken. As examples of this are the increased amount of funding for European PPP projects being provided by the European Central Bank, and worldwide by the World Bank.
- *Not a core competence*: many PPP initiatives involved the contractors becoming involved in projects in which they had no previous experience. Examples included construction firms becoming involved in rail infrastructure management and in running hospitals. These areas require specialist knowledge and skills that took the new PPP contractors by surprise and had not been allowed for in the costing.
- *Corruption allegations*: Critics of PPP point to the political lobbying activities of PPP contractors, and the consultancies advising them, to ensure projects are awarded to them. This has affected many countries to the extent that the Organisation for Economic Cooperation and Development (OECD) hosted a special conference in this in 2007.
- *Underperformance:* post investment audit reports frequently observe that services provided under PPP are inferior to the corresponding service provided by the state directly. This is often blamed on poor contracts that enable the provider to escape obligations, cut corners and charge for extras. However there is also the general view that as well as cutting unnecessary costs (a key justification of PPP) there is also the temptation for contractors to chip away at essential costs too.
- *Collapse of the provider:* several PPP contractors have gone bankrupt. In the UK the most recent and high profile example was rail and school infrastructure provider Jarvis plc in April 2010. This leaves an essential project either incomplete or the facilities management in the hands of the liquidator who no longer has any obligations under the contracts signed by the failed contractor.

What impact do PFI projects have on the Statement of Comprehensive Income and the Statement of Financial Position of a firm like BZCS?

The Examiner has set this Pre-seen up so that BZCS does not own the PFI asset. It seems to belong to BeeZed or possibly to BZBBS. Therefore in effect BZCS contracts with the SPV as it would with any other client. It builds the hospital or school and will charge costs and revenues to the project in the usual way. It will appear as Sales Revenue and Cost of Sales in the Statement of Comprehensive Income and any work in progress at year end will be placed in Trade receivables as work for which revenues are due but which have not been invoiced or settled yet.

Paras 4-6 **How do the risks of the contractor vary between these three forms of contract?**

More details of these contracts can be found in *IAS 11 – Construction Contracts*.

1. *Fixed price contracts:* these are also referred to a Firm Fixed Price (FFP), lump sum or Fixed Fee (FFC) contracts. The construction company takes all the risk for the project taking a different amount of time and costing a different amount of money than it estimated at the tendering stage. This risk can be upside (it costs less) or downside (it costs more and/or runs into penalty payments for lateness). Trying to win the tender may encourage the contractor to enter a low bid, but this can lead to a devastating loss later, or a search for ways to save costs which in turn may adversely affect the quality of the finished project. Several FFC contractors have become bankrupt as a consequence of FFP contracts, particularly where the design for the building featured new technologies and features which presented difficulties during the construction phase.

2. *Cost-plus contracts:* also called Time and Materials contracts (T&M) they reduce risk to the contractor by allowing them to recover any adverse usage or rate variances. The 'agree profit element' can be expressed as a fixed percentage of the actual contact cost, or as a fixed fee to be added to the actual contract cost. Sometimes the contract may contain refinements such as a guaranteed maximum contract cost, a bonus to the contractor for on-time or early completion, or an agreement for the client and the contractor to share any eventual cost savings.

3. *Long-term PFI contracts:* the risks are isolated within the SPV which will usually have its own financing arrangements and be responsible for managing its own debts. Because they are in-effect leasing an asset or renting the service of it to the public body the SPV bears all the risks of fixed price contracts plus the operating risks for the years thereafter. For example a builder may contract to build and maintain a hospital for 20 years at a set fee per patient bed. They bear the risk of subsequent increases in construction costs and delays, rises in finance costs (for example a rise in the costs of debt), and increases in maintenance costs, for example of maintenance staff and materials, heating costs, local property taxes and so on. They also run risks from variations in the use of the asset such as a decision to reduce patient numbers. The PPP contracts may be drafted to reduce these risks such as by adding in an annual increase in charges linked to movement in a price index, or a guaranteed volume of usage by the public sector client. One common risk with PFI contracts has been subsequent changes of specification by the client. This can include requests for extra space or features which, although outside the contract, plunge the contractor into a damaging public relations battle in which the contractor is portrayed as opportunistic and an enemy of the public interest. Another risk is where the public sector client fails to perform their part of the deal, such as not quickly granting planning permissions for the new building (or for conversion of the former building to an alternative use), or arranging the efficient moving of staff and equipment from the old premises to the new premises.

Finally PFI contracts feature significant *political risk*. One recent example if this was in the UK where a huge PFI/PPP initiative Partnerships for Schools (PfS) was set up and announced a project to invest in new schools, the Building Schools for the Future programme (BSF), in March 2010. This was severely curtailed in July 2010 by the newly-elected coalition government, leading to the cancellation of 715 potential PFI projects.

Para 7 **Why is a bid price agreed only at Step 4 given that the detailed bid was prepared at Step 2?**

Tenders for construction projects will not be as simple as tenders to provide janitorial supplies or office stationery. The precise specification for the new building will not have been determined until Stage 4. Instead the initial tender, at Steps 1 & 2, is more like a Request For a Proposal (RFP) or, in the case of a PFI these are called Preliminary Invitations To Negotiate (PITN). The client provides a broad outline of what it wants and the contractors will use this to produce initial non-binding tenders. The purpose of this is to give the client an indication of the potential suitability of each contractor, taking into account their interpretation of the brief, the skills and experience they outline in their tender, and the skeleton price they propose.

This 'beauty parade' will involve a one or two pass selection process involving meetings, presentations and discussions at the end of which the 'preferred contractor' will be announced and a time limit set on how long the client will work with this contractor in order to reach a final deal before it decides whether to throw the contract open to competition again.

The 'preferred contractor' will be the one whom the client feels it can work with best. This decision will weigh up costs but also the experience, stability and attitudes of the contractors.

The firm price will emerge after long weeks of clarification and negotiation between the client and this preferred contractor.

What techniques have you studied in your CIMA exams so far that might be used by contractors during this process?

This process will use the tendering techniques covered in the present *E1 Enterprise Operations* syllabus (previously within *P4 Organisational Management and Information Systems*) and the project management techniques covered in *E2 Enterprise Management* (previously *P5 Integrated Management*). These include:

- The tender process;

- Issues in supplier selection: experience, stability, cost, relationship, CSR;

- Work breakdown structures: to divide the project as a whole down into tasks and deliverables;

- Resource budgets: to identify the amount of each resource needed for each task and project (eg man/hours, tonnes of concrete, days that a tower crane will be needed on site). This may involve the construction of resource histograms and Gantt charts;

- Network analysis: to identify the sequence and timings of each task and from this to identify critical paths and control milestones;

- Risk management: identification of risk factors and strategies to treat these risks;

- Techniques of project management: appointment of project team and project manager, project planning, use of project management software, methods of control and expediting

- Post investment audits: identification of causes of departures from plan and lessons to be learned.

You are unlikely to be asked detailed questions about these on exam day but you will be expected to be familiar with the terminology and the tasks involved since, for the purposes of this exam, you are assumed to be working for BZCS.

What management accounting information will the contractor require from its management accountants?

In preparing a tender the management accountant will be expected to provide the Bid Manager (see paragraph 55) with the following information:
Data on the likely costs of each of the resources. These will be drawn from the costs being incurred by projects at present, from recent projects, and from surveys of the market and tenders from sub-contractors.

- *Information on the costs and availability of funding*: this will require a cash flow forecast for the project that incorporates the timing of the project, the credit being offered by suppliers and subcontractors, and assessment of the lending sources available to the project and the costs of that borrowing.

- *Commentary on the validity of the assumptions being made.* It is not the job of the management accountant to venture times and quantities for construction projects. That is the professional skill provided by specialist quantity surveyors, project managers and engineers. However it is reasonable for the management accountant to compare these estimates with the rates and usage of past projects and to ask questions where they seem out of line.

- *Information on likely tender prices submitted by rivals*: to win the tender it is essential that BZCS is not unduly more expensive than other bidders. The likely bid prices of rivals can be gauged by considering the actual tender prices of past projects (usually announced in construction magazines such as *Construction News* and *Building*), the recent competitive bids submitted by BZCS where the rivals won the contract (it would not be usual to obtain details if a rivals actual bid since these usually remain confidential under the terms of a tender), and a consideration of the financial and strategic position of rivals, for example how desperate are they for work or would they low-ball on price this time to get a strategic foot-hold in a promising sector which their strategy requires them to target? Some competitor accounting may be possible, for example assessing their likely costs of design teams, specialist equipment, capital and overheads.

What ethical issues may be raised during the process described?

The T4 exam awards 10 marks for analysis and recommendations concerned with ethical issues introduced in the Unseen material on exam day. Several ethical issues may arise during bidding:

- *Collusion with rival bidders*: in April 2008 the UK Office of Fair Trading named 112 construction firms it believed to have colluded in inflating tender process for public sector contracts, at the expense of billions of pounds of UK tax payers money and allegedly with the complicity of the public servants involved. This included all the biggest PPP contractors. Similar practices were discovered in 2009 in Montreal and the problem is believed to be endemic in the sector. Those who admit the practice claim that often it is *cover pricing* ie putting in a high bid that has no chance of being accepted because the contractor is too busy to take on the work at the moment but still wants to be included in the list of bidders to be considered in the future for other projects. This is explicitly included in paragraphs 49-51 of the BZCS Pre-seen material.

- *Collusion with clients*: contractors may form arrangements with staff at the potential client to get a favourable result in return for a commission. This commission looks like a bribe and is paid for the tender list excluding a rival, accepting an inflated price, or drafting a contract that gives the contractor elbow-room to increase charges later.

- *Low-balling:* this would be submitting a very low price at the start in order to exclude rivals and enter negotiations. After this has been done the eventual price will rise. The contractor was being dishonest in its original bid and had no intention of accepting work at that rate.

- *Making use of parallel labour market:* the contractor may price the contract low by relying on the use of low-skilled or informal labour sources. In some countries this involves avoiding paying income taxes and social insurance contributions, whilst in others it can extend to virtual slave labour. In May 2009 Human Right Watch drew attention to collusion between contractors and government agencies to use repressive labour laws in United Arab Emirates to enable gross exploitation of building workers.

- *Misleading commitments in tender:* Appendix 4 and paragraphs 34-41 of the Pre-seen material refer to the CSR commitments of BZCS. These commitments to health and safety, environmental pollution, treatment of staff, energy efficient design and so on are usually essential to winning contacts from clients with similar commitments to CSR. It is possible that the contractor does not have a strong intention of actually following these through.

Para 8 **How might the information in this paragraph be used in the exam?**

Your role in the exam is that of a management accountant working for BZCS. It is quite possible that you might be asked to use additional data provided to calculate the cost impact of a change in construction specification and to make recommendations on the price change to be made to accommodate it.

Para 9 **What is the significance of BZCS being part of a listed company?**

Para 12 tells us that your exam is only concerned with BZCS and not with the whole of its holding company, BeeZed. In para 18 and in Appendix 2 we are told that BZCS is a 100% subsidiary of BeeZed. The Pre-seen material does not provide the information we would require to assess the financial condition of BeeZed as a whole, nor to establish how much of BeeZed's profits and revenues are contributed by BZCS.

The value of a listed company's shares depend on the markets expectations on the amounts and timings of BeeZed's future cash flows.

BZCS depends on BeeZed for its finance. Paragraph 19 also refers to this. Appendix 2 shows that at the end of its 2010 financial year it owed €125m of loans to BeeZed. It appears to pay interest at 5.55% (2010 finance expense of €7.5m on average loans of €135m: €125m+€145m/2).

Winning new contracts will presumably increase the share price providing the markets believe that they will result in a profit to BeeZed as a whole.

If BZCS runs into difficulties with a construction project, such as delays and/or cost overruns, then this can be expected to harm BeeZed's share price and market value. This will add urgency to any steps to turn a project around or to quantify the potential effect on year end profit of a delay or cost over

Paras 10-12 **What potential significance can be attached to the Examiner telling us about the two other divisions of BeeZed if these are not going to be the subject of the exam?**

The Pre-seen makes clear that the case involves only BZCS, the construction and project management part of BeeZed. Several interpretations can be put on this:

- *The Examiner is keeping things simple for you:* the Examiner is focusing you on just construction and project management and not other potential aspects of the business. This will make industry research more simple, and also means that in evaluating projects in the exam you would only need to consider the profits from building the project, and not have to worry about incomes and costs from future management.

- *The Examiner intends to exam you on placing a valuation on BZCS:* by keeping BZCS separate with its own Income Statement and Statement of Financial Position, right down to its own tax rates and cash flows, the Examiner could be setting the scene for an exam day Unseen in which the Board of BeeZed is considering selling-off BZCS, or accepting an offer for it from another construction company, and in which you are required to calculate a range of values for BZCS using net assets, earnings and cash flow methods.

- *The Examiner intends to explore issues of cross-subsidisation and performance evaluation:* para 11 makes clear that PFI contracts are signed by the holding company, BeeZed and then it will agree how revenues (and costs) are divided between BZCS and BZBSS.

    This raises the issues of interface agreements. These agreements are signed between the members of an SPV, here BZCS and BZBSS and, potentially other contractors that have joined. The agreement specifies how revenue and costs will be allocated and who pays for any problems, overruns etc. Even within a holding company structure the MDs of BZCS and BZBSS would have an interest in ensuring as much of the revenue as possible comes to them but as many of the costs go to the other as can be arranged. This would boost the profits of their division and help their bonus and promotion prospects. The value of a hospital project to BeeZed as a whole will be 20+ years of cash flows from construction and into facilities management. Therefore a tender price will contain both parts and there may be a temptation to make little profit on the construction part, but to make it up by having a high facilities management charge. Under this scenario the NPV of the project would be high but it might not be in the interests of the construction division to accept it. This point seems to be alluded to later in para 26.

Similar issues arise when the project specification changes. For example is a change in specification to a hospital results in a greater number of rooms this will increase the costs to the construction division, but increase the revenues of the facilities management division. This raises the question of who should pay for the change: the client or the facilities management division?

Finally if a project goes wrong there are issues of who bears the cost. Suppose the project for the new hospital is running 18 months behind. The client will not be happy and may be entitled to charge penalty fees for not having a hospital. But the facilities management arm may also charge fees connected to its incomes being delayed by 18 months.

Para 13 **What new information is introduced in this paragraph?**

Most of this paragraph emphasises the point already made, that the financial information relates only to BZCS and concerns only revenues and costs from construction activities.

The new information is the reference to the *three critical success factors* for BZCS being its reputation for *quality,* for *safety* and for *delivering projects on time.*

These three critical success factors could be seen as in opposition. For example if a project is running late the project manager may choose to take short-cuts on quality or safety in order to hit the deadline.

Para 14 **How does the balance of business in this paragraph affect our assessment of the likely risks and returns of BZCS?**

At first glance this appears to be a well-diversified portfolio that seeks to secure business in six areas. However there are a number of significant risk factors:

Speculative commercial building: the Office Buildings Division differs from the business described in paragraph 7 because it is involved in speculative construction as well as construction under tender. This means it takes the risk on buying land, gaining planning permissions, building and then selling, or letting, the space. In a recession of the sort affecting 2008-2010 this is a very poor sector to be involved in as firms do not readily take-on new office or business accommodation. These could be assets of falling value that are sitting on the division's accounts and reducing profits through impairment charges and interest costs.

Sophisticated environmental projects: as already mentioned, fixed price tenders for projects with new technologies are a common source of financial loss for construction companies.

Energy projects: gas storage facilities and power stations are projects with high intrinsic risks such as from explosions and leakages. One current and interesting development has been the re-emergence of nuclear energy as a technology and the role of PFI/PPP in this. In Feb 2010 a PFI initiative was announced by the US state of Georgia, in April 2010 Romanian PPP EnergoNuclear sought funding for a second station, and in December 2010 the Philippines government announced it is considering including nuclear power stations within PPP.

It is noticeable that BZCS is not presently involved in house-building, neither for the private sector nor for public housing. This is a high margin but, as recent years have shown, a volatile business. In this BeeZed resembles real-world firms Balfour Beatty, Carillion, de-merged from general builder Tarmac, and Taylor Woodrow. The latter de-merged its housing and civil engineering divisions in 2007 by combining its housing with Wimpy homes to form Taylor Wimpy, leaving the remaining 49% Taylor Woodrow International to become a subsidiary of French construction and facilities giant Vinci.

Para 15 **Does your role in this exam mean you will be reporting to one of these 6 Commercial Directors?**

Appendix 1 shows that the finance function does not report to the Commercial Director of a division. Instead you will probably report to the Finance Director. However paragraphs 26 – 30 tell us that the management accounting function prepares project accounts which are reviewed by the responsible Project Manager and will be presented each month to the Commercial Manager of the appropriate division and, in case of significant problems, to the main BZCS Board. It seems possible that in the exam you may be called on to produce a report to assist the Project Manager present a review of performance or explanation of a problem.

Paragraph 33 confirms that Project Managers are assisted by Finance Department in preparing monthly reports by the end of day 3 after each month end.

In paragraph 55 we are told about Bid Managers, Post Completion Managers, and Sales and Marketing Managers in each division. It is possible that the Examiner may ask you to prepare some documents for one of these.

Paras 16-20   **What new information is introduced in these paragraphs?**

These paragraphs repeat earlier comments about the independence of BZCS and signpost us to the Appendices.

Para 19 stands out for its reference to the holding company, BeeZed, using external bank loans. This is presumably to alert us to the problems of the banking sector potentially spilling-over into the availability of finance for BeeZed. In October 2010 The Bank of England published its quarterly *Trends in Lending* survey which remarked on generally higher lending to business with the exception of lending to construction sector which had fallen £5.7bn in the previous year. The same occurred during 2009 in the USA which led construction firms to turn to private equity finance to raise $12bn to enable them to finish projects.

Paras 21-23   **What might the Examiner have had in mind by including data on geographical analysis of revenues?**

- *To illustrate BZCS's dependence on two geographical regions*: the pie chart shows that the percentages of total revenue accounted for by the four regions were Europe 54.4%, USA 29%, Middle East 8.7% and Rest of World 7.7% (€690:369:110:98/€1,267). The business is very dependent on economies that are undergoing a credit crunch from the banking crisis and from public spending cuts. These have been principally a response to market concerns about the credit-worthiness of government debt in Europe (the so-called *European contagion*) and USA fears of rapidly increasing inflation.

- *To illustrate that a Pie chart can be created in Excel:* in Autumn 2010 CIMA added a Student Support Guide to the T4 section of the CIMA website. This dealt with ways to answer the section (b) requirement of the exam, the requirement for a second document demonstrating effective communication. For the first time in the history of the exam it was suggested that this could require graphs or charts created from data in Excel and attached to a letter or email. The examples provided were of a time-series graph and a histogram, but it seems equally plausible that the Examiner might expect a pie chart and this could be part of a PowerPoint presentation. Given that sitters in May will include candidates sitting the exam using conventional pen-and-paper this suggests that a requirement to use Excel will be reserved for the exam on March 1st where all candidates will be using PCs. *It is recommended that you try to recreate the diagram in paragraph 23 using Excel and ensure you can import it into a Word document.* Also consider how you might use the diagram functions in Excel to display the data in paragraph 25.

Para 25   **How profitable is BZCS? Are its profits sufficient?**

According to the table in paragraph 25 BZCS made an operating profit of €34.7 million in 2010. This same figure appears in Appendix 2 where the Statement of Financial Position reveals capital employed of €434.5mn. Therefore in 2010 BZCS achieved a return on capital employed of 8% (€34.7m/€434.5m), marginally ahead of the 5.5% it pays on its debt (see comments on paragraph 9 above).

The margins vary between the 6 divisions:

Division	Operating margin	Proportion of total revenue	Proportion of total profits
Office Buildings	3.9%	17.4%	24.5%
Sports Facilities	2.3%	11.5%	9.8%
Environmental Projects	2.2%	15.3%	12.1%
Infrastructure Projects	4.6%	28.8%	48.4%
Community Projects	0.6%	16.9%	3.7%
Energy Projects	0.4%	10.3%	1.4%
Total	**2.7%**	**100%**	**100%**

This table indicates:
- The profits of BZCS are heavily dependent on its Infrastructure Projects division
- Two divisions: Community Projects and Energy Projects together account for 27.2% of revenues but only 5.1% of profits. These may be strategic investments at the *Problem Child* stage, or they could be *Dogs*. At present they reduce BZCS's margins and profitability significantly and, without close control over costs, could slip into a loss-making position.
- That overall margins are tight and represent a limited amount of profit for the taking of significant risk. This is something true of the construction sector as a whole.

Given that each division has its own Commercial Director (paragraph 15) these differing financial performances may be a reflection of their managerial performance, or it may be attributable to different levels of competition in each sector of the construction industry.

Para 26 **Does this paragraph have any impact on how we evaluate the 6 divisions of BZCS?**

This paragraph returns us to considering the issue of cross-subsidisation already discussed in relation to paragraphs 10-13 above. As a group BeeZed earns contribution from the facilities management conducted by its BZBBS subsidiary. In quoting for building projects it may decide to instruct BZCS to enter a low quote in order to win the project, and then seek to earn higher profits from the facilities management contract over the next 10 to 30 years. For example the low margins from the Community Projects Division may be compensated for by high returns from maintaining the hospitals, health centres, universities and schools.

Such a cross subsidization may enable group profit maximization, but it could lead to dysfunctional decisions by BZCS based on the analysis of paragraph 25, for example to tender higher prices for Community Projects or even to close the division in order to raise the overall profitability of the BZCS subsidiary.

You may recall this problem from your studies of transfer prices. Potential solutions to this problem include:

- *Substitution of shadow prices:* BeeZed could agree to base evaluation of BZCS and its divisions upon revenues and profits that include an additional book entry for the profits enjoyed on the facilities management contract.

- *Central subsidy:* the Board of BeeZed could agree to provide BZCS with an annual remittance of revenue in recognition of the profit it lost by tendering a low price for the initial construction project.

It should be noted that if BZCS is indulging in cross-subsidisation and using this to charge low prices on construction tenders it could be accused of *predatory pricing*. This refers to the practice of charging deliberately low, sometimes uneconomic, prices in order to force rivals out of the industry and to create a barrier to entry that will allow the successful firm to raise prices later. The practice, if proven to have occurred, is unlawful in many countries and can lead to fines.

In practice it is very hard to prove such a case because contractors will argue that it is merely healthy competition. Also that there is no economic rationale behind it because once the contractors begin to raise prices they will attract competitors back into the market.

For BeeZed to seek to use cross-subsidisation it would need to be sure that it could write long-term and advantageous facilities management contracts. Often the SPV contains the construction contractor, say BZCS, and the facilities management provider, say BZBBS. But the client may seek to separate this by refusing to agree to a facilities management contract that could become excessively expensive later. They may insist on regular break clauses, or that rates be set with reference to external benchmarks.

An internet search reveals that, regrettably, many client bodies, for example local authorities, find it necessary to issue guidelines to staff on how to detect overcharging by facilities management providers, in particular overcharging on staff time and for work that didn't take place.

For example, in November 2009: Surry County Council served notice on one named contractor that it would terminate its road maintenance contracts in 2011 following audits that revealed overcharging of up to £1m in a year and poor workmanship 'In the same year [2006], an audit report criticised "unacceptable standards of workmanship" in Surrey, and an investigation showed one of its road work gangs had only completed 57 minutes of labour in an eight-hour day.

The conclusion seems to be that the level of scrutiny and control exercised over construction bids is not matched by similar scrutiny and control over the ensuing 10 to 30 years of facilities management expenditure and that it is possible for an unscrupulous contractor to pad their earnings later.

Paras 27-30 **Why has the Examiner included this detail on costing and management accounting?**

This exam places you in the role of a management accountant at BZCS. Therefore this is the system that you help to operate and you should be familiar with it.

Project accounting is commonly used in the construction sector. It requires that all invoices and costs be allocated to a unique project number. Similarly any payments received will be allocated to the same project.

What issues are raised by the allocation of non-project based overhead costs?

The allocation of non-project based overheads to the projects affects the operating profits in paragraph 25 (the total operating profit of €34.7m in paragraph 25 also appears in Appendix 2 and so is calculated after deduction of all operating costs). This opens the possibility that the margins of the 6 divisions could be affected by these non-production overheads.

The Pre-seen material doesn't state the amount or nature of these costs. If they are needed in the exam they will be expressly given in the Unseen material on exam day. However we can see that according to Appendix 2 Administrative expenses were €22m in 2010, equivalent to 38.8% of Gross profit. Not all of these would be attributable directly to projects. But its does suggest that the non-project costs are likely to be significant.

Appendix 1 shows that some of these non-project based overhead costs will include finance and IT, procurement, PR and HR.

Suppose one non-project overhead is administrative support from Procurement for tenders and that this is allocated according to number of tenders submitted by the division. If the Energy Projects division has submitted lots of tenders, but has not secured many contracts, this could lead to the low operating margins of the division. This should lead the Commercial Director to question why his division is generating the costs of tenders without enjoying more success.

However treating the overhead costs in this way is only valid if they are *attributable* to the activities of the division, ie that they rise and fall according to how much the division makes use of them. If the administrative costs of BZCS were fixed and not increased by being used for tender preparation then allocating them to a division would invite dysfunctional decision-making. The Commercial Director might decide to prepare less tenders, to avoid the costs, and leave the administrative staff idle but still costing the same, whilst the revenues of the division fall due to lack of new contracts.

This gives rise to three potential dysfunctional effects that could arise from inappropriate treatment of non-project based overheads:

1. *Project pricing errors.* BZCS will seek to recover all its costs from the tenders it wins, either by including them in the fixed price bids or adding them into the costs for the cost-plus awards. If the allocation of non-project overheads is skewed towards a particular division this will increase its costs and hence may make its tenders uncompetitive. At the same time the remaining divisions may escape overheads and not recover them sufficiently from the prices they charge.

2. *Divisional performance evaluation errors.* Divisions that receive the bulk of the non-project overheads will report lower operating profit margins. This may lead to the Commercial Director missing-out on bonuses and promotion and could lead to unnecessary attempts to cut costs or close divisions.

3. *Failure to control non-project overheads.* If an overhead is allocated to a division the Commercial Director may seek to reduce the cost by economising on the division's use of the resources concerned. This is consistent with the principles of good cost management. However if the allocation of overhead is arbitrary, say according to sales turnover, then the Commercial Director cannot take reasonable actions to control it. This means that no-one is controlling the total overhead cost and it may rise each year and reduce the total profit of BZCS.

It should be noted that the organizational structure in Appendix 1 will be effective from January 2011. This means that the allocation of non-project overheads used to derive the table in paragraph 25 will be on a different basis from the way that costs will be allocated by the time of your exam. This may change the margins of the 6 Divisions.

What cost drivers might be used to allocate the non-project based overhead costs?

There is no indication in the Pre-seen case study of how BZCS does this. If it is important in the exam it will be stated explicitly.
The basic principles of Activity Based Costing are:

- Overhead costs should all be assigned to activity pools. In the case of BZCS these pools might include such things as tendering, health and safety assurance, financial control, information services, procurement and so on.

- For each activity pool a cost driver should be identified that bears a close relation to the activities in the pool and hence the costs caused by the activity. Taking the example of the pools above these drivers might be number of tenders, number of sites operated, number of projects and number of purchase orders.

- An overhead allocation rate should be arrived at by dividing the forecast total overhead in each activity pool by the forecast volume of drivers for the coming period

- Overheads should be allocated to division according to number of drivers they generate (eg the number of tenders they issue)

- Overheads can be controlled by divisions making less use of the drivers (eg issuing less purchase orders through buying in larger quantities each time) providing the fall in activity is matched by reductions in resources devoted to the activity (ie some procurement staff will need to be laid-off as the number of purchase orders falls).

Past T4 exams have required candidates to re-calculate costs and returns using new ABC rates and drivers.

What is the potential significance to your examination of the monthly reporting described in paragraph 30?

It seems likely that you may be required to produce a presentation like this on exam day. It is worth noting the types of report detailed in this paragraph and paragraph 28

- Statement of contract revenue and costs to date. This would involve allocation of direct costs and non-project overhead costs discussed above.
- Evaluation of effect of significant operational problems or successes. This seems to be a reference to variance analysis.
- Forecast of contract revenue and costs to end of project – broken down into financial years (ie pre Sept 30th and post Sept 30th) .
- Impact of approved changes on revenues and costs. This would seem to point to revised forecasts and variances.

This presentation would be prepared for the Commercial Director, or perhaps the Project Manager. The Examiner will expect you to make this presentation intelligible to non-accountants and perhaps to include drafts of slides and diagrams developed from Excel.

Para 31   **Is BZCS set for growth in 2011?**

The data given here suggests that the upturn for 2011 predicted in paragraph 1 has come early to BZCS. They have a year-on-year increase in revenues of 30% at September 30th 2010.

It also demonstrates the very long-term nature of contracts and that the profits of BZCS will be slow to recover. Paragraph 47 refers to contract duration often spanning more than 2 years.

This paragraph indicates that BZCS's order book a year earlier, at September 30th 2009, stood at €1,846m (100/130 x €2,400m). But according to paragraph 22 the total revenue for year end 2010 was €1,267m. This is below the order book revenue figure. This is because the order book shows the total value of the projects in hand, whilst the financial accounts show the value that can be attributed to the financial year

Paragraph 48 tells us that in December 2010 BZCS has 14 projects operational or which 10 will be due for completion during 2011 and 4 during the following year. This raises the possibility that that €2,400m referred to in paragraph 31 may be largely the tail of contracts secured in 2008 or 2009 and not a sign of a rush of new contracts. Paragraph 44 seems to refer to increased competition making it harder for BZCS to win new contacts.

In paragraph 28 we are told that monthly management accounts seek to apportion costs and revenues into the relevant financial years.

This should remind us of the provisions of 'IAS 11 – Construction Contracts'. In brief the amount of costs and revenues that can be recorded at year-end for an on-going contract will be assessed using a *percentage of completion method.* This is done in one of two ways

1. *Work certified method*: Work certified to date ÷ total contract price; or
2. *Cost method*: Total costs incurred to date ÷ total contract costs.

Problems occur when trying to use percentage of completion methods for fixed price and cost-plus contracts because to apply the method the accountants must be able to reliably estimate the future costs of the project and the timing to completion in order to be reasonably certain that the benefits will come to the firm.

In the context of the T4 examination this presents the Examiner with an opportunity to assess a number of potential ethical issues relating to your role as a management accountant. BZCS is a division of a listed company, BeeZed. BeeZed will wish to publish financial statements and perhaps also profit forecasts to reassure its investors. On exam day you might find yourself under pressure to flatter financial accounts by:

- not attributing all the costs incurred by the project to the financial accounting period
- not provisioning for remedial work, a cost, that you know needs to be done
- overlooking the late-running of a project to bring more of the projected earnings into the present financial year

Paras 32-33   **How is financial control exercised in BZCS?**

The main financial controls come from the Project Manager, assisted by the Finance function and using the BZPM system. The BZPM system provides three controls:

1. *Process Standardisation*: the system imposes controls on how projects are set up, documented and tracked.
2. *Document control*: it produces standard documents and stores them.
3. *Cost control*: the Pre-seen makes clear that the BZPM generates the backbone of the management accounts.

One limitation of the system seems to be the need for manual intervention to convert the cash-based accounts of the BZPM system to reports based on the accruals conventions used in financial reporting.

Another limitation, which we will return to under paragraph 58, is that BZPM doesn't seem to interface with the work of the new central Procurement Department through providing transparency over the supply chain of BZCS.

What implications may the information in this paragraph have for your exam?

You may be presented with data from the BZPM system and asked to manipulate in to produce a month-end report.

Given that the March 2011 exam takes place on March 1st it seems reasonable to set this as a task ready for a presentation two days later.

Paras 34-42   **How comprehensive is BZCS' commitment to Corporate Social Responsibility?**

Real-world rivals to BZCS all have sections on their websites devoted to CSR commitments.

A benchmark for European contractors like BZCS is the April 2010 report of the European Commission sponsored Building Responsible Competitiveness project Guidelines to Enhance CSR in the Construction Sector.

This report indicates best practice in the following areas:

1. *Health and Safety*

    The report advocates:

    - Training programs for workers to increase awareness and knowledge on health and safety issues, also tailored to immigrant workers speaking different languages
    - Control systems to ensure the application of safety standards, internally and in the supply chain
    - Use of cutting-edge and safer equipment
    - Improve employees health by physical activities and warm-up exercises
    - Increased transparency and control along the supply chain
    - Develop partnerships with external consultants and local experts to assess and intensify necessary actions in the field of health and safety
    - Use of healthy building materials

2. *Eco-compatibility*

    The main focuses here are on reduction of CO_2 emissions from the supply chain and the buildings, noise reduction, avoidance of waste and creating aesthetically appropriate buildings. It notes that 40% of EU energy consumption is attributable to buildings. It is clear that the construction industry is principally being asked to make better buildings more than just act in a socially-responsible manner in how it sets about building them.

    The report recommends:

    - Eco-compatible conception of buildings (green buildings)
    - Sustainable management of construction processes and materials life-cycles to optimize resource-efficiency, waste management, transport etc.
    - Implementation of environmental and sustainability management system standards into the supply chain
    - Stakeholder engagement with regards to the adoption of sustainable practices during the working process (use of equipment etc.)
    - Research and Development investments

3. *Responsible supply-chain management*

    The report points out that CSR cannot be limited to the boundaries of the construction firm alone. This is because construction is a uniquely networked industry through sub-contracting, extended supply chains and so on.

    The report urges:

    - Responsible selection of suppliers via a set of specific CSR criteria and correspondent implementation mechanisms
    - Monitoring and evaluation systems for suppliers
    - Awareness-raising and proactive supplier engagement on the promotion of socially responsible behaviour
    - Limitation to the number of sub-contractors.

4. *Equal opportunities*

This applies to the workforces of the contractors and the need for appropriate recognition of the need for balanced participation across both genders, and all relevant ethnic groups
The report recommends

- Integration of equal opportunity policies into the company's organizational principles and internal governance (action plan, code of conduct, trainings for human resources managers)
- Tools for work - family life balance via supporting structures and facilitations (flexible working hours, reintegration after maternity/paternity leave via training, financial contributions)

The policies of BZCS seems to cover all areas in the guidelines and reiterated in the *BZCS's Mission Statement and CSR Initiatives* at Appendix 4.

Will CSR benefit the business of BZCS?

Four types of argument are advanced for firms adopting policies on CSR:

1. *Moral obligation*: firms are corporate citizens and, like all citizens, should do the right thing and be a good neighbour;
   Sustainability: business has stewardship over the assets of the World and must ensure these are preserved and available, as far as possible, for the benefits of future generations;

2. *License to operate*: all firms require the permissions of governments and regulators to carry on business. Not fulfilling CSR obligations endangers this and may lead to withdrawal of licenses or the imposition of conditions that will be hard to comply with;

3. *Reputation:* the image and brand of the business will be strengthened by having good CSR credentials and this will win business and investment.

It seems likely that BZCS will benefit most under the License to Operate and Reputation arguments.

Para 43 **Does having a separate Bid Manager and Project Manager raise any control issues for BZCS?**

The skills needed to manage bids and to manage projects may be different and it will make sense for BZCS to separate them.

However this leaves two potential issues for BZCS:

1. *Do bids accurately reflect the likely costs of the project?* It will be necessary for the Project Manager, or the finance team advising the Project Manager, to ensure that the best and most up-to-date estimates of rates and times are provided to the bid team.

2. *Do Bid Managers suffer a conflict of interest?* Bid Managers will presumably seek to win contracts and may be offered incentives such as bonuses based on the number and value if bids. Given that they rarely have responsibility for ensuring the project comes in on time and within budget this may tempt them to submit unrealistic tenders which then cannot be finished on time or within budget.

Para 44	**What implications would failing to gain government contracts have for BZCS?**
	The analysis of the table in paragraph 25 shows that the majority of BZCS' profits come from this sector. This is due to the high margins available.
Paras 45-46	**Has BZCS spread its risks effectively?**
	The statement in paragraph seems to suggest a diverse client portfolio. However the range of contract values described in paragraph 47 could mean that a larger range of clients is still consistent with a large reliance on a few key clients, or a particular sector.
	The table in paragraph 25 demonstrates that BZCS is still heavily reliant on its Infrastructure Projects division which, paragraph 14 tells us, is road building and airports. These are likely to be projects for the government and hence reliant on government budgets.
	The reference to the London 2012 Olympic Games may remind us of the risk attached to time-critical projects. The embarrassment of overruns on projects including the Wembley Stadium and the late completion of the athletes village for the 2010 Commonwealth Games in Dehli underline this concern.
	This said a report by the UK National Audit Office in February 2010 stated that 'the Venues and infrastructure for the 2012 London Olympic and Paralympic Games are on track to be delivered on time for the Games and the cost is currently forecast to be within the £9,325 million budget for the Games announced in March 2007'.
Paras 47-48	**Does BZCS have sufficient new contracts to sustain its business?**
	Paragraph 47 tells us that BZCS normally has 12-20 projects in hand in progress at a time. Paragraph 48 tells us it presently has 14 projects and that 10 will be complete within a year.
	Making the simplifying assumption that all projects take 2 years this means that tenders in 2009 generated 10 contracts for BZCS but that in 2010 it generated only 4. This suggests that BZCS may face a sharp downturn in its monthly revenues as 2011 progresses and projects are finished unless the remaining 4 contracts are substantially bigger then average or that there are plenty of new contracts for BZCS to begin.
Paras 49-51	**What may the impacts of the OFT investigation be on BZCS and its industry?**
	The OFT has the power to fine a firm up to 10% of its global turnover if it is found to have contravened competition laws.
	In September 2009 the OFT levied fines totaling £129.5m on 103 construction firms found guilty of illegal bid-rigging. The largest fines were as follows:

Firm	Fine
Kier Group plc	£17,894,438
Interserve plc	£11,634,750
Try, Accord and Galliford	£8,333,329
Ballast Nedham	£8,333,116
Bowmer and Kirkland	£7,574,736
Concentra Ltd	£6,720,551
John Sisk and Son	£6,191,627
Connaught Partnerships	£5,568,868
Carillion JM Ltd (after 45% leniency)	£5,375,689
Balfour Beatty (after 50% leniency)	£5,197,004
Pearce Construction	£5,188,846

According to the OFT Press Release

The OFT has concluded that the firms engaged in illegal anti-competitive bid-rigging activities on 199 tenders from 2000 to 2006, mostly in the form of 'cover pricing'.

Cover pricing is where one or more bidders in a tender process obtains an artificially high price from a competitor. Such cover bids are priced so as not to win the contract but are submitted as genuine bids, which gives a misleading impression to clients as to the real extent of competition. This distorts the tender process and makes it less likely that other potentially cheaper firms are invited to tender.

In 11 tendering rounds, the lowest bidder faced no genuine competition because all other bids were cover bids, leading to an even greater risk that the client may have unknowingly paid a higher price.

The OFT also found six instances where successful bidders had paid an agreed sum of money to the unsuccessful bidder (known as a 'compensation payment'). These payments of between £2,500 and £60,000 were facilitated by the raising of false invoices.

The infringements affected building projects across England worth in excess of £200 million including schools, universities hospitals, and numerous private projects from the construction of apartment blocks to housing refurbishments.

Eighty-six out of the 103 firms received reductions in their penalties because they admitted their involvement in cover pricing prior to today's decision.

According to its powers the OFT could levy a fine of up to €126m from BZCS (10% x €1,267m turnover). According to paragraph 50 BZCS admitted collusion over one successful bid and expects leniency.

However the management of BZCS does not seem to fully appreciate the nature of the OFT's interest. It will not levy the fine solely in respect of the bid in which BZCS was successful. If BZCS had submitted cover prices, and received compensations payments, to assist other contractors to win other bids then this too is a distortion of competition, illegal, and will be taken into consideration when setting a fine.

It could also be noted that the compensation payments involved raising false invoices which is a fraud and lay attract the attention of the taxation authorities.

Having been found guilty of cover pricing may not exclude BZCS from tendering for further contracts. The OFT, in its Press Release of 2009, included the following statement:

Related guidance issued today by the OFT in conjunction with the Office of Government Commerce cautions procurers against excluding the infringing firms from future tenders, as the practice of cover pricing was widespread in the construction industry and those that have already faced investigation can now be expected to be particularly aware of the competition rules.

In effect it says that these firms will have learned their lesson and will not infringe the rules again.

One approach available to BZCS is to manage the public relations and investor fall-out and to implement improvements. The highest-fined firm, Kier, responded to the OFT fines in the following terms

Kier Regional Limited has now been found by the OFT to have breached the Competition Act 1998 in respect of three tenders between 2001 and 2005. As a result, the OFT has fined Kier £17.9m (calculated by reference to its worldwide group turnover). At no point has the OFT alleged or found that Kier paid or received any compensation payments.

Kier is totally committed to ensuring that the practice of cover pricing and anti-competitive behaviour more generally is totally driven out of the construction industry and we have been leading the drive by the UK Contractors Group (UKCG) to ensure that a new industry wide code of conduct governing competitive behaviour is implemented.

Kier has strengthened its processes and procedures through a comprehensive programme of internal and external audit and training, so as to ensure that anti-competitive practices do not occur anywhere in the Group.

Source: Kier Press Release 22.9.09

In August 2009 the UK Contractors Group (which has 20 members drawn from the largest contractors) and the National Federation of Builders jointly launched a code of conduct on how members should comply with the UK competition laws.

On the same day as OFT announced its fines in the UK the Australian Competition and Consumer Commission (ACCC) accused three construction companies of price fixing and deceptive conduct in tendering for government construction projects in Queensland.

Para 52 **What will be the effect on the costs, profits and CSR of BZCS making greater use of subcontractors?**

Greater use of subcontractors will reduce the fixed costs of BZCS by making them into variable costs. If there are fewer or less valuable contracts in future it means that BZCS will not need to pay staff to stand idle.

Sub-contracting may create problems for the assurance of CSR (quality, safety, equality etc) because the control of this lies with the subcontractors. Paragraph 52 does not suggest that BZCS has taken on additional staff to monitor supply chain compliance. In fact paragraphs 56 – 58 suggests there is no supply-chain management function in BZCS, merely procurement.

This raises potential for an examination featuring breakdowns in CSR at BZCS and a question mark over the sincerity of its commitment to the undertakings in Appendix 4.

Para 53 **What are the implications for the marketing activities if BZCS of seeking more private sector contracts?**

Marketing and sales will need to focus on making relationships with new sorts of clients. Public sector contracts will be awarded by central or local government departments and will require a transparent bidding process. For example in the UK the Office of Government Commerce (part of the UK Treasury) has laid down detailed procedures and scoring checklists that public bodies must adhere to when awarding contracts. All European public sector contracts above a financial threshold must be advertised in the Official Journal of the European Union (www.ojeu.com) a daily e-publication that gives access to a portal that describes tenders.

Private sector contracts will be awarded by diverse organizations and the tendering process will vary. Contract leads are often published in trade magazines such as Construction News and are based on announcements of tenders, planning applications, and contract invitations. There are also portals available, such as www.tendersdirect.co.uk. However BZCS will wish to form relationships with *referral markets* such as the practices of architects, quantity surveying and specialist contractors.

Para 54 **What may be the reasons for the Examiner setting January 1st 2011 as the date for the new structure to come into effect?**

This date enables the Examiner to provide up-dates on the effects in the Unseen material on exam day in March or May. You should not be surprised to be confronted with:

- Difficulties in making the new structure work
- Significantly different financial information on costs and revenues of each division
- A requirement to calculate ways of allocating the costs of these new functions to the different projects and divisions (recalling paragraph 27 where we are told ABC is used to allocate non-project overhead costs)

Para 55 **How many Project Managers did BZCS need at the end of 2010?**

According to paragraph 48, BZCS had 14 live projects at the end of December 2010. Therefore it needed 14 Project Managers.

Paras 56-58 **What benefits will BZCS expect to get from centralised procurement?**

The benefits are likely to be

- better control over purchases (eg quality, price, cash flow and credit and financial control over authorization and avoidance of defalcations of money or materials)
- higher bulk discounts
- better CSR compliance by using only approved suppliers that have good policies and procedures in place.

Recalling your earlier studies of purchasing in *E1 Enterprise Operations* (formerly *P4 Organisational Management and Information Systems*) it can be seen that BZCS seems to be at a relatively low stage on the *Strategic Positioning Tool* of Reck and Long. This model suggested that the maturity of the purchasing and supply-chain management (PSM) of a firm can be gauged on a four-stage scale of Passive, Independent, Supportive and Integrative. BZCS seems to have made the transition from Passive to Independent by centralising purchasing in 2011. The main justification seems to have been cost-savings (para 58).

To gain greater maturity this would need to evolve into a fuller strategic role by offering greater *Support* (say by using supply chain management to help streamline operations on site and to discharge CSR objectives) and then to *Integration*, for example by giving BZCS access to leading edge contractors or enabling it to position itself distinctively in a sector of the market.

One issue to consider is the carbon impact if BZCS decides to buy materials from a distant supplier in order to obtain a better price, but then ships the material a long distance to site.

What difficulties may BZCS experience from centralised procurement?

It is likely that BZCS will suffer teething troubles by switching so quickly to centralised purchasing. These may come to light in the exam-day Unseen material.

The difficulties are likely to revolve around:

- *Inflexibility of supply*: for example Project Managers not being able to rely on using the precise materials they are familiar with. This could lead to increased remedial work due to faulty installations and so on
- *Delays in obtaining delivery*. This may result from failures to plan ahead, or disruption to supply chains where previously materials would have been obtained locally.
- *Wrong specifications of material*. The Project Manager will know what they require but adding in a central purchasing function opens the chance for the wrong thing to be ordered

- *Increased costs of monitoring supply-chain*. The BZPM system described in paragraph 32 doesn't seem to have a facility for making the supply-chain transparent. It allows Project Managers to input data and progress but doesn't seem to be an extranet solution that will allow suppliers and transport contractors to update it with the whereabouts of the supplies that the project manager is relying on.

A further problem may be the inability of local contracts to make use of local suppliers. Appendix 4 contains commitments such as 'increasing the use of locally sourced resources' and 'investing in the communities in which we operate'. Centralised procurement can still place orders with suppliers local to the construction site, but there will be a tendency for procurement to stick with familiar suppliers, especially if they are trying to simplify supply chains and gain bulk discounts.

BZCS also needs to consider whether it would be more likely to win contracts if it committed to using local suppliers. In granting planning permission and funding public bodies frequently undertake a cost-benefit analysis of the project that will consider the indirect benefits of the project such as the impact on local employment and incomes of the construction phase.

How could the role of the Procurement Department be improved?

The new centralised function seems to fall short of the Integrative role advocated by Reck and Long. This can be underlined by considering Cousins' *Strategic Supply Wheel*.

Cousins characterizes the relationship of a firm like BZCS to its suppliers as being on a scale between *opportunistic* (ie bargaining to take short-term advantage of suppliers and to get low prices) and *collaborative* (ie a longer term relationship featuring mutual trust and commitment and joint problem solving). Cousins says that a range of *relationship concepts* denote the relationship of BZCS to its suppliers. These are organisational structure, portfolio of relationships, cost-benefit analysis, skills and competences, and performance measures.

One area of the Pre-seen in which there is evidence of a lack of integration is at paragraphs 32 -33 where the BZPM project management system is described. There is no clear indication that the Procurement Department is integrated within this system. Indeed Appendix 1 shows BZCS's IT Manager reporting to the Finance Director. This would seem to imply that the main purpose of systems like BZPM is financial control rather that supporting operations. It is also an entirely internal system and is not visible to suppliers.

In the short run, as a minimum, BZPM should provide transparency on order status. Project Managers will wish to be able to view the status of the orders for materials they are depending upon because centralised procurement means they can no-longer be sure the order has been placed and are no longer in a position to call up the supplier and quote order numbers. Achieving such transparency would require some *process improvements* to be made.

In the longer-run proper integration might be better achieved by *Business Process Re-engineering*. The Procurement Department could be replaces by full e-procurement under which the project details and progress entered in BZPM could be configured as an extranet solution available to designated suppliers, and used to trigger orders, synchronise deliveries to the location and time when they are needed, and monitor and log the supply-chain transactions and supplier performance.

Useful free resources on improving business integration in construction are provided by Constructing Excellence (www.constructingexcellence.org.uk)

Appendix 1 **Why has the case writer introduced these changes from January 1ˢᵗ 2011?**

These changes may give rise to issues that arise in the Unseen material on exam day:

New overhead cost allocations

- Managers for whom you may be asked to prepare reports
- Requirements for suggestions of improvements to resolve issues that have arisen.

What further improvements could be made to this new organisational structure?

Improvement could include

- Promotion of the IT Manager to IT Director: IS/IT has a strategic role in BZCS if it were used for supply chain integration. This could include linking the BZPM system to an extranet solution to improve communication with suppliers and sub-contractors. It could also be used to automatically conduct financial transactions. By leaving the IT Manager reporting to the Financial Director BZCS runs the risk of IS/IT being limited to being an aspect of financial control and also takes away the potential seniority of the Information Management function.

- BZCS will need to be able to adopt a client as well as a project focus. Under the new structure they are attached to the type of project. However the client of an Infrastructure Project, say a local branch of public administration, might also be the client for a Community Project. Projects may also overlap, for example building a new business park (Office Buildings Division) may be part of a town plan that also requires roads and drainage (Infrastructure and Environmental Project Divisions) and possibly some social facilities (Community Projects Division) A client may expect to enjoy a consistency of service and not to be passed between various Sales & Marketing Managers and Project Managers. This implies some element of a matrix structure may need to evolve to cope with common projects and clients.

- Upgrade the role of the Procurement Director to one that involves a responsibility of the supply chain as a whole.

2.1 Summary of key points from pre-seen information

A key skill in this exam is being able to extract the important information from the data you are given. Here are the key points from the BZCS construction case Pre-seen material:

The business environment of BZCS

The Pre-seen material refers to the depressed state of the construction industry (para 1), the increased competitive pressure this brings and the tightening-up of selection criteria (para 44), and the potential fall-out from investigations into price-fixing in the industry (paras 49-51). This means that work will be harder to find and is likely to be less profitable.

The T4 (TOPCIMA) examination is a real world exam and you are required to research some information about the real environment.

The credit crunch: many commercial banks have been bailed out by governments and international monetary authorities partly as a consequence of their previous lending to property development firms that left the banks holding un-saleable properties and bad loans. Bank lending is low and banks are suspicious of lending for property development.

Structural deficit reduction: many European governments have austerity budgets to reduce the size of their national debts. This is because banks have been expressing doubts about the credit-worthiness of the bonds and bills issued by some governments. This will reduce spending by states on construction.

Recession: reduced private sector investment and government expenditure threaten a downward multiplier effect on demand in economies leading to rising unemployment and further reductions in investment. This will particularly hit the construction sector. The effect will come through slowly because some large projects have already started and will provide work for several more years, but there will be an immediate impact on new contracts as less receive funding and come up for tender. However the recovery may also be slower in the construction sector.

Financial performance of BZCS

BZCS is a wholly-owned subsidiary of BeeZed. The overall Return on Capital Employed of BZCS is about 11% (Appendix 2: Operating profit/Capital employed €34.7m/€186 + 125). However without having statements of financial position for its 6 divisions it is not possible to confirm that each division is contributing to shareholder wealth.

Para 23 demonstrates that BZCS is strongly reliant on Europe and USA for its revenues (shares of total revenue: Europe 54%, USA 29%). This suggests that despite having many projects around the world (para 13) the most valuable ones are in Europe and USA. Para 48 states that BZCS has 14 projects in progress at 31st December 2010.

Para 25 details the revenues and operating profits of the six Commercial Divisions of BZCS. This data can be evaluated as follows:

Division	Operating margin %	Proportion of total revenue	Proportion of total profits
Office Buildings	3.9%	17.4%	24.5%
Sports Facilities	2.3%	11.5%	9.8%
Environmental Projects	2.2%	15.2%	12.1%
Infrastructure Projects	4.6%	28.8%	48.4%
Community Projects	0.6%	16.9%	3.8%
Energy Projects	0.4%	10.2%	1.4%
Total	**2.7%**	**100%**	**100%**

This demonstrates the following things:

BZCS's profits depend on Infrastructure Projects (48.4% of total) and Office Buildings (24.5%) Divisions. These sectors of the market are potentially under threat from the present economic environment of BZCS. Infrastructure includes roads and airports and these usually require state funding. State funding is being cut across Europe as governments struggle to reduce their borrowing. Office building requires a buoyant economy and is likely to be a depressed market in the wake of the global financial crisis.

Several divisions are barely profitable: Community Projects and Energy Projects account for 27.1% of revenues but only 5.2% of profits. The former includes health and schools and the latter includes power stations. In times of reduced government spending and recession the markets will become very competitive and margins could be squeezed further.

Future performance of BZCS

Interpretation of the financial information for BZCS is complicated by several factors:

Backward looking: financial reporting information is always historic. With BZCS an additional point is that because contracts last several years the level of revenues and profits in 2010 are largely a result of tender wins from 2007 and 2008. Para 48 tells us that BZCS has 14 live contracts at the start of 2011 of which 10 will be completed by the end of the year. The order book detailed in para 31 includes the remaining revenue to be received from these 14 contracts and so the 30% improvement over September 2009 is not necessarily a lead indicator of BZCS's future growth, but rather a lagging indicator of good contract winning performance several years ago.

Sharing of project returns: paras 11, 13 and 26 state that other subsidiaries of BeeZed (the holding company) get benefit from the projects that BZCS builds. This could mean that BZCS will be encouraged to provide a low price for a tender to win the tender and therefore make a low profit, and its sister company will make a high profit from resulting management and maintenance work.

Future liabilities: para 28 refers to monthly allocation of revenues and costs to projects. However unlike a shop, which will have sales revenues to record each month, the revenues of a construction project are infrequent and may be paid in stages, as each phase is completed and signed-off, or will be paid at the end. During the intervening months the management accountant will estimate revenues on the basis of the percentage of the project (or phase) that has been completed and pro-rate the revenue accordingly. If unforeseen problems arise that will delay the project, or increase costs, then the previous statements of profits will have been too high.

Management accounting issues facing BZCS

In the exam room you will be required to take the role of a management accountant working for BZCS. This means you will probably be asked to comment on, and make recommendations about, management accounting issues.

The management accounting issues in this Pre-seen are:

- **The need to assist with preparing monthly reports:** these are referred to in para 30. Reports are presented to the Commercial Director of the division by the Project Managers. Sometimes they are presented to BZCS Board. Para 33 states that the Finance Department assists them in this. Each Project Manager has a single project to look after (para 55). Paras 28 and 32 state this month-end report compares actual costs (including accruals) against budget, and forecasts against budget, and para 30 tells us that the non-financial elements of this report will include safety issues, for example those referred to in para 38.

  The examiner could ask you to prepare the financial elements of a month-end report, such as calculating costs and variances from data. This could be extended to include indicators on safety performance. A second requirement could be to produce a draft of slides, or some briefing notes and diagrams, to assist the Project Manager to deliver this report and to explain the assumptions, variances, and their implications.

- **Allocation of non-project based overhead costs:** para 27 describes direct cost allocation to projects under a project costing system but states that non-project based overhead costs are allocated using Activity Based Costing techniques (ABC). Appendix 1 and paras 52-58 describe a new organisational structure that has come into effect on 1st January 2011. This indicates that non-project overhead costs will include the costs of providing the functions controlled by the Finance Director, Procurement Director, Public Relations and Marketing Director, and Human Resources Director, and within each Division, the costs of the Post Completion Manager (*note:* Appendix 1 specifically states that the Project, Bid and Sales Managers are specific to projects, but does not state this for the Post Completion Manager, while para 55 refers to a single Post Completion Manager within each division having responsibility for all projects).

  This raises a number of potential issues that could feature in the Unseen material on exam day:

  Recalculation of project or divisional profits using new cost data: para 25 shows divisional profit to 30th September 2010. This would have been based on cost accounting under the former structure of BZCS and not the new structure from 1st January 2011. Presumably the forecasts for existing projects at 30th September 2010 were based on the former cost centres too. In the examination your Unseen material could contain new cost driver data and you might be required to assess the profitability of the project, or division, using the new data.

  Identifying the right drivers for each cost: para 27 refers to 'appropriate cost drivers' but doesn't state what these are. Given that the restructuring is recent, these drivers may not have been decided yet. Procurement costs could be driven by number of orders, diversity of inputs used, and number of suppliers. Finance overheads could be driven by time spent preparing reports for each Project Manager. Human resource management costs are typically allocated according to number of staff members, but also might have an element of time for situations where a project or division has protracted issues;

  Commenting on the appropriateness of the cost drivers: the uses and effects of the new cost drivers could be open to criticism from you. Project Managers and Commercial Directors will wish to avoid incurring costs. For example Project Managers may try to conduct more purchasing themselves to avoid central procurement costs (para 57 says they can do this providing they order things for which no global contract has been negotiated), or use sub-contractors rather than employees to avoid human resource overheads;

Impacts of overhead allocation on cost management: the point of ABC is not just *cost allocation* (ie a tidying-up exercise that seeks to put the cost somewhere) but also *cost attribution* (ie identifying and therefore controlling the things that cause the cost). If the cost drivers are correctly chosen then ABC can be an effective cost control technique. For example imagine Project Managers are poorly organised and as a consequence generate lots of small, last minute orders. This will increase costs in the Procurement Department through needing more staff (and desks, PCs, office space etc) and increasing overtime payments. By charging this overhead to Project Managers on the basis of number of orders (perhaps with a penalty rate for last minute orders) it will encourage the Project Managers to consolidate requirements into a smaller number of large orders. This can reduce the costs of procurement *providing BZCS is then willing to reduce the size of its Procurement Department*. If BZCS doesn't reduce the size (and therefore costs) of the department as order numbers fall then all that will happen is the activity cost per order will rise as the same overhead is divided by a smaller number of orders and ABC will have achieved nothing.

Relevance of overheads to project assessment: allocating overheads to projects reduces the return from those projects or, when bidding for work, increases the price of the tender. If these costs include non-relevant costs (ie do not lead to additional cash flows as a consequence of the project) then strictly speaking they should not be used for pricing decisions nor for accepting or rejecting contracts. If it's proved that the project makes a contribution (ie revenue in excess of variable costs) then it should be undertaken because the contribution helps pay some of the overheads. In the long run BZCS could not stay in business when the revenue from every project covered is just the variable costs but not the overheads because it would be loss making. But in the short run, if work is scarce, profits would be reduced by turning down projects with contributions that didn't cover overheads, or by losing tenders through trying to price tenders high enough to cover overheads. This issue was specifically included in the September 2010 T4 examination.

- **Budgeting for changes:** changes to project specifications and the need to assess the costs of changes is referred to in paras 8, 28, and 32. These changes come from client requests and with additional data provided in the Unseen material on exam day, could form the basis of a requirement.

- **Fixed price contracts:** para 4 describes these. The effect of fixed price is to transfer the project risks from the client to the contractor. If the contractor can reduce costs below the original budget it gains extra profit, but if costs rise above forecast they must bear the losses. The costs of building a standard accommodation block for a hospital or a health centre may be more certain because the contractor has data from similar past projects to base quotes on. But in the real world complex contracts include building roads and bridges over new terrain, tunnelling, sports stadiums with complex roofing, and office blocks of radical design. In some well-publicised cases, contractors have lost money from fixed price contracts and then taken legal action against subcontractors for non-performance, and against the client or designers for withholding critical information at the time the tender was constructed, or not giving promised access or other assistance to the project.

Management issues facing BZCS

- **Need to win contracts:** para 31 states BZCS's order book is 30% up year on year but para 1 states that any upturn in work in the sector is not expected until the start of 2011. This does not mean that BZCS is ahead of the wave of new orders. Rather it can be explained by the fact that the order book measures revenue. This includes the value of work remaining from existing contracts. Para 48 states that by the end of 2010 BZCS has 14 contracts in progress of which 10 will end within a year. 14 contracts is below average for BZCS, which, according to para 47, usually has 12 to 20 contracts (average 16 contracts). Para 44 implies that BZCS may find it harder to win contracts due to tighter selection criteria threatening its 'preferred supplier status' with European governments. The restructuring detailed in paras 52 – 58 may have been undertaken to insulate BZCS from a downturn in business through cutting its costs of purchases and shifting its fixed costs out to sub-contractors. But it still needs profitable contracts to cover the costs of its remaining 10,100 employees, and other costs such as the €7.5m of finance costs, and the €88m of depreciation (Appendix 3) if it is to avoid falling into losses.

- **Corporate Social Responsibility:** Appendix 4 and paras 34 – 41 detail BZCS's commitments to CSR. Health and safety is a top priority, but so are environmental issues such as waste management (para 40) and low emissions buildings (para 41). Real world construction firms often add CSR objectives relating to workforce fair pay and diversity (particularly improving the participation by women in a traditionally masculine industry) and responsibility to the communities in which they build. These are briefly covered in Appendix 4. It is very likely that CSR compliance is amongst the strict criteria insisted on by clients (para 44). Having promised these things to clients it must deliver on them. Some CSR will have direct financial benefits, such as reduced transport costs, fewer claims for industrial injury, less disruption to projects from safety problems and so on. But in a tighter commercial environment the Bid Managers may promise CSR performance to win contracts on which the Project Manager will seek to cut corners later. One specific problem here is the use of sub-contractors. They may be selected on grounds of cost and without proper consideration for their CSR credentials. It is noticeable that BZCS doesn't seem to have any senior manager with responsibility for CSR. Another potential problem is the drawing up of lists of 'preferred suppliers' by the Procurement Department (para 58) which, it seems, is mainly driven by the need to cut costs. This may be too narrow a focus to also deliver CSR.

- **Managing its new supply-chain:** the restructuring has created a central Procurement Department to replace direct ordering from site by Project Managers. This has been justified on the grounds of cost reductions (para 57) and something described as 'better control over purchases' (para 57). This might refer to quality assurance and ability to audit supplier performance. It might equally imply avoidance of fraud by Project Managers and their teams. But BZCS seems to have an immature approach to purchasing and supply based on cost minimisation. Mature approaches would consider supply-chain integration with small numbers of suppliers being selected on the basis of their ability to deliver on time, quality, collaboration, and, to a lesser extent, cost. One particular sign of this immaturity of BZCS is in the discussion of its project management system BZPM (paras 32-33). BZPM seems to be an accounting system that draws data down from work planning and scheduling. There is no mention of BZPM showing the status of orders and deliveries, still less an extranet that would allow suppliers and sub-contractors to monitor progress and likely demands, to synchronise deliveries and to manage the performance of their work teams. In reality BZCS may find the costs it saves by central procurement will be lost again through Project Managers chasing orders, deliveries and work teams, and through delays to work resulting from muddle. Delays will also cost BZCS revenue as on-time projects are critical success factors for winning future business (para 13). Some system development of the BZPM system may be necessary. Given that BZCS's IT Manager reports to the Financial Director, you may be requested to comment on the value of such improvements.

- **Change management:** the restructuring described in paras 52-58 and Appendix 1 is very recent although it seems to have taken place in two stages. The move to sub-contracting took place in 2009 and early 2010 whilst the move to central procurement is more recent. These are therefore at different stages in the change process with sub-contracting needing to re-freeze (Lewin) whilst procurement is still between unfreezing and change. It is not clear whether the remaining structure of Bid Managers, Sales and Marketing Managers and Project Managers in para 55 is a recent change. It seems more likely that further change is needed because the divisional structure deals with common clients and issues separately in each division. A given public client might well want office buildings, roads and energy projects and expect a joined-up service from BZCS rather than to be passed between, or quarrelled over by, different Commercial Directors. Similarly knowledge on bids, technologies, supplier performance and energy conservation should be shared. The divisional silos of BZCS may not encourage this.

- **Managing the outcome of the bid tendering investigation**: the material in paras 49 – 51 is based on a real enquiry by the UK's Office of Fair Trading in 2009 that uncovered pricing collusion between 103 contractors when tendering for public sector (state) contracts. The outcome was fines of up to £17m per contractor and a response by the industry to restore confidence by establishing a code of ethics and guidelines on how to stay within the competition laws in the future. But collusion is rife in the culture of the construction industry, as the OFT recognised. BZCS must brace itself for a fine. This fine will not be based in the value of the single UK hospital contract it won, but on the effect of its collusion on every contract that may have led to the winning bidder receiving an inflated fee due to the lack of real competition. It must also have an internal response available to ensure it can show that it has taken steps to stop Bid Managers and others from continuing this practice. Its Public Relations and Marketing Director (Appendix 1) will need to have words of apology and assurances ready to give the media and the clients it hopes to win tenders from in the future.

2.2 Looking ahead

The Examiner has built some themes into this Pre-seen that could be developed and examined as issues in the Unseen materials. However, you should not necessarily expect to see them in the unseen material, and you should *never* try to question spot issues fir the T4 (TOPCIMA) un-seen case study.

Remember, your role is as a management accountant in BZCS. You are more likely to be required to carry out calculations and make practical recommendations on highlighted issues than to be asked to produce fresh strategies for BZCS.

Tender price for a new contract

The Unseen may provide details of a new building or contract, including some rates and prices for inputs and work. You may be required to evaluate the project and suggest a tender price using the data given but also making appropriate comments on potential risks, the availability of finance, and the value of having some understanding of the likely tender prices of rivals based on an arm's-length understanding of their past bids, costs and strategic objectives. Avoidance of collusion could form the basis of an ethical aspect to this.

Calculation of overruns and recommend how to deal with them

You could be given data on standard times, quantities and rates for the project and also the actual times, quantities and rates. You may have to calculate variances and to identify ways to bring the project back on budget.

Month end report on a project

You could be given financial data to time apportion into the month (and/or year end) and be required to prepare a month end analysis and a forecast to year end. This could include commentary and also an additional requirement that you structure it as a presentation suitable for use in a teleconference.

Variation to a contract

Clients can change contracts but must pay the extra costs involved. You could be asked to calculate the extra costs. An additional requirement might be to put this in a letter, email or presentation suitable for someone to take to the client.

Ethical issues

Possible ethical issues, to be discussed in Section 5 of your answer, include maintaining CSR through the supply chain, dealing with problems on projects where there is a trade-off between CSR or honesty and profit, or dealing with collusion. An interesting and relevant twist here might include your obligations as a Chartered Management Accountant. You may be asked to be involved in something unethical or become aware of such a thing. You may have to consider when and how you should whistle-blow.

Exam skills

Now you have worked through the detail of the case, take time to think what the most important information is from the data you have been given.

Make a summary of the key points from the Pre-seen material. Can you summarise the key points and issues facing BZCS into a one-page business summary?

Also, make sure you undertake an overall strategic analysis of the pre-seen material. You should always prepare a SWOT analysis, and a stakeholder analysis as part of your preparation, but the material in this case suggests internal issues like project management or organisational structure could also be important so you need to take account of these as well.

Remember it is vital you analyse all the different aspects of the information you are given in the case study scenario:

Analyse the numbers – Review any numerical and financial data (profitability, cashflow, working capital, liquidity, gearing, investment ratios)

Environmental analysis – PESTEL analysis; stakeholders (Mendelow's matrix)

Business environment and competitive strategy – Type of industry (product / industry life cycle); Five forces; generic strategies. What do you know about key customers and suppliers? What do you know about the business' marketing strategy?

> Does your analysis of these aspects of the business identify any potential **opportunities** and **threats**?

Products and services – Product range, features, quality, demand; Product portfolio

Value – How does the business add value? Value chain; distinctive competencies.

Information systems and processes – How is IT used in the business strategy; how does the business use e-commerce; what do you know about the business' IT systems? Does the IT set up present any business or security risks?

Management information and control systems – How are activities and resources controlled? What do you know about the management accounting or management information systems?

Performance measures – Have you identified the critical success factors and / or the key performance indicators? Could you produce a balanced scorecard?

Organisation – What is the organisational structure and culture; Who are the key personnel? Are there any personnel and HRM issues?

Investor objectives – What is the capital structure and what are the investor's objectives? What do you know about share price and the value of the business? What do you know about the business' capital? (shares; debt; cost of capital)

> Does your analysis of these aspects of the business identify any **strengths** and **weaknesses**?

Then also think about:

New developments – what new projects may the company be considering? New product development, acquisitions, divestments, new information systems, new organisation structure, new processes?

However, you should NOT be question spotting here; you should simply be thinking of what possible new business projects have been suggested in the preseen material.

Once you have completed your detailed analysis, then **synthesise** what you know:

Produce a position statement

- Mission statement
- Competences and CSF's
- Key business risks
- SWOT analysis – prioritising key S, W, O & T.
- Key business issues
- Balanced scorecard

And draw these points together into your one page business summary:

BUSINESS SUMMARY: Name of company			
Nature of business :........................ Current mission	Turnover	CFSs for success in industry • •	
Distinctive competence			
Major stakeholder objective			
ANALYSIS BACKUP			
Key financial data: trends		External : 5 forces	
Gross profit Net profit ROCE Other	Estimated value of business	P E S T	1 Barriers 2 Substitutes 3 Customers 4 Suppliers 5 Company
Gearing Cash Operating cycle		Internal • Capacity • Structure • Information • Other	
Worrying indicators			
Competitive strategy: Cost leadership/Differentiation/Focus/'stuck in the middle'			
Customers – Key data			

SYNTHESIS

SWOT (Items of high importance)		RISKS: (High importance)	Time
0	0	1	
1	1	2	
2	2	3	
3	3		
Weaknesses	Threats		
1	1	4	
2	2		
3	3	5	

Key issues (High importance)	Time	Selection of possible business projects (High importance)	
1		1	
2		2	
3		3	
4		4	
5		5	
6		Possible discount rate	

BZCS: unseen and requirements

This chapter contains the unseen material and requirements from the March 2011 exam.

We have produced a suggested answer to the exam in Chapter 16.

The requirement for this exam mirrors the type of requirement you should expect in your exam: a report worth up to 90 marks, followed by a smaller, secondary requirement worth up to 10 marks (with the 10 marks being awarded for Logic.)

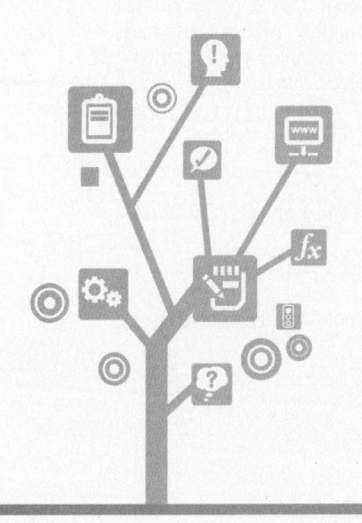

15

March 2011

BZCS - Construction company case – Unseen material provided on examination day

Additional (unseen) information relating to the case is given on pages 15 to 19.

Read all of the additional material before you answer the question.

ANSWER THE FOLLOWING QUESTION

You are the Management Accountant of BZCS.

The Commercial Director of the Sports Facilities Division has asked you to provide advice and recommendations on the issues facing this division of BZCS.

Question 1 part (a)

Prepare a report that prioritises, analyses and evaluates the issues facing the Sports Facilities Division of BZCS and makes appropriate recommendations.

(Total marks for Question 1 part (a) = 90 Marks)

Question 1 part (b)

In addition to your analysis in your report for part (a), you should draft an email to the Commercial Director of the Sports Facilities Division on the advantages and disadvantages of attempting to complete the Binnet City sports complex project before the end of December 2011, together with your recommendation on this issue.

Your email should contain no more than 10 short sentences.

(Total marks for Question 1 part (b) = 10 Marks)

Your script will be marked against the T4 Part B Case Study Assessment Criteria shown on the next page.

Assessment Criteria

Criterion	Maximum marks available
Analysis of issues (25 marks)	
Technical	5
Application	15
Diversity	5
Strategic choices (35 marks)	
Focus	5
Prioritisation	5
Judgement	20
Ethics	5
Recommendations (40 marks)	
Logic	30
Integration	5
Ethics	5
Total	**100**

BZCS - Construction company case – unseen material provided on examination day

Read this information before you answer the question

Sports complex in Binnet

BZCS won the contract to build a replacement sports complex in the European City of Binnet to serve its population of 400,000. The project is funded wholly by the local government. The existing local sports complex is over 30 years old and must close by 31 December 2011, as it does not meet new European Health and Safety standards, which will be effective from 1 January 2012. The contract is to build a multi-functional sports complex on a new site, with indoor sports facilities for a range of sports, a gym, an indoor 50 metre swimming pool and outdoors athletics facilities. BZCS, or any part of the BeeZed group, will not be involved with on-going maintenance of this sports complex.

BZCS has been involved with this proposed project for over 2 years and submitted its bid in October 2009. Work was originally scheduled to start in December 2009. However the local government of Binnet delayed its selection of the construction company. BZCS only signed contracts in September 2010. The contract is for a fixed price of €64.0 million. The contract includes a clause for penalties for late delivery by BZCS. The penalties comprise a fixed penalty of €3.0 million if the sports complex is not fully completed and delivered by 31 December 2011 (week 52), even if the project is delivered 1 day late. There are further penalties of €0.1 million for each week the sports complex is delivered late beyond week 52 of 2011.

The plans prepared for the bid in October 2009 were based on costs totalling €57.6 million which generated an operating profit for BZCS of €6.4 million, a 10% operating profit margin.

Change in Project Manager

When the contract was signed in September 2010, BZCS appointed a Project Manager. Work on site commenced in October 2010. The project plan was to deliver the completed project by October 2011 and to work 5.5 (five and a half) days per week, which is normal in this industry. A clause in the contract with Binnet's local government stated that BZCS would only be allowed to work 7 days each week for a maximum of 22 weeks during the contract period.

The Project Manager responsible for the Binnet sports complex has recently resigned and he left BZCS on 4 February 2011, after serving his 1 month's notice period. BZCS's senior management were slow to appoint a successor as they considered this project was running as planned. All of BZCS's Sport Facilities Division's Project Managers had been allocated to other projects, including to Olympic Games construction projects. A new Project Manager, Roger Pebble, has now been appointed. He had previously been a Project Manager in BZCS's Community Projects Division. He arrived on site yesterday, Monday 28 February 2011.

Procurement issues

Roger Pebble has identified that a number of activities that should have taken place by now have not occurred. This includes placing the order for the agreed specification of the sports complex's glass panels. These are to be made from special glass that retains heat, which will reduce heat loss from the building. These should have been ordered in early January 2011. The specialist supplier has stated that there is a 16 week lead time. There are no alternative suppliers for these specialised glass panels. Furthermore, alternative suppliers of standard glass panels cannot deliver any quicker.

The new centralised Procurement Department was set up on 1 January 2011. The new Procurement Director had thought that this order for the glass panels had already been placed by the Project Manager before he left BZCS. With the changeover to the central Procurement Department, and then the resignation of the previous Project Manager, this key contract has not been placed with the supplier.

The contracted specification for the interior of the sports complex includes high usage of recycled materials and wooden flooring using wood from sustainable forests. However, it has been identified that the lead time from one particular supplier is longer than previously advised. Therefore, obtaining these materials may cause a further delay to the completion of the project unless the orders are placed this week. Any possible delay in ordering these materials is not included in the 12 weeks for Activity H shown below.

Sports complex project running late

Roger Pebble has reviewed the project's progress on site and he has used BZCS's project management system to prepare a critical path analysis. The critical path analysis is shown in Appendix 5 to this unseen material (Appendices 1- 4 are included in the Pre-seen material). He has discovered that the project has not been well managed and that the project is running late. He communicated his concerns to his line manager, BZCS's Commercial Director for the Sports Facilities Division. BZCS's Commercial Director for the Sports Facilities Division has asked Roger Pebble to work with you, the Management Accountant, to assess what activities still need to happen and also to prepare an update on the project's profitability.

Roger Pebble has also identified an activity that had not been included in the original costings. This is Activity B, which is additional external drainage and is forecast to cost €0.9 million.

Some of the activities shown below are dependent on others. For example, the table below indicates that Activity C cannot begin until Activity A is complete. The critical path in Appendix 5 is based on the activities below which are required to complete the sports complex:

Activity	Description of activity	Preceding activity	Duration	Cost of each activity
			Weeks	€ million
A	Order for sports centre glass panels	-	16	9.0
B	Inadequate external drainage – new drainage to be installed	-	2	0.9
C	Completion of the roof and installation of glass panels to make the building water tight	A	8	3.6
D	Construction of all interior walls and construction of the swimming pool	C	4	2.2
E	Initial fixing of electrics and water supplies	D	3	2.0
F	Construction of all outdoor athletics facilities	B	8	4.2
G	Outdoor spectators' stand constructed	B	3	1.6
H	All interior construction completed	E	12	5.2
I	Final fix of electrics and water supplies	H	5	4.0
J	Swimming pool completed, filled and tested	I	3	7.8
K	Construction of final road surface, car parking and landscaping	F and G	2	1.2
	Totals		66 weeks	€41.7 m

The BZPM (BZCS's Project Management system) has prepared the forecast costs for each activity up to completion, based on the originally planned number of BZCS's employees allocated to this project and sub-contractors' existing contracts. The manpower costs included in each of the above activities cannot be reduced.

It is now the first week in March 2011 (week 9) and next week is the start of week 10.

Up to and including the end of the current week (week 9), the actual cumulative expenditure (including accruals) for this project is €16.4 million.

Proposals to use additional manpower resources

BZCS has a choice to incur higher costs by using additional manpower resources (both its own employees and sub-contractors) to try to deliver the project by the end of week 50 in 2011, allowing a possible further slippage of 2 weeks before the contract penalty payments would be imposed. Roger Pebble has not yet informed the local government of Binnet of the potential delay, as he is waiting for a decision by the Commercial Director of the Sports Facilities Division on what possible action could be taken to bring forward the completion date.

There are 3 proposals. It should be noted that alternatives 1 and 2 are mutually exclusive.

Proposal 1 – Working 7 days each week
To increase the working week from 5.5 days to a full 7 day working week for all employees and sub-contractors currently on site. The additional cost, for working 7 full days each week, i.e. to generate an extra 1.5 days each week, is €90,000 per week. This option could only operate for a maximum of 22 weeks, generating an extra 33 days in total. Proposal 3 below, using additional manpower can be used together with this proposal.

Proposal 2 – Overtime working
To pay overtime to employees and sub-contractors currently on site, in addition to the normal 5.5 working days each week. Normal working hours are 40 hours per week. With 11 hours overtime per week, this would approximately generate an additional 1.5 days over each working week. The total overtime that would be incurred each week is forecast to cost an additional €100,000 per week, covering all employees and sub-contractors on site. This option cannot be used at the same time as Proposal 1, shown above.

Proposal 3 – Additional manpower
To increase the number of manpower resources (some of BZCS's employees but mainly sub-contractors) allocated to this project. This would cost €350,000 for each week saved.

Roger Pebble considers that irrespective of whichever of the above 3 proposals is used to bring the project forward, that all employees and sub-contractors on site should be awarded a bonus if the sports complex is completed by the end of week 50. The bonus is forecast to cost €200,000 in total.

The Commercial Director of the Sports Facilities Division has asked you, as Management Accountant, to work with the new Project Manager, Roger Pebble. He has asked you to report back on the following, assuming all actions start from the beginning of week 10:

(i) To calculate the week number when the sports complex will be completed, assuming no additional manpower or extra hours are worked on the project.

(ii) To calculate the forecast full cost of the project and the operating profit for the project, assuming no additional manpower or extra hours are worked on the project.

(iii) To calculate the additional costs for each of the above 3 proposals to provide additional manpower resources so as to deliver the project by week 50 of 2011, at the latest.

(iv) To calculate the revised operating profit for the project for each of the above 3 proposals to provide additional manpower resources with, and without, the proposed bonus.

Project management IT system

BZCS's Commercial Director of the Sports Facilities Division is concerned that BZCS's project management IT system, BZPM, has not been sufficiently effective at managing the Binnet project. It appears that BZPM produced its usual monthly reports including warning reports and emails to the Project Manager who left the company at the start of February 2011. The system also allowed the Project Manager to over-ride warnings and adjust the critical path for activities that the Project Manager had considered had been undertaken, such as the lack of the placement of the order for glass panels. BZPM currently shows that the order for the glass panels was placed in January 2011, despite the fact that the order had not been placed.

Roger Pebble, as well as other BZCS Project Managers, has often complained about the lack of confidence Project Managers have with some of the data held in BZPM. Sometimes purchases of materials or sub-contractors' invoices are allocated against the incorrect project number or the incorrect activity within a project. Some Project Managers are doubtful about the accuracy of some of the data in BZPM and keep their own records.

The Commercial Director of the Sports Facilities Division has asked you, as Management Accountant, to work with the new Project Manager, Roger Pebble, to report on how BZPM could be improved.

Disposal of construction site waste

BZCS uses specialist sub-contractors to dispose of waste from its building sites in a safe and responsible way. Across most European countries, BZCS's sub-contractor for site waste disposal is Waste ZX. The rolling annual contract with Waste ZX was renewed in January 2011 but the renewed contract now excludes the disposal of soil and plants. The Procurement Director appointed a new sub-contractor, Earth YT, in January 2011 which specialises in the disposal of soil and plants at a lower cost than previously charged by Waste ZX.

Some environmental protesters have recently publicised significant damage to a lake near to the city of Binnet as a result of the dumping of vast quantities of soil and plants which have blocked the flow of water from the river leading into the lake. The environmental protesters are blaming Earth YT.

BZCS's Public Relations and Marketing Director has been involved in an internal investigation following the adverse publicity. He has discovered that some of the dumped soil has originated from BZCS's building sites, including the sports complex project in the city of Binnet. He is planning to recommend to the BZCS Board that BZCS cancels its contract with Earth YT immediately. He is also recommending to the BZCS Board that BZCS should refuse to accept any responsibility for the clearing up of the river and lake.

Appendix 5

**Critical path analysis for the City of Binnet sports complex
– as at end week 9 2011**

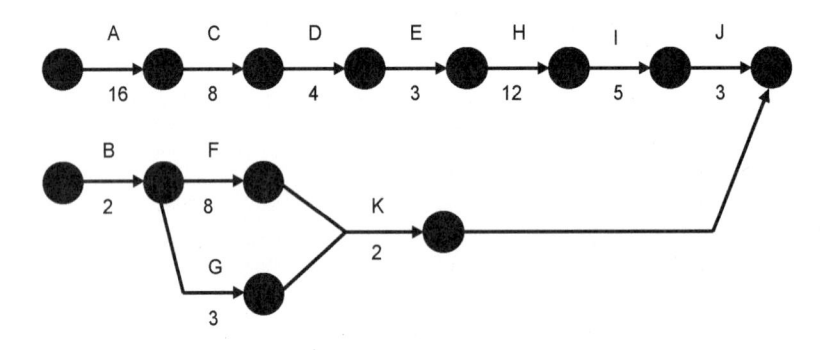

```
     A          C          D          E          H          I          J
 ●──────●──────●──────●──────●──────●──────●──────●──────●
     16         8          4          3         12          5          3

     B          F
 ●──────●──────●
     2          8     ╲
                       ╲       K
                        ●──────●───────────────────╲
                       ╱       2                    ╲
                      ╱                              ╲
                   G ╱                                ╲
                 ●                                     →
                    3
```

Note: All numbers shown above are the time taken, in weeks, to complete each activity.

End of unseen material

APPLICABLE MATHS TABLES AND FORMULAE

Present value table

Present value of 1.00 unit of currency, that is $(1 + r)^{-n}$ where r = interest rate; n = number of periods until payment or receipt.

Periods (n)	1%	2%	3%	4%	5%	6%	7%	8%	9%	10%
1	0.990	0.980	0.971	0.962	0.952	0.943	0.935	0.926	0.917	0.909
2	0.980	0.961	0.943	0.925	0.907	0.890	0.873	0.857	0.842	0.826
3	0.971	0.942	0.915	0.889	0.864	0.840	0.816	0.794	0.772	0.751
4	0.961	0.924	0.888	0.855	0.823	0.792	0.763	0.735	0.708	0.683
5	0.951	0.906	0.863	0.822	0.784	0.747	0.713	0.681	0.650	0.621
6	0.942	0.888	0.837	0.790	0.746	0705	0.666	0.630	0.596	0.564
7	0.933	0.871	0.813	0.760	0.711	0.665	0.623	0.583	0.547	0.513
8	0.923	0.853	0.789	0.731	0.677	0.627	0.582	0.540	0.502	0.467
9	0.914	0.837	0.766	0.703	0.645	0.592	0.544	0.500	0.460	0.424
10	0.905	0.820	0.744	0.676	0.614	0.558	0.508	0.463	0.422	0.386
11	0.896	0.804	0.722	0.650	0.585	0.527	0.475	0.429	0.388	0.350
12	0.887	0.788	0.701	0.625	0.557	0.497	0.444	0.397	0.356	0.319
13	0.879	0.773	0.681	0.601	0.530	0.469	0.415	0.368	0.326	0.290
14	0.870	0.758	0.661	0.577	0.505	0.442	0.388	0.340	0.299	0.263
15	0.861	0.743	0.642	0.555	0.481	0.417	0.362	0.315	0.275	0.239
16	0.853	0.728	0.623	0.534	0.458	0.394	0.339	0.292	0.252	0.218
17	0.844	0.714	0.605	0.513	0.436	0.371	0.317	0.270	0.231	0.198
18	0.836	0.700	0.587	0.494	0.416	0.350	0.296	0.250	0.212	0.180
19	0.828	0.686	0.570	0.475	0.396	0.331	0.277	0.232	0.194	0.164
20	0.820	0.673	0.554	0.456	0.377	0.312	0.258	0.215	0.178	0.149

Periods (n)	11%	12%	13%	14%	15%	16%	17%	18%	19%	20%
1	0.901	0.893	0.885	0.877	0.870	0.862	0.855	0.847	0.840	0.833
2	0.812	0.797	0.783	0.769	0.756	0.743	0.731	0.718	0.706	0.694
3	0.731	0.712	0.693	0.675	0.658	0.641	0.624	0.609	0.593	0.579
4	0.659	0.636	0.613	0.592	0.572	0.552	0.534	0.516	0.499	0.482
5	0.593	0.567	0.543	0.519	0.497	0.476	0.456	0.437	0.419	0.402
6	0.535	0.507	0.480	0.456	0.432	0.410	0.390	0.370	0.352	0.335
7	0.482	0.452	0.425	0.400	0.376	0.354	0.333	0.314	0.296	0.279
8	0.434	0.404	0.376	0.351	0.327	0.305	0.285	0.266	0.249	0.233
9	0.391	0.361	0.333	0.308	0.284	0.263	0.243	0.225	0.209	0.194
10	0.352	0.322	0.295	0.270	0.247	0.227	0.208	0.191	0.176	0.162
11	0.317	0.287	0.261	0.237	0.215	0.195	0.178	0.162	0.148	0.135
12	0.286	0.257	0.231	0.208	0.187	0.168	0.152	0.137	0.124	0.112
13	0.258	0.229	0.204	0.182	0.163	0.145	0.130	0.116	0.104	0.093
14	0.232	0.205	0.181	0.160	0.141	0.125	0.111	0.099	0.088	0.078
15	0.209	0.183	0.160	0.140	0.123	0.108	0.095	0.084	0.079	0.065
16	0.188	0.163	0.141	0.123	0.107	0.093	0.081	0.071	0.062	0.054
17	0.170	0.146	0.125	0.108	0.093	0.080	0.069	0.060	0.052	0.045
18	0.153	0.130	0.111	0.095	0.081	0.069	0.059	0.051	0.044	0.038
19	0.138	0.116	0.098	0.083	0.070	0.060	0.051	0.043	0.037	0.031
20	0.124	0.104	0.087	0.073	0.061	0.051	0.043	0.037	0.031	0.026

Cumulative present value of 1.00 unit of currency per annum, Receivable or Payable at the end of each year for n years $\left[\frac{1-(1+r)^{-n}}{r}\right]$

Periods (n)	1%	2%	3%	4%	5%	6%	7%	8%	9%	10%
1	0.990	0.980	0.971	0.962	0.952	0.943	0.935	0.926	0.917	0.909
2	1.970	1.942	1.913	1.886	1.859	1.833	1.808	1.783	1.759	1.736
3	2.941	2.884	2.829	2.775	2.723	2.673	2.624	2.577	2.531	2.487
4	3.902	3.808	3.717	3.630	3.546	3.465	3.387	3.312	3.240	3.170
5	4.853	4.713	4.580	4.452	4.329	4.212	4.100	3.993	3.890	3.791
6	5.795	5.601	5.417	5.242	5.076	4.917	4.767	4.623	4.486	4.355
7	6.728	6.472	6.230	6.002	5.786	5.582	5.389	5.206	5.033	4.868
8	7.652	7.325	7.020	6.733	6.463	6.210	5.971	5.747	5.535	5.335
9	8.566	8.162	7.786	7.435	7.108	6.802	6.515	6.247	5.995	5.759
10	9.471	8.983	8.530	8.111	7.722	7.360	7.024	6.710	6.418	6.145
11	10.368	9.787	9.253	8.760	8.306	7.887	7.499	7.139	6.805	6.495
12	11.255	10.575	9.954	9.385	8.863	8.384	7.943	7.536	7.161	6.814
13	12.134	11.348	10.635	9.986	9.394	8.853	8.358	7.904	7.487	7.103
14	13.004	12.106	11.296	10.563	9.899	9.295	8.745	8.244	7.786	7.367
15	13.865	12.849	11.938	11.118	10.380	9.712	9.108	8.559	8.061	7.606
16	14.718	13.578	12.561	11.652	10.838	10.106	9.447	8.851	8.313	7.824
17	15.562	14.292	13.166	12.166	11.274	10.477	9.763	9.122	8.544	8.022
18	16.398	14.992	13.754	12.659	11.690	10.828	10.059	9.372	8.756	8.201
19	17.226	15.679	14.324	13.134	12.085	11.158	10.336	9.604	8.950	8.365
20	18.046	16.351	14.878	13.590	12.462	11.470	10.594	9.818	9.129	8.514

Periods (n)	11%	12%	13%	14%	15%	16%	17%	18%	19%	20%
1	0.901	0.893	0.885	0.877	0.870	0.862	0.855	0.847	0.840	0.833
2	1.713	1.690	1.668	1.647	1.626	1.605	1.585	1.566	1.547	1.528
3	2.444	2.402	2.361	2.322	2.283	2.246	2.210	2.174	2.140	2.106
4	3.102	3.037	2.974	2.914	2.855	2.798	2.743	2.690	2.639	2.589
5	3.696	3.605	3.517	3.433	3.352	3.274	3.199	3.127	3.058	2.991
6	4.231	4.111	3.998	3.889	3.784	3.685	3.589	3.498	3.410	3.326
7	4.712	4.564	4.423	4.288	4.160	4.039	3.922	3.812	3.706	3.605
8	5.146	4.968	4.799	4.639	4.487	4.344	4.207	4.078	3.954	3.837
9	5.537	5.328	5.132	4.946	4.772	4.607	4.451	4.303	4.163	4.031
10	5.889	5.650	5.426	5.216	5.019	4.833	4.659	4.494	4.339	4.192
11	6.207	5.938	5.687	5.453	5.234	5.029	4.836	4.656	4.486	4.327
12	6.492	6.194	5.918	5.660	5.421	5.197	4.988	7.793	4.611	4.439
13	6.750	6.424	6.122	5.842	5.583	5.342	5.118	4.910	4.715	4.533
14	6.982	6.628	6.302	6.002	5.724	5.468	5.229	5.008	4.802	4.611
15	7.191	6.811	6.462	6.142	5.847	5.575	5.324	5.092	4.876	4.675
16	7.379	6.974	6.604	6.265	5.954	5.668	5.405	5.162	4.938	4.730
17	7.549	7.120	6.729	6.373	6.047	5.749	5.475	5.222	4.990	4.775
18	7.702	7.250	6.840	6.467	6.128	5.818	5.534	5.273	5.033	4.812
19	7.839	7.366	6.938	6.550	6.198	5.877	5.584	5.316	5.070	4.843
20	7.963	7.469	7.025	6.623	6.259	5.929	5.628	5.353	5.101	4.870

FORMULAE

Valuation Models

(i) Irredeemable preference share, paying a constant annual dividend, d, in perpetuity, where P_0 is the ex-div value:

$$P_0 = \frac{d}{k_{pref}}$$

(ii) Ordinary (Equity) share, paying a constant annual dividend, d, in perpetuity, where P_0 is the ex-div value:

$$P_0 = \frac{d}{k_e}$$

(iii) Ordinary (Equity) share, paying an annual dividend, d, growing in perpetuity at a constant rate, g, where P_0 is the ex-div value:

$$P_0 = \frac{d_1}{k_e - g} \text{ or } P_0 = \frac{d_0[1+g]}{k_e - g}$$

(iv) Irredeemable (Undated) debt, paying annual after tax interest, $i(1-t)$, in perpetuity, where P_0 is the ex-interest value:

$$P_0 = \frac{i[1-t]}{k_{dnet}}$$

or, without tax:

$$P_0 = \frac{i}{k_d}$$

(v) Future value of S, of a sum X, invested for n periods, compounded at $r\%$ interest:

$$S = X[1+r]^n$$

(vi) Present value of £1 payable or receivable in n years, discounted at $r\%$ per annum:

$$PV = \frac{1}{[1+r]^n}$$

(vii) Present value of an annuity of £1 per annum, receivable or payable for n years, commencing in one year, discounted at $r\%$ per annum:

$$PV = \frac{1}{r}\left[1 - \frac{1}{[1+r]^n}\right]$$

(viii) Present value of £1 per annum, payable or receivable in perpetuity, commencing in one year, discounted at $r\%$ per annum:

$$PV = \frac{1}{r}$$

(ix) Present value of £1 per annum, receivable or payable, commencing in one year, growing in perpetuity at a constant rate of g% per annum, discounted at r% per annum:

$$PV = \frac{1}{r - g}$$

Cost of Capital

(i) Cost of irredeemable preference capital, paying an annual dividend, d, in perpetuity, and having a current ex-div price P_0:

$$k_{pref} = \frac{d}{P_0}$$

(ii) Cost of irredeemable debt capital, paying annual net interest, $i(1-t)$, and having a current ex-interest price P_0:

$$k_{dnet} = \frac{i[1-t]}{P_0}$$

(iii) Cost of ordinary (equity) share capital, paying an annual dividend, d, in perpetuity, and having a current ex-div price P_0:

$$k_e = \frac{d}{P_0}$$

(iv) Cost of ordinary (equity) share capital, having a current ex-div price, P_0, having just paid a dividend, d_0, with the dividend growing in perpetuity by a constant g% per annum:

$$k_e = \frac{d_1}{P_0} + g \quad \text{or} \quad k_e = \frac{d_0[1+g]}{P_0} + g$$

(v) Cost of ordinary (equity) share capital, using the CAPM:

$$k_e = R_f + [R_m - R_f]\beta$$

(vi) Weighted average cost of capital, k_0:

$$k_0 = k_e \left[\frac{V_E}{V_E + V_D} \right] + k_d \left[\frac{V_D}{V_E + V_D} \right]$$

BZCS: answer

This is the suggested answer to the **March 2011** unseen and requirement, written by BPP Learning Media. Your report will be different to this and may analyse some different issues. This is as it should be, there is no one correct answer.

However, if you fail to prioritise the key issues, you will find it very difficult to pass the exam.

Note: our solution is a comprehensive solution to this exam, and reflects the length and depth of solutions provided by CIMA's examiners. As such, this solution aims to provide guidance on how each issue in the unseen could have been tackled, but this makes the solution longer than an answer which could have been submitted in an exam. In our experience, candidates submit scripts of around 2,500 words in the exam.

We have also included a suggested marking scheme developed by BPP Learning Media from the Post Exam Guides and Script Reviews following the exam.

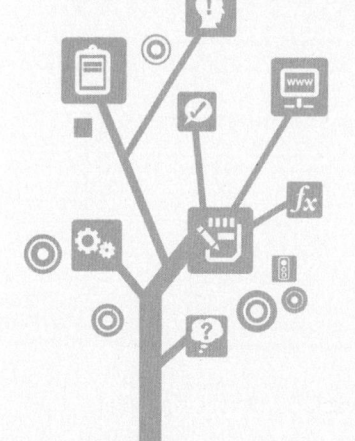

Review the marking grid carefully to see where the Examiner awarded marks, and therefore the sorts of things you can improve in your answers to ensure you score as many marks as you can.

Once you have answered this case study and reviewed our answer, you are also strongly advised to read through the CIMA examiner's **post-exam guide**. The post-exam guides are available in the 'Study resources' section for T4 on the *cimaglobal.com* website.

Much of the information in the post-exam guide will be specific to this March 2011 case (rather than the case you will face in your exam). However, the post-exam guides do also include some more general comments on candidates' scripts, and the guides highlight some common errors, including omissions, which candidates make, and any common weaknesses they show. If you have shown some of the same weaknesses in your practice exams to date, these are points you need to address before you sit your real exam.

Answer to Question 1a

REPORT

To: Commercial Director: Sports facilities Division: BZCS

From: Management Accountant

Date: 1st March 2011 (Week 9)

Contents

1. Introduction
2. Terms of reference
3. Prioritisation of issues facing Sports facilities Division
4. Discussion of the main issues facing Sports facilities Division
5. Ethical considerations facing Sports facilities Division
6. Recommendations on the main issues facing Sports facilities Division
7. Conclusion

Appendices

A. SWOT analysis
B. Motivation theory - Herzberg
C. Stakeholder analysis
D. Budgeted costs and profits of Binnet project
E. Additional costs of labour proposals
F. Revised operating profits
G. Email to Commercial Director

1 Introduction

The Sports Facilities Division must finish the Binnet sports complex by week 52 or face financial penalties. It may be prudent to consider week 50 as the target completion date to allow for further slippage. This means there are between 41 and 43 weeks to complete the project against a critical path that shows 51 weeks of activities are needed to finish the project.

This need to complete the Binnet sports complex is the context against which the decisions below must be made.

2 Terms of reference

This report was commissioned by the Commercial Director: Sports facilities Division to prioritise, analyse and evaluate the issues facing the division and offer appropriate recommendations.

3 Prioritisation of issues facing Sports facilities Division

The issues below have been prioritised based on the potential impact each could have on the division. A full SWOT analysis is presented in Appendix A.

3.1 Sports complex project running late – first priority

This contract must be finished by the end of week 52, on 31st December 2011. The network analysis in Appendix 5 shows a minimum project time of 51 weeks (16+8+4+3+12+5+3). However the first activity on the critical path, Activity A: the ordering of the glass roof panels, has been delayed by 9 weeks and now will not begin until week 10. Therefore there are 43 weeks remaining until the project must be completed, and 51 weeks of work still to do. This project is set to overshoot by 8 weeks. If the target is to finish by the end of week 50, we need to reduce project time by 10 weeks.

Failure to complete by week 52 will lead to a fixed penalty of €3m and a further €0.1m per additional week. Therefore, on the basis of the above overshoot, this project faces penalties of €3.8m, equivalent to 59% of the budgeted operating profit (€3.8m/€6.4m where operating profit is 10% of €64m = €6.4m).

This is a very significant reduction in profit that will have significant *impact* on the division's profit and its reputation for on-time delivery. It is also extremely *urgent* because further delays will cost a further €0.1m per week.

Therefore this issue has been given first priority.

3.2 Procurement issues – second priority

Two immediate procurement issues are outstanding: ordering the glass panels and ordering the recycled materials. Delay in either decision would extend the time needed for this project beyond the 51 weeks' minimum time in the network analysis.

Delay will impact on penalty payments at a rate of €0.1m per extra week, and therefore decisions are urgently needed.

These issues have been given priority two because despite extreme urgency, they are not the only issues that must be addressed to avoid the huge penalties for missing the week 52 completion date.

3.3 Proposals to use additional manpower resources – third priority

To bring the project back on track, three proposals have been made to increase manpower resources.

It is essential that some of the activities on the critical path be 'crashed' below their planned duration if this project is to be finished on time. The proposals result in significant *impact* on labour resources, but at significant increases in costs.

This decision is less *urgent* as, according to the network analysis, no activities on the critical path involving labour will begin until after the 16 weeks needed for the roofing panels to arrive. Therefore it has been given priority three.

3.4 Project management IT system – fourth priority

The failures over this project have highlighted limitations in the BZPM system and have led to an overall loss of confidence in it. There is also the possibility that other projects in the division or in the company as a whole are running late or are being accounted for incorrectly.

There is potential risk here. However the *impact* is less immediate and obvious than the late running of the Binnet project and it is more *urgent* that the known threats be dealt with.

Therefore this issue has been given fourth priority.

3.5 Other issues facing Sports facilities Division

There are issues of lesser importance which have not been prioritised in this report as they are seen as less urgent and as having minor impact on the division. These include:

- Disposal of construction site waste – this may cause delays and some cost increase but is not as significant as the issues above.

- Change in Project Manager – this raises issues about effective scrutiny and succession planning which will be dealt with in the discussion of the BZPM system.

Ethical issues facing the division will be discussed in a separate section.

4 Discussion of the main issues facing Sports facilities Division

4.1 Sports complex project running late – first priority

At present the forecast overshoot will lead to at least a €3.8m penalty, equivalent to 61% of the budgeted operating profit.

Option 1 – allow project to overrun

Assuming that the 51 weeks forecast can be delivered without further slippage, the *benefits* of this option are mainly that it would save higher outlays on manpower resources and other expediting payments and activities.

The *drawbacks* are that the division would incur penalty payments of €3.8m and probably more. Further slippage is likely, as in December the project will run into the traditional European holidays around Christmas and New Year, which could mean it loses a further 2 weeks.

It would also harm BZCS's reputation for on-time delivery, one of its critical success factors.

The 2011 profits of the division would need to be written down as the future value of this project would fall by the amount of the fines and also in recognition that, at Sept 30th, a lower percentage of the project would be complete than had been budgeted.

Option 2 – seek variation to the contract or recompense from contractors

Fixed-price contracts often give rise to legal actions over where liability or blame lies. This has been a continuing feature of the UK's Wembley Stadium project where, 4 years after its opening, lead contractor Multiplex is presently suing in support of its allegation that it was not shown critical details on steel roofing members at the time it bid.

In this case BZCS might be able to attribute the late running in part to the late signing of contracts, or subsequent need for additional external drainage if this can be shown to have been unclear at the time of the bid. It is possible that BZCS may also be able to find other areas where the bid was compromised or the operations hampered by the client.

The *advantages* of this legal approach is that it may convince the client to forgo some part of the penalties rather than face lengthy, expensive and uncertain legal cases later.

The *disadvantages* are that at least part of the fault lies within BZCS and the industry will become aware of this. BZCS may get a reputation as an incompetent contractor that uses litigation to bully its clients. It could lose the cases and lose future work too.

Option 3 – expedite the project

Various options have been suggested and are analysed in the sections below.

In addition to the extra manpower resources and performance bonuses to manpower the division could consider payments to others on the critical path to crash activity times. For example it could make extra payments to the providers of the glass panels and, if critical, the providers of recycled materials.

The activities on the critical path could be reviewed to see if any could be started earlier, for example can the interior walls be started (Activity D) before the whole roof is finished (Activity C)?

Given the failings in the BZPM system, an additional layer of reporting should be considered, such as a weekly presentation by the Project Manager for Binnet to the Commercial Director.

The *advantages* of expediting the project and bringing it in on time are that penalty payments will be avoided. It will also maintain BZCS's reputation for on-time delivery and thereby safeguard additional work. Following the revelations of problems with the Wembley Stadium project Multiplex was in effect compelled to relinquish its shares in a company that had contracts to build the 2012 London Olympic Village after the sponsors expressed concerns over the viability of the company. The shares were sold to Westfield, a rival builder which has completed the village.

The *drawbacks* are that some of the options will be costly.

Other issues

There are questions to be asked about the circumstances that led to this project being accepted and whether BZCS is equipped to manage the risks of fixed price contracts.

4.2 Procurement issues – second priority

There are two purchases outstanding: for specialised glass panels and for recycled materials. Lack of either set of component will delay the project and lead to significant financial penalties.

Option 1 – order glass panels

It is not clear that these have been ordered yet. There is no quicker alternative to the present supplier. Costs could be saved by ordering lower specification glass, thus recouping some of the profit following penalties. However this would be at the risk of subsequent legal action for non-fulfilment of contract and would also be unethical.

The supplier could be contacted and a quicker delivery negotiated in return for a bonus payment or enhanced fee. As things presently stand the contract is set to be 8 weeks overdue and miss the week 50 target by 10 weeks. This means that each week the supplier will save at least €100,000 in penalty payments from the 16 week lead time. Significant reductions in lead time could potentially do away with the need for enhanced labour payments and possibly even avoid the €3m penalty clause.

The specialist supplier could be encouraged to prioritise the BZCS order, or to employ special working.

If the project could be re-planned, as suggested in 4.1 above, it may be possible to have some panels on site earlier and so complete parts of the building to allow later jobs to be expedited, say the completion and filling of the pool, which at present adds 3 weeks to project time.

Option 2 – order recycled materials

Failure to order these within a week will add further delay to the project. Again cheaper substitutes may arrive quicker and be cheaper but would lead to a risk of subsequent legal action against BZCS as well as maybe being ethically inappropriate.

Ordering these immediately would maintain budgeted times and costs.

Given that these are time-critical and that all slippage time has been exceeded, it may be prudent to place clear delivery dates, with penalties for breach, into the contract to purchase and possibly also a bonus for on-time delivery.

4.3 Proposals to use additional manpower resources – third priority

The information requested is as follows:

(i) The project is presently forecast to take 51 weeks (16+8+4+3+12+5+3) to complete from the submission of order for the roof panels. This means the project will not be complete until week 60 (week 9 plus 51 weeks) – or rather week 8 of 2012.

(ii) Appendix D shows that forecast profits are €5.9m before penalties and €2.1m after penalties if the project is delayed to week 60.

(iii) Appendix E shows forecast extra labour costs to be €3.38m for Proposal 1 plus additional labour (Proposal 3) as required, €3.7m for Proposal 2 and €3.5m for Proposal 3 on its own.

(iv) Appendix F shows the revised operating profits requested. These range from €2.2m (Proposal 2) to €2.52m (Proposal 1 plus additional labour) before bonus, which is the same value under all proposals.

These proposals can be further evaluated using the Suitability, Acceptability and Feasibility framework of Johnson, Scholes and Whittington.

Suitability

Proposal 1 is not suitable by itself. This is because Proposal 1 delivers only 33 extra days of labour after which the opportunity is exhausted due to the constraints on 7 day working in the contract. This is equivalent to 6 extra working weeks (33/5.5) which on its own is not sufficient to make up the 10 weeks' late running of the contract (assuming a week 50 target). The deficit is 4 weeks, which could be made up using additional labour at €1.4m but reducing operating profit to €2.52m.

Proposal 2 requires 37 weeks worth of overtime in the next 41 weeks to deliver completion by week 50.

Proposal 3 is apparently able to deliver a very flexible labour resource sufficient to finish the project on time.

Acceptability

Proposal 1 plus additional labour as required results in the highest total operating profit, €2.52m.

Proposal 2 is the most expensive option of the three, reducing operating profit to €2.2m.

Proposal 3 is the most flexible and can allow for variations in labour at each stage of the project and to catch up any further slippage. It leads to an operating profit of €2.4m which is marginally less than the €2.52m from a combination of Proposal 1 with a further 4 weeks from additional manpower.

Considering the cost per extra labour day: Proposal 1 costs €60,000 per day (€90,000 x 22 weeks /33 days); Proposal 2 costs €66,667 per day (€100,000/1.5 days); Proposal 3 costs €63,636 per day (€350,000/5.5).

Feasibility

The calculations above imply that demand for labour is evenly spread throughout the project. In reality, the project lifecycle suggests that peak labour demand may come at the middle of a project and then tail off. Also there is only a limited use for labour at the moment as we are due to wait 16 weeks for glass panels before work can begin on the activities on the critical path. Activities B, F, G and K, 15 days in total, will absorb the regular workforce during the wait for the panels. There is no point in using overtime to finish these activities sooner as they are not on the critical path.

There must also be a question over expecting labour productivity to remain constant if the 22 weeks of 7 day working is continuous. Workers will become tired, have periods of illness and so on. There will be delays to the project that will leave workers idle.

The recommendation by Roger Pebble that a bonus be paid to the team will cost €200,000. It would seem inappropriate to pay this to the staff of sub-contractors as it is the sub-contractors' job to hit targets. However paying this bonus is less expensive than an alternative, paying €350,000 for a week's extra labour. The sum could be set aside for payment if the project hits the week 50 deadline or used to buy extra labour if it becomes clear the deadline will be missed otherwise.

According to motivation theory such as Herzberg (Appendix B), this will bring greater effort.

4.4 Project management IT system – fourth priority

The problems of project management extend beyond the BZPM system.

The specific problems of the system appear to be:

- Ability of Project Managers to over-ride the data in the system
- Apparently recording orders that have not taken place (eg glass panels)
- Misallocation of costs to projects

These appear to be human errors rather than technical errors.

Action 1 – restrict ability to adjust system

At present Project Managers, and perhaps others, can manipulate the system. Restricting ability to change entries to head office staff would stop this and remove the system from the influence of day-to-day contingencies.

This would have the *advantage* that it would require the Project Manager to justify the request for a change which, in itself, provides a discipline and a chance for scrutiny.

The *disadvantage* would be that it would lead to additional layers of procedure and staff to undertake changes. It would also run the risk that Project Managers might choose to disregard the system entirely and use private, parallel systems, and thereby further lose transparency.

Action 2 - Incorporate BZPM data into month-end reports

A fault seems to be that the outgoing Project Manager was able to ignore warnings from the system, because the warnings went to the Project Manager alone. A second level of scrutiny, such as the system reporting to the Commercial Director or a management accountant, would enable these warnings to be queried at the month end.

To make this effective it would be essential that PMs could not suppress information by adjusting the system to hide problems.

Action 3 – Improve the inputting of data to the system

The inputting of data is faulty. This is damaging confidence and the usefulness of the system. Managers keeping private systems is a waste of resources and moves the BZCS further from transparency.

Data inputting can be improved by better training and internal controls.

4.5 Other issues facing Sports facilities Division

These are issues of lesser importance which have not been prioritised in this report as they are seen as less urgent and as having minor impact on the division.

5 Ethical considerations facing Sports facilities Division

5.1 Disposal of construction site waste

The commission of a contractor, Earth YT, which dumps waste irresponsibly is a breach of responsibility by BZCS. Given that BZCS has statements of CSR in this area (Appendix 4) the latter are misleading if adequate safeguards are not put in place.

The suggestion by the PR and Marketing Director that BZCS should refuse to accept responsibility is a further breach of duty.

BZCS holds itself out as having commitments to the natural environment. It is clear that these took second place to a cheaper quotation from Earth YT against Waste ZX. Such cost saving is only short-term if it necessitates later cleaning up and damages public relations. The environmental protesters need to be kept satisfied (Mendelow matrix: Appendix C) to avoid this escalating.

BZCS should interview Earth YT immediately and demand that it clears up the dumped soil. This should be accompanied by an analysis of legal obligations under its contract with BZCS.

In the event that Earth YT does not comply, the contract should be terminated as soon as possible under its terms. Meanwhile BZCS should pay to have the soil removed.

A public statement should be made on this as soon as possible to avoid the environmental protesters taking direct action and disrupting construction work or harming BZCS's public image further.

Future contracts should have specific clauses forbidding this kind of behaviour by contractors.

5.2 Treatment of workforce

There are various proposals to increase the working weeks of employees and sub-contractors to bring the Binnet project back on target.

There may also be a temptation to cut corners to save time.

Forcing staff to work extra time against their will is oppressive and unfair treatment of staff. The firm also has a duty of care to its staff, and to staff of sub-contractors, to ensure they are not endangered from misjudgements by themselves or others due to tiredness or rushing. Again BZCS has made health and safety commitments as part of its CSR programme.

BZCS should offer additional weekend days to staff but should be prepared to accept that some staff will not wish to take it. Staff should volunteer rather than be compelled. Steps should also be taken to ensure that the staff at sub-contractors are volunteers and not conscripts.

This suggests that Proposal 1 is more ethical because it limits the amount of overtime to 22 weeks and uses additional temporary manpower too. It means that employees can decline weekend work without endangering the contract.

It is recommended that weekend work be advertised on site notice boards and that staff can sign up for it voluntarily and without pressure.

5.3 Short-cuts on project

Due to the difficulties it is obvious that the profit from this project will be below budget. In these circumstances there may be a temptation to save costs by cutting corners. Examples include doing away with recycled materials in favour of cheaper materials, or not finishing to the usual standards, skimping on testing and so forth.

Taking short cuts is dishonest if it means not doing what the contract specifies. It is also unfair and could lead to safety issues and abrogation of duty of care to users and staff.

It is recommended that the Post Completion Manager be requested to look out for short cuts on the Binnet project due to the temptation for the PM and sub-contractors to recoup time and costs by short cuts.

6 Recommendations on the main issues facing Sports facilities Division

6.1 Sports complex project running late – first priority

The division should take all reasonable steps to expedite the project and to deliver the Binnet sports complex on time.

This is because the financial and reputation risks of late delivery are considerable and potentially avoidable. It is hard to remove the stigma of failure of the sort that has made Multiplex synonymous with the 2 year overshoot and losses it incurred at Wembley. It will rebound on the other 5 divisions of BZCS too. The furore over last-minute issues at the XIX Commonwealth Games village at Delhi in 2010 underlines this.

BZCS should investigate whether clients or contractors are partly to blame for the delays and hence whether it can mitigate losses.

It is recommended that the Commercial Director:

- Instructs Roger Pebble to conduct a review of the present project plan to see where the present critical path can be crashed most effectively.

- Instructs the bid manager to review the bid process and identify any information that has subsequently come to light that could have been material at the time of the original bid submission. This should be reported to the Commercial Director who can then take advice on potential legal recourse.

- Instructs Roger Pebble to review project management weekly and have a weekly meeting with the Commercial Director to update on progress.

6.2 Procurement issues – second priority

It is recommended that both orders be placed at the earliest opportunity and certainly within a week.

Both contracts should contain incentives for the components to be delivered on time, or better, in order to avoid further slippage.

For the specialist panels it is clear that any improvement to the 16 week lead time would be significantly advantageous to BZCS. An appropriate incentive payment should be offered for delivering early. A fee of €100,000 per week can be justified because it is the potential cost of the weekly penalty, and possibly higher if the reduction in lead time helps BZCS avoid the fixed €3m penalty as well.

The recycled material deliveries will need to be scheduled against the revised project plan. It is recommended that buffer inventories be established in case of demand running ahead. This will avoid workers being idle. Achievement of delivery and quality targets should be made a condition of the contract with penalties for delay, and bonuses for hitting them.

There is however no benefit from having excessive materials on site before they are needed. Synchronisation to the revised plan is essential. John Laing found that having materials arriving early during the building of the Cardiff Millennium Stadium led to a shortage of space and delayed works, eventually buckling the roof when it was decided to store materials on top.

Negotiations must be handled discreetly without revealing the problems of the division. Intimating the severity of the potential penalty payments to be paid by BZCS will risk the suppliers holding out for bigger fees and bonus payments.

The need for a more transparent and reliable purchasing process will be dealt with in relation to recommendations for the BZPM system below.

6.3 Proposals to use additional manpower resources – third priority

It is recommended that Proposal 1 and Proposal 3 be used, that is 7 day working plus additional manpower.

This is recommended because they are the two cheapest ways to increase labour. The amount of weekend working will depend firstly on the proportion of staff agreeing to work weekends. Secondly it will depend on whether lead times for ordering the panels can be reduced. If not, it would be necessary to work 22 out of 25 weekends to meet the week 50 target (50 – 9 – 16), which will not allow sufficient workforce recuperation.

The additional labour is available to supplement as needed because the building industry allows daily and weekly contracts for labour.

It is recommended that the €200,000 bonus be held aside as a bonus for completion by week 50 as this will help the workforce and sub-contractors focus on the delivery date. The sum should be reallocated to additional manpower in weeks 51 and 52 if the week 50 deadline is missed.

This bonus should be paid only to workers who have worked on the project for 20 weeks or more before completion date. This avoids legal issues with workers who have departed earlier, and with the unfairness of rewarding late joiners who would not have made a big difference.

The Project Manager should immediately notify staff and contractors of the availability of weekend working and ensure acceptances are gained. As stated above, the actual weekends will not commence until delivery of the glass panels and will be based on the demands of the revised project plan.

The Project Manager should notify employment agencies of the likely demand for labour on the project in order that they can identify suitable pools of staff.

6.4 Project management IT system – fourth priority

It is recommended that PMs are no longer allowed to adjust the BZPM system and instead have read-only privileges. This is recommended because at present the PMs are able to suppress inconvenient data. This compromises transparency and the reliability of reports.

It is recommended that staff at headquarters be permitted to make changes in response to requests from PMs and that these requests for change be recorded. This is recommended as a discipline on PMs through a segregation of duties.

It is recommended that outputs from the BZPM system be part of the month-end pack sent to PMs. This is recommended because it ensures that PMs will be called to account for any problems with the project by the Commercial Director of their Division.

These recommended changes go beyond the Sports Facilities Division and should be implanted in all divisions of BZCS. It is thus also recommended that the Commercial Director brings the recommendations in this section of the report to the attention of the Finance Director and suggests that the FD works with the IT Manager to implement better internal controls.

6.5 Other issues facing BZCS

These are issues of lesser importance which have not been prioritised in this report as they are seen as less urgent and as having minor impact on the division.

7 Conclusion

It is essential that the Binnet project be completed on time to avoid fines and losses. The apparent causes of these problems and the inadequacies of the project management system need to be addressed for the future.

Appendix A: SWOT analysis

Strengths	Weaknesses
• Reputation for quality and delivery • Flexible cost base through sub-contracting	• Misuse of project management system • Poor management of fixed price contract • Poor assessment of suppliers (eg Earth YT)
Opportunities	**Threats**
• Future projects	• Late running of Binnet project leading to penalty payments • Further problems with other projects due to poor internal controls • Loss of future contracts due to reputation for late delivery if Binnet is late

Appendix B: Motivation theory - Herzberg

Herzberg identifies two factors in motivation:

- Hygiene factors: these assure moderate motivation. They include pay, supervisor relations, company policy and workmates.

- Motivating factors: these bring forward superior effort. They include challenge, achievement and recognition.

Providing a bonus to the group for achieving a week 50 deadline represents a challenge and also recognition. It will be motivating.

Appendix C: Stakeholder analysis

Mendelow identifies 4 stakeholder groups

- Minimal effort: low interest and low power – eg day paid labourers

- Keep informed: low power, high interest – eg sports fans

- Keep satisfied: high power, low interest – eg local community

- Key players: high power, high interest – eg BZCS Managing Director and Board, local government of Binnet

The environmental protesters are likely to be Keep Satisfied due to their power to influence local opinion through the press and perhaps to disrupt construction by demonstrations.

Appendix D: Budgeted costs and profits of Binnet project

Forecast without additional labour costs (pre penalty payments)

Budgeted costs = €57.6m

Actual and forecast costs (including drainage in forecast costs) = €41.7m + €16.4m = €58.1m

Additional costs = €0.5m

	€m
Fixed revenue as per contract	64.0
Budgeted cost as per contract	(57.6)
Additional costs	(0.5)
Forecast profit before penalties	**5.9**
Penalty for missing week 52 deadline	(3.0)
Penalty for overshoot (week 60 – week 52) x €0.1m per week	(0.8)
Forecast profit after penalties	**2.1**

Appendix E: Additional costs of labour proposals

Working 7 days each week

€90,000 x 22 weeks of 7 day working = €1.98m

Equates to 22 x (1.5/5.5) full weeks work = 6 full weeks work

Thus cost of additional manpower required (using Proposal 3 figures) = €350,000 x 4 weeks = €1.4m

Total cost = €1.98m + €1.4m = €3.38m

Overtime working

10 full weeks work required

Equates to 10 x (5.5/1.5) overtime weeks = 37 overtime weeks

€100,000 x 37 overtime weeks = €3.7m

Additional manpower

€350,000 x 10 weeks (Week 60 – Week 50 = 10 weeks) = €3.5m

Appendix F: Revised operating profits

Working 7 days each week

Without bonus €5.9m - €3.38m = €2.52m
With bonus €2.52m - €0.2m = €2.32m

Overtime working

Without bonus €5.9m - €3.7m = €2.2m

With bonus €2.2m - €0.2m = €2.0m

Additional manpower

Without bonus €5.9m - €3.5m = €2.4m

With bonus €2.4m - €0.2m = €2.2m

Appendix G: Email to Commercial Director

Answer to Question 1b

To: Commercial Director : Sports Facilities Division
From: Management Accountant
cc   Financial Director

Binnet City Sports Stadium

Statement of facts

At present this project is set to overrun its contract completion date, in Week 52, by 8 weeks.

This over-run will render us liable to penalties of €3.8m and will reduce expected profit to €1.7m against budgeted profit of €6.4m.

This has been due to problems in project management that have resulted in a critical order for glass panels not having been placed, at the expense of 9 lost working weeks on a 51 week contract.

Assessment

The advantages of allowing the overrun are that we avoid paying extra costs to catch up.

The disadvantages are that profits will be reduced by the penalty payments and we may suffer a loss of reputation due to late delivery.

Recommendations

The project must be completed by the end of December 2011. The plan should set a target of completion by the end of Week 50 in 2011, to allow for limited overrun.

The project should be re-planned to identify opportunities to crash activities on the critical path and to attempt to run some in parallel.

Additional labour should be provisioned based on an amount of 7 day working supplemented as needed by additional hiring.

Close attention should be given to other projects due to inherent failings in project management systems that this has exposed.

Yours

Management Accountant

Marking Grid for March 2011 Real Exam

Criteria	Issues to be discussed	Marks	Total marks available for criterion
Technical	SWOT/PEST/Ansoff/Porter's 5 forces/Porter's generic strategies/Mendelow/Suitability, Acceptability, Feasibility/ BCG/Balanced Scorecard/Life cycle analysis/Marketing knowledge, motivation theory 1 mark for EACH technique demonstrated.	1 each max 5	Max = 5
Application	SWOT – to get full 3 marks the script must include all the Top 4 issues	1–3	Max = 15
	Other Technical Knowledge applied to case material in a meaningful relevant way – on merit	1–2 Max 5 for application of theory	
	Calculations:		
	Forecast project overrun (days)	1	
	Full cost of project without additional labour	1	
	Additional costs of 3 proposals	6	
	Revised operating profits under 3 proposals	3	
	Additional calculations on merit	Max 3	
	Total marks available (but max = 15)	19	
Diversity	Display of sound business awareness and relevant real life examples related to case	1–2 marks each example used on merit	Max = 5
Focus	**Major issues to be discussed:**		Max = 5
	Sports complex running late	1	
	Procurement problems	1	
	Proposals for additional manpower	1	
	Project management IT system	1	
	Disposal of construction waste	1	
	Project manager replacement		
	Total marks available	5	
Prioritisation	5 marks if 4 issues are prioritised in the correct order. Deduct 1 mark for each issue placed lower than place in correct ranking	5	Max = 5
Judgement	4 key and 1 minor issues available for detailed analysis in this case:		Max = 20
	Marks on merit based on depth of analysis and commercially realistic comments		
	Sports complex running late: financial impact, reputation risk, potential remedies: re-plan, legal remedies	1–6	
	Procurement problems: place orders, incentives for suppliers, ensure penalties for late delivery, issues leading to this	1–6	
	Proposals for additional manpower: flexibility, dependence on revised plan, effectiveness of bonus	1–6	

Criteria	Issues to be discussed	Marks	Total marks available for criterion
	Project management IT system: issues in present system, potential controls, issues of autonomy of Project Manager versus control and transparency, group wide issue	1–4	
	Disposal of construction waste: potential reputation risk, potential for demonstrators causing delays	1–2	
	Project manager: need for succession planning, issues of culpability	1–2	
	Total marks available (but max = 20)	26	
Integration	Judge script holistically and whether recommendations follow on logically from analysis of the issues and refers to data in appendices. How well written is the report: professional language ?	1–2 if weak 3–5 if script is good	Max = 5
Logic	**Recommendations:** (Marks on merit. Max 1 mark if only an unjustified recommendation is given)		
	Sports complex running late: essential to hit target, logical suggestions and action plans	0–7	
	Procurement problems: immediate placing of orders, stipulate SLAs, refinements to system, tracking and scrutiny	0–6	
	Proposals for additional manpower: balanced decision recognising uneven demand for labour in projects and need for flexibility	0–6	Max = 30 Q1 – 20 Q2 – 10
	Project management IT system: group issue, process improvement	0–5	
	Disposal of construction waste: clear up and publicise, inclusion in SLA of CSR	0–2	
	Project manager: need for deputies, succession plans	0–2	
	Total marks available (but max = 20)	28	
QUESTION 1(b)	Maximum of 2 marks for each heading. Answer must include financial implications and a clear conclusion. Marks reduced by 1 for each sentence in excess of 10	10	
	Total marks available	10	
Ethics	Ethical issues in case include: • Disposal of site waste • Treatment of staff • Short-cuts	Up to 5 for identification and discussion of issues Up to 5 for recommendations on how to address those issues	Max = 10
Total			100

BPP comment on this exam:

This exam was extremely challenging because, at first glance, it created the impression that there was only one issue. Moreover, the numerical analysis was drawn from an area that is not covered at strategic level (critical path analysis).

However, as you started to consider the exam in more detail, you should have been be able to pick out a number of separate commercial issues, which were all signaled by a heading in the case.

Possibly more importantly though, this exam serves as a reminder that the T4 (TOPCIMA) case could take many different styles, and so you should not try to predict what new information the unseen case for your exam will contain.

Papy: pre-seen data

This chapter includes the 'pre-seen' data for Papy supermarkets, which was examined in September and November 2011.

Remember, the **paragraph numbering has been added by BPP** for ease of reference later. The actual pre-seen material you get from CIMA will not have the paragraphs numbered.

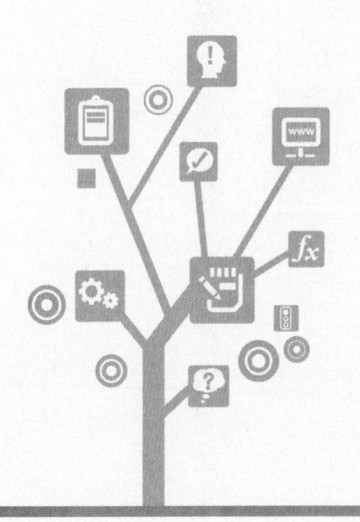

T4 – Part B Case Study Examination

For examinations on Wednesday 31 August 2011 and on Thursday 24 November 2011

PRE-SEEN MATERIAL, PROVIDED IN ADVANCE FOR PREPARATION AND STUDY FOR THE EXAMINATIONS IN SEPTEMBER AND NOVEMBER 2011.

INSTRUCTIONS FOR POTENTIAL CANDIDATES

This booklet contains the pre-seen case material for the above examinations. It will provide you with the contextual information that will help you prepare yourself for the examinations.

The Case Study Assessment Criteria, which your script will be marked against, is included on page 16.

You may not take this copy of the pre-seen material into the examination hall. A fresh copy will be provided on the examination day.

Unseen material will be provided on the examination day; this will comprise further context and the examination question.

The examination will last for three hours. You will be allowed 20 minutes reading time **before the examination begins** during which you should read the question paper and, if you wish, make annotations on the question paper. However, you will **not** be allowed, **under any circumstances**, to either begin writing or using your computer to produce your answer or to use your calculator during the reading time.

You will be required to answer ONE question which may contain more than one element.

PC examination only: Your computer will contain two blank files – one Word and an Excel file. Please ensure that you check that the file names for these two documents correspond with your candidate number.

Contents of this booklet:	Page
Pre-seen material – Papy sustainable trading	2
Pre-Seen Appendices 1 - 6	9
Case Study Assessment Criteria	16

Sustainable trading in the supermarket industry

The supermarket industry

1. There are many large international companies which operate supermarkets in a range of countries around the world using globally recognised brand names. Most of the supermarket chains have a large market share in their home country and have expanded to other countries both by acquisition and by organic growth. There have been many acquisitions of smaller supermarket chains in order to achieve greater economies of scale and to expand the promotion of the supermarket brand globally.

2. Most of the large supermarkets sell a wide range of products with food items comprising less than 75% of revenues. Non-food items include household and electrical goods as well as clothing and shoes.

3. The trend in the past was to build and operate larger and larger stores with the view that most people would make the journey to a large supermarket to shop. However, over the last decade there has been a reversal in this trend with the opening (mainly through acquisition) of smaller "convenience" stores enabling people to shop locally. A small "convenience" store is defined as a small retail store which is open long hours offering a limited range of food and household products and is located in city centre or suburban residential areas. Within city centres, these convenience stores have generated increasingly high sales levels. This has encouraged supermarket chains to operate a portfolio of smaller "convenience" stores as well as large supermarket stores.

4. Some global food retailers operate a range of brands and have a portfolio of several types of stores, ranging from very large "hypermarkets" to smaller "convenience" local stores. A "hypermarket" is defined as a very large retail store which combines a grocery supermarket and a department store, situated at out-of-town locations and generally having a sales area of over 20,000 square metres.

5. The global supermarket industry is highly competitive and most brands compete primarily on price. There have been many changes in the way supermarkets operate over the last decade. These innovations include internet shopping, wider ranges of organic produce, wider ranges of non-food products and the expansion of "own brand" products and "value" ranges. "Own brand" products are food and household products which display the brand name of the store selling it rather than that of the company which made it. "Value" ranges are defined as goods sold at substantially lower prices than other comparable products under "own brand value range" labels, so that the target customers consider that they are getting exceptional value for money.

Background information on sustainable trading

6. Sustainable trading is defined as "a trading system that does not harm the environment or deteriorate social conditions while promoting economical growth" (source: European Union (EU) website).

7. Sustainable trading is also often related to the reduction in carbon emissions which is acknowledged to be an important factor linked to climate change. It is now argued that climate change is one of the greatest threats facing mankind.

8. Climate change is being caused by the build up of greenhouse gases (GHGs) in the atmosphere from human activities, primarily the burning of fossil fuels, to provide the energy for the goods and services that we use every day.

9. There are several gases that contribute to the greenhouse effect and the best known is carbon dioxide. These other gases have different effects, and are usually measured and reported as the equivalent amount of carbon dioxide. For the purposes of this case, all gases are described as "GHGs" or "Carbon emissions" although they include the equivalent amount of other harmful gases.

10 The supermarket industry has been slow to react to the need for sustainable trading as there has been a period of intense price competition and the focus of most supermarkets has been on maintaining customer loyalty and profitability. All global supermarket chains measure and report a range of statistics concerning their sustainability or "green" credentials, but some have not incorporated sustainability into their strategic plans.

11 Currently, around 2,500 organisations globally now measure and disclose their carbon emissions and climate change strategies. It is recognised that retail businesses can play an important role in tackling climate change but many businesses are slow to respond to the challenges. In a recent survey, it was found that 85% of Chief Executives believe that companies do integrate the measurement of sustainability into their businesses. However, only 64% of Chief Executives considered that their companies do so effectively. Clearly there is enormous scope for improvement by companies to monitor and improve their levels of sustainable trading.

12 A recent assessment of 500 global companies which have set themselves carbon emission reduction targets shows that only 19% of these companies have shown significant carbon emission reductions. The opinion of researchers demonstrates that the response of companies to make significant reductions is "not equal to the global sustainability challenges faced". Therefore there is huge scope for large reductions in carbon emissions if companies are focussed on achieving real change in the way that they operate.

Carbon credits

13 Carbon credits and carbon markets are part of the international attempt to reduce the growth of carbon emissions, which is primarily carbon dioxide. One carbon credit is equal to one tonne of carbon dioxide (or equivalent gases). One tonne is equivalent to around 1,000 kilograms (kg). All measurements of carbon emissions in this case study are shown in kg.

14 Carbon credits were created following the Kyoto Protocol in 1997 which aims to reduce carbon emissions. Since that date more than 180 countries have ratified their agreement to reduce the volume of carbon emissions.

Papy supermarkets

15 The Papy supermarket brand was formed in the early 1950's in a European country and was initially a family-run business. It was listed on the stock exchange of its home country in 1960. The number of stores operated by the Papy group has grown considerably since.

16 The Papy supermarket chain now operates in its home European country as well as in 7 other European countries. It does not currently operate outside of Europe. Its Board considers that there is plenty of room for the company to grow within Europe, where its supply chain is established and works efficiently. It does not offer Internet shopping at present.

17 A summary of Papy's key personnel is shown in **Appendix 1** on pages 9 and 10.

18 The Papy chain had 1,156 stores operational at 31 December 2010. These stores generated total sales revenues of over €12,900 million in the financial year ended 31 December 2010. The operating profit was €658 million.

19 Within the portfolio of 1,156 stores, 414 stores are large supermarkets, with an average store size of 2,800 square metres. The remaining 742 Papy stores are small convenience stores.

20 A summary of Papy's stores and statistics is shown in **Appendix 2** on page 11.

Papy's recent history

21 Over the last 10 years, trading conditions have been very competitive, but Papy has shown an increase in profits and earnings per share (EPS) each year. The company has not opened many large supermarkets in the last 10 years, but it has expanded the number of small convenience stores from 360 to 742 stores at 31 December 2010.

22 The company operates a dual pricing policy whereby some products are slightly higher priced at the small convenience stores, although still competitively priced. Customer numbers have increased across all stores in the last 5 years. Furthermore, the number of customers who regularly shop at Papy stores, as measured by loyalty card usage, has increased.

23 During 2010, the average sales revenue of all customers has shown a small increase when expressed as revenue per visit. For example, in supermarket stores, the average sales revenue per customer per visit was €121.10 in the year ended 31 December 2010, which is a small increase on the revenue per customer per visit of €118.75 for the year ended 31 December 2009.

Financials and shares

24 Papy generated sales revenue of €12,911 million in the financial year ended 31 December 2010, with a gross profit of €2,608 million (20.2%). Its operating profit was €658 million, a margin of 5.1%, up from 4.9% in the year ended 31 December 2009, due to both a small growth in the gross margin and a small reduction in the administration costs as a percentage of sales revenue.

25 The earnings per share (EPS) for the year ended 31 December 2010 was €4.544 (year to 31 December 2009 EPS was €4.219). This is an increase of 7.7%.

26 An extract from the accounts for Papy is shown in **Appendix 3** on page 12.

27 Papy's Cash Flow Statement for the year ended 31 December 2010 is shown in **Appendix 4** on page 13.

28 There are 100 million shares in issue and 200 million authorised shares. The majority are held by large investors including institutional investors and the founding family has retained only around 5% of the shares.

29 Papy operates an employee share scheme which rewards all of its employees with free shares dependent on the achievement of individual store profitability targets as well as the achievement of a range of group financial targets. Papy's employee share scheme currently purchases shares already in issue to meet the requirements for shares given to employees. The total cost of shares given to Papy's employees is included in administrative expenses in the Statement of Comprehensive Income.

Sustainable trading

30 There are many facets to sustainable trading in the supermarket industry. Some of Papy's competitors, especially the largest global supermarket companies, have already started to address the need to become more sustainable companies. The facets of sustainable trading include the following:

31
- Reductions in energy consumption
- Reduction in carbon emissions
- Use of alternative sources of power
- Reduction in waste and improved levels of recycling
- Reduction in the volume of free plastic carrier bags given to customers
- Being a responsible employer and improving the well-being of employees
- Providing training to employees to enhance their career development

- Paying a fair price to suppliers
- Sourcing products from suppliers which are also trying to be responsible and sustainable in the ways in which they operate
- Sourcing of paper and wooden products from recycled sources as well as from companies which operate sustainable forests
- Inspecting the working conditions at supplier sites and taking action where they do not meet company standards
- Selection and assistance to Papy's supply chain companies to enhance their sustainable trading credentials
- Reviving local rural life with the opening of convenience stores in small communities.

Competitor analysis

32 Papy is operating in a competitive market in a total of 8 European countries. It is difficult to assess Papy's overall market share across the European countries in which it operates. However, in its "home" country, Papy has a market share of around 19% and it is within the top 3 supermarket chains, based on sales revenues, in this country.

33 The table below compares some key performance indicators of Papy against 3 of its competitors based on data extracted from the annual accounts and report for the latest available financial year.

	Papy	Competitor 1	Competitor 2	Competitor 3
Revenue (total group) € million (see Note 1 below)	12,911	53,900	64,020	11,820
Operating profit margin	5.1%	5.9%	3.4%	4.8%
Number of stores – Europe only (end of year figures)	1,156	2,576	5,420	1,046
Market share in "home" country (see Note 2 below)	19.0%	22.9%	28.9%	22.0%
Change in market share over last year	+ 0.3%	+ 0.1%	+ 0.8%	+ 0.2%
Free disposable plastic bags (shown as per square metre of sales area)	549	506	266	580
Carbon emissions (GHGs) (shown as kilograms (kg) per average square metre of sales area)	1,042	681	243	1,005

34

35 Notes to the table above:

1. Revenue figures for each of the competitors include revenues generated from Internet shopping and revenues generated outside of Europe.

2. Market share in "home" country reflects a different "home" country for each of the competitors.

Recent Boardroom changes

36 Tobias Otte had been Papy's Chief Executive for 12 years. However, due to poor health over the last 2 years, he had not given his full attention to the need for changes within the Papy group. The most notable area where Papy has fallen behind its competitors is in the monitoring and targeted reduction of energy and carbon emissions.

37 Tobias Otte retired in March 2011 and the in-coming Chief Executive, Lucas Meyer, is renowned for his ability to bring about change within the companies for which he has worked. His first action on arrival was to obtain Board approval for a new Board position of Corporate Affairs Director. He was then instrumental in recruiting Arif Karp, who had been working as a consultant advising companies on how to reduce carbon emissions and to improve the performance measures for these companies' corporate social responsibilities.

38 An extract from a recent press announcement by Papy's new Chief Executive is shown in **Appendix 5** on page 14.

39 Arif Karp joined Papy on 20 June 2011. He is currently establishing the range and the quality of the data currently being collected by Papy and assessing the integrity of the data. He plans to form a team to prepare and implement new proposals.

Corporate Social Responsibilities

40 Papy has made significant progress in many of the areas of its Corporate Social Responsibilities and in the last year it has had some major achievements but the group still faces many challenges. Papy's CSR responsibilities have been split into 5 sections which are:

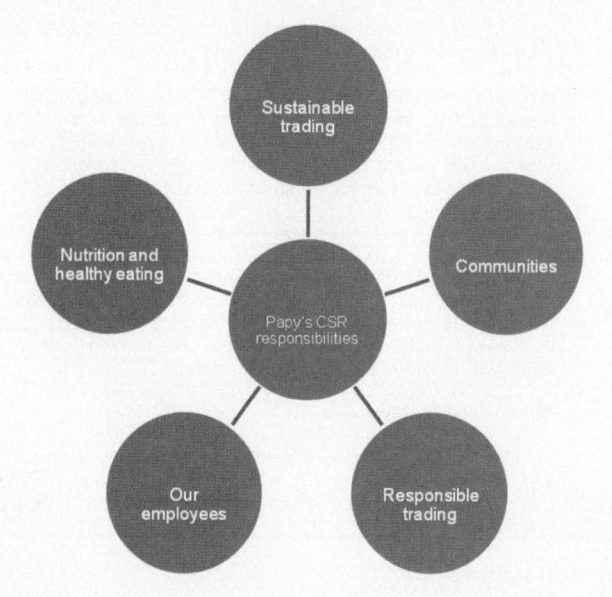

- Sustainable trading
- Communities
- Responsible trading
- Our employees
- Nutrition and healthy eating

(Papy's CSR responsibilities)

Sustainable trading

41 The biggest challenge facing Papy, as well as many other companies worldwide in a wide range of industries, is sustainable trading and the impact of its operations on the environment and on climate change. Papy currently has targets for its carbon emissions, which are measured as "carbon emissions in kilograms (kg) per square metre of sales area".

42 Papy is also reducing its waste materials and is improving the volume and range of materials that it recycles. Papy is committed to reducing the volume and types of packaging for its products in order to reduce waste.

43 The availability of free disposable bags at checkouts is being discouraged and customers in some countries have been offered free re-usable shopping bags. Papy has reduced the weight and the type of plastic used in the manufacture of its carrier bags and is actively encouraging customers to re-use bags, including a credit to customers' loyalty cards for re-using carrier bags.

Some of Papy's current sustainability measures are shown in **Appendix 6** on page 15.

Communities

44 In respect of the communities in which Papy operates, it has established a range of community and school projects and supports a range of charities. Additionally, Papy's employees are encouraged to participate in community projects, both voluntarily and through paid secondments, to lend Papy's skills to enhance community and charitable projects.

Responsible trading

45 Papy would like to be considered as a responsible retailer which treats its suppliers and its customers fairly. During the last year, Papy expanded its range of ethically sourced products, both "Fair Trade" labelled products and other ethically sourced products. "Fair Trade" labelled products are defined as those produced by an organised social movement which helps small-scale farmers in developing countries to obtain better trading conditions than they could achieve individually, and ensures a fair price is paid to producers in order for them to earn a living wage.

46 Papy only procures fish from suppliers which meet the criteria set out in the international fishing industry's guide to responsible purchasing practices.

47 In a survey of Papy's supply chain, over 90% of suppliers considered they are treated with respect by Papy and that a fair price was negotiated. Some of Papy's suppliers have entered into longer-term contracts than in the past, in order to reflect Papy's commitment, loyalty and support to agricultural producers worldwide. Papy also inspects the working conditions at supplier sites to ensure compliance with its policy for suppliers' working conditions.

Employees

48 Papy has almost 97,000 full-time equivalent (FTE) employees. Papy values its employees and has many dedicated training centres to enhance their skills. Papy is developing more managerial level employees in each of the countries in which it operates, in order to help to build upon its successful expansion. It has also been training its employees in order to raise their awareness of environmentally-friendly actions.

Nutrition and healthy eating

49 Nutrition and healthy eating is another important CSR responsibility in which Papy is keen to find and promote the right message to help its customers make more healthy eating choices. Papy has expanded its ranges of healthy eating products and 100% of products are labelled with nutritional values.

IT systems

50 Papy has a range of sophisticated and integrated IT systems which range from logistics to finance systems. Papy's procurement IT systems are linked to over 70% of its suppliers. Orders are tracked from supplier to distribution depots and onto each store location using the latest scanning IT solutions.

51 Because of Papy's significant growth throughout Europe in recent years and the increase in the number of stores in operation, Papy's IT Director, Ziad Abbill, has needed to invest heavily in IT

hardware and software solutions. This ensures that the IT capacity is more than adequate to cope with the forecast growth in the volume of goods procured, control of inventory (which is so important in the food retailing industry as products have a short shelf life) and retail transactions.

52 To meet the requirements of consumer legislation, Papy's computerised tills need to ensure all special offers, both group and local store offers, are correctly reflected in prices charged to its customers.

53 Ziad Abbill is currently having discussions with Arif Karp on the possible need for an Environmental Management System (EMS). This type of IT system would be used to capture and report on a wide range of non-financial data. This could help Papy's management team to track and report on a range of issues concerning sustainable trading.

Carbon emissions

54 The Papy chain of supermarkets generates carbon emissions in many ways and reports these under sustainable trading within Papy's CSR responsibilities (shown on page 6). Papy's carbon emissions are generated in the following ways:

1. Heating, cooling and lighting at stores and distribution depots
2. Moving products to the stores
3. Construction of new stores

55 Furthermore, carbon emissions are generated by suppliers in Papy's supply chain. Additionally, Papy's customers generate their own carbon footprint by travelling to and from Papy stores and also in the way they use the products bought and dispose of its packaging. Arif Karp also recognises that the majority of the carbon emissions which are generated in the manufacture or processing of the products that Papy sells, originate from its supply chain. He would like to educate and encourage Papy's suppliers in order to assist them to reduce their carbon emissions.

56 Until recently, Papy's Board has set targets for reductions in carbon emissions in an unstructured way with no real definition of what actions are required in order to make significant reductions. Therefore, whilst the spirit of reductions has been embraced by Papy's management team, there has been no overall strategy developed in order to achieve the reductions. Whilst there has been a range of initiatives, which include more efficient logistics for deliveries to stores, reduced packaging and the increased use of rail transportation rather than road, there has not been an integrated approach on a large scale to tackle and reduce Papy's carbon emissions.

57 The new Chief Executive, Lucas Meyer, wants to change the way in which the Papy chain of stores operates, so that it can reduce its carbon emissions and become a more sustainable retailing company. Therefore, Arif Karp considers that Papy needs to set targets for the coming years and to plan how reductions in carbon emissions could be achieved.

Appendix 1 (page 1)

Papy's key personnel

Non-executive Chairman - Dmitry Baludia
Dmitry Baludia, aged 58, became Non-executive Chairman in January 2010. Prior to this he held an executive position on the Papy Board as Operations and Logistics Director. He was instrumental in Papy's expansion into the 7 European countries in which it now operates. He has worked for Papy for over 22 years. Prior to this he held a senior role in another food retailing company.

Chief Executive - Lucas Meyer (newly appointed)
— Tobias Otte (retired)

Tobias Otte, aged 55, was the Chief Executive of Papy for 12 years and he retired due to ill-health in March 2011 after a period of poor health over the last 2 years.

Lucas Meyer, aged 47, was appointed Chief Executive on 1 May 2011. He previously held the role of Chief Executive for a major European clothing retailer for 4 years. Prior to this role he had been the Finance Director for a global sportswear brand. The Board considers that his experience in non-food retailing will bring new knowledge to Papy. He is also known for his ability to bring about change and to introduce new ideas in the companies he has worked for. The new Chief Executive believes that the Papy group of supermarkets has not been taking its Corporate Social Responsibility seriously enough. He has been key in the creation of a new Board role of Corporate Affairs Director.

Operations and Logistics Director - Rafael Lucci
Rafael Lucci, aged 42, has worked for Papy for only 5 years. He joined as the Operations and Logistics Manager in one of the European countries that Papy expanded into 5 years ago. He has proved himself to be a good manager and has worked closely with Ziad Abbill, the IT Director, to introduce new IT solutions to improve operational efficiency and to save costs. He was promoted to his current position in January 2010 when Dmitry Baludia became Non-executive Chairman.

Corporate Affairs Director – Arif Karp
Arif Karp, aged 43, was appointed to this new role on 20 June 2011, in order to initiate change within Papy. Arif Karp was previously in the role of a consultant for a leading global consultancy company which advised companies on how to reduce carbon emissions and to improve their performance measures in respect of their corporate social responsibilities. This consultancy company agreed to allow him to take up this position at Papy without serving all of his notice period, as it believed that he would bring good publicity for the consultancy group with the work that he will undertake at Papy. He has worked with Lucas Meyer in his previous role and they have a good respect for each other's skills.

Finance Director – Abdul Yarkol
Abdul Yarkol, aged 55, has been Papy's Finance Director for 8 years after a member of the founding Papy family retired. He has been frustrated at the lack of leadership over the last 2 years, due to the ill-health of the now retired Chief Executive, Tobias Otte.

IT Director – Ziad Abbill
Ziad Abbill, aged 38 and the youngest Board member, has been on the Papy Board for 2 years. He has proved himself as a committed, highly motivated individual who has overseen a number of significant changes in Papy's IT systems. He is well liked and respected as he has the ability to listen to the needs of the system's users.

Marketing Director – Karen Wagnes
Karen Wagnes, aged 52, was appointed to the Papy Board 6 years ago having held various managerial roles in marketing and store management for Papy in the preceding 6 years. She had previously worked in a marketing role for a competing supermarket company.

Appendix 1 (page 2)

Papy's key personnel (continued)

65 *Human Resources Director – Simona Papy*
Simona Papy, aged 45, joined the Papy Board 3 years ago. She is a member of the founding Papy family and has worked in many roles throughout the company including a period as store manager at one of the largest of the Papy chain of supermarkets. In this role she identified the importance of staff motivation and took a post-graduate course in Human Relations. She worked in a senior role in the HR department for several years before she was appointed, on merit, as HR Director, when the previous HR Director left the company.

66 *Non-executive directors*
Papy has 7 Non-executive directors

67 *CSR Manager – Suzanna Nec*
Suzanna Nec, aged 54, has worked for Papy for over 30 years and has been the CSR Manager reporting to the Papy Board for the last 12 years but is not a Board Director. She has been involved in a period of great change for the company and has many skills to offer. However, the new Chief Executive, Lucas Meyer, did not consider that she had the skill set required to be appointed to the new role of Corporate Affairs Director. She reports directly to Arif Karp.

Appendix 2

Summary of Papy's stores and statistics

	Year ended 31 December 2009 Actual	Year ended 31 December 2010 Actual	Year ended 31 December 2011 Latest full year forecast
Number of stores:			
Start of year			
Supermarkets	400	406	414
Small convenience stores	700	716	742
Total	1,100	1,122	1,156
New store openings:			
Supermarkets	6	8	8
Small convenience stores	30	32	22
Total	36	40	30
Closures:			
Supermarkets	0	0	0
Small convenience stores	14	6	4
Total	14	6	4
End of year:			
Supermarkets	406	414	422
Small convenience stores	716	742	760
Total	1,122	1,156	1,182
Average for the year			
Supermarkets	403	410	418
Small convenience stores	708	729	751
Total	1,111	1,139	1,169
Total sales area (all stores) (square metres)			
- end year	1,351,600	1,381,800	1,409,600
- average for the year	1,340,800	1,366,700	1,395,700
Average sales revenue per square metre of sales area €	9,427	9,447	9,468
Average sales revenue per FTE employee €	132,293	133,356	133,771

Appendix 3

Extract from Papy's Statement of Comprehensive Income, Statement of Financial Position and Statement of Changes in Equity

Statement of Comprehensive Income	Year ended 31 December 2010 € million	Year ended 31 December 2009 € million
Revenue	12,911.0	12,640.0
Cost of sales	10,303.0	10,099.0
Gross profit	2,608.0	2,541.0
Administrative expenses	1,950.0	1,921.0
Operating profit	658.0	620.0
Finance income	17.3	14.9
Finance expense	69.4	72.3
Profit before tax	605.9	562.6
Tax expense (effective tax rate is 25%)	151.5	140.7
Profit for the period	454.4	421.9

Statement of Financial Position	As at 31 December 2010 € million	€ million	As at 31 December 2009 € million	€ million
Non-current assets (net)		3,247.0		3,396.0
Current assets				
Inventory	1,072.0		1,086.0	
Trade receivables	336.0		322.0	
Cash and cash equivalents	603.9		480.0	
Total current assets		2,011.9		1,888.0
Total assets		5,258.9		5,284.0
Equity and liabilities				
Equity				
Share capital	100.0		100.0	
Share premium	635.0		635.0	
Retained earnings	1,369.4		1,105.0	
Total Equity		2,104.4		1,840.0
Non-current liabilities				
Long term loans		870.0		1,020.0
Current liabilities				
Trade payables	2,133.0		2,283.3	
Tax payables	151.5		140.7	
Total current liabilities		2,284.5		2,424.0
Total equity and liabilities		5,258.9		5,284.0

Note: Paid in share capital represents 100 million shares of €1.00 each at 31 December 2010

Statement of Changes in Equity For the year ended 31 December 2010	Share Capital € million	Share premium € million	Retained earnings € million	Total € million
Balance at 31 December 2009	100.0	635.0	1,105.0	1,840.0
Profit	-	-	454.4	454.4
Dividends paid	-	-	190.0	190.0
Balance at 31 December 2010	100.0	635.0	1,369.4	2,104.4

Appendix 4

Cash Flow Statement

	Year ended 31 December 2010	
	€ million	€ million
Cash flows from operating activities:		
Profit before taxation (after Finance costs (net))		605.9
Adjustments:		
Depreciation	541.0	
Finance costs (net)	52.1	
		593.1
(Increase) / decrease in inventories	14.0	
(Increase) / decrease in trade receivables	(14.0)	
Increase / (decrease) in trade payables (excluding taxation)	(150.3)	
		(150.3)
Cash generated from operations		1,048.7
Finance costs (net) paid	(52.1)	
Tax paid	(140.7)	
		(192.8)
Cash generated from operating activities		855.9
Cash flows from investing activities:		
Purchase of non-current assets (net)	(392.0)	
Cash used in investing activities		(392.0)
Cash flows from financing activities:		
Repayment of loans	(150.0)	
Dividends paid	(190.0)	
Cash flows from financing activities		(340.0)
Net increase in cash and cash equivalents		123.9
Cash and cash equivalents at 31 December 2009		480.0
Cash and cash equivalents at 31 December 2010		603.9

Appendix 5

Press report on Papy's announcement to become more sustainable

Date: 24 June 2011

The new Chief Executive of Papy, Lucas Meyer, announced yesterday his intention for the Papy chain of supermarkets to change the way in which it operates, in order to become a more sustainable business.

He stated "the Papy chain will incorporate sustainability in its strategy and it will also promote the need for a more sustainable attitude in the food retailing business, both to customers and to its own supply chain". He further commented "Papy should take a greater responsibility for the effect it has on the environment in which it operates".

Lucas Meyer further stated that "with fossil fuel due to run out in 40 years time there has never been a greater need for action. We can no longer wait for Governments to legislate to force change upon us. We should not be complacent and wait for our competitors to spur us into taking actions".

He continued by stating "We, at Papy, are going to make changes in the way that we operate that will affect our supply chain and our customers. However, we feel that the changes we will make in the coming months, and years, are the right way to operate a business in the long-term. We are confident that our loyal customers will see that what we plan to do will help Papy to trade in a much more sustainable way. We aim to reduce carbon emissions and make changes in order to become a business that can maintain its long-term presence in this industry".

Lucas Meyer added "in order to survive in the competitive food retailing market we must change. Innovation is the key to our future success".

By the end of trading on 23 June 2011, Papy's share price had risen to €38.80 per share.

Appendix 6

Some of Papy's current Sustainability Indicators for the period 2008 to 2010

Energy consumption

Energy consumption (kWh per square metre of sales area)

Year	kWh per square metre of sales area
2008	911
2009	880
2010	858

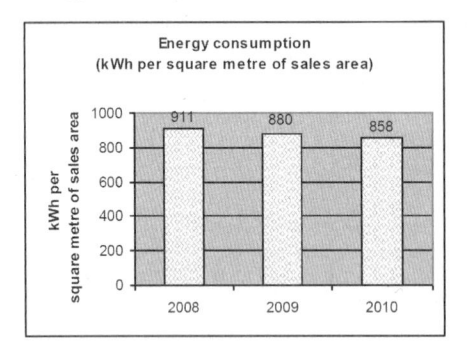

The reported measure is the average kilowatt hours (kWh) divided by the total number of square metres of sales area.

Free disposable plastic bags

The reported measure is the number of free disposable plastic bags purchased by Papy and given to customers at checkouts, divided by the total number of square metres of sales area.

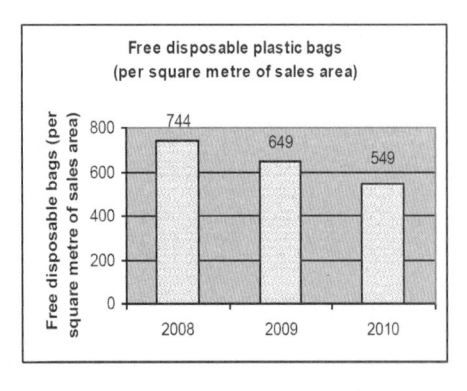

Free disposable plastic bags (per square metre of sales area)

Year	Free disposable bags per square metre of sales area
2008	744
2009	649
2010	549

Carbon emissions

Carbon emissions in kg per square metre of sales area

Year	Kg of Carbon emissions per square metre of sales area
2008	1,109
2009	1,077
2010	1,042

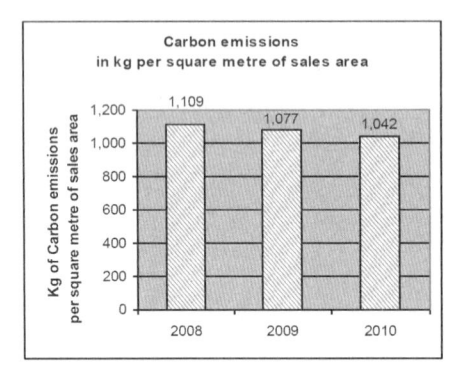

This is the consolidated total of all carbon emissions in kilograms (kg) (including Papy's stores' and warehouses' energy consumption and the transportation of products to stores) divided by Papy's average sales area (in square metres) for each year.

The reported measure is carbon emissions in kilograms (kg) per square metre of sales area.

This measure excludes carbon emissions generated by Papy's supply chain.

End of pre-seen material

Papy: some help from BPP

After you have read and marked up the case, remember it is important to work through and analyse the pre-seen material in detail, before summarising the key points.

This chapter is designed to help you as you work through the pre-seen material, and highlights the sorts of question you should be asking as you do.

Again, though, remember that in conjunction with your detailed reading of the case you must also be preparing a general strategic analysis of Papy as you analyse the pre-seen material: for example, SWOT analysis, stakeholder analysis, consideration of Porter's generic strategies, change management and corporate social responsibility.

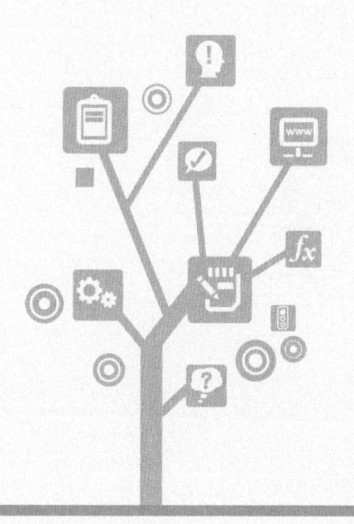

And don't forget that once you have worked through all the pre-seen material you must then synthesise what you know, as we showed you in Chapter 10 in the Zubinos case.

Remember, you should ultimately be aiming to summarise the key findings from your analysis of pre-seen material into a one-page business summary.

Finally, remember that the BPP Learning Media toolkit for your paper will provide you with detailed activities which help you analyse the pre-seen material specifically related to your exam.

topic list

1 Reading the case in detail

2 Analysis of the case

1 Reading the case in detail

Sustainable trading in the supermarket industry

The supermarket industry

1. There are many large international companies which operate supermarkets in a range of countries around the world using globally recognised brand names. Most of the supermarket chains have a large market share in their home country and have expanded to other countries both by acquisition and by organic growth. There have been many acquisitions of smaller supermarket chains in order to achieve greater economies of scale and to expand the promotion of the supermarket brand globally.

2. Most of the large supermarkets sell a wide range of products with food items comprising less than 75% of revenues. Non-food items include household and electrical goods as well as clothing and shoes.

3. The trend in the past was to build and operate larger and larger stores with the view that most people would make the journey to a large supermarket to shop. However, over the last decade there has been a reversal in this trend with the opening (mainly through acquisition) of smaller "convenience" stores enabling people to shop locally. A small "convenience" store is defined as a small retail store which is open long hours offering a limited range of food and household products and is located in city centre or suburban residential areas. Within city centres, these convenience stores have generated increasingly high sales levels. This has encouraged supermarket chains to operate a portfolio of smaller "convenience" stores as well as large supermarket stores.

4. Some global food retailers operate a range of brands and have a portfolio of several types of stores, ranging from very large "hypermarkets" to smaller "convenience" local stores. A "hypermarket" is defined as a very large retail store which combines a grocery supermarket and a department store, situated at out-of-town locations and generally having a sales area of over 20,000 square metres.

5. The global supermarket industry is highly competitive and most brands compete primarily on price. There have been many changes in the way supermarkets operate over the last decade. These innovations include internet shopping, wider ranges of organic produce, wider ranges of non-food products and the expansion of "own brand" products and "value" ranges. "Own brand" products are food and household products which display the brand name of the store selling it rather than that of the company which made it. "Value" ranges are defined as goods sold at substantially lower prices than other comparable products under "own brand value range" labels, so that the target customers consider that they are getting exceptional value for money.

Background information on sustainable trading

6. Sustainable trading is defined as "a trading system that does not harm the environment or deteriorate social conditions while promoting economical growth" (source: European Union (EU) website).

7. Sustainable trading is also often related to the reduction in carbon emissions which is acknowledged to be an important factor linked to climate change. It is now argued that climate change is one of the greatest threats facing mankind.

8. Climate change is being caused by the build up of greenhouse gases (GHGs) in the atmosphere from human activities, primarily the burning of fossil fuels, to provide the energy for the goods and services that we use every day.

9. There are several gases that contribute to the greenhouse effect and the best known is carbon dioxide. These other gases have different effects, and are usually measured and reported as the equivalent amount of carbon dioxide. For the purposes of this case, all gases are described as "GHGs" or "Carbon emissions" although they include the equivalent amount of other harmful gases.

Page 2 of the Pre-seen

Paras	
1-2	What do these paragraphs tell us about the competitive pressures and competitive strategies in the supermarket industry?
	What are the implications of these competitive pressures and competitive strategies for Papy supermarkets?
3-5	Why do supermarkets follow the strategies of opening convenience stores, offering differentiated product ranges, offering on-line shopping and selling non-food items?
	Does Papy supermarkets follow all three strategies?
	Which strategies of real-world supermarkets are not mentioned in these paragraphs?
6-9	What issues might a supermarket focus on in order to improve its 'sustainable trading' performance?

10 The supermarket industry has been slow to react to the need for sustainable trading as there has been a period of intense price competition and the focus of most supermarkets has been on maintaining customer loyalty and profitability. All global supermarket chains measure and report a range of statistics concerning their sustainability or "green" credentials, but some have not incorporated sustainability into their strategic plans.

11 Currently, around 2,500 organisations globally now measure and disclose their carbon emissions and climate change strategies. It is recognised that retail businesses can play an important role in tackling climate change but many businesses are slow to respond to the challenges. In a recent survey, it was found that 85% of Chief Executives believe that companies do integrate the measurement of sustainability into their businesses. However, only 64% of Chief Executives considered that their companies do so effectively. Clearly there is enormous scope for improvement by companies to monitor and improve their levels of sustainable trading.

12 A recent assessment of 500 global companies which have set themselves carbon emission reduction targets shows that only 19% of these companies have shown significant carbon emission reductions. The opinion of researchers demonstrates that the response of companies to make significant reductions is "not equal to the global sustainability challenges faced". Therefore there is huge scope for large reductions in carbon emissions if companies are focussed on achieving real change in the way that they operate.

Carbon credits

13 Carbon credits and carbon markets are part of the international attempt to reduce the growth of carbon emissions, which is primarily carbon dioxide. One carbon credit is equal to one tonne of carbon dioxide (or equivalent gases). One tonne is equivalent to around 1,000 kilograms (kg). All measurements of carbon emissions in this case study are shown in kg.

14 Carbon credits were created following the Kyoto Protocol in 1997 which aims to reduce carbon emissions. Since that date more than 180 countries have ratified their agreement to reduce the volume of carbon emissions.

Papy supermarkets

15 The Papy supermarket brand was formed in the early 1950's in a European country and was initially a family-run business. It was listed on the stock exchange of its home country in 1960. The number of stores operated by the Papy group has grown considerably since.

16 The Papy supermarket chain now operates in its home European country as well as in 7 other European countries. It does not currently operate outside of Europe. Its Board considers that there is plenty of room for the company to grow within Europe, where its supply chain is established and works efficiently. It does not offer Internet shopping at present.

17 A summary of Papy's key personnel is shown in **Appendix 1** on pages 9 and 10.

18 The Papy chain had 1,156 stores operational at 31 December 2010. These stores generated total sales revenues of over €12,900 million in the financial year ended 31 December 2010. The operating profit was €658 million.

19 Within the portfolio of 1,156 stores, 414 stores are large supermarkets, with an average store size of 2,800 square metres. The remaining 742 Papy stores are small convenience stores.

20 A summary of Papy's stores and statistics is shown in **Appendix 2** on page 11.

PART C PRACTICE TOPCIMA CASES
18: Papy: some help from BPP

Paras	
10-12	How may the issues in these paragraphs be used to create questions on exam day?
13-14	Why are carbon credits and carbon markets relevant to Papy's sustainability objectives?
15-16	How might the information in these paragraphs be used in the exam?
17-20	What financial analysis might these paragraphs lead you to suggest?

Papy's recent history

21 Over the last 10 years, trading conditions have been very competitive, but Papy has shown an increase in profits and earnings per share (EPS) each year. The company has not opened many large supermarkets in the last 10 years, but it has expanded the number of small convenience stores from 360 to 742 stores at 31 December 2010.

22 The company operates a dual pricing policy whereby some products are slightly higher priced at the small convenience stores, although still competitively priced. Customer numbers have increased across all stores in the last 5 years. Furthermore, the number of customers who regularly shop at Papy stores, as measured by loyalty card usage, has increased.

23 During 2010, the average sales revenue of all customers has shown a small increase when expressed as revenue per visit. For example, in supermarket stores, the average sales revenue per customer per visit was €121.10 in the year ended 31 December 2010, which is a small increase on the revenue per customer per visit of €118.75 for the year ended 31 December 2009.

Financials and shares

24 Papy generated sales revenue of €12,911 million in the financial year ended 31 December 2010, with a gross profit of €2,608 million (20.2%). Its operating profit was €658 million, a margin of 5.1%, up from 4.9% in the year ended 31 December 2009, due to both a small growth in the gross margin and a small reduction in the administration costs as a percentage of sales revenue.

25 The earnings per share (EPS) for the year ended 31 December 2010 was €4.544 (year to 31 December 2009 EPS was €4.219). This is an increase of 7.7%.

26 An extract from the accounts for Papy is shown in **Appendix 3** on page 12.

27 Papy's Cash Flow Statement for the year ended 31 December 2010 is shown in **Appendix 4** on page 13.

28 There are 100 million shares in issue and 200 million authorised shares. The majority are held by large investors including institutional investors and the founding family has retained only around 5% of the shares.

29 Papy operates an employee share scheme which rewards all of its employees with free shares dependent on the achievement of individual store profitability targets as well as the achievement of a range of group financial targets. Papy's employee share scheme currently purchases shares already in issue to meet the requirements for shares given to employees. The total cost of shares given to Papy's employees is included in administrative expenses in the Statement of Comprehensive Income.

Sustainable trading

30 There are many facets to sustainable trading in the supermarket industry. Some of Papy's competitors, especially the largest global supermarket companies, have already started to address the need to become more sustainable companies. The facets of sustainable trading include the following:

31
- Reductions in energy consumption
- Reduction in carbon emissions
- Use of alternative sources of power
- Reduction in waste and improved levels of recycling
- Reduction in the volume of free plastic carrier bags given to customers
- Being a responsible employer and improving the well-being of employees
- Providing training to employees to enhance their career development

Paras	
21-23	Does the rise in profits and EPS prove that Papy is following a successful strategy?
	Why might the revenue per visit have increased?
24-27	Does the information in these paragraphs suggest Papy is doing well?
28	What is the significance of this information on share ownership?
29	Why would Papy operate this employee share scheme and does it promote higher shareholder wealth?
	Is it usual for firms to buy shares back from the open market to give to employees?
30-31	How many of these facets of sustainable trading are addressed by Papy at the moment?
	How might the examiner use this list to create questions per exam day?

- Paying a fair price to suppliers
- Sourcing products from suppliers which are also trying to be responsible and sustainable in the ways in which they operate
- Sourcing of paper and wooden products from recycled sources as well as from companies which operate sustainable forests
- Inspecting the working conditions at supplier sites and taking action where they do not meet company standards
- Selection and assistance to Papy's supply chain companies to enhance their sustainable trading credentials
- Reviving local rural life with the opening of convenience stores in small communities.

Competitor analysis

32 Papy is operating in a competitive market in a total of 8 European countries. It is difficult to assess Papy's overall market share across the European countries in which it operates. However, in its "home" country, Papy has a market share of around 19% and it is within the top 3 supermarket chains, based on sales revenues, in this country.

33 The table below compares some key performance indicators of Papy against 3 of its competitors based on data extracted from the annual accounts and report for the latest available financial year.

	Papy	Competitor 1	Competitor 2	Competitor 3
Revenue (total group) € million (see Note 1 below)	12,911	53,900	64,020	11,820
Operating profit margin	5.1%	5.9%	3.4%	4.8%
Number of stores – Europe only (end of year figures)	1,156	2,576	5,420	1,046
Market share in "home" country (see Note 2 below)	19.0%	22.9%	28.9%	22.0%
Change in market share over last year	+ 0.3%	+ 0.1%	+ 0.8%	+ 0.2%
Free disposable plastic bags (shown as per square metre of sales area)	549	506	266	580
Carbon emissions (GHGs) (shown as kilograms (kg) per average square metre of sales area)	1,042	681	243	1,005

34

35 Notes to the table above:

1. Revenue figures for each of the competitors include revenues generated from Internet shopping and revenues generated outside of Europe.

2. Market share in "home" country reflects a different "home" country for each of the competitors.

PART C PRACTICE TOPCIMA CASES 18: Papy: some help from BPP *321*

Paras	
32	What is the relevance of % market share?
33-35	Is Papy one of Europe's larger supermarkets? Which of Papy's competitors is performing the best? How might the information in this table be turned into the subject of a question on exam day?

Recent Boardroom changes

36 Tobias Otte had been Papy's Chief Executive for 12 years. However, due to poor health over the last 2 years, he had not given his full attention to the need for changes within the Papy group. The most notable area where Papy has fallen behind its competitors is in the monitoring and targeted reduction of energy and carbon emissions.

37 Tobias Otte retired in March 2011 and the in-coming Chief Executive, Lucas Meyer, is renowned for his ability to bring about change within the companies for which he has worked. His first action on arrival was to obtain Board approval for a new Board position of Corporate Affairs Director. He was then instrumental in recruiting Arif Karp, who had been working as a consultant advising companies on how to reduce carbon emissions and to improve the performance measures for these companies' corporate social responsibilities.

38 An extract from a recent press announcement by Papy's new Chief Executive is shown in **Appendix 5** on page 14.

39 Arif Karp joined Papy on 20 June 2011. He is currently establishing the range and the quality of the data currently being collected by Papy and assessing the integrity of the data. He plans to form a team to prepare and implement new proposals.

Corporate Social Responsibilities

40 Papy has made significant progress in many of the areas of its Corporate Social Responsibilities and in the last year it has had some major achievements but the group still faces many challenges. Papy's CSR responsibilities have been split into 5 sections which are:

- Sustainable trading
- Communities
- Responsible trading
- Our employees
- Nutrition and healthy eating

(centre: Papy's CSR responsibilities)

Sustainable trading

41 The biggest challenge facing Papy, as well as many other companies worldwide in a wide range of industries, is sustainable trading and the impact of its operations on the environment and on climate change. Papy currently has targets for its carbon emissions, which are measured as "carbon emissions in kilograms (kg) per square metre of sales area".

PART C PRACTICE TOPCIMA CASES   18: Papy: some help from BPP   323

Paras	
36-38	What is likely to be the impact of the replacement of Tobias Otte by Lucas Meyer?
39	How might the information in this paragraph affect exam day?
40-41	What new information is introduced in these paragraphs? Why are the facets of CSR presented as a diagram?

42 Papy is also reducing its waste materials and is improving the volume and range of materials that it recycles. Papy is committed to reducing the volume and types of packaging for its products in order to reduce waste.

43 The availability of free disposable bags at checkouts is being discouraged and customers in some countries have been offered free re-usable shopping bags. Papy has reduced the weight and the type of plastic used in the manufacture of its carrier bags and is actively encouraging customers to re-use bags, including a credit to customers' loyalty cards for re-using carrier bags.

Some of Papy's current sustainability measures are shown in **Appendix 6** on page 15.

Communities

44 In respect of the communities in which Papy operates, it has established a range of community and school projects and supports a range of charities. Additionally, Papy's employees are encouraged to participate in community projects, both voluntarily and through paid secondments, to lend Papy's skills to enhance community and charitable projects.

Responsible trading

45 Papy would like to be considered as a responsible retailer which treats its suppliers and its customers fairly. During the last year, Papy expanded its range of ethically sourced products, both "Fair Trade" labelled products and other ethically sourced products. "Fair Trade" labelled products are defined as those produced by an organised social movement which helps small-scale farmers in developing countries to obtain better trading conditions than they could achieve individually, and ensures a fair price is paid to producers in order for them to earn a living wage.

46 Papy only procures fish from suppliers which meet the criteria set out in the international fishing industry's guide to responsible purchasing practices.

47 In a survey of Papy's supply chain, over 90% of suppliers considered they are treated with respect by Papy and that a fair price was negotiated. Some of Papy's suppliers have entered into longer-term contracts than in the past, in order to reflect Papy's commitment, loyalty and support to agricultural producers worldwide. Papy also inspects the working conditions at supplier sites to ensure compliance with its policy for suppliers' working conditions.

Employees

48 Papy has almost 97,000 full-time equivalent (FTE) employees. Papy values its employees and has many dedicated training centres to enhance their skills. Papy is developing more managerial level employees in each of the countries in which it operates, in order to help to build upon its successful expansion. It has also been training its employees in order to raise their awareness of environmentally-friendly actions.

Nutrition and healthy eating

49 Nutrition and healthy eating is another important CSR responsibility in which Papy is keen to find and promote the right message to help its customers make more healthy eating choices. Papy has expanded its ranges of healthy eating products and 100% of products are labelled with nutritional values.

IT systems

50 Papy has a range of sophisticated and integrated IT systems which range from logistics to finance systems. Papy's procurement IT systems are linked to over 70% of its suppliers. Orders are tracked from supplier to distribution depots and onto each store location using the latest scanning IT solutions.

51 Because of Papy's significant growth throughout Europe in recent years and the increase in the number of stores in operation, Papy's IT Director, Ziad Abbill, has needed to invest heavily in IT

Paras	
42-43	What steps could Papy take in order to reduce waste packaging and to encourage recycling?
	Evaluate the methods being used by Papy to reduce its measured use of plastic bags and suggest additional methods.
44	How could this commitment to communities be measured for reporting purposes?
45-47	What would constitute irresponsible trading?
	What are ethically sourced products?
	Is anything missing from this list of responsible practices?
48	Why is training staff to do their jobs regarded as being CSR when it would seem to be essential for carrying on business?
49	Why has Papy concerned itself with healthy eating?
50-51	How vital is IT to Papy?

hardware and software solutions. This ensures that the IT capacity is more than adequate to cope with the forecast growth in the volume of goods procured, control of inventory (which is so important in the food retailing industry as products have a short shelf life) and retail transactions.

52 To meet the requirements of consumer legislation, Papy's computerised tills need to ensure all special offers, both group and local store offers, are correctly reflected in prices charged to its customers.

53 Ziad Abbill is currently having discussions with Arif Karp on the possible need for an Environmental Management System (EMS). This type of IT system would be used to capture and report on a wide range of non-financial data. This could help Papy's management team to track and report on a range of issues concerning sustainable trading.

Carbon emissions

54 The Papy chain of supermarkets generates carbon emissions in many ways and reports these under sustainable trading within Papy's CSR responsibilities (shown on page 6). Papy's carbon emissions are generated in the following ways:

1. Heating, cooling and lighting at stores and distribution depots
2. Moving products to the stores
3. Construction of new stores

55 Furthermore, carbon emissions are generated by suppliers in Papy's supply chain. Additionally, Papy's customers generate their own carbon footprint by travelling to and from Papy stores and also in the way they use the products bought and dispose of its packaging. Arif Karp also recognises that the majority of the carbon emissions which are generated in the manufacture or processing of the products that Papy sells, originate from its supply chain. He would like to educate and encourage Papy's suppliers in order to assist them to reduce their carbon emissions.

56 Until recently, Papy's Board has set targets for reductions in carbon emissions in an unstructured way with no real definition of what actions are required in order to make significant reductions. Therefore, whilst the spirit of reductions has been embraced by Papy's management team, there has been no overall strategy developed in order to achieve the reductions. Whilst there has been a range of initiatives, which include more efficient logistics for deliveries to stores, reduced packaging and the increased use of rail transportation rather than road, there has not been an integrated approach on a large scale to tackle and reduce Papy's carbon emissions.

57 The new Chief Executive, Lucas Meyer, wants to change the way in which the Papy chain of stores operates, so that it can reduce its carbon emissions and become a more sustainable retailing company. Therefore, Arif Karp considers that Papy needs to set targets for the coming years and to plan how reductions in carbon emissions could be achieved.

Paras	
52-53	What changes to IT systems are likely in the near future?
54-57	What is the potential relevance of the list of ways in which Papy generates carbon to your exam? How might Papy educate its suppliers on carbon emissions? What effect would internet shopping have on Papy's carbon footprint?

Appendix 1 (page 1)

Papy's key personnel

Non-executive Chairman - Dmitry Baludia
Dmitry Baludia, aged 58, became Non-executive Chairman in January 2010. Prior to this he held an executive position on the Papy Board as Operations and Logistics Director. He was instrumental in Papy's expansion into the 7 European countries in which it now operates. He has worked for Papy for over 22 years. Prior to this he held a senior role in another food retailing company.

Chief Executive - Lucas Meyer (newly appointed)
- Tobias Otte (retired)

Tobias Otte, aged 55, was the Chief Executive of Papy for 12 years and he retired due to ill-health in March 2011 after a period of poor health over the last 2 years.

Lucas Meyer, aged 47, was appointed Chief Executive on 1 May 2011. He previously held the role of Chief Executive for a major European clothing retailer for 4 years. Prior to this role he had been the Finance Director for a global sportswear brand. The Board considers that his experience in non-food retailing will bring new knowledge to Papy. He is also known for his ability to bring about change and to introduce new ideas in the companies he has worked for. The new Chief Executive believes that the Papy group of supermarkets has not been taking its Corporate Social Responsibility seriously enough. He has been key in the creation of a new Board role of Corporate Affairs Director.

Operations and Logistics Director - Rafael Lucci
Rafael Lucci, aged 42, has worked for Papy for only 5 years. He joined as the Operations and Logistics Manager in one of the European countries that Papy expanded into 5 years ago. He has proved himself to be a good manager and has worked closely with Ziad Abbill, the IT Director, to introduce new IT solutions to improve operational efficiency and to save costs. He was promoted to his current position in January 2010 when Dmitry Baludia became Non-executive Chairman.

Corporate Affairs Director – Arif Karp
Arif Karp, aged 43, was appointed to this new role on 20 June 2011, in order to initiate change within Papy. Arif Karp was previously in the role of a consultant for a leading global consultancy company which advised companies on how to reduce carbon emissions and to improve their performance measures in respect of their corporate social responsibilities. This consultancy company agreed to allow him to take up this position at Papy without serving all of his notice period, as it believed that he would bring good publicity for the consultancy group with the work that he will undertake at Papy. He has worked with Lucas Meyer in his previous role and they have a good respect for each other's skills.

Finance Director – Abdul Yarkol
Abdul Yarkol, aged 55, has been Papy's Finance Director for 8 years after a member of the founding Papy family retired. He has been frustrated at the lack of leadership over the last 2 years, due to the ill-health of the now retired Chief Executive, Tobias Otte.

IT Director – Ziad Abbill
Ziad Abbill, aged 38 and the youngest Board member, has been on the Papy Board for 2 years. He has proved himself as a committed, highly motivated individual who has overseen a number of significant changes in Papy's IT systems. He is well liked and respected as he has the ability to listen to the needs of the system's users.

Marketing Director – Karen Wagnes
Karen Wagnes, aged 52, was appointed to the Papy Board 6 years ago having held various managerial roles in marketing and store management for Papy in the preceding 6 years. She had previously worked in a marketing role for a competing supermarket company.

PART C PRACTICE TOPCIMA CASES   18: Papy: some help from BPP   329

Paras	
58-64	Why might the case writer have introduced biographical details of named individuals into the pre-seen material?
	Does the Chairman have the right background for the role he has been appointed to?
	Is this an experienced or an inexperienced Board?
	Can any significance be attached to the reduced terms of notice on which Papy recruited Arif Karp?
	Do the previous jobs of the Directors provide any pointers to future directions for Papy?

Appendix 1 (page 2)

Papy's key personnel (continued)

65
Human Resources Director – Simona Papy
Simona Papy, aged 45, joined the Papy Board 3 years ago. She is a member of the founding Papy family and has worked in many roles throughout the company including a period as store manager at one of the largest of the Papy chain of supermarkets. In this role she identified the importance of staff motivation and took a post-graduate course in Human Relations. She worked in a senior role in the HR department for several years before she was appointed, on merit, as HR Director, when the previous HR Director left the company.

66
Non-executive directors
Papy has 7 Non-executive directors

67
CSR Manager – Suzanna Nec
Suzanna Nec, aged 54, has worked for Papy for over 30 years and has been the CSR Manager reporting to the Papy Board for the last 12 years but is not a Board Director. She has been involved in a period of great change for the company and has many skills to offer. However, the new Chief Executive, Lucas Meyer, did not consider that she had the skill set required to be appointed to the new role of Corporate Affairs Director. She reports directly to Arif Karp.

Paras	
65-67	Do these paragraphs cast doubt on the quality of corporate governance at Papy's? Why has the detail about Suzanna Nec been included?

Appendix 2

Summary of Papy's stores and statistics

	Year ended 31 December 2009 Actual	Year ended 31 December 2010 Actual	Year ended 31 December 2011 Latest full year forecast
Number of stores:			
Start of year			
Supermarkets	400	406	414
Small convenience stores	700	716	742
Total	1,100	1,122	1,156
New store openings:			
Supermarkets	6	8	8
Small convenience stores	30	32	22
Total	36	40	30
Closures:			
Supermarkets	0	0	0
Small convenience stores	14	6	4
Total	14	6	4
End of year:			
Supermarkets	406	414	422
Small convenience stores	716	742	760
Total	1,122	1,156	1,182
Average for the year			
Supermarkets	403	410	418
Small convenience stores	708	729	751
Total	1,111	1,139	1,169
Total sales area (all stores) (square metres)			
- end year	1,351,600	1,381,800	1,409,600
- average for the year	1,340,800	1,366,700	1,395,700
Average sales revenue per square metre of sales area €	9,427	9,447	9,468
Average sales revenue per FTE employee €	132,293	133,356	133,771

Appx	
2	What is the average sales area of a convenience store?
	Are convenience stores always a success?
	What is the potential significance of the inclusion of average numbers of stores for the year and how is it arrived at?
	Are the trends of indicators of sales revenue per m^2 of sales area and per FTE encouraging?

Appendix 3

**Extract from Papy's Statement of Comprehensive Income,
Statement of Financial Position and Statement of Changes in Equity**

Statement of Comprehensive Income	Year ended 31 December 2010 € million	Year ended 31 December 2009 € million
Revenue	12,911.0	12,640.0
Cost of sales	10,303.0	10,099.0
Gross profit	2,608.0	2,541.0
Administrative expenses	1,950.0	1,921.0
Operating profit	658.0	620.0
Finance income	17.3	14.9
Finance expense	69.4	72.3
Profit before tax	605.9	562.6
Tax expense (effective tax rate is 25%)	151.5	140.7
Profit for the period	454.4	421.9

Statement of Financial Position	As at 31 December 2010 € million	€ million	As at 31 December 2009 € million	€ million
Non-current assets (net)		3,247.0		3,396.0
Current assets				
Inventory	1,072.0		1,086.0	
Trade receivables	336.0		322.0	
Cash and cash equivalents	603.9		480.0	
Total current assets		2,011.9		1,888.0
Total assets		5,258.9		5,284.0
Equity and liabilities				
Equity				
Share capital	100.0		100.0	
Share premium	635.0		635.0	
Retained earnings	1,369.4		1,105.0	
Total Equity		2,104.4		1,840.0
Non-current liabilities				
Long term loans		870.0		1,020.0
Current liabilities				
Trade payables	2,133.0		2,283.3	
Tax payables	151.5		140.7	
Total current liabilities		2,284.5		2,424.0
Total equity and liabilities		5,258.9		5,284.0

Note: Paid in share capital represents 100 million shares of €1.00 each at 31 December 2010

Statement of Changes in Equity For the year ended 31 December 2010	Share Capital € million	Share premium € million	Retained earnings € million	Total € million
Balance at 31 December 2009	100.0	635.0	1,105.0	1,840.0
Profit	-	-	454.4	454.4
Dividends paid	-	-	190.0	190.0
Balance at 31 December 2010	100.0	635.0	1,369.4	2,104.4

PART C PRACTICE TOPCIMA CASES 18: Papy: some help from BPP

Appx 3

Is Papy's profitability improving or falling and what factors are contributing to this?

Evaluate Papy's use of working capital

Evaluate Papy's Return on Capital Employed

Should Papy invest in new stores?

Appendix 4

Cash Flow Statement

	Year ended 31 December 2010	
	€ million	€ million
Cash flows from operating activities:		
Profit before taxation (after Finance costs (net))		605.9
Adjustments:		
Depreciation	541.0	
Finance costs (net)	52.1	
		593.1
(Increase) / decrease in inventories	14.0	
(Increase) / decrease in trade receivables	(14.0)	
Increase / (decrease) in trade payables (excluding taxation)	(150.3)	
		(150.3)
Cash generated from operations		1,048.7
Finance costs (net) paid	(52.1)	
Tax paid	(140.7)	
		(192.8)
Cash generated from operating activities		855.9
Cash flows from investing activities:		
Purchase of non-current assets (net)	(392.0)	
Cash used in investing activities		(392.0)
Cash flows from financing activities:		
Repayment of loans	(150.0)	
Dividends paid	(190.0)	
Cash flows from financing activities		(340.0)
Net increase in cash and cash equivalents		123.9
Cash and cash equivalents at 31 December 2009		480.0
Cash and cash equivalents at 31 December 2010		603.9

PART C PRACTICE TOPCIMA CASES 18: Papy: some help from BPP

Appx	
4	Is Papy cash positive?

Appendix 5

Press report on Papy's announcement to become more sustainable

Date: 24 June 2011

The new Chief Executive of Papy, Lucas Meyer, announced yesterday his intention for the Papy chain of supermarkets to change the way in which it operates, in order to become a more sustainable business.

He stated "the Papy chain will incorporate sustainability in its strategy and it will also promote the need for a more sustainable attitude in the food retailing business, both to customers and to its own supply chain". He further commented "Papy should take a greater responsibility for the effect it has on the environment in which it operates".

Lucas Meyer further stated that "with fossil fuel due to run out in 40 years time there has never been a greater need for action. We can no longer wait for Governments to legislate to force change upon us. We should not be complacent and wait for our competitors to spur us into taking actions".

He continued by stating "We, at Papy, are going to make changes in the way that we operate that will affect our supply chain and our customers. However, we feel that the changes we will make in the coming months, and years, are the right way to operate a business in the long-term. We are confident that our loyal customers will see that what we plan to do will help Papy to trade in a much more sustainable way. We aim to reduce carbon emissions and make changes in order to become a business that can maintain its long-term presence in this industry".

Lucas Meyer added "in order to survive in the competitive food retailing market we must change. Innovation is the key to our future success".

By the end of trading on 23 June 2011, Papy's share price had risen to €38.80 per share.

Appx	
5	What was Papy's PE ratio on 23rd June 2011?

Does anything in Lucas Meyer's announcement add anything to our understanding of this pre-seen material?

Was Lucas Meyer's announcement well-received by investors? |

Appendix 6

Some of Papy's current Sustainability Indicators for the period 2008 to 2010

Energy consumption

Energy consumption
(kWh per square metre of sales area)

Year	kWh per square metre of sales area
2008	911
2009	880
2010	858

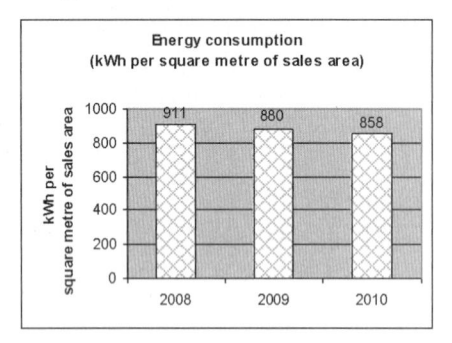

The reported measure is the average kilowatt hours (kWh) divided by the total number of square metres of sales area.

Free disposable plastic bags

The reported measure is the number of free disposable plastic bags purchased by Papy and given to customers at checkouts, divided by the total number of square metres of sales area.

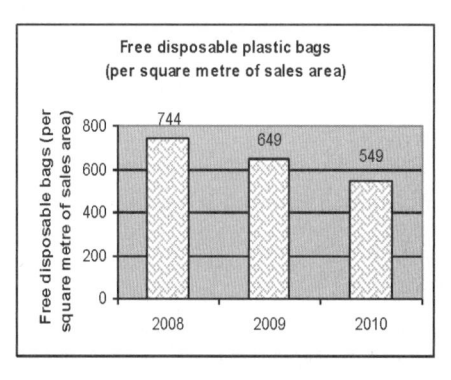

Free disposable plastic bags
(per square metre of sales area)

Year	Free disposable bags (per square metre of sales area)
2008	744
2009	649
2010	549

Carbon emissions

Carbon emissions
in kg per square metre of sales area

Year	Kg of Carbon emissions per square metre of sales area
2008	1,109
2009	1,077
2010	1,042

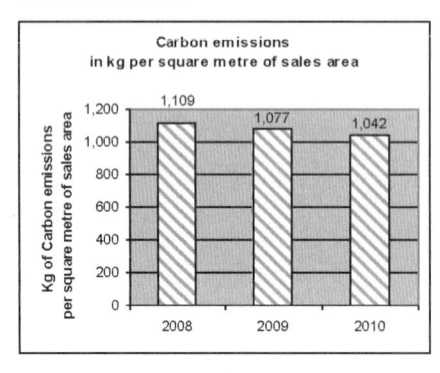

This is the consolidated total of all carbon emissions in kilograms (kg) (including Papy's stores' and warehouses' energy consumption and the transportation of products to stores) divided by Papy's average sales area (in square metres) for each year.

The reported measure is carbon emissions in kilograms (kg) per square metre of sales area.

This measure excludes carbon emissions generated by Papy's supply chain.

End of pre-seen material

Appx	
6	What is the purpose of the data and presentation in this appendix? Is Papy improving its performance under these measures?

Your script will be marked against the T4 Part B Case Study Assessment Criteria shown below.

Criterion	Maximum marks available
Analysis of issues (25 marks)	
Technical	5
Application	15
Diversity	5
Strategic choices (35 marks)	
Focus	5
Prioritisation	5
Judgement	20
Ethics	5
Recommendations (40 marks)	
Logic	30
Integration	5
Ethics	5
Total	100

2 Analysis of the case

In this section, we provide an analysis of the pre-seen material: in effect, providing answers to the questions we have raised in the previous section.

Paras 1-2 **What do these paragraphs tell us about the competitive pressures and competitive strategies in the supermarket industry?**

These paragraphs demonstrate that the supermarket industry is very competitive, is globalised, and that supermarkets are expanding by combining the Ansoff strategies of Product Development (25% or revenue coming from non-food items) and Market Development ('expanded to other countries').

It also makes the point that these strategies are based around three components:

- Achievement of economies of scale
- Use of globally-recognised brand names (it is made clear this refers to the store name as a brand rather then the brands of the products it sells)
- Acquisition of smaller chains of stores

What are the implications of these competitive pressures and competitive strategies for Papy supermarkets?

It is clear that Papy has also expanded globally because it has stores in 8 European countries (para 16) but that it remains a smaller player (para 34 reveals it has at least 2 significantly larger rivals). This suggests that it may not enjoy the economies of scale that its larger rivals do and therefore may suffer if it allows itself to be cornered into a price-sensitive segment of the market.

Paras 3-5 **Why do supermarkets follow the strategies of opening convenience stores, offering differentiated product ranges, offering on-line shopping and selling non-food items?**

All four strategies are intended to increase sales revenue but also to increase gross margins.

Convenience stores derive purchasing and brand economies of scale from the larger supermarket chain. They are able to use these to compete effectively with the family-run corner shops that previously serviced the out-of-hours market and local market. The supermarket-owned convenience stores can change higher prices than the supermarket for the same items, and will limit stock to the higher contribution products.

The differentiated product ranges, from value ranges to premium own-brand range, increase revenues by allowing price discrimination. The more affluent shopper elects to buy the premium range, whilst the budget-conscious shopper can elect to buy value ranges. It also provides the opportunity to encourage the shopper to trade up from own-brand value or regular ranges to premium branded product. Organic food products appeal to small segments of the market who might otherwise buy from niche channels such as from box schemes for organic food, or health food stores such as Holland and Barrett. For the majority of the market organic food is a premium price product which they may trade up to if the circumstances are right. Having supermarket specific private label brands also provides the supermarket with bargaining power over the manufacturers of these fast-moving consumer goods (FMCGs) because the supermarket can claim that its private label branded tea, fruit drink, ready meals and so on are at least as popular as the supplier's proprietary branded product. It is also likely that the wide range acts as a barrier to entry against more focused retailers such as discount warehouse chains below and premium niche stores above (in UK terms, against Aldi or Lidl and also against Waitrose, Booths, and Marks and Spencer).

On-line shopping appears to be more convenient for the shopper and may permit the selling of the same products at higher prices than in-store. It may enhance brand because the on-line experience of one may help lock in the customer. For some chains it helps overcome a lack of ground-based outlets in an area. However much of the motive seems to be defensive. Many supermarkets take the view that although on-line shopping is a parallel chain to their shops which just duplicates costs without increasing revenues, if they don't offer on-line shopping then they will lose out to a rival that did offer it. There is also the view that having an on-line shopping presence is a 'chip in the game' in case on-line shopping reaches a tipping point with the use of smartphones, tablets and smart appliances that turn it into the predominant mode of FMCG shopping.

Non-food items may provide higher margins but also provide access to other parts of the customers' budgets. These range from pots and pans, through clothing, audio and electronic products, and on to services such as insurance, telephony and contact lens supply. Several supermarket operators now judge their commercial success in terms of shares of total consumer spending rather than just share of food sales. In economics terms the supermarkets are able to gain economies of scale and economies of scope from this wider offering. The economies of scale come from their purchasing power and also from the fact that these extra items are sold through existing channels where the costs of the stores, warehousing and promotion are already paid. The economies of scope result from the wider range benefiting from the store brand and acting as a magnet for customers. For example people may go to the shop to buy clothing and then also buy food on impulse.

Does Papy supermarkets follow all three strategies?

No. Papy doesn't have on-line shopping (para 16) and there is no specific mention of Papy stocking organic food.

Which strategies of real-world supermarkets are not mentioned in these paragraphs?

Every T4 pre-seen has to simplify the industry to make the case study exam manageable. But also you are expected to show some knowledge of the industry in order to judge or suggest new directions for Papy. Several strategies of supermarkets seem to have been left out:

Food only stores: supermarkets like Marks and Spencer have opened these near railway stations, in busy office areas, and in service stations to capture the lunchtime 'sandwich' market and also the market for top-up groceries and ready meals.

Stores in stores: several supermarkets offer branches inside motorway services and service stations, inside hospitals and residential homes.

Fair Trade products: many supermarkets feature ranges of these and in one case, the UK Co-operative, makes a selling point of the ethics of its trading. Para 45 refers to Papy offering ethically-sourced products, including Fair Trade labelled products.

Loyalty programmes: most supermarkets have loyalty schemes which give shoppers a choice of free items or tickets to days out in return for spending. Para 22 later refers to Papy's operation of a loyalty card scheme.

Catalogue shopping: supermarkets use their stores to distribute large catalogues of household goods for direct ordering. In the UK Tesco has been a leader in this.

On-line non-food shopping: the supermarkets use their websites and brand to attract orders for consumer durables such as washing machines.

Paras 6-9 **What issues might a supermarket focus on in order to improve its 'sustainable trading' performance?**

Sustainability is a very elastic concept. The EU definition in Paragraph 6 refers to sustainable trading as not harming either the environment or the social conditions. This is a broad concept of sustainability and could be used to imply that supermarkets should not undertake activities that would harm farmers or local small shops, as well as not increasing greenhouse gases.

The case writer seems to narrow sustainability down to carbon emissions in paras 7 to 14, but the broader 'facets' are described later in para 31 and under the banner of Corporate Social Responsibility (para 40).

In essence supermarkets need to focus on:

- **Energy usage** in their operations and in the supply chain. This will include store design and insulation, logistics, use of refrigeration and lighting. The sources of energy used may be significant, for example whether lorries run on petrol, LPG or biomass fuels.

- **Waste and emissions**. This will include packaging, carrier bags, disposal of unsold product, noise and effluent from operations in the supply chain such as refrigeration gases, run-off from abattoirs and so on.

- **Employment policies**. Paying proper attention to workforce diversity (age, gender, ethnic group, disability and so on), pay and conditions, rest breaks, management approach, personal development and so on. This may be extended to the conditions of workers in the firms that supply the supermarket.

- **Fair terms for suppliers**. This involves fair prices, payment terms, not rejecting consignments on spurious quality grounds, advance notification of termination of contracts.

- **Sourcing sustainably produced inputs**. This is very broad and ranges from packaging material from sustainable forests to foods that are Rainforest Alliance Certified.

- **Supporting the community it operates in**. This will encompass purchasing from local businesses, providing jobs to local workers but also includes providing stock to village shops or local delivery rounds, charitable giving, avoidance of disruption and noise from deliveries, product sales and traffic to and from the shops.

Paras 10-12 **How may the issues in these paragraphs be used to create questions on exam day?**

There seem to be three issues embedded in these paragraphs:

Whether sustainability is consistent with a successful competitive strategy. Para 10 tells us that supermarkets have dragged their feet on sustainability by preferring to focus on consumer loyalty and profits. This implies that sustainability by supermarkets is not something that consumers value within a brand and neither does it improve profits.

This runs contrary to the thinking of two UK retailers, Marks and Spencer and Co-operative, who have sought to make sustainability a part of their brand credentials.

What needs to be measured in order to impact on carbon emissions. Para 12 reveals that even where carbon emission targets are set, they don't lead to an appreciable reduction in emissions. This could imply that the targets are too slack to have a real impact, or perhaps are targeting what is easy to achieve rather than the impact of the significant sources of carbon emissions.

How to use performance measures to drive change in processes and strategies. Para 11 records that although 85% of CEOs believe their firms have sustainability measures only 64% believe they are effective. The case writer draws the obvious conclusion in the closing sentence – that there is scope for better monitoring to improve sustainability.

To summarise, the case writer has signalled three potential topics for discussion in the exam:

- Sustainability and competitive advantage
- Improved monitoring of sustainable performance (this seems to be broader that carbon emissions)
- Supermarkets becoming 'focussed on achieving real change in the way that they operate'

The T4 exam requires you to assume the role of a newly-qualified Chartered Management Accountant within Papy supermarkets. Given this role it is unlikely that you will be asked to describe change management in detail, nor to give your opinion on competitive strategy. It is more likely that you will be asked to suggest or evaluate measures of sustainability and that you may be expected to do this within the context of the competitive strategy that has been decided.

Paras 13-14 **Why are carbon credits and carbon markets relevant to Papy's sustainability objectives?**

These paragraphs are very important to understanding this case study.

The first thing to memorise is that a carbon credit is equal to 1,000kg of carbon gases. Sometimes also called an *emission allowance* the carbon credit is therefore a basic unit of account.

The pre-seen simplifies matters. The Kyoto protocol set targets for the four greenhouse gases carbon dioxide, methane, nitrous oxide, sulphur hexafluoride, and also two groups of gases believed to damage the ozone layer, hydroflurocarbons and perflurocarbons. The six are converted into CO_2 equivalents in determining reductions in emissions. Each participating country accepted a base line level for their annual output of these gases in 1990. Of these, 37 countries (the so-called Annex 1 countries) signed up to making targeted reductions in emissions by 2012. This leads to a series of annual emission allowances for each country. The country then allocates these between the firms in the country as in effect 'permissions to pollute' but with the implication that the allocation will fall each year and that firms will be fined for exceeding their permitted emissions.

These are 'tradable permits' and this leads to a carbon market. Firms that are likely to exceed their permitted carbon emissions seek to buy surplus permits from firms that have not reached their maximum permitted emissions. This creates a financial incentive for firms to invest in changes to processes that will reduce carbon emissions because some of the costs of these can be offset by selling surplus carbon permits on the carbon market.

The sustainability objectives of Papy are affected in two ways depending on its present carbon emissions:

If Papy exceeds its carbon allowances, it will incur costs in buying additional permits to pollute. Better sustainability would help reduce its costs through lower cost of permits and also lower cost of buying energy.

Papy may be able to achieve additional revenues from selling surplus permits or using the proceeds from selling the permits to fund improvements to its processes aimed at reducing its carbon footprint.

Paras 15-16 **How might the information in these paragraphs be used in the exam?**

These paragraphs could throw up a number of potential scenarios for the real exam:

- An evaluation of opportunities to open Papy supermarkets in further European countries
- An evaluation of opportunities to open Papy's first supermarket outside Europe
- An evaluation of a proposal for Papy to begin offering internet shopping

In the exam evaluation of strategic options should be undertaken using the Suitability, Acceptability, Feasibility model of Johnson and Scholes. Given the pre-seen emphasises the sustainability objectives of Papy you may be required to consider the Acceptability of the option in terms of its impact on carbon emissions or other targets, or its suitability against general goals relating to other aspects of sustainability.

The case writer specifically mentions the supply chain being 'established' and 'efficient' in Europe. Managing stores outside Europe would extend this supply chain and may involve taking on new suppliers. The sustainability credentials of Papy could be tarnished by the increased transport distances, perhaps the greater use of air cargo, and the difficulty in ensuring that suppliers are following sustainable practices themselves.

Paras 17-20 **What financial analysis might these paragraphs lead you to suggest?**

Detailed analysis will be conducted when we move on to consider the Appendices.

However using Appendix 3 enables the calculation of the 2010 operating margin of Papy at 5.1% (€658m/€12,911m). We might wish to assess whether this is a rising or falling trend using earlier years. We would also be interested in relating profit to the investment base of Papy using ROCE.

Segmental analysis could be undertaken on the relative profitability of the two sizes of store to evaluate which type of store Papy should concentrating on opening in future.

It is notable that Papy does not appear to have any hypermarkets

PART C PRACTICE TOPCIMA CASES   18: Papy: some help from BPP   347

Paras 21-23 **Does the rise in profits and EPS prove that Papy is following a successful strategy?**

Falling profits generally reflect a failing strategy or adverse business climate. Papy has rising profits. This may be an indicator of success. Before this is confirmed it would be necessary to ensure that the increase was greater than inflation, and that this was profit on a like-for-like basis. If the rise in profit has occurred solely because of extra stores then it may not have been sufficient to justify the investment in the new stores.

Rising Earnings Per Share is also regarded as a good sign. If this was due to expansion funded by debt then again there is no assurance that the extra earnings justify the costs of expansion. This criticism is modified by the fact that earnings are calculated post interest and tax. Therefore if EPS rises it means that the rise in gross earnings is at least sufficient to pay the additional interest on any borrowings used to fund the expansion, but it still may not be a sufficient return for shareholders.

Why might the revenue per visit have increased?

One influencing factor may be inflation. The rise in spending per customer between 2009 and 2010 is 2.0% (€121.10/€118.75 x 100%) which is below the rate of inflation in most Eurozone countries over the same period.

The revenues will be determined by the number of shoppers multiplied by the average spend per visit. Paras 22 and 23 say both have increased. This may be a consequence of the increased number of convenience stores in Papy's portfolio because, as para 22 tells us, the prices are slightly higher in convenience stores.

The higher average spend per visit may reflect the fact that customers are buying a wider range of products from Papy and not from other retailers.

Paras 24-27 **Does the information in these paragraphs suggest Papy is doing well?**

Rising operating margin and rising profit are the signs of a healthy company. The fact that gross margin has increased indicates that the investment in convenience stores and non-food products is helping Papy to succeed in a 'very competitive' market (para 21).

The improvement in operating margin is also partly due to a fall in administrative costs. Whilst welcome, the problem with profit rises due to administrative cost reductions is that there is a limit to how long a firm can find more costs to cut. The rise in gross margin therefore is probably more encouraging than the cost reductions.

This reference to administrative costs could be a hint that the exam will ask you to discuss the value of off-shoring some administrative activities to reduce costs further.

Para 28 **What is the significance of this information on share ownership?**

Papy has only issued half of its authorised share capital. This means that it can issue significant amounts of extra shares without passing resolutions through General Meetings to increase authorised share capital. This may be significant if the examiner sets an exam day Unseen involving Papy considering taking over another supermarket.

The shares are mainly held by large and institutional investors. This means that they will take a commercial view of Papy and require it to maximise shareholder wealth. The family may have other goals for Papy, but with only 5% of the shares the family's influence will be limited, even though the HR Director, Simona Papy, is a family member.

Using stakeholder analysis (Mendelow) it could be said that the large institutional shareholders are 'key players' whereas the Papy family are merely 'keep informed'.

Para 29 **Why would Papy operate this employee share scheme and does it promote higher shareholder wealth?**

This scheme may be offered for one or more of the following reasons:

- Motivate staff to improve the profits of their store. Although individual store employees are unable to influence the share price, this scheme rewards them by giving shares for hitting profit targets at the store.

- Give staff a stake in the success of Papy. Staff might feel resentful if they see profits rising and share prices rising but with none of the benefit coming to them. Having shares allows them to participate in the success they helped to generate.

- Improve staff retention. It is not clear how this scheme operates. It could be that staff are given shares in their own name, in which case they could still benefit from them after they leave Papy. However many schemes lodge the shares in trust for the employees and give them dividends whilst they work for the firm, but nothing after they leave the firm. This latter scheme can help improve staff retention.

Is it usual for firms to buy shares back from the open market to give to employees?

This arrangement is unusual. Most firms have an amount of authorised capital set aside which is issued when the decision is taken to give staff more shares. Papy has only issued half its authorised share capital (para 28), hinting maybe that the unissued remainder is to be used for other purposes.

Paras 30-31 **How many of these facets of sustainable trading are addressed by Papy at the moment?**

According to Appendix 6 Papy monitors energy consumption, use of disposable plastic bags, and carbon emissions. Paras 40-49 indicate that Papy is also engaged in reducing packaging, proving support to community and school projects, sourcing products from ethically sound suppliers (including fish which is specifically mentioned) treating suppliers well, developing employees, and encouraging healthy eating.

Therefore Papy does not seem to be pursuing alternative energy sources, responsible procurement, or opening rural shops.

How might the examiner use this list to create questions for exam day?

The examiner might develop questions on exam day such as:

- Asking you to evaluate proposals to add further policies and projects in the list to Papy's existing sustainability activities, perhaps in the hope of gaining competitive advantage

- Setting business problems where the more profitable options conflict with sustainability in one of these areas, or there is a conflict between sustainability objectives, for example increased use of local suppliers to reduce transportation resulting in decreased use of suppliers in developing countries

- Asking you to evaluate or recommend performance measures for monitoring progress and performance in any of these areas.

Para 32 **What is the relevance of % market share?**

In the Boston Consulting Group matrix *relative* market share is used as a proxy measure for competitive strength. This paragraph suggests that Papy may have two rivals bigger than itself in its 'home country' (being 'within the top three' implies it is third largest although strictly speaking the biggest provider is also within the top three).

Therefore taking market share as an **indicator of success** we would have to conclude that Papy was not doing very well. This is a dangerous conclusion however, because there could be **non-competing groups** in the market. For example a premium positioned supermarket may well be smaller than a budget positioned supermarket but they don't compete. A provider of local convenience stores is not significantly threatened by a larger operator of hypermarkets. One of the problems of using data on market share is that there will always be problems in defining what the term 'market' means.

Market share, according to Boston Consulting Group, is also a **cause of competitive success**. This is because larger market share requires greater production volumes. Greater production volumes allow lower costs through the benefit of greater economies of scale and experience effects. Given that we are told that the supermarket industry is 'very competitive' (para 21) this may require the supermarkets to achieve lower costs in order to protect their margins against falling prices. This analysis seems to be borne out by the earlier report that the supermarket industry is consolidating, as larger supermarkets buy-up smaller chains (para 1).

It is worth remembering that Porter criticised the importance BCG placed on costs as the only source of competitive advantage by pointing out that some firms produced high rates of profit by strategies of **differentiation** or **focus**. A 19% share of the market is significant, being larger than the UK's Asda, Sainsbury's and Morrisons (17%, 16% and 13% respectively in March 2011). However a competitor with a smaller share than Papy's may not be at a disadvantage against larger rivals if it has a differentiated position in the market, such as Waitrose's premium quality or Co-Operative's convenience/ethical positions in the UK (4% and 9% shares respectively) compared with the more general value positioning of market leader Tesco (31% share).

The difficulty of **defining scope of market** is intensified when product range is considered. For example in the UK Waitrose and Co-operative do not sell clothes or consumer durables. This raises the problem of comparing like-with-like.

Also where supermarkets span national boundaries it is possible that a firm that is the large internationally, such as Aldi with 8,133 stores, may be bigger than others globally, but may be relatively small within country markets such as the UK. (Aldi has 422 UK stores and is ranked 9th with a 2.8% share)

Paras 33-35 **Is Papy one of Europe's larger supermarkets?**

This is impossible to say from the data given, but unlikely when we consider real world data in chapter 2. The table includes revenue from outside Europe which Papy does not have but Competitors 1 and 2 may have. It also credits on-line shopping which Papy does not have (para 16). Within Europe, or in any one of its 8 European country locations, Papy could conceivably be bigger than its rivals.

Which of Papy's competitors is performing the best?

The following table show that Competitor 1 has the highest operating profits of the four.

	Papy	Competitor 1	Competitor 2	Competitor 3
Operating profit (Revenue x Operating margin)	€658m	€3,180m	€2,177m	€567m

The table makes further comparisons impossible because the profits and revenues are from all stores, Europe and beyond and include internet shopping, but the store numbers cited are Europe only. The marker shares are also of potentially different home countries.

The only other points we can make are:

- Competitor 2 has the highest increase in market share. It also has the lowest margin, which could suggest that it is a discounter gaining share in a recession-struck World economy. But this is only a supposition as the figures could mean it is a premium-priced supermarket that is very poor at controlling its operating costs.

- Competitor 2 is also the most environmentally active with the lowest carbon footprint and lowest volume of disposable plastic bags (this ignores the alternative interpretation that it has large empty floor areas that don't sell very much!).

How might the information in this table be turned into the subject of a question on exam day?

This table is likely to be important for exam day. Based on past TOPCIMA exams it may be developed in several ways:

Takeover or merger of Papy with a competitor. Suppose Papy offered to merge with Competitor 3 by offering to exchange one Papy share for each of the shares in Competitor 3. *Assume* you are told that Competitor 3 has 100m shares. Would this be in the interests of Papy's shareholders? On purely financial grounds it would not. The operating profit per share of Papy is €6.58 (€658m/100m) whereas Competitor 3 has an operating profit per share of €5.67 (€567m/100m). The earnings of Papy's shareholders would be diluted, as we can see if we combine the profits of the two firms and divide by the higher number of issued shares. The total profits would be €1,225m and the total issued shares would be 200m, giving an operating profit per share of €6.125 (€1,225m/200m) which is a fall from €6.58 per share for Papy shareholders. This financial analysis also overlooks the potential increased costs of integration (unifying name, integrating supply chain, standardising pay and conditions, integrating systems and IT and so on). These would depress profits further for some years. But it also doesn't give credit for the effects of synergy in the long run from rationalisation of stores where they compete in the same area, shared technical benefits (if, for example, Competitor 3 could contribute expertise in internet shopping to the combined group), and the defensive benefit of stopping another firm buying Competitor 3 and boosting its market strength further. As a Chartered Management Accountant working for Papy these are impacts you could be expected to weigh up in the advice you offer Papy's management.

Benchmarking. The data in the table is not detailed enough to allow much benchmarking, but it could be added to in the Unseen material on exam day. We can already see that Papy is not doing well in terms of carbon emissions and disposable plastic bags. But to what extent is Competitor 2's rapid growth attributable to its better ecological credentials? Is the reason for its lower profit margins something to do with the short term costs of reducing carbon emissions, the long term costs of paying suppliers better prices or from it being more choosy about the ecological credentials of its suppliers?

Paras 36-38 What is likely to be the impact of the replacement of Tobias Otte by Lucas Meyer?

This is a typical device used by this particular case writer. The pre-seen signals changes are about to happen and this should lead us to consider what sorts of effects they may have on the exam day Unseen material and requirements.

The obvious impact will be an increased focus on carbon emissions. This is the 'most notable' area in which Papy has fallen behind (para 36) but para 34 shows it has also fallen behind two rivals in offering too many plastic bags.

The case writer has an opportunity to set requirements relating to the benefits of pursuing a low carbon footprint.

PART C PRACTICE TOPCIMA CASES 18: Papy: some help from BPP 351

It is however important not to suffer tunnel vision when interpreting this pre-seen material. A new incoming CEO might also wish to review other aspects of the strategy set by Tobais Otte in the past 12 years such as whether:

- Increased openings of convenience stores has been the right step (para 21)
- It should invest in internet shopping (para 16)
- It should merge with another store chain
- It should expand into the growth economies beyond Europe (para 16)
- You could be asked to evaluate and report on these matters.

Para 39 How might the information in this paragraph affect exam day?

This looks like a strong hint that your role on exam day will be as part of the team that implements new data collection and reporting systems. Arif Karp's background is in carbon emissions reduction (para 37) but also includes 'corporate social responsibilities', which implies he has a broader scope of interest beyond Papy's carbon footprint.

As far as we can see Arif Karp is 'currently' forming his team. The current date may be assumed to be mid July 2011. Therefore by exam day on 31 August, and certainly by 24 November, there may be data ready to evaluate and report on.

Paras 40-41 What new information is introduced in these paragraphs?

These paragraphs remind us that CSR means more to Papy than merely carbon emissions. The diagram represents the 'facets' of sustainable trading introduced in para 31. In para 31 they were introduced as things Papy's competitors are doing. Here we are told that Papy aims to do them too, that it has had some 'major achievements' but also that it faces 'many challenges' still (para 40).

Why are the facets of CSR presented as a diagram?

The diagram is a an easy reminder of the scope of sustainability. It should be easy to remember the five facets (or 'sections') with the mnemonic SCREN

Sustainable
Communities
Responsible
Employees
Nutrition

It also could be the template of a CSR balanced scorecard which might be developed as part of the work to be carried out by Arif Karp's team (para 39).

Paras 42-43 What steps could Papy take in order to reduce waste packaging and to encourage recycling?

There is a difference between reducing waste and encouraging recycling.

Reducing waste packaging requires a reduction in the packaging on the products themselves, and the packaging used in transit. This could include reducing the physical dimensions of the product, reducing the gauge of the packaging (ie make it thinner and so reduce the tonnage used per year), encouraging suppliers to change volume of products to reduce packaging (for example doubling the capacity of a bottle of bath oil or soft drink would not require double the surface area of packaging), encouraging refills rather than completely new containers of product (this is used in replacement purchase items such as instant coffee, cleaning solutions, liquid detergents and hand soaps), and replacing tins, boxes and bottles with smaller sachets or flexible wrapping (used for fruit drinks, pet food, ground coffee, biscuits). The decision to request suppliers to deliver stock secured to pallets with webbing rather than supply in boxes would also reduce packaging.

Encouraging recycling requires that packaging be made of recyclable content. Therefore packaging such as glass, aluminium, tinned cans and cardboard are more readily recycled than plastic packaging, which is often burned. At store level the boxes (or 'cases') that foods are delivered in can be recycled and suppliers encouraged to use these.

No supermarkets have yet introduced schemes to incentivise customers to return packaging of the sort characterised in the past by children scouring the neighbourhood for soft drink bottles in order to recover the deposit paid on them by the original purchaser. Such schemes are used at large public events such as music festivals to encourage some of the audience to wander around collecting towers of cardboard beer cups to cash in for free drinks.

Evaluate the methods being used by Papy to reduce its measured use of plastic bags and suggest additional methods.

The reference to Papy changing the type of plastic in carrier bags is perhaps a reference to introducing bio-degradable plastic bags in which an enzyme in the plastic is activated by prolonged darkness, such as being buried in a landfill site, and devours the plastic. Para 43 also mentions reducing the weight of bags, perhaps by making them smaller or less thick.

These initiatives would not impact on Papy's policy of reducing bags used because Papy measures number of bags, not the gross weight of the bags nor whether they are biodegradable or not.

The policies of issuing free, or discounted, reusable shopping bags has been operated by Tesco and others. The loyalty scheme is also practised by several supermarkets. Other supermarkets train staff to ask if the customer requires a bag rather than merely issuing them on the assumption that they do. Several stores, notably Marks and Spencer, charge customers for bags to discourage their use.

The difficulty with discouraging customers from using fresh bags is that it can be seen by the customer as mean-spiritedness not be offered a bag, or worse to be charged for one. It perhaps illustrates the gulf between firms' focus on sustainability and the shopping publics' appreciation of the supermarkets' reasons and efforts to reduce bag use.

Para 44   **How could this commitment to communities be measured for reporting purposes?**

Papy seems to have a narrow perception of helping communities that is limited to doing good works. It doesn't appear to include matters such as supporting local suppliers, ensuring local employment or avoiding disruption to lifestyles such as by limiting delivery times to social hours or stamping out sales of alcohol to local youth.

In past TOPCIMA case studies this case writer has provided measures based on number of full-time equivalent worker days (FTE) donated or provided to local projects.

Another approach might be to specify classes of projects (environmental improvement, helping the elderly, participation in fundraising for local causes and so on) and require each store to report its contribution each year under each heading.

Paras 45-47   **What would constitute irresponsible trading?**

Supermarkets and other shops have attracted criticism in recent years for the following practices:

- Paying unrealistic prices for products at below production costs
- Demanding retrospective discounts on products already bought
- Unilateral reductions to contracted purchase prices without consultation
- Late payment and exploitative credit terms
- Rejections of consignments of product on spurious quality grounds to avoid supermarkets over-purchasing or sometimes to punish suppliers that have spoken out about their poor treatment by supermarkets

- Demands for suppliers to 'voluntarily' contribute to charitable schemes being run by the supermarket
- Buying from suppliers that indulge in unethical treatment of employees, contractors and other suppliers
- Buying from suppliers that use unsustainable methods of farming and production, or which deprive local population of access to land, water or energy
- Offering unsustainably low prices in order to force smaller local stores out of business

What are ethically sourced products?

The pre-seen provides a clear description of Fair Trade products (para 45). In past TOPCIMA cases this case writer has introduced issues into the Unseen material where firms discover that the products they have been selling as Fair Trade are actually misrepresented.

Other aspects of ethically sourced products could include:

- Products purchased without taint of corruption by suppliers to win the contracts, such as paying inducement to Papy's buyers
- Products not being produced in a way that harms the environment. Part of the attraction of organic produce (vegetables, fruit, cereals, eggs, meat and so on) is that it has been grown, harvested and reared without use of artificial fertilisers, pesticides or antibiotics that might then create problems for the environment or health in the future. Organic food may have a Soil Association kitemark, or in other cases a Rain Forest Alliance endorsement
- Partnerships with suppliers in developing countries gives something back to the community such as education, housing and health care to improve quality of life and to help move the society beyond reliance on low value primary produce
- Fair wages and decent working conditions at suppliers facilities. Many supermarkets require that suppliers sign undertakings to this effect, or that they sign up to recognised treaties such as the Ethical Trading Initiative. Para 47 refers to Papy proactively inspecting supplier facilities. In some real-world cases this audit process has lacked independence because the inspections are carried out by the stores buyers during contract negotiations and the buyers have sometimes been accused of colluding with suppliers to turn a blind eye to breaches in return for better prices. These better prices enable the buyer to receive a bonus payment from their store for good performance.

Is anything missing from this list of responsible practices?

Papy might wish to consider the distance that products have travelled. It has commitment to reducing carbon emissions which might be assisted by buying locally where possible rather than relying on air freight and overland lorry distribution.

Para 48 **Why is training staff to do their jobs regarded as being CSR when it would seem to be essential for carrying on business?**

Enhancing skills amongst the local labour force enables Papy to give more senior jobs to staff from the host country. This improves local incomes and improves Papy's diversity performance.

Para 48 may also indicate Papy's HR strategy. When it enters a new country it appears to use expatriate staff to manage the business initially, whilst developing local managerial talent. Once local management are competent this releases managers to enable Papy to extend into new areas.

Para 49 **Why has Papy concerned itself with healthy eating?**

In recent years there has been growing concern about the long term health effects of increased consumption of processed foods. These foods are high in fats and carbohydrates which, if consumed to excess, can lead to obesity and conditions such as diabetes. Similarly the presence of high salt levels has been indicated as a contributor to kidney disease. Finally the 'five a day' mantra has become popular as a way to ward off other ailments and diseases.

Concerns over body shape and fitness also drive consumers' concerns about what they are eating.

Therefore Papy would see that there is a market for healthy food, as well as it being socially responsible to make clear the content of the foods and to ensure there are healthy choices available.

Paras 50 - 51   **How vital is IT to Papy?**

The description of the IT systems in these paragraphs show that Papy has a Supply Chain Management system (SCM) in place. The supplier tag the products with bar code stickers ('latest scanning IT solutions') to check them in and out at each stage of the supply chain. It also handles retail transactions (para 51) so it can be assumed that this refers to point of sale scanning.

Using the models of IT portfolios developed by Peppard/McFarlan the SCM system is Key Operational/Factory. It has high present significance but that investment to date has solely been to expand its reach and capacity as Papy grows (para 51).

Paras 52-53   **What changes to IT systems are likely in the near future?**

Para 52 refers to the legal requirement that prices are accurately reflected at the check-out. This paragraph seems a little out of place and may be the case writer putting down a marker that will enable Unseen material to be set on exam day that reveals the system has been overcharging customers. This would be a priority issue, as it has consequences for reputation risk as well as legal and ethical implications.

The mention of Arif Karp strengthens the theme in the pre-seen of the need to have performance measures for the aspects to sustainability ie non-financial data. You could be required to suggest suitable measures for this.

Another change, hinted at in para 16, is that IT systems may need to be developed to permit internet shopping. As well as a website interface this would require an ability to provide indications of which items are in stock, special discounts and so on. In the UK supermarkets vary in how they operate their internet shopping. Some link the system to regional distribution warehouses which provides a wider range of products and better stock availability. Others operate a central order portal, but then leave it to local stores to fulfil the order. This has the effect that customers often order items that are out of stock at the local store (or perhaps not stocked at all), leading to customer frustration and arbitrary product substitutions by the staff at the store.

Once internet shopping is introduced it would permit Papy to sell a much wider range of products than can presently be carried in the store. Using its brand strength and loyalty scheme it could offer consumer durables, furniture, and electronic goods to customers.

One application of IT that is not apparently in use at Papy is purchasing portals. These are where Papy posts a requirement for a quantity of a given product and suppliers bid to fill the order. This has been a notable trend in fresh food supply.

Paras 54-57   **What is the potential relevance of the list of ways in which Papy generates carbon to your exam?**

This pre-seen makes frequent references to Papy's intention to introduce targets and measures for carbon emissions. This is again reinforced in para 57.

The list provides a starting point for such measures: energy use by store appliances, distance travelled by goods, and the energy efficiency of new stores. It is not a complete list because para 55 extends the causes to include the manufacturing activities of suppliers and the journeys to the stores by customers.

How might Papy educate its suppliers on carbon emissions?

Providing briefing documents, courses or computer based training might be a start. But these would only be effective if the suppliers had an interest in implementing the recommendations. More effective methods might include:

- **Requiring suppliers to achieve certification under ISO 14001**, the environmental management system standard by a certain date as a condition for receiving further orders from Papy. Achieving certification under ISO 14001 would require that the supplier undertook an end-to-end review of the environmental impacts of what it does, set up procedures to monitor this, and undertake actions to minimise any environmental harm.

- **Request measures of carbon emissions from suppliers on a regular basis**. Based on the adage 'what gets measured is what gets done' this would encourage the suppliers to understand their environmental impact better.

What effect would internet shopping have on Papy's carbon footprint?

Recent research has concluded that internet shopping will reduce the carbon footprint of supermarkets like Papy.

In July 2009 the UK's Chartered Institute of Logistics and Transport produced a report that revealed the 'last mile' of the supply chain, from store to home, generates more carbon than all the prior upstream logistics activities in the supply chain. The key finding of the report reads *'A 50-mile delivery round by van produces 21,665g of CO2. When this is divided equally among the 120 [average per van] drops [of shopping to homes], each drop is responsible for 181g of CO2; a standard return shopping trip by car of 12.8 miles, however, generates 4,274g of CO2, 24 times more than the average home delivery drop'.*

Therefore introducing internet shopping would be a positive move in reducing Papy's carbon footprint.

Paras 58-64 ### Why might the case writer have introduced biographical details of named individuals into the pre-seen material?

This case writer does not always include biographical details. When they are included it seems to be for the following reasons:

- **To give you a role in the exam that involves reporting to one of them**. As a management accountant you might assume you would be reporting to Abdul Yarkol or one of his reports. But you could find that you are asked to report to Arif Karp and therefore need to be able to identify who he is and what his role is.

- **To reward your familiarisation with the pre-seen**. In your report you should use the names of these individuals rather than just their roles.

- **It allows the case writer to insinuate other details about the people into the case.** These can then be used to develop threads in the Unseen material on exam day. We will examine a few of these below.

Does the Chairman have the right background for the role he has been appointed to?

The likely answer is that Dmitry Baludia does not have the right background. The job of Chairman is to run the Board, whilst the CEO and Executive Directors run the business. He has 22 years experience of Papy but none in running a Board. Investors may question his ability to keep the interests of the Board balanced. In addition he did not meet, when appointed, the independence criteria that the UK Corporate Governance Code states a Chairman should fulfil, as he was previously an Executive Director of Papy.

Is this an experienced or an inexperienced Board?

On the whole the Board is relatively new in the job. In relation to Rafael Lucci the case writer says he has worked for Papy for 'only 5 years'. This suggests that in the case writer's view 5 years is a short time. Using this yardstick it's worth noting that Lucas Meyer, Arif Karp, Ziad Abbill and Simona Papy all have less than 5 years' experience on the Board, and several of these joined the Board from positions outside Papy.

The overall impression is of a board with good industrial experience. Lucas Meyer has 4 years CEO experience with Papy as his second CEO appointment.

Arif Karp has a strong background in CSR, emissions management, and CSR measures although this seems narrow compared to the breath of a portfolio called Corporate Affairs. For example Papy might suffer a public relations issue such as contaminated fuel sold at its pumps damaging car engines of the sort for which Tesco paid out compensation of £8m to 15,000 motorists in 2007 after a poorly managed PR response.

The Board as a whole seems to be ready to make changes under its new CEO. However none seems to have any experience outside Europe with the possible exception of Arif Karp.

Can any significance be attached to the reduced terms of notice on which Papy recruited Arif Karp?

One interpretation might be that his previous employers were glad to see him go. However that does not appear to be the case here. Arif Karp has already worked elsewhere with Lucas Meyer and so would not have been offered a job if he was not an effective manager. In addition his previous employers hope to gain reflected glory from Arif's achievements at Papy.

A possible interpretation is one of conflict of interests. Having been appointed, it would be suspicious if Arif Karp then began relying on his previous employers to provide expensive consultants to assist him. Raising an issue like this in the Unseen material could permit the examiner to assess your appreciation of ethical issues. Ethics is worth 10 marks.

Do the previous jobs of the Directors provide any pointers to future directions for Papy?

The main pointers are:

- CEO has a background in clothing retailing. This could point to Papy introducing or increasing its range of clothing items.

- Arif Karp has been employed to improve CSR and in particular monitor and reduce carbon emissions.

Paras 65-67 **Do these paragraphs cast doubt on the quality of corporate governance at Papy's?**

The appointment of a member of the founding family to a Board role could look like favouritism and a breach of the normal codes on appointments. However the case writer does make clear she was appointed on merit, not on family name. It is interesting to speculate why the case writer chose to make the HR Director a family member. It may be a deliberate trap for the unwary to waste time deliberating. Or possibly in the Unseen material there may be ethical dilemmas presented to Simona Papy in which she is asked to dismiss staff to whom the family is loyal, or in which her professional duty conflicts with the interests of family shareholders.

Papy has 7 non-executive directors in a Board with 7 executive directors which is an appropriate balance.

The Board seems to be missing a Company Secretary, although perhaps there is one not counted as a Director and so not mentioned.

Why has the detail about Suzanna Nec been included?

CSR is an important theme in this pre-seen, so she may have been included to give an extra name to be cited in the Unseen or in your report.

Suzanna Nec is unlikely to be happy given that she was passed over for Board appointment. The case writer may be suggesting that Suzanna Nec is likely to suffer conflict with Arif Karp.

Appendix 2

What is the average sales area of a convenience store?

In 2010 the total sales area of Papy was 1,381,800 square metres at end of year. Para 19 tells us that the average area of a large supermarket is 2,800 square metres and that Papy has 414 large supermarkets (this is the 2010 year end amount). Therefore the 742 small convenience stores provided 222,600m^2 (1,381,800 m^2 – 414 large supermarkets x 2,800 m^2 each), equivalent to 300m^2 each.

This calculation illustrates the sort of calculation you might need to do in the exam to then go on to compare new data relating to emissions, of carrier bag use, per type of store.

Are convenience stores always a success?

According to Appendix 2 Papy has closed some convenience stores in 2009 and 2010, although it has opened more than it closed in both years.

What is the potential significance of the inclusion of average numbers of stores for the year and how is it arrived at?

This use of averages is a favourite trick of this case writer and we must ensure we are clear on how to use these numbers.

For 2010 the average number of Supermarkets was 410. This is the average of the number at the start of the year, 406 (the 2009 end of year total will be the number at the start of 2010) and the number at the end of 2010, 414 – (ie 406+414/2 = 410 stores).

Many of the activity drivers in this pre-seen are expressed in rates per m^2. Sales revenues are expressed per m^2 of store space, and para 34 expresses plastic bag use and carbon emissions per m^2 of store space. It is important, when forecasting how changing the number of store may impact on Papy, to use the average number of stores and not the year end number.

For example in 2010 Appendix 2 states that average sales revenue per square metre of store space was €9,447 per m^2. Multiplying this by the average store area for 2010 gives a total revenue for 2010 of €129.11m (€9,447 x 1,366,700) which agrees to the total revenue figure given for 2010 in Appendix 3. However if we had multiplied the average revenue by the year end store area of 1,381,800 then it would have overestimated sales revenue to be €130.54m (1,381,800 m^2 x €9,447).

Are the trends of indicators of sales revenue per m^2 of sales area and per FTE encouraging?

A quick glace at the indicators is encouraging. They seem to be rising.

However the rate of increase is discouraging. Growth in average sales revenue per m^2 of sales space was 0.21% (€9,447 – €9,427/€9,427 x 100%) between 2009 and 2010 and is forecast to be 0.22% (€9,468 – €9,447/€9,447 x 100%) between 2010 and 2011. This is considerably less than the rate of inflation across Europe and hence shows that *real* sales revenue per m^2 of sales space is actually falling. Similarly the rise in sales revenue per FTE was 0.80% (€133,356 – €132,293/€132,293 x 100%) between 2009 and 2010 and is forecast to fall to a growth rate of 0.31% (€133,771 – €133,356/€133,356 x 100%) between 2010 and 2011.

This means that the sales growth and profit growth of Papy are being generated by a firm that is suffering declining real sales and declining efficiency in its use of staff.

Appendix 3 **Is Papy's profitability improving or falling and what factors are contributing to this?**

Papy's net profit ratio has risen from 3.3% to 3.5% between 2009 and 2010 (2009: €421.9m/€12,640m. 2010: €454.4m/€12,911m.).

This has been attributable to a rise in operating ratio from 4.9% to 5.1% (2009: €620m/€12,640m. 2010 €658m/€12,911m – confirmed in para 24) due to a very small rise in the gross margin from 20.1% to 20.2% (2009: €2,541m/€12,640m. 2010: €2,608m/€12,911m) and a small improvement in administrative cost efficiency with only 15.1% of turnover being taken as administrative costs in 2010 compared to 15.2% in 2009 (2009: €1,921m/€12,640m. 2010 €1,950m/€12,911m).

Another contributor to improved net profits has been a €5.3m improvement in the firms net finance expense from (€57.4m) in 2009 to (€52.1m) in 2010 (2009: €72.3m - €14.9m. 2010: €69.4m - €17.3m).

Evaluate Papy's use of working capital

Papy's cash position has improved from €480.0m to €603.9m (26%) and its long term loans have fallen by €150m (15%).

Papy has improved its use of working capital by reducing total inventory by €14m (1.3%: €14m/€1,086m), which is highlighted further by the improved rates of inventory turnover from 39.25 days to 37.98 days (2009: €1,086m/€10,099m x 365. 2010: €1,072m/€10,303m x 365). This may be the effect of better inventory control systems.

However elsewhere the working capital cycle has deteriorated. Trade receivables have increased in total by €14m and actual credit given has increased from 9.3 days to 9.5 days (2009: €322m/€12,640m x 365. 2010 €336m/€12,911m x 365). Trade payables have also fallen by €150.3m in total, or from 82.5 days to 75.6 days (2009: €2,283.3m/€10,099m x 365. 2010: €2,133m/€10,303m x 365).

Evaluate Papy's Return on Capital Employed

Given that ROCE is Earnings before finance expense and tax/ Total equity and liabilities minus current liabilities

2009 = 22.2% (€620m + €14.9m/€5,284m - €2,424m)

2010 = 22.7% (€658m + €17.3m/€5,258.9m - €2,284.5m)

Should Papy invest in new stores?

Papy seems to be under-investing in new assets.

In 2010 Papy redeemed €150m of loans. The rate of interest being paid on these loans can be estimated as 7.3% (being the 2010 finance expense of €69.4m being paid for an average loan balance of €945m: ie €1,020m+€870m/2).

Given that Papy earns 22.7% ROCE on its assets, its shareholders would benefit if it borrowed more loans at 7.3% and invested the proceeds in more stores, rather than reducing the rate of store openings in order to use cash to repay loans.

PART C PRACTICE TOPCIMA CASES   18: Papy: some help from BPP   359

Appendix 4 **Is Papy cash positive?**

Appendix 4 shows that Papy's operations generated €855.9m of cash in 2010.

Investment and renewal in existing stores and in opening 40 new stores absorbed €392m of cash, leaving sufficient to pay dividends and to redeem debt.

Appendix 5 **What was Papy's PE ratio on 23rd June 2011?**

The 2010 EPS of Papy was €4.544 (para 25). The share price on 23rd June 2011 was €38.80. Therefore the PE ratio was 8.54 times (€38.80/€4.544)

Does anything in Lucas Meyer's announcement add anything to our understanding of this pre-seen material?

The statement largely confirms the points made earlier in the pre-seen. Meyer wishes to adopt a strategy to improve Papy's sustainability.

The only surprise was his mention of fossil fuels running out. Reduction of carbon emissions is done to reduce the global warming effect, not to conserve scare fossil fuels. Burning oil, gas and coal do in themselves create carbon dioxide in a way that wind energy or nuclear energy do not. But the emphasis of this case has been on reducing emissions by using less energy, not reducing emissions by changing the sources of energy used. Para 31 states that changing energy sources is something competitors are doing, but this is not mentioned in the commitments of Papy in para 41.

Was Lucas Meyer's announcement well-received by investors?

On first reading it seems strange that the date of the press report is 24 June 2011, while the rise in the share price was to the end of the previous day, 23 June 2011. However, the first line of the press release refers to the announcement as having happened yesterday i.e. 23 June so it would appear that Luca Meyer's announcement has had a positive effect on the share price.

We cannot be sure that by exam day the investors will still be in support of Papy's new sustainable business model.

Appendix 6 **What is the purpose of the data and presentation in this appendix?**

This data seems to serve two purposes:

Firstly it reminds us of two of the measures of sustainability introduced in para 34. The measure of energy consumption is an additional measure. Note that the title of Appendix 6 is that these are 'Some' of the Indicators used, suggesting there may be others, which may be included in the Unseen.

Secondly it may be a hint about presentation of data for the exam day for candidates taking the exam on a PC. A CIMA guidance article issued in September 2010 stated that candidates could be expected to produce summary data in the form of charts or diagrams using Excel. Ensure you could recreate the diagrams in Appendix 6.

Is Papy improving its performance under these measures?

Papy is improving its performance under all three measures.

2.1 Summary of key points from the pre-seen material

A key skill in this exam is being able to extract the important information from the data you are given. Here are the key points from the Papy sustainable trading Pre-seen material:

The business environment of Papy

The Pre-seen makes clear that Papy operates in a very competitive industry featuring 'intense price competition' (para 10). It is also a global industry in which the larger supermarkets are acquiring the smaller ones (para 1). The table in paragraph 34 shows operating profit margins between 3.4% and 5.9%. Appendix 3 reveals that Papy had a gross margin of 20% in 2010 (€2,608m/€12,911m).

The marketplace seems to feature three sizes of stores: hypermarkets with sales areas of over 20,000 m^2, supermarkets with an average size of 2,800 m^2, and small convenience stores which, in Papy's case, have an average size of 300 square metres[1]. At present Papy does not operate hypermarkets (para 19).

Papy appears to be one of the smaller players in the industry. It has a 19% share of its home market, which seems to rank it third largest in the country (para 32). It is also the third largest amongst the firms detailed in the table in paragraph 34. It also does not at present operate outside of Europe and its Board seems to wish to focus on Europe and not to extend beyond it (para 16).

The T4 examination is a real world exam and you are required to research some information about the real environment. Some relevant points from the real world of supermarkets that you may like to consider are:

Internet shopping: this has been adopted by many UK supermarkets including Tesco, Asda, Sainsbury's, Waitrose and Marks and Spencer. It has not been adopted by price competitive supermarkets like Morrisons, Iceland and Farmfoods. Neither does the Co-operative offer it, although it does offer a home delivery service for items selected and paid for in store. Papy doesn't offer it at present (para 16) and therefore research into what is offered, and why some supermarkets do not offer it, may be valuable.

Emissions and sustainable trading: this is a major part of the Pre-seen material and the websites of most major supermarkets refer to policies on sustainability. For some, like Tesco, the commitment appears in the corporate information section of the site rather than in the main selling area, whereas Marks and Spencer mentions recycling on its customer home page and there are links to pages about its Plan A initiative. It is worth considering which stakeholders real-world supermarkets are targeting with their sustainability policies, investors, customers, or both? Also look at what they are doing.

Industry segments: the supermarket industry seems to segment into premium, mid-market and budget segments. There are some mass market providers, such as Tesco and Sainsbury's in the UK. There are also others with premium positions, such as Waitrose and Booths, and discounters such as Aldi. Consider the different modes of competition they use. Firms like Asda and Morrisons feature prominently in price check comparisons and feature 'housewives' and popular celebrities in their advertisements whilst others employ famous chefs. Most research seems to point to a splitting of the market between the hypermarket discounters like Aldi, which has been growing in the UK at a rate of 16% pa, and premium brands like Waitrose which has enjoyed up to 20% growth. This has left the mass market players squeezed into fighting it out with each other, each offering low prices combined with quality.

Supplier issues: there has been an increasing focus on the tactics used by supermarket buyers to extract lower prices from suppliers in order to keep prices competitive and profits rising. These tactics have included asking for discounts retrospectively, breaking agreements by unilaterally imposing price cuts, demanding contributions to supermarkets' good causes, extending credit periods and punishing producers by turning away consignments of fresh produce on spurious grounds of low quality. These tactics have achieved the greatest attention where they are used on providers of fresh produce such as milks, eggs, meat, and fruit. UK supermarkets are subject to the Groceries (Supply Chain Practices) Market

---

[1] At December 31st 2010 Papy had 1,156 stores of which 414 were large supermarkets and 742 were convenience stores (para 19). Appendix 2 states that at 31st December 2010 Papy's total sales area was 1,381,800 m^2. Of this area 1,159,200m^2 was provided by supermarkets (414 stores x 2,800 m^2) leaving 222,600 m^2 being provided by its 742 convenience stores, an average of 300 m^2 each (222,600 m^2/742 stores).

Investigation Order 2009, which came into force in February 2010, following a lengthy investigation by the Competition Commission. It requires fair treatment of suppliers. Many industry articles suggest the order has been ineffective because suppliers are still frightened to speak out against their treatment by supermarkets.

International issues: Papy operates solely within Europe and that seems to be where it wishes to expand. The Pre-seen was issued in July 2011 in an economic environment in which the governments of several countries in Europe are being forced to cut spending, dismiss state employees, and change benefit entitlements in order to reduce borrowing to qualify for financial assistance from other central banks and from the International Monetary Fund. This will cause recession and instability. Which European countries would you recommend it invested in, and which should it avoid? Are there better investments to be made in developing countries and what are real world supermarkets doing? For example Tesco's biggest market outside the UK is South Korea. It plans to quadruple its size in China by opening further hypermarkets, and is also engaged in refurbishments and openings across some Eastern European countries.

Themes in the Pre-seen material for Papy

The title of this Pre-seen is Papy sustainable trading. On exam day you will receive additional Unseen material and the requirements of the exam. These will build on themes in the Pre-seen material.

The main themes in the Pre-seen material are:

- Sustainable trading and shareholder value
- Use of sustainable trading for competitive advantage
- Measuring performance of sustainable trading
- Change management in Papy

Other themes may be introduced on exam day in the Unseen material.

Sustainable trading and shareholder value

The majority of the shares in Papy are held by institutional investors (para 28). This means that the dominant stakeholder group will want Papy to maximise shareholder wealth. Appendix 5 tells us that the new CEO of Papy, Lucas Meyer, has announced that he intends to 'change the way it operates, in order to become a more sustainable business'.

Appendix 5 is a news report published on the day following Lucas Meyer's announcement on 23 June. It shows that the share price of Papy rose. This presumably indicates investors welcomed and approved of the new strategy of sustainability.

Sustainability may be expected to improve shareholder value in several ways:

- **Reduce operating costs by encouraging savings**. This Pre-seen points to energy savings (para 31 and Appendix 6), disposable packaging (para 42) and disposable plastic bags (para 43 and Appendix 6) as particular targets.

- **Carbon credits**. Paragraphs 13 and 14 discuss carbon credits and carbon markets. Under the Kyoto Protocol major countries were allotted a maximum number of carbon credits to share out amongst firms in their country. These countries agreed to a progressive reduction in carbon credits each year. Each government allocates these credits to firms within its country. If a firm exceeds the number of units it has been allocated it must buy more credits on the carbon markets, or apply to government to obtain more. Firms that do not use their entire allocation of credits can sell them for cash on the carbon market.

    Therefore investing to reduce its carbon emissions may save Papy money by not requiring it to buy extra credits and perhaps may give it a source of revenue from selling its surplus credits.

- **Waste disposal costs**. This point is not drawn out in the Pre-seen but is worth mentioning. To reduce waste going into landfill the European Union introduced, in 1996, the first of a number of anti-landfill measures. One was the Packaging Waste Directive which makes firms responsible for the waste they introduce into the supply chain. This means that Papy will be deemed responsible for introducing a certain amount of packaging into the chain, such as boxes, wrappers, tin cans, bottles and bags. It will be required to demonstrate that it has arranged for the recycling or destruction of an equivalent amount. It does this by purchasing Packaging Waste Recovery Notes (PRN's) from professional recycling and recovery firms that specialise in collecting such waste packaging. If Papy can reduce the amount of packaging and waste it creates it can reduce the money it spends on these.

- **Avoidance of litigation and fines**. Sustainability is a requirement increasingly enshrined in law. Failure to act to improve it can lead to prosecutions and fines.

- **Attracting ethical investment funds**. Share prices are determined by demand for the shares. Social Responsible Investment funds (SRIs) have doubled in size since 2007 to about 6.3% of all assets under investment in 2010 (*source: Financial Times October 17th 2010*). If Papy can improve its sustainability credentials it may attract investment from these funds which will increase its share price. Becoming a 'green chip' share is good public relations too. Perhaps the rise in its share price on 23 June was market sentiment anticipating this effect in the longer term and buying ahead.

- **Easier entry to new countries**. Having a good CSR record may make foreign governments, or local government bodies, view Papy's planning applications more favourably.

- **Attracting more customers and charging higher prices**. If sales revenues and margins increase then this will also raise profits. This brings us to the next theme in this Pre-seen material, sustainability and competitive advantage.

Use of sustainable trading for competitive advantage

Paragraph 1 states that the main routes to competitive advantage in the supermarket industry are economies of scale and the supermarket's brand. Paragraph 10 refers to 'intense price competition'.

The Pre-seen tells us that Papy has a 19% share of its home market and appears to be in third place (para 32). The table in para 34 shows it is 20% the size of Competitor 1 and 24% the size of Competitor 2 (€12,911m divided by €64,020m and €53,900m respectively). Therefore it has a *low relative market share* and will struggle to gain the economies of scale enjoyed by its rivals. Given that its products are 'competitively priced' (para 22), this suggests it has to follow the prices set by market leaders. It will be at the mercy of cost leaders in the industry.

Porter is famous for identifying the alternative strategy of Differentiation. This is a source of competitive advantage, and therefore superior profitability, for firms that cannot be cost leaders. Differentiation in supermarkets can be on the basis of quality of food, convenience, product range and so on. The Pre-seen does not give a clear picture of whether Papy has a differentiated position. The fact that it charges competitive prices suggests it doesn't. It tells us that in the past 10 years Papy has focused on opening more small convenience stores rather than large supermarkets (para 21). It seems to imply that the higher prices charged in these stores (para 22) have been responsible for its increasing profits over the decade (para 21). Customer volumes have been rising over the past 5 years (para 22) but this will in part be due to the greater number of stores it has opened. The like-for-like spend seems to have risen by 2% in 2010 according to paragraph 23 (€121.10/€118.75), which is lower than the rate of inflation in many European countries, below the 2.7% rate of food price inflation across Europe during 2010 and certainly below the 4.2% rate of food price inflation in the UK (*source: Investor magazine*).

Lucas Meyer seems to wish for Papy to catch up with, and to jump ahead of, competitors in its development of a sustainable business. He refers to 'promoting the need for a more sustainable attitude in the food retailing business..to customers' (Appendix 5) and goes on to say its 'loyal customers' will be the ones who see what Papy is doing and will help it trade in a more sustainable way.

This is a gamble. Paragraph 10 tells us that supermarkets have not been quick to put their undertakings about sustainable trading into practice because they have focused instead on 'maintaining customer loyalty and profitability'. This seems to imply that they believe sustainability might work against loyalty and profitability. It's tempting to think this may be because it involves raising prices, telling customers what is good for them, and then charging the customer for a carrier bag to carry their shopping home in. It also seems to assume that shoppers will be influenced by a supermarket's treatment of suppliers and the environment. Households may be more concerned with making their budget stretch in a recession-struck economy.

Real world supermarkets like Marks and Spencer and the Co-operative have sought to gain market share by emphasising their sustainability credentials. They appeal to a small section of the overall supermarket shopper population and certainly far less than the 19% presently shopping with Papy.

Lucas Meyer is not experienced in food retailing (para 59). He has sold clothing and sportswear in the past. They are both markets that deal in luxuries, where brands are important. Food is a necessity and generally accounts for a much larger proportion of the household budget. Lucas Meyer's 'new knowledge' may be wishful thinking.

Measuring the performance of sustainable trading

Appendix 6 provides three measures of sustainability, energy consumption, carbon emissions, and issue of free plastic bags. Arif Karp joined on 20 June 2011, the month before the Pre-seen was released. He has experience in 'performance measures for....corporate social responsibilities' (para 37), is presently reviewing the quality and integrity of data in Papy (para 39), and is in discussions with Ziad Abbill about introducing an Environmental Management System (EMS) to track more non-financial data (para 53). He has the support of the CEO, Lucas Meyer (para 61) and considers that targets for carbon emissions (and perhaps other aspects of sustainability) need to be set (para 57).

In your role as a Chartered Management Accountant working for Papy you could be expected to advise on such measures and the ways to capture the data. You could also be expected to evaluate the data gathered. You might also be asked to evaluate the investment in setting up an EMS by comparing its costs with the potential cost savings and other benefits it might lead to.

There is very little additional information in the Pre-seen on this aspect of the case. However paragraph 55 makes clear that this needs to extend to the manufacturers of the products Papy sells, and also its logistics arrangements (para 56). If Papy wishes to reduce its carbon footprint it also needs to consider the carbon generated by its customers in travelling to and from its stores (para 55). This could be affected by internet shopping. Research by the Chartered Institute of Logistics and Transport suggests customers travelling to shop create 26 times more carbon emissions than if they obtained the same goods by internet shopping.

Although the Pre-seen strongly hints at carbon emissions, the facets of sustainable trading are much wider and are detailed in paragraphs 41 to 49. Arif Karp also seeks to improve these (para 61) and so may require measures for these too.

Change management in Papy

Lucas Meyer had been in the post for little more than 2 months at the time the Pre-seen was released. He is known as a CEO who brings about change (para 59). His announcement in Appendix 5, the views attributed to Arif Karp in paragraph 55, and the approach to nutrition and healthy eating (para 49) all include terms like 'educate' and 'messages' These may remind you of particular techniques of change management.

The proposals of Lucas Meyer would represent significant change for Papy. The table in paragraph 34 shows that Papy has the highest carbon emissions of the four supermarkets featured, and also the second to worst level of issuing disposable bags.

From your CIMA studies you will be aware of the approaches to change management identified by writers such as Kotter and Schlesinger and Lewin. You may also be aware that later books by Kaplan and Norton on the role of the Balanced Scorecard emphasised performance measures as an agent of change.

Using a popular framework, Lewin's Force Field theory, it's possible to see the driving forces for change towards sustainability as Lucas Meyer, competitors, legislation on the environment, fair trading and food standards. The resisting forces may be customer attitudes, shareholder desire for profits, the ability of suppliers to meet the standards required, and perhaps Dmity Baludia whose background seems to be in the conventional non-sustainable ways of doing business (para 58).

You should be prepared to advise on these aspects of bringing in new methods and performance measures.

Other issues

Although the Pre-seen focuses strongly on sustainability there are other issues that are worth noting.

Potential acquisitions: paragraph 1 states that supermarkets grow by acquisitions. The table in paragraph 34 shows that Competitor 3 is smaller and less profitable than Papy. Merging them could reduce costs and bring other synergies. One simple example of synergy is that Papy could increase Competitor 3's operating profits by €35m (€11,820m x 5.1% – 4.8%). The statement, in paragraph 28, that Papy has 200m authorised shares but only 100m issued shares would allow the Board to offer new equity in Papy in exchange for shares in Competitor 3.

Home shopping: Papy doesn't presently offer this (para 16). If the Unseen asks for an evaluation of moving into internet shopping any advice you offer should balance increased market coverage, lower emissions and improved convenience and customer loyalty against cannibalisation of the business of its small convenience stores and competing for the scarce IT resources which already need heavy investment to keep up with store openings (para 51) and the possible demand for an EMS (para 53).

Ethics: the T4 exam awards 10 marks for discussion of ethical issues. These are normally introduced in the Unseen information. They could include managers taking inducements for awarding contracts to suppliers, unethical treatment of suppliers or staff, or discovery of wrong food labelling (all have featured in past CIMA case study exams). There may be larger issues to discuss such as the ethics of holding out commitments to sustainability which are not actually being put into practice (para 10) or the role you play being compromised by pressure from management to evaluate projects according to their impact on sustainability rather than, say, shareholder wealth.

PART C PRACTICE TOPCIMA CASES   18: Papy: some help from BPP   365

Exam skills

Now you have worked through the detail of the case, make sure you also do an overall strategic analysis of the pre-seen material.

For example, have you prepared (and prioritised) a SWOT analysis?

Have you prepared a stakeholder analysis?

Have you identified the key business issues and risks facing Papy?

And can you summarise the key findings from your analysis into a one-page business summary?

Remember it is vital you analyse all the different aspects of the information you are given in the case study scenario:

Analyse the numbers – Review any numerical and financial data (profitability, cashflow, working capital, liquidity, gearing, investment ratios)

Environmental analysis – PESTEL analysis; stakeholders (Mendelow's matrix). CSR issues?

Business environment and competitive strategy – Type of industry (product / industry life cycle); Five forces; generic strategies. What do you know about key customers and suppliers? What do you know about the business' marketing strategy?

> Does your analysis of these aspects of the business identify any potential **opportunities** and **threats**?

Products and services – Product range, features, quality, demand; Product portfolio. How will sustainability issues influence Papy's products and services?

Value – How does the business add value? Value chain; distinctive competencies. Again, what impact could sustainability issues and CSR have here?

Information systems and processes – How is IT used in the business strategy; how does the business use e-commerce; what do you know about the business' IT systems? Does the IT set up present any business or security risks?

Management information and control systems – How are activities and resources controlled? What do you know about the management accounting or management information systems?

Performance measures – Have you identified the critical success factors and / or the key performance indicators? Could you produce a balanced scorecard?

Organisation – What is the organisational structure and culture; Who are the key personnel? Are there any personnel and HRM issues?

Investor objectives – What is the capital structure and what are the investor's objectives? What do you know about share price and the value of the business? What do you know about the business' capital? (shares; debt; cost of capital)

> Does your analysis of these aspects of the business identify any **strengths** and **weaknesses**?

Then also think about:

New developments – what new projects may the company be considering? New product development, acquisitions, divestments, new information systems, new organisation structure, new processes?

However, you should NOT be question spotting here; you should simply be thinking of what possible new business projects have been suggested in the pre-seen material.

Once you have completed your detailed analysis, then **synthesise** what you know:

Produce a position statement

- Mission statement
- Competences and CSF's
- Key business risks
- SWOT analysis – prioritising key S, W, O & T.
- Key business issues
- Balanced scorecard

And draw these points together into your one page business summary:

BUSINESS SUMMARY: Name of company			
Nature of business :........................ Current mission	Turnover	CFSs for success in industry • •	
Distinctive competence			
Major stakeholder objective			
ANALYSIS BACKUP			
Key financial data: trends		External : 5 forces	
Gross profit Net profit ROCE Other	Estimated value of business	P E S T	1 Barriers 2 Substitutes 3 Customers 4 Suppliers 5 Company
Gearing Cash Operating cycle		Internal • Capacity • Structure	
Worrying indicators		• Information • Other	
Competitive strategy: Cost leadership/Differentiation/Focus/'stuck in the middle'			
Customers – Key data			

SYNTHESIS

SWOT (Items of high importance)		RISKS: (High importance)	Time
0	0	1	
1	1	2	
2	2	3	
3	3		
Weaknesses	Threats		
1	1	4	
2	2		
3	3	5	

Key issues (High importance)	Time	Selection of possible business projects (High importance)	
1		1	
2		2	
3		3	
4		4	
5		5	
6		Possible discount rate	

Papy: unseen and requirements

This chapter contains the unseen material and requirement from the September 2011 exam.

We have produced a suggested answer to this exam in Chapter 20.

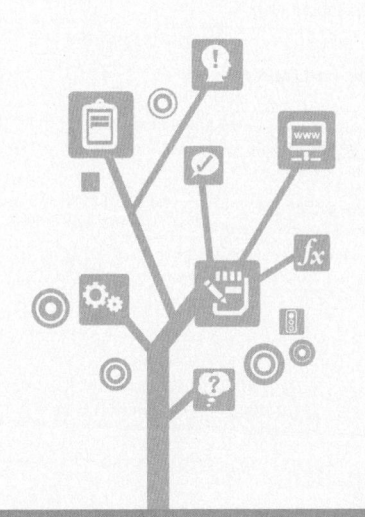

September 2011

Papy – Sustainable trading – Unseen material provided on examination day

Additional (unseen) information relating to the case is given on pages 19 to 22.

Read all of the additional material before you answer the question.

ANSWER THE FOLLOWING QUESTION

You are the Management Accountant of Papy.

Lucas Meyer, Chief Executive, has asked you to provide advice and recommendations on the issues facing Papy.

Question 1 part (a)
Prepare a report that prioritises, analyses and evaluates the issues facing Papy and makes appropriate recommendations.

(Total marks for Question 1 part (a) = 90 Marks)

Question 1 part (b)
In addition to your analysis in your report for part (a), Lucas Meyer, Chief Executive, has asked you to prepare a presentation to the Papy Board, on the savings in carbon emissions that could be achieved by the replacement freezer cabinet proposal and the solar panels proposal.

Your presentation should contain no more than 5 bullet points, including your recommendation, and 1 graph (a column chart or a bar chart or a line chart).

This graph, as an attachment to your presentation, should show Papy's carbon emissions expressed as "kilogram (kg) per square metre of sales area" for each of the 5 years 2009 to 2013. Your graph should include the savings in carbon emissions that could be achieved if Papy were to implement both of the above 2 proposals.

(Total marks for Question 1 part (b) = 10 Marks)

Your script will be marked against the T4 Part B Case Study Assessment Criteria shown below.

Criterion	Maximum marks available
Analysis of issues (25 marks)	
Technical	5
Application	15
Diversity	5
Strategic choices (35 marks)	
Focus	5
Prioritisation	5
Judgement	20
Ethics	5
Recommendations (40 marks)	
Logic	30
Integration	5
Ethics	5
Total	100

Papy - Sustainable trading in the supermarket industry – unseen material provided on examination day
Read this information before you answer the question

New team established

Arif Karp, Corporate Affairs Director, has been tasked to establish a multi-disciplinary team to help Papy become more sustainable and to reduce carbon emissions. This new team includes you, the Management Accountant, as well as representatives from marketing, store management and logistics. He is still selecting some team members.

Carbon emissions targets

Papy's published carbon emissions for the last 2 years, measured in kilograms (kg), are:

	2009 Published	2010 Published
Published levels of carbon emissions (kg million)	1,444	1,424
Actual total sales area (square metres)	1,340,800	1,366,700
Published carbon emissions (kg per square metre)	1,077	1,042

At a recent Board meeting, Arif Karp, advised that his initial research had identified that the published levels of carbon emission figures for 2009 (1,444 million kg) and 2010 (1,424 million kg), shown above, are understated and should be increased by 5%.

Lucas Meyer, Chief Executive, stated at this Board meeting that he considers that the forecast figures, shown in the table below, are far too high. Papy's latest forecast for carbon emissions, which have been revised for the understatement of 5% identified by Arif Karp, are as follows:

	2011 Forecast	2012 Forecast	2013 Forecast
Forecast levels of carbon emissions (kg million)	1,427	1,351	1,274
Forecast total sales area (square metres)	1,395,700	1,425,400	1,457,000
Forecast carbon emissions (kg per square metre)	1,022	948	874

The forecast figures in the table above exclude the effects of the 2 proposals set out below.

Lucas Meyer proposes a target reduction in carbon emissions for 2012 based on a 25% reduction from the revised 2010 levels (that is 1,042 kg per square metre which needs to be updated for the understatement). Lucas Meyer's proposed target for 2013 is based on a reduction of 15% from the new 2012 target. All targets are based upon the measurement of "carbon emissions per square metre of sales area".

Lucas Meyer has assured the Board that financing for capital investment projects to reduce carbon emissions will be given a top priority. Lucas Meyer has asked Arif Karp to identify suitable investment projects to help deliver his proposed target reductions in carbon emissions.

The terms of Arif Karp's employment includes a performance related bonus linked to the level of the reduction in Papy's carbon emissions and waste materials over the next few years.

Arif Karp has asked you to calculate the revised level of carbon emissions for 2009 and 2010 and the new target levels of carbon emissions, based on Lucas Meyer's proposed target reductions, for 2012 and 2013. He has also asked you to comment on whether the new 2013 target is attainable with the proposals set out on the next 2 pages.

September 2011   T4 Part B Case Study

Proposal to change freezer cabinets

The freezer cabinets in Papy's supermarkets and small convenience stores include several different models and sizes procured from a small range of manufacturers. They also vary as to when they were purchased and installed. Papy's usual policy is to replace them every 8 years.

There has recently been a 2 month trial in 30 supermarkets using low carbon technology freezer cabinets, supplied by one of Papy's existing freezer cabinet manufacturers. This trial confirmed that these freezer cabinets would result in a substantial reduction in energy usage and carbon emissions.

The proposal is to replace the current freezer cabinets in a substantial number of Papy stores during the rest of this year, so they are all fully operational from 1 January 2012 onwards. Papy has sufficient cash available to finance the capital costs of this proposal.

Relevant data for this proposal is:

- To change the freezer cabinets at 400 supermarket stores
- To change the freezer cabinets at 100 small convenience stores
- Electricity costs would be reduced by €60,000 each year for each supermarket store and by €18,000 each year for each small convenience store.
- Capital costs would be €200,000 for each supermarket store and €50,000 for each small convenience store.
- Reduction in carbon emissions due to the proposed new freezer cabinets is forecast to be 110,000 kg each year for each supermarket store and 30,000 kg each year for each small convenience store.

Some of the existing freezer cabinets that will be removed are not fully depreciated. The net book value is €25.0 million and it is forecast that they would have no realisable value.

The trial showed a small drop in the volume of sales of frozen food products, as customers have to open the glass doors to access the frozen food products with the new freezer cabinets, rather than simply reaching into the freezers as previously. The forecast gross margin for sales of frozen food products for each supermarket store is €560,000 for each year. This figure is forecast to remain unchanged over the next 5 years.

The trial data showed the following reduction in the gross margin for each supermarket store:

- 60% of supermarket stores showed a fall of 3%
- 30% of supermarket stores showed a fall of 5%
- 10% of supermarket stores showed no change

It is forecast that sales volumes for all of the 400 supermarket stores will fall in accordance with the trial information shown above but that sales volumes for all of 100 small convenience stores will remain unchanged.

It should be assumed that capital expenditure is eligible for 100% tax relief, received 1 year in arrears at the tax rate of 25%. All other cash flows are eligible for tax relief at the tax rate of 25% and that tax is paid, or refunded, 1 year in arrears. The Finance Director has set a criterion for the appraisal of this proposal, and has stated that for acceptance of this proposal the undiscounted payback should be less than 5 years. However, the Finance Director has some reservations about the appropriateness of this appraisal method.

Proposal for solar panels

Arif Karp would like most of Papy's supermarket stores that are located in southern Europe, which experience high levels of sunshine, to be fitted with solar panels on the roofs of these supermarket stores in order to generate solar powered electricity. Depending on the location of the store, it is forecast that up to 30% of each of the store's electricity requirement could be produced by the solar panels. This would save electricity costs and also reduce the stores' carbon emissions. Solar panels will not currently be installed for any small convenience stores.

It is proposed that 200 supermarket stores that are located in Southern Europe would have solar panels installed over a 2 year period, at the rate of 100 supermarkets each year.

The proposal generates an NPV of €91 million at a risk adjusted post-tax cost of capital of 9% when evaluated over a 10 year period. The discounted payback period is within 8 years.

The capital cost of installing solar panels for each supermarket store is €3 million.

It is proposed that the capital cost will be funded by new debt. Abdul Yarkol, Finance Director, considers that Papy's gearing (defined as debt to debt plus equity) is significantly lower than some of its competitors, which have gearing ratios of around 40%. He is currently in negotiations with banks but other sources of finance may also be required.

There is some discussion in Arif Karp's team as to whether Papy should invest in solar panels for as many as 200 supermarket stores in the next 2 years or whether Papy should wait. The technology for solar panels is improving, allowing a greater amount of electricity to be generated by each solar panel. Improved solar panel technology, which could be 20% more effective than the current technology, is likely to be commercially available in 2017.

Arif Karp wants this proposal to invest in solar panels for 200 supermarket stores to proceed as soon as possible. He considers that any investment undertaken now could easily be upgraded to use the newer technology solar panels as they become available.

The reduction in carbon emissions as a direct result of this investment is forecast to be an average of 900,000 kg for each year for each supermarket store.

For simplicity, it should be assumed that if this proposal is approved, then the capital expenditure for the solar panels for the first 100 supermarket stores will be incurred in 2011. The benefits from the electricity savings and carbon emission reductions from these 100 stores with solar panels will begin in 2012. The second 100 supermarket stores will be installed in late 2012 and the carbon reductions will begin in 2013.

Measurement of waste materials

Papy currently measures waste materials, including packaging materials for products delivered to stores, by volume. However, Arif Karp considers that the weight of waste materials would be a more helpful measurement. The statistics for waste materials for last year and the latest forecast figures for 2011 and 2012 are as follows:

Waste materials from all stores	2010 Actual	2011 Forecast	2012 Forecast
By volume (millions of cubic metres)	450	430	409
By weight (kg million)	110	95	70

Papy publishes an annual Corporate Social Responsibility report which includes statistics on sustainability issues, including waste materials. Arif Karp proposes that all statistics for waste material reduction should be based on weight, and not volume.

September 2011   21   T4 Part B Case Study

Management of change

Arif Karp has requested all store managers to collect a new range of non-financial data effective from 1 September 2011. This data is to be submitted monthly, on spreadsheets, to his team for collation and analysis. Arif Karp would like to implement a dedicated IT system for capturing this non-financial data. However, many of Papy's senior management team have not replied to any of his requests concerning the sources of information for data for this proposed new IT system and the general response is that they are too busy. Therefore, Arif Karp has appointed external consultants to help to specify the requirements for this new IT system. These external consultants have expertise in IT systems but lack specialist knowledge of the supermarket industry.

Many employees either do not know, or understand, what Arif Karp and his team are trying to achieve. Most employees are focused on their specific job responsibilities and in meeting the current financial targets. They do not understand the reasons for change and are resistant to taking on the extra work that store managers have passed to them to do.

Currently targets include a range of measures, including waste reduction and speed of products to stores, but principally targets have been financial measures such as revenues and operating profit for each store. Some of the senior management team, as well as some store managers, are sceptical about the cost of the initiatives being considered and that the demands of reducing carbon emissions will raise costs. They believe that the pressure to deliver increased profits will ultimately take precedence over reductions in carbon emissions. They further believe that this is just a temporary phase for Papy and that Arif Karp will be unable to deliver substantial reductions in carbon emissions, and that he will consequently leave Papy.

Arif Karp is frustrated about the lack of support given to him and his team from both the senior management team, including some Board members, as well as store managers. He recognises the urgency in changing attitudes within Papy in order to meet revised carbon emission targets and become more sustainable.

You should discuss what actions are required in order to help bring about change in employees attitudes and to minimise employees' resistance to change.

Cancellation of 2 supplier contracts

As part of a review of sales and the level of waste from unsold fresh produce, Papy has established that sales have reduced for a small range of fresh products supplied under 2 contracts. The level of waste currently being experienced has eroded Papy's gross profit margins for these products significantly.

Rafael Lucci, Papy's Operations and Logistics Director, is proposing to cancel these 2 contracts when they expire in 3 months time. These 2 contracts are with farming co-operatives in Africa which produce fresh fruit under the "Fair Trade" label. The "Fair Trade" label is defined as an organised social movement which helps small-scale farmers in developing countries to obtain better trading conditions than they could achieve individually, and ensures that a fair price is paid to producers in order for them to earn a living wage.

End of unseen material

APPLICABLE MATHS TABLES AND FORMULAE

Present value table

Present value of 1.00 unit of currency, that is $(1 + r)^{-n}$ where r = interest rate; n = number of periods until payment or receipt.

Periods (n)	1%	2%	3%	4%	5%	6%	7%	8%	9%	10%
1	0.990	0.980	0.971	0.962	0.952	0.943	0.935	0.926	0.917	0.909
2	0.980	0.961	0.943	0.925	0.907	0.890	0.873	0.857	0.842	0.826
3	0.971	0.942	0.915	0.889	0.864	0.840	0.816	0.794	0.772	0.751
4	0.961	0.924	0.888	0.855	0.823	0.792	0.763	0.735	0.708	0.683
5	0.951	0.906	0.863	0.822	0.784	0.747	0.713	0.681	0.650	0.621
6	0.942	0.888	0.837	0.790	0.746	0705	0.666	0.630	0.596	0.564
7	0.933	0.871	0.813	0.760	0.711	0.665	0.623	0.583	0.547	0.513
8	0.923	0.853	0.789	0.731	0.677	0.627	0.582	0.540	0.502	0.467
9	0.914	0.837	0.766	0.703	0.645	0.592	0.544	0.500	0.460	0.424
10	0.905	0.820	0.744	0.676	0.614	0.558	0.508	0.463	0.422	0.386
11	0.896	0.804	0.722	0.650	0.585	0.527	0.475	0.429	0.388	0.350
12	0.887	0.788	0.701	0.625	0.557	0.497	0.444	0.397	0.356	0.319
13	0.879	0.773	0.681	0.601	0.530	0.469	0.415	0.368	0.326	0.290
14	0.870	0.758	0.661	0.577	0.505	0.442	0.388	0.340	0.299	0.263
15	0.861	0.743	0.642	0.555	0.481	0.417	0.362	0.315	0.275	0.239
16	0.853	0.728	0.623	0.534	0.458	0.394	0.339	0.292	0.252	0.218
17	0.844	0.714	0.605	0.513	0.436	0.371	0.317	0.270	0.231	0.198
18	0.836	0.700	0.587	0.494	0.416	0.350	0.296	0.250	0.212	0.180
19	0.828	0.686	0.570	0.475	0.396	0.331	0.277	0.232	0.194	0.164
20	0.820	0.673	0.554	0.456	0.377	0.312	0.258	0.215	0.178	0.149

Periods (n)	11%	12%	13%	14%	15%	16%	17%	18%	19%	20%
1	0.901	0.893	0.885	0.877	0.870	0.862	0.855	0.847	0.840	0.833
2	0.812	0.797	0.783	0.769	0.756	0.743	0.731	0.718	0.706	0.694
3	0.731	0.712	0.693	0.675	0.658	0.641	0.624	0.609	0.593	0.579
4	0.659	0.636	0.613	0.592	0.572	0.552	0.534	0.516	0.499	0.482
5	0.593	0.567	0.543	0.519	0.497	0.476	0.456	0.437	0.419	0.402
6	0.535	0.507	0.480	0.456	0.432	0.410	0.390	0.370	0.352	0.335
7	0.482	0.452	0.425	0.400	0.376	0.354	0.333	0.314	0.296	0.279
8	0.434	0.404	0.376	0.351	0.327	0.305	0.285	0.266	0.249	0.233
9	0.391	0.361	0.333	0.308	0.284	0.263	0.243	0.225	0.209	0.194
10	0.352	0.322	0.295	0.270	0.247	0.227	0.208	0.191	0.176	0.162
11	0.317	0.287	0.261	0.237	0.215	0.195	0.178	0.162	0.148	0.135
12	0.286	0.257	0.231	0.208	0.187	0.168	0.152	0.137	0.124	0.112
13	0.258	0.229	0.204	0.182	0.163	0.145	0.130	0.116	0.104	0.093
14	0.232	0.205	0.181	0.160	0.141	0.125	0.111	0.099	0.088	0.078
15	0.209	0.183	0.160	0.140	0.123	0.108	0.095	0.084	0.079	0.065
16	0.188	0.163	0.141	0.123	0.107	0.093	0.081	0.071	0.062	0.054
17	0.170	0.146	0.125	0.108	0.093	0.080	0.069	0.060	0.052	0.045
18	0.153	0.130	0.111	0.095	0.081	0.069	0.059	0.051	0.044	0.038
19	0.138	0.116	0.098	0.083	0.070	0.060	0.051	0.043	0.037	0.031
20	0.124	0.104	0.087	0.073	0.061	0.051	0.043	0.037	0.031	0.026

September 2011   T4 Part B Case Study

Cumulative present value of 1.00 unit of currency per annum, Receivable or Payable at the end of each year for n years $\left[\dfrac{1-(1+r)^{-n}}{r}\right]$

Periods (n)	1%	2%	3%	4%	5%	6%	7%	8%	9%	10%
1	0.990	0.980	0.971	0.962	0.952	0.943	0.935	0.926	0.917	0.909
2	1.970	1.942	1.913	1.886	1.859	1.833	1.808	1.783	1.759	1.736
3	2.941	2.884	2.829	2.775	2.723	2.673	2.624	2.577	2.531	2.487
4	3.902	3.808	3.717	3.630	3.546	3.465	3.387	3.312	3.240	3.170
5	4.853	4.713	4.580	4.452	4.329	4.212	4.100	3.993	3.890	3.791
6	5.795	5.601	5.417	5.242	5.076	4.917	4.767	4.623	4.486	4.355
7	6.728	6.472	6.230	6.002	5.786	5.582	5.389	5.206	5.033	4.868
8	7.652	7.325	7.020	6.733	6.463	6.210	5.971	5.747	5.535	5.335
9	8.566	8.162	7.786	7.435	7.108	6.802	6.515	6.247	5.995	5.759
10	9.471	8.983	8.530	8.111	7.722	7.360	7.024	6.710	6.418	6.145
11	10.368	9.787	9.253	8.760	8.306	7.887	7.499	7.139	6.805	6.495
12	11.255	10.575	9.954	9.385	8.863	8.384	7.943	7.536	7.161	6.814
13	12.134	11.348	10.635	9.986	9.394	8.853	8.358	7.904	7.487	7.103
14	13.004	12.106	11.296	10.563	9.899	9.295	8.745	8.244	7.786	7.367
15	13.865	12.849	11.938	11.118	10.380	9.712	9.108	8.559	8.061	7.606
16	14.718	13.578	12.561	11.652	10.838	10.106	9.447	8.851	8.313	7.824
17	15.562	14.292	13.166	12.166	11.274	10.477	9.763	9.122	8.544	8.022
18	16.398	14.992	13.754	12.659	11.690	10.828	10.059	9.372	8.756	8.201
19	17.226	15.679	14.324	13.134	12.085	11.158	10.336	9.604	8.950	8.365
20	18.046	16.351	14.878	13.590	12.462	11.470	10.594	9.818	9.129	8.514

Periods (n)	11%	12%	13%	14%	15%	16%	17%	18%	19%	20%
1	0.901	0.893	0.885	0.877	0.870	0.862	0.855	0.847	0.840	0.833
2	1.713	1.690	1.668	1.647	1.626	1.605	1.585	1.566	1.547	1.528
3	2.444	2.402	2.361	2.322	2.283	2.246	2.210	2.174	2.140	2.106
4	3.102	3.037	2.974	2.914	2.855	2.798	2.743	2.690	2.639	2.589
5	3.696	3.605	3.517	3.433	3.352	3.274	3.199	3.127	3.058	2.991
6	4.231	4.111	3.998	3.889	3.784	3.685	3.589	3.498	3.410	3.326
7	4.712	4.564	4.423	4.288	4.160	4.039	3.922	3.812	3.706	3.605
8	5.146	4.968	4.799	4.639	4.487	4.344	4.207	4.078	3.954	3.837
9	5.537	5.328	5.132	4.946	4.772	4.607	4.451	4.303	4.163	4.031
10	5.889	5.650	5.426	5.216	5.019	4.833	4.659	4.494	4.339	4.192
11	6.207	5.938	5.687	5.453	5.234	5.029	4.836	4.656	4.486	4.327
12	6.492	6.194	5.918	5.660	5.421	5.197	4.988	7.793	4.611	4.439
13	6.750	6.424	6.122	5.842	5.583	5.342	5.118	4.910	4.715	4.533
14	6.982	6.628	6.302	6.002	5.724	5.468	5.229	5.008	4.802	4.611
15	7.191	6.811	6.462	6.142	5.847	5.575	5.324	5.092	4.876	4.675
16	7.379	6.974	6.604	6.265	5.954	5.668	5.405	5.162	4.938	4.730
17	7.549	7.120	6.729	6.373	6.047	5.749	5.475	5.222	4.990	4.775
18	7.702	7.250	6.840	6.467	6.128	5.818	5.534	5.273	5.033	4.812
19	7.839	7.366	6.938	6.550	6.198	5.877	5.584	5.316	5.070	4.843
20	7.963	7.469	7.025	6.623	6.259	5.929	5.628	5.353	5.101	4.870

FORMULAE

Valuation Models

(i) Irredeemable preference share, paying a constant annual dividend, d, in perpetuity, where P_0 is the ex-div value:

$$P_0 = \frac{d}{k_{pref}}$$

(ii) Ordinary (Equity) share, paying a constant annual dividend, d, in perpetuity, where P_0 is the ex-div value:

$$P_0 = \frac{d}{k_e}$$

(iii) Ordinary (Equity) share, paying an annual dividend, d, growing in perpetuity at a constant rate, g, where P_0 is the ex-div value:

$$P_0 = \frac{d_1}{k_e - g} \text{ or } P_0 = \frac{d_0[1+g]}{k_e - g}$$

(iv) Irredeemable (Undated) debt, paying annual after tax interest, $i(1-t)$, in perpetuity, where P_0 is the ex-interest value:

$$P_0 = \frac{i[1-t]}{k_{dnet}}$$

or, without tax:

$$P_0 = \frac{i}{k_d}$$

(v) Future value of S, of a sum X, invested for n periods, compounded at $r\%$ interest:

$$S = X[1+r]^n$$

(vi) Present value of £1 payable or receivable in n years, discounted at $r\%$ per annum:

$$PV = \frac{1}{[1+r]^n}$$

(vii) Present value of an annuity of £1 per annum, receivable or payable for n years, commencing in one year, discounted at $r\%$ per annum:

$$PV = \frac{1}{r}\left[1 - \frac{1}{[1+r]^n}\right]$$

(viii) Present value of £1 per annum, payable or receivable in perpetuity, commencing in one year, discounted at $r\%$ per annum:

$$PV = \frac{1}{r}$$

(ix) Present value of £1 per annum, receivable or payable, commencing in one year, growing in perpetuity at a constant rate of $g\%$ per annum, discounted at $r\%$ per annum:

$$PV = \frac{1}{r-g}$$

Cost of Capital

(i) Cost of irredeemable preference capital, paying an annual dividend, d, in perpetuity, and having a current ex-div price P_0:

$$k_{pref} = \frac{d}{P_0}$$

(ii) Cost of irredeemable debt capital, paying annual net interest, $i(1-t)$, and having a current ex-interest price P_0:

$$k_{dnet} = \frac{i[1-t]}{P_0}$$

(iii) Cost of ordinary (equity) share capital, paying an annual dividend, d, in perpetuity, and having a current ex-div price P_0:

$$k_e = \frac{d}{P_0}$$

(iv) Cost of ordinary (equity) share capital, having a current ex-div price, P_0, having just paid a dividend, d_0, with the dividend growing in perpetuity by a constant $g\%$ per annum:

$$k_e = \frac{d_1}{P_0} + g \quad \text{or} \quad k_e = \frac{d_0[1+g]}{P_0} + g$$

(v) Cost of ordinary (equity) share capital, using the CAPM:

$$k_e = R_f + [R_m - R_f]\beta$$

(vi) Weighted average cost of capital, k_0:

$$k_0 = k_e \left[\frac{V_E}{V_E + V_D}\right] + k_d \left[\frac{V_D}{V_E + V_D}\right]$$

Papy: answer

This is the suggested answer to the **September 2011** unseen and requirement, written by BPP Learning Media. Your report will be different to this and may analyse different issues. This is as it should be, there is no one correct answer. Nonetheless, if you fail to prioritise the key issues you will find it very difficult to pass your T4 (TOPCIMA) exam.

We have also included a suggested marking scheme developed by BPP Learning Media from the Post Exam Guides and Script Reviews following the real exam.

Review this marking grid carefully to see where the Examiner awarded marks, and therefore the sorts of things you can improve in your answers to ensure you score as many marks as possible.

Once you have answered this case study and reviewed our answer, you may also find it useful to read through the CIMA examiner's **post-exam guide**. The post-exam guides are available in the 'Study resources' section for T4 on the *cimaglobal.com* website.

Much of the information in the post-exam guide will be specific to this particular September 2010 case (rather than the case you will face in your exam). However, the post-exam guides do also include some more general comments on candidates' scripts, and the guides highlight some common errors, including omissions, which candidates make and common weaknesses they show. If you have shown some of the same weaknesses in your practice exams to date, these are points you need to address before you sit your real exam.

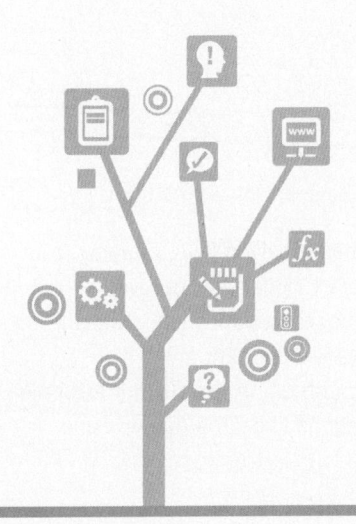

Answer to Question 1a

REPORT

To: Lucas Meyer: CEO Papy

From: Management Accountant

Date: 31st August 2011

Contents

1 Introduction
2 Terms of reference
3 Prioritisation of issues facing Papy
4 Discussion of the main issues facing Papy
5 Ethical considerations facing Papy
6 Recommendations on the main issues facing Papy
7 Conclusion

Appendices

A SWOT analysis
B Stakeholder analysis
C Force Field analysis (Lewin)
D Revised emission targets
E Carbon reductions from investments
F Evaluation of freezer proposal

1 Introduction

Papy has announced a strategy to improve its sustainability which has been received favourably by investors. The credibility of senior management will depend on Papy's ability to deliver improved sustainability. The discovery by Arif Karp that past emissions are 5% higher than published, makes it even more important that Papy makes real progress. This will be particularly important given the increased financial implications of excessive carbon emissions in many countries. In the UK, for example, the Carbon Reduction Commitment scheme (CRC) is targeted at organisations like supermarkets and levies tax revenues based on emissions.

2 Terms of reference

This report was commissioned by the Chief Executive of Papy to prioritise, analyse and evaluate the issues facing the company and offer appropriate recommendations.

3 Prioritisation of issues facing Papy

The issues below have been prioritised based on the potential impact each could have on Papy. A full SWOT analysis is presented in Appendix A.

3.1 Carbon emission targets – first priority

The reputation of the Board of Papy depends on its ability to progress with its strategy of sustainability. The forecast reduction in carbon between 2011 and 2013 is 14% (1- 874/1022), some way below the targets set by the CEO. Achieving these targets is the context for the issues discussed below.

This issue has been given first priority because achieving these targets will have enormous impact on Papy's operations and on its reputation. It is also urgent because steps need to be taken immediately.

3.2 Management of change – second priority

The lack of general understanding and support for the strategy will hamper its success. This pervades from shop floor to senior management. If not dealt with, it will lead to non-implementation or reluctant implementation of initiatives, staff turnover, and a lack of good local ideas coming forward.

This issue has been given second priority because it is fundamental to Papy's chances of becoming more sustainable. If Papy is to invest hundreds of millions successfully, its workforce must enthusiastically implement the strategy for change.

3.3 Proposal for solar panels – third priority

The proposal to put solar panels on to 200 stores over 2 years involves total capital expenditure of €600m (200 × €3m). It will potentially reduce carbon emissions and so contribute to achieving the new emissions targets. The first phase of capital expenditure appears to be scheduled for 2011 and therefore a decision is needed urgently.

Therefore this issue has been given third priority.

3.4 Proposal to change freezer cabinets – fourth priority

This proposal requires Papy to replace freezers at 500 locations by 1 January 2012. The capital expenditure will be €85m and the changeover could reduce gross margins by up to 5%. It can reduce emissions and help Papy achieve its targets.

This issue has a significant financial impact. To meet the deadline, a decision is needed soon. However the lower capital outlay and lower emission reduction compared to solar panels has led to this being given fourth priority.

3.5 Other issues facing Papy

There are issues of lesser importance which have not been prioritised in this report as they are seen as less urgent and as having less impact on the business. These are:

- Cancellation of two supplier contracts
- Management of waste materials

Ethical issues facing the division will be discussed in a separate section.

4 Discussion of the main issues facing Papy

4.1 Carbon emission targets– first priority

Appendix D shows the revised targets for Papy's carbon emissions. The revised data is as follows in kg per square metre:

- 2009 1,131
- 2010 1,094
- Target 2012 821
- Target 2013 697

Papy faces a significant challenge in reaching the new targets. Between 2010 and 2011 the total carbon emissions per square metre over total sales area should fall by 72kg (1,094 – 1,022), equivalent to 6.6% (72/1,094). The targets require emissions to fall by 201kg between 2011 and 2012 (1,022 – 821) and by 124kg by 2013 (821 – 697). These are greater forecast reductions than Papy has achieved in past years.

Appendix D shows that the targeted 15% improvement on these forecasts requires that an additional 127kg million be saved in 2012 and 177kg million in 2013.

Appendix E shows that the freezer cabinets will reduce emissions per square metre over total sales area by 33kg in 2012 and 32kg in 2013, and solar panels will reduce emissions by 63kg in 2012 and 124kg in 2013. This would mean an overall reduction in emissions per square metre over total sales area of 96kg in 2012 and 156kg in 2013.

Therefore neither the 2012 nor 2013 revised targets are attainable with just the two investment proposals set out. More savings are needed.

Therefore in 2012 sustainable additional carbon savings of 31kg per square metre (127 – 96) will be needed to hit the target and an additional 21kg (177 – 156) in 2013.

Option 1 – revise the targets to make them attainable

The targets for 2012 and 2013 cannot be met by just undertaking the two investments set out. Reducing the targets, would make them attainable.

The *advantages* of this option would be that it would reduce the investment costs of finding further ways to reduce carbon. It would also avoid any reputation risk to Papy resulting from missing targets it had published.

The *disadvantages* of this would be that it would disappoint investors who expected the sustainability strategy to bring larger reductions and instead will be promised reductions of 6% in 2012. Another disadvantage is that it would leave Papy vulnerable to the costs of carbon taxes, such as the UK's CRC, which would reduce profits.

Option 2 – find additional ways to reduce carbon

So far this discussion has focused on just the two investments as ways to reduce carbon. There are other techniques besides investing in fridges and solar panels. These include using LED lighting in stores, reducing in-store refrigeration by encouraging home delivery of frozen items, conversion of delivery vehicles to bio-fuels, liquefied gas or electricity.

Such initiatives require the involvement of management and suppliers in deciding how to reduce carbon, and the support of stakeholders like staff and customers. This has been the approach of Marks and Spencer with its Plan A.

The *advantages* of this option are that it will retain shareholder support, avoid carbon taxes and also give Papy a competitive advantage in the market place.

The *disadvantages* are that it may initially be costly and, as seems to have happened in Papy already, run against the culture of the firm, leading to poor implementation.

4.2 Management of change – second priority

Various change models can be used to assess and deal with the resistance to the sustainability strategy.

According to Lewin, change situations can be understood as a battle between two groups of forces, driving forces and resisting forces. These are detailed in Appendix C.

There are various options that can be pursued.

Option 1 – Management development

Senior management is unsure of the reasons for the new strategy. This can be addressed by management development including away-days where Lucas Meyer and Arif Karp can outline their ideas and invite guest speakers and consultants to speak.

The *advantages* of this option are that it will help overcome misunderstanding and ignorance of the strategy. It will also provide an opportunity for managers to question the Board on their intentions.

The *disadvantages* are that the meetings may disrupt the operations of Papy by taking management away from their responsibilities. It will cost money to accommodate the managers and pay for their travel. There is also the danger that the meetings could degenerate into an argument if managers retain deep-seated opposition to the new strategy.

Option 2 – Staff communications

Staff at shop level can make a difference to the success of the strategy by how they communicate it to customers, ensure that energy is not wasted, and so on. Also, as Appendix B shows, staff are in the 'keep informed' section of Mendelow's matrix.

The *advantages* of staff communication include improved implementation of the strategy, reduced resistance and the encouragement of participation.

The *disadvantages* are that it will involve cost and may leave some staff uninterested or cynical about the project.

Option 3 – Revised performance measurement system

At present Papy lacks a performance management system that reports systematically on non-commercial targets such as impacts associated with emissions and energy use. This leads to a focus on commercial targets that are measurable, such as customer footfall, revenue and costs.

Changing the system to include measures of non-commercial performance will help to focus managers and staff on the fulfilment of the new strategy according to the maxim 'what gets measured gets done'.

The *advantages* of this option are that it will provide monitoring information on the success of implementation of strategy to allow control. Another advantage is that it will help motivate staff by giving feedback on the success of their efforts and perhaps a basis for performance related payments.

The *disadvantages* are that increasing the number of performance measures can confuse management when the measures are not congruent, such as where installing freezers reduces sales and margin. It will also increase the costs of control by demanding additional systems to capture data and to report information.

4.3 Proposal for solar panels – third priority

This proposal can be evaluated using the SAF framework of Johnson, Scholes and Whittington.

Suitability

Papy has a strategy both to reduce its energy use and to reduce its carbon emissions. These solar panels will contribute to both objectives. Additionally energy prices are rising continually, as fossil fuels deplete and energy politics force the prices of the remaining supplies up. Using less bought-in energy helps shield Papy against these forces.

Although there is a potential for a more effective solar panel in 2017, delay to this investment would make it harder for Papy to hit its 2012 and 2013 emissions targets.

Acceptability

The project has an NPV of €91m which appears to make it acceptable to investors. Some doubt should be cast on the use of a 9% cost of capital. This is mainly because the size of the project is large, €600m (€3m x 200 stores). If the project was financed by debt alone, it would increase Papy's capital gearing from its present 29% to 41% (€870.0/€2,974.4: €1,470.4/€3,574.4). To compensate investors for the higher risk caused by this higher gearing the project should perhaps be evaluated at a higher cost of capital. The NPV of the project investment is €575.1m (€300m x (1 + 0.917)) and the NPV of the project is €91m, which means that it is 15.8% sensitive to its discount rate (91/575.1). If a higher cost of capital was used, this project would have a negative NPV and therefore not be acceptable to shareholders.

The payback is around 8 years which exceeds the 5 years set by the Finance Director for the freezer cabinet investment. However the FD uses a discounted payback target for the solar panels whereas the 5 year payback quoted for the freezer cabinets is undiscounted.

Feasibility

There seems to be some doubt that banks will provide the entire €600m finance required for this project. Additional sources of finance might be needed. Papy held €603.9m of cash at the end of 2010, up from €480m in 2009. Between the two years it generated €855.9m cash from operating activities. Although some of these cash flows will have been set aside for new stores and refurbishments there will be some surplus funds available. Furthermore the manufacturers of the solar panels may be able to provide a lease finance option.

If a situation of capital rationing develops because funds are not available the Board should consider the carbon reduction per Euro invested. For solar panels this is 0.3kg per year (900,000kg/€3,000,000). For freezer cabinets it is 0.55kg for supermarkets (110,000kg/€200,000).

4.4 Proposal to change freezer cabinets – fourth priority

This proposal can also be evaluated using SAF analysis.

Suitability

The new freezers are suitable because they will contribute to the reduction of carbon emissions by the start of 2012. There may be other benefits, such as energy use reduction and providing a better working environment for staff who tend to suffer from the cold working conditions created by open front 'dairy' freezers.

Acceptability

This requires that the project be acceptable to some key stakeholders. A stakeholder analysis is presented in Appendix B. This shows that management, investors and suppliers are the key players here.

Appendix F shows the financial assessment of this proposal. This shows that it will payback during 2016, before the end of the 5th year, the criterion set by the Finance Director.

There are a number of limitations to this analysis. One major limitation is the assumption that energy costs will stay constant. In reality they will probably rise and this would move the payback earlier. There is also no allowance made for the potential costs of carbon taxes on the emissions caused by the energy usage which, if accounted for, would also increase annual savings and so reduce the time to payback.

The €7.39m lost margin from customers being unwilling to open the doors may be an over-estimate. The pilot was conducted in supermarkets when rival supermarkets continued to offer open fridges. It is likely that all supermarkets will adopt these new cabinets with the effect that customers will become accustomed (or at least resigned) to using them in the same way as they have adapted to self-checkout tills.

Payback is itself a faulty appraisal method. It ignores the total financial return to the project by focusing instead on how long it would take to recover the initial investment. Evaluating this proposal using the investment criterion applied to the solar panels option reveals a net present value of €27.34m over 10 years on €85m of capex, giving a return of €0.32 (27.34/85) compared to the €0.15 from solar panels (91/600). This shows it is a profitable investment that is superior to the solar panels.

Feasibility

Changing over 400 supermarkets and 100 stores in 4 months is an ambitious project, particularly as November and December are peak frozen food shopping periods in Europe in the run up to Christmas. There is no guarantee that original equipment manufacturers will have the ability to supply so many new freezers in the time available.

As has been noted above, raising the capital of €85m will be an additional burden on top of the €600m needed for solar panels.

4.5 Other issues facing Papy

There have not been discussed due to lack of time.

5 Ethical considerations facing Papy

5.1 Measurement of waste materials

Arif Karp has proposed changing measurement from volume to weight.

Arif Karp has a conflict of interest in making this suggestion because he is paid a bonus based on reductions in carbon emissions and waste. His duty is to help Papy achieve sustainability goals, not to maximise his own income.

The table shows that waste reductions of 4.9% are forecast if measured by volume (430-409/430) but 26.3% if measured by weight (95-70/95).

There are arguments for either measure since volume reflects the disposal problem of waste whereas weight indicates the resources wasted.

To avoid this conflict of interest either Arif Karp's bonus should be re-based to avoid him gaining from this change, or the decision to change measure should be taken independently.

It is recommended that an independent consultant be appointed to make recommendations on how waste should be measured.

5.2 Cancellation of 2 supplier contracts

This issue poses Papy with two conflicting ethical obligations.

The ethical duty of fairness would suggest that the African co-operatives should be supported and the contracts extended. Papy also has a CSR commitment to support fair prices.

The ethical duty of honesty would be compromised by continuing to use the co-operatives. Papy presents itself as seeking to reduce its environmental impact and therefore it should seek to reduce waste.

Better marketing by Papy of the products could reduce waste by increasing demand. Stressing their Fair Trade origins may help here.

It is recommended that Papy works with the co-operatives to find ways of reducing waste. This probably means better forecasting of demand to avoid unsold inventory, and using dynamic pricing and special offers to clear back-inventory of fresh produce.

6 Recommendations on the main issues facing Papy

6.1 Carbon emission targets – first priority

It is recommended that Papy revises the 2012 emission target to be more attainable but that it aims to beat this target and achieve significant reductions in carbon emissions over the coming years.

This is recommended because it balances the need for Papy to make real progress towards its sustainability objectives whilst also ensuring that its targets are realistic and that it does not lose credibility as a consequence of missing them.

It is recommended that the 2012 target be revised to 910kg per square metre which is a 4% reduction against the original forecast (910/948). This target therefore stretches performance, but avoids making an unrealistic commitment.

To reach this revised target it will be essential that the investment in solar panels and in freezers goes ahead.

It is proposed that Arif Karp charges his new multi-disciplinary team to identify further initiatives to reduce carbon emissions. This may include involving other stakeholders such as suppliers.

It is important that the change management process described elsewhere in this report is carried out to ensure ideas are generated and are implemented.

6.2 Management of change – second priority

Recommendation 1

This report recommends that a programme of management development is undertaken to help achieve senior support for the new strategy.

This is recommended because senior managers will be responsible for explaining the new strategy to other staff and for monitoring the implementation of the strategy in their areas of responsibility.

It is recommended that a series of mid-week conferences be scheduled across the countries Papy operates in. These should be attended by store managers, warehouse managers and other office holders. The conferences should be addressed by Lucas Meyer and Arif Karp but also be workshop based to enable managers to translate the broad policies into actions for their particular areas of responsibility.

Recommendation 2

This report recommends a communications strategy be set up to explain and update all staff on the strategy.

This is recommended because effective implementation of the strategy requires it to be understood and supported at all levels.

To do this a series of standard presentations should be developed to be delivered by team leaders in each department or function. There should be quarterly meetings to update the staff on recent developments. This could be backed up by a special site on the Papy intranet.

Recommendation 3

It is recommended that a new performance measurement system be established.

This is recommended because staff and managers will be motivated to achieve the targets they are set. If the targets include ones related to sustainability this will cause staff to pursue those goals too.

Creating these new measures will necessitate the creation of a special working party to identify the key processes in Papy that impact on the emissions and energy usage. The critical functions should be identified and metrics established for each. A data gathering system for each should be set up and the resulting data provided to the EMS for reporting.

6.3 Proposal for solar panels – third priority

It is recommended that the purchase of solar panels be undertaken providing the finance can be raised and that the effects of this are not sufficient to increase the cost of capital significantly.

This is because the proposal is financially acceptable and will make a significant contribution to reducing Papy's carbon footprint.

In the event that capital is not sufficient then priority should be given to freezer cabinets because the carbon savings per Euro are higher from freezer cabinets than from solar panels (0.55kg compared to 0.3kg).

The first step must be to secure financing, which is presently being investigated by Abdul Yarkol.

Plans need to be drawn up to put installations into the stores. It is recommended that these be prioritised on the basis of which stores use most energy and therefore the initial 100 hundred stores must be identified quickly to avoid delay to this project.

Given the significant amount of capex involved, and the fact that investments like these will be essential to achieving carbon reductions in the future, it is recommended that a post-investment audit be undertaken after the first year to ensure that the savings and costs are as forecast.

6.4 Proposal to change freezer cabinets – fourth priority

It is recommended that Papy install the freezers in supermarkets as suggested by the proposal. However a pilot should be conducted at convenience stores before finally committing to installing the new freezers in these too.

This is recommended because it will be an essential part of meeting the 2012 and 2013 carbon reduction targets. The proposal pays back within 5 years, has a positive NPV and makes a contribution to attaining the goal of reducing carbon emissions. Delaying some introductions until the existing freezers were obsolete would avoid the €25m write off of assets, and hence reduction in profit. Given the priorities of the board to reduce emissions this may be a secondary consideration.

It is recommended that orders be placed with the manufacturers to secure the supply of the freezers and that this be synchronised with a project plan to roll out the new freezers across the stores.

A pilot project should be arranged for the convenience stores, to be completed by the end of the November, to validate the forecast savings and margin reductions used in the calculation in Appendix F.

Future store buildings and refurbishments should be specified with the new freezers.

Care should be taken over the disposal of the old freezers as some freezers contain gases that can damage the environment.

6.5 Other issues facing Papy

These have not been discussed due to lack of time.

7 Conclusion

It is essential that the sustainability project of Papy be progressed. The recommendations in this report assist this.

Appendix A: SWOT analysis

Strengths	Weaknesses
• Supportive investors • New CEO	• Third in the market • Culture opposed to change to sustainability
Opportunities	**Threats**
• Solar panels project • New freezer project • New measurements for waste materials • Increased awareness about climate change	• Resistance to carbon reduction targets and policies • Bad publicity from cancellation of African contracts

Appendix B: Stakeholder analysis

Mendelow identifies 4 stakeholder groups. These can be applied to the freezer proposal

- Minimal effort: low interest and low power – eg casual shoppers
- Keep informed: low power, high interest – eg regular shoppers, staff, media
- Keep satisfied: high power, low interest
- Key players: high power, high interest – eg investors, management of Papy, suppliers of freezers.

Appendix C: Force Field analysis (Lewin)

Lewin identifies two forces in a change situation:

- Driving forces: these are perceived as making the change happen. They include the influence of Lucas Meyer and Arif Karp, environmental regulation and pollution taxes, and the expectations of investors.

- Resisting forces: these are perceived as obstacles to change. These include lack of understanding of the implications of sustainability, control systems that emphasis financial returns over emissions, lack of training.

Appendix D: Revised emission targets

kg per square metre	2009	2010	2011	2012	2013
Original published level	1,077	1,042			
Revised level (+5%)	1,131	1,094			
Forecast levels			1,022	948	874
New target				821	697
Variance				(127)	(177)

Appendix E: Carbon reductions from investments

	2011	2012	2013
Freezer cabinets			
Number of supermarkets		400	400
Number of convenience stores		100	100
Carbon savings from supermarkets (400 × 0.11)		44	44
Carbon savings from convenience stores (100 × 0.03)		3	3
Total saving kg million		47	47
Saving kg per square metre over total sales area (W1)		33	32
Solar panels			
Number of installations during the year	100	100	
Number of stores with solar panels in year		100	200
Carbon saving per installation kg million		0.90	0.90
Total saving kg million		90	180
Saving kg per square metre over total sales area (W2)		63	124
Combined savings kg per square metre		96	156

Workings

(W1): Savings from freezers divided by total forecast area of Papy stores 2012 & 2013

   eg 2012: 47,000,000kg/1,425,400 square metres = 33kg per square metre

(W2): Savings from panels divided by total forecast area of Papy stores 2012 & 2013

   eg 2012: 90,000,000kg/1,425,400 square metres = 63kg per square metre

Appendix F: Evaluation of freezer proposal

€m		2012	2013 - 2021
Savings			
Supermarket electricity (€60K × 400)		24	24
Convenience store electricity (€18K × 100)		1.8	1.8
		25.8	25.8
Lost margin in supermarkets (€560K × 400 × (60% × 3% + 30% × 5% + 10% × 0%))		7.39	7.39
Profit impact		18.41	18.41
Post tax return (2012: + €85m × 25%, 2013 -2021 - €18.41m × 25%)		39.66	13.81
Payback €m			
Capital costs			
Supermarkets (400 × €200K)	80		
Convenience stores (100 × €50K)	5		
Amount left to payback 2011	85		
2012	45.34		
2013	31.53		
2014	17.72		
2015	3.91		

2016	(9.9)
NPV	
PV of post tax return	
13.81 x (6.418 – 0.917)	75.97
39.66 x 0.917	36.37
	112.34
less capex	85.00
NPV	*27.34*

Answer to Question 1b

Presentation to Papy Board

Carbon Emissions 2012-2013

- Table shows new emission targets for 2012 and 2013 to be 821kg mill per m^2 and 697kg mill per m^2

- These will require that we reduce emissions per m^2 below forecast by a further 127kg mill in 2012 and 177kg mill in 2013

- Investment in solar panels and freezers will reduce emissions by 96kg mill per m^2 in 2102 and 156kg mill per m^2 in 2013. Leaving a shortfall against target of 31kg mill in 2012 and 21kg mill in 2013 to be made up by other initiatives

- Reducing our emissions in 2013 to 32% lower than our 2011 emissions is very ambitious and will require more than just the two investments in solar panels and freezers to accomplish.

- It is recommended that both investments are undertaken and that, in addition, further carbon-reducing projects be identified.

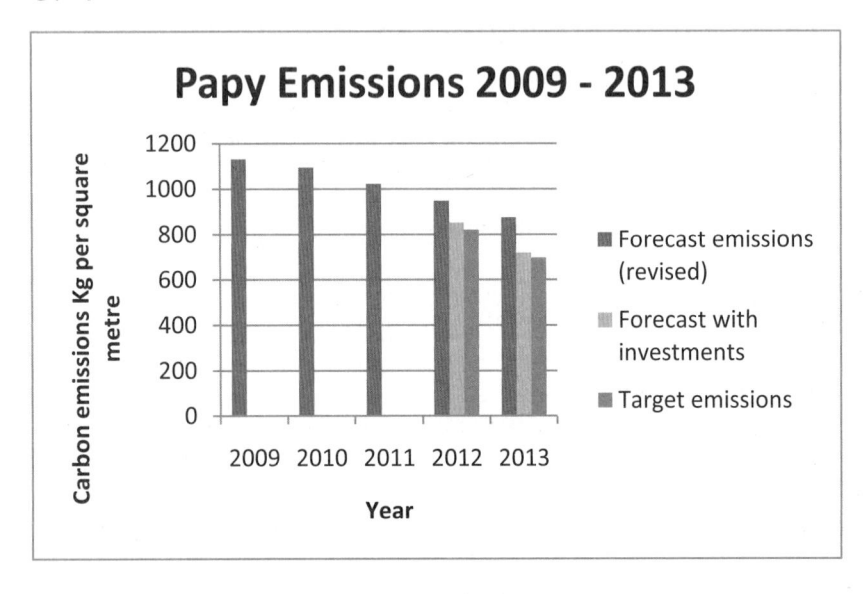

Marking Grid for September 2011 Real Exam

Criteria	Issues to be discussed	Marks	Total marks available for criterion
Technical	SWOT/PEST/Ansoff/Porter's 5 forces/Porter's generic strategies/Mendelow/Suitability, Acceptability, Feasibility/ BCG/Balanced Scorecard/Life cycle analysis/Marketing knowledge, motivation theory 1 mark for EACH technique demonstrated.	1 each max 5	Max = 5
Application	SWOT – to get full 3 marks the script must include all the Top 4 issues	1–3	Max = 15
	Other Technical Knowledge applied to case material in a meaningful relevant way – on merit	1–2 Max 5 for application of theory	
	Calculations: Revised emission forecasts and targets and calculation of variances pre and post investments	Up to 4 marks	
	Evaluation of emissions impact of investment projects on emissions per m^2	Up to 5 marks	
	Payback evaluation of freezer investment	Up to 5 marks	
	Other calculations on merit	Up to 4 marks	
	Total calculation marks available 18	Max 10 for calculations	
Diversity	Display of sound business awareness and relevant real life examples related to case	1–2 marks each example used on merit	Max = 5
Focus	**Major issues to be discussed:**		Max = 5
	New carbon emission targets	1	
	Change management	1	
	Solar panels	1	
	Freezer cabinets	1	
	Measurement of waste	1	
	Cancellation of supplier contracts		
	Total marks available	5	

Criteria	Issues to be discussed	Marks	Total marks available for criterion
Prioritisation	5 marks if 4 issues are prioritised in the correct order with sequence of top two interchangeable. Deduct 1 mark for each issue placed lower than place in correct ranking.	5	Max = 5
Judgement	4 key and 2 minor issues available for detailed commercial analysis in this case:		
	Marks on merit based on depth of analysis and commercially realistic comments		
	New carbon emission targets: recognition that they are ambitious given past performance, remaining gap after investments, consideration of having lower targets, proposals for improvement.	Up to 6 marks	
	Change management: crucial to hitting targets, needed to support new CEO, potential conceptualisation of reasons for resistance and remedies, dangers of ineffective change management	Up to 6 marks	Max = 20
	Solar panels: SAF assessment in light of new targets, problems with use of 9% cost of capital, discussion of 2017 technology (delay, length of appraisal horizon should be reduced).	Up to 5 marks	
	Freezer cabinets: SAF assessment in light of new targets, problems with use of payback, data based on supermarkets not convenience stores	Up to 5 marks	
	Measurement of waste: not key target, arguments for and against based on environmental impact of volume against quantity	Up to 2 marks	
	Cancellation of contracts: need to reduce waste as a target, potential reputation risk of cancelling contract, ways of reducing waste to restore profits,	Up to 2 marks	
	Total marks available (but max = 20)	26	
Integration	Judge script holistically and whether recommendations follow on logically from analysis of the issues and refers to data in appendices. How well written is the report: professional language?	1–2 if weak 3–5 if script is good	Max = 5

Criteria	Issues to be discussed	Marks	Total marks available for criterion
Logic	**Recommendations:**		
	(Marks on merit. Max 1 mark if only an unjustified recommendation is given)		
	New carbon emission targets: maintain targets/minor revision recommended. Role of investments and culture change in hitting them, regular reporting and communication of targets via balanced scorecard, briefings	Up to 6 marks	
	Change management: prioritise action, employment of change strategies (eg change agent, education and communication) set timescales, incentivisation, involvement of stakeholders	Up to 6 marks	
	Solar panels: recommend accept, identify suppliers, choose initial sites, post-investment audit	Up to 4 marks	Max = 30 Q1 – 20 Q2 – 10
	Freezer cabinets: recommend accept, more info on convenience stores, identify suppliers, communicate with customers to reduce lost sales	Up to 4 marks	
	Measurement of waste: recommend remain with weight pending independent advice, publicise reasons for any change to stakeholders, rebase bonus of Karp's bonus against new measure	Up to 2 marks	
	Cancellation of supplier contracts: review of product profitability to reduce waste and costs, decide following that.	Up to 2 marks	
	Total marks available (but max = 20)	24	
QUESTION 1(b)	3 marks for correct graph based on data derived		
	1 mark per bullet point to maximum of 5	10	
	2 marks for clear recommendation on both proposals		
	Total marks available	10	
Ethics	Cancellation of supplier contract	Up to 5 for identification and discussion of issues	
	See If advocacy by Arif Karp to change waste measures which will affect bonus		Max = 10
		Up to 5 for recommendations on how to address those issues	
Total			100

Jot toys: pre-seen data

This chapter includes the 'pre-seen' data for Jot toy manufactuer, examined in March 2012.

Howver, please note the **paragraph numbering has been added by BPP** for ease of reference. The 'real' pre-seen material you get from CIMA will not have the paragraphs numbered.

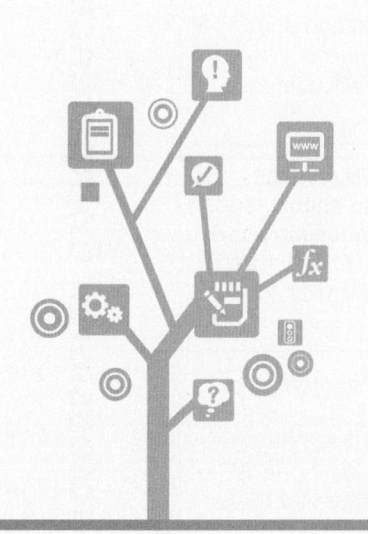

CIMA

T4 – Part B Case Study Examination

For examinations on Tuesday 28 February 2012 and on Thursday 24 May 2012

PRE-SEEN MATERIAL, PROVIDED IN ADVANCE FOR PREPARATION AND STUDY FOR THE EXAMINATIONS IN FEBRUARY AND MAY 2012.

INSTRUCTIONS FOR POTENTIAL CANDIDATES

This booklet contains the pre-seen case material for the above examinations. It will provide you with the contextual information that will help you prepare yourself for the examinations.

The Case Study Assessment Criteria, which your script will be marked against, is included on page 16.

You may not take this copy of the pre-seen material into the examination hall. A fresh copy will be provided on the examination day.

Unseen material will be provided on the examination day; this will comprise further context and the examination question.

The examination will last for three hours. You will be allowed 20 minutes reading time **before the examination begins** during which you should read the question paper and, if you wish, make annotations on the question paper. However, you will **not** be allowed, **under any circumstances**, to either begin writing or using your computer to produce your answer or to use your calculator during the reading time.

You will be required to answer ONE question which may contain more than one element.

PC examination only: Your computer will contain two blank files – one Word and an Excel file. Please ensure that you check that the file names for these two documents correspond with your candidate number.

Contents of this booklet:	Page
Pre-seen material – Jot – toy Case	2
Pre-Seen Appendices 1 - 6	11
Assessment Criteria	16

© The Chartered Institute of Management Accountants 2012

Jot – toy case

Industry background

1. There is a large number of companies of various sizes which design and sell toys to retailers globally. Most toy companies outsource the manufacture of their toys and currently 86% of the world's toys are manufactured in China. Most of the rest of the world's toys are manufactured in other Asian countries, with only low volumes of products manufactured in Europe and the USA.

2. The toy market is divided up into a variety of sectors, by children's age range and the type of toy. There are different sectors with toys aimed for babies under one year old, children aged 1 to 3 years and pre-school children of 3 to 5 years. There is a further sector for children of school age of 5 years and upwards. Additionally the toy market is broken down into categories of toys. Research has shown that children aged 2 to 4 years old receive the most toys in quantity but that the most money is spent on toys for the 6 to 8 year age group.

3. The current trend in toy sales is towards electronic toys and computer assisted learning. Many of these electronic toys are highly developed to be attractive to children. Sales of traditional toys and games have achieved relatively low growth in the European market over the last 10 years, whereas electronic toys and merchandise from popular films and TV programmes have seen reasonable growth. Merchandise from films and TV programmes are licensed to toy manufacturers or toy retailers which can achieve high short-term profits depending on the licensing arrangement and the volume of sales. However, fashion trends are difficult to predict and toy retailers can be left with large volumes of unsold inventories if the toys are unpopular or less in demand than originally anticipated.

4. The toy market is highly seasonal and is dominated by the pre-Christmas sales period. Typically, around 30% to 55% of toy sales occur in the fourth quarter of the calendar year (October to December).

5. China has established itself as a high quality, low-cost manufacturing base for a wide range of consumer products for global markets. It does not, as yet, principally design and create new products, but instead is capable of manufacturing products that have been created by Western companies. It is necessary for the companies which create the designs, whether the product is a toy, a range of clothing or a computer chip, to ensure that the design is protected by registering the design for intellectual property rights (IPR's). However, in many instances small changes can be made so that "copies" of the design do not breach the IPR. Legal protection of IPR's is becoming increasingly important in today's global markets, where resources are sourced in one area of the world, manufactured into finished products in another area (principally in China and other Asian countries) and then sold in other geographical markets.

6. Most toy retailers procure a range of products from many different toy companies. There is a wide range of companies, from small to very large multi-national companies, which operate as toy design and distributing companies. These companies design, patent or license the toys and then outsource the manufacture to specialist toy manufacturers. The toy companies then sell their products to toy retailers.

7. There are several global toy fairs each year which attract buyers from toy retailers across the world. One of the largest toy fairs is held in Hong Kong in January each year, where new toys are launched for the following Christmas market. Other global toy fairs are held in Europe, Russia and the USA, also early in the calendar year. At these toy fairs, buyers will assess and choose which of the new toys may achieve high sales. The toy fairs attract a wide range of exhibitors which are launching new toys, both large listed companies and small companies.

8. The level of sales achieved by many toy companies will often depend on orders generated from buyers attending these international toy fairs. Therefore, it is important that prototype toys and marketing literature is ready in order to meet the requirements of these global buyers at the start of each calendar year.

Jot

9   The Jot brand was established in 1998 by husband and wife team Jon and Tani Grun. The company initially designed a small range of toys which were manufactured in their home European country. These toys proved to be very popular in their home country and Jon Grun then expanded the range of products.

10 By 2003, within five years of starting Jot, the founders were encouraged to see Jot's products ordered by many large toy retailers across Europe. By this stage the company had grown considerably, and had annual sales of almost €2 million. Commencing in 2004, Jot started outsourcing all of its manufacturing to a range of manufacturing companies in China in order to reduce its cost base and to enable the company to price its products more competitively.

11 By the end of 2010 sales revenue exceeded €8 million and the company had achieved substantial sales revenue growth each year. Jot has seen its sales revenue grow by 16% in the year ended 31 December 2010 and by almost 18% in the year to 31 December 2011 (unaudited figures).

12 A summary of Jot's key personnel is shown in **Appendix 1** on page 11.

Jot's product range

13 Jot currently has a relatively small range of 34 products aimed at only 2 age groups. These are the pre-school age group of 3 to 5 year olds and the next age group of 5 to 8 year olds. It currently does not produce any toys aimed at babies aged less than one, toddlers aged less than 3 years old or children aged over 8 years old.

14 Jot's products include a range of toys designed by the company, for which it holds the IPR's, as well as some licensed toys, for which it pays a license fee to the companies which hold the IPR's. Jot's products mainly include electronic features and this is seen as one of the strengths of its products.

15 Jot currently launches around 5 totally new products each year. It also enhances certain aspects of some of its other products to refresh their appearance and features. It also has a range of toys that sell consistently well and have not changed materially for a few years.

16 Jot's products for the 3 to 5 year old age group include:
- Construction toys with sound effects and electronic actions.
- Learning products such as mini-computers which ask questions and the child responds by pressing different keys.
- Toy vehicles some of which have electronic features such as sounds and lights.
- Plastic toys which have "animatronics" to make the toys move, for example, toy dinosaurs.
- Toy cameras.
- Electronic learning products to aid learning the alphabet and basic maths skills.
- Licensed soft play toys based on film and TV programme characters.
- Licensed plastic figures, cars and machines based on film and TV programme characters, some of which include electronic features that generate movements and sounds, including theme tunes.

17 Jot's products for the 5 to 8 year old age group include:
- Toy cameras and video cameras.
- Dolls and action figures, some of which move and make sounds.
- Small hand-held games boxes for playing computer games and educational learning products to improve maths and readings skills.
- A range of games and educational learning products for the hand-held games boxes.

18 Jot's products are sold to toy retailers for between €7 and €38. These are Jot's selling prices to toy retailers. Most of the retailers will then sell these toys at a large mark-up, which can be as much as 50% to 100%, i.e. a toy procured from Jot at €10 could be retailed to the end customer at €20.

19 In the year ended 31 December 2011 Jot's actual sales volumes (unaudited) were over 706,000 units across Jot's entire range of products. The total sales revenue for the year ended 31 December 2011 (unaudited) was €9,866,000, which resulted in an average selling price of just under €14 per unit. Over 80% of Jot's product sales are sold to retailers for €20 or less.

Financials and shares

20 Jot has achieved a high annual growth in sales, with sales revenue reaching €9,866,000 in the year ended 31 December 2011 (unaudited), a growth of 17.9% from 2010 (€8,371,000 sales revenue for year ended 31 December 2010). Additionally, it has achieved an operating profit margin of 5.58% in the year to 31 December 2011, a rise from the previous year's profit margin of 5.41%.

21 An extract from Jot's accounts (unaudited) for the year ended 31 December 2011 is shown in **Appendix 2** on page 12.

22 Jot's Statement of Cash Flows for the year ended 31 December 2011 (unaudited) is shown in **Appendix 3** on page 13.

23 Jot is a young, growing company which is dependent on loan finance. Jot has three bank loans totalling €1,600,000, each at an interest rate of 10% per year, which are due for repayment as follows:
- Bank loan of €500,000 due in January 2014.
- Bank loan of €500,000 due in January 2015.
- Bank loan of €600,000 due in January 2020.

24 Jot's bank has been very responsive to the company's needs for cash in order to fund its growth but has indicated that at the present time it would not be able to provide any additional long-term finance.

25 Jot has an overdraft facility of €1,500,000, which the bank has stated is the maximum limit. The current cost of its overdraft is at an interest rate of 12% per year. At 31 December 2011, Jot's overdraft was €960,000.

26 Jot's business is highly seasonal with a significant proportion of sales occurring in quarters 3 and 4. As Jot builds up its inventory in preparation for higher levels of sales in quarters 3 and 4, cash flow is negative during the second half of the year. This is because outsourced manufacturing for the majority of all products occurs mainly from the end of quarter 2, during all of quarter 3 and the beginning of quarter 4.

27 Jot is a private limited company and not listed on any stock exchange. It has 40,000 shares in issue, each of €1 par value. The company has an authorised share capital of 200,000 shares. To date, the Board of Jot has not declared any dividends. The shares are held as follows:

	Number of shares held at 31 December 2011	Percentage shareholding %
Jon Grun	12,000	30
Tani Grun	12,000	30
Alana Lotz	8,000	20
Boris Hepp	4,000	10
Michael Werner	4,000	10
Total	40,000	100

Production of toys

28   Jot has its own in-house team of designers who are involved in designing toys that are unique, innovative and fun to play with. The production of new toys is split into two stages. Firstly, the design stage involves the design team developing a new toy and after it has been approved, the second stage is where the operations team is responsible for contracting an outsourced manufacturer for the mass production of each product.

29   The head of Jot's design team is Alana Lotz, Product Development Director. She is responsible for researching the market trends in toys globally and establishing the availability of new innovative technology which could be incorporated into new toy designs. This is what helps to make Jot's product range innovative and at the "cutting edge" of new technology, as the products incorporate new technology electronic chip components.

30   Research and development work on new product development usually occurs between May and December each year so that the new products have been fully tested ready for the annual launch of Jot's new range of toys each January. Jot currently launches 5 totally new products each year and the development costs are generally between €0.1 and €0.25 million for each new product. The total design and development costs are around €1.2 million each year. This is included in administration expenses in Jot's statement of comprehensive income.

31   Jot has just finalised its range of new products for 2012, so as to allow time to produce marketing literature and prepare prototypes ready for the global toy fairs being held in January to March 2012 in various locations around the world.

32   The design team develops all new products through the following stages:

- Brainstorming for new ideas.
- Designing a new product using Jot's CAD / CAM IT system.
- Production of first prototype.
- Market research and improvements through to production of second prototype.
- Sign off by design and management team.
- Application for intellectual property rights (IPR's) for each product design.

33   Jot uses a specialised company, based in Europe for the manufacture and testing of all prototype products and there are often two or three stages involved before the prototype product is produced to the satisfaction of the designers. Only when each product is signed off by the design and management team can Jot's legal team apply for the IPR's for the product design. Then the approved new product designs go into production by outsourced manufacturers.

34   The designs are then electronically transferred to Jot's operations team headed up by Michael Werner, Operations Director, for the selection and appointment of outsourced manufacturers. The stages in the production process are as follows:

- Designs are sent electronically to outsourced manufacturers for tender.
- Outsourced manufacturer(s) selected and appointed and volumes and delivery deadlines for production agreed.
- Packaging designs and artwork are prepared and approved.
- Production samples are reviewed by Jot's in-house Quality Assurance team located both in Europe and in Asia.
- Production is commenced to meet agreed volume and delivery deadlines.

35   Michael Werner is responsible for the selection, appointment and monitoring of Jot's outsourced manufacturers and all aspects of the management of the outsourced manufacturing process for Jot's products. Jot's products are all manufactured by a small number of specialised outsourced manufacturing companies which are all based in China. Jot is responsible for shipments of all products from its outsourced manufacturers to its warehouses or sometimes directly to customers.

Outsourced manufacturers

36 Currently Jot uses 20 off-shore outsourced manufacturing companies. Off-shore outsourced manufacturing is defined as shifting work to foreign, distant companies in order to reduce production costs. Some of the outsourced manufacturers are small companies each of which manufactures just one of Jot's products. Some of the larger outsourced manufacturing companies make several of Jot's products. All of these outsourced manufacturing companies do not work exclusively for Jot but manufacture toys, as well as other products, for a number of international companies. All of Jot's outsourced manufacturers are based in China.

37 When a product design has been approved and the IPR applied for, Michael Werner will send the product design with an indication of the number of products to be manufactured and the timescale for shipment, to a small range of outsourced manufacturers for them to tender for the manufacture of the product. Jot often asks the same outsourced manufacturing companies, which it has used previously, to tender for the manufacture of its new product designs each year. Therefore, there is a high level of "repeat business" and a good level of understanding and commitment established between Jot, based in Europe, and its outsourced manufacturers based in China.

38 When the tenders have been received, Michael Werner and his team review the outsourced manufacturing companies' submissions and then select the outsourced manufacturer to be appointed. Jot's designers and sales team will have already decided on an indicative selling price, so the unit price to be charged to Jot by the outsourced manufacturing company is often the determining factor when making the decision of which outsourced manufacturing company to use. Whilst other factors are considered, such as quality and ability to deliver the required volume of products to the required timescale, it is the unit price which is important in order to achieve the planned level of gross margin. Gross margin is defined as sales revenue less the outsourced manufacturing cost of units sold and excludes all other costs.

39 Jot's design team already knows the cost of making each product, based on the list of components required, so it is the cost of manufacturing that will vary between the different tenders. Generally, in most tenders, the unit prices quoted by different outsourced manufacturers are quite close to each other.

40 Most of Jot's products are manufactured using basic raw materials, such as plastic and electronic components for the toys and plastic and paper products for their packaging. The majority of Jot's products require a range of electronic components. These components are readily available from a variety of sources but are subject to price fluctuations. Each product design will specify which, and how many, of each component type is required. Some of the electronic components are specialised and contain "application-specific integrated circuits" (ASIC components) which are procured from specialist suppliers. Jot does not have any agreements with these specialised suppliers as all components, including ASIC components, are procured directly by the outsourced manufacturer appointed to manufacture each of Jot's products. Some of Jot's outsourced manufacturers, which manufacture a range of electronic products for Jot and other companies, have on-going supply contracts in place for several key components, which helps them to price their products competitively.

41 The timescales each year for the production of Jot's products is for tenders to be submitted and manufacturers appointed by the end of May. The major proportion of manufacturing occurs between June and early November each year. The last of the manufacturing occurs in early November to enable time for the products to be shipped to Jot's warehouses in Europe and the USA, or sometimes directly to Jot's customers, in time to meet the Christmas sales peak. All three of Jot's warehouses are leased.

42 Over the last 10 to 15 years many companies have outsourced their manufacturing to companies in China. However, with wage rates in China increasing, some companies have started to consider "near-shoring". Near-shoring is defined as the transfer of business processes to companies in a nearby country. Therefore, if Jot were to consider near-shoring, this would result in having some outsourced manufacturers based in Europe.

Sales

43 Jot's sales revenue for the year ended 31 December 2011 (unaudited) was €9,866,000. The geographical analysis of these sales is shown as follows:

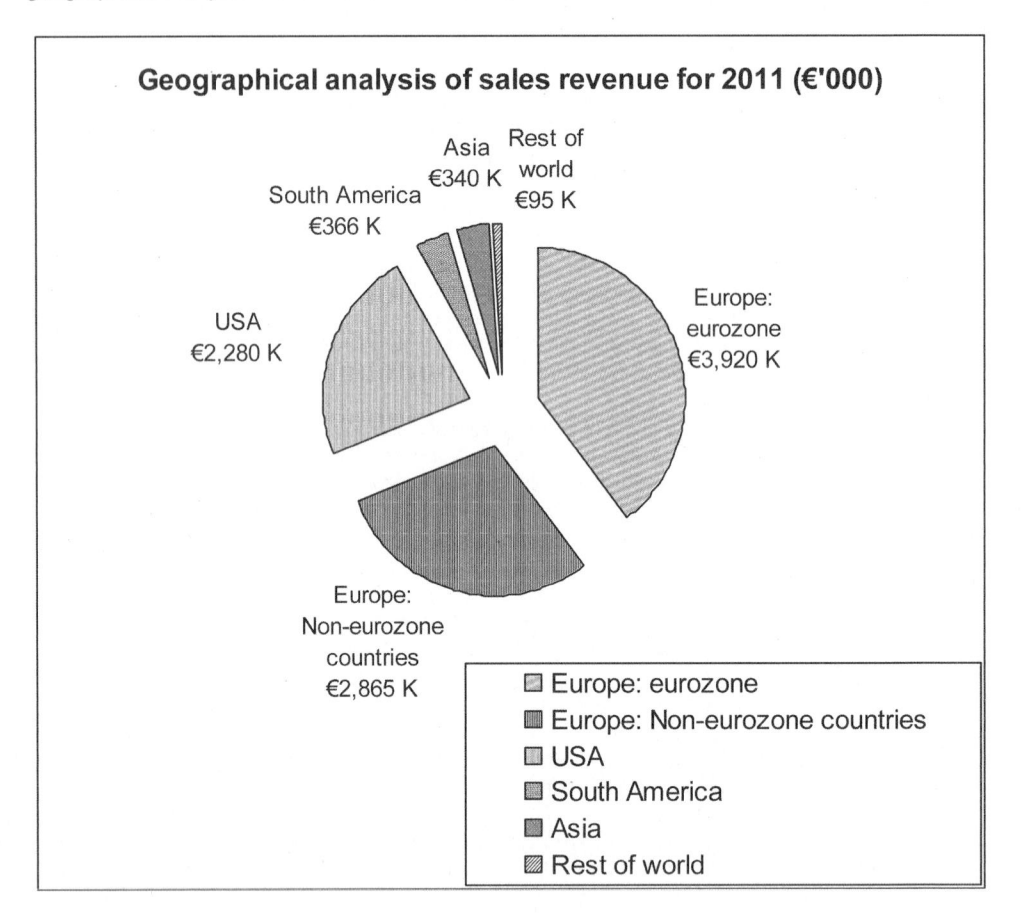

Geographical analysis of sales revenue for 2011 (€'000)

- Europe: eurozone €3,920 K
- Europe: Non-eurozone countries €2,865 K
- USA €2,280 K
- South America €366 K
- Asia €340 K
- Rest of world €95 K

44 Jot's customers are mainly:

- Retailers – these include large toy retailers as well as supermarket chains and other retailers
- Distributors – these distributors purchase Jot's products and sell them on to a wide range of smaller retailers.

45 Jot currently has three warehouses, two in Europe and one in the USA. Usually all products are shipped from each of Jot's outsourced manufacturers directly to one of Jot's three warehouses. In some instances, products are shipped directly to customers.

46 Jot's terms of sale are for payment within 30 days of invoice. Invoices are produced automatically, on a daily basis, based on information transferred to the sales ledger from the inventory control IT system. However, Jot is very dependent on sales to large retailers, which often do not pay until at least 60 days after the invoice date. Jot has little influence over these retailers and does not want to jeopardise future sales by chasing them too aggressively.

47 Sales of Jot's toys are highly seasonal as shown in the quarterly analysis of sales in **Appendix 4** on page 14.

48 In the year ended 31 December 2011, sales in quarter 3 (July to September) were 25% of annual sales and sales in quarter 4 (October to December) were 51% of annual sales.

49 Jot's sales are highly dependent on seven large retailers. These seven large companies comprise toy retailers, large international supermarket retailers, department stores and one on-line retailer. Over 68% of Jot's sales in the financial year ended 31 December 2011 were to these 7 customers based in Europe and the USA. These key customers place their main orders in May or June each year and sometimes earlier. If individual products are selling well or the retailers consider sales may be higher than they originally thought, then the retailers would place additional orders with Jot. This could happen at any time between June through to late October.

50 The remaining 32% of sales are to distributors as well as small and medium sized retailers around the world. Jot currently has around 350 customers in total, including the 7 large customers.

51 With the placement of orders from its large customers and the many smaller customers early in the year, Jot is able to place firm orders with its outsourced manufacturers with a reasonable degree of certainty of sales levels. However, there is always a balancing act between placing a large order to meet committed and expected sales and not holding enough inventory.

Licensed toys

52 Jot currently has 12 product lines which are licensed products from popular film and TV programmes for the manufacture and sale of toys. Licensed products are defined as toys which use a logo, design or character from a film or TV programme and the owner of the IPR will license each product under a strict licensing agreement, whereby a royalty is paid to the owner of the IPR for each unit manufactured. A licensed product is where the TV or film company owns the intellectual property rights (IPR's) for the characters and licenses the manufacture and sale of the products to another company in exchange for a license fee for each item produced (whether sold or not).

53 A fixed license fee is paid to the licensor in accordance with the licensing contract, and the fee is usually paid at the time Jot places an order with its outsourced manufacturer. The fee is between 5% and 10% of Jot's selling price to retailers.

54 Anna Veld, Licensing Director, joined Jot in 2009 and has negotiated all of the licensed products that Jot currently sells. She is very experienced in this field and in liaison with both Sonja Rosik and Boris Hepp, she has identified products for Jot to develop and sell. Licensed products now account for almost 10% of Jot's sales, in terms of the number of units sold.

Inventory control

55 Michael Werner is responsible for logistics and inventory control. There is always a difficult decision to be made when placing orders with outsourced manufacturers, between ordering too much inventory and not selling it and the opposite of losing sales because of lack of inventory. This is further exacerbated due to the seasonal nature of sales, which are predominantly made in quarters 3 and 4 of each calendar year.

56 At the start of each calendar year, any unsold inventory for products that Boris Hepp, Sales Director, considers to be out of date, are offered to Jot's customers at substantially reduced prices to clear them and the inventory value is written down. There are a few products which are sold on a regular basis throughout each year and their inventory value is not written down.

57 Inventory counts at the end of the financial year are reconciled with Jot's IT inventory control system and any discrepancies are written off. Jot's inventory is valued at the lower of cost or realisable market value, based on a first-in, first-out basis. Inventory value is based only on out-sourced manufacturing contracted charges, using the unit price from manufacturer's invoices, unless the realisable value is lower.

58 Inventory also includes a reserve for the write-down in value in respect of slow-moving and obsolete products. This valuation is based upon Jot's management team's review of inventories taking into account for each product the estimated future sales demand, anticipated product selling prices, expected product lifecycle and products planned for discontinuation. The valuation for inventory write down is reviewed quarterly. At 31 December 2011 the write-down reserve was €0.124 million. This is netted off against the value of the current inventory of products held in Jot's warehouses.

The Jot brand

59 The Jot brand name is synonymous with quality electronic toys. Jot's products are innovative and appealing to the targeted age groups. Sonja Rosik, Marketing Director, joined Jot three years ago when the role was separated from that of the Sales and Marketing Director, leaving Boris Hepp, Sales Director, free to concentrate on securing sales in wider geographical markets.

60 Marketing has become increasingly important in the promotion of new products. No longer can a company rely on a good product being identified by the key buyers for large retailers. It is of vital importance to market new products before, during and after the global toy fairs, which are held in several locations in the January to March period of each year. The toy fairs can often "make or break" the success of each new product and the need to gain a positive reaction from buyers, based on sample products, is very important.

61 The launch plans for new products and the marketing support Jot's customers receive can have an impact on the reaction of buyers at the global toy fairs. A significant volume of sales orders arise directly from these toy fairs and Sonja Rosik's team has made a very strong contribution to achieving positive press reports for new products and providing buyers with good quality and clear marketing literature. Boris Hepp is very pleased with Sonja Rosik and her team, which helps his sales team to secure firm sales orders for Jot's products.

62 Additionally, Sonja Rosik, has been working on the establishment of links and promotion of the Jot brand in new geographical markets as well as further market penetration in Europe and the competitive USA market.

IT systems

63 Tani Grun appointed an external IT consultancy company some years ago to provide the IT systems required for Jot's growing business. However, some of the systems are not ideal and do not provide Jot's management team with all of the data that it requires. There is also some replication of data between different IT systems.

64 The Finance Department operates a multi-currency nominal ledger and integrated sales and purchase ledgers. However, these IT systems do not accept data directly from any of Jot's other IT systems. The Finance Department also operates a fixed assets register.

65 Jot outsources the logistics of its products, both the movement of manufactured products and the sales to customers, to a global logistics company. This company operates a fast efficient service and with the increase in sales volumes over the last few years, a reduction on the unit costs has recently been negotiated. The outsourced logistics company provides Jot with access to all tracking and logistics data for products moving into Jot's three warehouses and prepares reports on products which have been shipped directly to customers.

66 The data concerning goods delivered to Jot's three warehouses is transferred electronically to Jot's inventory control system. This database system generates despatch notes for all orders that are fulfilled from each warehouse. The majority of customer deliveries are fulfilled from Jot's warehouses and not directly from the manufacturer. The despatch note data is transferred electronically to the Finance Department in order to raise invoices to customers for goods despatched. Information on customer orders which are delivered directly from the manufacturer is transferred by the outsourced logistics company to the Finance Department, in order to raise invoices.

67 All product designs and product drawings, which include a detailed listing of all parts and components, are prepared using a standard CAD / CAM IT system. This allows direct interface with Jot's outsourced manufacturers. This ensures that each new product design can be transferred to the appointed outsourced manufacturer's IT systems when the product is ready for manufacture, thereby eliminating any delays and confusion over the exact product specification and design.

Target markets for growth

68 Jot would like to expand its sales by specifically targeting other areas of the world, including the Russian and the Asian markets. These two specific markets have a growing demand for the types of product that Jot sells. Sonja Rosik has visited several countries in Jot's target markets and met with retailers and distributors of children's toys. She has been working with Michael Werner to establish distribution links for these markets and to arrange delivery of products direct to customers based in Asia, rather than have its products shipped to Jot's European warehouses for onward shipping back to Asia.

69 When Jot first entered the USA market in 2006, it was caught unawares by the higher than expected volume of demand and spent almost a year trying to meet the growth in demand for the products ordered. Jot has since discovered that it is necessary to manufacture larger numbers of each product, in order to ensure that its products are available if demand exceeds its expected supply levels, before launching into new geographical markets.

70 Extracts from Jot's 5-year plan is shown in **Appendix 5** on page 15.

71 The 5-year plan shows growth in sales revenue at 17% for 2012 and around 13% to 14% for the remaining 4 years of the plan period as well as a small growth in operating profit margins.

Corporate social responsibilities and product safety

72 Jot's management team is aware of the importance of its corporate social responsibilities (CSR) but so far it has not officially published what it does or how it will improve its CSR plans. This is an area which Michael Werner and Alana Lotz plan to develop in the next year, so that Jot can publish its CSR achievements and targets.

73 However, Jon Grun has always impressed on all of Jot's employees and managers the importance of its products exceeding, rather than simply conforming to, the required safety standards.

74 European Union (EU) law requires that all toys which are to be sold in any EU country must carry the "CE" marking. The "CE" marking confirms that "Certification Experts" have carried out all applicable testing to identify hazards and assess risks, in order to determine that the products meet the required product safety regulations of the EU. The "CE" marking may be on the toys themselves or on their packaging. In the EU a toy is defined as "any product or material designed or clearly intended for use in play by children of less than 14 years of age".

75 These EU safety regulations apply to all companies based in the EU which supply toys anywhere in the EU, and apply to all companies, whether they are manufacturers, importers, wholesalers, retailers or hirers. It is the responsibility of the toy company and the manufacturer to ensure that the product meets the safety regulations and that the "CE" marking is fixed on the product. Jot cannot delegate this responsibility.

Appendix 1
Jot's key personnel

Jon Grun – Managing Director

76 Jon Grun, aged 48, is an engineer and has worked in a variety of large companies designing electrical products. He always wanted to establish his own company and was inspired to start the Jot toy company in 1998 when his children were young, as he felt there was a gap in the market for innovative, educational toys. Jon Grun owns 30% of the shares in issue.

Tani Grun – Finance and IT Director

77 Tani Grun, aged 44, is married to Jon Grun. She is a CIMA accountant and worked for some large companies in senior roles before taking on the Finance Director role for Jot when it was formed in 1998. Initially she worked part-time, but as the company has grown, she is finding the role more challenging. She is considering recruiting a new person to take responsibility for IT for Jot as she considers that outside experience is necessary to move the company forward. Currently, many of Jot's IT solutions are out-sourced. Tani Grun owns 30% of the shares in issue.

Alana Lotz – Product Development Director

78 Alana Lotz, aged 44, has been Tani Grun's friend for many years and trained as a design engineer and then worked for a global toy manufacturer for 12 years. Tani Grun recruited her when Jot was established in 1998 and she has been a leading force in the expansion of the range of new toys and in the recruitment and retention of Jot's design team. She holds 20% of the shares in issue.

Sonja Rosik, Marketing Director

79 Sonja Rosik, aged 35, was recruited in 2009 when the role of Marketing Director was separated from the previous role of Sales and Marketing Director. She has brought a wealth of new ideas and dynamism to Jot's marketing and has helped to expand Jot's products to new geographical markets. She does not own any shares.

Boris Hepp – Sales Director

80 Boris Hepp, aged 42, joined Jot in 2003 when sales in Europe were starting to grow rapidly. He held the joint role of Sales and Marketing Director until 2009, when the Board decided that he would be best employed in concentrating on capturing sales in new markets. Boris Hepp had known Jon Grun for many years before he joined Jot and was very impressed at how quickly the company had grown. Boris Hepp holds 10% of the shares in issue which he purchased when he joined Jot in 2003.

Michael Werner – Operations Director

81 Michael Werner, aged 50, is responsible for all operations, including management of outsourced manufacturing, logistics and inventory control. All stages from the handover of each product design through to delivery to Jot's customers are under Michael Werner's control. He joined Jot in 2008 from a large European based electrical company. He enjoys meeting the challenges faced by Jot's growth and also the freedom to manage operations without the large corporate culture that he found frustrating. He holds 10% of the shares in issue which he purchased when he joined Jot in 2008.

Anna Veld - Licensing Director

82 Anna Veld, aged 37, has extensive knowledge of licensing agreements from her previous roles working for a global film company which licensed its merchandising products and she has also worked for a large toy manufacturer. She has been instrumental in increasing the number of licensed products that Jot sells. She does not own any shares.

Viktor Mayer - HR manager

83 Viktor Mayer, aged 55, joined Jot in 2011 on a part-time basis to help with HR matters, which Jon Grun used to manage with the help of an outsourced HR agency.

Appendix 2

Extract from Jot's Statement of Comprehensive Income, Statement of Financial Position and Statement of Changes in Equity

Statement of Comprehensive Income	Year ended 31 December 2011 (Unaudited) €'000	Year ended 31 December 2010 €'000
Revenue	9,866	8,371
Cost of sales	6,719	5,615
Gross profit	3,147	2,756
Distribution costs	552	478
Administrative expenses	2,044	1,825
Operating profit	551	453
Finance income	13	12
Finance expense	213	201
Profit before tax	351	264
Tax expense (effective tax rate is 30%)	105	79
Profit for the period	246	185

Statement of Financial Position	As at 31 December 2011 (Unaudited) €'000	€'000	As at 31 December 2010 €'000	€'000
Non-current assets (net)		750		721
Current assets				
Inventory	542		470	
Trade receivables	4,065		3,173	
Cash and cash equivalents	21		29	
Total current assets		4,628		3,672
Total assets		5,378		4,393
Equity and liabilities				
Equity				
Issued share capital	40		40	
Share premium	90		90	
Retained earnings	802		556	
Total Equity		932		686
Non-current liabilities				
Long term loans		1,600		1,600
Current liabilities				
Bank overdraft	960		790	
Trade payables	1,781		1,238	
Tax payables	105		79	
Total current liabilities		2,846		2,107
Total equity and liabilities		5,378		4,393

Note: Paid in share capital represents 40,000 shares of €1.00 each at 31 December 2011

Statement of Changes in Equity For the year ended 31 December 2011 (Unaudited)	Share capital €'000	Share premium €'000	Retained earnings €'000	Total €'000
Balance at 31 December 2010	40	90	556	686
Profit	-	-	246	246
Dividends paid	-	-	-	-
Balance at 31 December 2011	40	90	802	932

Appendix 3

Statement of Cash Flows

	Year ended 31 December 2011 (Unaudited)	
	€'000	€'000
Cash flows from operating activities:		
Profit before taxation (after Finance costs (net))		351
Adjustments:		
Depreciation	240	
Finance costs (net)	200	
		440
(Increase) / decrease in inventories	(72)	
(Increase) / decrease in trade receivables	(892)	
Increase / (decrease) in trade payables (excluding taxation)	543	
		(421)
Finance costs (net) paid	(200)	
Tax paid	(79)	
		(279)
Cash generated from operating activities		91
Cash flows from investing activities:		
Purchase of non-current assets (net)	(269)	
Cash used in investing activities		(269)
Cash flows from financing activities:		
Increase in bank overdraft	170	
Dividends paid	0	
Cash flows from financing activities		170
Net (decrease) in cash and cash equivalents		(8)
Cash and cash equivalents at 31 December 2010		29
Cash and cash equivalents at 31 December 2011		21

Appendix 4

Quarterly analysis of sales for 2009 to 2011

		Qtr 1 Jan - Mar	Qtr 2 Apr - June	Qtr 3 Jul – Sept	Qtr 4 Oct - Dec	Total
2011 Actual (unaudited)	Sales €'000 %	988 10%	1,380 14%	2,490 25%	5,008 51%	9,866 100%
2010 Actual	Sales €'000 %	730 9%	1,250 15%	2,360 28%	4,031 48%	8,371 100%
2009 Actual	Sales €'000 %	548 8%	1,010 14%	2,025 28%	3,622 50%	7,205 100%

Appendix 5

Extracts from Jot's 5 year plan

	Actual (Unaudited) 2011	Plan 2012	Plan 2013	Plan 2014	Plan 2015	Plan 2016
Revenue €'000	9,866	11,568	13,124	14,791	16,840	19,260
Gross margin	31.9%	32.3%	32.6%	32.9%	33.2%	33.6%
Operating profit €'000	551	694	820	961	1,137	1,348
Operating profit	5.6%	6.0%	6.2%	6.5%	6.8%	7.0%
Number of unit sales '000	706.3	868.5	977.5	1,102.0	1,240.0	1,405.0
Number of countries products to be sold in	22	23	25	28	32	36
Number of new products to be launched each year	5	6	7	8	9	10

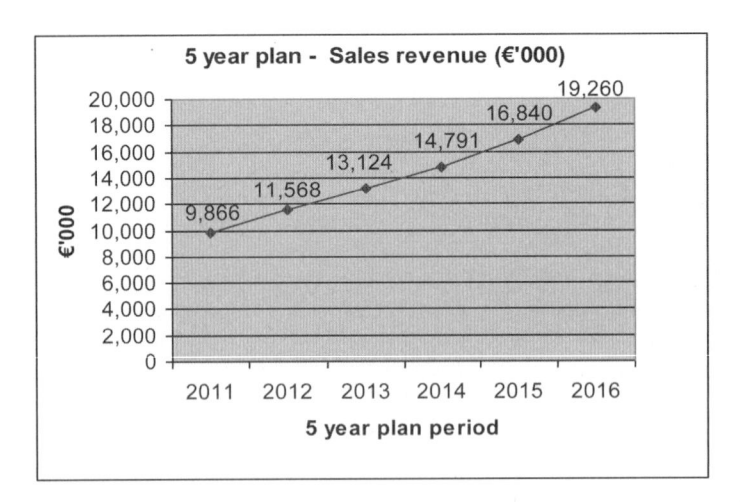

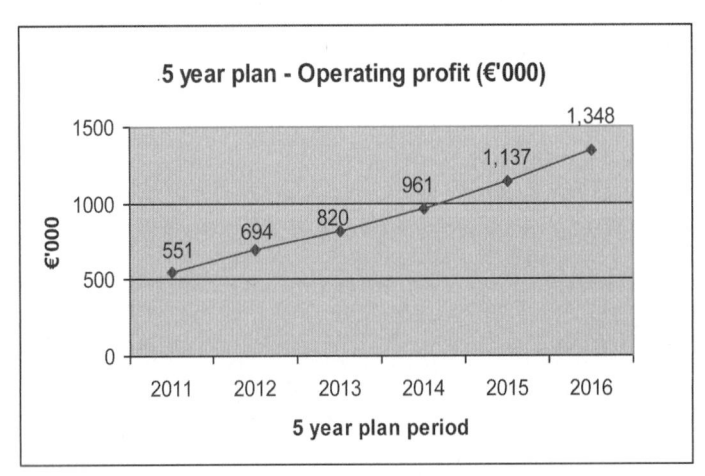

5 year plan - Sales revenue (€'000)

- 2011: 9,866
- 2012: 11,568
- 2013: 13,124
- 2014: 14,791
- 2015: 16,840
- 2016: 19,260

5 year plan - Operating profit (€'000)

- 2011: 551
- 2012: 694
- 2013: 820
- 2014: 961
- 2015: 1,137
- 2016: 1,348

End of Pre-seen material

Jot toys: some help from BPP

As we have highlighted in the previous practice cases, make sure you work methodically through the detail of the pre-seen, analysing the information you are given.

However, once again, remember that as you work through the case you should also be preparing some more general strategic analysis of 'Jot toys' as you analyse the pre-seen material: in particular, SWOT analysis, stakeholder analysis, and portfolio analysis.

And don't forget that once you have worked through the pre-seen material you should then synthesise what you know. Remember, you should ultimately be aiming to summarise the findings of your analysis of the pre-seen material into a one-page business summary.

Finally, remember that the BPP Learning Media toolkit for your paper will provide you with detailed activities which help you analyse the pre-seen material specifically related to your exam.

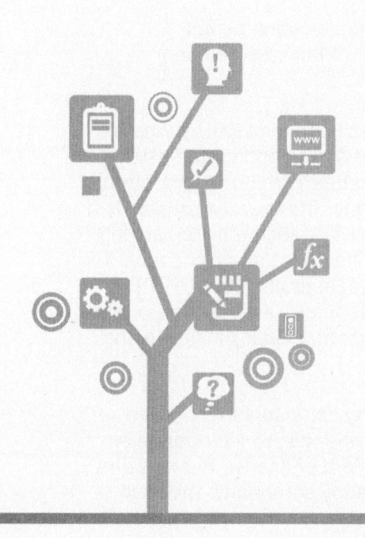

topic list

1 Reading the case in detail

2 Analysis from BPP Learning Media

1 Reading the case in detail

Jot – toy case

Industry background

1. There is a large number of companies of various sizes which design and sell toys to retailers globally. Most toy companies outsource the manufacture of their toys and currently 86% of the world's toys are manufactured in China. Most of the rest of the world's toys are manufactured in other Asian countries, with only low volumes of products manufactured in Europe and the USA.

2. The toy market is divided up into a variety of sectors, by children's age range and the type of toy. There are different sectors with toys aimed for babies under one year old, children aged 1 to 3 years and pre-school children of 3 to 5 years. There is a further sector for children of school age of 5 years and upwards. Additionally the toy market is broken down into categories of toys. Research has shown that children aged 2 to 4 years old receive the most toys in quantity but that the most money is spent on toys for the 6 to 8 year age group.

3. The current trend in toy sales is towards electronic toys and computer assisted learning. Many of these electronic toys are highly developed to be attractive to children. Sales of traditional toys and games have achieved relatively low growth in the European market over the last 10 years, whereas electronic toys and merchandise from popular films and TV programmes have seen reasonable growth. Merchandise from films and TV programmes are licensed to toy manufacturers or toy retailers which can achieve high short-term profits depending on the licensing arrangement and the volume of sales. However, fashion trends are difficult to predict and toy retailers can be left with large volumes of unsold inventories if the toys are unpopular or less in demand than originally anticipated.

4. The toy market is highly seasonal and is dominated by the pre-Christmas sales period. Typically, around 30% to 55% of toy sales occur in the fourth quarter of the calendar year (October to December).

5. China has established itself as a high quality, low-cost manufacturing base for a wide range of consumer products for global markets. It does not, as yet, principally design and create new products, but instead is capable of manufacturing products that have been created by Western companies. It is necessary for the companies which create the designs, whether the product is a toy, a range of clothing or a computer chip, to ensure that the design is protected by registering the design for intellectual property rights (IPR's). However, in many instances small changes can be made so that "copies" of the design do not breach the IPR. Legal protection of IPR's is becoming increasingly important in today's global markets, where resources are sourced in one area of the world, manufactured into finished products in another area (principally in China and other Asian countries) and then sold in other geographical markets.

6. Most toy retailers procure a range of products from many different toy companies. There is a wide range of companies, from small to very large multi-national companies, which operate as toy design and distributing companies. These companies design, patent or license the toys and then outsource the manufacture to specialist toy manufacturers. The toy companies then sell their products to toy retailers.

7. There are several global toy fairs each year which attract buyers from toy retailers across the world. One of the largest toy fairs is held in Hong Kong in January each year, where new toys are launched for the following Christmas market. Other global toy fairs are held in Europe, Russia and the USA, also early in the calendar year. At these toy fairs, buyers will assess and choose which of the new toys may achieve high sales. The toy fairs attract a wide range of exhibitors which are launching new toys, both large listed companies and small companies.

8. The level of sales achieved by many toy companies will often depend on orders generated from buyers attending these international toy fairs. Therefore, it is important that prototype toys and marketing literature is ready in order to meet the requirements of these global buyers at the start of each calendar year.

Page 2 of the Pre-seen

Paras	
1-2	Why has the examiner given this general information on the global toy industry? How will it be useful in the exam?
	Which of the market segments is the most valuable?
3	What are the implications of this paragraph for the marketing strategy of Jot?
4	What are implications of this seasonality for Jot?
5	What might the examiner be expecting you to conclude about a toy firm depending on China for production of its toys?
6-8	What do these paragraphs convey about the way that toy firms add value?
	Does the fact that Jot is a small firm have any significance to its prospects for commercial success?
	What factors are critical to the commercial success of a toy company?

Jot

9 The Jot brand was established in 1998 by husband and wife team Jon and Tani Grun. The company initially designed a small range of toys which were manufactured in their home European country. These toys proved to be very popular in their home country and Jon Grun then expanded the range of products.

10 By 2003, within five years of starting Jot, the founders were encouraged to see Jot's products ordered by many large toy retailers across Europe. By this stage the company had grown considerably, and had annual sales of almost €2 million. Commencing in 2004, Jot started outsourcing all of its manufacturing to a range of manufacturing companies in China in order to reduce its cost base and to enable the company to price its products more competitively.

11 By the end of 2010 sales revenue exceeded €8 million and the company had achieved substantial sales revenue growth each year. Jot has seen its sales revenue grow by 16% in the year ended 31 December 2010 and by almost 18% in the year to 31 December 2011 (unaudited figures).

12 A summary of Jot's key personnel is shown in **Appendix 1** on page 11.

Jot's product range

13 Jot currently has a relatively small range of 34 products aimed at only 2 age groups. These are the pre-school age group of 3 to 5 year olds and the next age group of 5 to 8 year olds. It currently does not produce any toys aimed at babies aged less than one, toddlers aged less than 3 years old or children aged over 8 years old.

14 Jot's products include a range of toys designed by the company, for which it holds the IPR's, as well as some licensed toys, for which it pays a license fee to the companies which hold the IPR's. Jot's products mainly include electronic features and this is seen as one of the strengths of its products.

15 Jot currently launches around 5 totally new products each year. It also enhances certain aspects of some of its other products to refresh their appearance and features. It also has a range of toys that sell consistently well and have not changed materially for a few years.

16 Jot's products for the 3 to 5 year old age group include:
- Construction toys with sound effects and electronic actions.
- Learning products such as mini-computers which ask questions and the child responds by pressing different keys.
- Toy vehicles some of which have electronic features such as sounds and lights.
- Plastic toys which have "animatronics" to make the toys move, for example, toy dinosaurs.
- Toy cameras.
- Electronic learning products to aid learning the alphabet and basic maths skills.
- Licensed soft play toys based on film and TV programme characters.
- Licensed plastic figures, cars and machines based on film and TV programme characters, some of which include electronic features that generate movements and sounds, including theme tunes.

17 Jot's products for the 5 to 8 year old age group include:
- Toy cameras and video cameras.
- Dolls and action figures, some of which move and make sounds.
- Small hand-held games boxes for playing computer games and educational learning products to improve maths and readings skills.
- A range of games and educational learning products for the hand-held games boxes.

PART C PRACTICE TOPCIMA CASES | 22: Jot toys: some help from BPP | **415**

Paras	
9-12	What is the purpose of the information in these paragraphs?
	Does Jot have an appropriate product portfolio?
	Which products are likely to give Jot the best financial returns?
13-17	How could Jot extend this product portfolio?

18 Jot's products are sold to toy retailers for between €7 and €38. These are Jot's selling prices to toy retailers. Most of the retailers will then sell these toys at a large mark-up, which can be as much as 50% to 100%, i.e. a toy procured from Jot at €10 could be retailed to the end customer at €20.

19 In the year ended 31 December 2011 Jot's actual sales volumes (unaudited) were over 706,000 units across Jot's entire range of products. The total sales revenue for the year ended 31 December 2011 (unaudited) was €9,866,000, which resulted in an average selling price of just under €14 per unit. Over 80% of Jot's product sales are sold to retailers for €20 or less.

Financials and shares

20 Jot has achieved a high annual growth in sales, with sales revenue reaching €9,866,000 in the year ended 31 December 2011 (unaudited), a growth of 17.9% from 2010 (€8,371,000 sales revenue for year ended 31 December 2010). Additionally, it has achieved an operating profit margin of 5.58% in the year to 31 December 2011, a rise from the previous year's profit margin of 5.41%.

21 An extract from Jot's accounts (unaudited) for the year ended 31 December 2011 is shown in **Appendix 2** on page 12.

22 Jot's Statement of Cash Flows for the year ended 31 December 2011 (unaudited) is shown in **Appendix 3** on page 13.

23 Jot is a young, growing company which is dependent on loan finance. Jot has three bank loans totalling €1,600,000, each at an interest rate of 10% per year, which are due for repayment as follows:
- Bank loan of €500,000 due in January 2014.
- Bank loan of €500,000 due in January 2015.
- Bank loan of €600,000 due in January 2020.

24 Jot's bank has been very responsive to the company's needs for cash in order to fund its growth but has indicated that at the present time it would not be able to provide any additional long-term finance.

25 Jot has an overdraft facility of €1,500,000, which the bank has stated is the maximum limit. The current cost of its overdraft is at an interest rate of 12% per year. At 31 December 2011, Jot's overdraft was €960,000.

26 Jot's business is highly seasonal with a significant proportion of sales occurring in quarters 3 and 4. As Jot builds up its inventory in preparation for higher levels of sales in quarters 3 and 4, cash flow is negative during the second half of the year. This is because outsourced manufacturing for the majority of all products occurs mainly from the end of quarter 2, during all of quarter 3 and the beginning of quarter 4.

27 Jot is a private limited company and not listed on any stock exchange. It has 40,000 shares in issue, each of €1 par value. The company has an authorised share capital of 200,000 shares. To date, the Board of Jot has not declared any dividends. The shares are held as follows:

	Number of shares held at 31 December 2011	Percentage shareholding
		%
Jon Grun	12,000	30
Tani Grun	12,000	30
Alana Lotz	8,000	20
Boris Hepp	4,000	10
Michael Werner	4,000	10
Total	40,000	100

Paras	
18-19	What is the significance of this mark-up?
	Why are we told that 80% of toys are sold for €20 or less?
20-26	Do you consider Jot to have good financial management?
	Why might the current overdraft figures be misleading?
	What issues may Jot face in 2012 and after as it seeks to grow its business?
	How could its cash flow and working capital management be improved?
27	What is the significance of this information on share ownership?
	Should Jot seek to raise venture capital?

Production of toys

28 Jot has its own in-house team of designers who are involved in designing toys that are unique, innovative and fun to play with. The production of new toys is split into two stages. Firstly, the design stage involves the design team developing a new toy and after it has been approved, the second stage is where the operations team is responsible for contracting an outsourced manufacturer for the mass production of each product.

29 The head of Jot's design team is Alana Lotz, Product Development Director. She is responsible for researching the market trends in toys globally and establishing the availability of new innovative technology which could be incorporated into new toy designs. This is what helps to make Jot's product range innovative and at the "cutting edge" of new technology, as the products incorporate new technology electronic chip components.

30 Research and development work on new product development usually occurs between May and December each year so that the new products have been fully tested ready for the annual launch of Jot's new range of toys each January. Jot currently launches 5 totally new products each year and the development costs are generally between €0.1 and €0.25 million for each new product. The total design and development costs are around €1.2 million each year. This is included in administration expenses in Jot's statement of comprehensive income.

31 Jot has just finalised its range of new products for 2012, so as to allow time to produce marketing literature and prepare prototypes ready for the global toy fairs being held in January to March 2012 in various locations around the world.

32 The design team develops all new products through the following stages:

- Brainstorming for new ideas.
- Designing a new product using Jot's CAD / CAM IT system.
- Production of first prototype.
- Market research and improvements through to production of second prototype.
- Sign off by design and management team.
- Application for intellectual property rights (IPR's) for each product design.

33 Jot uses a specialised company, based in Europe for the manufacture and testing of all prototype products and there are often two or three stages involved before the prototype product is produced to the satisfaction of the designers. Only when each product is signed off by the design and management team can Jot's legal team apply for the IPR's for the product design. Then the approved new product designs go into production by outsourced manufacturers.

34 The designs are then electronically transferred to Jot's operations team headed up by Michael Werner, Operations Director, for the selection and appointment of outsourced manufacturers. The stages in the production process are as follows:

- Designs are sent electronically to outsourced manufacturers for tender.
- Outsourced manufacturer(s) selected and appointed and volumes and delivery deadlines for production agreed.
- Packaging designs and artwork are prepared and approved.
- Production samples are reviewed by Jot's in-house Quality Assurance team located both in Europe and in Asia.
- Production is commenced to meet agreed volume and delivery deadlines.

35 Michael Werner is responsible for the selection, appointment and monitoring of Jot's outsourced manufacturers and all aspects of the management of the outsourced manufacturing process for Jot's products. Jot's products are all manufactured by a small number of specialised outsourced manufacturing companies which are all based in China. Jot is responsible for shipments of all products from its outsourced manufacturers to its warehouses or sometimes directly to customers.

Paras	
28-33	How important is Jot's new product development process to its financial performance?
	Is it a flexible and efficient process?
	How are prototypes made?
	How are the prototypes used?
	Is the process clearly focused on generating financial benefits?
	Are the toys safe?
34-35	How critical is Michael Werner to Jot?
	Why does Jot have QA staff in Asia?

Outsourced manufacturers

36 Currently Jot uses 20 off-shore outsourced manufacturing companies. Off-shore outsourced manufacturing is defined as shifting work to foreign, distant companies in order to reduce production costs. Some of the outsourced manufacturers are small companies each of which manufactures just one of Jot's products. Some of the larger outsourced manufacturing companies make several of Jot's products. All of these outsourced manufacturing companies do not work exclusively for Jot but manufacture toys, as well as other products, for a number of international companies. All of Jot's outsourced manufacturers are based in China.

37 When a product design has been approved and the IPR applied for, Michael Werner will send the product design with an indication of the number of products to be manufactured and the timescale for shipment, to a small range of outsourced manufacturers for them to tender for the manufacture of the product. Jot often asks the same outsourced manufacturing companies, which it has used previously, to tender for the manufacture of its new product designs each year. Therefore, there is a high level of "repeat business" and a good level of understanding and commitment established between Jot, based in Europe, and its outsourced manufacturers based in China.

38 When the tenders have been received, Michael Werner and his team review the outsourced manufacturing companies' submissions and then select the outsourced manufacturer to be appointed. Jot's designers and sales team will have already decided on an indicative selling price, so the unit price to be charged to Jot by the outsourced manufacturing company is often the determining factor when making the decision of which outsourced manufacturing company to use. Whilst other factors are considered, such as quality and ability to deliver the required volume of products to the required timescale, it is the unit price which is important in order to achieve the planned level of gross margin. Gross margin is defined as sales revenue less the outsourced manufacturing cost of units sold and excludes all other costs.

39 Jot's design team already knows the cost of making each product, based on the list of components required, so it is the cost of manufacturing that will vary between the different tenders. Generally, in most tenders, the unit prices quoted by different outsourced manufacturers are quite close to each other.

40 Most of Jot's products are manufactured using basic raw materials, such as plastic and electronic components for the toys and plastic and paper products for their packaging. The majority of Jot's products require a range of electronic components. These components are readily available from a variety of sources but are subject to price fluctuations. Each product design will specify which, and how many, of each component type is required. Some of the electronic components are specialised and contain "application-specific integrated circuits" (ASIC components) which are procured from specialist suppliers. Jot does not have any agreements with these specialised suppliers as all components, including ASIC components, are procured directly by the outsourced manufacturer appointed to manufacture each of Jot's products. Some of Jot's outsourced manufacturers, which manufacture a range of electronic products for Jot and other companies, have on-going supply contracts in place for several key components, which helps them to price their products competitively.

41 The timescales each year for the production of Jot's products is for tenders to be submitted and manufacturers appointed by the end of May. The major proportion of manufacturing occurs between June and early November each year. The last of the manufacturing occurs in early November to enable time for the products to be shipped to Jot's warehouses in Europe and the USA, or sometimes directly to Jot's customers, in time to meet the Christmas sales peak. All three of Jot's warehouses are leased.

42 Over the last 10 to 15 years many companies have outsourced their manufacturing to companies in China. However, with wage rates in China increasing, some companies have started to consider "near-shoring". Near-shoring is defined as the transfer of business processes to companies in a nearby country. Therefore, if Jot were to consider near-shoring, this would result in having some outsourced manufacturers based in Europe.

Paras	
36-38	What comments can you make about the way Jot single-sources its toys?
	Are there any issues for Jot's protection of its IPR's?
	Why does Jot use the same suppliers year after year?
	How could e-procurement help Jot?
39	What significance can be attached to the prices being close together?
	Does Jot change manufacturers often?
40	Why are components subject to price fluctuations?
	What are the potential implications of these fluctuations for Jot?
	What benefits might Jot get from having direct agreements with component suppliers?
	What drawbacks might Jot suffer if it decided to source components itself and pass them on to manufacturers?
41	How might this paragraph affect the May exam?
	What significance may be given to the statement that Jot's warehouses are leased?
42	What benefits might Jot enjoy from having some manufacturers near-shore?
	What drawbacks might Jot suffer from having some manufacturers near-shore?

Sales

43 Jot's sales revenue for the year ended 31 December 2011 (unaudited) was €9,866,000. The geographical analysis of these sales is shown as follows:

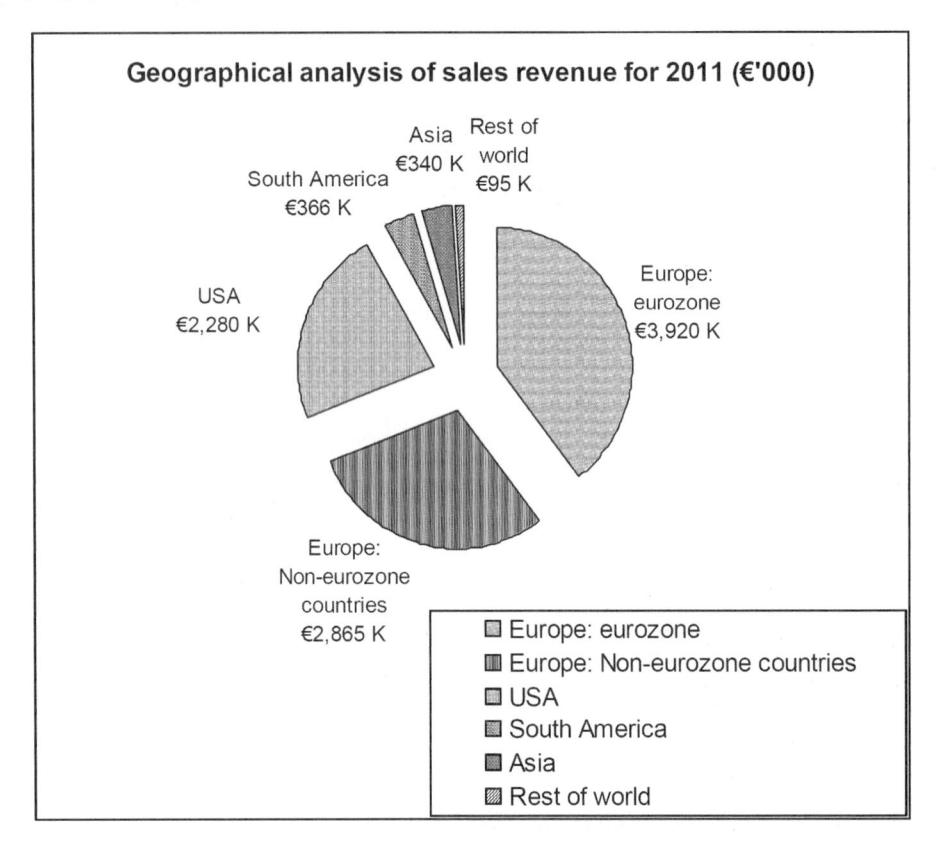

Geographical analysis of sales revenue for 2011 (€'000)

- Europe: eurozone €3,920 K
- Europe: Non-eurozone countries €2,865 K
- USA €2,280 K
- South America €366 K
- Asia €340 K
- Rest of world €95 K

44 Jot's customers are mainly:

- Retailers – these include large toy retailers as well as supermarket chains and other retailers
- Distributors – these distributors purchase Jot's products and sell them on to a wide range of smaller retailers.

45 Jot currently has three warehouses, two in Europe and one in the USA. Usually all products are shipped from each of Jot's outsourced manufacturers directly to one of Jot's three warehouses. In some instances, products are shipped directly to customers.

46 Jot's terms of sale are for payment within 30 days of invoice. Invoices are produced automatically, on a daily basis, based on information transferred to the sales ledger from the inventory control IT system. However, Jot is very dependent on sales to large retailers, which often do not pay until at least 60 days after the invoice date. Jot has little influence over these retailers and does not want to jeopardise future sales by chasing them too aggressively.

47 Sales of Jot's toys are highly seasonal as shown in the quarterly analysis of sales in **Appendix 4** on page 14.

PART C PRACTICE TOPCIMA CASES

Paras	
43-45	Calculate the percentage of total sales revenue from Jot's top four regional markets
	Why has the examiner presented this data as a pie chart rather than a table?
	Which client groups will give Jot the highest margins?
	How might e-commerce help Jot serve some of these client segments?
46	How good is credit control at Jot?
	How could credit control at Jot be improved?
47-48	What is the significant of this statement about seasonal sales?

48 In the year ended 31 December 2011, sales in quarter 3 (July to September) were 25% of annual sales and sales in quarter 4 (October to December) were 51% of annual sales.

49 Jot's sales are highly dependent on seven large retailers. These seven large companies comprise toy retailers, large international supermarket retailers, department stores and one on-line retailer. Over 68% of Jot's sales in the financial year ended 31 December 2011 were to these 7 customers based in Europe and the USA. These key customers place their main orders in May or June each year and sometimes earlier. If individual products are selling well or the retailers consider sales may be higher than they originally thought, then the retailers would place additional orders with Jot. This could happen at any time between June through to late October.

50 The remaining 32% of sales are to distributors as well as small and medium sized retailers around the world. Jot currently has around 350 customers in total, including the 7 large customers.

51 With the placement of orders from its large customers and the many smaller customers early in the year, Jot is able to place firm orders with its outsourced manufacturers with a reasonable degree of certainty of sales levels. However, there is always a balancing act between placing a large order to meet committed and expected sales and not holding enough inventory.

Licensed toys

52 Jot currently has 12 product lines which are licensed products from popular film and TV programmes for the manufacture and sale of toys. Licensed products are defined as toys which use a logo, design or character from a film or TV programme and the owner of the IPR will license each product under a strict licensing agreement, whereby a royalty is paid to the owner of the IPR for each unit manufactured. A licensed product is where the TV or film company owns the intellectual property rights (IPR's) for the characters and licenses the manufacture and sale of the products to another company in exchange for a license fee for each item produced (whether sold or not).

53 A fixed license fee is paid to the licensor in accordance with the licensing contract, and the fee is usually paid at the time Jot places an order with its outsourced manufacturer. The fee is between 5% and 10% of Jot's selling price to retailers.

54 Anna Veld, Licensing Director, joined Jot in 2009 and has negotiated all of the licensed products that Jot currently sells. She is very experienced in this field and in liaison with both Sonja Rosik and Boris Hepp, she has identified products for Jot to develop and sell. Licensed products now account for almost 10% of Jot's sales, in terms of the number of units sold.

Inventory control

55 Michael Werner is responsible for logistics and inventory control. There is always a difficult decision to be made when placing orders with outsourced manufacturers, between ordering too much inventory and not selling it and the opposite of losing sales because of lack of inventory. This is further exacerbated due to the seasonal nature of sales, which are predominantly made in quarters 3 and 4 of each calendar year.

56 At the start of each calendar year, any unsold inventory for products that Boris Hepp, Sales Director, considers to be out of date, are offered to Jot's customers at substantially reduced prices to clear them and the inventory value is written down. There are a few products which are sold on a regular basis throughout each year and their inventory value is not written down.

57 Inventory counts at the end of the financial year are reconciled with Jot's IT inventory control system and any discrepancies are written off. Jot's inventory is valued at the lower of cost or realisable market value, based on a first-in, first-out basis. Inventory value is based only on out-sourced manufacturing contracted charges, using the unit price from manufacturer's invoices, unless the realisable value is lower.

PART C PRACTICE TOPCIMA CASES   22: Jot toys: some help from BPP   **425**

Paras	
49-50	What significance is there in Jot having customers of different sizes?
	How would Customer Profitability Analysis help Jot to improve its financial performance?
	How could Jot carry out CPA?
	Why are we told about the time when orders are placed and when repeat orders may be submitted?
51	At what point in the year does Jot get the first idea of how popular its ranges are going to be in 2012?
52-54	How might the examiner set a requirement involving licensed toys?
	How important is Anna Veld to Jot?
55	What does this paragraph add to our understanding of Jot's operations and position?
56-58	What do these paragraphs covey about the product life cycle of Jot's products?
	How significant is the inventory write down reserve for 2011?

58 Inventory also includes a reserve for the write-down in value in respect of slow-moving and obsolete products. This valuation is based upon Jot's management team's review of inventories taking into account for each product the estimated future sales demand, anticipated product selling prices, expected product lifecycle and products planned for discontinuation. The valuation for inventory write down is reviewed quarterly. At 31 December 2011 the write-down reserve was €0.124 million. This is netted off against the value of the current inventory of products held in Jot's warehouses.

The Jot brand

59 The Jot brand name is synonymous with quality electronic toys. Jot's products are innovative and appealing to the targeted age groups. Sonja Rosik, Marketing Director, joined Jot three years ago when the role was separated from that of the Sales and Marketing Director, leaving Boris Hepp, Sales Director, free to concentrate on securing sales in wider geographical markets.

60 Marketing has become increasingly important in the promotion of new products. No longer can a company rely on a good product being identified by the key buyers for large retailers. It is of vital importance to market new products before, during and after the global toy fairs, which are held in several locations in the January to March period of each year. The toy fairs can often "make or break" the success of each new product and the need to gain a positive reaction from buyers, based on sample products, is very important.

61 The launch plans for new products and the marketing support Jot's customers receive can have an impact on the reaction of buyers at the global toy fairs. A significant volume of sales orders arise directly from these toy fairs and Sonja Rosik's team has made a very strong contribution to achieving positive press reports for new products and providing buyers with good quality and clear marketing literature. Boris Hepp is very pleased with Sonja Rosik and her team, which helps his sales team to secure firm sales orders for Jot's products.

62 Additionally, Sonja Rosik, has been working on the establishment of links and promotion of the Jot brand in new geographical markets as well as further market penetration in Europe and the competitive USA market.

IT systems

63 Tani Grun appointed an external IT consultancy company some years ago to provide the IT systems required for Jot's growing business. However, some of the systems are not ideal and do not provide Jot's management team with all of the data that it requires. There is also some replication of data between different IT systems.

64 The Finance Department operates a multi-currency nominal ledger and integrated sales and purchase ledgers. However, these IT systems do not accept data directly from any of Jot's other IT systems. The Finance Department also operates a fixed assets register.

65 Jot outsources the logistics of its products, both the movement of manufactured products and the sales to customers, to a global logistics company. This company operates a fast efficient service and with the increase in sales volumes over the last few years, a reduction on the unit costs has recently been negotiated. The outsourced logistics company provides Jot with access to all tracking and logistics data for products moving into Jot's three warehouses and prepares reports on products which have been shipped directly to customers.

66 The data concerning goods delivered to Jot's three warehouses is transferred electronically to Jot's inventory control system. This database system generates despatch notes for all orders that are fulfilled from each warehouse. The majority of customer deliveries are fulfilled from Jot's warehouses and not directly from the manufacturer. The despatch note data is transferred electronically to the Finance Department in order to raise invoices to customers for goods despatched. Information on customer orders which are delivered directly from the manufacturer is transferred by the outsourced logistics company to the Finance Department, in order to raise invoices.

PART C PRACTICE TOPCIMA CASES 22: Jot toys: some help from BPP

Paras	
59-62	How important is Sonja Rosik to Jot's commercial success?
	Can Jot rely on Sonja Rosik staying with the company?
63-67	What factors make Jot's IT systems 'not ideal'?
	How could Jot improve its IT systems?

67 All product designs and product drawings, which include a detailed listing of all parts and components, are prepared using a standard CAD / CAM IT system. This allows direct interface with Jot's outsourced manufacturers. This ensures that each new product design can be transferred to the appointed outsourced manufacturer's IT systems when the product is ready for manufacture, thereby eliminating any delays and confusion over the exact product specification and design.

Target markets for growth

68 Jot would like to expand its sales by specifically targeting other areas of the world, including the Russian and the Asian markets. These two specific markets have a growing demand for the types of product that Jot sells. Sonja Rosik has visited several countries in Jot's target markets and met with retailers and distributors of children's toys. She has been working with Michael Werner to establish distribution links for these markets and to arrange delivery of products direct to customers based in Asia, rather than have its products shipped to Jot's European warehouses for onward shipping back to Asia.

69 When Jot first entered the USA market in 2006, it was caught unawares by the higher than expected volume of demand and spent almost a year trying to meet the growth in demand for the products ordered. Jot has since discovered that it is necessary to manufacture larger numbers of each product, in order to ensure that its products are available if demand exceeds its expected supply levels, before launching into new geographical markets.

70 Extracts from Jot's 5-year plan is shown in **Appendix 5** on page 15.

71 The 5-year plan shows growth in sales revenue at 17% for 2012 and around 13% to 14% for the remaining 4 years of the plan period as well as a small growth in operating profit margins.

Corporate social responsibilities and product safety

72 Jot's management team is aware of the importance of its corporate social responsibilities (CSR) but so far it has not officially published what it does or how it will improve its CSR plans. This is an area which Michael Werner and Alana Lotz plan to develop in the next year, so that Jot can publish its CSR achievements and targets.

73 However, Jon Grun has always impressed on all of Jot's employees and managers the importance of its products exceeding, rather than simply conforming to, the required safety standards.

74 European Union (EU) law requires that all toys which are to be sold in any EU country must carry the "CE" marking. The "CE" marking confirms that "Certification Experts" have carried out all applicable testing to identify hazards and assess risks, in order to determine that the products meet the required product safety regulations of the EU. The "CE" marking may be on the toys themselves or on their packaging. In the EU a toy is defined as "any product or material designed or clearly intended for use in play by children of less than 14 years of age".

75 These EU safety regulations apply to all companies based in the EU which supply toys anywhere in the EU, and apply to all companies, whether they are manufacturers, importers, wholesalers, retailers or hirers. It is the responsibility of the toy company and the manufacturer to ensure that the product meets the safety regulations and that the "CE" marking is fixed on the product. Jot cannot delegate this responsibility.

Paras	
68 - 71	What changes is Jot considering making to its supply chain arrangements to serve these target markets?
	What lessons from its USA experience should Jot bear in mind before it expands into Russia or into Asian markets?
	Why does the examiner refer to the 5 year plan here?
72-75	What might be contained in the CSR policies of a toy company?
	How might the examiner base an exam day issue on product safety?

Appendix 1
Jot's key personnel

Jon Grun – Managing Director

76 Jon Grun, aged 48, is an engineer and has worked in a variety of large companies designing electrical products. He always wanted to establish his own company and was inspired to start the Jot toy company in 1998 when his children were young, as he felt there was a gap in the market for innovative, educational toys. Jon Grun owns 30% of the shares in issue.

Tani Grun – Finance and IT Director

77 Tani Grun, aged 44, is married to Jon Grun. She is a CIMA accountant and worked for some large companies in senior roles before taking on the Finance Director role for Jot when it was formed in 1998. Initially she worked part-time, but as the company has grown, she is finding the role more challenging. She is considering recruiting a new person to take responsibility for IT for Jot as she considers that outside experience is necessary to move the company forward. Currently, many of Jot's IT solutions are out-sourced. Tani Grun owns 30% of the shares in issue.

Alana Lotz – Product Development Director

78 Alana Lotz, aged 44, has been Tani Grun's friend for many years and trained as a design engineer and then worked for a global toy manufacturer for 12 years. Tani Grun recruited her when Jot was established in 1998 and she has been a leading force in the expansion of the range of new toys and in the recruitment and retention of Jot's design team. She holds 20% of the shares in issue.

Sonja Rosik, Marketing Director

79 Sonja Rosik, aged 35, was recruited in 2009 when the role of Marketing Director was separated from the previous role of Sales and Marketing Director. She has brought a wealth of new ideas and dynamism to Jot's marketing and has helped to expand Jot's products to new geographical markets. She does not own any shares.

Boris Hepp – Sales Director

80 Boris Hepp, aged 42, joined Jot in 2003 when sales in Europe were starting to grow rapidly. He held the joint role of Sales and Marketing Director until 2009, when the Board decided that he would be best employed in concentrating on capturing sales in new markets. Boris Hepp had known Jon Grun for many years before he joined Jot and was very impressed at how quickly the company had grown. Boris Hepp holds 10% of the shares in issue which he purchased when he joined Jot in 2003.

Michael Werner – Operations Director

81 Michael Werner, aged 50, is responsible for all operations, including management of outsourced manufacturing, logistics and inventory control. All stages from the handover of each product design through to delivery to Jot's customers are under Michael Werner's control. He joined Jot in 2008 from a large European based electrical company. He enjoys meeting the challenges faced by Jot's growth and also the freedom to manage operations without the large corporate culture that he found frustrating. He holds 10% of the shares in issue which he purchased when he joined Jot in 2008.

Anna Veld - Licensing Director

82 Anna Veld, aged 37, has extensive knowledge of licensing agreements from her previous roles working for a global film company which licensed its merchandising products and she has also worked for a large toy manufacturer. She has been instrumental in increasing the number of licensed products that Jot sells. She does not own any shares.

Viktor Mayer - HR manager

83 Viktor Mayer, aged 55, joined Jot in 2011 on a part-time basis to help with HR matters, which Jon Grun used to manage with the help of an outsourced HR agency.

Paras	
76-83	Does Jot's product portfolio carry though Jon's 1998 assessment of the market opportunity?

Is Tani Grun suffering work overload and what could be the impact of this?

How do you assess the contribution made by Alana Lotz to the strategic position of Jot?

What are the differences between Sales and Marketing as business functions? |

Appendix 2

**Extract from Jot's Statement of Comprehensive Income,
Statement of Financial Position and Statement of Changes in Equity**

Statement of Comprehensive Income	Year ended 31 December 2011 (Unaudited) €'000	Year ended 31 December 2010 €'000
Revenue	9,866	8,371
Cost of sales	6,719	5,615
Gross profit	3,147	2,756
Distribution costs	552	478
Administrative expenses	2,044	1,825
Operating profit	551	453
Finance income	13	12
Finance expense	213	201
Profit before tax	351	264
Tax expense (effective tax rate is 30%)	105	79
Profit for the period	246	185

Statement of Financial Position	As at 31 December 2011 (Unaudited) €'000	€'000	As at 31 December 2010 €'000	€'000
Non-current assets (net)		750		721
Current assets				
Inventory	542		470	
Trade receivables	4,065		3,173	
Cash and cash equivalents	21		29	
Total current assets		4,628		3,672
Total assets		5,378		4,393
Equity and liabilities				
Equity				
Issued share capital	40		40	
Share premium	90		90	
Retained earnings	802		556	
Total Equity		932		686
Non-current liabilities				
Long term loans		1,600		1,600
Current liabilities				
Bank overdraft	960		790	
Trade payables	1,781		1,238	
Tax payables	105		79	
Total current liabilities		2,846		2,107
Total equity and liabilities		5,378		4,393

Note: Paid in share capital represents 40,000 shares of €1.00 each at 31 December 2011

Statement of Changes in Equity For the year ended 31 December 2011 (Unaudited)	Share capital €'000	Share premium €'000	Retained earnings €'000	Total €'000
Balance at 31 December 2010	40	90	556	686
Profit	-	-	246	246
Dividends paid	-	-	-	-
Balance at 31 December 2011	40	90	802	932

Appx	
2	How has Jot's gross margin changed between 2010 and 2011?

Appendix 3

Statement of Cash Flows

	Year ended 31 December 2011 (Unaudited)	
	€'000	€'000
Cash flows from operating activities:		
Profit before taxation (after Finance costs (net))		351
Adjustments:		
Depreciation	240	
Finance costs (net)	200	
		440
(Increase) / decrease in inventories	(72)	
(Increase) / decrease in trade receivables	(892)	
Increase / (decrease) in trade payables (excluding taxation)	543	
		(421)
Finance costs (net) paid	(200)	
Tax paid	(79)	
		(279)
Cash generated from operating activities		91
Cash flows from investing activities:		
Purchase of non-current assets (net)	(269)	
Cash used in investing activities		(269)
Cash flows from financing activities:		
Increase in bank overdraft	170	
Dividends paid	0	
Cash flows from financing activities		170
Net (decrease) in cash and cash equivalents		(8)
Cash and cash equivalents at 31 December 2010		29
Cash and cash equivalents at 31 December 2011		21

Appx	
3	Is Jot a cash generating business?

Appendix 4

Quarterly analysis of sales for 2009 to 2011

		Qtr 1 Jan - Mar	Qtr 2 Apr - June	Qtr 3 Jul – Sept	Qtr 4 Oct - Dec	Total
2011 Actual (unaudited)	Sales €'000 %	988 10%	1,380 14%	2,490 25%	5,008 51%	9,866 100%
2010 Actual	Sales €'000 %	730 9%	1,250 15%	2,360 28%	4,031 48%	8,371 100%
2009 Actual	Sales €'000 %	548 8%	1,010 14%	2,025 28%	3,622 50%	7,205 100%

Appx	
4	What is the value of this Appendix?

Appendix 5

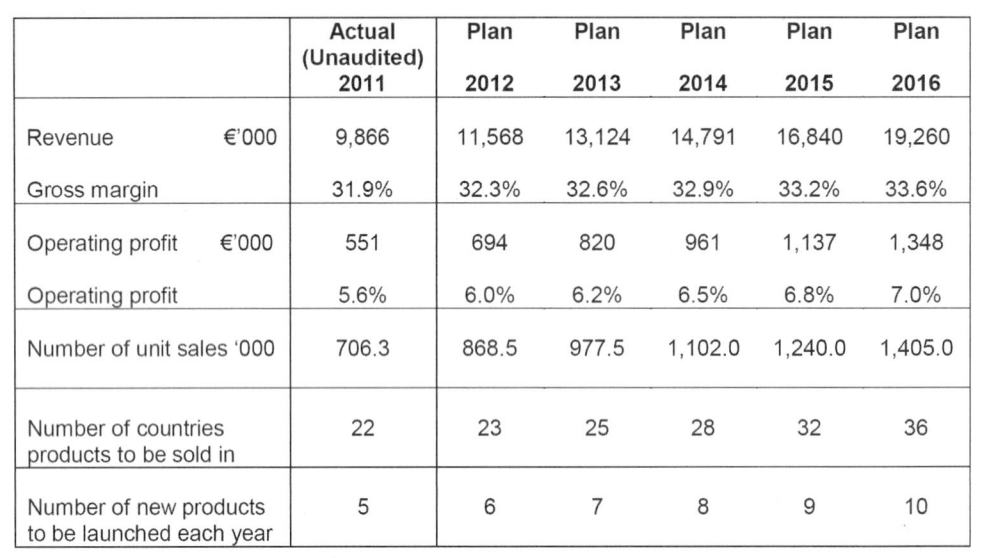

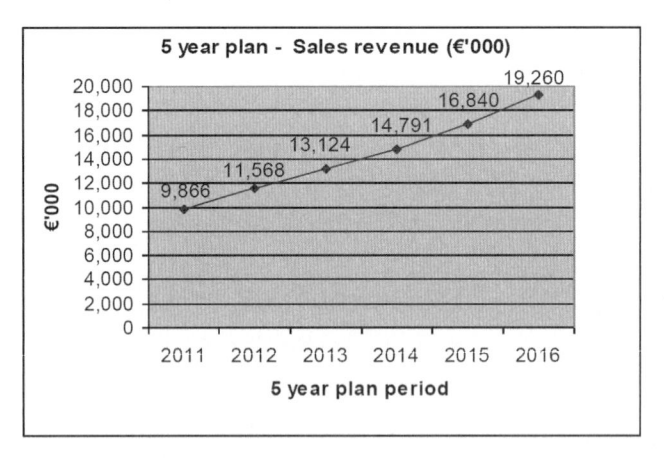

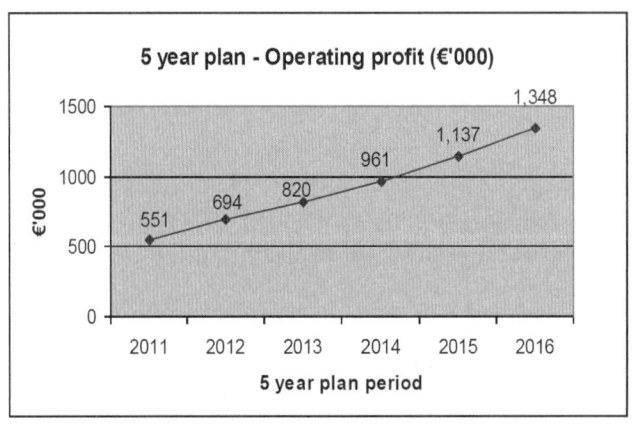

Extracts from Jot's 5 year plan

	Actual (Unaudited) 2011	Plan 2012	Plan 2013	Plan 2014	Plan 2015	Plan 2016
Revenue €'000	9,866	11,568	13,124	14,791	16,840	19,260
Gross margin	31.9%	32.3%	32.6%	32.9%	33.2%	33.6%
Operating profit €'000	551	694	820	961	1,137	1,348
Operating profit	5.6%	6.0%	6.2%	6.5%	6.8%	7.0%
Number of unit sales '000	706.3	868.5	977.5	1,102.0	1,240.0	1,405.0
Number of countries products to be sold in	22	23	25	28	32	36
Number of new products to be launched each year	5	6	7	8	9	10

5 year plan - Sales revenue (€'000)

Year	Revenue
2011	9,866
2012	11,568
2013	13,124
2014	14,791
2015	16,840
2016	19,260

5 year plan - Operating profit (€'000)

Year	Operating profit
2011	551
2012	694
2013	820
2014	961
2015	1,137
2016	1,348

End of Pre-seen material

Appx 5

What is the value of this Appendix?

Activity: SWOT Analysis

Finally: complete a SWOT analysis for Jot using the following Pro-forma

Strengths	Weaknesses
Opportunities	Threats

2 Analysis from BPP Learning Media

In this section, we provide an analysis of the pre-seen material: in effect, providing answers to the questions we have raised in the previous section.

Paras 1-2 Why has the examiner given this general information on the global toy industry? How will it be useful in the exam?

The examiner puts a lot of effort into researching industry background information. It is accurate, if simplified, and gets you started on understanding the toy industry. This is because, for the purposes of the exam, you are assumed to be working in the finance team at Jot and therefore would have some knowledge of the industry.

Chapter 2 of this TOPCIMA Toolkit provides more research information for you. The examiner expects you to conduct, and will give you marks for, original industry research of your own.

A good source of research material is www.globaltoynews.com which has a free archive of very useful articles.

The ways you should use this industry information in the examination are to:

- Comment on the suitability of courses of action being considered by Jot. For example would you recommend that Jot shifted toy production to Europe, given that 'most of the world's toys are made in Asia'? Not without very good reasons

- Help you generate ideas to solve Jot's problems. You might be able to recommend a course of action to Jot which is the same as a real world firm has done

- Help you justify your recommendations. In effect you can tell the Board of Jot 'this would work because it worked for company x'

Which of the market segments is the most valuable?

The 6-8 years segment seems to be the more valuable because of the greater sales revenue it generates for sales of a smaller volume of toys compared to the 2-4 years (it's not clear what happens with 5 year olds). However this is not certain because the toys for 6-8s could be more complex and costly to make.

Para 3 What are the implications of this paragraph for the marketing strategy of Jot?

This paragraph accurately describes the main trend in the toy market towards electronically enabled toys. It presents them as the growth segment of the market with the two remaining segments, traditional toys and games, being mature or even in decline.

Jot has a distinctive competence and reputation in electronic toys (para 59). This seems to have been the segment that appealed to Jot's founder and managing director (para 76). This means that the growth of this segment of the market may benefit Jot by enabling it to follow a strategy of Differentiation Focus in a very crowded market in which it is a very small player.

This paragraph also presents the market for merchandising based on films and TV programmes as less stable and more risky. Any marketing strategy based on this market relies upon being able to identify blockbuster films or programmes in advance, being able to bid for the license rights, and being able to come up with toys that can exploit the brief global interest in the characters and vehicles in the films or programmes. For a firm like Jot, which is small, the risks are probably too great because it lacks the depth of capital and secure earnings streams needed to be involved in speculative investment in license rights. It also lacks global coverage. This segment is better served by the major manufacturers like Hasbro and Mattel.

At this point it would be useful for you to do some research on what toys are available for each segment, and what these electronic toys look like. A walk down the aisles of a large toy store would be helpful. Here are some useful links where toys are indexed by age group and by type:

www.woolworths.co.uk/toys (on-line retail company owned by Shop Direct, formed after the demise of Woolworths high street stores)

www.amazon.co.uk/toys

www.toysrus.co.uk

www.argos.co.uk/toys

Para 4   **What are implications of this seasonality for Jot?**

This seasonality is referred to repeatedly in the pre-seen material (see also paras 26, 47, 55, and Appendix 4). Note that in 2011 Jot made 51% of its revenues in Quarter 4 (Appendix 4 €5008k/€9866k) and 76% in Quarters 3 and 4 together (€2490k+€5008k/€9866k). Some of the following implications of this seasonality are also drawn out in the pre-seen:

- High risk: Jot depends on a narrow selling season of 3 months to get a financial return on its investments in product development and inventories. If it has invested in too many of the wrong toys it will get into financial trouble.

- Cash flow impacts: Jot has outgoings all year on maintaining warehouses and conducing research and marketing. From June it builds inventories ready for the Christmas boom. This means it suffers negative cash flows in the second half of each year and depends on bank credit to sustain it.

- Unused capacity: Jot maintains warehouses, staff and IT systems all year that are capable of coping with a huge rush in demand in the final quarter of the year. Although manufacturing and logistics are outsourced by Jot it still has significant fixed costs remaining.

Para 5   **What might the examiner be expecting you to conclude about a toy firm depending on China for production of its toys?**

Para 10 tells us that Jot outsources all its final production runs to China but it uses a single European company for developing prototypes and testing (para 33).

There seem to be four issues embedded in these paragraphs:

- **Low cost manufacturing.** China is traditionally a cheap location for manufacturing products where technology is limited and where the main labour cost is assembly and packing. Given that 86% of the world's toys are made in China (para 1) it follows that any firm that does not go to China would potentially be at a severe cost disadvantage;

- **Piracy of Intellectual Property Rights (IPR's).** These IPR's are what make the toy special and able to attract a premium price. But China has a poor reputation for respect of IPR's. Its manufacturers deal with many toy firms and so there will be a ready route to market for pirated designs. These are marketed quite openly – often from internet sites registered in Western markets. See for example http://toyhell.com/bootlegtransformers.html

- **Lack of flexibility.** The fact that Jot uses one European firm to build all its prototypes, but uses numerous Chinese firms to make its final production runs demonstrates that Jot needs the geographical proximity and skills of the European partner. The fact that there are cultural obstacles in communication with China, and the geographical distance delays deliveries, means that Chinese manufacturers can only produce to finished designs, cannot provide variations, and cannot offer Just-In-Time supply.

- **Proximity to growth markets.** According to para 43 the majority of Jot's sales are in Europe and USA. Both are significant distances from China. It is worth recalling that the growth economies are assumed to be Brazil, Russia, India and China (BRIC countries). Para 68 states that Jot is targeting Russia and Asia over the next 5 years. Russia borders China and China is part of Asia. Jot may be moving its business nearer to its Chinese manufacturers and therefore reducing the significance of geographical distance.

It is also worth recalling that there are always question marks over the desirability of China as a production location. In late 2011 the Chinese government introduced further repressive policies that denied civil liberties, Europe and USA have an on-going trade dispute with China over exchange rates and market access, and there are perpetual concerns over the conditions of work in Chinese factories that seem to be manifesting themselves in very high suicide rates amongst Chinese factory workers. Firms like Hasbro have been very proactive in developing 'safe play' policies on 'manufacturing ethics' to deal with poor working conditions and so deflecting the inevitable criticism from interest groups (www.csr.hasbro.com)

Paras 6-8 **What do these paragraphs convey about the way that toy firms add value?**

These paragraphs portray toy companies as network organisations that depend on their toy designs and marketing activities to add value and make profits. All the rest of the value system is provided by other firms, notably manufacturers and retailers.

Does the fact that Jot is a small firm have any significance to its prospects for commercial success?

Jot had sales turnover of €9.9m in 2011. By contrast Hasbro had turnover, in 2009, of $4070m (€3044m, using average 2009 exchange rate). Jot is very small by comparison.

According to Toys Industries of Europe (TIE), the trade association for the European toy industry, 'around 80% of the [European toy manufacturing] sector is composed of small and medium-sized enterprises (SMEs), which have less than 50 employees'. (www.tietoy.org),

This suggests that smaller businesses like Jot are not uncommon or unsuccessful. In strategic theory such as the work of the Boston Consulting Group that emphasised the importance of relative market share, the main benefits of large market size are:

Economies of scale: these are mainly in production, logistics and marketing;

- Experience effects: the reductions in the costs of operation gained by learning from the lesson taught by having made and sold lots of the product in the past;

- Economies of scope: these arise from having a large portfolio of products that mutually support each other, for example by having both video games and action figures, or making the products attractive to a retailer because they can offer everything that is needed;

- Access to capital: the larger firm usually has better access to equity markets and better credit ratings on its borrowings.

Porter identified that strategies of Differentiation enabled firms to produce outstanding profitability despite not having these cost advantages. A sub-set of this, characterised by small firms like Jot, is Differentiation Focus. The firm concentrates on becoming distinctive and valuable in a small niche.

Para 29 refers to Jot's products being 'innovative and at the 'cutting edge' of new technology'.

Jot may be able to avoid price competition from low cost players if it builds a niche position in electronic and educational toys.

What factors are critical to the commercial success of a toy company?

The critical success factors would seem to be:

- Dynamism: TIE reports that, in Europe, 60% of revenue is generated by toys that are new on the market that year. This requires awareness of opportunities, good research and development, and quick time to market;

- Success at global trade fairs: paragraph 8 makes clear that many orders come from trade fairs held in the first 3 months of the year. Para 31 tells us that Jot has finalised its toys for 2012 and is on target in its preparations for the toy fairs. However we do not know whether these are the toys that the market will want. Apparently this will not be confirmed until May when orders from the large retailers start coming in (para 49). However by the time of the 28 February exam the firm would have some initial indication of how good its new toys are.

- Appropriate price and costs: like any firm, a toy firm needs to be able to make the toy at the price that will sell it, but also be able to make it and supply it at a cost that gives a decent margin to itself and its owners.

Paras 9-12 **What is the purpose of the information in these paragraphs?**

These paragraphs are really just introducing Jot and do not contain important facts. You are taking the exam in 2012, so past history is not very important. The main messages to take from these paragraphs are: Jot has been in business for 14 years.

- It has grown organically and successfully.
- It is closely controlled by the husband and wife team that founded it and may still depend on them.

It might be interesting to speculate whether the examiner intends to introduce issues of the problems of small firms growing, such as explored in Greiner's Growth Model, or perhaps the breakdown of internal controls as growth outstripping management controls. But the remainder of the pre-seen does not return to these themes with the exception, as we shall see, of some working capital problems, and role overload being suffered by Tani Grun, Jot's Finance Director.

Paras 13-17 **Does Jot have an appropriate product portfolio?**

The product portfolio is detailed in paras 16 and 17. There seem to be three broad groups:

- Educational and learning products utilising complex programmes and functionality. These seem to be similar to the real world Nintendo DS hand console and more specifically the products of the Hong Kong firm Video Technology Ltd (VTech) or some of the products of French manufacturer Lexibook. These three real-world firms are much bigger than Jot however. Note that Jot makes both the hand-held game boxes and ranges of software to use on them.

- Toys with electronic features: these are basically plastic toys that talk back or move.

- Licensed-in toys figures: these are dolls and soft play toys.

We could take the view that this portfolio is too broad for Jot. Its reputation is for electronic educational toys, so it is difficult to see how 'toy vehicles with sounds and lights', or things like toy cameras, plastic figures and soft play toys fit with this or are considered 'innovative and at the 'cutting edge' of new technology'. (para 29).

Which products are likely to give Jot the best financial returns?

The pre-seen does not provide a breakdown of earnings and costs by product. This may be provided, if relevant, in the unseen material on exam day.

However it seems likely that the better margins will be on the electronic learning products. This is for three reasons:

- They are likely to be more attractive to parents and others who wish to help children develop. This will enable a premium price to be charged.

- They will provide earnings over longer periods of time than, say, an action figure based on a recent feature film would. This will repay the research and development costs better.

There will not be payments to license holders as there will be with the soft play toys and plastic figures.

The electronic learning products are probably better for cross-selling and on-selling too. Selling a toy fire engine won't immediately lead to a demand for another toy from Jot. But a hand-held games box (console) will lead to demands for additional games and programmes. In the same way selling a good 'key maths skills' programme may lead to sales of 'key spelling skills' if the series is the same. This improves return to investments in product design and marketing.

- The reference to established products in para 15 suggests that some of its cash flows do depend on products that require little development expenditure.

How could Jot extend this product portfolio?

The pre-seen implies, in para 13, that Jot might consider developing toys for children over 8 and for children under 3.

Real world firm VTech does not extend to these groups, and this may be significant. It seems to stay in the area where it can add value to play, and without being drawn into developing fully functioning tablets and PC's.

It is unlikely that Jot has much distinctive to offer the under 3's. Jots products speak and move, but the under 3's are principally learning motor skills and language skills. It is doubtful that Jot has anything special to assist these. Lexibook has products for children from birth to 3, but these are cot lights and bath toys.

Certainly Jot could move up the age ranges further. It could thereby lengthen the period of earnings it can get from customers acquired at younger ages and recoup more of the research and marketing costs for its consoles.

Jot could learn from Nintendo's experiences since the launch of the Nintendo DS in 2004. This seems to have taken Nintendo from being a games and toys manufacturer towards the grown-ups market too, notably with its Touch! Generations software, that provides brain training, healthy eating advice, and e-books. Jot may like to consider doing the same.

Jot does not produce home games consoles like the X-Box 360, Nintendo Wii or PS3. These are not toys as such, and it is a very crowded market, but there might be an opportunity to license some of its educational content to these larger producers.

Paras 18-19 **What is the significance of this mark-up?**

The mark-up is an indicator of the buyer power enjoyed by the retailer. Jot would wish to keep as much as possible of the €20 received as retail sales revenue. The fact that sometimes, when mark-up is 100%, that Jot keeps as little at 50% of the revenue shows that retailers have high buyer power.

Also be careful of mark-up and margin. The examiner may be intending setting a question that uses both concepts. If the supply price of the toy is €10 and shop adds a 50% mark-up the retail price will be €15, ie 150% of its base price. Therefore the €5 margin enjoyed by the shop will be 33% of the retail price (50%/150%: 33% x €15 = €5). We will return to this in the discussion of para 38 below.

Note that the mark-up ranges from 50% to 100%. There are several possible reasons the examiner included this:

- This may reflect different degrees of buyer power between large and small retailers (see paras 49-50).

- It may provide the basis for an exam day requirement involving assessing Direct Product Profitability or Customer Account Profitability, as some products/clients may be more profitable that others.

- It may be intended as a reflection that some of Jot's toys cannot command the same high mark-ups as others. It is tempting to think that low mark-ups are available on generic soft toys and plastic figures, and higher mark-ups are on educational electronic toys. Alternatively it may arise from the lower mark-up products being the ones in the later stages of their product life cycle, and the higher mark-up ones being the newer products (which the real-world TIE report referred to above also states).

- The exam may feature a decision by some retailers to de-list (stop stocking) the lower mark-up toys due to their low profitability.

Why are we told that 80% of toys are sold for €20 or less?

The examiner writes a factually-based case study. Therefore this, and the mark-ups discussed above, may be in the Pre-seen solely because they are an accurate reporting of the facts.

However this looks more deliberate and could be an invitation to consider Direct Product Profitability.

Given that 20% of toys cost more than €20, but the average price of the toys is €14 per unit, there must be significant percentage selling at prices below €10.

Note the examiner is talking about sale prices here not revenues. The examiner does not conclusively say '80% of sales revenues are generated by toys that sell for less than €20', although the average price of €14 demonstrates that a lot of sales revenue is coming from low price toys.

This means that the majority of Jot's output has a maximum retail price of €40 (ie maximum €20 sale price plus maximum 100% retailer mark-up). Inspection of the websites recommended above will show that electronic learning toys retail at far more than €40. For example children's tablet games computers from VTech and LeapPad retail for in excess of €100.

We will see later that Jot has capacity constraints due to lack of working capital. It also has ambitious plans to boost sales and margins in the next 5 years. At present it devotes 80% of its activity to low revenue products. The Pareto Rule has been used to imply that 80% of the earnings of most firms may come from 20% of their activities.

The examiner may be reminding you of this in the pre-seen, and is intending to set exam requirements and involving focusing Jot on the 20% of items that sell for more than €20.

A final point on para 19, and reminding you that this is a management accounting exam. The decision-making at Jot is driven by gross margins, which it calculates as 'sales revenue less the outsourced manufacturing costs of units sold and excludes all other costs' (see para 38, italics added). From an Activity Based Costing/Activity Based Management (ABC/ABM) perspective this is dangerous to proper financial control. A low value item, like a €10 toy, will produce very little contribution, but the activities of designing it, contracting with manufacturers to make it, shipping and holding it in inventory, processing orders and invoicing for it, will all generate costs (overheads) which are not set against the margin on the product. Para 63 refers to some of Jot's IT systems as 'not ideal and do not provide Jot's management team with all the data it requires'. This could refer to poor cost analysis.

The examiner may be setting an exam requirement involving on cost attribution and recalculation of product profitability. This has been a topic in several previous T4 exams.

PART C PRACTICE TOPCIMA CASES   22: Jot toys: some help from BPP   **447**

Paras 20-26 **Do you consider Jot to have good financial management?**

The rising sales and rising operating profit margins reflect good financial management. Considering the recession across Europe and USA in 2010 and 2011 (and due to deepen in 2012), the performance is very good.

The high dependence on loan finance is not surprising for a firm in the early stages of growth, but Jot has been in business for 14 years and may be at a point that it needs to raise additional equity.

Jot has an operating profit margin of 5.58% (para 20), yet pays overdraft interest at 12% (para 25) and uses this to finance its inventories for Quarters 3 and 4 and some of the next Quarter 1. So interest payment is in excess of 6% (12%/2 quarters) on inventory and trade receivables. The operating margins on its lower value products may come very close to being insufficient to pay for the costs of the finance used to support them.

Why might the current overdraft figures be misleading?

Jot has an overdraft of €960k at 31 December 2011. This will be the peak overdraft for the year. It should fall sharply over the months between the end of December and the date of the first exam on 28 February 2012.

Jot uses the overdraft to pay manufacturers, and research and development teams, to design and to manufacture products during the year. The manufacturers receive payment from the end of July. The majority of toys are sold in Quarter 4 to retailers and distributors but payment is not received for 60+ days (para 46). Therefore most of the cash from the toy sales will not be received until 2012.

What issues may Jot face in 2012 and after as it seeks to grow its business?

The refusal by its bank to lend further credit reflects the widespread caution amongst banks to lend to businesses due to banks having suffered severe reserve depletion in the global banking crisis that began in 2007.

In the short term this means that Jot has only €540k additional credit remaining above the amount it needed to support its 2011 operations. Jot's Statement of Financial Position (Appendix 2) shows that its overdraft rose €170k between 2010 and 2011 year ends, and its cash position fell €8k. It ended the year with a need for €178k extra cash.

The Statement of Cash Flows (Appendix 3) shows that Jot's operations generated €91k of cash but the purchase of non-current assets, at a cost of €269k, meant it needed to borrow extra finance. This seems to have been mainly replacement investment ie €269k of purchase, less €240k of depreciation, gives the €29k increase between 2010 and 2011 of non-current assets shown in the Statement of Financial Position.

However its 5 year plan (Appendix 5) shows that Jot intends to finance the development of 7 new products during 2012 to be launched in 2013, up from 6, to finance entry into a new country, and to increase its sales from €9,866k to €11,568k (17%). This may strain its capital base.

There is also a danger that Jot may find that some of its retailers do not pay what they owe. Consider the following December 2011 report from the UK's Association of Business Recovery Specialists (R3);

"Earlier this year, R3's Business Distress Index showed the retail sector was experiencing significantly higher signs of distress than any other sector, with this sector more likely than any other to be concerned about their debt levels (41%).

The figures showed that six in ten (58%) retailers were experiencing a decrease in profit which was 24% higher than the cross sector average. Close to half (48%) of retailers had suffered a fall in sales volume and a quarter of retailers said they were having cash flow difficulties – 9% more than the cross-sector average.

December's quarterly rent day will prove a key test for many retailers, as they could translate into potential insolvencies at the start of 2012."

BPP LEARNING MEDIA

Woolworths, a toy retailer, went broke in late 2008 and left suppliers unpaid. The examiner might inflict a similar blow on Jot in the unseen material for the 28 February exam. This would deplete Jot's cash position as well as demanding a writing down of its Current assets (Trade receivables) with a consequent reduction in the pre-tax profits.

How could its cash flow and working capital management be improved?

Cash flow and working capital management could be improved by:

Reduce the amount of inventory. This could mean ceasing to stock some low profit lines. More ambitiously, improve stock turnover by arranging with manufacturers to produce later and supply directly to the retailers.

- Improve use of supplier credit.
- Reduce the credit taken by clients.
- Find products to make and sell in the first three quarters of the year. Jot seems to be locked into the Christmas cycle, whereas some types of electronic toys, such as new video game programs, are successfully released and sold mid-year.

Para 27   What is the significance of this information on share ownership?

There are four stand-out points from this paragraph:

- Jot is a private and unquoted company. This restricts its access to capital because it cannot at present sell shares to third parties due to the lack of a ready market.

- There is a delicate balance amongst the shareholders. Jon and Tani Grun, a married couple, together control the company with 60% of the equity. But if they opposed each other on some point of policy then either would need an alliance with 2 or more other shareholders to gain control. This has been an element in past real TOPCIMA exams and this same examiner once set unseen material in which a married couple with a similar shareholding position entered divorce proceedings.

- The shareholders have not received any dividend in up to 14 years since obtaining shares in Jot. But paying dividends would reduce Jot's ability to reinvest cash into its growth. Even so some shareholders may be getting impatient for dividends and may try to force the issue.

- Jot has authorised capital of 160,000 shares greater then its issued capital. This is not unusual in a firm. But it does mean that Jot could allot additional shares to another director or an incoming investor without going through a complex legal process to increase its authorised capital.

Should Jot seek to raise venture capital?

Jot will need to raise additional capital to carry out its 5 year plan (Appendix 5). This plan intends that revenues and unit sales approximately double in 5 years, and that Jot expands its operations to a further 14 countries. We are later told that these will be Russia and some Asian countries (para 68).

The operating profits of Jot are also set to more than double in 5 years. This would help to make Jot an attractive investment for venture capitalists.

However taking on venture capital would raise several issues for Jot:

- Loss of control. At present Mr and Mrs Grun control the firm they created. Venture capitalists would wish to have a considerable say in the running of Jot. They would probably expect to have 30%-50% of the equity and would also require that legal agreements be signed that bind Jot to certain financial targets, consultation processes and even a date for it to be sold or quoted on a market.

- Non-shareholders need to be considered. Appendix 1 states that 2 Directors are not shareholders. If Jot issues shares to venture capitalists, and if it is believed that in 5 years time all shareholders will get a significant sum for their shares when the company is sold, then these 2 Directors will become unsettled and envious. This issue has been a feature in previous TOPCIMA pre-seens.

- Some directors may not agree with Jot being partly-managed by external investors. Appendix 1 shows that Jon Grun and Michael Werner both seem to prefer smaller firms and a sense of ownership.

- Is the 5 year plan realistic? A venture capitalist will base its investment on the figures in the plan. It will expect the targets to be hit, and will agitate for change if they are not. There may be ratchets on its equity stake that will operate if the targets are not hit in order to give it a bigger share of the earnings and ownership if the firm under-performs. Before selling away their firm the directors need to be sure the plan is realistic.

Taking on venture capital is a big strategic step. Your role is as a management accountant. It is unlikely in the real world, and in the exam, that you would be asked to arrange this. However in the exam you could be asked to comment on the adequacy of the share price being offered by the venture capitalist, and/or to explain to management the consequences of having venture capital.

Para 28-33 How important is Jot's new product development process to its financial performance?

Para 29 states that Jot's products are 'innovative and at the 'cutting edge' of new technology'. This is underlined later by the statement that 'the Jot brand is synonymous with quality electronic toys' (para 59). The importance placed on new product development (NPD) by Jot to achieve its growth plans is justified by the statement 'the current trend in toy sales is towards electronic toys and computer assisted learning'(para 3).

NPD is the source of Jot's competitive advantage. It is in a market with a product life cycle that is pushed along by the tidal wave of Web 2.0 technologies. It has to invest to stay current. Getting ahead of the wave will help it to gain adoptions and lock in customers. This is in the same way Nintendo Wii did when it was the first games console to offer multidimensional player interaction via motion detection, or Apple did with its first i-Phone. Early adopters bought it, now have an investment in it and will not readily switch to X-Box Connect or Android phones.

This will give the following financial benefits:

- Enable entry into premium-priced segments of the market where early adopters want the latest, and best, toys

- Enable Jot to register IPR's that will protect the products against copying, thus increasing sales volumes and prices against copy-cat rivals

Extend the lifecycle of legacy products by freshening them up with new features and interactivity

- Offset buyer power because retailers will not seriously jeopardise their sales by resisting the price and not stocking this year's 'must have' toy

- Gain a bridgehead in a market by selling the hand console, with new features (eg like Nintendo 3DS) and then capitalising on this for many years by selling the games and software to run on it

- Gain repeat purchases from existing and loyal customers with legacy handsets who want to have the new ones.

It should be noted that in 2011 Jot spent €1.2m on NPD, which is 12% (€1,200k/€9,866k) of its revenues. This means that it could become a target for cost cutting and cash conservation. You need to be prepared to evaluate such measures numerically but also to make reference to the potential importance of NPD in maintaining Jot's earnings and market position.

Is it a flexible and efficient process?

One puzzle in this pre-seen is what the NPD team does between December and May. Para 31 tells us its work for the 2012 range is complete before January, and para 30 tells us that NPD work begins in May. That does not seem very efficient. Presumably the examiner intends this to mean that the team develops new products in the light of the acceptance of the previous new products for which the big orders arrive from May each year (para 49).

This means that NPD takes 8 months to complete, and is driven by the buying cycle of the toy industry. It doesn't seem to require continuous or quicker NPD because it believes the buying decisions are made each January to March (para 8).

However Nintendo does not rely solely on Christmas sales. Here is how it harnessed its NPD (and pricing) to smooth its cash flows from Nintendo 3DS during 2011:

'The Nintendo 3DS was released in Japan on February 26, 2011; in Europe on March 25, 2011; in North America on March 27, 2011; and in Australia on March 31, 2011. On July 28, 2011, Nintendo announced a major price drop starting August 12. In addition, consumers who bought the system at its original price gained access to ten free Nintendo Entertainment System games starting September 1, 2011 and 10 free Game Boy Advance games starting December 16, 2011, from the Nintendo eShop.' (*source Wikipedia*)

In a previous T4 case involving fast fashion this examiner described the transformation to the apparel industry in the real world brought by the decisions of retailers, notably Zara, to move away from the practice of 4 set seasons of clothes each year, and to move to one of rapid and continual innovation. This increased the number of annual visits made by customers from 6 per year to 17 per year, and hence improved total sales revenues of both retailers and manufacturers. You may like to suggest similar thinking to Jot.

Continuous and smart NPD would require some changes to Jot's present process.

One worrying aspect of the present process at Jot is that manufacturing considerations don't seem to come into play until the second stage of the process. This might affect the ultimate costs of production of the products. However the pre-seen clearly implies that the design team of Jot do have a very good idea, during this phase, of what something may cost to make (para 39) so perhaps the examiner is not intending to make this an issue in the exam.

How are prototypes made?

Making prototypes is a specialist process which, like many small firms in the toy industry, Jot outsources. Real world firms that provide this service include First Cut (www.firstcut.eu) and JH May (www.jhmay.com).

Jot has its own CAD/CAM systems (paras 32 and 67) on which toys are designed in 3D. Most CAD/CAM systems output exploded diagrams of parts, design drawings and, most importantly, data streams to instruct 3D laser equipment how to cut the toy components (or the moulds to make them) out of solid materials. The CAD/CAM systems can also subject the on-screen designs to virtual stress testing such as dropping, squashing and throwing to assess the point at which something shatters. Some CAD/CAM applications have protocols programmed in such as minimum component sizes to avoid creating toys with choke hazards.

CAD/CAM systems are intelligent systems. They will suggest ideas to the designer where simplifications to the design, such as removal of a fiddly part or to use the same component in 2 places rather than having 2 marginally different components doing the same job, could make the final product easier and cheaper to make and perhaps also simplify the stocking of replacement parts.

Jot will provide electronic files of its design to its prototyping firm to be made into 3D models and eventually into working prototypes.

How are the prototypes used?

The early prototypes will be tested initially for functionality in a laboratory. This will check how robust it is, whether it works, battery life and so on. Later prototypes will be shown to target customers, children and their parents, in focus groups to evaluate responses and to help the team understand how the toy might be used and what promotional messages might sell it.

Beta version prototypes, ie penultimate versions, will be shown at trade fairs to retailers and their feedback sought. Generally the public will be invited to a special day at each fair to get large scale last minute opinions.

Following this the final versions of the product are designed, along with packaging and accessories, ready for Jot to put out to tender in May.

Is the process clearly focused on generating financial benefits?

Assuming the above comments are correct, and cost considerations are kept in mind throughout, this process seems aimed at creating products that yield a good financial return. This is borne out by the growth record of Jot's earnings in para 19.

One favourable aspect of the process is the emphasis given to market research on prototypes. This ensures the final toy has some potential to gain market acceptance and that will lead to higher sales volumes and better margins.

Are the toys safe?

Jot uses the same firm to prototype as it does to test. This is also a practice in the real world. Firms like My Toy Testing (www.mytoytesting.com) offer this service.

The regulations around toy testing are returned to in paras 72-75 of the pre-seen. It concludes with the statement 'Jot cannot delegate this responsibility' (para 75). This seems to imply that examiner anticipates making an unsafe toy an issue in one of the exams.

Paras 34-35 ### How critical is Michael Werner to Jot?

Michael Werner seems to be one of the most critical members of the Jot team. His job is to ensure the right products are available, at the right cost, in the right places, at the right time. But para 27 shows he has only 10% of the shares in Jot.

Why does Jot have QA staff in Asia?

The most likely explanation is that these staff are actually based in China and visit the factories of the 20 outsourced manufacturers (para 36).

Alternatively they may be inspecting product going to Asian markets which may have different specification from European and USA products. But this seems unlikely due to the currently low volumes sold in Asia (para 43).

Paras 36-38 ### What comments can you make about the way Jot single-sources its toys?

Jot asks 'a small range' of its 20 outsource suppliers to quote and then places the entire order with one of them. This raises several issues:

- By single-sourcing it becomes dependant on one manufacturer for all its stocks of a toy. This makes it vulnerable to production problems at the factory, and also it lacks flexibility. We know that demand for toys is uncertain. If Jot underestimates demand it will depend on its sole manufacturer having spare capacity in order to increase availability. If it had multi-sourced it would have a better chance of squeezing out extra output;

- Single-sourcing may enable it to obtain lower prices due to giving one factory the entire production run;
- Single-sourcing may reduce logistics costs because it will allow bulk shipping of the toy from one single location;
- Single sourcing reduces the costs of quality assurance inspections, order and payment processing and so on.

Are there any issues for Jot's protection of its IPR's?

China has a poor reputation for protecting IPR's and is well known as the source of 'bootleg' toys. This is often accomplished by advertising toys on portals such as www.made-in-china.com which has thousands of toys listed. By sourcing from China Jot exposes itself to copying.

The practice of asking several suppliers to quote also has the disadvantage that the designs of the toy have been given to manufacturers who ultimately will not make it. The manufacturers would be in a position to share the designs with other toy firms. This could lead to clone and bootleg products.

Protecting IPR's is expensive and Jot is a small firm. Given the short selling season, and the huge number of national markets, any infringement of IPR's would not lead to effective outlawing of sales of the bootleg product before the season was long-past. This leaves Jot with the expensive process of trying to reclaim damages by assessing the revenues it may have lost due to the bootleg version being available.

Why does Jot use the same suppliers year after year?

There are probably 4 reasons for this:

- Habit: parts of the pre-seen suggest that the management of Jot feels it has been successful and doesn't want to change a winning business model. Setting up new supply arrangements will be costly and time consuming and would seem to be unnecessary.

- Predictability: para 39 tells us that Jot knows the prices of components and manufacturing when designing toys. It knows these from its previous dealings with the manufacturers. Also it will have sifted-out poorly performing manufacturers over the years and now probably has confidence in the 20 it uses.

- Transaction costs: the systems of Jot are linked to the systems of the manufacturers (paras 34 and 67) as probably also are the systems of its logistics partner (para 65). Adding additional suppliers will mean a cost of extending these systems to them. We are told that Jot's systems are not up to date (para 63). Other transaction costs would include the costs of conducting quality assurance visits and, depending on Jot's future policies on Corporate Social Responsibility (CSR) referred to in para 72, the costs of ethical compliance audits too.

- Security: by placing regular orders with each supplier Jot may obtain more security over its IPR's. A supplier that is given designs but then no orders may see no drawbacks in pirating the design. But a manufacturer that has regular orders from Jot may be unlikely to risk future work by infringing IPR's.

How could e-procurement help Jot?

Jot could consider using an online exchange (or trading hub) to obtain tenders from a wider range of manufacturers. This portal could allow the download of designs and specifications, and the upload of tenders.

This could be a portal set up by Jot itself. But this would be expensive, need maintenance and require marketing to ensure manufacturers know it exists.

There are two types of online exchange, available to Jot:

- Request for quotation - an invitation to suppliers to provide a quote for a specific Jot product. These exchanges are run by consortiums of toys and other plastic good design firms, or by third parties;

- Request for bid - an invitation from manufacturers to buyers like Jot to bid for a specific product or production capacity that they can provide;

Exchanges like Commport (www.commport.com) also offer transaction services such as ordering, invoicing and payment.

The difficulties with e-procurement are the assurance of quality and reliability of supply. Safeguarding these can impose additional costs of assurance on Jot that it does not presently pay for using its established providers.

Para 39 **What significance can be attached to the prices being close together?**

This may mean any of the following:

- Prices are similar because the manufacturers simply assemble bought-in components, which are a set price, and they have roughly similar labour costs and margins.

- Prices are similar because the manufacturers also know the 'going rates' that Jot is accustomed to paying from the prices they receive from Jot for other toys.

- The manufacturers are in collusion to fix the tenders and they share the work between them.

Does Jot change manufacturers often?

We are told that it has 20 suppliers and often asks the same ones to tender each year (para 37).

Jot produces 5 or 6 new lines of toy each year. It also has legacy toys that it places repeat orders for.

It would seem that Jot will have little incentive to change suppliers of the legacy toys because prices are usually quite close and the established manufacturer should have demonstrated ability under the other purchasing mix criteria: adequate quality, volume and meeting of timescale (para 38).

This might lead to Jot paying too much for the manufacture of legacy toys.

Para 40 **Why are components subject to price fluctuations?**

'Fluctuations' suggest the movements of component prices are both up *and* down. The most likely explanation for this is foreign exchange movements.

What are the potential implications of these fluctuations for Jot?

The implications for Jot are:

- Possibly very little. The outsourced manufacturer has quoted a firm price and it will bear the risk if component prices change unexpectedly this year.

- Jot needs to hedge its foreign exchange exposure to avoid depreciation in the Euro, making toys produced outside Europe more expensive and denting its operating margins.

- Jot may find that it produces products at a loss during 2012 if these fluctuations on component prices increase finished toy costs considerably.

- It calls into question whether the design team accurately knows the cost of making a toy during the design stage (para 39) and therefore whether it can be sure it will make the margins it anticipates.

What benefits might Jot get from having direct agreements with component suppliers?

The main benefits would be:

- It could protect its IPR's better in respect of ASIC components because it would control which firm had access to its designs;

- It could multi-source its purchases of toys because it would be able to allow more suppliers to have access to the same components. This could achieve lower prices for manufacture of the final toy, and would also allow it to spread work to increase flexibility in times of unexpected high demand;

- It might be able to stop bootlegging of its toys by ensuring that the ASICs are strictly controlled and don't fall into the hands of manufacturers that are willing to infringe its IPR's, in the same way as the Coca Cola Company controls its licensees by not giving them the secret recipe to its syrup.

What drawbacks might Jot suffer if it decided to source components directly and pass them on to manufacturers?

The main drawback might be a higher unit cost of component because, as the pre-seen says, its outsource manufacturers gain economies of scale that Jot would not get because they source for more than one set of toys.

A second drawback would be that a manufacturer could argue that defects in the toys were the responsibility of Jot because it provided poor components.

This step would also involve Jot in the extra transactions costs of identifying, contracting with, and conducting exchange with even more suppliers.

Para 41 **How might this paragraph affect the May exam?**

This paragraph hints at supplier selection being an issue in the May exam. It could also be in the March exam on 28 February.

It might also be an opportunity for the examiner to set issues involving:

- Deciding whether a product is still profitable to sell;
- Creating a cash flow forecast until end of year or even until end of Quarter 1 2012.

What significance may be given to the statement that Jot's warehouses are leased.

This could convey that:

- Jot cannot borrow against them to raise capital, say by mortgage or debenture.

- Some of Jot's administrative expenses are its lease payments which would disappear if it outsourced warehousing (but instead it would incur contract payments to its outsourced warehousing partner).

- Jot could outsource warehousing without having to sell industrial buildings which makes outsourcing more feasible providing a break clause in the leases is forthcoming.

Para 42 **What benefits might Jot enjoy from having some manufacturers near-shore?**

This paragraph looks like a hint for the exam, possibly the May exam because para 41 says suppliers are selected in May.

The benefits of having a European manufacturer would be:

- More ready and swift replenishment of inventories. Para 41 describes manufacturers starting making toys for Jot in early June and continuing to early November. This seems to indicate a 6 week minimum supply time (early November to mid December after which the Christmas sales boom would tail off). This is probably due to the long time needed to get inventory from China. A manufacturer in Europe could supply in a couple of weeks, rather than a couple of months. This would help avoid lost sales;

- Better working capital management. There would be a shorter working capital cycle, due to faster delivery, and the potential to reduce over-ordering because Jot could relay on swift replenishment from Europe. This would reduce demand for, and the cost of, working capital;

- Reduced exchange rate risk. Para 43 shows that the majority of Jot's sales take place in Europe, and that the largest amount of these is with Eurozone countries. If Jot contracted with a manufacturer in the Eurozone it would offset some of its foreign exchange exposure by receiving revenues and paying costs in the same currency.

- Better Corporate Social Responsibility. Manufacturers in Europe will be bound by the laws on health and safety, minimum wages, and non-discrimination. They will also have to abide by laws and expectations on environmental emissions and other 'green' issues.

What drawbacks might Jot suffer from having some manufacturers near-shore?

The drawbacks of having a European manufacturer would be:

- Probably higher unit costs that will put Jot at a competitive disadvantage against the 86% of toys made in China (para 1);

- Possible need to embrace multi-sourcing, which could increase transaction costs and reduce cost savings from economies of scale. Presently Jot gives one manufacturer the entire responsibility for a given range (para 38). Using European near-shore manufacture for replenishment stocks would involve Jot in having 2, or more, suppliers of the same toy. Otherwise Jot would need to designate a near-shore manufacturer for particular product ranges, and leave the other ranges in China.

Paras 43-45 Calculate the percentage of total sales revenue from Jot's top four regional markets

- Europe Eurozone: 39.7% (€3,920k/€9,866k)
- Europe Non-Eurozone: 29.0% (€2,865k/€9,866k)
- USA: 23.1% (€2,280k/€9,866k)
- South America: 3.7% (€366k/€9,866k)

Why has the examiner presented this data as a pie chart rather than a table?

One reason may be because it is more visual and makes clear the importance of Jot's two key markets and the massive importance of Europe, taken as a whole. This chart is provided immediately after the discussion of near-shoring to Europe. It shows that Europe as a whole provides 68.7% of Jot's total sales revenue. This enhances the case for near-shoring to Europe.

In the September and November 2011 exams the examiner required candidates to provide data as a line graph. A pie chart would be easier to draw in Excel, which suggests that it might be required in the March 2012 exam (on 28 February) because all candidates then will be taking exams on a PC.

Note Appendix 5 provides two line graphs using the data from the table in the same Appendix. Again this may be a hint. Note that in the May exam some candidates will be sitting conventionally. But all should have rulers with them and should be able to draw line graphs like these from data they have calculated,

Which client groups will give Jot the highest margins?

If this is important in the exam the examiner will give precise data in the unseen material. However we shall see that Client Profitability Analysis seems to be a theme in this pre-seen, and this is the first time we have encountered it.

It's impossible to say which clients will return the better margins:

- Large retailers (para 49 mentions 7 in particular) will probably use bargaining power to push prices down and demand longer to pay. But also they may be cheaper to supply because they will order in bulk, allow direct supply from the outsourced manufacturer (para 45), require a small number of delivery drops, and involve less transaction costs of order handling, invoicing and credit control.
- Other retailers are smaller and may provide a better price but will have higher transaction costs.
- Distributors will pay low prices. This is because they will wish to place a mark-up on the toys before they supply them to the small retailer, and the small retailer will need a mark-up too. This will put pressure on Jot. They are likely to be expensive to supply due to uncertain order volumes and high transaction costs that need to be recovered from relatively small volumes of sales, compared to the sales to large retailers.

Note that Jot monitors in particular gross margin, defined as revenue less price paid to manufacturer (para 38 and Appendix 5). The transaction costs of selling to the different segments of client would not be deducted before calculation of gross margin. It could lead Jot to supply some clients at prices, and in quantities, that are actually loss-making.

A more sensitive cost analysis, using activity based drivers, might reveal more information.

How might e-commerce help Jot serve some of these client segments?

e-commerce could reduce the costs of servicing small client accounts and potentially allow Jot to sell direct to some, rather than sacrifice margin by giving a cut to the distributors.

Jot could create a web site, or portal, that would allow retailers to input orders directly, and to track their orders. If Jot provided this via an outsource party then it could also include payments systems and automated documentation.

Para 46 ### How good is credit control at Jot?

This paragraph states that invoices are produced automatically based on information transferred from the inventory control system to the sales ledger. Yet para 64 tells us that the sales ledger system 'does not accept data directly from any of Jot's other systems'. This suggests that the sales ledger relies on manual entry of the details from the despatch notices issued by its warehouses.

The first problem for credit control is the delay in issuing invoices which will not be immediate. This could add a few days to the working capital cycle at peak times.

Another point to note is that it's not clear how it enters deliveries made direct to retailers from outsourced manufacturers (para 45) as these might not be entered in the inventory system.

There will also be inaccuracy and cost generated by having to enter despatches manually into the sales ledger.

Credit controls over some larger retailers are poor and poor payers are not chased aggressively. They do not pay until 'at least' 60 days after invoice date. This implies that some may take even longer to pay than 60 days.

How could credit control at Jot be improved?

There are various techniques that could be employed:

- More proactive chasing of invoices that are overdue
- Scaled retrospective discounts for on-time payment which are removed if the payment is late
- Denial of further supply to clients with overdue accounts
- Selling of trade receivables to a debt factor to allow them to collect and for Jot to receive money sooner from the factor

Paras 47-48 **What is the significant of this statement about seasonal sales?**

This is repetition of a point made earlier (paras 4 and 26). This means it is probably something very important to understand for your exam. See debrief to para 4 above.

Paras 49-50 **What significance is there in Jot having customers of different sizes?**

Jot has 'around 350 customers in total' of whom 7 account for 68% of its sales revenues. The remaining 32% of revenues is generated by 343 customers. Note that these include distributors who will be supplying several shops, so the number of shops that stock Jot toys will be greater than 350.

If we consider the gross profits for 2011 were €3,147k (Appendix 2) we can say that the average gross profit generated by each of the large clients was €306k (€3,147k x 68% /7), and the average gross profit from each of the remaining 343 customers was €2.9k (€3,147k x 32% /343).

These are average figures. It may be that the largest of the 7 big customers, say Toys R' Us, or Amazon buys twice as much as the smallest of the big customers, say Tesco, and there will be substantial variations between the sales revenues and profits from the 343 smaller customers.

But even these average figures allow us to make the following points:

- The loss of a single large retailer would potentially put Jot on the edge of making losses. In 2011 the operating profit of Jot was €551k so the loss of gross profit of say €306k from one large retailer during 2011 would have dented the operating profits by taking them down to €245k. Finance costs are fixed so the profit before tax would have fallen to €45k, (€245k + €13k - €213k) compared to €351k, a decline of 87% (1- €45k/€351k). *Please note this calculation assumes that administrative expenses would not decline as sales fell which may not be the case if Jot responded effectively to the loss of the large client.*

- Jot may have unprofitable customers. The above calculations allocate gross profits between customers pro-rata to turnover. But in fact Jot may find that its 7 clients generate 68% of turnover but, say, 80% of operating profits. In other words, some of the smaller customers are unprofitable due to the high costs of servicing them. As discussed under para 43-45, it's very possible that a number of the unprofitable customers are distributors rather than retailers.

How would Customer Profitability Analysis help Jot to improve its financial performance?

A limitation of the data we have is that we cannot see what makes up distribution costs and administrative expenses which, in 2011, totalled €2,596k (€552k + €2,044k), equivalent to 83% of gross profits (€2,596k/€3,147k).

Costs may differ widely between clients. For example:

- The need to operate warehouses may be due to the need to hold stocks to service smaller customers which order in small quantities, whilst the large retailers are able to receive bulk shipments direct from the outsourced manufacturer;

- The finance costs of €213k may be partly generated by the need to hold inventory to serve the unpredictable demands from smaller customers (note the 'key customers' place orders in May or June and sometimes earlier – para 49);

- The distribution expenses may be high because of the costs of despatching relatively small volumes of toys to small customers;

- The administrative expenses could be inflated by the costs of order handling, creation of packing notes, invoices and so on, for small volume orders. The time and persons needed to do these processes for an order will be the same whether it is for 10 toys or 100,000 toys.

This statements above about likely differences in profitability between large and small clients is pure speculation. It could be the large clients that are unprofitable. If it is important to the exam then data will be given in the unseen material on exam day.

However this does point to the need for Customer Profitability Analysis (CPA). The benefits would be:

- It would enable Jot to identify its most profitable customers and ensure that it retains them;

- It would help identify the reasons for the poor profitability of the remainder. This could point to ways to engineer processes to give better profits, such as electronic ordering or minimum order quantities;

- It would identify customers who are unprofitable. This could lead to the prices they are charged being increased to a level where they either become profitable or cease to buy from Jot.

How could Jot carry out CPA?

Strictly speaking CPA requires a full Activity Based Costing/Management (ABC/M) analysis to be carried out. This would involve a management accountant implementing the following process:

- Obtaining management support and resources (eg time from regular duties, temporary staff, consultancy advice) to carry out the analysis;

- Create cost pools by establishing what the key processes at Jot are (eg sales ordering, order entry, tender processing, product research and testing and so on);

- Assign costs to the pools by re-analysing cost codes into their constituent parts, for example taking 'administration wages', asking what percentage of administration time falls into each of the cost pools and then assigning the 'administration wages' pro rata to the pools. These are usually the overhead costs.

- Identify an appropriate driver for each pool. This will be an activity which has a strong relationship to the conduct of the things in the pool, for example number of new products, number of sales visits, number of orders for the cost pools of research and development, sales costs, and order processing respectively.

- Assess how much each customer generates the activities, and therefore the total overheads, that serving them has generated in a year.

- Compare the overhead attributable to them with the gross margin attributable to sales to the customer over the year. This will reveal their Customer Account Profitability.

The examiner may set a requirement asking you to explain this process and its benefits. You might wish to make the following points:

- Jot probably lacks the data history on clients to enable a tracking of the activities generated by each client.

- To do this Jot would need a Customer Relationship Management system (CRM) to track interactions, which it does not have at present (paras 64-67). It would be costly to implement and would absorb its scarce capital.

- Conducting a fresh analysis will take a year because activities and orders run on a one year cycle due to Jot having a seasonal business – ie sales activities in January to March, tenders in May, order placing in June to October and so on. It would also be an expensive use of time.

- As a small firm it would be prohibitively expensive to calculate a CPA for each of its 350+ customers. It should focus on the top 7 and then sample the top, middle, and bottom of the remaining 343, ranked by sales volume.

- Jot could make some immediate headway by asking relevant staff to give their opinions of the customers who they process most orders from, get more calls and queries from, or who need most chasing to pay. A simple technique for small firms is to assign, by impression, the letters A to D to clients for 'value' and numbers 1 to 4 for 'amount of time and trouble dealing with them'. Then focus on the high value customers (A1's), consider losing the worst ones (D4's) and then re-engineer the remainder to take them to A1 by taking steps to increase their value and/or to reduce the trouble and time in dealing with them. The A-D ratings could be based on 2011 sales data.

The benefits of CPA would be:

- Better identification of which clients to focus on and which to value engineer

- Clearer understanding of what drives costs. Many ABC/M investigations lead to immediate improvements to business processes once the true costs of present activities becomes clear to management

- Will act as a catalyst for change in how customers are managed

- Will help develop marketing strategy for the future by focusing Jot on developing products and marketing activities that attract profitable customers rather than just sales revenues and volumes

Why are we told about the time when orders are placed and when repeat orders may be submitted?

This seems to underline the problem Jot has in forecasting its sales volumes. In May/June it does not know the final figure for the volumes of each toy that will be ordered between then and the end of October. This forces it into a choice, spelled out in para 51, between

- Ordering generously to get lower unit cost. However this also absorbs working capital and it risks having unsold inventory at year end which will be sold at a deep discount (para 56).

- Ordering conservatively but risking higher unit costs for small repeat orders and/or lost sales due to stock-outs

Para 51   **At what point in the year does Jot get the first idea of how popular its ranges are going to be in 2012?**

This is a very hard paragraph to interpret.

Early in the year would normally imply some time in the first Quarter, perhaps immediately following the trade fairs. But it refers to large customers placing orders early in the year, which seems to contradict the statement in para 49 that they place their orders in May or June 'or sometimes earlier'.

The best interpretation would be that:

- Trade fairs predominantly get sales orders from small customers. This does suggest that Jot might attribute the costs of attendance at trade fairs to the CPA of smaller customers, but not larger ones who would be visited by Jot or invited to special showings.

- By March (or indeed the exam date of 28 February) Jot will have a fair idea of which products are Stars and which are Dogs in its portfolio.

However it is very hard to make sense of the statement that early in the year Jot has a 'reasonable degree of certainty' about its future sales and so could place orders with outsource manufacturers. If this is the case why does paras 41 and 49 refer to May and June?

This seems to be a device by the examiner to allow the March exam (on 28 February), as well as the May exam, to contain issues requiring you to advise on supplier selection or carry out financial forecasting for the year.

Paras 52 - 54 How might the examiner set a requirement involving licensed toys?

These paragraphs seem to have been written to enable the examiner to set a requirement for you to evaluate an offer to Jot of a license to make toys based on a new film or TV series.

This financial calculation could require

- Calculation of profit from the license. This would involve consideration of revenues, costs and license fees. It is noticeable that the license is 'for each unit produced' rather than being based on gross revenue or net revenue. Recall para 18 and the discussion of 'mark-up' and 'margin';

- Cash flow forecast for the product. The examiner could provide a cash flow forecast for 2012 and ask you to adjust it for the inclusion of the new licensed product;

- Net present value of the proposal. This is less likely because sales of toys based on films get the majority of their income within a few months of the release of the film (and then the DVD) and then tail off. NPV tends to be reserved for projects with several years of earnings. There is no cost of capital in the pre-seen so if the examiner provides a cost of capital in the exam it would imply that an NPV is required.

In any assessment of buying a license the following points should be stressed:

- Very high uncertainty around whether the film will be a success. In 2011 the DC Comics-based film 'The Green Lantern' was judged the 5th worst box office flop (comparing cost of making the film with first month sales revenue from viewings). Bad timing, bad reviews, and bad direction will quickly leave Jot with unsold toys that will never be wanted, yet they have paid a per-unit fee to make the toys they now have to destroy;

- Follow on value. If a film is a success then there will be a sequel and that can generate new demands for the toys. Consider Star Wars, Toy Story, Shrek, Mission Impossible and so on. TV series will have many seasons of new programmes if they are good, for example Dr Who, The Simpsons and so on. Others can be re-launched later, for example Sesame Street/The Muppet Show, or have spin off's, such as Puss In Boots from Shrek;

- New marketing channels. Many of the licensed toys become give aways with children's meals. Could Jot consider supplying a huge a fast food chain as a new type of customer?

- Need to ensure exclusivity. Jot does not seem to have truly global coverage (paras 43 and 68). Therefore it would not be wise for it to tender for the global rights to a license. This means that whilst it may have sole rights for Europe or USA, there is a danger that another license holder might import products into those markets to rival them. Also there should be clarity on where the license applies. For example, Jot may be happy for another firm to have a license to make clothing based on the same film, but not one to make computer software.

How important is Anna Veld to Jot?

Anna is one of the most recent recruits to the Board of Jot (she and Sonja Rosik were both appointed in 2009 – para 79) and seems to have built up the licensed toy business up to 10% in less than 2 years. Because they are short life cycle products, there will always be a need for new licenses to replace the ones that have gone past peak earnings.

It is worrying, and a weakness of Jot, that Anna holds no shares (para 82). This means she may not benefit financially from the eventual success of Jot. In past exams the examiner has used lack of share ownership as a pretext to set unseen material in which the Director has left for a better offer, or where the Director appears to be considering leaving.

Paras 55 **What does this paragraph add to our understanding of Jot's operations and position?**

This paragraph adds nothing new. It is purely repetition of points we have noted from earlier paragraphs.

This is very encouraging. It means the examiner wants us to understand this point. So it has been repeated for emphasis.

Paras 56-58 **What do these paragraphs covey about the product life cycle of Jot's products?**

Only 'a few products' are sold on a regular basis throughout the year'. This suggests that most of Jot's products have relatively short life cycles.

How significant is the inventory write down reserve for 2011?

The write down reserve is €0.124m. This is 18.6% (€124k/€124k+542k – Appendix 2 shows inventory already written down) of the original carrying cost of inventory at year end.

Other ways to look at this is to say that it is 1.8% of the total cost of sales for 2011 (€124k/€6,719k), or 1.3% of total sales revenue (€124k/€9,866k).

This appears to be a fairly modest overestimation of demand for the toys, given the uncertainties of the market.

But to put this into perspective, Jot's 2011 operating profit margin of 5.6% (Appendix 5) could have been 6.9% (5.6% + 1.3%) if this write down had been avoided.

Paras 59-62 **How important is Sonja Rosik to Jot's commercial success?**

Sonja Rosik has responsibility for three key areas that are important to Jot's success:

- Developing links with new target markets for Jot in Russia and Asian countries (para 68)
- Providing marketing literature crucial to getting sales (paras 8 and 61)
- Handling public relations (PR) such as getting press articles

She is described as having brought a 'wealth of new ideas and dynamism to Jot's marketing and helped to expand Jot's products to new geographical markets' (para 79)

The 5 year plan (Appendix 5) forecasts growing revenues and expansion into further countries.

Therefore Sonja Rosik may be crucial to the delivery of Jot's 5 year plan.

Can Jot rely on Sonja Rosik staying with the company?

Sonja joined in 2009, the same year as Anna Veld. Neither own shares and so have no stake in the success of Jot.

- She is also the youngest member of the Board and seems to be described as a person with energy and purpose. This may be the examiner's indication that Sonja may clash with the longer-serving Directors.

Paras 63-67 **What factors make Jot's IT systems 'not ideal'?**

These paragraphs suggest the following limitations to Jot's IT systems:

- They may be out of date because they are some years old – Jot was founded in 1998, at the time of the first e-commerce in Europe. The systems may use obsolete languages and applications that hinder integration with new applications and outside systems.

- They are not subject to on-going system development. The use of an external consultant means expertise was lacking in house and, despite intentions, no expert has been employed since (para 77). This again can explain lack of integration between systems.

- There is replication of data. This is worrying because some systems don't integrate. This means that a detail such as a customer record, inventory position, or unit price might be wrong on one system. A single database would be better.

- The systems don't integrate. The system uses 'despatch notes' which suggests some paper-based elements. They are possibly re-keyed into the finance system. This means manual transfer of data with inevitable inaccuracies, lags in updating data, in particular in the finance system, and inability to interrogate data because financial information is divorced from inventory and logistics information. This reduces the information available to make management decisions on product and customer profitability.

- Lack of integration makes supply chain improvement very difficult. 2012 approaches to Supply Chain Management (SCM) require end to end transparency of information to partners, information to be real time and up to date, and transfer of information to be electronic. The Jot system is a long way from this. This deficiency is remedied by having warehouses to hold stock, reliance on third party systems, and additional inventory to cope with orders as late as October.

However the CAD/CAM system seems to be better as it seems to be used to communicate with the manufacturer and tester of the prototypes (para 32) and also with the outsourced manufacturers (para 67).

How could Jot improve its IT systems?

The improvements needed would be very expensive and would need to smooth the supply chain and improve management information:

- A Customer Relationship Management System (CRM) to handle enquires, sales force management, receive orders and manage promotion. This could include a website of information with an ability for customers to order directly;

- A Supply Chain Management System to pass orders to manufacturers, including to the firms that provide them with components, packaging and so on, triggered by the receipt of an order. This would also provide invoicing to customers and orders to logistics partners. For items held in warehouses rather than delivered direct from factory to customer there would be a real time stock report that could be displayed via extranet to customers and through websites;

But the costs of these systems is far beyond the financial resources of Jot. Therefore it may wish to consider:

- Leasing space on systems operated by third parties. This so-called 'cloud' solution would be very attractive to a firm with high capacity utilisation in Quarters 1 and 2, but limited use in Quarters 3 and 4.

- Transfer responsibility for 'fulfilment' completely to a business partner to enable Jot to focus solely on toy design, marketing and customer management.

Paras 68-71 **What changes is Jot considering making to its supply chain arrangements to serve these target markets?**

Jot is considering using third parties to distribute its toys, and also to supply direct from factory to retailer.

This is presumably because Jot cannot afford to set up warehouse operations there, and that it lacks potential sales volumes to justify them.

Anticipate exam requirements asking you to evaluate alternative distributors, and to advise on what steps need to be taken to ensure appropriate Service Level Agreements (SLA's) are in place.

What lessons from its USA experience should Jot bear in mind before it expands into Russia or into Asian markets?

These are potentially enormous markets geographically and in terms of population size. The USA experience shows that they would need enormous stocks unless Jot can set up a supply chain that does not rely on stocks, in the same way that firms like Dell have.

Dell waits for orders to be placed and then has SCM systems and partnership arrangements to make the product within days. This requires that suppliers are situated near its markets. Dell originally supplied the whole of Europe from its plant in Limerick, Republic of Ireland before, in 2009, shifting production to a new plant at Lodz in Poland. Since 2010 Dell has sold many of its factories to other manufacturers, including the Polish factory, and has relied on contract manufacturing arrangements.

One clear issue from the USA experience is that for Jot to serve its large markets by stockpiling inventory will demand huge amounts of working capital that it does not have.

Why does the examiner refer to the 5 year plan here?

There are probably two reasons why the examiner has included it here:

- To remind candidates that delivery of the 5 year plan relies on Jot being successful in entering its target markets. Appendix 5 shows that it anticipates revenue and margin growth, and a significant increase in the number of countries in which it operates. This emphasises the importance of retaining Sonja and Anna.

- To emphasise the point that Jot is in severe danger of overtrading because it will not have sufficient capital to support the planned expansion. This means that it will have to get additional working capital and/or find ways to economise on its use of capital.

Paras 72-75

What might be contained in the CSR policies of a toy company?

Most of the discussion in these paragraphs seems to concern CSR as simply product safety. This is obviously very important. But real-world firm Hasbro has a much wider perspective. (www.csr.hasbro.com)

Hasbro firstly makes 'stakeholder engagement' central to the development and delivery of CSR. It listens to what communities, regulators, customers, suppliers and interest groups want to say and seeks to respond. It also expects its business partners to support its aims.

Hasbro makes clear that it expects its stakeholders to behave ethically. This means to be fair, honest, just, and truthful. It forbids bribes, bullying, misleading claims and so on.

Hasbro arranges CSR engagements under three headings:

Product Safety

This includes the makeup of the product, the materials used in it and its packaging, its safety in use. It also extends this into the role models being portrayed by some toys, and their encouragement of appropriate values. Children are impressionable and will take social cues from toys and games. Hence real-world concern over violent toys, dolls based on unfeasibly slender and predominantly fair-skinned girls (as pilloried by the Malibu Stacey motif in The Simpsons), and encouragement of sedentary lifestyles in front of games boxes leading to obesity (but not Wii Fit).

Manufacturing Ethics

This refers to the payment and treatment of staff at the firm and at its partners. It includes materials used and their impact on the health of the workforce. It may extend to issues such as the impact of the manufacturing plants on local communities, anti-discrimination in hiring and promotion decisions, and positive action to make a difference through provision of housing, education or contract to local businesses.

Environmental Sustainability

This is the lifecycle of the product from the origins of the materials used to make it and its packaging (oil in the case of plastics), through to the end of life of the product and its recycling and/or disposal. It focuses on carbon emissions (ie polluting gases from the energy used in production and transportation), the effect of degradation of the product (eg plastic is not usually biodegradable, and electronic circuits and batteries contain radioactive elements and poisons), the impact of its production and administrative facilities on the natural environment (harm to Greenfield areas, appearance, congestion and so on).

Be prepared to advise Jot on what may be included in its CSA policy.

How might the examiner base an exam day issue on product safety?

Past T4 examinations have featured the following issues around safety:

- Discovery of an unsafe product and the requirement to advise management what to do about it
- Decisions on launching a profitable new product but where there are some unresolved safety issues
- Advising on response to bad PR resulting from the firm selling a bad product
- Advising on defending or settling a legal case for product liability, often with expected values as the basis of a minor calculation.

Paras 76-83 — **Does Jot's product portfolio carry though Jon's 1998 assessment of the market opportunity?**

Para 3 also reinforces Jon Grun's judgement.

The product portfolio described in paras 16-17 seems to contain a lot of products that would not be classed as innovative and educational.

Is Tani Grun suffering work overload and what could be the impact of this?

This could lead to:

- A loss of financial control in Jot (eg over cash flow and/or debtor control)
- More delegation to you as a management accountant at Jot (ie more opportunities for the examiner to set high level questions for you to answer)
- Sudden disappearance of Tani Grun because of stress (ie a problem issue in the unseen material)
- Difficulties in implementing new IT solutions and/or weaknesses in Jot's existing systems

How do you assess the contribution made by Alana Lotz to the strategic position of Jot?

The description of Alana seems to suggest she has been an asset to Jot. However:

- She may be responsible for an extension of the range beyond the original market opportunity identified by Jon Grun.
- Her shareholding of 20% seems to have been given to her, possibly when Jot was founded and she joined. All subsequent director-shareholders are described as having bought their shares. This may suggest underlying tensions, with Alana being perceived by others, particularly Sonja and Anna, as being unfairly favoured by the Gruns.
- Her shareholding, and close friendship with Tani Grin, does potentially create a 50% block holding, voting in one direction if the Board fell into dispute.

What are the differences between Sales and Marketing as business functions?

In general terms sales is concerned with selling the product that the firm makes. The activities of Boris Hepp, Sales Manager of Jot, will include;

- Input into annual budgeting process through forecasting sales revenue and margins

- Management of field sales force team
- Liaison with customers
- Personal management of key accounts
- Input into preparation of promotional literature
- Input into organisation of Jot's appearance at trade fairs

Historically, Marketing has developed in many firms from Sales as a separate function. This seems to have happened at Jot in 2009. The tasks of a Marketing Director would be more strategic and be concerned with:

- Identification and evaluation of markets and potential new markets
- Evaluation and management of product portfolio
- Evaluation and management of client portfolio
- Input into new product development to ensure products meet needs of target customers
- Management of the Jot brand and promotional message
- Product pricing and distribution strategy

There are two features of the marketing role at Jot that may be problematic:

- Although a source of 'new ideas' Sonja Rosik does not seem to be involved in new product development (para 32);
- Sonja does not hold any shares. This may make her seem junior to Boris Hepp who has bought shares and who has 6 years more experience that Sonja;

Appendix 2 **How has Jot's gross margin changed between 2010 and 2011**

Jot's gross margin has fallen slightly, from 32.9% to 31.9% (2010: €2,756k/€8,371k, 2011 €3,147k/€9,866k).

This casts doubt on Jot's 5 year plan forecasts which forecasts rising gross margins.

Appendix 3 **Is Jot a cash generating business?**

The Statement of Cash Flows shows that Jot generated €91k cash from operating activities. This was eliminated by the €269k expenditure on non-current assets.

The answer to the question posed, on whether Jot is cash generating or not depends on what the expenditure on non-current assets comprised. The key point is whether it was a one-off in 2011, or whether it will happen again in 2012.

Non-current assets include buildings, plant and machinery, IT systems, vehicles and licenses, and capitalised development spending.

We are told that Jot does not own its warehouses but rather leases them (para 41). It also does not manufacture. Depreciation of €240k of non-current assets is 33.3% of their 2010 year end book value (€240k/€721k), which seems high. Possible explanations are:

- This includes writing down of license agreements
- This includes writing down of capitalised design expenditure

The €269k of expenditure on non-current assets during 2011 could include capitalisation of investment in design, or in the purchase of new licenses by Anna Veld.

If it is either of these then it may recur in 2012 because Jot will design 7 new toys during 2012 for sale in 2013 (Appendix 5) and new licenses too. This would mean Jot 's growth is cash negative.

However the €269k could have been a one-off expenditure on new non-current assets, in which case it may not recur during 2012. In this case Jot is possibly cash generative after all.

The pre-seen allows either interpretation. If it is important, the unseen will make it clear on exam day.

Appendix 4 **What is the value of this Appendix?**

This appendix seems merely to emphasise the point about seasonal sales.

Appendix 5 **What is the value of this Appendix?**

The key messages from this Appendix seem to be that:

- Jot has an aggressive growth strategy.

- Growth is to be accomplished by product development and market development (Ansoff).

- Despite higher forecast margins over the 5 years, the average price per toy will fall from €13.97 (€9.866k/706.3k). €13.71(€19,260k/1,405.0k). This does not suggest that Jot will be seeking premium priced markets.

You may be asked to construct a graph in the exam, for example using Excel if you are sitting the computer-based exam.

Solution to activity : SWOT Analysis

Strengths	Weaknesses
In-house design team producing an innovative product range at the cutting edge of new technology, Alana Lotz (Head of design) appears to be a key employee (para 29) Jot's organisation structure appears to be flexible (manufacturing and IT are outsourced) which will allow it to focus on its core business Jot is profitable company (Appendix 2) with a strong brand with a good reputation for quality (para 59)	Lack of access to funds to finance expansion (paras 20-26) Credit control (para 46) failing to achieve 30 day payment terms Some key staff have no shareholding (e.g. Anna Veld Licensing Director and Sonia Rosik Marketing Director) IT systems are not ideal and seem unlikely to be able to produce information needed to make management decisions on product and customer profitability (paras 63-67) Lack of formal CSR procedures (paras 72-75)
Opportunities	**Threats**
Trend towards toys & computer assisted learning (para 3) New markets in Asia and Russia (paras 68-71)	Risk of a decline in the value of the euro, causing the cost of purchasing from Chinese suppliers to rise (para 35) Buyer power - especially from its 7 large retail customers e.g. risk of cash flow issues due to late payment by major customers (para 49) Economic downturn affecting Christmas sales

2.1 Summary of Key Points from pre-seen information

A key skill in this exam is being able to extract the important information from the data you are given. Here are the key points from the Jot toys Pre-seen material:

The business environment of Jot

Jot is a small toy company in an industry which features a small number of large toy manufacturers, such as Hasbro and Mattel, and a relatively small number of very large retailers including Toys R'Us, Amazon, Tesco, Wal-Mart and so on. This said the real world industry does feature a very large number of small to medium sized manufacturers. The small firms survive by being good at innovation in toy development.

The market is very seasonal, with the majority of sales to households taking place at Christmas. This means that retailers and distributors require delivery of inventories from September to December each year. This is reflected in the pattern of Jot's quarterly sales figures in Appendix 4.

The market also requires a high level of product innovation due to the short life cycle of many toys. Although there are some toys and games that have relatively long life cycle, such as Lego, Barbie and so on, most become obsolete due to either their technological functionality becoming dated and/or the characters and films on which they are based become no longer popular with children.

These factors create the following business environment dynamics:

- **Strong seasonality** of cash flows as toy manufacturers build inventory for sales in the final 2 quarters of the year;

- **High investment in product research and development,** for example Jot spends 12% of its turnover and 38% of its gross profit on research and development each year (para 30);

- **High degrees of uncertainty about forecast sales** at the start of each year due to many firms depending on the success of its new product launches in January to March toy fairs;

- **Strong buyer power** exercised by large retailers and distributors which require toys firms to keep production costs low by outsourcing to China. This buyer power can be off-set only by finding alternative direct distribution methods, such as internet downloads of software, or by producing this year's 'must-have' toy that becomes a social craze in one or more countries. In the past these have included Tracy Island/Thunderbirds toys (Matchbox/Mattel) and Tamagotchi cyber pets (Bandai).

Themes in the Jot Pre-seen material

Management of working capital: Jot is cash negative during the second half of the year (para 26) and at the end of 2011 it held trade receivables (debtors) of €4,065k and inventory of €542k, a total of €4,607k of which €1,781k is financed by trade payables, leaving €2,826k to be financed by Jot. This is probably its peak borrowing, caused by the seasonality of the industry. It is financed in the main by a bank overdraft of €960k and bank loans of €1,600k. Jot plans to increase its sales in 2012 by 17% to €11,568k (1-€11,568k/€9,866k – Appendix 5) and so, this could lead to a 17% rise in its working capital needs, ie a further €480k (€2,826k x 17%). Jot also intends to develop 7 new products during 2012 for launch in 2013, rather than staying at the level of 6 new products as it developed during 2011 (Appendix 5) requiring extra investment of between €100k and €250k (para 30). This means Jot may require at least €580k more capital in 2012 than it used in 2011 (€480k + €100k).

But at the end of 2011 Jot had used up all its bank loans and all but €540k of its maximum overdraft. It will not have sufficient working capital to meet the goals in its 5 year plan. Jot needs to improve its working capital management, and get additional forms of finance, to help it meet its goals.

Order quantities: Jot appoints outsourced manufacturers by the end of May and manufacturing takes place between June and November (para 41). The costs of ordering too much inventory are tied up working capital and having to sell it below cost due to not having sold it all (paras 56-57). The potential costs of ordering too little at the start are higher unit price, re-order costs, and lost revenue from turning away sales. This is a trade off, and it is referred to several times in the Pre-seen material. This is likely to be a question in one of the real exams. The problem could be resolved by adopting just-in-time (or lean supply) approaches, and having near-shore manufacturers (para 42) would reduce supply lead times compared to relying on Chinese factories.

Supplier selection: Jot uses 20 outsourced manufacturers from China (para 36) and gives a single one of these the entire responsibility for producing any given toy (para 38 reads 'the outsourced manufacturer'). Some of these 20 manufacturers only make one product (para 36). This means that Jot is single-sourcing each product which may help it get lower prices due to the manufacturer passing on economies of scale. But it also means that its flexibility is reduced because it relies on the sole manufacturer of the toy having capacity to cope with late orders. Also the tenders do not achieve widely different prices (para 39) but they do cause costs of transactions to rise and Jot may not be aware of this. Jot bases its supplier selection decisions on achieving planned gross margin (para 38). Gross margin is sales price minus price paid to manufacturer. It ignores all the transactions costs of handling tenders, ordering and tracking, and account settlement. Having 20 suppliers, some making only one toy, but enjoying no significant price reductions as a result may be a non-value adding approach. Perhaps close partnerships with a few manufacturers would give better prices and less transactions costs. Suppliers are not evaluated on their Corporate Social Responsibility (CSR) status which may need to change given that Jot is bringing forward a CSR policy in 2012 (para 72).

Protecting IPR's: (without some special features to make them valuable and special toys are just lumps of plastic). These features include brand names, special images, connection with films or TV programmes, or special functionality. All these should be protected by Intellectual Property Rights (IPR's) and it is these that gives Jot its margins. Jot may also potentially be held responsible for the IPR's it buys-in as licences (paras 52-54) and the licensor may seek damages if Jot does not protect them. There are several potential weaknesses in Jot's IPR protections: it does not register IPR's until quite late in its design phase (para 32) and after it has given the plans to the prototype maker, and after the toy has been subject to market research; Chinese manufacturers have a poor record in respecting the IPR's of western firms; the components and ASIC's are sourced by the outsourced manufacturers (para 40); and Jot is too poor a company to afford legal action to protect its IPR's.

Unfocused product portfolio: Jot has a reputation for quality electronic toys (para 59) and was established to exploit a gap in the market for 'innovative, educational toys' (para 76) it is well-placed to ride the wave of the trend towards such toys in the market as a whole (para 3). Its present product portfolio seems to contain toys that are not especially differentiated (paras 16-17) and, presumably, this could account for the fact that their prices and the mark-ups available to retailers vary so widely (para 18). Jot may be incurring transactions costs in supplying toys that outweigh the revenues from selling them. With increasing numbers of toys being developed, and new countries to be entered (Appendix 5) Jot may need to assess the profitability of each toy and make decisions on which toys are truly valuable. This suggests that it should conduct Product Profitability Analysis (PPA).

Unfocused client portfolio: Jot has over 350 customers or whom the top 7 provide 68% of Jot's total sales revenue, or an average of €958.4k each (€9,866k x 68%/7) whilst the remaining 344+ customers provide an average revenue of €9.18k (€9,866k x 32%/344). But each client generates costs due to order-taking, account management and so on. It would seem that Jot may have unprofitable customers and should conduct Customer Profitability Analysis (CPA) to identify its key accounts and to find ways of engineering up the profitability of the low value accounts.

IT systems: Jots IT systems were set up 'some years ago' and are a little dated (para 63). There is no IT specialist in the management team (para 77), the systems are not integrated, and Jot relies on its logistics partner for key information. There is no mention of any e-commerce systems, such as catalogues, product information, or web pages for small retailers to place orders. There is no e-procurement system or Customer Relationship Management system (CRM). Because the financial systems do not take direct input from the other systems it means that end-to-end management of their supply chain will be difficult.

Real world toy firms like Habsbro have invested in Enterprise Resource Planning systems (ERP) to overcome this. Hasbro uses SAP Business One as part of its 2 tier ERP system to help it track customers and arrange fulfilment of orders (http://www.youtube.com/watch?v=BIOPwRJA-Yc) . However Jot is far too small and under-capitalised to afford to invest in an ERP solution of its own. This opens the possibility of outsourcing its information systems completely, or forming partnerships with suppliers who can offer this.

New sources of earnings: the Pre-seen states that Jot doesn't produce toys for the under-3's or the over 8's (para 13). The latter may be an attractive new market for leveraging Jot's expertise in electronic and learning toys. Firms like Nintendo have accessed these markets very effectively using the Nintendo DS handheld consoles, and these run software, such as brain training, that means they appeal to adults too. The software market is appealing to firms like Jot because it creates a tail of follow-on earnings to help it capitalise on its earlier sales of handsets. Also software can be downloaded directly from the manufacturer which is a low cost supply solution with no need to share margin with the retailers.

New countries: Jot 's 5 year plan shows it expanding from serving 22 countries in 2011 to serving 36 by 2016 (Appendix 5). The target markets are 'Russia and the Asian Markets'(para 68). The experience it had in USA suggests that entering such large markets will demand huge working capital. That is probably the reason why Jot is intending to enter the market by working with local partners (para 68). Jot will need to adapt products to local markets (languages, imagery and so on) and will increased risk due to exposure to new currencies and political/legal regimes.

Exam skills

Now you have worked through the detail of the case, take time to think what the most important information is from the data you have been given.

Make a summary of the key points from the Pre-seen material. Can you summarise the key points and issues facing Jot into a one-page business summary?

Also, make sure you undertake an overall strategic analysis of the pre-seen material. You should always prepare a SWOT analysis, and a stakeholder analysis as part of your preparation, but the material in this case suggests that issues such as new product development, supply chain management and customer profitability analysis could also be important, so you need to take account of these as well.

Remember it is vital you analyse all the different aspects of the information you are given in the case study scenario:

Analyse the numbers – Review any numerical and financial data (profitability, cashflow, working capital, liquidity, gearing, investment ratios)

Environmental analysis – PESTEL analysis; stakeholders (Mendelow's matrix); CSR issues?

Business environment and competitive strategy – Type of industry (product / industry life cycle); Five forces; generic strategies.

What do you know about key customers and suppliers? Customer profitability analysis? Supply chain management?

What do you know about the business' marketing strategy?

> Does your analysis of these aspects of the business identify any potential **opportunities** and **threats**?

Products and services – Product range, features, quality, demand; Product profitability. Product portfolio.

Value – How does the business add value? Value chain; distinctive competencies or capabilities? (Links to supply chain management?)

Information systems and processes – How is IT used in the business strategy; how does the business use e-commerce; what do you know about the business' IT systems? Does the IT set up present any business or security risks? Or does it present any opportunities (eg e-procurement)?

Management information and control systems – How are activities and resources controlled? What do you know about the management accounting or management information systems?

Performance measures – Have you identified the critical success factors and / or the key performance indicators? Could you produce a balanced scorecard?

Organisation – What is the organisational structure and culture; Who are the key personnel? Are there any personnel and HRM issues?

Investor objectives – What is the capital structure and what are the investor's objectives? What do you know about share price and the value of the business? What do you know about the business' capital? (shares; debt; cost of capital)

> Does your analysis of these aspects of the business identify any **strengths** and **weaknesses**?

Then also think about:

New developments – what new projects may the company be considering? New product development, acquisitions, divestments, new information systems, new organisation structure, new processes?

However, you should NOT be question spotting here; you should simply be thinking of what possible new business projects have been suggested in the pre-seen material.

Once you have completed your detailed analysis, then **synthesise** what you know:

Produce a position statement

- Mission statement
- Competences and CSF's
- Key business risks
- SWOT analysis – prioritising key S, W, O & T.
- Key business issues
- Balanced scorecard

And draw these points together into your one page business summary:

BUSINESS SUMMARY: Name of company				
Nature of business :......................... Current mission		Turnover	CFSs for success in industry	
			•	
			•	
Distinctive competence				
Major stakeholder objective				
ANALYSIS BACKUP				
Key financial data: trends		External : 5 forces		
Gross profit Net profit ROCE Other	Estimated value of business	P E S T	1 Barriers 2 Substitutes 3 Customers 4 Suppliers 5 Company	
Gearing Cash Operating cycle		Internal • Capacity • Structure • Information • Other		
Worrying indicators				
Competitive strategy: Cost leadership/Differentiation/Focus/'stuck in the middle'				
Customers – Key data				

SYNTHESIS

SWOT (Items of high importance)		RISKS: (High importance)	Time
0	0	1	
1	1	2	
2	2	3	
3	3		
Weaknesses	Threats		
1	1	4	
2	2		
3	3	5	

Key issues (High importance)	Time	Selection of possible business projects (High importance)	
1		1	
2		2	
3		3	
4		4	
5		5	
6		Possible discount rate	

Jot toys: unseen and requirements

This chapter contains the unseen material and requirements from the March 2012 exam.

We have produced a suggested answer to the exam in Chapter 24.

The requirement for this exam mirrors the type of requirement you should expect in your exam: a report worth up to 90 marks, followed by a smaller, secondary requirement worth up to 10 marks (with the 10 marks being awarded for Logic.)

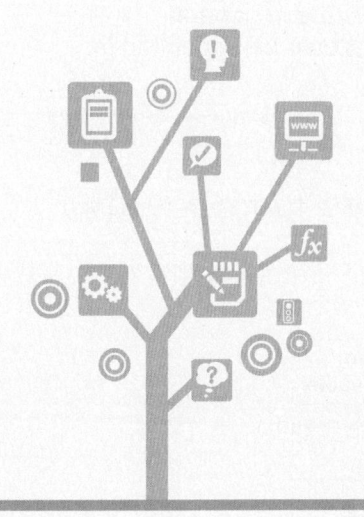

Jot – toy case – Unseen material provided on examination day

Additional (unseen) information relating to the case is given on pages 19 to 22.

Read all of the additional material before you answer the question.

ANSWER THE FOLLOWING QUESTION

You are the Management Accountant of Jot.

Jon Grun, Managing Director, has asked you to provide advice and recommendations on the issues facing Jot.

Question 1 part (a)
Prepare a report that prioritises, analyses and evaluates the issues facing Jot and makes appropriate recommendations.

(Total marks for Question 1 part (a) = 90 Marks)

Question 1 part (b)
In addition to your analysis in your report for part (a), Tani Grun, Finance and IT Director, has asked you to draft an email to Jot's management team. This email should set out the key criteria for the selection of outsourced manufacturers in general, together with your recommendation on which manufacturer(s) should be appointed for products YY and ZZ.

Your email should contain no more than 10 short sentences.

(Total marks for Question 1 part (b) = 10 Marks)

Your script will be marked against the T4 Part B Case Study Assessment Criteria shown below.

Assessment Criteria

Criterion	Maximum marks available
Analysis of issues (25 marks)	
Technical	5
Application	15
Diversity	5
Strategic choices (35 marks)	
Focus	5
Prioritisation	5
Judgement	20
Ethics	5
Recommendations (40 marks)	
Logic	30
Integration	5
Ethics	5
Total	**100**

Jot - toy case– unseen material provided on examination day

Read this information before you answer the question

VP "own brand" proposal

A major toy retailer based in the USA, VP, has taken a keen interest in the growth of Jot and is impressed with its innovative products and their quality. VP is one of Jot's seven main customers and it sells most of Jot's product range. VP is Jot's main customer in the USA with over 90% of its sales in this geographical area. The remainder of sales in the USA are generated by many small retailers. Total sales to VP in 2011 were just over €2.0 million, out of Jot's total sales of €9.866 million in the year ended 31 December 2011.

VP wishes to increase its range of "own brand" labelled products. VP's Procurement Director has recently met with Jon Grun, Managing Director, and has proposed that Jot produces a range of toys using VP's "own brand" labelling. This proposal would be for a 5 year period starting 1 January 2013 (the start of Year 1). The proposal is summarised as follows:

- Jot would design, manage the outsourced manufacturing process and produce an agreed range of products which would be labelled and packaged using VP's "own brand" rather than the Jot brand.

- All VP "own brand" products would be sold only in the USA.

- VP would place firm orders for the "own brand" products in March each year and VP would bear the risk of any unsold inventory. Currently VP places several orders between March and September each year.

- Jot would design 1 product exclusively for VP each calendar year. VP would pay a fee for this exclusive product of €0.25 million each year which is forecast to just cover the design and pre-production costs.

- VP would pay a reduced price, compared to Jot's current selling prices, for each VP "own brand" product. VP has requested a price reduction of 20% across all products. Jot's current average selling price of products to VP is €14.00 per unit. This is forecast to stay the same for the next 5 years.

- VP forecasts that sales volumes of the "own brand" products would increase by 50% every year for the 5 year period, due to extensive marketing (paid for by VP), from its current level of 145,000 units for 2012.

- Shipping costs are currently €0.40 per unit, payable by Jot. This is forecast to stay the same for the next 5 years.

The average manufacturing cost of products sold to VP is currently €9.50 per unit. This is forecast to stay the same for the next 5 years. However, Michael Werner, Operations Director, considers that Jot will be able to secure a price reduction from its outsourced manufacturers of 5% due to the extra volumes for the proposed VP "own brand" products.

Alternatively, if Jot decides not to pursue the "own brand" proposal with VP, Jot forecasts that sales volumes to VP could grow at 12% each year from its current level of 145,000 units, at an average selling price of €14.00 per unit. This is forecast to stay the same for the next 5 years.

Tani Grun, Finance and IT Director, considers that an appropriate pre-tax cost of capital is 10%.

Quality problem

Anna Veld, Licensing Director, has secured the licensing arrangement for a range of action figures based on a new children's film which is due to be released in July 2012. Planned sales for 2012 are 80,000 units in total, although if the film is a box office success, sales could be higher. The license fee is €0.70 per unit and is payable on *all* units manufactured (irrespective of whether the manufactured units are scrapped, sold or held in inventory).

Following tenders and subsequent negotiations, Jot appointed outsourced manufacturer Q (Q), which is based in China, to produce 80,000 units of these licensed products. Jot has used Q once before with no problems. The manufacturing process uses the technology called "injection moulding" where master moulds for each of the action figure are made to reproduce all of the products. Michael Werner personally inspected and signed off the master moulds in January 2012 and production commenced.

The first shipment of 10,000 units arrived at one of Jot's warehouses in Europe in February 2012 and on inspection, it has been established that the products do not meet Jot's quality standards. Michael Werner contacted Q and insisted that all production be stopped immediately. In the meantime, a further 10,000 units have been manufactured. No payments have yet been made to Q.

Michael Werner has now visited Q's factory and he has established that the manufacturing process has been rushed and the plastic used was of poor quality. Jot's contract had not specified the details of the plastic to be used as Q had made acceptable quality products for Jot previously. Michael Werner has discussed these problems with the Managing Director of Q and was told "at the contracted manufacturing price of €6.00, this is the best that Jot will get". The Managing Director of Q reminded Michael Werner that it had originally tendered a price per unit of €7.00. However, Michael Werner put pressure on Q to reduce the price down to €6.00 through tough negotiations. The Managing Director of Q has confirmed that his company could produce better quality products but only if Jot agrees to the realistic price of €7.00 per unit.

An alternative outsourced manufacturer, P (P), has now tendered a cost per unit of €7.10. Jot has not used this outsourced manufacturer before but its quality of production is known to be very good. However, Michael Werner is concerned that new moulds would need to be made by P before manufacturing can commence. Jot requires delivery of all 80,000 units by the end of May 2012 to enable it to transport them to its customers.

Marketing material

Sonja Rosik, Marketing Director, is aware that the marketing promotional literature for one of Jot's newly launched electronic products, which is aimed at the 5-8 year old age range, gives the impression of having several features which the product does not actually have.

Sales orders have been placed by some of Jot's customers and the product is currently being manufactured. The packaging for the product also contains slightly misleading information and claims. Jon Grun, Managing Director, is very annoyed about the incorrect marketing literature and packaging. He recalls that when Jot was a smaller company he personally signed off all marketing literature. He has asked Michael Werner, Operations Director, to investigate what can be done about the packaging for this product, both for future production as well for the first consignment of products that have recently been delivered to one of Jot's European warehouses. Jot has not yet despatched any sales orders to its customers.

Jon Grun considers that Sonja Rosik has been negligent in allowing this exaggeration of features to be incorporated incorrectly into the marketing material and the packaging of this product. Sonja Rosik does not understand why Jon Grun is so annoyed about what she considers to be a minor error in the marketing material. She has stated that "no one will really notice that the toy does not do this". Jon Grun is considering asking Sonja Rosik to resign.

Manufacturing problems

All of Jot's products are currently produced by 20 outsourced manufacturing companies. Except for the production of prototype and trial products, all outsourced manufacturing is located in China. In the middle of February 2012, an earthquake hit the area in China where two of Jot's outsourced manufacturers' factories are located. The two factories and much of the surrounding area have sustained significant damage. It is envisaged that these two outsourced manufacturers will be unable to re-build their factories and supply any products to Jot, or to their other customers, until at least the start of 2013. The two outsourced manufacturers produced products YY and ZZ for Jot and had not manufactured any of these products in 2012 before the earthquake occurred. The planned data for these two products is as follows:

	Forecast volumes required for 2012	Selling price	Current contracted manufacturing charge to Jot
	Units	€ per unit	€ per unit
Product YY	120,000	9.00	7.05
Product ZZ	30,000	12.00	7.44

Over the last 2 weeks, Michael Werner, Operations Director, has invited tenders from outsourced manufacturers for products YY and ZZ for delivery of products to meet sales forecasts for 2012.

All of Jot's existing outsourced manufacturers *except one* (Manufacturer A), have confirmed that they do <u>not</u> have any spare capacity to manufacture any additional products for Jot in 2012.

Michael Werner has narrowed down the tenders received from outsourced manufacturers to three alternative outsourced manufacturers, which are summarised as follows:

	Manufacturer A	Manufacturer B	Manufacturer C
Current manufacturer for Jot	Yes	No	No
Tendered manufacturing charge per unit:			
Product YY € per unit	8.00	6.60	7.05
Product ZZ € per unit	7.60	6.60	7.75
Manufacturing set-up costs to be charged to Jot:			
Product YY €	Zero (in unit cost)	€60,000	€12,000
Product ZZ €	Zero (in unit cost)	€30,000	€12,000
Shipping & transportation cost € per unit	€0.40	€0.60	€0.02
Location	China (near to earthquake area)	A different Asian country	Eastern Europe
Quality of production (established from initial tests and references)	Reasonable	Reasonable	Very good
Jot's view of each company's corporate social responsibility (CSR) status	Some problems	Some problems	Acceptable
Maximum available capacity in 2012 (for both products YY and ZZ in total in any combination)	120,000 units	180,000 units	100,000 units

March 2012

Inventory

The accounts for the year ended 31 December 2011 are currently being audited. The inventory valuation in the Statement of Financial Position is €542,000 which is net of a write-down reserve of €124,000 in respect of some slow moving products. However, the external auditors are concerned about the valuation of three specific slow-moving products, which have already been written-down in value. These are shown in the table below:

Products	Inventory volumes Units	Current written-down valuation € per unit
Product BB	4,900	6.30
Product CC	2,680	12.50
Product FF	1,200	7.00

At the start of each calendar year any unsold inventory for products which Boris Hepp, Sales Director, considers are out of date are offered to Jot's customers at substantially reduced prices to clear the inventory of them. This has not been done this year.

One of the external auditors has met with Boris Hepp about these three products. Boris Hepp stated that he considers that he could sell the remaining products BB and CC at the following revised values but that product FF was "worthless".

- Product BB – revised valuation €2.50 per unit
- Product CC – revised valuation €5.00 per unit

The auditor reported the outcome of his meeting with Boris Hepp to Tani Grun and the auditor has insisted that Tani Grun amends the accounts for the year ended 31 December 2011 to reflect these reduced inventory values.

Tani Grun is worried about the extent of these revised inventory valuations. She simply does not believe Boris Hepp's very pessimistic valuations. Tani Grun has told Boris Hepp that he must revise the valuations to a higher level and that he must inform the auditors that his comments and valuations were incorrect.

End of unseen material

APPLICABLE MATHS TABLES AND FORMULAE

Present value table

Present value of 1.00 unit of currency, that is $(1 + r)^{-n}$ where r = interest rate; n = number of periods until payment or receipt.

Periods (n)	1%	2%	3%	4%	5%	6%	7%	8%	9%	10%
1	0.990	0.980	0.971	0.962	0.952	0.943	0.935	0.926	0.917	0.909
2	0.980	0.961	0.943	0.925	0.907	0.890	0.873	0.857	0.842	0.826
3	0.971	0.942	0.915	0.889	0.864	0.840	0.816	0.794	0.772	0.751
4	0.961	0.924	0.888	0.855	0.823	0.792	0.763	0.735	0.708	0.683
5	0.951	0.906	0.863	0.822	0.784	0.747	0.713	0.681	0.650	0.621
6	0.942	0.888	0.837	0.790	0.746	0705	0.666	0.630	0.596	0.564
7	0.933	0.871	0.813	0.760	0.711	0.665	0.623	0.583	0.547	0.513
8	0.923	0.853	0.789	0.731	0.677	0.627	0.582	0.540	0.502	0.467
9	0.914	0.837	0.766	0.703	0.645	0.592	0.544	0.500	0.460	0.424
10	0.905	0.820	0.744	0.676	0.614	0.558	0.508	0.463	0.422	0.386
11	0.896	0.804	0.722	0.650	0.585	0.527	0.475	0.429	0.388	0.350
12	0.887	0.788	0.701	0.625	0.557	0.497	0.444	0.397	0.356	0.319
13	0.879	0.773	0.681	0.601	0.530	0.469	0.415	0.368	0.326	0.290
14	0.870	0.758	0.661	0.577	0.505	0.442	0.388	0.340	0.299	0.263
15	0.861	0.743	0.642	0.555	0.481	0.417	0.362	0.315	0.275	0.239
16	0.853	0.728	0.623	0.534	0.458	0.394	0.339	0.292	0.252	0.218
17	0.844	0.714	0.605	0.513	0.436	0.371	0.317	0.270	0.231	0.198
18	0.836	0.700	0.587	0.494	0.416	0.350	0.296	0.250	0.212	0.180
19	0.828	0.686	0.570	0.475	0.396	0.331	0.277	0.232	0.194	0.164
20	0.820	0.673	0.554	0.456	0.377	0.312	0.258	0.215	0.178	0.149

Periods (n)	11%	12%	13%	14%	15%	16%	17%	18%	19%	20%
1	0.901	0.893	0.885	0.877	0.870	0.862	0.855	0.847	0.840	0.833
2	0.812	0.797	0.783	0.769	0.756	0.743	0.731	0.718	0.706	0.694
3	0.731	0.712	0.693	0.675	0.658	0.641	0.624	0.609	0.593	0.579
4	0.659	0.636	0.613	0.592	0.572	0.552	0.534	0.516	0.499	0.482
5	0.593	0.567	0.543	0.519	0.497	0.476	0.456	0.437	0.419	0.402
6	0.535	0.507	0.480	0.456	0.432	0.410	0.390	0.370	0.352	0.335
7	0.482	0.452	0.425	0.400	0.376	0.354	0.333	0.314	0.296	0.279
8	0.434	0.404	0.376	0.351	0.327	0.305	0.285	0.266	0.249	0.233
9	0.391	0.361	0.333	0.308	0.284	0.263	0.243	0.225	0.209	0.194
10	0.352	0.322	0.295	0.270	0.247	0.227	0.208	0.191	0.176	0.162
11	0.317	0.287	0.261	0.237	0.215	0.195	0.178	0.162	0.148	0.135
12	0.286	0.257	0.231	0.208	0.187	0.168	0.152	0.137	0.124	0.112
13	0.258	0.229	0.204	0.182	0.163	0.145	0.130	0.116	0.104	0.093
14	0.232	0.205	0.181	0.160	0.141	0.125	0.111	0.099	0.088	0.078
15	0.209	0.183	0.160	0.140	0.123	0.108	0.095	0.084	0.079	0.065
16	0.188	0.163	0.141	0.123	0.107	0.093	0.081	0.071	0.062	0.054
17	0.170	0.146	0.125	0.108	0.093	0.080	0.069	0.060	0.052	0.045
18	0.153	0.130	0.111	0.095	0.081	0.069	0.059	0.051	0.044	0.038
19	0.138	0.116	0.098	0.083	0.070	0.060	0.051	0.043	0.037	0.031
20	0.124	0.104	0.087	0.073	0.061	0.051	0.043	0.037	0.031	0.026

Cumulative present value of 1.00 unit of currency per annum, Receivable or Payable at the end of each year for n years $\left[\dfrac{1-(1+r)^{-n}}{r}\right]$

Periods (n)	1%	2%	3%	4%	5%	6%	7%	8%	9%	10%
1	0.990	0.980	0.971	0.962	0.952	0.943	0.935	0.926	0.917	0.909
2	1.970	1.942	1.913	1.886	1.859	1.833	1.808	1.783	1.759	1.736
3	2.941	2.884	2.829	2.775	2.723	2.673	2.624	2.577	2.531	2.487
4	3.902	3.808	3.717	3.630	3.546	3.465	3.387	3.312	3.240	3.170
5	4.853	4.713	4.580	4.452	4.329	4.212	4.100	3.993	3.890	3.791
6	5.795	5.601	5.417	5.242	5.076	4.917	4.767	4.623	4.486	4.355
7	6.728	6.472	6.230	6.002	5.786	5.582	5.389	5.206	5.033	4.868
8	7.652	7.325	7.020	6.733	6.463	6.210	5.971	5.747	5.535	5.335
9	8.566	8.162	7.786	7.435	7.108	6.802	6.515	6.247	5.995	5.759
10	9.471	8.983	8.530	8.111	7.722	7.360	7.024	6.710	6.418	6.145
11	10.368	9.787	9.253	8.760	8.306	7.887	7.499	7.139	6.805	6.495
12	11.255	10.575	9.954	9.385	8.863	8.384	7.943	7.536	7.161	6.814
13	12.134	11.348	10.635	9.986	9.394	8.853	8.358	7.904	7.487	7.103
14	13.004	12.106	11.296	10.563	9.899	9.295	8.745	8.244	7.786	7.367
15	13.865	12.849	11.938	11.118	10.380	9.712	9.108	8.559	8.061	7.606
16	14.718	13.578	12.561	11.652	10.838	10.106	9.447	8.851	8.313	7.824
17	15.562	14.292	13.166	12.166	11.274	10.477	9.763	9.122	8.544	8.022
18	16.398	14.992	13.754	12.659	11.690	10.828	10.059	9.372	8.756	8.201
19	17.226	15.679	14.324	13.134	12.085	11.158	10.336	9.604	8.950	8.365
20	18.046	16.351	14.878	13.590	12.462	11.470	10.594	9.818	9.129	8.514

Periods (n)	11%	12%	13%	14%	15%	16%	17%	18%	19%	20%
1	0.901	0.893	0.885	0.877	0.870	0.862	0.855	0.847	0.840	0.833
2	1.713	1.690	1.668	1.647	1.626	1.605	1.585	1.566	1.547	1.528
3	2.444	2.402	2.361	2.322	2.283	2.246	2.210	2.174	2.140	2.106
4	3.102	3.037	2.974	2.914	2.855	2.798	2.743	2.690	2.639	2.589
5	3.696	3.605	3.517	3.433	3.352	3.274	3.199	3.127	3.058	2.991
6	4.231	4.111	3.998	3.889	3.784	3.685	3.589	3.498	3.410	3.326
7	4.712	4.564	4.423	4.288	4.160	4.039	3.922	3.812	3.706	3.605
8	5.146	4.968	4.799	4.639	4.487	4.344	4.207	4.078	3.954	3.837
9	5.537	5.328	5.132	4.946	4.772	4.607	4.451	4.303	4.163	4.031
10	5.889	5.650	5.426	5.216	5.019	4.833	4.659	4.494	4.339	4.192
11	6.207	5.938	5.687	5.453	5.234	5.029	4.836	4.656	4.486	4.327
12	6.492	6.194	5.918	5.660	5.421	5.197	4.988	7.793	4.611	4.439
13	6.750	6.424	6.122	5.842	5.583	5.342	5.118	4.910	4.715	4.533
14	6.982	6.628	6.302	6.002	5.724	5.468	5.229	5.008	4.802	4.611
15	7.191	6.811	6.462	6.142	5.847	5.575	5.324	5.092	4.876	4.675
16	7.379	6.974	6.604	6.265	5.954	5.668	5.405	5.162	4.938	4.730
17	7.549	7.120	6.729	6.373	6.047	5.749	5.475	5.222	4.990	4.775
18	7.702	7.250	6.840	6.467	6.128	5.818	5.534	5.273	5.033	4.812
19	7.839	7.366	6.938	6.550	6.198	5.877	5.584	5.316	5.070	4.843
20	7.963	7.469	7.025	6.623	6.259	5.929	5.628	5.353	5.101	4.870

FORMULAE

Valuation Models

(i) Irredeemable preference share, paying a constant annual dividend, d, in perpetuity, where P_0 is the ex-div value:

$$P_0 = \frac{d}{k_{pref}}$$

(ii) Ordinary (Equity) share, paying a constant annual dividend, d, in perpetuity, where P_0 is the ex-div value:

$$P_0 = \frac{d}{k_e}$$

(iii) Ordinary (Equity) share, paying an annual dividend, d, growing in perpetuity at a constant rate, g, where P_0 is the ex-div value:

$$P_0 = \frac{d_1}{k_e - g} \text{ or } P_0 = \frac{d_0[1+g]}{k_e - g}$$

(iv) Irredeemable (Undated) debt, paying annual after tax interest, $i(1-t)$, in perpetuity, where P_0 is the ex-interest value:

$$P_0 = \frac{i[1-t]}{k_{dnet}}$$

or, without tax:

$$P_0 = \frac{i}{k_d}$$

(v) Future value of S, of a sum X, invested for n periods, compounded at $r\%$ interest:

$$S = X[1+r]^n$$

(vi) Present value of £1 payable or receivable in n years, discounted at $r\%$ per annum:

$$PV = \frac{1}{[1+r]^n}$$

(vii) Present value of an annuity of £1 per annum, receivable or payable for n years, commencing in one year, discounted at $r\%$ per annum:

$$PV = \frac{1}{r}\left[1 - \frac{1}{[1+r]^n}\right]$$

(viii) Present value of £1 per annum, payable or receivable in perpetuity, commencing in one year, discounted at $r\%$ per annum:

$$PV = \frac{1}{r}$$

(ix) Present value of £1 per annum, receivable or payable, commencing in one year, growing in perpetuity at a constant rate of $g\%$ per annum, discounted at $r\%$ per annum:

$$PV = \frac{1}{r-g}$$

Cost of Capital

(i) Cost of irredeemable preference capital, paying an annual dividend, d, in perpetuity, and having a current ex-div price P_0:

$$k_{pref} = \frac{d}{P_0}$$

(ii) Cost of irredeemable debt capital, paying annual net interest, $i(1-t)$, and having a current ex-interest price P_0:

$$k_{dnet} = \frac{i[1-t]}{P_0}$$

(iii) Cost of ordinary (equity) share capital, paying an annual dividend, d, in perpetuity, and having a current ex-div price P_0:

$$k_e = \frac{d}{P_0}$$

(iv) Cost of ordinary (equity) share capital, having a current ex-div price, P_0, having just paid a dividend, d_0, with the dividend growing in perpetuity by a constant $g\%$ per annum:

$$k_e = \frac{d_1}{P_0} + g \quad \text{or} \quad k_e = \frac{d_0[1+g]}{P_0} + g$$

(v) Cost of ordinary (equity) share capital, using the CAPM:

$$k_e = R_f + [R_m - R_f]\beta$$

(vi) Weighted average cost of capital, k_0:

$$k_0 = k_e\left[\frac{V_E}{V_E + V_D}\right] + k_d\left[\frac{V_D}{V_E + V_D}\right]$$

Jot toys: answer

This is the suggested answer to the **March 2012** unseen and requirement, written by BPP Learning Media. Your report will be different to this and may analyse some different issues. This is as it should be, there is no one correct answer. However, if you fail to prioritise the key issues, you will find it very difficult to pass the exam.

Note: our solution is a comprehensive solution to this exam, and reflects the length and depth of solutions provided by CIMA's examiners. Therefore this solution aims to provide guidance on how each issue in the unseen could have been tackled. It does not represent the length of answer that could have been submitted in an exam.

In our experience, candidates submit scripts of around 2,500 words in the exam.

We have also included a suggested marking scheme developed by BPP Learning Media from the Post Exam Guides and Script Reviews following the exam.

Once you have answered this case study and reviewed our answer, you may also find it useful to read through the CIMA examiner's post-exam guide. The **post-exam guides** are available in the 'Study resources' section for T4 on the *cimaglobal.com* website.

Much of the information in the post-exam guide will be specific to this March 2012 case (rather than the case you will face in your exam). However, the post-exam guides do also include some more general comments on candidates' scripts, and the guides highlight some common errors, including omissions, which candidates make, and any common weaknesses they show. If you have shown some of the same weaknesses in your practice exams to date, these are points you need to address before you sit your real exam.

Answer to Question 1a

REPORT

To: Jon Grun, Managing Director, Jot

From: Management Accountant

Date: March 2012

Contents

1. Introduction
2. Terms of reference
3. Identification and prioritisation of issues
4. Approaches to resolving the main issues
5. Ethical issues
6. Recommendations
7. Conclusion

Appendices

A. SWOT analysis
B. Costs of resolving manufacturing problems
C. Evaluation of VP own brand proposal

1 Introduction

According to the European Commission report of 2011 the toy industry of Europe is mainly made up of small and medium size enterprises such as Jot. The 27 countries of the EU were responsible for €1.05 billion of exports of toys to non-EU countries. This justifies Jot's drive towards seeking market expansion in Russia and Asia.

The largest sector in the EU is for pre school children (3 to 5 age group) which accounts for some 20% of the total value of toys sold in the region.

2 Terms of reference

The Management Accountant has been requested to produce this report to identify and evaluate the issues facing Jot and offer appropriate recommendations.

3 Identification and prioritisation of issues

The issues below are prioritised based on their importance in terms of the impact and urgency they have on Jot. A SWOT analysis is included in Appendix A.

3.1 Quality problem – first priority

The poor quality of the first consignment of action figures leaves Jot needing to arrange a supply of 80,000 units by the end of May 2012 or risk missing the main volume of sales at the time of the launch of the film. The launch is only 3 months away which is a very short time to secure a supplier, check samples and receive delivery given that low cost manufacturing in China requires a shipping time of several months to reach European and US markets. The potential cost of this is €134,000 (20,000 units at €6.00 manufacturing cost + €0.70 license fee) if these units have to be paid for.

The urgency of the need to find alternative supplies makes this first priority.

3.2 Manufacturing problems – second priority

Jot needs to find alternative suppliers to make products YY and ZZ. Some of the quoted costs are higher than budgeted and this will affect actual profits of Jot.

This disruption to supply will affect the ability of Jot to provide products in the peak selling periods of Q3 and Q4 2012. This is less urgent than issue 1 which requires supplies by end of May 2012.

This is therefore issue number 2.

3.3 VP own brand proposal – third priority

VP provides over 20% of Jot's annual revenue and is Jot's only significant customer in the USA. This customer alone is budgeted to provide €2,030,000 revenue in 2012 (145,000 x €14) and is therefore extremely financially significant. There is also the need to avoid upsetting VP and losing a massive customer.

There is no time scale for this decision and it will not affect supply until 2013. Therefore it is less urgent than the previous 2 issues.

It is therefore issue number 3.

3.4 Inventory write down – fourth priority

This write down is of limited significance to Jot because it has no immediate cash impacts and Jot does not have external investors who will be unsettled by the adjustment although the bank and perhaps some customers may be concerned.

The principal concern is how these items were overvalued in the first place. Jot needs to find out whether, after allowing for the write-down of unsold stock, the lines produced a profit and what lessons can be learned for the future. This may affect ordering decisions due to commence in May 2012.

It is therefore issue number 4.

3.5 Other issues facing Jot

There are issues of lesser immediate concern which have not been prioritised in this report.

Marketing material: This will be discussed as an ethical issue in a separate discussion of ethics in section 5 of this report.

4 Approaches to resolving the main issues

4.1 Quality problem – first priority

There are several issues raised by the poor quality of the first batch of products. These are:

- Obtaining reliable supplies by the end of May
- Whether to scrap the 20,000 units, and if these are not scrapped, whether to produce the other 60,000 units at the reduced quality

- Whether to pay the €120,000 (€6 x 20,000 units) for the 20,000 made so far if the units are scrapped
- Whether it is possible to avoid paying the license fee of €14,000 on these units (€0.70 x 20,000 units)

if the units are scrapped.

Option 1 – sell the low quality units

This would require that Jot relaxes its quality standards.

The *advantages* of this option are that it would avoid paying license fees on units that were not sold. It would also avoid some of the increased costs of switching to a different supplier. It would also avoid any disputes over paying for these initial products. If all 80,000 units were supplied at this reduced quality it would provide a higher total contribution.

The *disadvantages* of this option would be the harm to Jot's brand reputation if it became associated with lower quality products. There would also be the costs of managing returns and refunds if shops received quantities of the toy back from customers. This loss of credibility may lead to licensors being unwilling to offer Jot licenses in future.

As far as future production is concerned, Jot has to decide which supplier to choose. The discussion below is on the basis that Jot decides that the 20,000 units have to be remade.

Option 2 – stay with Q but improve quality of future units

It seems likely that Q will seek to avoid taking the blame for these poor units by blaming the actions of Michael Werner in forcing the price down. A negotiated settlement may be better than one that results in Q ceasing to supply the toy and resorting to the courts to get the €120,000 it will claim it is owed (€6 x 20,000 units).

The *advantages* of this option would be that it would not necessitate the costs of producing new moulds. It would also be swifter because Q has moulds and production capacity scheduled. It would also be €8,000 cheaper than transferring production to the alternative manufacturer which will require €7.10 per unit (€7.10-€7 x 80,000). Finally it would also maintain goodwill with Q which otherwise may take legal action for payment, and damages for breach of contract, whilst also possibly selling the rejected volumes of toys on the illegal market.

The *disadvantages* of this option are that Q is likely to insist on full payment for the units it has made before remaking them and/or making the remainder. This will weaken Jot's legal and bargaining position over avoiding paying for the low quality units. It would also reduce actual profit by €80,000 against budget (€7-€6 x 80,000). Finally it is doubtful that Q can produce to the required quality. Q is blaming the low price for the poor quality of these units, rather than any failing by itself. Jot has only used Q once before and it's possible that Q was more rigorous that time and this time has become complacent.

Option 3 – use alternative supplier

The *advantages* of this option would be that it would leave Jot free to refuse to pay Q, or reach agreement on a reduced fee. It would also enable Jot to consider taking legal action for damages against Q, although the involvement of Michael Werner in reducing the cost may mean that such an action would fail. The level of quality is also more likely to be assured from an alternative supplier.

The *disadvantages* of this option are that it would be slower, because moulds need to be made. It will also be more expensive due to the costs of the moulds and the €0.10 per unit higher cost compared to the quoted price from Q. It would also leave Q unhappy and in possession of 10,000 units of unsold toys which may leak into the market and undermine sales of Jot's official version.

4.2 Manufacturing problems – second priority

The total sales at risk is €1,440,000 (120,000 x €9 + 30,000 x €12). The total gross profit at risk is €370,800 (120,000 x €9 - €7.05 + 30,000 x €12 - €7.44), equivalent to 12.4% of 2012 planned revenue (€1,440k/€11,568k) and 9.9% of 2012 planned gross profit (€370.8k/€11,568k x 32.3%).

Appendix B shows the total costs of using the alternative manufacturers.

Manufacturer A

The *advantages* of Manufacturer A are that it produces Product ZZ most cheaply, and Jot has experience of dealing with A. This may reduce the costs of inspection and quality control as well as transaction costs such as ordering, invoicing, arranging shipping and so on.

The *disadvantages* of Manufacturer A are that it is the most expensive producer of Product YY and that its location may make it vulnerable to a further earthquake in the region. It also does not have sufficient capacity to make both toys. It also has a poor CSR status.

Manufacturer B

The *advantages* of Manufacturer B are that it has sufficient capacity to make both toys. It is also not in the earthquake zone. It has a reasonable quality rating.

The *disadvantages* of Manufacturer B are that it is the most expensive producer of Product ZZ. It also has a poor CSR status.

Manufacturer C

The *advantages* of Manufacturer C are that it is a cheaper producer of Product YY than the other firms (and may also be cheaper than the original manufacturer if using the original manufacturer would have led to transport costs of €0.4 per unit like Manufacturer A from the same area). This is due to its closeness to Jot's main markets in Europe. This also brings potential benefits of quicker replenishment and lower inventories which may enhance profits further by avoiding lost sales through avoiding stock-outs, and less costs of working capital and inventory management. Choosing Manufacturer C would provide a valuable first step in near-shoring for Jot. This is enhanced by its excellent quality. It also has acceptable CSR status.

The *disadvantages* of Manufacturer C are that it is only able to make 83% of the required quantity of Product YY, in which it is the best value. It is the second most expensive producer of Product ZZ, although there is little to choose between the three manufacturers in financial terms for this product.

4.3 VP own brand proposal– third priority

The opportunity to provide own-brand product to VP can be evaluated using the Suitability, Acceptability and Feasibility framework of Johnson, Scholes and Whittington.

Suitability

Jot has limited working capital and we have found the expansion into the USA has strained this.

VP is asking for one toy made especially for it. It is not clear whether this new toy will be additional to VP's normal level of purchases and hence represents a doubling of VP's purchases, or whether it will replace regular purchases.

It would appear that VP is in effect requesting that Jot supplies it directly rather than buy the same toy alongside the remaining US clients.

Granting VP exclusivity increases Jot's reliance on VP. At the end of the 5 year contract Jot would face considerable buyer power (Porters 5 forces) from VP who would have replaced Jot's brand by its own, and could then contract with other toy makers, or design and commission its own toys, and cut Jot out.

Acceptability

Appendix C shows that the VP own brand proposal has a net present value of €3,585,240 compared to €3,138,030 from continuing with Jot's present branding. This mean the own label proposal is financially better by €447,000.

There may be further benefits if Jot decides to cease providing other stores and to rely on VP as its sole distribution channel in the USA. This would include closing the US warehouse operation, reduction in sales and marketing spending, and the costs of the working capital tied up in inventory. This would release the costs and capital involved for use in supporting the growth in other markets featured in our 5 year plan.

The smaller stores will object to being denied these exclusive toys because it will take custom even more to VP. However the small stores have limited stakeholder power because in total they account for only 10% of US business and turnover of about €280,000 in 2011 (USA total €2,280,000 minus VP's €2,000,000). Therefore they need only be kept informed of Jot's decision (Mendelow's matrix: high interest, low power).

Exclusive supply arrangements are unlikely to be deemed a breach of competition law in the USA.

The contract poses some risks to Jot because it depends on VP continuing in business and not going bankrupt as Woolworth plc did in the UK in 2008 despite having a very large share of the toy market.

However the contract also reduces risk because VP will place firm orders and therefore not leave Jot to carry the commercial risk of whether a toy will be a success or not.

Feasibility

The offer seems feasible in that the 2012 sales are in line with the historical sales to VP. However the 50% per annum growth looks ambitious and needs to be explained. Is this assuming that each new toy will sell 50% more than the one launched in the previous year? Or is the level of sales in 2014 50% higher because the extra 50% is the on-going tail of sales from the toy launched in 2013?

4.4 Inventory write down – fourth priority

The value of the proposed inventory write down is €47,120 (1,200 x €7 + 2,680 x €12.50-€5.00 + 4,900 x €6.30 - €2.50).

The inventory values will not affect revenues. The toys will sell for the price they achieve and Jot will receive the money. An overvaluation will not increase the income, and an undervaluation will not reduce it.

Option 1 – ignore the auditor's request for an impairment of inventory values

The *advantages* of this would be that it would avoid a fall in Jot's 2011 profits and year end value.

The *disadvantages* of this would be that it would lead to a qualified audit report and possibly the resignation of the auditors. This would alarm the bank and other users of Jot's accounts, such as large clients who would conduct a risk assessment of Jot before relying on it for supply of key products.

Option 2 – replace original values with Boris Hepp's values

The *advantages* of this would be that it would avoid an argument with the auditors. It would also potentially be more accurate as Boris Hepp is presumably the best placed person to judge the realisable value of inventory.

The *disadvantages* of this would be the €47,120 reduction in 2011 profit. Because Jot is unquoted and has no external shareholders this is less serious than it would be for a quoted firm. The profit reduction does not reduce cash, but it does force the Board to recognise that the cash it might have anticipated from selling this inventory will not be appearing. There is no mention of bank covenants on loans linked to profits or asset values. However the bank will presumably receive Jot's accounts and may be dismayed that operating profits have fallen by 8.5% (€47.1k/€551k) and total assets by 0.88%(€47.1k/€5,378k).

Option 3 – replace original values with revised but generous values

The *advantages* of this would be to reduce the impact on the profits and assets of Jot.

The *disadvantages* of this would be that it would further compromise the integrity of the accounts. The auditors will respond badly to made-up figures and may conclude that the past errors have been more than oversight, and instead reflect poor controls and a poor respect for the truth. The auditors may also recognise that Tani Grun has used oppressive behaviour to insert the values she prefers, and this may lead to further problems with the auditors.

Option 4 – Sell the stock as a fire sale

The inventory could be offered to existing customers at reduced prices. Alternatively the items could be offered in a trade sale. Grey market dealers specialise in buying distress stocks and selling them at low prices through networks of retail chains, market traders, and catalogue stores.

The *advantages* of this would be to liquidate the capital in the inventory and obtaining cash. It would also provide an accurate valuation of 'net realisable value'.

The *disadvantages* of this would be that it would reduce the value of the Jot brand.

4.4 Other issues facing Jot

There are issues of lesser immediate concern which have not been prioritised in this report.

5 Ethical issues

5.1 Integrity and objectivity of the accounting system

Why this is an ethical issue

As a member of CIMA Tani Grun is subject to the CIMA ethical code. To seek to influence the values put on inventory comes close to infringing the principles of integrity and objectivity. The values in the accounting system, and accounts, should be arm's length objective values and not values based on the personal opinion of, or convenience to, management.

Also Tani Grun seems to be acting unfairly to Boris Hepp by saying she simply does not believe his 'pessimistic' valuations. Boris Hepp is the expert and his judgement should not be called into question without evidence that he may be mistaken. For Tani Grun to do otherwise is oppressive.

Recommendation

Unless Tani Grun is able to bring evidence forward to the contrary, the values suggested by Boris Hepp should be accepted.

5.2 Marketing material

Why this is an ethical issue

Jot has an ethical duty to be truthful and not misleading in the information it provides. Sonja Rosik's response that no-one will notice is unacceptable. For Jot knowingly to promote products falsely is tantamount to lying.

Recommendation

The misconception should be corrected. This could be done by fixing a sticker to each box to list the features correctly. The promotional literature should be recalled and reissued, or customers should be advised of the error before they place their order.

A letter or email should be sent to all stockists explaining the error and a refunds policy instituted to ensure disgruntled buyers can get their money back.

5.3 Attitude to Sonja Rosik

Why this is an ethical issue

Jon Grun is considering asking Sonja Rosik to resign over the errors in the promotional literature. He seems to be speaking from annoyance. This is unfair and unjust.

It is unjust because Sonja has not had the opportunity to explain how the error happened. For example there may have been a late change to product specification after the prototypes were made of which she was not made aware. In this case the blame would justly belong elsewhere.

It is unfair because it is summary and disproportionate. To sack a director over one error is wrong.

Recommendation

No immediate action should be taken against Sonja Rosik. Instead she should be asked to put right the errors and then to prepare a report to the Board explaining how the errors happened.

The Board may consider reprimanding Sonja if she is found to be at fault, but it should be no more than a reprimand.

This issue, and the behaviour of Tani Grun towards Boris Hepp, suggests that the Board of Jot might benefit from a short course in corporate governance and ethics of the sort run by the Institute of Directors (IoD).

6 Recommendations

6.1 Quality problem – first priority

Recommendations

It is recommended that Jot continues to source this toy from manufacturer Q, but subject to the manufacturer achieving strict quality targets for which a bonus of up to €1 per toy will be paid.

It is recommended that Jot approaches the licensor and offers verified destruction of the 20,000 units in return for forgiveness of, or reduction in, the €14,000 fee payable.

Reasons for recommendations

Remaining with Q will assure supply more quickly than turning to an alternative supplier. This is due to the need for moulds to be made, equipment set up, and initial batches checked. It will also give Q an interest in dealing more favourably with the matter of payment for the 20,000 units made so far and also in destroying properly the 10,000 inventory in its possession. Q is also the cheaper supplier which will help protect profits.

Approaching the licensor is recommended in order to mitigate some of the costs of these initial low quality 20,000 units.

Actions

Michael Werner should open urgent negotiations with Q to resolve this problem. This could be done by videoconference. He should avoid admitting any culpability for the poor units as this would restrict his negotiating room.

Michael Werner should negotiate to have Q make the entire 80,000 units for a fee of €480,000 (€6 x 80,000) but be prepared to negotiate a bonus of up to €80,000 for on-time delivery of the consignment and its quality reaching a stated level. This gives Q a contract of up to €560,000 in value, plus any upside there may be if the film is a box office success. This upside should be emphasised.

Jot's Asian quality assurance manager should attend Q's factory to verify the improved quality of the first new batch of these toys.

Michael Werner should seek to negotiate an orderly resolution to the issue of the €120,000 payment for the 20,000 poor quality units. One approach might be to seek to make the €560,000 order dependant on Q agreeing to forfeit this. Q is unlikely to accept this but it may come back with a counter-offer below the €120,000.

Anna Veld, Licensing Director, should approach the licensor to explain the background of the problem and seek a reduction of, or forgiveness for, the license fee owed by Jot.

Secure destruction of the 20,000 low quality units should be arranged, with a certificate issued by the disposal firm. This may help satisfy the licensor that the toys have been destroyed.

6.2 Manufacturing problems – second priority

Recommendations

It is recommended that 100,000 units of Product YY be ordered from Manufacturer C.

It is recommended that 30,000 units of Product ZZ be ordered from Manufacturer A.

The further 20,000 units of Product YY should be ordered from Manufacturer A. Jot should seek to rely on the zero set up cost being good for 20,000 units. This is reasonable given that A charges no set up cost for 30,000 units of Product ZZ.

Reasons for recommendations

Manufacturer C is the cheapest source of Product YY. This is due to the lower transport costs. The 100,000 units will cost €719,000.

Topping up the additional 20,000 units from Manufacturer A will cost a further €168,000 (€8.4 x 20,000), giving a total cost for the 120,000 units of €887,000. This is less that the cost of either A or B producing them.

Buying from C also provides a first step for Jot in near-shoring, and the reduced distance from the manufacturer will improve inventory management and reduce carbon emissions.

Manufacturer A is the cheapest available producer of Product ZZ at €240,000

The original sourcing arrangements were due to cost €1,129,200 (120,000 x €7.05 + 30,000 x €7.44 + 150,000 x €0.4. This assumes no set up costs and same transport costs as from Manufacturer A.) These new sourcing arrangements will cost €1,127,000 (€887,000 + €240,000) a favourable cost, and profit variance against forecast of €2,200.

The risk remains that Jot is still reliant to some extent on manufacturers in an earthquake zone. However these recommendations mitigate the risks by shifting the production of 100,000 units, worth €900,000 revenue, away and leaving just €540,000 in the area of the earthquake (20,000 units at €9 and 30,000 units at €12: €180,000 + €360,000). To have moved production entirely away from the earthquake area would have required Jot to use Manufacturer B for both products. Therefore it is recommended that Jot absorbs the remaining risk for the present year.

Actions

Manufacturer C should be contacted and an order agreed for 100,000 units of Product YY. This order should be made conditional on the factory visit by Jot being satisfactory and the first batch meeting quality standards.

Michael Werner should instruct the European quality assessor to visit C's factory within the next month.

Michael Werner should speak to the management of C to assess whether it may be possible to increase its output from 100,000 units to the full 120,000 units, for example by providing an incentive payment to increase overtime working or productivity. This bonus could be up to €26,600 (20,000 units at the difference between the costs of manufacture and transport from A compared to C: ie €8.40 - €7.07).

Prior to final placing of orders with A an assessment should be made of the likelihood of a repeat earthquake in the area. It is likely that several manufacturing trade associations will be commissioning reports on this for their members.

Orders for the 30,000 units of Product ZZ should be placed with A. Depending on the outcome of the offer to C for extra units, a further order for 20,000 units of YY may also be placed.

The logistics partner of Jot, and its finance and IT team, will need to be informed of the appointment of C.

6.3 VP own brand proposal– third priority

Recommendations

It is recommended that the own brand offer from VP is accepted.

It is recommended that a review is taken of the remaining non-VP sales in USA with a view either to withdraw from these or supply via alternative channels such as appointing a US firm to act as agent, or complementary importing by another toy company.

Reasons for recommendations

The offer from VP has a higher financial value to Jot than continuing independently.

The entry by Jot into the USA has failed to gain any other significant clients but has used capital in setting up a warehouse. Retaining VP and using the resources in other markets may help Jot grow faster.

Actions

Jot should ask VP for a specimen contract for its lawyers to review. VP is likely to have one already and it would save the costs of Jot paying to have a new one drafted. Also VP is very unlikely to consider the use of a supplier's contract.

This contact should be carefully reviewed. In particular the ownership of designs, whether Jot can sell the same toys outside USA under its own name, termination clauses and so forth should be scrutinised.

A review of the profitability of supplying the remaining market should be undertaken with a view to making a decision in the fourth quarter of 2012 on the continuation of the US operation. This should consider the prospects for winning any further large retailers in the US such as Wal Mart, Toys R'Us or Amazon.

Alana Lotz should make provision for the design of an extra toy for the VP contract. Whether this is additional to the 7 already due for launch in 2013 will depend on whether Jot is allowed to sell the VP toy outside USA under Jot's own brands.

This contract should remain confidential until late 2012 in order to give Jot time to decide the future of its US operations and of its staff there.

6.4 Inventory write down – fourth priority

Recommendations

It is recommended that Boris Hepp's inventory values be used in the 2011 final accounts.

It is recommended that inventory control policies be reviewed to reveal slow moving items earlier and at a time when they might still be sold for a reasonable price.

Reasons for recommendations

Boris Hepp's valuations are likely to be the most reliable give that he has contact with the market.

The impact is not sufficiently material to justify any further expert opinions or a quarrel with the auditors.

It is also important to establish the integrity of the accounts, especially given Jot's high reliance on bank lending and its future needs for finance. This requires a clean audit report.

Actions

The auditors should be contacted by Tani Grun and informed that the revised values provided by Boris Hepp will stand.

The items should be offered for sale and an attempt made to clear them. This includes FF which may still yield some revenue.

The process of inventory control should be reviewed to ensure slow moving items are identified in a timely way and promoted, and not re-ordered, to avoid the overhang of unsold stock.

6.5 Other issues facing Jot

There are issues of lesser immediate concern which have not been prioritised in this report.

7 Conclusion

This report has examined the issues facing Jot and has made appropriate recommendations on them. Some decisions need to be made immediately while others can be reviewed at a later date.

Appendix A SWOT analysis

Strengths	Weaknesses
• Rapid growth • Strong brand • Reputation for innovation and quality	• Poor monitoring of slow-moving stock • Lack of checking of claims in marketing materials • Poor supplier selection processes
Opportunities	**Threats**
• VP own brand proposal	• Lack of quality product for license deal • Complaints about misleading marketing material • Loss of supply due to earthquake • Profit and asset impairment due to inventory revaluation

Appendix B Costs of Resolving Manufacturing Problems

	YY	ZZ
Forecast volume (000)	120	30
Manufacturer A		
Manufacturing cost per unit	8	7.6
Shipping cost per unit	0.4	0.4
Total variable cost per unit	8.4	8
Total variable costs (€000)	1008.0	240.0
Set up cost	0.0	0.0
Total costs	1008.0	240.0
Manufacturer B		
Manufacturing cost per unit	6.6	6.6
Shipping cost per unit	0.6	0.6
Total variable cost per unit	7.2	7.2
Total variable costs (€000)	864	216
Set up cost	60	30
Total costs	924	246
Forecast volume (000)	100	30
Manufacturer C		
Manufacturing cost per unit	7.05	7.75
Shipping cost per unit	0.02	0.02
Total variable cost per unit	7.07	7.77
Total variable costs (€000)	707	233.1
Set up cost	12	12
Total costs	719	245.1

Appendix C - Evaluation of VP Own Brand Proposal

	2012	2013	2014	2015	2016	2017
VP Own Brand						
Sales volume (000)	145.00	217.50	326.25	489.38	734.06	1,101.09
Contribution per unit (11.20-9.025)		2.175	2.175	2.175	2.175	2.175
Gross margin €000		473.06	709.59	1,064.39	1,596.59	2,394.88
Shipping costs		-87.00	-130.50	-195.75	-293.63	-440.44
Total proceeds		386.06	579.09	868.64	1,302.96	1,954.44
DF@ 10%		0.909	0.826	0.751	0.683	0.621
PV (€000)		350.93	478.33	652.35	889.92	1,213.71

Total PV
€3,585,240

Jot Brand						
Sales volume (000)	145.00	162.40	181.89	203.71	228.16	255.54
Contribution per unit (14-9.50)		4.50	4.50	4.50	4.50	4.50
Gross margin €000		730.80	818.50	916.72	1,026.72	1,149.93
Shipping costs		-64.96	-72.76	-81.49	-91.26	-102.22
Total proceeds		665.84	745.74	835.23	935.46	1,047.71
DF@ 10%		0.909	0.826	0.751	0.683	0.621
PV (€000)		605.25	615.98	627.26	638.92	650.63

Total PV
€3,138,030

* the design costs have been ignored in the VP Own Brand calculation because the outflow of €250,000 is eliminated by the €250,000 inflow from the payment by VP

QUESTION 1(B) - EMAIL

To: Management Team

From: Management Accountant

Date: March 2012

Selection of outsourced suppliers

Recent events have led to a need to clarify the factors that must be considered when selecting suppliers:

General Criteria for selecting suppliers

Capacity: the supplier must be able to provide the required volume of products within the required time frame.

Quality: the products must meet the quality requirements of Jot. The recent problems with action figures from Q show that overlooking this is a false economy.

Price: the price being charged by the supplier must yield an adequate gross margin.

Transport costs: these are significant. In the case of Manufacturer B they are around a further 10% on top of manufacturing costs.

Risk: we should consider avoiding placing orders with manufacturers in areas subject to earthquakes, floods, and other natural disasters.

CSR: in the absence of a decided policy by Jot we should seek assurance on general ethical requirements of decent working conditions and pay, and also that the materials and production processes are sustainable.

Product YY and ZZ

Following the earthquake damage to the original manufacturer, it is recommended that the orders be placed as follows:

Product YY: 100,000 from Manufacturer C and 20,000 from Manufacturer A (subject to C being unable to produce them).

Product ZZ: 30,000 units from Manufacturer A.

These have been recommended because it will create an overall favourable cost and profit variance of €2,200 against the original supplier. It will also allow Jot to experiment with near sourcing.

Marking Grid

Criteria	Issues to be discussed	Marks	Total marks available for criterion
Technical	SWOT/PEST/Ansoff/Porter's 5 forces/Porter's generic strategies/Mendelow/Suitability, Acceptability, Feasibility/ BCG/Balanced Scorecard/Life cycle analysis/Marketing knowledge 1 mark for EACH technique demonstrated.	1 each max 5	Max = 5
Application	SWOT – to get full 3 marks the script must include all the Top 4 issues	1–3	Max = 15
	Other Technical Knowledge applied to case material in a meaningful relevant way – on merit	1–2 Max 5 for application of theory	
	Calculations:		
	Comparison of costs of three manufacturers for YY and ZZ	6	
	NPVs of VP own brand and Jot brand	6	
	Other relevant calculations on merit	5	
	Total marks available (but max = 15)	22	
Diversity	Display of sound business awareness and relevant real life examples related to case	1 mark each example used on merit	Max = 5
Focus	1 mark for each commercial issue well discussed (5 marks if 4 issues well discussed) Quality problem Manufacturing problems VP own brand proposal Inventory Marketing material		Max = 5
Prioritisation	5 marks if top 2 issues from solution are in top 2	5	Max = 5
	Reduce by 1 mark for each place a top 2 issue falls below issue number 2 – eg if manufacturing problems is number 1 but quality problem is issue 4 then 3 marks awarded (5 minus 2)		

Criteria	Issues to be discussed	Marks	Total marks available for criterion
Judgement	Marks on merit based on depth of analysis and linked to central themes of profit and growth of Jot		
	Quality problem: urgency for end of May, time needed for moulds, issue Werner's culpability, unfamiliarity of P, need to negotiate invoice payment, negotiate license payment, danger of leakage of 10,000 rejected units	1–7	
	Manufacturing problems: issues of risk of relying on China, opportunity to experiment with near-shoring, limited importance of CSR in decision, green miles	1–6	Max = 20
	VP own brand proposal: key client, vulnerability to buyer power, chance to make partial withdrawal from USA, growth assumptions, other costs and savings, reduction of risk	1–6	
	Inventory: role of auditor, dangers of down-valuation, impact on banks, issues of poor control	1–3	
	Marketing material: reputation risk, potential costs of refunds, loss of client goodwill	1–3	
	Total marks available (but max = 20)	25	
Logic	**Recommendations:**		
	(Marks on merit. Max 1 mark if only an unjustified recommendation is given)		
	Quality problem: clear decision on sound rationale that recognises the balance between speed and resolution of money owed and liability. (Case can be made for choosing P or Q).	1–6	
	Manufacturing problems: clear decision on selection of supplier(s) based on sound rationale that recognises the balance between cost, risk, and chance to try near-shoring	1–6	Max = 30 Q1a – 20 Q1b – 10
	VP own brand proposal: clear decision based on sound rationale that balances present forecast earnings against loss of autonomy and buyer power	1–5	
	Inventory: recommendation to go with Hepp values, investigate reasons for poor inventory control, reassurance of bank and auditors	1–3	
	Marketing material: clear decision based on sound rational that recognises the balance between cost of correction/recall against reputation risk and loss of goodwill	1–3	
	Total marks available (but max = 20)	23	

PART C PRACTICE TOPCIMA CASES　　　　　　　　　　　　　　　　24: Jot toys: answer　　**499**

Criteria	Issues to be discussed	Marks	Total marks available for criterion
QUESTION 1(b)	Up to 2 marks for brevity of presentation		
	1 mark for each valid point selection criterion		
	Additional 2 marks overall if criteria related to experience of issues in the unseen material	10	
	Up to 2 marks for clear recommendation on choice of manufacturer(s)		
	Total marks available	10	
Integration	Judge script holistically and whether recommendations follow on logically from analysis of the issues and refers to data in appendices. How well written is the report: professional language?	1–2 if weak 3–5 if script is good	Max = 5
Ethics	Ethical issues in case include: Misrepresentation in marketing material Unfair attitude towards Sonja Rasik Integrity of accounts Unfair and oppressive treatment of Boris Hepp	Up to 5 for identification and discussion of issues Up to 5 for recommendations on how to address those issues	Max = 10
Total			100

EGC: Specimen exam paper

This chapter includes the Specimen exam paper which CIMA issued for the 2010 syllabus.

This chapter contains both pre-seen and unseen material so is an example of all the case study material you will receive.

It also provides another illustration of the type of requirements you are likely to face in your exams: with a 90 mark requirement followed by a 10 mark one.

However, we have included this paper to summarise the type of case study and requirement you should expect in your exams, rather than as an additional Practice case study.

Accordingly, we have not provided a detailed analysis for it, nor a BPP solution.

However, if you want to see the Examiner's answers to this Specimen Paper they are available on CIMA's website: www.cimaglobal.com

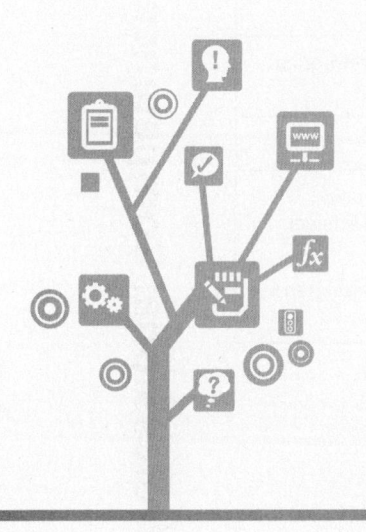

CIMA

T4 – Part B Case Study Examination
Specimen Examination Paper

Instructions to candidates

You are allowed three hours to answer this question paper.
You are allowed 20 minutes reading time **before the examination begins** during which you should read the question paper and, if you wish, make annotations on the question paper. However, you will **not** be allowed, **under any circumstances**, to open the examination answer book and start writing or to use your calculator during the reading time.
This booklet contains the examination question and both the pre-seen and unseen elements of the case material.
Answer the question on page 13, which is detachable for ease of reference. The Case Study Assessment Criteria are also included on page 14.
Maths Tables and Formulae are provided on pages 20 to 23.
Write your full examination number, paper number and the examination subject title in the spaces provided on the front of the examination answer book. Also write your contact ID and name in the space provided in the right hand margin and seal to close

Contents of this booklet:	Page
Pre-seen material – Electricity Generating Corporation	2 - 8
Pre-seen Appendices A – D	9 - 12
Question requirement and Assessment criteria	13 - 14
Unseen material	15 - 18
Unseen Appendix E	19
Maths Tables and Formulae	20 - 23

T4 Test of Professional Competence - Part B Case Study Exam

BPP LEARNING MEDIA

The Electricity Generating Corporation

Introduction

The Electricity Generating Corporation (EGC) is located in a democratic Asian country. EGC was established as a nationalised industry many years ago. Its home Government at that time had determined that the provision of the utility services of electricity generation and gas production should be managed directly by boards which were accountable directly to Government. In theory, nationalised industries should be run efficiently, on behalf of the public, without the need to provide any form of risk-related return to the funding providers. In other words, EGC, along with other nationalised industries is a non-profit making organisation. This, the Government claimed at the time, would enable prices charged to the final consumer to be kept low.

Industry structure

EGC operates 12 coal fired power stations across the country and transmits electricity through an integrated national grid system which it manages and controls. It is organised into three regions, Northern, Eastern and Western. Each region generates electricity which is sold to 10 private sector electricity distribution companies which are EGC's only customers. The 10 distribution companies are the suppliers of electricity to final users including households and industry within the country and are not under the management or control of EGC. They are completely independent companies owned by shareholders.

The three EGC regions transmit the electricity they generate into the national grid system. A shortage of electricity generation in one region can be made up by taking from the national grid. This is particularly important when there is a national emergency, such as exceptional weather conditions. However, there have been times when EGC has not been able to fully satisfy demand and this has led to power cuts. The charges for electricity generated by EGC are regulated by the Government. EGC sells the electricity it generates to the 10 distribution companies at a uniform price. The 10 distribution companies then sell the electricity they purchase from EGC to the final customer. The Government requires EGC to maintain electricity generation at all times and has in the past guaranteed that its costs will be met in full by the central Government treasury.

The nationalised utility industries were set up in a monopolistic position. As such, no other providers of these particular services were permitted to enter the market within the country. Therefore, EGC is the sole generator of electricity in the country. The electricity generating facilities, in the form of the 12 coal fired power stations were all built over 15 years ago and some date back to before EGC came into being. The structure of EGC is that it has a Management Board headed by a Managing Director who reports to senior civil servants in the Government's Ministry of Energy.

Financing of EGC

The Government uses its own cash-based accounting system for all the nationalised industries, EGC included. EGC draws funding directly from the Government on a regular basis to cover its cash requirements for its capital needs and any shortfall in its operating costs. The Government does not operate an accruals-based accounting system for the nationalised industries.

When EGC was formed, a large amount of Government cash funding was required initially to give it financial stability. The model of financing which emerged for EGC was one that resulted in its costs being guaranteed. As EGC is the monopoly generator of electricity in the country it charges the price approved by the Government to the 10 private sector electricity distribution companies. Any overall financial deficit EGC incurs is made up through additional Government funding. In practice, EGC continues to be a large cash consumer of Government funds. While recognising that it provides funds for capital equipment and renewals, the Government's aim is that EGC should at least cover its operating costs from revenue earned from the 10 private sector electricity distribution companies.

There has been no other source of funding for EGC other than income from the 10 private sector electricity distribution companies and funds provided directly from the Government. The Government however, has now instituted a loan system to cover expenditure when EGC needs more cash than it collects in revenue. The argument the Minister of Energy has made is that the Government cannot simply provide unlimited funds for EGC. Any further demands for cash by EGC beyond what it collects in revenue can only be met by loans from the Government. No funding can be obtained from any other source.

The loan facilities have been established to emphasise the principle that any additional funding from the Government is a liability to EGC and that it must pay interest on the loan and eventually pay back the capital sum. This principle was established by the Government in a drive to introduce a more commercial basis to EGC's financing. Government loans have no fixed repayment dates and are made to EGC at a preferential rate of interest, fixed at 2% below the Government-set bank rate.

Recently, the Minister of Energy has stated that productivity, return on assets and good stewardship of public funds are of high importance in managing all the nationalised industries. This is a particular challenge for EGC as it is subject to inflationary pressure which has increased in the country over the last year, and its Government-approved prices are set for a period on the basis of a low, rather than a commercial, price. The response of EGC's Managing Director has been that the role of the Management Board is to maintain the provision of electricity generation at any cost rather than maximising investment returns or providing value for money.

Introduction of commercial accounting practices at EGC

At the request of the Minister of Energy, a pro forma set of accounts incorporating an income statement, balance sheet, cash flow statement and a statement of the changes in equity have been produced for 2007/8 and 2008/9. This is the first time EGC has prepared accounts using commercial accounting principles. The purpose of these accounts is to illustrate how EGC's financial position would appear in a commercial environment. Extracts from this set of pro forma accounts are shown at **Appendices A and B.** Within these pro forma accounts some of EGC's loans have been "notionally" converted by the Government into ordinary shares in a further attempt to illustrate how EGC's financial reports would appear using the accepted format of commercial accounting principles. Financing costs are only payable on the Government loans as shown in the balance sheet.

The pro forma accounts show a loss for the year ended 31 March 2009. Being a nationalised industry and effectively the first set of "commercially based" accounts, there are no retained earnings brought forward into 2007/8. The "Other reserves" is a sum which was vested in EGC when it was first nationalised. This represents the initial capital stock valued on a historical cost basis from the former electricity generating organisations which became EGC when it was nationalised.

Capital market

EGC exists in a country which has a well developed capital market relating both to equity and loan stock funding. There are well established international institutions, which are able to provide funds and corporate entities are free to issue their own loan stock in accordance with internationally recognised principles.

Energy consumption within the country

Energy consumption has doubled in the country over the last 10 years. EGC continues to use coal fired power stations and now consumes most of the coal mined within the country.

Governance of EGC

The Managing Director of the Management Board of EGC reports to senior civil servants in the Ministry of Energy. There are no shareholders and ownership of the Corporation rests entirely with the Government. There is a formal annual meeting with senior Government officials at which the financial accounts of EGC are approved. Beyond this there are occasional informal meetings between members of the Management Board and Government officials, particularly when the Minister of Energy is required to present information relating to electricity generation to the country's Parliament.

Structure of EGC

All the staff employed by EGC are Government employees. The structure of EGC comprises a hierarchy of many levels of management authority. EGC is managed by the Management Board which comprises the Managing Director, the Directors of each of the Northern, Eastern and Western regions, a Technical Director, the Corporation Secretary and the Finance Director. With the exception of the Corporation Secretary and Finance Director, all the Management Board members are qualified electrical engineers.

Within the structure of EGC's headquarters, there are four support functions; engineering, finance, human resource management (HRM) and administration, each with its own chief officers, apart from HRM. The Senior HRM Officers and Chief Administrative Officer report to the Corporation Secretary. The Chief Accountant reports to the Finance Director and the Chief Engineer to the Technical Director. These functions are replicated in each region, each with its own regional officers and support staff. In the three regions, the Regional Accountants and their staff focus mainly on producing management accounting rather than financial accounting information. A structure chart and organisational staffing information is given at **Appendices C and D** for headquarters and a sample region which shows the engineering function under the heading of "Technical Staff" and "Engineering Staff", the finance function under the heading of "Finance Staff" and "Accountancy Staff", and HRM and administrative functions under the heading of "Secretariat Staff".

The number of professional engineering and operational staff has increased over the last 10 years in a period when demand for electricity has been increasing. The increase in operational employees has led to an increase in managerial and administrative staff at EGC. At EGC headquarters the management and administrative staff head count has increased to three times its level of a decade ago. In total, the number of staff employed by EGC at 31 March 2009 was 11,608 full time equivalent staff.

Management of EGC

The Managing Director and Regional Directors all studied in the field of electrical engineering at the country's leading university and have worked together for a long time. Although they did not all attend the university at the same time, they have a strong belief in the quality of their education. After graduation from university, each of the Regional Directors and the Managing Director started work at EGC in a junior capacity and then subsequently gained professional electrical engineering qualifications. They believe that the experience of working up through the ranks of EGC has enabled them to have a clear understanding of EGC's culture and the technical aspects of the industry as a whole.

The Management Board meets formally on a monthly basis but the Regional Directors and the Managing Director regularly meet together on a social level, outside the Management Board meetings at least once a month. One Regional Director was overheard to remark to his Regional Engineer that the only function of the Management Board meetings was to formally agree the decisions made by the Regional Directors and the Managing Director on the golf course.

The Technical Director is also a qualified electrical engineer but is not a graduate of the same university as the Managing Director and Regional Directors. She obtained a first class honours degree in Engineering with Business. After qualifying as an electrical engineer she took an MBA degree at a prestigious European university and is currently studying for a PhD in electrical engineering on a part-time basis. The Technical Director and the Finance Director tend to work closely together in attempting to introduce improvements in financial control within EGC.

The Corporation Secretary has held his post for 22 years and expects to retire in two years' time. He too has risen through the ranks of EGC, having first started working as a junior clerk in a regional office nearly 40 years ago. He studied hard and obtained a recognised qualification as a corporate secretary by undertaking correspondence courses. In his period of tenure he has been proud to provide the statutory returns as required by different Government ministries. He has always carried out the instructions of the Managing Directors of EGC without question as he has a strong sense of duty. Similarly, he expects total loyalty from the EGC headquarters staff who report to him.

The Finance Director is a graduate and a Fellow of CIMA. He has worked in several private enterprise organisations, engaged both in the retail and manufacturing sectors. Since he joined EGC in April 2009, he has been trying to introduce a system of budgetary control as he recognises that the Government is aiming to improve economy and efficiency while, at the same time, maintaining effectiveness in the nationalised industries as a whole. This initiative has been hampered by the fact that all the staff in the regions, including the finance staff, report to the relevant Regional Director and not the functional staff at headquarters.

At a recent Management Board meeting, the Managing Director made it clear to the Finance Director that, in his view, the main purpose of EGC is to maintain electricity generation whatever the financial implications. The Regional Directors and the Managing Director all agree that the Government will not reduce its commitment to funding EGC as this would threaten electricity generation. The Finance Director responded by reminding the members of the Management Board that now the Government is making loans not financial grants to EGC and that there is an obligation on EGC to repay these loans at some point in the future.

The Managing Director replied that:

"Irrespective of whether it is a loan or a gifted payment, the money is still found by Government and our job is to maintain electricity generation. It is not the role of the Management Board to worry about where the money comes from or in what form it arrives. We can leave that to the country's treasury."

The Managing Director then added to the Finance Director:

"Do you realistically expect the Government to demand repayment? I don't."

Decision making at EGC

Decision making within EGC is centralised. All decisions on capital expenditure are made by the Management Board and the Regional Directors are able to strongly influence these decisions. Operational decisions are made in each region. Any decision which requires non recurring expenditure over $5,000 must be made by the Regional Management Board. If the sum required is over $1 million, the decision is referred to the EGC Management Board. At EGC headquarters, decisions on expenditure relating to headquarters operations are delegated to the relevant EGC Management Board member but any non recurring expenditure over $5,000 must be referred to the Managing Director for approval. There is a strong culture throughout EGC of committee structures and of documentation being required to support almost any action or activity.

Power generation

EGC operates 12 coal fired power stations across the country. There is a well developed coal mining industry in the country but extraction is becoming more expensive. There is no other form of electricity generation in the country except for some wind turbine power experiments which only produce a small fraction of the country's electricity needs.

The Minister of Energy has stated that the country should progress towards more efficient and also renewable forms of power generation methods. This followed an announcement by the Prime Minister that the country needed to review how it could provide secure energy supplies and also reduce its impact on global warming.

Researchers in the country have cited France as an example of a country with a nationalised electricity industry which now generates most of its electricity from nuclear power. The country in which EGC is situated has no nuclear power stations.

Some members of the scientific community have concluded that the country will not be able to reduce its harmful emissions without developing a nuclear power generation programme. (The term "harmful emissions" in this context, refers to pollution coming out of electricity generating power stations which damage the environment.) The country's leading researcher into energy development has warned that without nuclear power generation, there will be increased usage of coal. This will generate ever more harmful emissions which will lead to an increase, not a decrease, in global warming. This will attract major criticism from other countries.

The researcher added that reliance on wave and solar power was not realistic as their development was not going to be speedy enough to replace existing power generation methods and meet the ever increasing demands for electricity. He did however acknowledge the potential benefit of using wind turbines as a means of environmentally friendly power generation. Another researcher has encouraged the Minister of Energy to clearly set out for the public how nuclear power can contribute to reducing harmful emissions.

In the past, EGC tended to over estimate demand and so over-capacity was built into the system, which led to higher costs. That position has now changed and there have been power cuts due to EGC sometimes being unable to fully satisfy demand. No new power stations have been built in the last 15 years.

EGC generates electricity using coal fired power stations. The Managing Director and Regional Directors of EGC are not very enthusiastic about other methods of electricity generation and have publicly stated their opposition to nuclear power. Their main concern has been on the grounds of public safety and the safe disposal of spent nuclear fuel. Quite apart from the very large capital investment which would be needed to establish nuclear power stations, they claim that the case for nuclear fuelled electricity production has not yet been proved. In particular, they argue that the cost of decommissioning a nuclear power station is very high.

Little research has been undertaken by EGC into alternative methods of power generation or the impact on the environment of continuing to use coal for fuel. The only research that has been done in the past was on ways of generating greater power yields from coal fuel sources. Unsurprisingly, much of this research has been funded by the country's coal production industry.

Price charged by EGC for electricity generated and EGC's cost structure

A kilowatt (kW) is a unit of energy, representing the rate at which energy is used or produced. EGC, in line with most electricity generators and suppliers in other countries, charges its customers by the kilowatt hour (kWh). A kWh is a unit of energy and represents one hour of electricity consumption at a constant rate of 1 kW. For example an electric fire rated at 1 kWh will consume 1 kW of electricity in one hour. The Government approved price charged by EGC for electricity in 2008/9 was $0·22 per kWh.

In total, in the financial year 2008/9 EGC generated and sold 60,000 million kilowatt hours of electricity to the 10 private sector distribution companies (compared with 58,000 million kilowatt hours in 2007/8).

The following costs were incurred by EGC in 2008/9 compared with 2007/8:

	2008/9 $ million	2007/8 $ million
Generating costs (including fuel)	10,145	9,874
Regional staff costs and overheads	845	812
Headquarters staff costs and overheads	820	780
Repairs and maintenance	228	268
Research and development	11	8
Operating leases	58	49
Total generating costs	12,107	11,791
Depreciation	799	650
Total operating costs incurred	12,906	12,441

Accounting system in operation at EGC

The accounting system that is in operation at EGC provides for a calculation of the total operating costs incurred in each region which includes the apportionment of headquarters staff costs and overheads. The cost accounts for EGC as a whole are produced annually. The method of apportionment of headquarters costs is simple. All headquarters costs are divided by three and charged equally to each region. The rationale for this system, which has been in operation since EGC was first established, is that since headquarters provides a service across all three regions, they should bear the actual costs incurred on an equal basis. It has been argued by the Regional Directors that this may not necessarily reflect the actual service provided to each region by headquarters in any one year. All research and development is carried out at headquarters and so these costs are charged equally to each region.

The Finance Director has expressed severe concerns about the lack of detailed management information. Consequently, he has asked the Regional Accountants to establish a working group, its task being to develop more detailed management accounting information.

The breakdown of operating costs across each of the three regions for 2008/9 is given below:

	Northern $ million	Eastern $ million	Western $ million	Total $ million
Generating costs	5,026	2,618	2,501	10,145
Regional staff costs and overheads	385	248	212	845
Headquarters staff costs and overheads	274	273	273	820
Repairs and maintenance	112	56	60	228
Research and development	4	4	3	11
Operating leases	0	35	23	58
Total generating costs	5,801	3,234	3,072	12,107
Depreciation	237	284	278	799
Total operating costs incurred	6,038	3,518	3,350	12,906

In addition $1,248 million was spent in 2008/9 on renewals of plant and equipment. Of this, $701 million was spent in the Northern Division, $320 million in the Eastern Division and $227 million in the Western Division. The renewals are necessary to keep the plant and equipment operational. These renewals enable EGC to maintain output at about the same level although there may be some variation in total output and generating capacity between years.

Electricity generation

The following table shows the generation of electricity by the 12 power stations operated by EGC in 2008/9 compared with the generated output in 2007/8:

	2008/9 Output produced	Utilisation of 100% capacity	Electricity generation at 100% capacity in 2008/9	2007/8 Output produced	Utilisation of 100% capacity
	kWh (million)	%	kWh (million)	kWh (million)	%
Northern Region:					
Station N1	2,644	46		2,950	51
Station N2	4,560	57		4,640	58
Station N3	7,207	67		6,538	61
Station N4	8,513	83		8,018	78
	22,924		34,761	22,146	
Eastern Region:					
Station E1	4,306	82		4,218	80
Station E2	2,548	71		2,531	71
Station E3	6,836	80		6,433	75
Station E4	8,194	87		7,909	84
	21,884		26,803	21,091	
Western Region:					
Station W1	3,931	76		3,796	73
Station W2	4,846	74		4,745	72
Station W3	4,202	83		4,113	81
Station W4	2,213	79		2,109	75
	15,192		19,585	14,763	

EGC as a whole generated close to the maximum amount of electricity in 2008/9 that they were capable of producing given the condition of some of the power stations. The total capacity of EGC's electricity generation if all its power stations operated at 100% efficiency all of the time with no breakdowns in 2008/9 was 81,149 million kWh.

Government drive for increased efficiency

The Minister of Energy has indicated to the Management Board members of EGC that the Government wishes to encourage more efficient methods of energy production. This includes the need to reduce production costs and reduce harmful emissions. The Government has limited resources for capital investment in energy production and wishes to be sure that future energy production facilities are more efficient and effective than at present.

The Minister of Energy is aware that the acceleration of the decline of the coal industry in another country resulted in the loss of many jobs in that country. This not only affected the coal industry itself but also other industries such as equipment suppliers, who were dependent on the survival of coal mining.

General election called

In a surprise move, the Prime Minister has called a general election. Among a number of other major proposals, the governing political party has proposed that one of its first tasks if re-elected would be to make the nationalised industries more efficient and accountable. The main opposition party has included the privatisation of all nationalised industries as a priority if it is elected. There are two main political parties in the country and while other political parties do exist and compete for seats in parliament, they have not been able to form a Government in the past. The probability that one of the two main political parties will win the election is therefore very high. A hung parliament, where no one political party has overall control, has a very low probability and can be ignored.

APPENDIX A

EXTRACTS FROM THE PRO FORMA ACCOUNTS OF THE ELECTRICITY GENERATING CORPORATION

INCOME STATEMENT

	Year ended 31 March 2009 $ million	Year ended 31 March 2008 $ million
Revenue	13,200	12,760
Total operating costs	12,906	12,441
Operating profit	294	319
Financing costs	(430)	(319)
Loss for the period	(136)	0

BALANCE SHEET

	At 31 March 2009 $ million	At 31 March 2008 $ million
Non-current assets (net)	15,837	15,388
Current assets		
Inventories	1,529	1,514
Receivables	2,679	2,491
Cash and cash equivalents	133	156
Total current assets	4,341	4,161
Total assets	20,178	19,549
Equity and reserves		
Ordinary shares	5,525	5,525
Losses	(136)	0
Other reserves	1,367	1,367
Total equity and reserves	6,756	6,892
Long-term liabilities (Government loans)	9,560	8,471
Current liabilities		
Payables	3,862	4,186
Total liabilities	13,422	12,657
Total equity and liabilities	20,178	19,549

APPENDIX B

CASH FLOW STATEMENT FOR THE YEAR ENDED 31 MARCH 2009

	$ million	$ million
Cash flows from operating activities:		
Loss		(136)
Adjustments for:		
Interest expense	430	
Depreciation	799	
(Increase)/decrease in inventories	(15)	
(Increase)/decrease in receivables	(188)	
Increase/(decrease) in payables	(324)	
		702
Cash generated from operations		566
Financing costs		(430)
Net cash from operating activities		136
Cash flows from investing activities:		
Purchase of non-current assets		(1,248)
(renewals of plant and equipment)		
Cash inflow/(outflow) before financing		(1,112)
Cash flows from financing activities:		
Proceeds from Government loans		1,089
Net decrease in cash and cash equivalents		(23)
Cash and cash equivalents at 31 March 2007		156
Cash and cash equivalents at 31 March 2008		133

STATEMENT OF CHANGES IN EQUITY FOR THE YEAR ENDED 31 MARCH 2009

	Share capital $ million	Other reserves $ million	Retained earnings $ million	Total $ million
Balance at 1 April 2008	5,525	1,367	0	6,892
Loss for the period			(136)	(136)
Balance at 31 March 2009	5,525	1,367	(136)	6,756

25: EGC: Specimen exam paper

APPENDIX C

STRUCTURE CHART AND STAFFING INFORMATION AT 31 MARCH 2008

EGC Management Board:

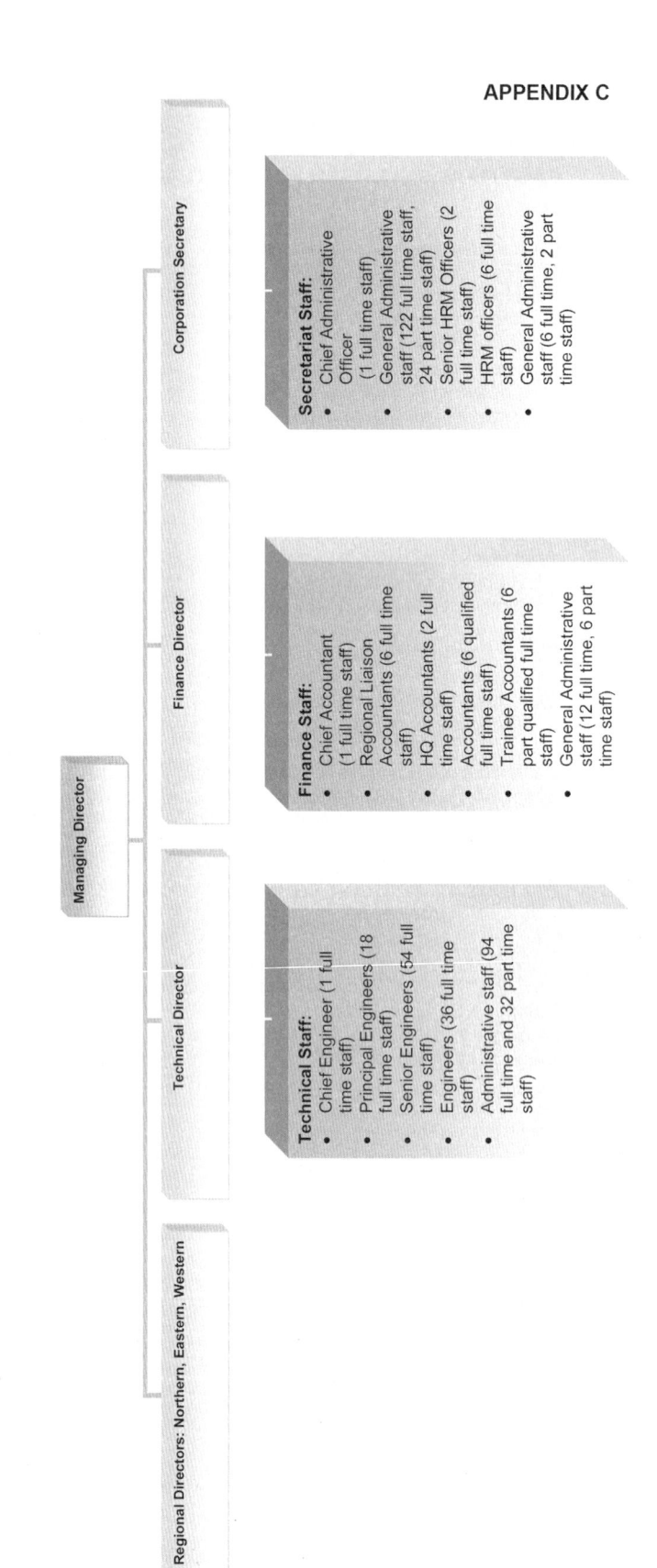

- Regional Directors: Northern, Eastern, Western
- Technical Director
- Managing Director
- Finance Director
- Corporation Secretary

Technical Staff:
- Chief Engineer (1 full time staff)
- Principal Engineers (18 full time staff)
- Senior Engineers (54 full time staff)
- Engineers (36 full time staff)
- Administrative staff (94 full time and 32 part time staff)

Finance Staff:
- Chief Accountant (1 full time staff)
- Regional Liaison Accountants (6 full time staff)
- HQ Accountants (2 full time staff)
- Accountants (6 qualified full time staff)
- Trainee Accountants (6 part qualified full time staff)
- General Administrative staff (12 full time, 6 part time staff)

Secretariat Staff:
- Chief Administrative Officer (1 full time staff)
- General Administrative staff (122 full time staff, 24 part time staff)
- Senior HRM Officers (2 full time staff)
- HRM officers (6 full time staff)
- General Administrative staff (6 full time, 2 part time staff)

APPENDIX D

Regional Management Board

Each of the three regions has the same structure. The Regional Director has responsibility for all staff within the region. The Regional Engineer, Regional Accountant and Regional Secretary all report directly to the Regional Director. The structure set out is for the Northern Region only. The staffing levels vary in each region.

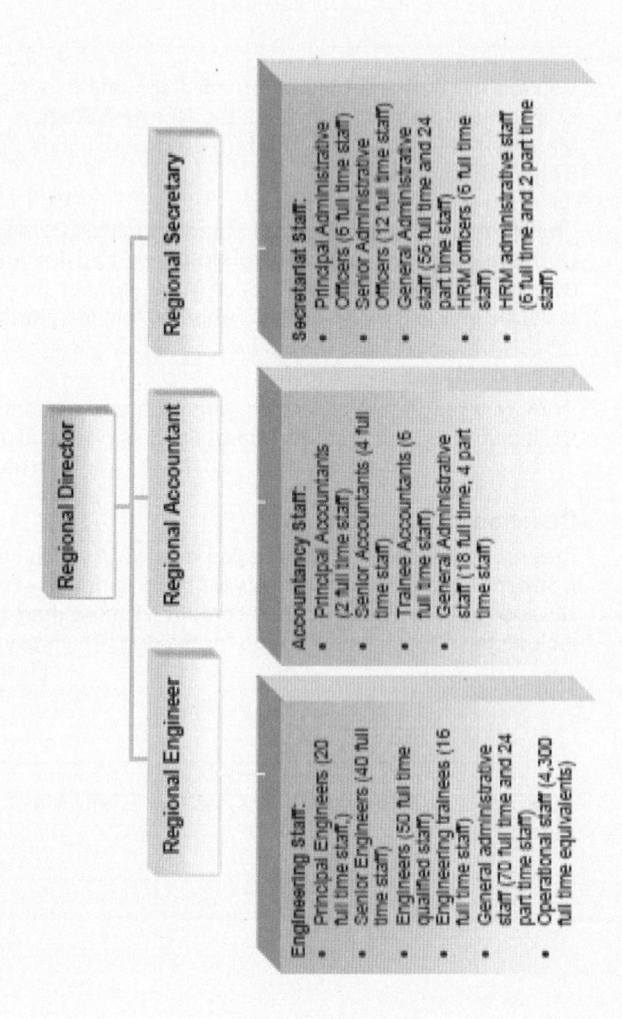

```
                    Regional Director
                           |
        ┌──────────────────┼──────────────────┐
  Regional Engineer  Regional Accountant  Regional Secretary
```

Engineering staff:
- Principal Engineers (20 full time staff.)
- Senior Engineers (40 full time staff)
- Engineers (150 full time qualified staff)
- Engineering trainees (16 full time staff)
- General administrative staff (70 full time and 24 part time staff)
- Operational staff (4,300 full time equivalents)

Accountancy staff:
- Principal Accountants (2 full time staff)
- Senior Accountants (4 full time staff)
- Trainee Accountants (6 full time staff)
- General Administrative staff (18 full time, 4 part time staff)

Secretariat staff:
- Principal Administrative Officers (6 full time staff)
- Senior Administrative Officers (12 full time staff)
- General Administrative staff (55 full time and 24 part time staff)
- HRM officers (6 full time staff)
- HRM administrative staff (6 full time and 2 part time staff)

End of Pre-Seen Material

Electricity Generating Corporation – Unseen material provided on examination day

Additional (unseen) information relating to the case is given on pages 15 to 19.

Read all of the additional material before you answer the question.

ANSWER THE FOLLOWING QUESTIONS

You are the Divisional Management Accountant in the Northern Division. The Northern Division was formerly known as the Northern Region. The post of Divisional Management Accountant was formerly known (in the pre-seen material) as the Regional Accountant.

The Northern Division General Manager (NDGM), recently appointed as head of the Northern Division, has asked you to provide advice and recommendations on the issues which the Northern Division Management Board must address, including how cultural change may be brought about within the Northern Division.

Question 1
Prepare a report that prioritises, analyses and evaluates the issues facing the Northern Division of EGC and makes appropriate recommendations.

(Total marks for question 1 = 90 Marks)

Question 2
Prepare two slides for presentation to NDGM which summarise the case from the Northern Division's point of view for making the investment proposed for power stations N1 and N2. Your slides should contain no more than 5 bullet points on each and include the financial justification for making the investment.

(Total marks for question 2 = 10 Marks)

Your script will be marked against the TOPCIMA Assessment Criteria shown on the next page.

Assessment Criteria

Criterion	Maximum marks available
Analysis of issues (25 marks)	
Technical	5
Application	15
Diversity	5
Strategic choices (35 marks)	
Focus	5
Prioritisation	5
Judgement	20
Ethics	5
Recommendations (40 marks)	
Logic	30
Integration	5
Ethics	5
Total	**100**

Electricity Generating Corporation – unseen material provided on examination day

Read this information before you answer the question

Structural change at EGC

The governing political party won the general election and immediately set about putting its pre-election proposals into action. One of the first announcements by the Prime Minister was that the Electricity Generating Corporation (EGC) must become more efficient and accountable. It will remain a single nationalised industry for now and will continue to be solely engaged in electricity power generation.

The previous Managing Director, Regional Directors and Corporation Secretary have all left the organisation. A new divisionalised structure for EGC was announced by the Minister of Energy. The Government's intention is that the new structure for EGC will provide more autonomy for decision making at divisional level. EGC now has a new Management Board, headed by a newly appointed Chairman. There is a new Divisional General Manager for each of the Northern, Eastern and Western divisions. All are members of the Management Board of EGC, as are the Finance Director and Technical Director and the new Corporation Secretary. The Chairman has made it very clear to Management Board members that EGC as a whole must undergo cultural change to become more efficient and accountable.

The Northern Divisional General Manager (NDGM) has established his divisional structure which includes a Divisional Management Accountant. This post was formerly known (in the pre-seen Appendix D) as the Regional Accountant.

Performance within the divisions of EGC

Each of the Northern, Eastern and Western divisions has its own management team, under the direction of its respective Divisional General Manager. The 10 private sector electricity distribution companies will continue to purchase their electricity as at present from EGC to supply the final users. The divisions may now compete on price for the sale of electricity to these 10 private sector electricity distribution companies. The Management Board of EGC is required by the Government to ensure that the three divisions generate electricity efficiently and economically and maintain sufficient volumes to meet demand effectively.

The Chairman has made it clear that in order to compete effectively with each other, the divisions all need to become more efficient in terms of reducing the cost of electricity generation. This includes a review of their staffing levels. The Chairman stated that strong financial control needs to be introduced within the divisions.

The Chairman also said the divisions need to provide management information to assist in the effective control of their costs. They must also satisfy the demands being made of them by the Government to introduce a range of performance measures. In addition, it is necessary for the divisions to demonstrate that they are meeting targets on reducing harmful emissions into the atmosphere.

Price and supply of generated electricity

The objective of the Government is to keep electricity prices as low as possible. Each of the three divisions of EGC now publishes on a daily basis the quantity of electricity it plans to generate each day and the price at which it will sell it to the 10 private sector electricity distribution companies. This means that price and supply from the three divisions may fluctuate on a daily basis and consequently supply may be controlled by the divisions to affect price.

Research and development

Currently all research and development is centrally controlled by EGC and the costs are charged equally across the divisions. Following the introduction of the divisional structure it is now proposed that the Divisional General Manager of the Eastern Division takes control of the entire research function for EGC.

The new Northern Divisional General Manager (NDGM), feels particularly frustrated that he is unable to obtain finance in order to carry out research. He is aware that there is much evidence showing how effective wind turbines would be if they were built in the Northern Divisional area.

Government programme for electricity generation by using wind power

The Government has now stated clearly that it will not tolerate nuclear power generation of electricity. Instead, the Minister of Energy has announced a very large programme for the installation of turbines driven by wind power, all of which will be established within the area of the Northern Division. These turbines will be phased in over a 4 year period and all will be operational by November 2013. When compared with existing methods of electricity generation, the new innovative wind turbines are expected to reduce harmful emissions per kilowatt hour (kWh) of electricity produced. Similarly, the Government expects that the wind turbines will effectively reduce overall electricity generation costs per kWh compared with the costs incurred at present by EGC.

When they are fully operational, the wind turbines will generate 12,000 million kWh of electricity in total each year in addition to the 60,000 million kWh generated by EGC in 2008/9. The generation of 60,000 million kWh of electricity may be taken as the maximum generating capacity in 2008/9 as it was so close to the limit of what EGC is actually capable of generating. The Government has stated that to meet expected demand, the country will only require the generation of 64,500 million kWh of electricity by November 2013, a 7·5% increase over the 2008/9 level of electricity generated. The operation of the wind turbines will enable some of the most inefficient coal fired power stations to be scaled down so that they will only be used as a reserve power source. This will significantly reduce variable running costs at each scaled down power station. The erection of the wind turbines will be carried out by a specialist building contractor, which has already been appointed.

The Government will provide funds for the initial capital cost of the wind turbines but has not yet decided who will operate and manage the programme. The Minister of Energy has stated that there will be only one organisation appointed to operate and manage the entire programme. He also said that he will need assurance that if the Northern Division of EGC is appointed to operate and manage the wind power generation programme, EGC as a whole must commit to achieving the following two targets:

1. Ensure the overall average cost of electricity generation is no more than $0·183 per kWh (at 2008/9 price levels) by November 2014. This target average cost applies across all forms of electricity generating methods including the use of coal or wind power. (The average operating cost per kWh in 2008/9 for EGC as a whole was $0·2151).

2. Produce a plan which enables the development of new technology which will provide for improved electricity generation with less waste, resulting in an overall reduction of harmful emissions by an average of 2% per year for 10 years commencing on 1 April 2010.

NDGM has made it clear to the Northern Division's Management Board that when the Government implements the wind turbine programme there may be a risk of job cuts if the Northern Division is not appointed to operate and manage the programme.

NDGM estimates that if the Northern Division were appointed to operate and manage the wind turbine power generation programme the total operating costs of the division, including apportioned headquarters overheads, at the 2008/9 price level, would be reduced. The forecast amount of this reduction in operating costs would be $570 million per year for each power station that is scaled down to become a reserve power source. This scaling down will not happen until November 2013 when all the wind turbines will be operational. This estimate takes full account of the total cost of operating the wind turbines and remaining coal fired power stations, including the savings from scaling down the power stations which are held in reserve. **Appendix E** provides information on output, capacity utilisation and costs relating to each of the power stations in the Northern Division in 2008/9.

Northern Division investment proposal

Each division is now an investment centre in its own right. The members of the Divisional Management Boards now have authority to make investments within prescribed limits normally up to $100 million. Projects which exceed $100 million must be approved by the EGC Management Board. EGC uses a cost of capital charge in line with the Government's rate of 6%. Capital funding to EGC will continue to be made by loans from the Government. Taxation can be ignored as EGC does not pay tax.

NDGM has agreed with EGC's Chairman and Finance Director that the total operating costs of generation in the Northern Division in 2008/9 of $6,038 million would be reduced in determining the controllable costs of the division. They have agreed that all except the headquarters staff costs and overheads of $274 million and research and development costs of $4 million, which were charged by headquarters, will be regarded as the controllable costs within the division.

Other information relating to the 2008/9 accounts:

	Northern Division $ million	EGC $ million
Non-current assets (net)	5,751	15,837
Total revenue	5,043	13,200
Total operating costs	6,038	12,906
Total controllable costs	5,760	12,906

An investment project which would be operational by 31 March 2010 is being considered by the Northern Division's Management Board. NDGM is very keen to improve the division's return on investment as he recognises that the other two divisions significantly outperform his own. EGC uses two investment criteria, Return on Investment and Residual Income. Return on Investment is defined as total revenue less total controllable costs expressed as a percentage of net non-current assets (as shown above).

This investment project involves a capital cost of $1,800 million (depreciated at 10% per year on a straight line basis) for equipment which would increase fuel efficiency and be introduced into power stations N1 and N2. This would reduce the amount of coal used and consequently significantly reduce harmful emissions from N1 and N2. In 2008/9, N1 and N2 accounted for 65% of the entire harmful emissions from the power stations in the Northern Division. (The Northern Division emitted 42% of the total harmful emissions for EGC as a whole in 2008/9). The project would enable staffing at these power stations to be reduced. It is estimated that the total savings generated by the introduction of this equipment, before depreciation, will be $315 million per year at 2008/9 price levels. This will commence immediately following the installation of the equipment.

NDGM is aware that some members of the EGC Management Board are not in favour of this investment project taking place as they expect the Northern Division to be appointed to operate and manage the wind turbine programme and consequently they believe that power stations N1 and N2 will be scaled down.

Earth tremor damage to power station N4

A report by geological researchers at the country's leading university has stated that buildings in the Northern Division are becoming increasingly subject to the threat of earth tremors. The report was clear that the area was not subject to serious earthquakes but only to the far less damaging earth tremors. There has been an increase in earth tremors within the area of the Northern Division. These have caused damage to the infrastructure in the area, including to power station N4. The Government has now introduced strict construction regulations requiring all new buildings to be able to withstand earth tremors. Any new power stations across the country will be subject to these construction regulations.

A structural report on the damage to power station N4 has concluded that it is safe and can continue to operate at the moment and should be able to do so for the next five years without any reduction of its generating capacity, even if earth tremor activity increases as expected. However, in order to guarantee continuity of its generating capacity after this period, repairs should be carried out within the five-year period. These will cost $1,500 million at the 2008/9 price level. As with other buildings whose capital cost was financed by the Government, power stations do not have any building repair or renewal insurance.

The power station, which produced 8,513 million kWh in 2008/9 or about 37% of the total electricity generated in the Northern Division, would have to close down for a period of six months while the repairs are carried out. These repairs would enable the power station to meet the new Government construction regulations and allow it to maintain its long term electricity generating levels at about 83% of capacity. (See **Appendix E**)

Divisional Management Accountant

As Divisional Management Accountant you are required to provide NDGM with immediate advice and recommendations on the issues which the Northern Divisional Management Board must address, including how cultural change may be brought about within the Northern Division. In addition, you are required to prepare two slides for presentation to NDGM, summarising the case for the investment proposal, including the financial justification, for power stations N1 and N2.

APPENDIX E

NORTHERN DIVISION'S OUTPUT, CAPACITY UTILISATION, TOTAL AND AVERAGE OPERATING COSTS IN 2008/9 AND COMPARISON OF TOTAL OPERATING COSTS ACROSS THE DIVISIONS

	2008/9 Output produced	Utilisation of 100% capacity	Total operating costs	Average operating costs per kWh
	kWh (million)	%	$ million	$
Northern Region:				
Station N1	2,644	46	1,051	0·398
Station N2	4,560	57	1,478	0·324
Station N3	7,207	67	1,708	0·237
Station N4	8,513	83	1,801	0·212
	22,924		6,038	

The total operating costs of the divisions and for EGC as a whole in 2008/9 were as follows:

	Northern $ million	Eastern $ million	Western $ million	EGC $ million
Total operating costs	6,038	3,518	3,350	12,906

The Government-approved price charged by EGC for electricity in 2008/9 was $0·22 per kWh.

APPLICABLE MATHS TABLES AND FORMULAE

Present value table

Present value of 1.00 unit of currency, that is $(1 + r)^{-n}$ where r = interest rate; n = number of periods until payment or receipt.

Periods (n)	1%	2%	3%	4%	5%	6%	7%	8%	9%	10%
1	0.990	0.980	0.971	0.962	0.952	0.943	0.935	0.926	0.917	0.909
2	0.980	0.961	0.943	0.925	0.907	0.890	0.873	0.857	0.842	0.826
3	0.971	0.942	0.915	0.889	0.864	0.840	0.816	0.794	0.772	0.751
4	0.961	0.924	0.888	0.855	0.823	0.792	0.763	0.735	0.708	0.683
5	0.951	0.906	0.863	0.822	0.784	0.747	0.713	0.681	0.650	0.621
6	0.942	0.888	0.837	0.790	0.746	0705	0.666	0.630	0.596	0.564
7	0.933	0.871	0.813	0.760	0.711	0.665	0.623	0.583	0.547	0.513
8	0.923	0.853	0.789	0.731	0.677	0.627	0.582	0.540	0.502	0.467
9	0.914	0.837	0.766	0.703	0.645	0.592	0.544	0.500	0.460	0.424
10	0.905	0.820	0.744	0.676	0.614	0.558	0.508	0.463	0.422	0.386
11	0.896	0.804	0.722	0.650	0.585	0.527	0.475	0.429	0.388	0.350
12	0.887	0.788	0.701	0.625	0.557	0.497	0.444	0.397	0.356	0.319
13	0.879	0.773	0.681	0.601	0.530	0.469	0.415	0.368	0.326	0.290
14	0.870	0.758	0.661	0.577	0.505	0.442	0.388	0.340	0.299	0.263
15	0.861	0.743	0.642	0.555	0.481	0.417	0.362	0.315	0.275	0.239
16	0.853	0.728	0.623	0.534	0.458	0.394	0.339	0.292	0.252	0.218
17	0.844	0.714	0.605	0.513	0.436	0.371	0.317	0.270	0.231	0.198
18	0.836	0.700	0.587	0.494	0.416	0.350	0.296	0.250	0.212	0.180
19	0.828	0.686	0.570	0.475	0.396	0.331	0.277	0.232	0.194	0.164
20	0.820	0.673	0.554	0.456	0.377	0.312	0.258	0.215	0.178	0.149

Periods (n)	11%	12%	13%	14%	15%	16%	17%	18%	19%	20%
1	0.901	0.893	0.885	0.877	0.870	0.862	0.855	0.847	0.840	0.833
2	0.812	0.797	0.783	0.769	0.756	0.743	0.731	0.718	0.706	0.694
3	0.731	0.712	0.693	0.675	0.658	0.641	0.624	0.609	0.593	0.579
4	0.659	0.636	0.613	0.592	0.572	0.552	0.534	0.516	0.499	0.482
5	0.593	0.567	0.543	0.519	0.497	0.476	0.456	0.437	0.419	0.402
6	0.535	0.507	0.480	0.456	0.432	0.410	0.390	0.370	0.352	0.335
7	0.482	0.452	0.425	0.400	0.376	0.354	0.333	0.314	0.296	0.279
8	0.434	0.404	0.376	0.351	0.327	0.305	0.285	0.266	0.249	0.233
9	0.391	0.361	0.333	0.308	0.284	0.263	0.243	0.225	0.209	0.194
10	0.352	0.322	0.295	0.270	0.247	0.227	0.208	0.191	0.176	0.162
11	0.317	0.287	0.261	0.237	0.215	0.195	0.178	0.162	0.148	0.135
12	0.286	0.257	0.231	0.208	0.187	0.168	0.152	0.137	0.124	0.112
13	0.258	0.229	0.204	0.182	0.163	0.145	0.130	0.116	0.104	0.093
14	0.232	0.205	0.181	0.160	0.141	0.125	0.111	0.099	0.088	0.078
15	0.209	0.183	0.160	0.140	0.123	0.108	0.095	0.084	0.079	0.065
16	0.188	0.163	0.141	0.123	0.107	0.093	0.081	0.071	0.062	0.054
17	0.170	0.146	0.125	0.108	0.093	0.080	0.069	0.060	0.052	0.045
18	0.153	0.130	0.111	0.095	0.081	0.069	0.059	0.051	0.044	0.038
19	0.138	0.116	0.098	0.083	0.070	0.060	0.051	0.043	0.037	0.031
20	0.124	0.104	0.087	0.073	0.061	0.051	0.043	0.037	0.031	0.026

Cumulative present value of 1.00 unit of currency per annum, Receivable or Payable at the end of each year for n years $\left[\frac{1-(1+r)^{-n}}{r}\right]$

Periods (n)	1%	2%	3%	4%	5%	6%	7%	8%	9%	10%
1	0.990	0.980	0.971	0.962	0.952	0.943	0.935	0.926	0.917	0.909
2	1.970	1.942	1.913	1.886	1.859	1.833	1.808	1.783	1.759	1.736
3	2.941	2.884	2.829	2.775	2.723	2.673	2.624	2.577	2.531	2.487
4	3.902	3.808	3.717	3.630	3.546	3.465	3.387	3.312	3.240	3.170
5	4.853	4.713	4.580	4.452	4.329	4.212	4.100	3.993	3.890	3.791
6	5.795	5.601	5.417	5.242	5.076	4.917	4.767	4.623	4.486	4.355
7	6.728	6.472	6.230	6.002	5.786	5.582	5.389	5.206	5.033	4.868
8	7.652	7.325	7.020	6.733	6.463	6.210	5.971	5.747	5.535	5.335
9	8.566	8.162	7.786	7.435	7.108	6.802	6.515	6.247	5.995	5.759
10	9.471	8.983	8.530	8.111	7.722	7.360	7.024	6.710	6.418	6.145
11	10.368	9.787	9.253	8.760	8.306	7.887	7.499	7.139	6.805	6.495
12	11.255	10.575	9.954	9.385	8.863	8.384	7.943	7.536	7.161	6.814
13	12.134	11.348	10.635	9.986	9.394	8.853	8.358	7.904	7.487	7.103
14	13.004	12.106	11.296	10.563	9.899	9.295	8.745	8.244	7.786	7.367
15	13.865	12.849	11.938	11.118	10.380	9.712	9.108	8.559	8.061	7.606
16	14.718	13.578	12.561	11.652	10.838	10.106	9.447	8.851	8.313	7.824
17	15.562	14.292	13.166	12.166	11.274	10.477	9.763	9.122	8.544	8.022
18	16.398	14.992	13.754	12.659	11.690	10.828	10.059	9.372	8.756	8.201
19	17.226	15.679	14.324	13.134	12.085	11.158	10.336	9.604	8.950	8.365
20	18.046	16.351	14.878	13.590	12.462	11.470	10.594	9.818	9.129	8.514

Periods (n)	11%	12%	13%	14%	15%	16%	17%	18%	19%	20%
1	0.901	0.893	0.885	0.877	0.870	0.862	0.855	0.847	0.840	0.833
2	1.713	1.690	1.668	1.647	1.626	1.605	1.585	1.566	1.547	1.528
3	2.444	2.402	2.361	2.322	2.283	2.246	2.210	2.174	2.140	2.106
4	3.102	3.037	2.974	2.914	2.855	2.798	2.743	2.690	2.639	2.589
5	3.696	3.605	3.517	3.433	3.352	3.274	3.199	3.127	3.058	2.991
6	4.231	4.111	3.998	3.889	3.784	3.685	3.589	3.498	3.410	3.326
7	4.712	4.564	4.423	4.288	4.160	4.039	3.922	3.812	3.706	3.605
8	5.146	4.968	4.799	4.639	4.487	4.344	4.207	4.078	3.954	3.837
9	5.537	5.328	5.132	4.946	4.772	4.607	4.451	4.303	4.163	4.031
10	5.889	5.650	5.426	5.216	5.019	4.833	4.659	4.494	4.339	4.192
11	6.207	5.938	5.687	5.453	5.234	5.029	4.836	4.656	4.486	4.327
12	6.492	6.194	5.918	5.660	5.421	5.197	4.988	7.793	4.611	4.439
13	6.750	6.424	6.122	5.842	5.583	5.342	5.118	4.910	4.715	4.533
14	6.982	6.628	6.302	6.002	5.724	5.468	5.229	5.008	4.802	4.611
15	7.191	6.811	6.462	6.142	5.847	5.575	5.324	5.092	4.876	4.675
16	7.379	6.974	6.604	6.265	5.954	5.668	5.405	5.162	4.938	4.730
17	7.549	7.120	6.729	6.373	6.047	5.749	5.475	5.222	4.990	4.775
18	7.702	7.250	6.840	6.467	6.128	5.818	5.534	5.273	5.033	4.812
19	7.839	7.366	6.938	6.550	6.198	5.877	5.584	5.316	5.070	4.843
20	7.963	7.469	7.025	6.623	6.259	5.929	5.628	5.353	5.101	4.870

Formulae

Valuation Models

(i) Irredeemable preference share, paying a constant annual dividend, d, in perpetuity, where P_0 is the ex-div value:

$$P_0 = \frac{d}{k_{pref}}$$

(ii) Ordinary (Equity) share, paying a constant annual dividend, d, in perpetuity, where P_0 is the ex-div value:

$$P_0 = \frac{d}{k_e}$$

(iii) Ordinary (Equity) share, paying an annual dividend, d, growing in perpetuity at a constant rate, g, where P_0 is the ex-div value:

$$P_0 = \frac{d_1}{k_e - g} \text{ or } P_0 = \frac{d_0[1+g]}{k_e - g}$$

(iv) Irredeemable (Undated) debt, paying annual after tax interest, $i(1-t)$, in perpetuity, where P_0 is the ex-interest value:

$$P_0 = \frac{i[1-t]}{k_{dnet}}$$

or, without tax:

$$P_0 = \frac{i}{k_d}$$

(v) Future value of S, of a sum X, invested for n periods, compounded at $r\%$ interest:

$$S = X[1+r]^n$$

(vi) Present value of £1 payable or receivable in n years, discounted at $r\%$ per annum:

$$PV = \frac{1}{[1+r]^n}$$

(vii) Present value of an annuity of £1 per annum, receivable or payable for n years, commencing in one year, discounted at $r\%$ per annum:

$$PV = \frac{1}{r}\left[1 - \frac{1}{[1+r]^n}\right]$$

(viii) Present value of £1 per annum, payable or receivable in perpetuity, commencing in one year, discounted at $r\%$ per annum:

$$PV = \frac{1}{r}$$

(ix) Present value of £1 per annum, receivable or payable, commencing in one year, growing in perpetuity at a constant rate of $g\%$ per annum, discounted at $r\%$ per annum:

$$PV = \frac{1}{r - g}$$

Cost of Capital

(i) Cost of irredeemable preference capital, paying an annual dividend, d, in perpetuity, and having a current ex-div price P_0:

$$k_{pref} = \frac{d}{P_0}$$

(ii) Cost of irredeemable debt capital, paying annual net interest, $i(1-t)$, and having a current ex-interest price P_0:

$$k_{dnet} = \frac{i[1-t]}{P_0}$$

(iii) Cost of ordinary (equity) share capital, paying an annual dividend, d, in perpetuity, and having a current ex-div price P_0:

$$k_e = \frac{d}{P_0}$$

(iv) Cost of ordinary (equity) share capital, having a current ex-div price, P_0, having just paid a dividend, d_0, with the dividend growing in perpetuity by a constant $g\%$ per annum:

$$k_e = \frac{d_1}{P_0} + g \quad \text{or} \quad k_e = \frac{d_0[1+g]}{P_0} + g$$

(v) Cost of ordinary (equity) share capital, using the CAPM:

$$k_e = R_f + [R_m - R_f]\beta$$

(vi) Weighted average cost of capital, k_0:

$$k_0 = k_e \left[\frac{V_E}{V_E + V_D} \right] + k_d \left[\frac{V_D}{V_E + V_D} \right]$$